WORKERS OF ALL COU

ized by Google LLC

KARL MARX

Theories of Surplus Value

PART III

LAWRENCE & WISHART LONDON
1972

Copyright © Lawrence & Wishart, 1972
SBN 85315 252 7

KARL MARX

THEORIES OF SURPLUS-VALUE

Volume IV of Capital

PART III

PROGRESS PUBLISHERS
Moscow

TRANSLATED FROM THE GERMAN
BY JACK COHEN AND S. W. RYAZANSKAYA
EDITED BY S. W. RYAZANSKAYA AND RICHARD DIXON

К. МАРКС

ТЕОРИИ ПРИБАВОЧНОЙ СТОИМОСТИ

(IV том «Капитала»)

Часть III

На английском языке

M $\frac{10101-324}{014(01)-75}$ 6-75

First printing 1971
Second printing 1975

PUBLISHERS' NOTE

This translation has been made from Karl Marx, *Theorien über den Mehrwert*, Teil 3, Dietz Verlag, Berlin, 1962. The arrangement of the material and the notes correspond on the whole to the Russian edition of Marx-Engels, *Collected Works*, Vol. 26, Part III, Moscow, 1964, prepared by the Institute of Marxism-Leninism in Moscow, where the manuscript of the work is kept.

We have attempted to keep the translation as closely as possible to the original. When, for the sake of clarity, it has been found necessary to insert a few words these are enclosed in square brackets. In order to avoid confusion, the square brackets occasionally used by Marx in the manuscript have been replaced either by pointed brackets ‹ › or, when the passages enclosed were longer, by braces { }.

Quotations from French, German and Italian authors are given in English in the text and are reproduced in the original language in the Appendix. In the case of British writers cited by Marx from a French source, the original English version appears in the text and the French translation used by Marx in the Appendix. Where an omission in a passage quoted has not been indicated by Marx, the ellipsis is enclosed in square brackets.

Other discrepancies between the quotations as recorded by Marx and as they appear in the original source, are mentioned in footnotes.

Words underlined by Marx, both in his own writing and in the extracts quoted by him, are set in italics, as are also titles of publications and foreign words customarily italicised (words underscored by two lines are set in spaced italics).

Chapter and section headings correspond in general to those of the Russian edition. Headings set in square brackets have been provided by the Institute of Marxism-Leninism in Moscow on the basis of formulations used by Marx in the chapter or section in question.

The numbers of Marx's notebooks are indicated by Roman numerals, those of the manuscript pages by Arabic numerals, which are separated from the text by vertical lines. As a rule these numbers are printed only at the beginning of the relevant portion of the manuscript, but where passages have been transposed the number of the manuscript page (and, when there is a change to another notebook, also the number of the notebook) is shown both at the beginning of the passage and at the end.

CONTENTS

[*CHAPTER XIX*] THOMAS ROBERT MALTHUS	13
[1. Malthus's Confusion of the Categories Commodity and Capital]	13
[2. Malthus's Vulgarised View of Surplus-Value]	18
[3. The Row Between the Supporters of Malthus and Ricardo in the Twenties of the 19th Century. Common Features in Their Attitude to the Working Class]	22
[4. Malthus's One-sided Interpretation of Smith's Theory of Value. His Use of Smith's Mistaken Theses in His Polemic Against Ricardo]	23
[5. Smith's Thesis of the Invariable Value of Labour as Interpreted by Malthus]	26
[6. Malthus's Use of the Ricardian Theses of the Modification of the Law of Value in His Struggle Against the Labour Theory of Value]	29
[7. Malthus's Vulgarised Definition of Value. His View of Profit as Something Added to the Price. His Polemic Against Ricardo's Conception of the Relative Wages of Labour]	31
[8. Malthus on Productive Labour and Accumulation]	34
[a)] Productive and Unproductive Labour	34
[b)] Accumulation	35
[9.] Constant and Variable Capital [According to Malthus] . . .	36
[10.] Malthus's Theory of Value [Supplementary Remarks] . . .	39
[11.] Over-Production, "Unproductive Consumers", etc.	40
[12. The Social Essence of Malthus's Polemic Against Ricardo. Malthus's Distortion of Sismondi's Views on the Contradictions in Bourgeois Production]	51
[13. Critique of Malthus's Conception of "Unproductive Consumers" by Supporters of Ricardo]	59
[14. The Reactionary Role of Malthus's Writings and Their Plagiaristic Character. Malthus's Apologia for the Existence of "Upper" and "Lower" Classes]	61
[15. Malthus's Principles Expounded in the Anonymous *Outlines of Political Economy*]	63

[CHAPTER XX] DISINTEGRATION OF THE RICARDIAN SCHOOL 69
  1. [Robert Torrens] 69
    [a) Smith and Ricardo on the Relation Between the Average Rate of Profit and the Law of Value] 69
    [b) Torrens's Confusion in Defining the Value of Labour and the Sources of Profit] 71
    [c) Torrens and the Conception of Production Costs] 79
  2. James Mill [Futile Attempts to Resolve the Contradictions of the Ricardian System] 84
    [a) Confusion of Surplus-Value with Profit] 85
    [b) Mill's Vain Efforts to Bring the Exchange Between Capital and Labour into Harmony with the Law of Value] 88
    [c) Mill's Lack of Understanding of the Regulating Role of Industrial Profit] 99
    [d)] Demand, Supply, Over-Production 100
    [e)] Prévost [Rejection of Some of the Conclusions of Ricardo and James Mill. Attempts to Prove That a Constant Decrease of Profit Is Not Inevitable] 104
  3. Polemical Writings 109
    a) [*Observations on Certain Verbal Disputes*. Scepticism in Political Economy] 110
    b) *An Inquiry into those Principles*... [The Lack of Understanding of the Contradictions of the Capitalist Mode of Production Which Cause Crises] 117
    c) Thomas De Quincey [Failure to Overcome the Real Flaws in the Ricardian Standpoint] 123
    d) Samuel Bailey 124
      [α) Superficial Relativism on the Part of the Author of *Observations on Certain Verbal Disputes* and on the Part of Bailey in Treating the Category of Value. The Problem of the Equivalent. Rejection of the Labour Theory of Value as the Foundation of Political Economy] 124
      [β) Confusion with Regard to Profit and the Value of Labour] 148
      [γ) Confusion of Value and Price. Bailey's Subjective Standpoint] 159
  4. McCulloch 168
    [a) Vulgarisation and Complete Decline of the Ricardian System under the Guise of Its Logical Completion. Cynical Apologia for Capitalist Production. Unprincipled Eclecticism] 168
    [b) Distortion of the Concept of Labour Through Its Extension to Processes of Nature. Confusion of Exchange-Value and Use-Value] 176
  5. Wakefield [Some Objections to Ricardo's Theory Regarding the "Value of Labour" and Rent] 187
  6. Stirling [Vulgarised Explanation of Profit by the Interrelation of Supply and Demand] 188

7. John Stuart Mill [Unsuccessful Attempts to Deduce the Ricardian Theory of the Inverse Proportionality Between the Rate of Profit and the Level of Wages Directly from the Law of Value] . . 190
   [a] Confusion of the Rate of Surplus-Value with the Rate of Profit. Elements of the Conception of "Profit upon Alienation". Confused Conception of the "Profits Advanced" by the Capitalist] . . 190
   [b] Apparent Variation in the Rate of Profit Where the Production of Constant Capital Is Combined with Its Working Up by a Single Capitalist] 213
   [c] On the Influence a Change in the Value of Constant Capital Exerts on Surplus-Value, Profit and Wages] 217
   [8. Conclusion] 237

[*CHAPTER XXI*] OPPOSITION TO THE ECONOMISTS (BASED ON THE RICARDIAN THEORY) 238

1. [The Pamphlet] *The Source and Remedy of the National Difficulties* 238
   [a] Profit, Rent and Interest Regarded as Surplus Labour of the Workers. The Interrelation Between the Accumulation of Capital and the So-called "Labour Fund"] 238
   [b] On the Exchange Between Capital and Revenue in the Case of Simple Reproduction and of the Accumulation of Capital] . . 246
   [c] The Merits of the Author of the Pamphlet and the Theoretical Confusion of His Views. The Importance of the Questions He Raises about the Role of Foreign Trade in Capitalist Society and of "Free Time" as Real Wealth] 252

2. Ravenstone. [The View of Capital as the Surplus Product of the Worker. Confusion of the Antagonistic Form of Capitalist Development with Its Content. This Leads to a Negative Attitude Towards the Results of the Capitalist Development of the Productive Forces] 257

3. Hodgskin 263
   [a] The Thesis of the Unproductiveness of Capital as a Necessary Conclusion from Ricardo's Theory] 263
   [b] Polemic Against the Ricardian Definition of Capital as Accumulated Labour. The Concept of Coexisting Labour. Underestimation of the Importance of Materialised Past Labour. Available Wealth in Relation to the Movement of Production] 266
   [c]] So-called Accumulation as a Mere Phenomenon of Circulation. (Stock, etc.—Circulation Reservoirs) 280
   [d] Hodgskin's Polemic Against the Conception that the Capitalists "Store Up" Means of Subsistence for the Workers. His Failure to Understand the Real Causes of the Fetishism of Capital] . . 290
   [e]] Compound Interest: Fall in the Rate of Profit Based on This 298
   [f] Hodgskin on the Social Character of Labour and on the Relation of Capital to Labour] 313
   [g] Hodgskin's Basic Propositions as Formulated in His Book — *Popular Political Economy*] 315

[h) Hodgskin on the Power of Capital and on the Upheaval in the Right of Property] ... 319
[4.] Bray as an Opponent of the Economists ... 319
[*CHAPTER XXII*] RAMSAY ... 326
[1. The Attempt to Distinguish Between Constant and Variable Capital. The View that Capital Is Not an Essential Social Form] 326
[2. Ramsay's Views on Surplus-Value and on Value. Reduction of Surplus-Value to Profit. The Influence Which Changes in the Value of Constant and Variable Capital Exert on the Rate and Amount of Profit] ... 328
[3. Ramsay on the Division of "Gross Profit" into "Net Profit" (Interest) and "Profit of Enterprise". Apologetic Elements in His Views on the "Labour of Superintendence", "Insurance Covering the Risk Involved" and "Excess Profit"] ... 353
[*CHAPTER XXIII*] CHERBULIEZ ... 362
[1. Distinction Between Two Parts of Capital—the Part Consisting of Machinery and Raw Materials and the Part Consisting of "Means of Subsistence" for the Workers] ... 362
[2. On the Progressive Decline in the Number of Workers in Relation to the Amount of Constant Capital] ... 364
[3. Cherbuliez's Inkling that the Organic Composition of Capital Is Decisive for the Rate of Profit. His Confusion on This Question. Cherbuliez on the "Law of Appropriation" in Capitalist Economy] 369
[4. On Accumulation as Extended Reproduction] ... 379
[5. Elements of Sismondism in Cherbuliez. On the Organic Composition of Capital. Fixed and Circulating Capital] ... 381
[6. Cherbuliez Eclectically Combines Mutually Exclusive Propositions of Ricardo and Sismondi] ... 396
[*CHAPTER XXIV*] RICHARD JONES ... 399
1. Reverend Richard Jones, *An Essay on the Distribution of Wealth, and on the Sources of Taxation*, London, 1831, Part I, Rent [Elements of a Historical Interpretation of Rent. Jones's Superiority over Ricardo in Particular Questions of the Theory of Rent and His Mistakes in This Field] ... 399
2. Richard Jones, *An Introductory Lecture on Political Economy etc.* [The Concept of the "Economical Structure of Nations". Jones's Confusion with regard to the "Labor Fund"] ... 413
3. Richard Jones, *Text-book of Lectures on the Political Economy of Nations*, Hertford, 1852 ... 419
[a) Jones's Views on Capital and the Problem of Productive and Unproductive Labour] ... 419
[b) Jones on the Influence Which the Capitalist Mode of Production Exerts on the Development of the Productive Forces. Concerning the Conditions for the Applicability of Additional Fixed Capital] ... 432
[c) Jones on Accumulation and Rate of Profit. On the Source of Surplus-Value] ... 445

ADDENDA

REVENUE AND ITS SOURCES. VULGAR POLITICAL ECONOMY 453
[1.] The Development of Interest-Bearing Capital on the Basis of Capitalist Production [Transformation of the Relations of the Capitalist Mode of Production into a Fetish. Interest-Bearing Capital as the Clearest Expression of This Fetish. The Vulgar Economists and the Vulgar Socialists Regarding Interest on Capital] 453
[2.] Interest-Bearing Capital and Commercial Capital in Relation to Industrial Capital. Older Forms. Derived Forms 468
[3. The Separation of Individual Parts of Surplus-Value in the Form of Different Revenues. The Relation of Interest to Industrial Profit. The Irrationality of the Fetishised Forms of Revenue] . . 473
[4. The Process of Ossification of the Converted Forms of Surplus-Value and Their Ever Greater Separation from Their Inner Substance—Surplus Labour. Industrial Profit as "Wages for the Capitalist"] 481
[5. Essential Difference Between Classical and Vulgar Economy. Interest and Rent as Constituent Elements of the Market Price of Commodities. Vulgar Economists Attempt to Give the Irrational Forms of Interest and Rent a Semblance of Rationality] 498
[6. The Struggle of Vulgar Socialism Against Interest (Proudhon). Failure to Understand the Inner Connection Between Interest and the System of Wage-Labour] 523
[7. Historical Background to the Problem of Interest. Luther's Polemic Against Interest Is Superior to That of Proudhon. The Concept of Interest Changes as a Result of the Evolution of Capitalist Relations] 527

APPENDICES

Quotations in French, German and Italian 543
Notes 564
Index of Authorities 581
Name Index 589
Subject Index 597

[CHAPTER XIX]

THOMAS ROBERT MALTHUS[1]

||XIII-753| The writings of Malthus which have to be considered here are:
1) *The Measure of Value Stated and Illustrated etc.*, London, 1823.
2) *Definitions in Political Economy etc.*, London, 1827 (as well as the same work published by *John Cazenove* in London in 1853 with Cazenove's "Notes and Supplementary Remarks").
3) *Principles of Political Economy etc.*, second ed., London, 1836 (first [edition] 1820 or thereabout, to be looked up).
4) Also to be taken into consideration the following work by a Malthusian[2] (i.e., a Malthusian in contrast to the Ricardians)—*Outlines of Political Economy etc.*, London, 1832.

[1. Malthus's Confusion of the Categories Commodity and Capital]

In his *Observations on the Effects of the Corn Laws etc.* (1814) Malthus still says the following about Adam Smith:

"Adam Smith[a] was evidently led into this train of argument from his habit of considering *labour*" (that is, the value of labour) "*as the standard measure of value* and corn as the measure of labour.... And that[b] neither labour nor any other commodity can be an accurate measure of real value in exchange, is now considered as one of the most incontrovertible doctrines of political economy; and indeed follows, [...] from the very definition of value in exchange" [pp. 11-12].

But in his *Principles of Political Economy* (1820), Malthus borrows this "standard measure of value" from Smith to use it

---

[a] In the manuscript "Doctor Smith" instead of "Adam Smith".—*Ed.*
[b] In the manuscript "That" instead of "And that".—*Ed.*

against Ricardo, though Smith himself never used it when he was really analysing his subject matter.[3] Malthus himself, in his book on the *Corn Laws* already referred to, adopted Smith's other definition concerning the determination of value by the quantity of capital (accumulated labour) and (immediate) labour necessary for the production of an article.

One cannot fail to recognise that both Malthus's *Principles* and the two other works mentioned, which were intended to amplify certain aspects of the *Principles*, were largely inspired by envy at the success of Ricardo's book[4] and were an attempt by Malthus to regain the leading position which he had attained by skilful plagiarism before Ricardo's book appeared. In addition, Ricardo's definition of value, though somewhat abstract in its presentation, was directed against the interests of the landlords and their retainers, which Malthus represented even more directly than those of the industrial bourgeoisie. At the same time, it cannot be denied that Malthus presented a certain theoretical, speculative interest. Nevertheless his opposition to Ricardo—and the form this opposition assumed—was possible only because Ricardo had got entangled in all kinds of inconsistencies.

The points of departure for Malthus's attack are, on the one hand, the origin of surplus-value[5] and [on the other] the way in which Ricardo conceives the equalisation of cost-prices[6] in different spheres of the employment of capital as a modification of the law of value itself [as well as] his continual confusion of profit with surplus-value (direct identification of one with the other). Malthus does not unravel these contradictions and *quid pro quos* but accepts them from Ricardo in order to be able to overthrow the Ricardian law of value, etc., by using this confusion and to draw conclusions acceptable to his protectors.

The real contribution made by Malthus in his three books is that he places the main emphasis on the *unequal* exchange between capital and wage-labour, whereas Ricardo does not actually explain how the exchange of commodities according to the law of value (according to the labour-time embodied in the commodities) gives rise to the unequal exchange between capital and living labour, between a definite amount of accumulated labour and a definite amount of immediate labour, and therefore in fact leaves the origin of surplus-value obscure (since he makes capital exchange immediately for labour and not for labour power). ||754| *Cazenove*, one of the few later disciples of Malthus, realises this and says in his preface to *Definitions etc.*, mentioned above:

> *Interchange of commodities* and *Distribution* (wages, rent and profit) must be kept distinct from each other ... the Laws of Distribution are not altogether dependent upon those relating to Interchange[a] ([T. R. Malthus, *Definitions in Political Economy*, ed. by John Cazenove, London, 1853,] Preface, pp. *vi* and *vii*).

Here this can only mean that the relation of wages to profit, the exchange of capital and wage-labour, of accumulated labour and immediate labour, do not *directly* coincide with the law of the interchange of commodities.

If one considers the *utilisation* of money or commodities as capital—that is, not their value but their capitalist *utilisation*—it is clear that *surplus-value* is nothing but the surplus of labour (the unpaid labour) which is commanded by capital, i.e., which the commodity or money commands over and above the quantity of labour it itself contains. In addition to the quantity of labour it itself contains (equal to the sum of labour contained in the elements of production of which it is made up, plus the immediate labour which is added to them), it buys a surplus of labour which it does not itself embody. This surplus constitutes the surplus-value; its size determines the rate of expansion of capital. And this surplus quantity of living labour for which it is exchanged is the source of profit. Profit (or rather surplus-value) does not result from the exchange of an amount of materialised labour for an equivalent amount of living labour, but from the portion of living labour which is appropriated in this exchange without an equivalent payment in return, that is, from unpaid labour which capital appropriates in this pseudo-exchange. If one disregards how this process is mediated—and Malthus is all the more justified in disregarding it as the intermediate link is not mentioned by Ricardo—if one considers only the factual content and the result of this process, then production of surplus-value, profit, transformation of money or commodities into capital, arises not from the fact that commodities are exchanged according to the law of value, namely, in proportion to the amount of labour-time which they cost, but rather conversely, from the fact that commodities or money (i.e., materialised labour) are

---

[a] Marx here summarises Cazenove's remarks.—*Ed.*

exchanged for *more* living labour than is embodied or worked up in them.

Malthus's sole contribution in the books mentioned is the emphasis he places on this point, which emerges all the less sharply in Ricardo as Ricardo always presupposes the finished product which is divided between the capitalist and the worker without considering exchange, the intermediate process which leads to this division. However, this contribution is cancelled out by the fact that he confuses the *utilisation* of money or the commodity as capital, and hence its *value* in the specific function of capital, with the *value of the commodity* as such; consequently he falls back in his exposition, as we shall see, on the fatuous conceptions of the Monetary System, on profit upon expropriation,[7] and gets completely entangled in the most hopeless confusion. Thus Malthus, instead of advancing beyond Ricardo, seeks to drag political economy back to where it was before Ricardo, even to where it was before Adam Smith and the Physiocrats.

"... in the same country, and at the same time, the exchangeable value of those commodities which can be resolved into labour and profits alone, would be accurately measured by the quantity of labour which would result from adding to the accumulated and immediate labour actually worked up in them the[a] varying amount of the profits on all the advances estimated in labour. But this must necessarily be the same as the quantity of labour which they will command" ([T. R. Malthus,] *The Measure of Value Stated and Illustrated*, London, 1823, pp. 15-16).

"... the labour which a commodity would command"[b] [is] "a standard measure of value" (op. cit., p. 61).

"... I had nowhere seen it stated" (that is, before his own book *The Measure of Value* appeared), "that the ordinary *quantity of labour* which a commodity will command must represent and measure *the quantity of labour worked up in it*, with the addition of profits" ([T. R. Malthus,] *Definitions in Political Economy etc.*, London, 1827, p. 196).

Mr. Malthus wants to include "profit" directly in the definition of *value*, so that it follows immediately from this definition, which is not the case with Ricardo. This shows that he felt where the difficulty lay.

Besides, it is particularly absurd that he declares the *value of the commodity* and its *realisation* as capital to be identical. When commodities or money (in brief, materialised labour) are

---

[a] The manuscript has "worked up in them+the".—*Ed.*
[b] The manuscript has "can command is" instead of "would command".—*Ed.*

exchanged as capital against living labour, they are always exchanged against a ||755| greater quantity of labour than they contain. And if one compares the commodity before this exchange on the one hand, with the product resulting from this exchange with living labour on the other, one finds that the commodity has been exchanged for its own value (equivalent) plus a surplus over and above its own value—the surplus-value. But it is therefore absurd to say that the value of a commodity is equal to its value plus a surplus over and above this value. If the commodity, as a commodity, is exchanged for other commodities and not as capital against living labour, then, insofar as it is exchanged for an equivalent, it is exchanged for the same quantity of materialised labour as is embodied in it.

The only notable thing is therefore that according to Malthus the profit exists already in the value of the commodity and that it is clear to him that the commodity always commands more labour than it embodies.

"... it is precisely because the labour which a commodity will ordinarily command measures the labour actually worked up in it with the addition of profits, that it is justifiable to consider it" (labour) "as a measure of value. If then *the ordinary value of a commodity* be considered as determined by *the natural and necessary conditions of its supply*, it is certain that the labour which it will ordinarily command is alone the measure of these conditions" ([T. R. Malthus,] *Definitions in Political Economy*, London, 1827, p. 214).

"*Elementary costs of Production.* An expression exactly equivalent to the conditions [...] of the supply" (*Definitions in Political Economy*, ed. by John Cazenove, London, 1853, p. 14).

"*Measure of the Conditions of* [...] *the Supply* [...]. The quantity of labour for which the commodity will exchange, when it is in its natural and ordinary state" (loc. cit., p. 14).

"... the quantity of labour which a commodity commands represents exactly the quantity of labour worked up in it, with the profits upon the advances, and does therefore really represent and measure those natural and necessary conditions of the supply, those elementary costs of production which determine value..." (op. cit., p. 125).

"... the demand for a commodity, though not proportioned to the *quantity* of any other commodity which the purchaser is willing and able to give for it, is really proportioned to the *quantity of labour* which he will give for it; and for this reason: the *quantity of labour which a commodity will ordinarily command*, represents exactly the effectual demand for it; because it represents exactly *that quantity of labour and profits united necessary to effect its supply*; while the *actual* quantity of labour which a commodity will command when it differs from the *ordinary* quantity, represents the excess or defect of demand arising from temporary causes" (op. cit., p. 135).

Malthus is right in this also. The conditions of *supply*, i.e., of the production or rather the reproduction of a commodity on the basis of capitalist production, are that it or its value (the money into which it is transformed) is exchanged in the process of its production or reproduction for more labour than is embodied in it, for it is only produced in order to realise a profit.

For example, a cotton manufacturer sells his calico. The condition for the supply of new calico is that he exchanges the money—the exchange-value of the calico—for more labour in the process of the reproduction of the calico than was embodied in it or than is represented by the money. For the cotton manufacturer produces calico as a capitalist. What he wants to produce is not calico, but profit. The production of calico is only a means for the production of profit. But what follows from this? The calico he produces contains more labour-time, more labour than was contained in the calico advanced. This surplus labour-time, this surplus-value, is also represented by a surplus product, i.e., *more* calico than was exchanged for labour. Therefore one part of the product does not replace the calico exchanged for labour, but constitutes surplus product which belongs to the manufacturer. Or, if we consider the whole product, each yard of calico contains an aliquot part, or its value contains an aliquot part, for which no equivalent is paid; this represents *unpaid* labour. If the manufacturer sells a yard of calico at its value, that is, if he exchanges it for money or for commodities which contain an equal amount of labour-time, he realises a sum of money, or receives a quantity of commodities which cost him nothing. For he sells the calico not for the labour-time for which he has paid, but for the labour-time embodied in the calico, and he did not pay for part of this labour-time. ||756| He receives, for example, labour-time equal to 12 shillings, but he only paid 8 shillings of this amount. When he sells it at its value, he sells it for 12 shillings, and thus gains 4 shillings.

[2. Malthus's Vulgarised View of Surplus-Value]

As far as the buyer is concerned, the assumption is that, under all circumstances, he pays *nothing but* the value of the calico. This means that he gives a sum of money which contains as much labour-time [as] there is in the calico. Three cases are possible. The buyer is a capitalist. The money (i.e., the value of the commodity) with which he pays, also contains a portion of unpaid labour. Thus, if one person sells unpaid labour, the other person buys with unpaid labour. Both realise unpaid labour—one as seller, the other as buyer. Or, the buyer is an independent producer. In this case he receives equivalent for equivalent. Whether the labour which the seller sells him in the shape of commodities is paid for or not, does not concern him. He receives as much materialised labour as he gives. Or, finally, he is a wage-worker. In this case also, like every other buyer—provided the commodities are sold at their value—he receives an equivalent for his money in the shape of commodities. He receives as much materialised labour in commodities as he gives in money. But for the money which constitutes his wages he has given more labour than is embodied in the money. He has replaced the labour contained in it along with surplus labour which he gives gratis. He paid for the money above its value, and therefore also pays for the equivalent of the money, the calico, etc., above its value. The cost for him as purchaser is thus greater than it is for the seller of any commodity although he receives an equivalent of the money in the commodity; but in the money he did not receive an equivalent of his labour; on the contrary, he gave more than the equivalent in labour. Thus the worker is the only one who pays for all commodities above their value even when he buys them at their value, because he buys money, the universal equivalent, above its value for labour. Consequently, no gain accrues to those who sell commodities to the worker. The worker does not pay the seller any more than any other buyer, he pays the value of labour. In fact, the capitalist who sells the commodity produced by the worker back to him, realises a profit on this sale, but only the same profit as he realises on every other buyer. His profit—as far as this worker is concerned—arises not from his having sold the worker the commodity *above* its value, but from his having previously bought it from the worker, as a matter of fact in the production process, *below* its value.

Now Mr. Malthus, who transformed the utilisation of commodities as capital into the value of commodities, quite consistently transforms all buyers into wage-workers, in other words he makes them all exchange with the capitalist not commodities, but immediate labour, and makes them all give back to the capitalist more labour than the commodities *contain*, while conversely, the capitalist's profit results from *selling all* the labour contained in the commodities when he has *paid* for only a portion of the labour contained in them. Therefore, whereas the difficulty with Ricardo [arises from] the fact that the law of commodity exchange does not directly explain the exchange between capital and wage-labour, but rather seems to contradict it, Malthus solves the difficulty by transforming the purchase (exchange) of commodities into an exchange between capital and wage-labour. What Malthus does not understand is the difference between the total sum of labour contained in a particular commodity and the sum of paid labour which is contained in it. It is precisely this difference which constitutes the source of profit. Further, Malthus inevitably arrives at the point of deriving profit from the fact that the seller sells his commodity not only *above* the amount it costs *him* (and the capitalist does this), but above what *it costs*; he thus reverts to the vulgarised conception of profit upon expropriation and derives surplus-value from the fact that the seller sells the commodity *above* its value (i.e., for more labour-time than is contained in it). What he thus gains as a seller of a commodity, he loses as a buyer of another and it is absolutely impossible to discover what profit is to be made in reality from such a general nominal price increase. ||757| It is in particular difficult to understand how society as a whole can enrich itself in this way, how a real surplus-value or surplus product can thus arise. An absurd, stupid idea.

Relying on some propositions of Adam Smith—who, as we have seen, naïvely expresses all sorts of contradictory elements and thus becomes the source, the starting-point, of diametrically opposed conceptions—Mr. Malthus attempts in a confused way, though on the basis of a correct surmise, and of the realisation of the existence of an unsolved difficulty, to counterpose a new theory to that of Ricardo and thus to maintain a "front rank" position. The transition from this attempt to the nonsensical, vulgarised conceptions proceeds in the following way.

If we consider the utilisation of a commodity as capital—that is, in its exchange for living, productive labour—we see that it commands—besides the labour-time it itself contains, i.e., besides the equivalent reproduced by the worker—surplus labour-time, which is the source of profit. Now if we transfer this *utilisation of the commodity* to its *value*, then each purchaser of a commodity must act as if he were a worker, that is, in buying it, besides the quantity of labour contained in the commodity, he must give for it a surplus quantity of labour. But since other purchasers, *apart from the workers*, are *not* related to commodities as workers (even when the worker appears as a mere purchaser, the old, original difference persists indirectly, as we have seen), it must be assumed that although they do not directly give more labour than is contained in the commodities, they give a value which contains more labour, and this amounts to the same thing. It is by means of this [quantity] of "surplus labour, or, what amounts to the same thing, the value of more labour", that the transition is made. In fact, it comes to this: the value of a commodity consists of the value paid for it by the purchaser, and this value is equal to the equivalent (the value) of the commodity plus a surplus over and above this value, surplus-value. Thus we have the vulgarised view that profit consists in a commodity being *sold more dearly than it was bought*. The purchaser buys it for more labour or for more materialised labour than it costs the seller.

But if the purchaser is himself a capitalist, a seller of commodities, and his money, his means of purchase, represents only goods which have been sold, then it follows that both have sold their goods too dearly and are consequently swindling each other, moreover they are swindling each other to the same extent, provided they both merely secure the average rate of profit. Where are the buyers to come from who will pay the capitalist the quantity of labour equal to that contained in his commodity plus his profit? For example, the commodity costs the seller 10 shillings. He sells it for 12 shillings. He thus commands labour not to the value of 10s. only, but of 2s. more. But the buyer also sells his commodity, which cost 10s., for 12s. So that each loses as a buyer what he gained as a seller. The only exception is the working class. For since the price of the product is increased beyond its cost, they can only buy back a part of that product, and thus another part of the product, or the price of another part of the product, constitutes profit for the capitalist. But as profit arises precisely from the fact that the workers can only buy back part of the product, the capitalist (the capitalist class) can never realise his profit as a result of demand from the workers, he cannot realise it by exchanging the whole product against the workers' wage, but rather by exchanging *the whole* of the workers' wage against only part of the product. Additional demand and additional buyers apart from the workers themselves are therefore necessary, otherwise there could not be any profit. Where do they come from? If they themselves are capitalists, sellers, then the mutual swindling within the capitalist class mentioned earlier occurs, since they mutually raise the nominal prices of their commodities and each gains as a seller what he loses as a buyer. What is *required* therefore are *buyers who are not sellers*, so that the capitalist can realise his profit and sell his commodities "at their value". Hence the necessity for landlords, pensioners, sinecurists, priests, etc., not to forget their menial servants and retainers. How these "purchasers" come into possession of their means of purchase ||758|, how they must first take part of the product from the capitalists without giving any equivalent in order to buy back less than an equivalent with the means thus obtained, Mr. Malthus does not explain. At any rate, what follows from this is his plea for the greatest possible increase in the unproductive classes in order that the sellers may find a market, a demand for the goods they supply. And so it turns out further that the author of the pamphlet on population[8] preaches continuous overconsumption and the maximum possible appropriation of the annual product by idlers, as a condition of production. In addition to the plea arising inevitably out of this theory, comes the argument that capital represents the *drive for abstract wealth*, *the drive to expand its value*, which can only be put into effect by means of a class of buyers representing the *drive to spend, to consume, to squander*, namely, the unproductive classes, who are buyers without being sellers.

[3. The Row Between the Supporters of Malthus and Ricardo in the Twenties of the 19th Century. Common Features in Their Attitude to the Working Class]

There developed on this basis a fine old row between the Malthusians and the Ricardians in the 20s (from 1820 to 1830 was in general the great metaphysical period in English political economy). Like the Malthusians, the Ricardians deem it necessary that the worker should not himself appropriate his product, but that part of it should go to the capitalist, in order that the worker should have an *incentive for production*, and that the development of wealth should thus be ensured. But they rage against the view of the Malthusians that landlords, state and church sinecurists and a whole lot of idle retainers must first lay hold—without any equivalent—of a part of the capitalist's product (just as the capitalist does in respect of the workers) therewith to buy their own goods from the capitalist with a profit for the latter, although this is exactly what the Ricardians affirm with regard to the workers. In order that accumulation may increase and with it the demand for labour, the worker must relinquish as much of his product as possible gratis to the capitalist, so that the latter can transform the net revenue, which has been increased in this way, back again into capital. The same sort [of argument is used by] the Malthusians. As much as possible should be taken away gratis from the industrial capitalists in the form of rent, taxes, etc., to enable them to sell what remains to their involuntary "shareholders" at a profit. The worker must not be allowed to appropriate his own product, otherwise he would lose the incentive to work, say the Ricardians along with the Malthusians. The industrial capitalist [the Malthusians say] must relinquish a portion of his product to the classes which only consume—*fruges consumere nati*[a]— in order that these in turn may exchange it again, on unfavourable terms, with the capitalist. Otherwise the capitalist would lose the incentive for production, which consists precisely in the fact that he makes a big profit, that he sells his goods far above their value. We shall return to this comic struggle later.

[4. Malthus's One-sided Interpretation of Smith's Theory of Value. His Use of Smith's Mistaken Theses in His Polemic Against Ricardo]

First of all, some evidence showing that Malthus arrives at a very common conception:

"Whatever may be the number of intermediate acts of barter which may take place in regard to commodities—whether the producers send them to China, or sell them in the place where they are produced: the question as to an adequate market for them, depends exclusively upon *whether the producers can replace their capitals with ordinary profits*, so as to enable them successfully to go on with their business. *But what are their capitals?* They are, as Adam Smith states, the tools to work with, the materials to work upon, and the means of commanding the necessary quantity of labour" [*Definitions in Political Economy*, ed. by Cazenove, London, 1853, p. 70].

(And this, he affirms, is all the labour worked up in the commodity. Profit is a *surplus* over and above the labour expended in the production of the commodity. In fact, therefore, a nominal surcharge over and above the cost of the commodity.) And in order that there may remain no doubt about his meaning,

---

[a] Those born to enjoy the fruits (Horace).—*Ed*

he quotes Colonel Torrens's *On the Production of Wealth* (Chap. VI, p. 349) approvingly as confirming his own views:

"... effectual demand consists in the power and inclination, on *the part of consumers*" ⟨the antithesis of buyers and sellers becomes that of consumers and producers⟩, ||759| "to give for commodities, either by immediate or circuitous barter, some greater proportion of all ingredients of capital than their production costs" ([R. Torrens, *An Essay on the Production of Wealth...*, London, 1821, p. 349, quoted by T. R. Malthus:] loc. cit., pp. 70-71).

And Mr. Cazenove himself, the publisher of, apologist for and commentator on the Malthusian *Definitions*, says:

"Profit does not depend on the *proportion in which commodities are exchanged with each other*"

⟨for if commodity exchange between capitalists alone were taken into account, the Malthusian theory, insofar as it does not speak of exchange with workers, who have *no* other commodity apart from their labour to exchange with the capitalist, would appear nonsensical [since profit would be] merely a reciprocal surcharge, a nominal surcharge on the prices of their commodities. Commodity exchange must therefore be disregarded and people who produce *no* commodities must exchange money⟩

"... (seeing that the same proportion may be maintained under every variety of profit) *but upon the proportion which goes to wages*, or is required to cover the prime cost, and which is in all cases determined by the degree in which the *sacrifice made by the purchaser* (or the *labour's worth which he gives*) in order to acquire a commodity, *exceeds that made by the producer, in order to bring it to market*" (op. cit., p. 46).

In order to achieve these wonderful results, Malthus has to make some very great theoretical preparations. First of all, seizing on that side of Adam Smith's theory according to which the value of a commodity is equal to the quantity of labour which it commands, or by which it is commanded, or against which it exchanges, he must cast aside all the objections raised by Adam Smith himself, by his followers and also by Malthus, to the effect that the *value* of a commodity—value [in general]—can be the measure of value.

The Measure of Value Stated and Illustrated (London, 1823) is a real example of feeble-minded thought, which winds its way in a casuistical and self-stupefying manner through its own inner confusion, and whose difficult, clumsy style leaves the unprejudiced and incompetent reader with the impression that the difficulty of making sense out of the confusion does not lie in the contradiction between confusion and clarity, but in a lack of understanding on the part of the reader.

Malthus has first of all to obliterate Ricardo's differentiation between "value of labour" and "quantity of labour"[9] and to reduce Smith's juxtaposition of the two to the one false aspect.

"... any given *quantity of labour* must be *of the same value as the wages* which command it, or for which it actually exchanges" (*The Measure of Value Stated and Illustrated*, London, 1823, p. 5).

The purpose of this phrase is to equate the expressions "*quantity of labour*" and "*value of labour*".

This phrase itself is a mere tautology, an absurd truism. Since *wages* or that "for which it" (i.e., a quantity of labour) "exchanges" constitute *the value* of this quantity of labour, it is tautologous to say: *the value* of a certain quantity of labour is equal to *the wages* or to the amount of money or commodities for which this labour exchanges. In other words, this means nothing more than: the exchange-value of a definite quantity of labour is equal to its exchange-value—otherwise called wages. But (apart from the fact that it is not labour, but labour-power, which exchanges directly for wages; it is this confusion that makes the nonsense possible) it by no means follows from this that a definite quantity of labour is equal to the quantity of labour embodied in the wages, or in the money or the goods which represent the wages. If a labourer works for 12 hours and receives the product of 6 hours labour as wages, then the product of the 6 hours constitutes the *value* of 12 hours labour (because the wages [represent] the exchangeable commodity for [12 hours labour]). It does not follow from this that 6 hours of labour are equal to 12 hours, or that the commodities in which 6 hours of labour are embodied [are] equal to the commodities in which 12 hours of labour are embodied. It does not follow that the value of wages is equal to the value of the product in which the labour is embodied. It follows only that the value of labour (because it is measured by the value of the labour-power, not by the labour carried out), the ||760| value of a given quantity of labour contains less labour than it buys; that, consequently, the *value of the commodities* in which this purchased labour is embodied, is very different from the value of the commodities with which this given quantity of labour was purchased, or by which it was commanded.

Mr. Malthus draws the opposite conclusion. Since the *value* of a given quantity of labour is equal to its value, it follows, according to him, that the value in which this quantity of labour is embodied is equal to the value of the wages. It follows further from this that the immediate labour (that is, disregarding the means of production) which is absorbed by and contained in a commodity, creates no greater value than that which is paid for it; [that it] only reproduces the value of the wages. The necessary consequence ensuing from this is that profit cannot be explained if the value of commodities is determined by the amount of labour embodied in them, but must rather be explained in some other way; provided the profit a commodity realises is to be included in the value of that commodity. For the labour worked up in a commodity consists 1) of the labour contained in the machinery, etc., used, which consequently reappears in the value of the product; 2) of the labour contained in the raw material used up. The amount of labour contained in these two elements before the new commodity is produced is obviously not increased merely because they become production elements of a new commodity. There remains therefore 3), the labour embodied in the wages which is exchanged for living labour. However, according to Malthus, this latter is not greater than the materialised labour against which it is exchanged. Hence, a commodity contains no portion of unpaid labour but only labour which replaces an equivalent. Hence it follows that if the value of a commodity were determined by the amount of labour embodied in it, it would yield no profit. If it does yield a profit, then this profit is a *surplus* in the price over and above the labour embodied in the commodity. Therefore, in order to be sold at its value (which includes the profit), a commodity must command a quantity of labour equal to the quantity of labour worked up in itself plus a surplus of labour representing the profit realised in the sale of the commodity.

[5. Smith's Thesis of the Invariable Value of Labour as Interpreted by Malthus]

Moreover, in order to make *labour*, not the quantity of labour required for production, but labour as a commodity, serve as a measure of value, Malthus asserts

"... *the constant value of labour*" (*The Measure of Value*, p. 29, note).
⟨There is nothing original in this; it is a mere paraphrase and further elaboration of a passage of Adam Smith's (l. I, ch. V, [*Recherches sur la nature et les causes de la richesse des nations,*] éd. Garnier, t. I, [Paris, 1802,] pp. 65-66).

"Equal quantities of labour, at all times and places, may be said to be of equal value to the labourer. In his ordinary state of health, strength, and spirits; in the ordinary degree of his skill and dexterity, he must always lay down the same portion of his ease, his liberty, and his happiness. The price which he pays must always be the same, whatever may be the quantity of goods which he receives in return for it. Of these, indeed, it may sometimes purchase a greater and sometimes a smaller quantity; but it is their value which varies, not that of the labour which purchases them. At all times and places, that is *dear* which it is difficult to come at, or which it costs much labour to acquire; and that *cheap* which is to be had easily, or with very little labour. Labour alone, therefore, never varying in its own value, is alone the ultimate and real standard by which the value of all commodities can at all times and places be estimated and compared."⟩ [*Wealth of Nations*, Vol. I, p. 36.][a]

⟨Further, Malthus's discovery—of which he is very proud and which he claims he was the first to make—namely, that value is equal to the quantity of labour embodied in a commodity plus a quantity of labour which represents the profit; [this discovery] seems likewise to be quite simply a combination of two sentences from Smith. (Malthus never escapes plagiarism.)

"The real value of all the different component parts of price, it must be observed, is measured by the quantity of labour which they can, each of them, purchase or command. Labour measures the value, not only of that part of the price which resolves itself into *labour*, but of that which resolves itself into *rent*, and of that which resolves itself into *profit*" ([*Wealth of Nations*, O.U.P., p. 55; Garnier,] t. I, l. I, ch. VI, p. 100).⟩

||761| Malthus writes in this context:

"In the former case of[b] the demand for labour, it appeared that the greater earnings of the labourer were occasioned,[c] not by a rise in the value of labour but by a fall in the value of the produce for which the labour was exchanged. And in the [...] case of an abundance of labour [...] the small earnings of the labourer were occasioned[c] by a rise in the value of the produce, and not by a fall in the value of [...] labour" (*The Measure of Value*, [London, 1823,] p. 35) (cf. pp. 33-35).

---

[a] This and the following passage from Adam Smith, which Marx quotes from Garnier's French translation, are printed in this volume according to Adam Smith, *Wealth of Nations*, Oxford University Press, London, 1928.— *Ed.*

[b] In the manuscript the word "Rises" takes the place of "In the former case of".—*Ed.*

[c] The word "caused" is used instead of "occasioned" in the manuscript.— *Ed.*

Bailey ridicules most excellently Malthus's *proof* that *the value of labour* is constant (Malthus's further demonstration, not that of Smith; [and] in general the sentence [about] the invariable value of labour):

"In the same way any article might be proved to be of invariable value; for instance, 10 yards of cloth. For whether we gave £5 or £10 for the 10 yards, the sum given would always be equal in value to the cloth for which it was paid, or, in other words, of invariable value in relation to cloth. But that which is given for a thing of invariable value, must itself be invariable, whence the 10 yards of cloth must be of invariable value ... it is just the same kind of futility to call wages invariable in value, because though variable in quantity they command the same portion of labour, as to call the *sum* given for a hat, of invariable value, because, although sometimes more and sometimes less, it always purchases the hat" ([Samuel Bailey,] *A Critical Dissertation on the Nature, Measures, and Causes of Value...*, London, 1825, pp. 145-47).

In the same work, Bailey bitingly derides the insipid, impressive-sounding tables with which Malthus "illustrates" his measure of value.

In his *Definitions in Political Economy* (London, 1827), in which Malthus gives full vent to his annoyance over Bailey's sarcasm, he seeks, amongst other things, to prove the *invariable value of. labour*, as follows:

"... there is one[a] large class of commodities, such as raw products, which in the progress of society tends to rise[b] as compared with labour [...] such as[c] manufactured articles, [...] fall; it may not be far from [...] truth to say, that [...] the average mass of commodities which a given quantity of labour will command in the same country, during the course of some centuries, may not very essentially vary" (*Definitions in Political Economy...*, London, 1827, p. 206).

Malthus's proof that a rise in the money price of labour must lead to an all-round rise in the money price of commodities is of just the same quality as his proof of the invariable value of labour:

"... if the money wages of labour universally rise, the value of money proportionally falls; and when the value of money falls ... the prices of goods always rise" (op. cit., p. 34).

It has to be proved that, when the value of money compared with labour falls, then the value of all commodities compared

---

[a] Instead of "there is one", the manuscript has "a".—*Ed.*
[b] Instead of "tends to rise", "rises" is used in the manuscript.—*Ed.*
[c] Instead of "such as", the words "whereas the" are used in the manuscript.—*Ed.*

with money rises, or that the value of money, not estimated in labour, but in the other commodities, falls. And Malthus proves this by presupposing it.

[6. Malthus's Use of the Ricardian Theses of the Modification of the Law of Value in His Struggle Against the Labour Theory of Value]

Malthus bases his polemic against Ricardo's definition of value entirely on the principles advanced by Ricardo himself, to the effect that variations[a] in the exchangeable values of commodities, independent of the labour worked up in them, are produced by the different composition of capital as resulting from the process of circulation—different proportions of circulating and fixed capital, different degrees of durability in the fixed capitals employed, different returns of circulating capitals. In short, on Ricardo's confusing cost-price with value and regarding the equalisation of cost-prices, which are independent of the mass of labour employed in the particular spheres of production, as modifications of value itself, thereby throwing the whole principle overboard. Malthus seizes on these contradictions in the determination of value by labour-time—contradictions that were first discovered and emphasised by Ricardo himself—not in order to solve them but in order to relapse into quite meaningless conceptions and to pass off the mere *formulation* of contradictory phenomena, their expression in speech, as their solution. We shall see the same method employed during the decline of the Ricardian school, i.e., by [James] Mill and McCulloch, who, in order to reason the contradictory phenomena out of existence, seek to bring them into direct conformity with the general law by gabble, by scholastic and absurd definitions and distinctions, with the result, by the way, that the foundation itself vanishes.

The passages in which Malthus uses the material provided by Ricardo against the law of value, and turns it against him, are the following:

"It is observed by Adam Smith that corn is an annual crop, butchers' meat a crop which requires four or five years to grow; and consequently, if we compare two quantities of corn and beef which are of equal exchangeable value, it is certain that a difference of three or four additional years profit

---

[a] From here the sentence is written in English in the manuscript.—*Ed.*

at fifteen per cent upon the capital employed in the production of the beef would, exclusively of any other considerations, make up in value for a much smaller quantity of labour, ||762| and thus we might have two commodities of the same exchangeable value, while the accumulated and immediate labour of the one was forty or fifty per cent less than that of the other. This is an event of daily occurrence in reference to a vast mass of the most important commodities in the country; and if profits were to fall from fifteen per cent to eight per cent, the value of beef compared with corn would fall above twenty per cent" (*The Measure of Value*, pp. 10-11).

Since capital consists of commodities, and a large proportion of the commodities which enter into it or constitute it have a price (or exchange-value in the ordinary sense) which consists neither of accumulated nor of immediate labour, but—insofar as we are discussing only this particular commodity—of a purely nominal increase in the value caused by the addition of the average profit, Malthus says:

"... labour is not the only element worked up in capital" (*Definitions etc.*, ed. by John Cazenove, p. 29).

"... what are the *costs of production*? ... the quantity of *labour in kind required to be worked up in the commodity*, and in the tools and materials consumed in its production *with such an additional quantity* as is equivalent to the ordinary profits upon the advances for the time that they have been advanced" (op. cit., pp. 74-75).

"On the same grounds Mr. Mill is quite incorrect, in calling capital hoarded labour. It may, perhaps, be called *hoarded labour and profits*; but certainly not hoarded labour alone, unless we determine to call profits labour" (op. cit., pp. 60-61).

"To say that the values of commodities are regulated or determined by the quantity of Labour and Capital necessary to produce them, is essentially false. To say that they are regulated *by the quantity of Labour and Profits* necessary to produce them, is essentially true" (op. cit., p. 129).

In this connection *Cazenove* adds a note on p. 130:

"The expression Labour and Profits is liable to this objection, that the two are not correlative terms,—labour being an agent and profits a result; the one a cause, the other a consequence. On this account *Mr. Senior* has substituted for it the expression *Labour and Abstinence*.... It must be acknowledged, indeed, that it is not the abstinence, but the *use* of the capital productively, which is the cause of profits" (according to Senior: "He who converts his revenue into capital, *abstains from the enjoyment* which its expenditure would afford him").

Marvellous explanation. The value of the commodity consists of the labour contained in it plus profit; [i.e.] of the labour contained in it and the labour not contained in it, but which must be paid for.

Malthus continues his polemic against Ricardo:

Ricardo's "proposition, that as the value of wages rises profits proportionably fall, cannot be true, except[a] on the assumption that commodities, which have the same quantity of labour worked up in them, are always of the same value, an assumption which probably will not be found to be true[b] in one case out of five hundred; and [...] from that [...] necessary state of things, which,[c] in the progress of civilisation and improvement, tends continually to increase the quantity of fixed capital employed, and to render more various and unequal the times of the returns of the circulating capital" (*Definitions etc.*, pp. 31-32).

(The same point is made on pp. 53-54 in Cazenove's edition where Malthus actually says:

"...that[d] natural [...] state of things...", falsifies Ricardo's measure of value because this state "... in the progress of civilisation and improvement, tends continually to increase the quantity of fixed capital employed, and to render more various and unequal the times of the returns of the circulating capital".)

"Mr. Ricardo [...] himself admits of considerable exceptions to his rule; but if we examine the classes which come under his exceptions, that is, where the quantities of fixed capital employed are different and of different degrees of duration, and where the periods of the returns of the circulating capital employed are not the same, we shall find that they are so numerous, that the rule may be considered as the exception, and the exceptions the rule" (op. cit., p. 50).

[7. Malthus's Vulgarised Definition of Value. His View of Profit as Something Added to the Price. His Polemic Against Ricardo's Conception of the Relative Wages of Labour]

In accordance with what has been said above, Malthus also declared value to be[10]:

"The estimation in which a commodity is held, founded upon its *cost to the purchaser* or the *sacrifice* which he must make in order to acquire it, which sacrifice is measured by the *quantity of labour that he gives in exchange for it, or what comes to the same thing*, by *the labour* which it will command" (op. cit., pp. 8-9).

Cazenove also emphasises as a difference between Malthus and Ricardo:

||763| "Mr. Ricardo has, with Adam Smith, adopted labour as the true standard of cost; but he has applied it to *producing* cost only. ... it is equally applicable as a measure of *cost to the purchaser*..." (op. cit., pp. 56-57).

[a] Instead of "cannot be true, except", the manuscript has "and vice versa, only true".—*Ed.*
[b] Instead of "an assumption which probably will not be found to be true", the manuscript has "and this is true".—*Ed.*
[c] Instead of "... from that ... necessary state of things, which", the manuscript has "indeed necessarily, because".—*Ed.*
[d] Instead of "that", the manuscript has "The".—*Ed.*

In other words: the value of a commodity is equal to the sum of money which the purchaser must pay, and this sum is best estimated in terms of the amount of ordinary labour which can be bought with it.* But what determines the sum of money is, naturally, not explained. It is the quite ordinary idea of the matter that is prevalent in everyday life. A mere triviality expressed in high-flown language. In other words, it means nothing more than that *cost-price* and *value* are identical, a confusion which, in the case of Adam Smith, and still more in the case of Ricardo, contradicts their real analysis, but which Malthus elevates into a law. It is the conception of value held by the philistine who, being a captive of competition, only knows the outward appearance of value. What then determines the cost-price? The capital outlay plus profit. And what determines profit? Where do the funds for the profit come from, where does the surplus product in which the surplus-value manifests itself come from? If it is simply a matter of a nominal increase of the money price, then nothing is easier than to increase the value of commodities. And what determines the value of the capital outlay? The *value* of the labour contained in it, says Malthus. And what determines this? The *value* of the commodities on which the wages are spent. And the value of these commodities? The value of the labour plus profit. And so we keep going round and round in a circle. Granting that the worker is in fact paid the value of his labour, that is, that the commodities (or sum of money) which constitute his wages are equal to the value of the commodities (or sum of money) in which his labour is realised, so that if he receives 100 thaler in wages he also adds only 100 thaler of value to the raw material, etc.—in short, to the capital outlay—then profit can only arise from a surcharge added by the seller over and above the *real* value of the commodity. All sellers do this. Thus, insofar as capitalists engage in exchange amongst themselves, nobody gains from this surcharge, and least of all is a surplus fund thus produced from which they can draw their revenue. Only the capitalists whose commodities are consumed by the working class will make a real and not an imaginary profit, by selling commodities back again to the workers at a higher price than they paid the workers for

---

* Malthus *presupposes* the *existence of profit* in order to be able to measure its value by an external standard. He does not deal with the question of the origin and intrinsic possibility of profit.

them. The commodities for which they paid the workers 100 thaler will be sold back again to them for 110 thaler. That means that they will only sell $^{10}/_{11}$ of the product back to the workers and retain $^{1}/_{11}$ for themselves. But what else does that mean but that the worker who, for example, works for 11 hours, gets paid for only 10 hours; that he is given the product of only 10 hours, while the capitalist receives one hour or the product of one hour without giving any equivalent. And what does it mean but that profit—as far as the working class is concerned—is made by their working for the capitalists *for nothing* part of the time, that therefore "the *quantity* of labour" does not come to the same as "the value of labour". The other capitalists however would only be making an imaginary profit, since they would not have this expedient.

How little Malthus understood Ricardo's first propositions, how completely he failed to comprehend that a profit is possible in other ways than by means of a surcharge is shown conclusively by the following passage:

"Allowing that the first commodities, if completed and brought into use immediately, might be the result of pure labour, and that their value would therefore be determined by the quantity of that labour; yet it is quite impossible that such commodities *should be employed as capital* to assist in the production of other commodities, *without the capitalist being deprived of the use of his advances for a certain period, and requiring a remuneration in the shape of profits.*

In the early periods of society, on account of the comparative scarcity of these advances of labour, this remuneration would be high, and would affect the value of such commodities to a considerable degree, owing to the high rate of profits. In the more advanced stages of society, the value of capital and commodities is largely affected by profits, on account of the greatly increased quantity of fixed capital employed, and the greater length of time for which much of the circulating capital is advanced before the capitalist is repaid by the returns. In *both cases,* the *rate at which commodities exchange with each other, is essentially affected by the varying amount of profits*" (*Definitions etc.*, ed. by Cazenove, p. 60).

The concept of *relative* wages is one of Ricardo's greatest contributions. It consists in this—that the *value of the wages* (and consequently of the *profit*) depends absolutely on the proportion of that part of the working-day during which the *worker works for himself* (producing or reproducing his wage) to that part of his time which belongs to the capitalist. This is important economically, in fact it is only another way of expressing the real theory of surplus-value.[11] It is important further in regard to the social relationship between the two ||764| classes. Malthus smells a rat and is therefore constrained to protest.

"No writer that I have met with, anterior to Mr. Ricardo, ever used the term *wages*, or real wages, as implying *proportions*."

(Ricardo speaks of the *value* of wages, which is indeed also presented as the part of the product accruing to the worker.[12])

Profits, indeed, imply proportions; and the *rate of profits has always justly been estimated by a percentage upon the value of the advances.*"

⟨What Malthus understands by *value of advances* is very hard, and for him even impossible, to say. According to him, the value of a commodity is equal to the advances contained in it plus profit. Since the advances, apart from the immediate labour, also consist of commodities, the value of the advances is equal to the advances in them plus profit. Profit thus equals profit upon the advances plus profit. And so on, *ad infinitum*.⟩

"But wages had uniformly been considered as rising or falling, not according to any *proportion* which they might bear to the whole produce obtained by a certain quantity of labour, but by the greater or smaller quantity of any particular produce received by the labourer, or by the greater or smaller power which such produce would convey, of commanding the necessaries and conveniences of life" (*Definitions etc.*, London, 1827, pp. 29-30).

Since the production of *exchange-value*—the increase of exchange-value—is the immediate aim of capitalist production, it is important [to know] how to measure it. Since the value of the capital advanced is expressed in money (real money or money of account), the rate of increase is measured by the amount of capital itself, and a capital (a sum of money) of a certain size—100—is taken as a standard.

"Profits of stock,"[a] says Malthus, "... consist of the difference between the value of the capital advanced, and the value of the commodity when sold or used" (op. cit., pp. 240-41).

[8. Malthus on Productive Labour and Accumulation]

[a)] Productive and Unproductive Labour

"... Revenue [...] is expended with a view to immediate support and enjoyment, and [...] capital [...] is expended with a view to profit" (op. cit., p. 86).

A labourer and a menial servant are "two instruments [...] used for purposes distinctly different, one to assist in obtaining wealth, the other to assist in consuming it" (op. cit., p. 94)[13].

---

[a] The manuscript gives "Profit of capital" instead of "Profits of stock".—*Ed.*

The following is a good definition of the productive labourer.

The productive labourer *directly "increases*[a] *his master's wealth" (Principles of Political Economy*, [second ed., London, 1836], p. 47, note).

In addition the following passage should be noted.

"The only productive consumption, properly so called, is the consumption or[b] destruction of wealth by capitalists with a view to reproduction.... The workman whom the capitalist employs certainly consumes that part of his wages which he does not save, as revenue, with a view to subsistence and enjoyment; and not as capital, with a view to production. *He is a productive consumer to the person who employs him,* and to the state, *but not, strictly speaking to himself" (Definitions*, ed. by Cazenove, p. 30).

[b)] Accumulation

"No political economist of the present day can by *saving* mean mere hoarding; and beyond this contracted and inefficient proceeding, no use of the term in reference to the national wealth can well be imagined, but that which must arise from a different application of what is saved, founded upon a real distinction between the different kinds of labour maintained by it" (*Principles of Political Economy*, [London, 1836,] pp. 38-39).

"*Accumulation of Capital.* The employment of a portion of revenue as capital. *Capital may therefore increase without an increase of stock or wealth*" (*Definitions*, ed. by Cazenove, p. 11).

"Prudential habits with regard to marriage carried to a considerable extent, among the labouring classes of a country mainly depending upon manufactures and commerce, *might injure it" (Principles of Political Economy*, [London, 1836,] p. 215).

This from the preacher of checks against over-population.

"It is the *want of necessaries* which mainly stimulates the labouring classes to produce luxuries; and were this stimulus removed or greatly weakened, so that the necessaries of life could be obtained with very little labour, instead of more time being devoted to the production of conveniences, there is every reason to think that less time would be so devoted" (op. cit., p. 334).

Most important for the exponent of the over-population theory, however, is this passage:

"... from the nature of a population, an increase of labourers cannot be brought into the market, in consequence of a particular demand, till after the lapse of sixteen or eighteen years, and the conversion of revenue into capital by saving, may take place much more rapidly; *a country is always liable* to *an increase in the quantity of the funds* for the maintenance of labour faster than the increase of population" (op. cit., pp. 319-20).

---

[a] The manuscript gives "augments" instead of "increases".—*Ed.*
[b] The manuscript has "and".—*Ed.*

[CHAPTER XIX]

||765| *Cazenove* rightly remarks:

"When capital is employed in *advancing to the workman his wages, it adds nothing to the funds for the maintenance of labour*, but simply consists in the application of a certain portion of [...] funds already in existence, to[a] the purposes of production" (*Definitions*, ed. by Cazenove, p. 22, note).

[9.] Constant and Variable Capital [According to Malthus]

"*Accumulated labour*". (It should really be called materialised labour, objectified labour.) "The[b] labour worked up in the raw materials and tools applied to the production of other commodities" (op. cit., p. 13).

In speaking of the labour worked up in commodities "... the labour worked up in the capital necessary to their production were[c] designated by the term *accumulated labour*, as contra-distinguished from the *immediate labour employed by the last capitalist*" (op. cit., pp. 28-29).

It is indeed very important to make this distinction. In Malthus, however, it leads to nothing.

He does make an attempt to reduce the surplus-value or at least its rate (which, by the way, he always confuses with profit and rate of profit) to its relation to variable capital, that part of capital which is expended on *immediate labour*. This attempt, however, is childish and could not be otherwise in view of his conception of value. In his *Principles of Political Economy* [second ed.], he says:

Supposing that the capital is expended only on wages, [if] "... a hundred pounds [is] expended in immediate labour, [...] the returns come in at the end of the year [...] £110, £120, or £130, it is evident that in each case the profits will be *determined by the proportion of the value of the whole produce which is required to pay the labour employed*. If the value of the produce in [the] market be £110, the proportion required to pay the labourers will be $^{10}/_{11}$ of the value of the produce, and profits will be ten per cent. If the value of the produce be £120, the proportion required to pay the labour employed will be[d] $^{10}/_{12}$, and profits will be twenty per cent. If [...] £130, the proportion required to pay the labour advanced will be $^{10}/_{13}$, and profits will be thirty per cent." [*Principles of Political Economy*, London, 1836, p. 267.] Supposing that "... the advances of the capitalist do not consist of labour alone [...] *the capitalist* [...] *expects an equal profit upon all the parts of the capital which he advances*. Let us suppose that a certain portion of the value of his advances, one-fourth for instance, consists of the wages of immediate labour, and[e] three-fourths consist of accumulated

---

[a] Instead of "to", the manuscript has "for".—*Ed.*
[b] The manuscript has "Accumulated labour=the".—*Ed.*
[c] The manuscript has "should be" instead of "were".—*Ed.*
[d] Instead of "required to pay the labour employed will be", the manuscript has "for labour".—*Ed.*
[e] The manuscript has "let us suppose $^1/_4$ of the advances for labour (immediate)" instead of the words used above.—*Ed.*

labour and profits, with any additions which may arise from rents, taxes or[a] other outgoings [...] it will be[b] strictly true that *the profits of the capitalist will vary with the varying value of this one-fourth of the[c] produce compared with the quantity of labour employed* [...] a farmer[d] employs in the cultivation [...] £2,000, £1,500 of which [...] in seed, keep of horses, wear and tear of his fixed capital, interest upon his fixed and circulating capitals, rents, tithes, taxes, etc. and £500 upon immediate labour, and [...] the returns [...] at the end of the year are worth[e] £2,400 [...] the farmer's profit will be £400, or twenty per cent.[f] And it is equally obvious that *if we took one-fourth of the value of the produce, namely £600, and compared it with the amount paid in the wages of immediate labour, the result would shew exactly the same rate of profits*" (loc. cit., pp. 267-68).

Here Malthus lapses into Lord Dundrearyism.[14] What he wants to do (he has an inkling that surplus-value, hence profit, has a definite relation to variable capital, the portion of capital expended on wages) is to show that "profits" are "determined by the proportion of the value of the whole produce which is required to pay the labour employed" [loc. cit., p. 267]. He begins correctly insofar as he assumes that the whole of the capital consists of variable capital, capital expended on wages. In this case, profit and surplus-value are in fact identical. But even in this case he confines himself to a very silly reflection. If the capital expended equals 100 and the profit is 10 per cent, the value of the product is, accordingly, 110 and the profit is $1/10$ of the capital expended (hence 10 per cent if calculated on the capital), and $1/11$ of the value of the total product, in the value of which its own value is included. Thus profit constitutes $1/11$ of the value of the total product and the capital expended forms $10/11$ of this value. In relation to the total, 10 per cent profit can be so expressed that the part of the value of the total product which is not made up of profit amounts to $10/11$ of the total product; or, a product of 110 which includes 10 per cent profit consists of $10/11$ outlay, on which the profit is made. This brilliant mathematical effort amuses him so much that he repeats the same calculation using a profit of·20 per cent, 30 per cent, etc. But so far we have merely a tautology. The profit is a percentage on the capital expended, the value of the total prod-

---

[a] The manuscript has "and" instead of "or".—*Ed.*
[b] The manuscript has "Then" instead of "it will be".—*Ed.*
[c] The manuscript has "his" instead of "of the".—*Ed.*
[d] The manuscript has "e.g. a farmer".—*Ed.*
[e] The manuscript has "are" instead of "are worth".—*Ed.*
[f] The manuscript has "his profit 400 on 2,000=20 per cent" instead of "the farmer's profit will be £400, or twenty per cent".—*Ed.*

uct includes the value of the profit and the capital expended ||766| is the value of the total product minus the value of the profit. Thus 110—10=100. And 100 is $^{10}/_{11}$ of 110. But let us proceed.

Let us assume a capital consisting not merely of variable but also of constant capital. "... the capitalist [...] expects an equal profit upon all the parts of the capital which he advances." This however contradicts the proposition advanced above that profit (it should be called surplus-value) is determined by the proportion of the capital expended on wages. But never mind. Malthus is not the man to contradict either the "expectations" or the notions of "the capitalists". But now comes his *tour de force*. Assume a capital of £2,000, three-quarters of which, or £1,500, is constant capital, one-quarter, or £500, is variable capital. The profit amounts to 20 per cent. Thus the profit equals £400 and the value of the product is £2,000 plus £400 =£2,400.[15] But what about Mr. Malthus's calculation? If one takes a quarter of the total product, it amounts to 600; a quarter of the capital expended is equal to 500, which is equal to the portion expended on wages; and 100, a quarter of the profit, which equals that part of the profit falling to this amount of wages. And this is supposed to prove that "the profits of the capitalist will vary with the varying value of this one-fourth of the[a] produce compared with the quantity of labour employed". It proves nothing more than that a profit of a given percentage, e.g. of 20 per cent, on a given capital—say of £4,000 — yields a profit of 20 per cent on each aliquot part of the capital; that is a tautology. But it proves absolutely nothing about a definite, *special*, distinguishing relationship of this profit to the part of the capital expended on wages. If, instead of [$^1/_4$] taken by Mr. Malthus, I take $^1/_{24}$ of the total product, i.e., 100 (out of 2,400), then this 100 contains 20 per cent profit, or $^1/_6$ of it is profit. The capital would be [£] $83^1/_3$ and the profit [£] $16^2/_3$. If the $83^1/_3$ were equal, for instance, to a horse which was employed in production, then it could be demonstrated according to Malthus's recipe that the profit would vary with the varying value of the horse or the $28^4/_5$ part of the total product.

Such are the wretched things Mr. Malthus comes out with when he stands on his own feet and cannot plagiarise Townsend,

---

[a] The manuscript has "his" instead of "of the".—*Ed.*

Anderson or anyone else. What is really remarkable and pertinent (apart from what is characteristic of the man) is the inkling that surplus-value must be calculated on the part of capital expended on wages.

⟨Given a definite rate of profit, the *gross profit*, the amount of profit, always depends on the size of the capital advanced. Accumulation, however, is then determined by the part of this amount which is reconverted into capital. But this part, since it is equal to the gross profit minus the revenue consumed by the capitalist, will depend not only on the value of the total profit, but on the cheapness of the commodities which the capitalist can buy with it; partly on the cheapness of the commodities which he consumes and which he pays for out of his revenue, partly on the cheapness of the commodities which enter into his constant capital. Wages here are assumed as given—since the rate of profit is likewise assumed as given.⟩

[10.] Malthus's Theory of Value [Supplementary Remarks]

The value of labour is supposed not to vary (derived from Adam Smith) but only the value of the commodities I acquire for it. Wages are, say, two shillings a day in one case, one shilling in another. In the first case, the capitalist pays out twice as many shillings for the same labour-time as in the second. But in the second case, the worker performs twice as much labour for the same product as in the first, since in the second case he works a whole day for one shilling and in the first case only half a day. Mr. Malthus believes that the capitalist pays sometimes more shillings, sometimes less, for the same labour. He does not see that the worker, correspondingly, performs either less or more labour for a given amount of produce.

"... giving more produce for a given quantity of labour, or getting more labour for a given quantity of produce, are one and the same thing in his" (Malthus's) "'view'; instead of being, as one would have supposed, just the contrary" (*Observations on Certain Verbal Disputes in Political Economy, Particularly Relating to Value, and to Demand and Supply*, London, 1821, p. 52).

It is stated very correctly in the same work (*Observations on Certain Verbal Disputes etc.*) that labour as a measure of value, in the sense in which Malthus borrows it from Adam Smith, would be just as good a measure of value as any other commodity and that it would not be so good a measure as money in fact is.

Here it would be in general a question only of a measure of value in the sense in which money is a measure of value.

||767| In general, it is never the *measure of value* (in the sense of money) which makes commodities commensurable (see Part I of my book, p. 45).[16]

"On the contrary, it is only the commensurability of commodities as materialised labour-time which converts gold into money."

Commodities as values constitute one *substance*, they are mere representations of the same substance—social labour. The *measure of value* (money) presupposes them as values and refers solely to the expression and size of this value. The *measure of value* of commodities always refers to the transformation of value into price and already presumes the value.

The passage in the *Observations* alluded to reads as follows:

Mr. Malthus says: "'In the *same* place, and at the *same* time, the different quantities of day-labour, which different commodities can command, will be exactly in proportion to their relative values in exchange', and vice versa.[17] If this is true of labour, it is just as true of anything else" (op. cit., p. 49). "Money does very well as a measure at the same time and place.... But it" (Malthus's proposition) "seems *not* to be true of labour. Labour is not a measure even at the same time and place. Take a portion of corn, such as is at the same time and place said to be of equal value with a given diamond; will the corn and the diamond, paid in specie, command equal portions of labour? It may be said [...] No; but the diamond will buy *money*, which will command an equal portion of labour ... the test is of no use, for it cannot be applied without being *rectified* by the application of the other test, which it professed to supersede. We can only infer, that the corn and the diamond will command equal quantities of labour, *because* they are of equal value, in money. But we were told to infer that two things were of equal value, because they would command equal quantities of labour" (loc. cit., pp. 49-50).

[11.] Over-Production, "Unproductive Consumers", etc.

Malthus's theory of value gives rise to the whole doctrine of the necessity for continually rising unproductive consumption which this exponent of over-population (because of shortage of food) preaches so energetically. The value of a commodity is equal to the value of the materials, machinery, etc., advanced plus the quantity of direct labour which the commodity contains; this, according to Malthus, is equal to the *value* of the wages contained in the commodity, plus a profit increment on these advances according to the general rate of profit. This nominal price increment represents the profit and is a condition of supply, and therefore of the reproduction of the commodity. These elements constitute the *price for the purchaser* as distinct from the *price for the producer*, and the price for the purchaser is the real value of the commodity. The question now arises—how is this price to be realised? Who is to pay it? And from what funds is it to be paid?

In dealing with Malthus we must make a distinction (which he has neglected to make). One section of capitalists produce goods which are *directly* consumed by the workers; another section produce either goods which are *only indirectly* consumed by them, insofar, for example, as they are part of the capital required for the production of necessaries, as raw materials, machinery, etc., or commodities which *are not consumed* by the workers *at all*, entering only into the revenue of the non-workers.

Let us first of all consider the capitalists who produce the articles which are consumed by the workers. These capitalists are not only buyers of labour, but also sellers of their own products to the workers. If the quantity of labour contributed by the worker is valued at 100 thaler the capitalist pays him 100 thaler. And this [according to Malthus] is the only value added to the raw material, etc., by the labour which the capitalist has bought. Thus the worker receives the value of his labour and only gives the capitalist an equivalent of that value in return. But although the worker nominally receives the value, he actually receives a smaller quantity of commodities than he has produced. In fact, he receives back only a part of his labour materialised in the product. Let us assume for the sake of simplicity—as Malthus does quite frequently—that capital consists only of capital laid out in wages. If 100 thaler are advanced to the worker in order to produce commodities, and these 100 thaler are the *value* of the labour purchased and the sole value which it adds to the product—then the capitalist sells these commodities for 110 thaler, and the worker, with his 100 thaler, can buy back only $^{10}/_{11}$ of the product; $^{1}/_{11}$ remains in the hands of the capitalist, to the value of 10 thaler, or the amount of surplus product in which this surplus-value of 10 thaler is embodied. If the capitalist sells the product for 120, then the worker receives only $^{10}/_{12}$ of the product and the capitalist $^{2}/_{12}$ of the product and its value. If he sells it for 130 (30 per cent), then the worker [receives] only $^{10}/_{13}$ and the capitalist $^{3}/_{13}$ of the product. If he sells it at 50 per cent profit, i.e., for 150, the worker receives $^2/_3$ and the ||768| capitalist $^1/_3$ of the product. The higher the price at which the capitalist sells, the lower the share of the worker, and the higher his own share in the value of the product and therefore also in the quantity of the product. And the less the worker can buy back of the value or of the product with the value of his labour. It makes no difference to the situation if, in addition to variable capital, constant capital is also advanced, for example, if, in addition to the 100 thaler wages, there is another 100 for raw materials, etc. In this case, if the rate of profit is 10, then the capitalist sells the goods for 220 instead of for 210 (namely, 100 constant capital and 120 the product of [direct] labour).

⟨*Sismondi's Nouveaux Principes etc.* first published in 1819.⟩

Here, as regards the *class of capitalists A*, who produce articles which are directly consumed by the workers—necessaries, we have a case where as a result of the nominal surcharge—the normal profit increment added to the price of the advances—a surplus fund is in fact created for the capitalist, since, in this roundabout way, he gives back to the worker only a part of his product while appropriating a part for himself. But this result follows not because he sells the entire product to the worker at the increased value, but precisely because the increase in the value of the product makes the worker unable to buy back the whole product with his wages, and allows him to buy back only part of it. Consequently, it is clear that demand by the workers can never suffice for the realisation of the surplus of the purchase price over and above the cost-price, i.e., the realisation of the profit and the "value" of the commodity. On the contrary, a profit fund only exists because the worker is unable to buy back his whole product with his wages, and his demand, therefore, does not correspond to the supply. Thus capitalist A has in hand a certain quantity of products of a certain value, 20 thaler in the present case, which he does not require for the replacement of the capital, and which he can now partly spend as revenue, and partly use for accumulation. N.B. The extent to which he has such a fund in hand depends on the value of the surcharge he adds over and above the cost-price and which determines the proportions in which he and the worker share the total product.

Let us now turn to the *class of capitalists B*, who supply raw materials, machinery, etc., in short constant capital, to class A. The capitalists of class B can sell *only* to class A, for they cannot sell their products back to the workers who have nothing to do with capital (raw material, machinery, etc.), or to the capitalists who produce luxury goods (all goods which are not necessaries and which are not commonly used by the labouring class), or to the capitalists who produce the constant capital required for the production of luxury goods.

Now we have seen that, in the capital advanced by A, 100 is included as constant capital. If the rate of profit is 10 per cent, the manufacturer of this constant capital has produced it at a cost-price of $90^{10}/_{11}$, but sells it for 100 ($90^{10}/_{11} : 9^{1}/_{11} = 100:10$). Thus he makes his profit by imposing a surcharge on class A. And thereby he receives from their product of 220, his 100 instead of only $90^{10}/_{11}$, with which, we will assume, he buys immediate labour. B does not by any means make his profit from his workers whose product, valued at $90^{10}/_{11}$, he cannot sell back to them for 100, because they do not buy his goods at all. Nevertheless, they are in the same position as the workers of A. For $90^{10}/_{11}$ they receive a quantity of goods which has only nominally a value of $90^{10}/_{11}$, for every part of A's product is made uniformly dearer, or each part of its value represents a smaller part of the product because of the profit surcharge.

(This surcharging can only be carried out up to a certain point, for the worker must receive enough goods to be able to live and to reproduce his labour-power. If capitalist A were to add a surcharge of 100 per cent and to sell commodities which cost 200 for 400, the worker would be able to buy back only a quarter of the product (if he receives 100). And if he needed half of the product in order to live, the capitalist would have to pay him 200. Thus he would retain only 100 (100 go to constant capital and 200 to wages). It would therefore be the same as if he sold the commodity for 300, etc.)

B makes his profit fund not (directly) through his workers, but through his sales to A. A's product not only serves to realise his profit, but constitutes his own profit fund. It is clear that A cannot realise the profit he makes on his workers by selling to B, and that B cannot provide sufficient demand for his product (enabling him to sell it at its value) any more than his own workers can. On the contrary, a retroaction takes place here. ||769| The more he raises the profit surcharge, the greater, in relation to his workers, is the portion of the total product which he appropriates and of which he deprives B.

Capitalist B adds a surcharge of the same size as A. B pays his workers $90^{10}/_{11}$ thaler as he did before, although they get less goods for this sum. But if A takes 20 per cent instead of 10 per cent, he [B] likewise takes 20 per cent instead of 10 per cent and sells for $109^1/_{11}$ instead of 100. As a result, this part of the outlay increases for A.

A and B may even be considered as a single class. (B belongs to A's expenditure and the more A has to pay to B from the total product, the less remains for him.) Out of the capital of $290^{10}/_{11}$, B owns $90^{10}/_{11}$ and A 200. Between them they expend $290\ ^{10}/_{11}$ and make a profit of $29^1/_{11}$. B can never buy back from A to the tune of more than 100 and this includes his profit of $9^1/_{11}$. As stated, both of them together have a revenue of $29^1/_{11}$.

As far as *classes C and D* are concerned, C being the capitalists who produce the constant capital necessary for the production of luxuries, and D being those who directly produce the luxuries, in the first place it is clear that the immediate demand for C is only formed by D. D is the purchaser of C. And C can only realise profit if he sells his goods to D too dearly by means of a nominal surcharge over and above the cost-price. D must pay C more than is necessary for C to replace all the constituent parts [of the cost-price] of his commodities. D for his part makes a profit surcharge partly on the advances made by C and partly on the capital expended directly on wages by D. From the profits which C makes out of D, he can buy some of the commodities made by D, although he cannot expend all his profit in this way, for he also needs necessaries for himself; and not only for workers for whom he exchanges the capital realised from D. In the first place, the realisation of the commodities by C depends directly on their sale to D; secondly, after that sale is effected, the value of the commodities sold by D cannot be realised as a result of the demand arising from C's profit, any more than the total value of A's commodities can be realised as a result of the demand coming from B. For the profit made by C is made out of D, and if C spends it again on commodities made by D instead of on others, his demand can still never be greater than the profit he makes out of D. It must always be much smaller than D's capital, than his total demand, and it never constitutes a source of profit for D (the most he can do is a little swindling of C by means of the surcharge on the goods he sells back to him) for C's profit comes straight out of D's pocket.

Further it is clear that, insofar as the capitalists—whether of class C or of D—mutually sell each other goods within each class, nobody gains anything or realises a profit thereby. A certain capitalist, M, sells to N for 110 thaler goods which cost only 100, but N does the same to M. After the exchange as before, each of them owns a quantity of goods the cost-price of which is 100. For 110 thaler each receives goods which cost only 100. The surcharge gives him no greater command over the goods of the other seller than it gives the other over his. And as far as value is concerned, it would be the same as if every M and N were to give himself the pleasure of baptising his commodities 110 instead of 100 without exchanging them at all.

It is clear further that [according to Malthus] the nominal surplus-value in D (for C is included in it) does not constitute real surplus product. The fact that the worker receives less necessaries for 100 thaler because of the surcharge imposed by A can, at first, be a matter of indifference to D. He has to expend 100 as he did before in order to employ a certain number of workers. He pays the workers the value of their labour and they add nothing more to the product, they only give him an equivalent. He can obtain a surplus over and above this equivalent only by selling to a third person and by selling his commodity above the cost-price.

In reality, the product of a mirror manufacturer [D] contains both surplus-value and surplus product just as that of the farmer. For his product contains unpaid labour (surplus-value) and this unpaid labour is embodied in the product just as much as is the paid labour. It is embodied in surplus product. One part of the mirrors costs him nothing although it has value, because labour is embodied in it in exactly the same way as in that part of the mirrors which replaces the capital advanced. This surplus-value exists as surplus product *before* the sale of the mirrors and is not [brought into being] only through this sale. If, on the contrary, the worker by his immediate labour had only provided an equivalent for the accumulated labour which he received in the form of wages, then neither ||770| the surplus product nor the surplus-value corresponding to it would exist. But according to Malthus, who declares that the worker only gives back an equivalent, things are different.

It is clear that class D (including C) cannot artificially create for itself a surplus fund in the same way as class A, namely, [by] selling their commodities back to the workers at a higher price than the workers were paid for producing them, thus appropriating part of the total product after replacing the capital expended. For the workers are not buyers of the goods made by D. No more can the surplus fund of this class [arise] from the sale of commodities or their mutual exchanges among the different capitalists of this class. It can be achieved only by the sale of their product to class A and to class B. [Because] the capitalists of class D sell commodities worth 100 thaler for 110, capitalist A can buy only $^{10}/_{11}$ of their product for 100 thaler and they retain $^{1}/_{11}$ of their output, which they can either consume themselves or exchange for commodities produced by other members of their own class D.

[According to Malthus] things happen in the following way to all capitalists who do not themselves directly produce necessaries and therefore do not sell back to the workers the major, or at least a significant, portion of their products.

Let us say that their constant capital is 100. If the capitalist pays another 100 in wages, he is paying the workers the value of their labour. To this 100 the workers add a value of 100, and the total value (the cost-price) of the product is therefore 200. Where then does the profit come from? If the average rate of profit is 10 per cent, then the capitalist sells goods worth 200 for 220. If he really sells them for 220, then it is clear that 200 is sufficient for their reproduction—100 for raw materials, etc., 100 for wages, and he pockets 20, which he can dispose of as revenue or use to accumulate capital.

But to whom does he sell the commodities at 10 per cent above their "production value", which, according to Malthus, is different from the "market value" or real value, so that profit, in fact, is equal to the difference between production value and sale value, equal to sale value minus production value? These capitalists cannot realise any profit through exchange or sale amongst themselves. If A sells B for 220 commodities worth 200, then B plays the same trick on A. The fact that these goods change hands does not alter either their value or their quantity. The quantity of goods which belonged formerly to A is now in the possession of B, and vice versa. The fact that what was previously 100 is now called 110, makes no difference. The purchasing power either of A or of B has in no way altered.

But, according to the hypothesis, these capitalists cannot sell their goods to the workers.

They must, therefore, sell them to the capitalists who produce necessaries. These, indeed, have a real surplus fund at their disposal resulting from their exchange with the workers.

The creation of a nominal surplus-value has, in fact, placed surplus product in their possession. And this is the only surplus fund which has existed up to now. The other capitalists can only acquire a surplus fund by selling their goods above their production value to those capitalists who possess a surplus fund.

As for the capitalists who produce the constant capital required for the production of necessaries, we have already seen that the producer of necessaries must perforce buy from them. These purchases enter into his production costs. The higher his profit, the dearer are the advances to which the same rate of profit is added. If he sells at 20 per cent instead of at 10 per cent, then the producer of his constant capital likewise adds 20 per cent instead of 10 per cent. And instead of demanding 100 for $90^{10}/_{11}$, he demands $109^1/_{11}$ or, in round figures, 110, so that the value of the product is now 210, 20 'per cent of which is 42, so that the value of the whole product is 252. Out of this the worker receives 100. The capitalist now receives more than $^1/_{11}$ of the total product as profit, whereas previously he received only $^1/_{11}$ when he sold the product for 220. The total amount of the product has remained the same, but the portion at the disposal of the capitalist has increased both in value and in quantity.

As for those capitalists who produce neither necessaries nor the capital required for their production, their profit [can] only be made by sales to the first two classes of capitalists. If the latter take 20 per cent, then the other capitalists will take [the same].

[Exchange by] the first class of capitalists and exchange between the two classes of capitalists are, however, two very different things. [As a result of exchange] with the workers, the first class has established a real surplus fund of necessaries (surplus product) which [as an increment] of capital is in their hands to dispose of, so that they can accumulate part of it and [spend] part of it [as revenue] either on necessaries or on luxuries. Surplus-value here, in fact, [represents] ||XIV-771| surplus labour and surplus product, although this is achieved [according to Malthus] by the clumsy, roundabout method of a surcharge on prices. Let us assume that the value of the product of the workers producing necessaries is, in fact, only equal to 100. Since, however, $^{10}/_{11}$ of this is sufficient to pay the wages, it follows that the capitalist only needs to spend $90^{10}/_{11}$, upon which he makes a profit of $9^1/_{11}$. But if he pays the workers 100 thaler and sells them the product for 110, under the illusion that value of labour and quantity of labour are identical, he still retains $1/_{11}$ of the product as he did previously. The fact that this is now worth 10 thaler instead of $9^1/_{11}$ represents no gain for him, for he has now advanced 100 thaler as capital, not $90^{10}/_{11}$.

But as far as the other classes of capitalists are concerned, they have no real surplus product, nothing in which surplus labour-time is embodied. They sell the product of labour worth 100 for 110 and merely by the addition of a surcharge this capital is supposed to be transformed into capital plus revenue.

But how stands the case now, as Lord Dundreary would say, between these two classes of capitalists?

The producers of necessaries sell surplus product[18] valued at 100 for 110 (because they paid 100 in wages instead of $90^{10}/_{11}$). But they are the only ones who have surplus product in their possession. If the other capitalists likewise sell them products valued at 100 for 110, then they do in fact replace their capital and make a profit. Why? Because necessaries to the value of 100 suffice for them to pay their workers, they can therefore keep 10 for themselves. Or rather because they in fact receive necessaries to the value of 100, but $10/_{11}$ of this is sufficient to pay their workers, since they are in the same position as capitalists in classes A and B. These, on the other hand, receive in return only an amount of produce representing a value of 100. The fact that its nominal cost is 110 is of no significance to them, for it neither embodies a greater amount quantitatively, as use-value, than was produced by the labour-time the 100 thaler contain, nor can it add 10 [thaler] to a capital of 100. This would be only possible if the commodities were resold.

Although the capitalists of both classes sell to one another for 110 commodities worth 100, only in the hands of the second class has 100 really the significance of 110. In actual fact, the capitalists of the first class only receive the value of 100 for 110. And they only sell their surplus product for a higher price because for the articles on which they spend their revenue they have to pay *more* than they are worth. In fact, however, the surplus-value realised by the capitalists of the second class is limited only to a share in the surplus product realised by the first class, for they themselves do not create any surplus product.

In connection with this increased cost of luxuries, it occurs just in time to Malthus that accumulation and not expenditure is the immediate object of capitalist production. As a result of this unprofitable trade, in the course of which the capitalists of class A lose a portion of the fruits wrung out of the workers, they are compelled to moderate their demand for luxuries. But if they do so, and increase their accumulation, then effective demand falls, the market for the necessaries they produce shrinks, and this market cannot expand to its full extent on the basis of the demand on the part of the workers and the producers of constant capital. This leads to a fall in the price of necessaries, but it is only through a rise of these prices, through the nominal surcharge on them—and in proportion to this surcharge—that the capitalists of class A are able to extract surplus product from the workers. If the price were to fall from 120 to 110, then their surplus product (and their surplus-value) would fall from $2/_{12}$ to $1/_{11}$, and consequently the market, the demand for the commodities offered by the producers of luxuries, would decline as well, and by a still greater proportion.

In the course of exchange with the second class, the first class sells real surplus product after having replaced its capital. The second class, on the other hand, merely sells its capital in order to turn its capital into capital plus revenue by this trade. The whole of production is thus only kept going (and this is especially the case with regard to its expansion) by means of *increasing the prices of necessaries*; to this, however, would correspond a price for luxuries in inverse proportion to the amount of luxuries actually produced. Class II, which sells for 110 goods of the value of 100, likewise does not gain by this exchange. For in actual fact, the 110 which it gets back is also only worth 100. But this 100 (in necessaries) replaces capital plus profit, while the other 100 [in luxuries] is merely called 110. Thus [it would] amount to class I receiving luxuries to the value of 100. It buys for 110 luxuries to the value of 100. For the other class, however, 110 is worth 110, because it pays 100 for the labour (thus replacing its capital) and therefore retains a surplus of 10.

||772| It is difficult to understand how any profit at all can be derived if those who engage in mutual exchange sell their commodities by overcharging one another at the same rate and cheating one another in the same proportion.

This incongruity would be remedied if, in addition to exchange by one class of capitalists with its workers and the mutual exchange between the capitalists of the different classes, there also existed a *third class of purchasers—a deus ex machina—*a class which paid the nominal value of commodities without itself selling any commodities, without itself playing the same trick in return; that is a class which transacted one phase only: M—C, but not M—C—M; [a class] which bought not in order to get its capital back plus a profit, but in order to consume the commodities; a class which bought without selling. In this case the capitalists would realise a profit not by exchange amongst themselves but 1) by exchange between them and the workers, by selling back to them a portion of the total product for the same amount of money as they paid the workers for the total product (after deducting the constant capital) and 2) from the portion of luxuries as well as necessaries sold to the third sort of purchaser. Since these pay 110 for 100 without selling 100 for 110 in their turn, a profit of 10 per cent would be made in actual fact and not simply nominally. The profit would be made in dual fashion by selling as little as possible of the total product back to the workers and as much as possible to the third class, who pay ready money, who, without themselves selling, buy in order to consume.

But buyers who are not at the same time sellers, must be consumers who are not at the same time producers, that is *unproductive consumers*, and it is this class of unproductive consumers which, according to Malthus, solves the problem. But these unproductive consumers must, at the same time, be consumers able to pay, constituting real demand, and the money they possess and spend annually must, moreover, suffice to pay not only the production value of the commodities they buy and consume, but also the nominal profit surcharge, the surplus-value, the difference between the market value and the production value. This class will represent consumption for consumption's sake in society, in the same way as the capitalist class represents production for production's sake, the one representing "the passion for expenditure", the other "the passion for accumulation" (see *Principles of Political Economy*, [second ed.,] p. 326). The urge for accumulation is kept alive in the capitalist class by the fact that their returns are constantly larger than their outlays, and profit is indeed the stimulus to accumulation. In spite of this enthusiasm for accumulation, they are not driven to over-production, or at least, not at all easily, since the *unproductive consumers* not only constitute a gigantic outlet for the products thrown on to the market, but do not themselves throw any commodities on to the market, and therefore, no matter how numerous they may be, they constitute no competition for the capitalists, but, on the contrary, all represent demand without supply and thus help to make up for the preponderance of supply over demand on the part of the capitalists.

But where do the annual financial resources of this class come from? There are, in the first place, the *landed proprietors*, who collect a great part of the value of the annual product under the title of rent and spend the money thus taken from the capitalists in consuming the goods produced by the capitalists, in the purchase of which they are cheated. These landed proprietors do not have to engage in production and do not on the average do so. It is significant, that insofar as they spend money on labour, they do not employ productive workers but *menial servants*, mere fellow-consumers of their fortune, who help to keep the prices of necessaries up, since they buy without helping to increase their supply or the supply of any other kind of commodity. But these landed proprietors do not suffice to create "an adequate demand". Artificial means must be resorted to. These consist of heavy *taxation*, of a mass of sinecurists in State and Church, of large armies, pensions, tithes for the priests, an impressive national debt, and from time to time, expensive wars. These are the "remedies" (*Principles of Political Economy*, [second ed.,] p. 408 et seq.).

The third class, proposed by Malthus as a "remedy", the class which buys without selling and consumes without producing, thus receives first of all an important part of the value of the annual product *without paying for it* and enriches the producers by the fact that the latter must first of all advance the third class money gratis for the purchase of their commodities, in order to draw it back again ||773| by selling the third class commodities above their value, or by receiving more value in money than is embodied in the commodities they supply to this class. And this transaction is repeated every year.

[12. The Social Essence of Malthus's Polemic Against Ricardo. Malthus's Distortion of Sismondi's Views on the Contradictions in Bourgeois Production]

Malthus correctly draws the conclusions from his basic theory of value. But this theory, for its part, suits his purpose remarkably well—an apologia for the existing state of affairs in England, for landlordism, "State and Church", pensioners, tax-gatherers, tenths, national debt, stock-jobbers, beadles, parsons and menial servants ("national expenditure") assailed by the Ricardians as so many useless and superannuated drawbacks of bourgeois production and as nuisances. For all that, Ricardo championed bourgeois production insofar as it [signified] the most unrestricted development of the social productive forces, unconcerned for the fate of those who participate in production, be they capitalists or workers. He insisted upon the *historical* justification and necessity of this stage of development. His very lack of a historical sense of the past meant that he regarded everything from the historical standpoint of his time. Malthus also wishes to see the freest possible development of capitalist production, however only insofar as the condition of this development is the poverty of its main basis, the working classes, but at the same time he wants it to adapt itself to the "consumption needs" of the aristocracy and its branches in State and Church, to serve as the material basis for the antiquated claims of the representatives of interests inherited from feudalism and the absolute monarchy. Malthus wants bourgeois production as long as it is not revolutionary, constitutes no historical factor of development but merely creates a broader and more comfortable material basis for the "old" society.

On the one hand, therefore, [there is] the working class, which, according to the population principle, is always redundant in relation to the means of life available to it, over-population arising from under-production; then [there is] the capitalist class, which, as a result of this population principle, is always able to sell the workers' own product back to them at such prices that they can only obtain enough to keep body and soul together; then [there is] an enormous section of society consisting of parasites and gluttonous drones, some of them masters and some servants, who appropriate, partly under the title of rent and partly under political titles, a considerable mass of wealth gratis from the capitalists, whose commodities they pay for above their value with money extracted from these same capitalists; the capitalist class, driven into production by the urge for accumulation, the economically unproductive sections representing prodigality, the mere urge for consumption. This is moreover [advanced as] the only way to avoid over-production, which exists alongside over-population in relation to production. The best remedy for both [is declared to be] over-consumption by the classes standing outside production. The disproportion between the labouring population and production is eliminated by part of the product being devoured by non-producers and idlers. The disproportion arising from over-production by the capitalists [is eliminated] by means of over-consumption by the owners of wealth.

We have seen how childishly weak, trivial and meaningless Malthus is when, basing himself on the weak side of Adam Smith, he seeks to construct a counter-theory to Ricardo's theory, which is based on Adam Smith's stronger sides. One can hardly find a more comical exertion of impotence than Malthus's book on value. However, as soon as he comes to practical conclusions and thereby once again enters the field which he occupies as a kind of economic Abraham a Santa Clara, he is quite at his ease. For all that, he does not abandon his innate plagiarism even here. Who at first glance would believe that Malthus's *Principles of Political Economy* is simply the Malthusianised translation of Sismondi's *Nouveaux Principes d'économie politique*? But this is the case. Sismondi's book appeared in 1819. A year later, Malthus's English caricature of it saw the light of day. Once again, with Sismondi, as previously with Townsend and Anderson, he found a theoretical basis for one of his stout economic pamphlets, in the production of which, incidentally, he also turned to advantage the new theories learned from Ricardo.

||774| While Malthus assailed in Ricardo that tendency of capitalist production which is revolutionary in relation to the old society, he took, with unerring parsonical instinct, only that out of Sismondi which is reactionary in relation to capitalist production and modern bourgeois society.

I exclude Sismondi from my historical survey here because a critique of his views belongs to a part of my work dealing with the real movement of capital (competition and credit) which I can only tackle after I have finished this book.

Malthus's adaptation of Sismondi's views can easily be seen from the heading of one of the chapters in the *Principles of Political Economy*:

"Of the Necessity of a Union of the Powers of Production with the Means of Distribution, in order to ensure a continued Increase of Wealth" ([second ed.,] p. 361).

[In this chapter it is stated:]

"... the powers of production [...] not alone [...] secure the creation of a proportionate degree of wealth. Something else seems to be necessary in order to call these powers fully into action. This is an effectual and unchecked demand for all that is produced. And what appears to contribute most to the attainment of this object, is, such a *distribution of produce*, and such an adaptation of this produce to the wants of those who are to consume it, as constantly to increase the exchangeable value of the whole mass" (*Principles of Political Economy*, [second ed.,] p. 361).

Furthermore, written in the same Sismondian manner and directed against Ricardo:

"... the *wealth* of a country depends partly upon the *quantity of produce* obtained by its labour, and partly upon such an adaptation of this quantity to the wants and powers of the existing population as is calculated to give it *value*. Nothing can be more certain than that it is not determined by either of them alone" (op. cit., p. 301).

"But where wealth and value are perhaps the most nearly connected, is in the *necessity of the latter to the production of the former* (loc. cit., p. 301).

This is aimed especially against Ricardo: Chapter XX, "*Value and Riches, Their Distinctive Properties*" [*On the Principles of Political Economy, and Taxation*, third ed., London, 1821, p. 320]. There Ricardo says, among other things:

"Value, then, essentially differs from riches, for value depends not on abundance, but on the difficulty or facility of production."

⟨Value, incidentally, can also increase with "the facility of production". Let us suppose that the number of men in a country rises from one million to six million. The million men worked 12 hours. The six million have so developed the productive powers that each of them produces as much again in 6 hours. In these circumstances, according to Ricardo's own views, wealth would have been increased sixfold and value threefold.⟩

"... riches do not depend on value. A man is rich or poor, according to the abundance of necessaries and luxuries which he can command.... It is through confounding the ideas of value and wealth, or riches that it has been asserted, that by diminishing the quantity of commodities, that is to say of the necessaries, conveniences, and enjoyments of human life, riches may be increased. If value were the measure of riches, this could not be denied, because by scarcity the value of commodities is raised; but ... if riches consist in necessaries and enjoyments, then they cannot be increased by a diminution of quantity" (op. cit., pp. 323-24).

In other words, Ricardo says here: wealth consists of *use-values* only. He transforms bourgeois production into mere production of use-value, a very pretty view of a mode of production which is dominated by *exchange-value*. He regards the specific form of bourgeois wealth as something merely formal which does not affect its content. He therefore also denies the contradictions of bourgeois production which break out in crises.

Hence his quite false conception of money. Hence, in considering the production process of capital, he ignores completely the circulation process, insofar as it includes the metamorphosis of commodities, the necessity of the transformation of capital into money. At any rate nobody has better and more precisely than Ricardo elaborated the point that bourgeois production is not production of wealth for the *producers* (as he repeatedly calls the workers) and that therefore the production of bourgeois wealth is something quite different from the production of "abundance", of "necessaries and luxuries" for the men who produce them, as this would have to be the case if production were only a means for satisfying the needs of the producers through production dominated by use-value alone. Nevertheless, the same Ricardo says:

"If we lived in one of Mr. Owen's parallelograms,[19] and enjoyed all our productions in common, then no one could suffer in consequence of abundance, but *as long as society is constituted as it now is*, abundance will often be injurious to producers, and scarcity beneficial to them" ([Ricardo], *On Protection to Agriculture*, fourth ed., London, 1822, p. 21).

||775| Ricardo regards bourgeois, or more precisely, capitalist production as the *absolute form* of production, whose specific forms of production relations can therefore never enter into contradiction with, or enfetter, the aim of production—abundance—which includes both mass and variety of use-values, and which in turn implies a profuse development of man as producer, an all-round development of his productive capacities. And this is where he lands in an amusing contradiction: when we are speaking of value and riches, we should have only society as a whole in mind. But when we speak of capital and labour, then it is self-evident that "gross revenue" only exists in order to create "net revenue". In actual fact, what he admires most about bourgeois production is that its definite forms—compared with previous forms of production—provide scope for the boundless development of the productive forces. When they cease to do this, or when contradictions appear within which they do this, he denies the contradictions, or rather, expresses the contradiction in another form by representing *wealth as such*—the mass of use-values in itself—without regard to the producers, as the *ultima Thule*.

Sismondi is profoundly conscious of the contradictions in capitalist production; he is aware that, on the one hand, its forms—its production relations—stimulate unrestrained development of the productive forces and of wealth; and that, on the other hand, these relations are conditional, that their contradictions of use-value and exchange-value, commodity and money, purchase and sale, production and consumption, capital and wage-labour, etc., assume ever greater dimensions as productive power develops. He is particularly aware of the fundamental contradiction: on the one hand, unrestricted development of the productive forces and increase of wealth which, at the same time, consists of commodities and must be turned into cash; on the other hand, the system is based on the fact that the mass of producers is restricted to the necessaries. Hence, according to Sismondi, crises are not accidental, as Ricardo maintains, but essential outbreaks—occurring on a large scale and at definite periods—of the immanent contradictions. He wavers constantly: should the State curb the productive forces to make them adequate to the production relations, or should the production relations be made adequate to the productive forces? He often retreats into the past, becomes a *laudator temporis acti*,[a] or he seeks to exorcise the contradictions by a different adjustment of revenue in relation to captial, or of distribution in relation to production, not realising that the relations of distribution are only the relations of production seen from a different aspect. He forcefully *criticises* the contradictions of bourgeois production but does not *understand* them, and consequently does not understand the process whereby they can be resolved. However, at the bottom of his argument is indeed the inkling that *new* forms of the appropriation of wealth must correspond to productive forces and the material and social conditions for the production of wealth which have developed within capitalist society; that the bourgeois forms are only transitory and contradictory forms, in which wealth attains only an antithetical existence and appears everywhere simultaneously as its opposite. It is wealth which always has poverty as its prerequisite and only develops by developing poverty as well.

We have now seen how nicely Malthus appropriates Sismondi. Malthus's theory is expressed in an exaggerated and even more nauseating form in *On Political Economy in connexion with the Moral State and Moral Prospects of Society*, second ed., London, 1832, by *Thomas Chalmers (Professor of Divinity)*. Here the parsonic element is more in evidence not only theoretically

---

[a] Eulogiser of the past (Horace, *Ars poetica*).—*Ed.*

but also practically, since this member of the Established Church defends it "economically" with its "loaves and fishes" and the whole complex of institutions with which this Church stands or falls.

The passages in Malthus (referred to above) having reference to the workers are the following:

"... the consumption and demand occasioned by the workmen employed in productive labour can never *alone* furnish a motive to the accumulation and employment of capital" (*Principles of Political Economy*, [London, 1836,] p. 315).

"No farmer will take the trouble of superintending the labour of ten additional men merely because his whole produce will then sell in the market at an advanced price just equal to what he had paid his additional labourers. There must be something in the previous state of the demand and supply of the commodity in question, or in its price, antecedent to and independent of the demand occasioned by the new labourers, in order to warrant the employment of an additional number of people in its production" (op. cit., p. 312).

"The demand created by the productive labourer himself can never be an *adequate* demand, ||776| because it does not go to the *full extent of what he produces. If it did, there would be no profit*, consequently no motive to employ him. The very *existence of a profit upon any commodity* presupposes a demand *exterior* to that of the labour which has produced it" (op. cit., p. 405, note).

"... as a great increase of consumption among the working classes must greatly increase the cost of production, it must lower profits, and diminish or destroy the motive to accumulate..." (loc. cit., p. 405).

"It is the *want of necessaries* which mainly stimulates the labouring[a] classes to produce luxuries; and were this stimulus removed or greatly weakened, so that the necessaries of life could be obtained with very little labour, instead of more time being devoted to the production of conveniences, there is every reason to think that less time would be so devoted" (op cit., p. 334).

Malthus is interested not in concealing the contradictions of bourgeois production, but on the contrary, in emphasising them, on the one hand, in order to prove that the poverty of the working classes is necessary (as it is, indeed, for this mode of production) and, on the other hand, to demonstrate to the capitalists the necessity for a well-fed Church and State hierarchy in order to create an adequate demand for the commodities they produce. He thus shows that for "... continued increase[b] of wealth" [op. cit., p. 314] neither increase of population nor accumulation of capital suffices (op. cit., pp. 319-20), nor "fertility of the soil"

---

[a] In the manuscript "working" instead of "labouring".—*Ed.*
[b] "Progress" instead of "increase" in the manuscript.—*Ed.*

(op. cit., p. 331), nor "labour-saving inventions", nor the extension of the "foreign markets" (op. cit., pp. 352 and 359).

"... both labourers and capital may be redundant, compared with the means of employing them profitably" (op. cit., p. 414 [note]).

Thus he emphasises the possibility of general over-production in opposition to the view of the Ricardians (inter alia op. cit., p. 326).

The principal propositions dealing with this matter are the following:

"... demand is always determined by *value*, and supply by *quantity*" (op. cit., p. 316, note).

Commodities are exchanged not only for commodities but also for productive labour and personal services and in relation to them, and also to money, there can be a general glut of commodities[a] (loc. cit.).

"... supply must always be proportioned to *quantity*, and demand to *value*" *(Definitions in Political Economy*, ed. by John Cazenove, London, 1853, p. 65 [note]).

"'It is evident,' says James Mill 'that whatever a man has produced, and does not wish to keep for his own consumption, is a stock which he may give in exchange for other commodities. His will, therefore, to purchase, and his means of purchasing, in other words, his demand, is [...] equal to the amount of what he has produced, and does not mean to consume.' ... It is quite obvious" [answers Malthus] "that his means of purchasing other commodities are not proportioned to the *quantity* of his own commodity which he has produced, and wishes to part with; but to its *value in exchange*; and unless the value of a commodity in exchange be proportioned to its quantity, it cannot be true that the demand and supply of every individual are always equal to one another" (loc. cit., pp. 64-65).

"If the demand of every individual were equal to his supply, in the correct sense of the expression, it would be a proof that he could always sell his commodity for the costs of production, including fair profits; and then even a *partial* glut would be impossible. The argument proves too much ... supply must always be proportioned to *quantity*, and demand to *value*" *(Definitions in Political Economy*, London, 1827, p. 48, note).

Here, by demand Mill understands the "means of purchasing" of the person who demands. But "... his[b] means of purchasing other commodities are not proportioned to the *quantity* of his own commodity which he has produced, and wishes to part with; but to its *value in exchange*; and unless the value of a commodity in exchange be proportioned to its quantity, it cannot be true that the demand and supply of every individual are always equal to one another" (loc. cit., pp. 48-49).

"It is still further from the truth"[c] for Torrens to say "'that increased supply is the one and only cause of increased effectual demand' [...]. If

---

[a] Marx summarises here the contents of a paragraph from Malthus's book *Principles of Political Economy*, London, 1836, p. 316.—*Ed.*

[b] In the manuscript "these" instead of "his".—*Ed.*

[c] In the manuscript "It is wrong" instead of "It is still further from the truth".—*Ed.*

it were, how difficult would it be for a society[a] to recover itself, under a temporary diminution of food and clothing. But [...][b] food and clothing [...] diminished in quantity will rise in value [...] the money-price of the remaining food and clothing will for a time rise in a greater degree than [in proportion to] the diminution of its quantity, while the money-price of labour may remain the same. The necessary consequence [...] the power of setting in motion a greater quantity of productive industry than before" (op. cit., pp. 59-60).

All a nation's commodities may fall compared with money or labour (op. cit., p. 64 et seq.). Thus a general glut of the market is possible (loc. cit.). Their prices can all fall below their production costs (loc. cit.).[c]

* * *

||777| For the rest, only the following passage from Malthus, which deals with the circulation process, need be noted.

"... if we reckon the value of the fixed capital employed as a part of the advances, we must reckon the remaining value of such capital at the end of the year as a part of the annual returns ... in reality his" (the capitalist's) "*annual advances consist only* of his circulating capital, the wear and tear of his fixed capital with the interest upon it, and the interest of that part of his circulating capital which consists of the money employed in making his annual payments as they are called for" (*Principles of Political Economy*, [second ed., London, 1836,] p. 269).

The *sinking fund*, i.e., the fund for wear and tear of the fixed capital, is, in my opinion, at the same time a fund for accumulation.

[13. Critique of Malthus's Conception of "Unproductive Consumers" by Supporters of Ricardo]

I wish to quote yet a few passages from a Ricardian book directed against Malthus's theory. As regards the attacks from the capitalist point of view which are made in the book against Malthus's unproductive consumers in general and landlords in particular I shall demonstrate elsewhere that they can be used word for word against the capitalists from the workers' standpoint. (This is to be included in the section "The Relationship Between Capital and Wage-Labour Presented from an Apologetic Standpoint".[20])

[An anonymous follower of Ricardo writes:]

---

[a] "Mankind" instead of "Society" in the manuscript.—*Ed.*
[b] In the manuscript "when" instead of the omitted words.—*Ed.*
[c] In this paragraph Marx paraphrases some of the ideas expressed by Malthus in his book *Definitions in Political Economy*, London, 1827, p. 64 et seq.—*Ed.*

"Considering, that an increased employment of capital will not take place unless a rate of profits equal to the former rate, or greater than it, can be ensured, and considering, that the mere addition to capital does not of itself tend to ensure such a rate of profits, but the reverse, Mr. Malthus, and those who reason in the same manner as he does, proceed to look out for some source, independent of and extrinsic to production itself, whose progressive increase may keep pace with the progressive increase of capital, and from which continual additional supplies of the requisite rate of profits may be derived" (*An Inquiry into those Principles, respecting the Nature of Demand and the Necessity of Consumption, lately advocated by Mr. Malthus etc.*, London, 1821, pp. 33-34).

According to Malthus, the "unproductive consumers" are such a source (loc. cit., p. 35).

"Mr. Malthus sometimes talks as if there were two *distinct funds*, capital and revenue, supply and demand, production and consumption, which must take care to keep pace with each other, and neither outrun the other. As if, *besides the whole mass of commodities produced*, there was required another mass, fallen from Heaven, I suppose, to purchase them with.... The fund for consumption, such as he requires, can only be had at the expense of production" (op. cit., pp. 49-50).

"We are continually puzzled, in his" (Malthus's) "speculations, between the object of increasing production and that of checking it. When a man is in want of a *demand*, does Mr. Malthus recommend him to pay some other person to take off his goods? Probably not" (op. cit., p. 55). Certainly yes.

"The object of selling your goods is to make a certain amount of money; it never can answer to part with that amount of money for nothing, to another person, that he may bring it back to you, and buy your goods with it: you might as well have just burnt your goods at once, and you would have been in the same situation" (op. cit., p. 63).

[He is] right in regard to Malthus. But because it is one and the same fund—"the whole mass of commodities produced"— which constitutes the production fund and the consumption fund, the fund of supply and the fund of demand, the fund of capital and the fund of revenue, it does not by any means follow that it is irrelevant how the total fund is divided between these various categories.

The anonymous author does not understand what Malthus means when he speaks of the "demand" of the workers being "inadequate" for the capitalist.

"... as to the *demand* from labour; that is, either the giving labour in exchange for goods, or ... in exchange[a] for present complete products, a future and accruing addition of value.... This is the real demand that it is material to the producers to get increased" (op. cit., p. 57).

What Malthus means is not the *offer of labour* (which our author calls *demand from labour*) but the demand for commodities

---

[a] In the manuscript "or ... the giving in exchange" instead of "or ... in exchange".—*Ed.*

which the wages the worker receives enable him to make, the money with which the worker buys commodities on the market. And Malthus rightly says of this demand that it can never be adequate to the supply of the capitalist. Otherwise the worker would be able to buy back the whole of his product with his wages.

||778| The same writer says:

"... the very meaning of an increased demand by them" (the labourers) "is a disposition to take less themselves, and leave a larger share for their employers; and if it be said[a] that this, by diminishing consumption, increases glut, I can only answer, that glut [...] is synonymous with high profits" (op. cit., p. 59).

This is meant to be witty, but in fact it contains the essential secret of "glut".

In connection with Malthus's *Essay on Rent*,[21] our author says:

"When Mr. Malthus published his *Essay on Rent*, it seems to have been partly with a view to answer the cry of 'No Landlords', which then 'stood rubric on the walls', to stand up in defence of that class, and to prove that they were not like *monopolists*. That rent cannot be abolished, that its increase is a natural concomitant, in general, of increasing wealth and numbers, he shewed; but neither did the vulgar cry of 'No Landlords' necessarily mean that there ought to be *no such thing* as rent, but rather that it ought to be equally divided among the people, according to what was called 'Spence's plan'.[22] But when he proceeds to vindicate landlords from the odious name of monopolists, from the observation of Smith, 'that they love to reap where they never sowed', he seems to be fighting for a *name*.... There is too much the air of an *advocate* in all these arguments of his" (op. cit., pp. 108-09).

[14. The Reactionary Role of Malthus's Writings and Their Plagiaristic Character. Malthus's Apologia for the Existence of "Upper" and "Lower" Classes]

Malthus's book *On Population* was a lampoon directed against the French Revolution and the contemporary ideas of reform in England (Godwin, etc.). It was an apologia for the poverty of the working classes. The *theory* was plagiarised from Townsend and others.

His *Essay on Rent* was a piece of polemic writing in support of the landlords against industrial capital. Its *theory* was taken from Anderson.

His *Principles of Political Economy* was a polemic work written in the interests of the capitalists against the workers and in

---

[a] In the manuscript "if it is said".—*Ed.*

the interests of the aristocracy, Church, tax-eaters, toadies, etc., against the capitalists. Its *theory* was taken from Adam Smith. Where he inserts his own inventions, it is pitiable. It is on Sismondi that he bases himself in further elaborating the theory. |XIV-778||

* * *

||VIII-345| {*Malthus* makes the following remarks, laced with his usual "profound philosophy", against any plan to provide the cottagers of England with cows (in the French translation of his *An Essay on the Principles of Population*, fifth ed., translated by P. Prévost, Genève, 1836, troisième éd., t. IV, pp. 104-05):

"It has been observed that those *cottagers*, who keep cows, are more industrious and more regular in their conduct, than those who do not.... Most of those who keep cows at present have purchased them with the fruits of their own industry. It is therefore more just to say that their industry has given them a cow, than that a cow has given them their industry" [Malthus, *An Essay on the Principles of Population*, fifth ed., Vol. 2, London, 1817, pp. 296-97].

And it is therefore correct that diligence in labour (together with the exploitation of other people's labour) has given cows to the parvenus amongst the bourgeoisie, while the cows give their sons the taste for idleness. If one took away from their cows not the ability to give milk, but to command other people's unpaid labour, it would be a very good thing for their taste for labour.

The selfsame "profound philosopher" remarks:

"But it is evident that all cannot be in the middle. Superior and inferior parts are in the nature of things absolutely necessary; and [...]" (naturally there can be no mean without extremes) "strikingly beneficial. If no man could hope to rise, or fear to fall in society; if industry did not bring with it its reward, and indolence its punishment; we could not expect to see that animated activity in bettering our condition, which now forms the masterspring ||346| of public prosperity" ([Malthus, *Principles of Population*, p. 303,] Prévost, p. 112).

Thus there must be lower classes in order that the upper ones may fear to fall and there must be upper classes in order that the lower ones may hope to rise. In order that indolence may carry its own punishment, the worker must be poor and the rentier and the landlord, so beloved of Malthus, must be rich. But what does Malthus mean by the reward of industry? As we shall see later, he means that the worker must perform part of his labour without an equivalent return. A wonderful stimulus, provided the "reward" and not hunger were the stimulus. What it all boils down to is that a worker may hope to exploit other workers some day.

Rousseau says: "The more monopoly spreads, the heavier do the chains become for the exploited."

Malthus, "the profound thinker", has different views. His supreme hope, which he himself describes as more or less utopian, is that the mass of the middle class should grow and that the proletariat (those who work) should constitute a constantly declining proportion (even though it increases absolutely) of the total population. This in fact is the *course* taken by bourgeois society.

"We might even venture," says Malthus, "to indulge a hope that at some future period the processes for abridging human labour, the progress of which has of late years been so rapid, might ultimately supply all the wants of the most wealthy society with less personal effort than at present; and *if they did not diminish the severity of individual exertion*" (he must go on risking just as much as before, and relatively more and more for others and less and less for himself), "might, at least, diminish the *number of those* employed in severe toil" ([Malthus, *Principles of Population*, p. 304,] Prévost, p. 113).} |VIII-346||

[15. Malthus's Principles Expounded in the Anonymous "Outlines of Political Economy"]

||XIV-778| A book in which Malthus's principles are elaborated is *Outlines of Political Economy; being a Plain and Short View of the Laws relating to the Production, Distribution, and Consumption of Wealth etc.*, London, 1832.

First of all the author[a] explains the practical reasons governing the opposition of the Malthusians to the determination of value by labour-time.

"That labour is the sole source of wealth seems to be a doctrine as dangerous as it is false, as it unhappily affords a handle to those who would represent all property as belonging to the working classes, and the share which is received by others as a robbery or fraud upon them" ([John Cazenove, *Outlines of Political Economy*, London, 1832,] p. 22, note).

In the following sentence it emerges more clearly than in Malthus that the author confuses the *value* of commodities with the *utilisation* of commodities, or of money as capital. In the latter sense it correctly expresses the origin of surplus-value.

---

[a] John Cazenove.—*Ed.*

"The *value of capital*, the quantity of labour which it is worth or will command, is [...] always greater than that which it has cost, and the difference constitutes the profit or remuneration to its owner" (op. cit., p. 32).

The following, too, which is taken from Malthus, is correct as an explanation of why profit is to be reckoned as part of the *production costs* of capitalist production:

"... profit upon the capital employed" 〈"unless this profit were obtained, there would be no adequate motive to produce the commodity"〉 "is an essential condition of the supply, and, as such, constitutes a component part of the *costs of production*" (loc. cit., p. 33).

In the following passage we have, on the one hand, the correct statement that profit directly arises out of the exchange of capital for labour, and on the other hand, the Malthusian thesis that profit is made in *selling*.

"... a man's profit does not depend upon his command of the *produce* of other men's labour, but upon his command of *labour itself*." (Here the correct distinction is made between the exchange of one commodity for another and the exchange of the commodity as capital for labour.) "If" (when the *value of money* falls) "he ||779| can sell his goods at a higher price, *while his workmen's wages remain unaltered*, he is clearly benefited by the rise, whether other goods rise or not. A smaller proportion of what he produces is sufficient to put that labour into motion, and a larger proportion consequently remains for himself" (op. cit., pp. 49-50).

The same thing happens when, for example, as a result of the introduction of new machinery, chemical processes, etc., the capitalist produces commodities below their old value and either sells them at their old value or, at any rate, above the individual value to which they have fallen. It is true that when this happens, the worker does not directly work a shorter period for himself and a longer one for the capitalist, but in the reproduction process, "a smaller proportion of what he produces is sufficient to put that labour into motion". In actual fact, the worker therefore exchanges a greater part of his immediate labour than previously for his own realised labour. For example, he continues to receive what he received previously, £10. But this £10, although it represents the same amount of labour to society, is no longer the product of the *same amount of labour-time* as previously, but may represent one hour less. So that, in fact the worker works longer for the capitalist and a shorter period for himself. It is as if he received only £8, which, however, represented the same mass of use-values as a result of the increased productivity of his labour.

The author remarks in connection with [James] Mill's arguments regarding the identity of demand and supply, discussed earlier[23]:

"The supply of each man depends upon the *quantity* which he brings to market: his demand for other things depends upon the *value* of his supply. The former is certain; it depends upon himself: the latter is uncertain; it depends upon others. The former may remain the same, whilst the latter may vary. A hundred quarters of corn, which a man brings to market, may at one time be worth thirty shillings, and at another time sixty shillings, the quarter. The *quantity or supply* is in both instances the same; but the man's demand or power of purchasing other things is twice as great in the latter as in the former case" (op. cit., pp. 111-12).

About the relationship of labour and machinery, the author writes the following:

"... when commodities are multiplied by a more judicious distribution of labour, no greater amount of demand than before is required in order to maintain all the labour which was previously employed;"

(How so? If the distribution of labour is more judicious, more commodities will be produced by the same labour; hence the supply will grow, and does its absorption not require an increased amount of demand? Does Adam Smith not rightly say that division of labour depends upon the extent of the market? In actual fact, the difference as regards demand from outside is the same except [that demand] on a larger scale [is required] when machinery is used. But "a more judicious distribution of labour" may require the same or even a greater number of labourers than before, while the introduction of machinery must under all circumstances diminish the proportion of capital laid out in immediate labour)

"whereas, when machinery is introduced, if there be not an increased amount of demand, or a fall in wages or profits, *some of the labour will undoubtedly be thrown out of employment* [....] let the case be supposed of a commodity worth £1,200, of which £1,000 consists of the wages of 100 men, at £10 each, and £200 of profits, at the rate of 20 per cent. Now, let it be imagined that the same commodity can be produced by the labour of 50 men, and a machine which has cost the labour of 50 men, and which requires the labour of 10 men to keep it in constant repair; the producer will then be able to reduce the price of the article to £800, and still continue to obtain the same remuneration for the use of his capital [....]

The wages of 50 men at £10, are £500
[The wages] of £10 to keep^a [the machine] in repair..........£100
Profit 20 per cent
    on circulating capital............................£500 } £200
    [...] on fixed capital............ ....£500 }
                    [Total]   £800"
                (op. cit., pp. 114-15).

---

^a In the manuscript "10 men to keep it" instead of "£10 to keep".—*Ed.*

⟨(The "10 men to keep it in [...] repair" represent here the annual wear and tear. Otherwise the calculation would be wrong, since the labour of repairing would then have to be added to the original production costs of the machinery.) Previously the manufacturer had to lay out £1,000 annually, but the product was [worth] £1,200. Now he has laid out £500 on machinery once and for all; he has not therefore to lay out this sum again in any other way. What he has to lay out is £100 annually for repairs and £500 in wages (since there are no raw materials in this example). He has to lay out only £600 per annum, but he makes a profit of £200 on his total capital just as he did previously. The amount and rate of profit remain the same as they were before. But his annual product amounts to only £800.⟩

"Those who used to pay £1,200 for the commodity will now have £400 to spare, which they can lay out either on something else, or in purchasing more of the same commodity. If it be laid out in ||780| the *produce* of immediate labour, it will give employment to no more than 33.4 men, whereas the number thrown out of employment by the introduction of the machine will have been 40, for—

The wages of 33.4 men at £10, are	£334
Profits 20 per cent	£ 66
Total	£400"

(loc. cit., pp. 114-16).

⟨In other words this means: If the £400 is expended on commodities which are the product of immediate labour and if the wages per man equal £10, then the commodities which cost £400 must be the product of less than 40 men. If they were the product of 40 men, then they would contain only *paid labour*. The value of labour (or the quantity of labour embodied in the wages) would be equal to the value of the product (the quantity of labour embodied in the commodity). But the commodities worth £400 contain *unpaid* labour, which is precisely what constitutes the profit. They must therefore be the product of less than 40 men. If the profit is 20 per cent. then only ⅚ of the product can consist of paid labour, that is, approximately £334 or 33.4 men at £10 per man. The other sixth, roughly £66, represents the unpaid labour. Ricardo himself has shown in exactly the same way that machinery itself, when its money price is as high as the price of the immediate labour it displaces, can never be the product of so much labour.[24]⟩

"If it" (i.e., the £400) "be laid out in the purchase of more of the same commodity, or of any other, where the same species and quantity of fixed capital were used, it would employ only 30 men, for—

The wages of 25 men at £10 each, are	£250
[The wages of] 5 men [at £10 each] to keep [it] in repair	£50
Profits on £250 circulated and £250 fixed capital . . .	£100
	£400"

(loc. cit., p. 116).

⟨That is to say, in the case where machinery is introduced, the production of commodities costing £800 involves an outlay of £500 on machinery. Thus for the production of £400 [worth of commodities] only £250 [is spent on machinery]. Furthermore, 50 workers are needed to operate machinery worth £500, therefore 25 workers ([their wages] amounting to £250) for machinery worth £250; further for repair (the maintenance of the machine) 10 men are needed if the machinery costs £500, consequently 5 men ([whose wages] come to £50) are needed for machinery costing £250. Thus [we have] £250 fixed capital and £250 circulating capital—a total of £500, on which there is a profit of 20 per cent amounting to £100. The product is therefore [made up of] £300 wages and £100 profit—£400. Thirty workers are employed in producing the commodities. Here it has been assumed all along that the capitalist who manufactures the commodities either borrows capital out of the (£400) savings which the consumers have deposited at the bank, or that—apart from the £400 which have been saved from the revenue of the consumers—he himself possesses capital. For clearly with a capital of £400 he cannot lay out £250 on machinery and £300 on wages.⟩

"When the total sum of £1,200 was spent on the produce of immediate labour, the division was £1,000 wages, £200 profits" (100 workers whose wages come to £1,000). "When it was spent partly in the one way and partly in the other ... the division was £934 wages and £266 profits" (i.e., 60 workers in the machine shop and 33.4 immediate labour making a total of 93.4 workers, whose wages come to £934), "and, as in the third supposition, when the whole sum was spent on the joint produce of the machine and labour, the division was £900 wages" (i.e., 90 workers) "and £300 profits" (loc. cit., pp. 114-17 [passim]).

||781| After the introduction [of the machine] the capitalist "certainly cannot employ as much labour as he did before, without accumulating further capital; but [...] the revenue which is saved by the consumers of the article after its price has fallen, will, by increasing their consumption of that or something else, create a demand for *some* though not for *all* the labour which has been displaced by the machine" (op. cit., p. 119 [note]).

"Mr. McCulloch [...] conceives that the introduction of machines into any employment *necessarily occasions an equal or greater demand for the disengaged labourers in some other employment.* [...] In order to prove this, he supposes that the annuity necessary to replace the value of the machine by the time it is worn out, will every year occasion an increasing demand for labour. But as the successive annuities added together up to the end of the term, can only equal the original cost of the machine, and the interest upon it during the time it is in operation, in what way it can ever create a demand for labour, beyond what it would have done had no machine been employed, it is not easy to understand" (loc. cit., pp. 119-20 [note]).

The sinking fund itself can, indeed, be used for accumulation in the interval when the wear and tear of the machine is shown in the books, but does not actually affect its work. But in any case, the demand for labour created in this way is much smaller than if the whole capital invested in machinery were laid out in wages, instead of merely the annual wear and tear. MacPeter is an ass—as always. This passage is only noteworthy, because it contains the idea that the sinking fund is itself a fund for accumulation.

[CHAPTER XX]

DISINTEGRATION OF THE RICARDIAN SCHOOL

1. [Robert Torrens]

[a) Smith and Ricardo on the Relation Between the Average Rate of Profit and the Law of Value]

||782| Robert Torrens, *An Essay on the Production of Wealth etc.*, London, 1821.

Observation of competition—the phenomena of production—shows that capitals of equal size yield an equal amount of profit on the average, or that, given the average rate of profit (and the term, average rate of profit, has no other meaning), the amount of profit depends on the amount of capital advanced.

Adam Smith has noted this fact. Its connection with the theory of value which he put forward caused him no pangs of conscience—especially since in addition to what one might call his esoteric theory, he advanced many others, and could recall one or another at his pleasure. The sole reflection to which this question gives rise is his polemic against the view which seeks to resolve profit into "wages of superintendence", since, apart from any other circumstance, the work of superintendence does not increase in the same measure as the scale of production and, moreover, the value of the capital advanced can increase, for instance, as a result of the dearness of raw materials, without a corresponding growth in the scale of production.[25] He has no immanent law to determine the *average profit* or its amount. He merely says that competition reduces this x.

Ricardo (apart from a few merely chance remarks) directly identifies profit with surplus-value everywhere. Hence with him, commodities sell at a *profit* not because they are sold *above* their value, but because they are sold *at their value*. Nevertheless, in considering *value* (in Chapter I of the *Principles*) he is the first to reflect at all on the relationship between the *determination of the value* of commodities and the phenomenon that capitals of equal size yield equal profits. They can only do this inasmuch as the commodities they produce—although *they are not sold at equal prices* (one can, however, say that their output has equal prices provided the value of that part of constant capital which is not consumed is added to the product)—yield the *same surplus-value*, the same surplus of price over the price of the capital outlay. Ricardo moreover is the first to draw attention to the fact that capitals of equal size are by no means of equal organic composition. The difference in this composition he defined in the way traditional since Adam Smith, namely as circulating and fixed capital, that is, he saw only the differences arising from the process of circulation.

He certainly does not directly say that it is a *prima facie* contradiction of the law of value that capitals of unequal organic composition, which consequently set unequal amounts of immediate labour in motion, produce commodities of the same value and yield the same surplus-value (which he identifies with profit). On the contrary he begins his investigation of value by assuming capital and a general rate of profit. He identifies *cost-price* with *value* from the very outset, and does not see that from the very start this assumption is a *prima facie* contradiction of the law of value. It is only on the basis of this assumption—which contains the main contradiction and the real difficulty—that he comes to a particular case, *changes in the level of wages*, their rise or fall. For the rate of profit to remain uniform the rise or fall in wages, to which corresponds a fall or rise in profit, must have unequal effects on capitals of different organic composition. If wages rise, then profits fall, and also the prices of commodities in whose production a relatively large amount of fixed capital is employed. Where the opposite is the case, the results are likewise opposite. Under these circumstances, therefore, the *"exchangeable values"* of the various commodities are not determined by the labour-time required for their respective production. In other words, this definition of an equal rate of profit (and Ricardo arrives at it only in individual cases and in this roundabout way) yielded by capitals of different organic composition *contradicts* the law of value or, as Ricardo says, constitutes an *exception* to it, whereupon Malthus rightly remarks that in the progress of ||783| industry, the rule becomes the exception and the exception the rule.[a] The contradiction itself is not clearly expressed by Ricardo, namely, not in the form: although one of the commodities contains

---

[a] See this volume, pp. 30-32. —*Ed.*

more unpaid labour than the other—for the amount of unpaid labour depends on the amount of paid labour, that is, the amount of immediate labour employed provided the rate of exploitation of the workers is equal—they nevertheless yield equal values, or the same surplus of unpaid over paid labour. The contradiction however occurs with him in a particular form: in certain cases, *wages*, variations in wages, affect the cost-price (he says, the exchangeable values) of commodities.

Equally, differences in the time of turnover of capital—whether the capital remains in the process of production (even if not in the labour process)[26] or in circulation for a longer period, requiring not more work, but more time for its turnover—these differences have just as little effect on the equality of profit, and this again contradicts (is, according to Ricardo, an *exception* to) the law of value.

He has therefore presented the problem very one-sidedly. Had he expressed it in a general way, he would also have had a general solution.

But his great contribution remains: Ricardo has a notion that there is a difference between value and cost-price, and, in certain cases, even though he calls them *exceptions* to the law of value, he formulates the contradiction that capitals of unequal organic composition (that is, in the last analysis, capitals which do not exploit the same amount of living labour) yield equal surplus-value (profit) and—if one disregards the fact that a portion of the fixed capital enters into the labour process without entering into the process that creates value—equal values, commodities of equal value (or rather [of equal] *cost-price*, but he confuses this).

[b) Torrens's Confusion in Defining the Value of Labour and the Sources of Profit]

As we have seen,[a] *Malthus* uses this [the contradiction described by Ricardo] in order to deny the validity of the Ricardian law of value.

At the very beginning of his book, *Torrens* takes this discovery of Ricardo as his point of departure, not, however, to solve the problem, but to present the "phenomenon" as the law of the phenomenon.

Supposing that capitals of different degrees of durability are employed: "If a woollen and a silk manufacturer were each to employ a capital of

---

[a] See this volume, pp. 14 and 29-31.—*Ed.*

£2,000; and if the former were to employ £1,500 in durable machines, and £500 in wages and materials; while the latter employed only £500 in durable machines, and £1,500 in wages and materials.... Supposing that a tenth of these fixed capitals is annually consumed, and that the rate of profit is ten per cent, then, as the results of the woollen manufacturer's capital of £2,000, must, to give him this profit, be £2,200, and as the value of his fixed capital has been reduced by the progress of production from £1,500 to £1,350, the goods produced must sell for £850. And, in like manner, as the fixed capital of the silk manufacturer is by the process of production reduced one-tenth, or from £500 to £450, the silks produced must, in order to yield him the *customary rate of profit* upon his whole capital of £2,000, sell for £1,750 ... when capitals equal in amount, but of different degrees of durability, are employed, the articles produced, *together with the residue of capital, in one occupation,* will be equal in exchangeable value to the things produced, and the residue of capital, *in another occupation*" ([R. Torrens, *An Essay on the Production of Wealth,* London, 1821,] pp. 28-29).

Here the phenomenon manifested in competition is merely mentioned, registered. Similarly a *"customary rate of profit" is presupposed* without explaining how it comes about, or even the feeling that this ought to be explained.

"*Equal capitals,* or, in other words, *equal quantities of accumulated labour, will often put in motion different quantities of immediate labour;* but neither does this furnish any exception to our general principle" (loc. cit., pp. 29-30),

namely, to the fact that the value of the product plus the residue of the capital not consumed, yield equal values, or, what is the same thing, equal profits.

The merit of this passage does not consist in the fact that Torrens here merely registers the phenomenon once again without explaining it, but in the fact that he defines the difference by stating that equal capitals set in motion unequal quantities of living labour, though he immediately spoils it by declaring it to be a "special" case. If the value is equal to the labour worked up, embodied in a commodity, then it is clear that—if the commodities are sold at their value—the surplus-value contained in them can only be equal to the unpaid, or surplus labour, which they contain. But this surplus labour—given the same rate of exploitation of the worker—cannot be equal in the case of capitals which put in motion different quantities of immediate labour, whether it is the immediate production process or the period of circulation which is the cause of this difference. It is therefore to Torrens's credit that he expresses this. What does he conclude from it? That here ||784| within capitalist production the law of value suddenly changes. That is, that the law of value, which is abstracted from capitalist production, contradicts capitalist phenomena. And what does he put in its place? Absolutely nothing but the crude, thoughtless, verbal expression of the phenomenon which has to be explained.

"In that early period of society"

(that is, precisely when exchange-value in general, the product as commodity, is hardly developed at all, and consequently when there is no law of value either)

"*the total quantity of labour, accumulated and immediate, expended on production*, is that [...] which [...] determines the quantity of one commodity which shall be received for a given quantity of another. When *stock* has *accumulated*, when *capitalists become a class distinct from labourers*, [...] when the person who undertakes any branch of industry, does not perform his own work, but advances subsistence and materials to others, then it is the *amount of capital*, or the *quantity of accumulated labour* expended in production, [...] which determines the exchangeable power of commodities (op. cit., pp. 33-34).

"As long as [these] two capitals [are] equal [the law of competition, always tending to equalise the profits of stock, will keep] their products of equal [...] value, *however we may vary the quantity of immediate labour which they put in motion*, or which *their products may require* [...] if we render these capitals unequal in amount, [the same law must render] their products of unequal value, though the total quantity of labour expended upon each, should be precisely equal" (op. cit., p. 39).

"... after the *separation of capitalists and labour*[ers], it is [...] the *amount of capital*, or quantity of accumulated labour, and not as *before this separation*, the sum of accumulated and immediate labour, expended on production, which determines the exchangeable value..." (loc. cit., pp. 39-40).

Here again, he merely states the phenomenon that capitals of equal size yield equal profits or that the cost-price of commodities is equal to the price of the capital advanced plus the average profit; there is at the same time a hint that—since equal capitals put in motion different quantities of immediate labour—this *phenomenon* is, *prima facie*, inconsistent with the determination of the value of commodities by the amount of labour-time embodied in them. The remark [made by Torrens] that this phenomenon of capitalist production only manifests itself when capital comes into existence—[when] the classes of capitalists and workers [arise, and] the objective conditions of labour acquire an independent existence as capital—is tautology.

But *how* the separation of the [factors necessary] for the production of commodities—into capitalists and workers, capital and wage-labour—upsets the law of value of commodities is merely "inferred" from the uncomprehended phenomenon.

Ricardo sought to prove that, apart from certain exceptions, the separation between capital and wage-labour does not change anything in the determination of the value of commodities. Basing himself on the exceptions noted by Ricardo, Torrens rejects the law. He reverts to Adam Smith (against whom the Ricardian demonstration is directed) according to whom the value of commodities was determined by the labour-time embodied in them "in that early period" when men confronted one another simply as owners and exchangers of goods, but not when capital and property in land have been evolved. This means (as I observed in Part I[27]) that the law which applies to commodities *qua* commodities, no longer applies to them once they are regarded as capital or as products of capital, or as soon as there is, in general, an advance from the commodity to capital. On the other hand, the product wholly assumes the form of a commodity only—as a result of the fact that the entire product has to be transformed into exchange-value and that also all the ingredients necessary for its production enter it as commodities—in other words it wholly becomes a commodity only with the development and on the basis of capitalist production. Thus the law of value is supposed to be valid for a type of production which produces no commodities (or produces commodities only to a limited extent) and not to be valid for a type of production which is based on the product as a commodity. The law itself, as well as the commodity as the general form of the product, is abstracted from capitalist production and yet it is precisely in respect of capitalist production that the law is held to be invalid.

The proposition regarding the influence of the separation of "capital and labour" on the determination of value—apart from the tautology that capital cannot determine prices so long as it does not as yet exist—is moreover a quite superficial translation of a fact manifesting itself on the surface of capitalist production. So long as each person works himself with his own tools and sells his product himself ⟨but in reality, the necessity to sell products on a ||785| social scale never coincides with production carried on with the producer's own means of production⟩, *his* costs comprise the cost of both the tools and the *labour* he performs. *The cost to the capitalist consists in the capital he advances*—in the sum of values he expends on production—*not in labour, which he does not perform*, and which only costs *him* what he pays for it. This is a very good reason for the capitalists to calculate and distribute the (social) surplus-value amongst themselves according to the size of their capital outlay and not according to the quantity of immediate labour which a given capital puts in motion. But it does not explain where the surplus-value—which has to be distributed and is distributed in this way—comes from.

Torrens adheres to Ricardo insofar as he maintains that the value of a commodity is determined by the quantity of labour, but he declares that [it is] only the *"quantity of accumulated labour"* expended upon the production of commodities which determines their value. Here, however, Torrens lands himself in a fine mess.

For example, the value of woollen cloth is determined by the *accumulated labour* contained in the loom, the wool, etc., and the wages, which constitute the ingredients of its production, *accumulated labour*, which, in this context, means nothing else but *embodied labour*, materialised labour-time. However, once the woollen cloth is ready and production is over, the immediate labour expended on the woollen cloth has likewise been transformed into accumulated or materialised labour. Then why should the value of the loom and of the wool be determined by the materialised labour (which is nothing but immediate labour embodied in an object, in a result, in a useful thing) they contain, and the value of the woollen cloth not be so determined? If the woollen cloth in turn becomes a component part of production in say dyeing or tailoring, then it is "accumulated labour", and the value of the coat is determined by the wages of the workers, their tools and the woollen cloth, the value of which is determined by the "accumulated labour" contained in it. If I regard a commodity as *capital*, that means in this context as a condition of production, then its value resolves itself into immediate labour, which is called "accumulated labour" because it exists in a materialised form. On the other hand, if I regard the same commodity as a commodity, as a product and result of the [production] process, then it is definitely not determined by the labour which is accumulated in it, but by the labour accumulated in its conditions of production.

It is indeed a fine vicious circle to seek to determine the value of a commodity by the value of the capital, since the value of the capital is equal to the value of the commodities of which it is made up.

James Mill is right as against this fellow when he says:

"*Capital is commodities.* If the value of commodities, then, depends upon the value of capital, it depends upon the value of commodities..." [James Mill, *Elements of Political Economy*, London, 1821, p. 74].

One thing more is to be noted here. Since [according to Torrens] the value of a commodity is determined by the value of the capital which produces it, or, in other words, by the quantity of labour, the labour accumulated and embodied in this capital, then only two possibilities ensue.

The commodity contains: first, the value of the fixed capital used up; second, the value of the raw material or the quantity of labour contained in the fixed capital and raw material; third, the quantity of labour which is materialised in the money or in the commodities which function as wages.

Now there are two [possibilities]:

The "accumulated" labour contained in the fixed capital and raw material remains the same after the process of production as it was before. As far as the third part of the "accumulated labour" advanced is concerned, the worker replaces it by his "immediate labour", that is, the "immediate labour" added to the raw material, etc., represents just as much accumulated labour in the commodity, in the product, as was contained in the wages. Or it represents more. If it represents more, the commodity contains more accumulated labour than the capital advanced did. Then profit arises precisely out of the surplus of accumulated labour contained in the commodity over that contained in the capital advanced. And the *value* of ||786| the commodity is determined, as previously, by the quantity of labour (accumulated plus immediate) contained in it (in the commodity the latter type of labour likewise constitutes accumulated, and no longer immediate, labour. It is immediate labour in the production process, and accumulated labour in the product).

Or [i.e., in the first case] immediate labour only represents the quantity [of labour] embodied in the wage, is only an equivalent of it. (If it were less than this, the point to be explained would not be why the capitalist makes a profit but how it comes about that he makes no loss.) Where does the profit come from in this case? Where does the surplus-value, i.e., the excess of the value of the commodity over the value of the component parts of production, or over that of the capital outlay, arise? Not in the production process itself—so that merely its realisation takes place in the process of exchange, or in the circulation process—but in the exchange process, in the circulation process. We thus come back to Malthus and the crude mercantilist conception of "profit upon expropriation". And it is this conception at which Mr. Torrens consistently arrives, although he is, on the other hand, sufficiently inconsistent to explain this *payable value* not by means of an inexplicable fund dropped down from the skies, namely, a fund which provides not only an equivalent for the commodity, but a surplus over and above this equivalent, and is derived from the means of the purchaser, who is always able to pay for the commodity above its value without selling it above its value—thus reducing the whole thing to thin air. Torrens, who is not as consistent as Malthus, does not have recourse to such a fiction, but, on the contrary, asserts that "effectual demand"—the sum of values paid for the product—arises from *supply* alone, and is therefore likewise a commodity; and thus, since the two sides are both buyers and sellers, it is impossible to see how they can mutually cheat one another to the same extent.

"The effectual demand for any commodity is always determined, and under any given rate of profit, is constantly commensurate with the quantity of the ingredients of capital, or of the things required in its production, which consumers may be able and willing to offer in exchange for it" (Torrens, *An Essay on the Production of Wealth*, London, 1821, p. 344).

"... increased supply is the one and only cause of increased effectual demand" (op. cit., p. 348).

Malthus, who quotes this passage from Torrens, is quite justified in protesting against it (*Definitions in Political Economy*, London, 1827, p. 59).[a]

But the following passages about *production costs*, etc., demonstrate that Torrens does indeed arrive at such absurd conclusions.

"*Market price*" (Malthus calls it "purchasing value") "must always include the customary rate of profit for the time being; [but] *natural price*, consisting of the *cost of production* or, in other words, of *the capital expended* in raising or fabricating commodities, cannot include the rate of profit" ([Torrens], op. cit., p. 51).

"The farmer [...] expends one hundred quarters of corn in cultivating his fields, and obtains in return one hundred and twenty quarters. In this case, twenty quarters, being the excess of produce above expenditure, constitute the farmer's profit; but it would be absurd to call this excess, or profit, a part of the expenditure".... Likewise "the master manufacturer [...] obtains in return a quantity of finished work. This finished work must possess a higher *exchangeable value* than the materials etc." (loc. cit., pp. 51-53).

[a] See this volume, p. 58.—*Ed.*

"Effectual demand consists in the power and inclination, *on the part of consumers* to give for commodities, either by immediate or circuitous barter, *some greater portion*[a] of all the ingredients of capital than their production costs" (op. cit., p. 349).

120 quarters of corn are most certainly more than 100 quarters. But—if one merely considers the use-value and the process it goes through, that is, in reality, the vegetative or physiological ||787| process, as is the case here—it would be wrong to say, not indeed, with regard to the 20 quarters, but with regard to the elements which go to make them up, that they do not enter into the *production process*. If this were so, they could never emerge from it. In addition to the 100 quarters of corn—the seeds—various chemical ingredients supplied by the manure, salts contained in the soil, water, air, light, are all involved in the process which transforms 100 quarters of corn into 120. The transformation and absorption of the elements, the ingredients, the conditions—the expenditure of nature, which transforms 100 quarters into 120—takes place in the *production process* itself and the elements of these 20 quarters enter into this process itself as physiological "expenditure", the result of which is the transformation of 100 quarters into 120.

Regarded merely from the standpoint of use-value, these 20 quarters are not mere profit. The inorganic components have been merely assimilated by the organic components and transformed into organic material. Without the addition of matter—and this is the physiological expenditure—the 100 qrs. would never become 120. Thus it can in fact be said even from the point of view of mere use-value, that is, regarding corn as corn—what enters into corn in inorganic form, as *expenditure*, appears in *organic* form, as the actual result, the 20 quarters, i.e., as the surplus of the corn harvested over the corn sown.

But these considerations, in themselves, have as little to do with the question of profit, as if one were to say that lengths of wire which, in the production process, are stretched to a thousand times the length of the metal from which they are fabricated, yield a thousandfold *profit* since their length has been increased a thousandfold. In the case of the wire, the length has been increased, in the case of corn, the quantity. But neither increase in length nor increase in quantity constitutes *profit*, which is

---

[a] In the manuscript, "proportion".—*Ed.*

applicable solely to exchange-value, although exchange-value manifests itself in a surplus product.

As far as exchange-value is concerned, there is no need to explain further that the value of 90 quarters of corn can be equal to (or greater than) the value of 100 quarters, that the value of 100 quarters can be greater than that of 120 quarters, and that of 120 quarters greater than that of 500.

Thus, on the basis of one example which has *nothing* to do with profit, with the surplus in the *value* of the product over the *value* of the capital outlay, Torrens draws conclusions about profit. And even considered physiologically, as use-value, his example is wrong since, in actual fact, the 20 quarters of corn which form the surplus product already exist in one way or another in the production process, although in a different form.

Finally, Torrens blurts out the brilliant old conception that profit is profit upon expropriation.

[c] **Torrens and the Conception of Production Costs**

One of Torrens's merits is that he has at all raised the controversial question: what are *production costs*. Ricardo continually confuses the *value* of commodities with their *production costs* (insofar as they are equal to the cost-price) and is consequently astonished that *Say*, although he believes that prices are determined by production costs, draws different conclusions.[28] Malthus, like Ricardo, asserts that the price of a commodity is determined by the cost of production, and, like Ricardo, he includes the profit in the production costs. Nevertheless, he defines value in a different way, not by the quantity of labour contained in the commodity, but by the quantity of labour it can command.

The ambiguities surrounding the concept of *production costs* arise from the very nature of capitalist production.

Firstly: The *cost to the capitalist* of the commodity (he produces) is, naturally, what it *costs him*. It costs him nothing—that is, he expends no value upon it—apart from the value of the *capital advanced*. If he lays out £100 on raw materials, machinery, wages, etc., in order to produce the commodity, it costs him £100, neither more nor less. Apart from the labour embodied in these advances, apart from the *accumulated labour* that is contained in the capital expended and determines the value of the commodities expended [in the production process], it costs him no labour. What the *immediate labour* costs him is the wages he pays for it. Apart from these wages, the immediate labour costs him nothing, and apart from immediate labour he advances nothing except the value of the constant capital.

||788| It is in this sense that Torrens understands production costs, and this is the sense in which every capitalist understands them when he calculates his profit, whatever its rate may be.

Production costs are here equated with the *outlay* of the capitalist, which is equal to the value of the capital advanced, i.e., to the quantity of the labour contained in the advanced commodities. Every economist, including Ricardo, uses *this* definition of production costs, whether they are called *advances* or *expenses*, etc. This is what Malthus calls the *producing price* as opposed to the purchaser's price. The transformation of surplus-value into *profit* corresponds to this definition of *expenses*.

Secondly: According to the first definition, the production costs are the price which the capitalist *pays* for the manufacture of the commodity during the process of production, therefore they are what the commodity costs *him*. But what the production of a commodity *costs* the capitalist and what the *production of the commodity itself costs*, are two entirely different things. The labour (both materialised and immediate) which the capitalist *pays* for the production of the commodity and the labour which is necessary in order to *produce* the commodity are entirely different. Their difference constitutes the difference between the value advanced and the value earned; between the purchase price of the commodity for the capitalist and its selling price (that is, if it is sold at its value). If this difference did not exist, then neither money nor commodities would ever be transformed into capital. The source of profit would disappear together with the surplus-value. The *production costs of the commodity itself* consist of the value of the capital consumed in the process of its production, that is, the quantity of materialised labour embodied in the commodity plus the *quantity of immediate labour* which is expended upon it. The *total amount* of "materialised" plus "immediate labour" consumed in it constitutes the *production costs of the commodity itself*. The commodity can only be produced by means of the industrial consumption of this quantity of materialised and immediate labour. This is the pre-condition for its emergence out of the process of production as a *product*, as a *commodity* and even as a use-value. And no matter how profit and wages may vary, these immanent production costs of the commodity remain the same so long as the technological conditions of the real labour process remain the same, or, what amounts to the same thing, as long as there is no variation in the existing development of labour productivity. In this sense, the *production costs of a commodity* are equal to its *value*. The living labour expended upon the commodity and the living labour paid by the capitalist are two different things. From the outset, therefore, the production costs of a commodity to the capitalist (his advances) differ from the *production costs of the commodity* itself, its value. The excess of its value (that is, what the commodity itself costs) over and above the value of the capital expended (that is, what it costs the capitalist) *constitutes the profit which, therefore, results not from selling the commodity above its value, but from selling it above the value of the advances the capitalist made.*

The production costs thus defined, *the immanent production costs* of the commodity, which are equal to its value, i.e., to the total amount of labour-time (both objectified and immediate) required for its production, remain the fundamental condition for its production and remain unchangeable so long as the productive power of labour remains unchanged.

Thirdly. I have however previously[29] shown that, in each separate branch of production or particular occupation, the capitalist does not by any means sell his commodities—which are also the product of a particular trade, occupation or sphere of production—at the value contained in them, and that, therefore, the amount of profit is not identical with the amount of surplus-value, surplus labour or unpaid labour embodied in the commodities he sells. On the contrary, he can, on the average, only realise as much surplus-value in the commodity as devolves on it as the product of an aliquot part of the social capital. If the social capital comes to 1,000 and the capital in a particular ||789| branch of production amounts to 100, and if the total amount of surplus-value (hence of the surplus product in which that surplus-value is embodied) equals 200, that is, 20 per cent, then the capital of 100 in this particular branch of production would sell its commodity for 120, whatever the value of the commodity, whether it is 120, or less or more; whether, therefore, the unpaid labour contained in his commodity forms a fifth of the labour expended upon it or not.

This is the *cost-price*, and when one speaks of *production costs* in the proper sense (in the economic, capitalist sense), then the term denotes the value of the capital outlay plus the value of the average profit.

It is clear that, however much the cost-price of an individual commodity may diverge from its value, it is determined by the *value* of the total product of the social capital. It is through the equalisation of the profits of the different capitals that they are connected with one another as aliquot parts of the aggregate social capital, and as such aliquot parts they draw dividends out of the common funds of surplus-value (surplus product), or surplus labour, or unpaid labour. This does not alter in any way the value of the commodity; it does not alter the fact that, whether its cost-price is equal to, or greater or smaller than, its value, it [the commodity] can never be produced *without its value* being produced, that is to say, without the total amount of materialised and immediate labour required for its production being expended upon it. This quantity of labour, not only of paid, but of unpaid labour, must be expended on it, and nothing in the general relationship between capital and labour is altered by the fact that in some spheres of production a part of the unpaid labour is appropriated by "brother capitalists"[30] and not by the capitalist who puts the labour in motion in that particular branch of industry. Further, it is clear that whatever the relation between the value and the cost-price of a commodity, the latter will always change, rise or fall, in accordance with the changes of value, that is to say, the quantity of labour required for the production of the commodity. It is furthermore clear that part of the profit must always represent surplus-value, unpaid labour, embodied in the commodity itself, because, on the basis of capitalist production, every commodity contains more labour than has been paid by the capitalist putting that labour in motion. Some part of the profit may consist of labour not worked up in a commodity produced in the particular branch of industry, or resulting from the given sphere of production; but, then, there is some other commodity, resulting from some other sphere of production, whose cost-price falls below its value, or in whose cost-price less unpaid labour is accounted for, paid for, than is contained in it.

It is clear, therefore, that although the cost-prices of most commodities must differ from their values, and hence the "costs of production" of these commodities must differ from the total quantity of labour contained in them, nevertheless, those costs of production and those cost-prices are not only determined by the values of the commodities and confirm the law of value instead of contradicting it, but, moreover, that the very existence of costs of production and cost-prices can be comprehended only on the basis of value and its laws, and becomes a meaningless absurdity without that premise.

At the same time one perceives how economists who, on the one hand, observe the actual phenomena of competition and, on the other hand, do not understand the relationship between the law of value and the law of cost-price, resort to the fiction that capital, not labour, determines the value of commodities or rather that there is no such thing as value.

||790| Profit enters into the *production costs of commodities*; it is rightly included in the "natural price" of commodities by Adam Smith, because, in conditions of capitalist production, the commodity—in the long run, on the average—is not brought to the market if it does not yield the cost-price, which is equal to the value of the advances plus the average profit. Or, as Malthus puts it—although he does not understand the origin of profit, its real cause—because the profit, and therefore the cost-price which includes it, is (on the basis of capitalist production) a condition of the *supply* of the commodity. To be produced, to be brought to the market, the commodity must at least fetch that market price, that cost-price to the seller, whether its own value be greater or smaller than that cost-price. It is a matter of indifference to the capitalist whether his commodity contains more or less unpaid labour than other commodities, if into its price enters as much of the general stock of unpaid labour, or the surplus product in which it is fixed, as every other equal quantity of capital will draw from that common stock. In this respect, *the capitalists are "communists"*. In competition, each naturally tries *to secure more than the average profit, which is only possible if others secure less*. It is precisely as a result of this struggle that the average profit is established.

A part of the surplus-value realised in profit, i.e., that part which assumes the form of interest on capital laid out (whether borrowed or not), appears to the capitalist as *outlay*, as *production cost* which he has as a *capitalist*, just as profit in general is the immediate aim of capitalist production. But in interest (especially on borrowed capital), this appears also as the actual precondition of his production.

At the same time, this reveals the significance of the distinction between the phenomena of production and of distribution. Profit, a phenomenon of distribution, is here simultaneously a phenomenon of production, a condition of production, a necessary constituent part of the process of production. How absurd it is, therefore, for John Stuart Mill and others to conceive bourgeois forms of production as absolute, but the bourgeois forms of distribution as historically relative, hence transitory. I shall return to this later. The form of production is simply the form of distribution seen from a different point of view. The specific features —and therefore also the specific limitation—which set bounds to bourgeois distribution, enter into bourgeois production itself, as a determining factor, which overlaps and dominates production. The fact that bourgeois production is compelled by its own immanent laws, on the one hand, to develop the productive forces as if production did not take place on a narrow restricted social foundation, while, on the other hand, it can develop these forces only within these narrow limits, is the deepest and most hidden cause of crises, of the crying contradictions within which bourgeois production is carried on and which, even at a cursory glance, reveal it as only a transitional, historical form.

This is grasped rather crudely but none the less correctly by Sismondi, for example, as a contradiction between production for the sake of production and distribution which makes absolute development of productivity impossible.

2. James Mill [Futile Attempts to Resolve the Contradictions of the Ricardian System]

||791| James Mill, *Elements of Political Economy*, London, 1821 (second ed., London, 1824).

Mill was the first to present Ricardo's theory in systematic form, even though he did it only in rather abstract outlines. What he tries to achieve is formal, logical consistency. The *disintegration* of the Ricardian school "therefore" begins with him. With the master what is new and significant develops vigorously amid the "manure" of contradictions out of the contradictory phenomena. The underlying contradictions themselves testify to the richness of the living foundation from which the theory itself developed. It is different with the disciple. His raw material is no longer reality, but the new theoretical form in which the master had sublimated it. It is in part the *theoretical disagreement of opponents of the new theory* and in part the *often paradoxical relationship of this theory to reality* which drive him to seek *to refute* his opponents and *explain away* reality. In doing so, he entangles himself in contradictions and with his attempt to solve these he demonstrates the beginning *disintegration of the theory* which he dogmatically espouses. On the one hand, Mill wants to present bourgeois production as the absolute form of production and seeks therefore to prove that its real contradictions are only apparent ones. On the other hand, [he seeks] to present the Ricardian theory as the absolute theoretical form of this mode of production and to disprove the theoretical contradictions, both the ones pointed out by others and the ones he himself cannot help seeing. Nevertheless in a way Mill advances the Ricardian view beyond the bounds reached by Ricardo. He supports the same historical interests as Ricardo—*those of industrial capital against landed property*—and he draws the practical conclusions from the theory—that of rent for example—more ruthlessly, against the institution of landed property which he would like to see more or less directly transformed into State property. This conclusion and this side of Mill do not concern us here.

[a) Confusion of Surplus-Value with Profit]

Ricardo's disciples, just as Ricardo himself, fail to make a distinction between *surplus-value* and *profit*. Ricardo only becomes aware of the problem as a result of the different influence which the variation of wages can exercise on capitals of different organic composition (and he considers different organic composition only with regard to the circulation process). It does not occur to them that, even if one considers not capitals in different spheres of production but *each* capital separately, insofar as it does not consist exclusively of variable capital, i.e., of capital laid out in wages only, rate of profit and rate of surplus-value are different things, that therefore profit must be a more developed, specifically modified form of surplus-value. They perceive the difference only insofar as it concerns equal profits—average rate of profit—for capitals in different spheres of production and differently composed of fixed and circulating ingredients. In this connection Mill only repeats in a vulgarised form what Ricardo says in Chapter I, "On Value" [*Principles of Political Economy*]. The only new consideration which occurs to him in relation to this question is this:

Mill remarks that *"time as such"* (i.e., not labour-time, but simply *time*) produces nothing, consequently it does not produce "value". How does this fit in with the law of value according to which capital, because it requires a longer time for its returns [to the manufacturer], yields, as Ricardo says, the same profit as capital which employs more immediate labour but returns more rapidly? One perceives that Mill deals here only with a quite individual case which, expressed in general terms, would read as follows. How does the cost-price, and the average rate of profit which it presupposes ||792| (and therefore also equal value of commodities containing very unequal quantities of labour), fit in with the fact that profit is nothing but a part of the labour-time contained in the commodity, the part which is appropriated by the capitalist without an equivalent? On the other hand, in the case of the average rate of profit and cost-price, criteria which are quite extrinsic and external to the determination of value are advanced, for example, that the capitalist whose capital takes longer to make its return because, as in the case of wine, it must remain longer in the production process (or, in other cases, longer in the circulation process) must be compensated for the time in which he cannot use his capital to produce value. But how can the time in which no value is produced create value?

Mill's passage concerning *"time"* reads:

"... time does nothing.[a] How then can it create value?[b] Time is a mere abstract term. It is a word, a sound. And it is the very same logical absurdity, to talk of an abstract unit measuring value, and of time creating it" (*Elements of Political Economy*, second ed., London, 1824, p. 99). [31]

In reality, what is involved in the *grounds for compensation* between capitals in different spheres of production is not the production of surplus-value, but *its division between different categories of capitalists*. Viewpoints are here advanced which have nothing whatever to do with *the determination of value as such*. Everything which compels capital in a particular sphere of production to renounce conditions which would produce a *greater amount of surplus-value* in other spheres, is regarded here as *grounds for compensation*. Thus, if more fixed and less circulating capital is employed, if more constant than variable capital is employed, if it must remain longer in the circulation process, and finally, if it must remain longer in the production process without being subjected to the labour process—a thing which always happens when breaks of a technological character occur in the production process in order to expose the developing product to the working of natural forces, for example, wine in the

---

[a] The manuscript has "time can do nothing".—*Ed.*
[b] The manuscript has "add to value" instead of "create value".—*Ed.*

cellar. Compensation ensues in all these cases and the last mentioned is the one which Mill seizes on, thus tackling the difficulty in a very circumscribed and isolated way. A part of the surplus-value produced in other spheres is transferred to the capitals more unfavourably placed with regard to the direct exploitation of labour, simply in accordance with their size (competition brings about this equalisation so that each separate capital appears only as an aliquot part of social capital). The phenomenon is very simple as soon as the relationship of surplus-value and profit as well as the equalisation of profit in a general rate of profit is understood. If, however, it is to be explained directly from the law of value without any intermediate link, that is, if the profit which a particular capital yields in a particular branch of production is to be explained on the basis of the surplus-value contained in the commodities it produces, in other words on the basis of the *unpaid labour* (consequently also on the basis of the labour directly expended in the production of the commodities), this is a much more difficult problem to solve than that of squaring the circle, which can be solved algebraically. It is simply an attempt to present that which does not exist as in fact existing. But it is in this *direct* form that Mill seeks to solve the problem. Thus no solution of the matter is possible here, only a sóphistic explaining away of the difficulty, that is, only *scholasticism*. Mill begins this process. In the case of an *unscrupulous blockhead* like *McCulloch*, this manner assumes a swaggering shamelessness.

Mill's solution cannot be better summed up than it is in the words of *Bailey*:

"The author[a] [...] has made a curious attempt to resolve the *effects of time* into *expenditure of labour*. 'If,' says he," (p. 97 of the *Elements*, second ed., 1824) "'the wine which is put in the cellar is increased in value one-tenth by being kept a year, one-tenth more of labour may be correctly *considered* as having been expended upon it.'... a fact can be correctly considered as having taken ||793| place only when it really has taken place. In the instance adduced, no human being, by the terms of the supposition, has approached the wine, or spent upon it a moment or a single motion of his muscles" ([Samuel Bailey,] *A Critical Dissertation on the Nature, Measures, and Causes of Value etc.*, London, 1825, pp. 219-20).

Here the contradiction between the general law and further developments in the concrete circumstances is to be resolved not by the discovery of the connecting links but by directly subordinating and immediately adapting the concrete to the abstract.

---

[a] In the manuscript, "Mr. Mill".—*Ed.*

This moreover is to be brought about by *a verbal fiction*, by changing the correct names of things. (These are indeed "verbal disputes", they are "verbal", however, because real contradictions which are not resolved in a real way, are to be solved by phrases.) When we come to deal with McCulloch, it will be seen that this manner, which appears in Mill only in embryo, did more to undermine the whole foundation of the Ricardian theory than all the attacks of its opponents.

Mill resorts to this type of argument only when he is quite unable to find any other expedient. But as a rule his method is quite different. Where the economic relation—and therefore also the categories expressing it—includes contradictions, opposites, and likewise the unity of the opposites, he emphasises the aspect of the *unity* of the contradictions and denies the *contradictions*. He transforms the unity of opposites into the direct identity of opposites.

For example, a commodity conceals the contradiction of use-value and exchange-value. This contradiction develops further, presents itself and manifests itself in the duplication of the commodity into commodity and money. This duplication appears as a process in the metamorphosis of commodities in which selling and buying are different aspects of a single process and each act of this process simultaneously includes its opposite. In the first part of this work, I mentioned that Mill disposes of the contradiction by concentrating only on the *unity* of buying and selling; consequently he transforms circulation into barter, then, however, smuggles categories borrowed from circulation into [his description of] barter.[32] See also what I wrote there about Mill's *theory of money*, in which he employs similar methods.[33]

In James Mill we find the unsatisfactory divisions—"Production", "Distribution", "Interchange", "Consumption".

[b) Mill's Vain Efforts to Bring the Exchange Between Capital and Labour into Harmony with the Law of Value]

Wages:

"Instead, however, of waiting till the commodity is produced, and [...] the value of it is realised, it has been found to suit *much better* the convenience of the labourers to receive their share *in advance*. The shape under which it has been found most convenient for all parties that they should receive it, is that of wages. When the share of the commodity which belongs to the labourer has been all received in the shape of wages, the commodity itself belongs to the capitalist, he having, in reality, bought the share of the labourer and paid for it in advance" ([James Mill, *Elements of Political Economy*, second ed., 1824, p. 41] *Elémens d'économie politique*, traduit de l'anglais par J. T. Parisot, Paris, 1823, pp. 33-34).[a]

It is highly characteristic of Mill that, just as *money* for him is an expedient invented for convenience' sake, *capitalist relations* are likewise invented for the same reason. These specific social relations of production are invented for "convenience'" sake. Commodities and money are transformed into capital because the worker has ceased to engage in exchange as a commodity producer and commodity owner; instead of selling commodities he is compelled to sell his labour itself (to sell directly his labour-power) as a commodity to the owner of the objective conditions of labour. This separation is the prerequisite for the relationship of capital and wage-labour in the same way as it is the prerequisite for the transformation of money (or of the commodities by which it is represented) into capital. Mill presupposes the *separation*, the *division*; he presupposes the relationship of capitalist and wage-worker, in order to present as a matter of convenience the situation in which the worker sells *no product*, no commodity, but his share of the product (in the production of which he has no say whatsoever and which proceeds *independently* of him) before he has produced it. ||794| Or, more precisely, the worker's share of the product is paid for—transformed into money—by the capitalist before the capitalist has disposed of, or realised, the product in which the worker has a share.

This view is aimed at circumventing the specific difficulty, along with the specific form of the relationship. Namely, the difficulty of the Ricardian system according to which the worker sells his *labour* directly (not his labour-power). The [difficulty can be expressed as follows]: the value of a commodity is determined by the labour-time required for its production; how does it happen that this law of value does not hold good in the greatest of all exchanges, which forms the foundation of capitalist production, the exchange between capitalist and labourer? Why is the quantity of materialised labour received by the worker as wages not equal to the quantity of immediate labour which he gives in exchange for his wages? To shift this difficulty, Mill transforms the labourer into a commodity owner who sells the

---

[a] This and the other passages taken by Marx from Parisot's translation of Mill's work are quoted in this volume from James Mill, *Elements of Political Economy*, London, 1824. These quotations are marked "Parisot" and the French text Marx used can be found in the Appendix of this volume.—*Ed.*

capitalist his *product, his commodity*—since his *share* of the product, of the commodity, is *his* product, his *commodity*, in other words, a value produced by him in the form of a particular commodity. He resolves the difficulty by transforming the transaction between capitalist and labourer, which includes the contradiction between materialised and immediate labour, into a common transaction between commodity owners, owners of materialised labour.

Although by resorting to this artifice Mill has indeed made it impossible for himself to grasp the specific nature, the specific features, of the proceedings which take place between capitalist and wage-worker, he has not reduced the difficulty in any way, but has increased it, because the peculiarity of the result is now no longer comprehensible in terms of the peculiarity of the commodity which the worker sells (and the specific featuie of this commodity is that its use-value is itself a factor of exchange-value, its use therefore creates a greater exchange-value than it itself contained).

According to Mill, the worker is a seller of commodities like any other. For example, he produces 6 yards of linen. Of these 6, 2 yards are assumed to be equal to the value of the labour which he has added. He thus sells 2 yards of linen to the capitalist. Why then should he not receive the full value of the 2 yards, like any other seller of 2 yards of linen, since he is now a seller of linen like any other? The contradiction with the law of value now expresses itself much more crassly than before. He does not sell a particular commodity differing from all other commodities. He sells labour embodied in a product, that is, a commodity which as such is not specifically different from any other commodity. If now the price of a yard [of linen]—that is, the quantity of money containing the same amount of labour-time as the yard [of linen] —is 2 shillings, why then does the worker receive 1 shilling instead of 2? But if the worker received 2 shillings, the capitalist would not secure any surplus-value and the whole Ricardian system would collapse. We would have to return to profit upon expropriation. The 6 yards would cost the capitalist 12 shillings, i.e., their value, but he would sell them for 13 shillings.

Or linen, and any other commodity, is sold at its value when the capitalist sells it, but *below* its value when the worker sells it. Thus the law of value would be destroyed by the transaction between worker and capitalist. And it is precisely in order to avoid this that Mill resorts to his fictitious argument. He wants to transform the relationship between worker and capitalist into the ordinary one between sellers and buyers of commodities. But why should not the ordinary law of value of commodities apply to this transaction? [It may be said however that] the worker is paid *"in advance"*. Consequently this is not after all the ordinary relationship of buying and selling commodities. What does this "payment in advance" mean in this context? The worker who, for example, is paid weekly, *"advances"* his labour and produces the share of the weekly product which belongs to him—his weekly labour embodied in a product—(both according to Mill's assumption and in practice) before he receives "payment" from the capitalist. The capitalist "advances" raw materials and machines, the worker the "labour", and as soon as the wages are paid at the end of the week, he *sells* a commodity, his commodity, his share of the total commodity, to the capitalist. But, Mill will say, the capitalist pays the 2 yards ||795| of linen due to the worker, i.e., turns them into cash, transforms them into money, before he himself sells the 6 yards and transforms them into money. But what if the capitalist is working on orders, if he sells the goods before he produces them? Or to express it more generally, what difference does it make to the worker—in this case the seller of 2 yards of linen—if the capitalist buys these 2 yards from him in order to sell them again, and not to consume them? Of what concern are the buyer's motives to the seller? And how can motives, moreover, modify the law of value? To be consistent, each seller would have to dispose of his commodities below their value, for he is disposing of his products to the buyer in the form of a use-value, whereas the buyer hands over value in the form of money, the cash form of the product. In this case, the linen manufacturer would also have to *underpay* the yarn merchant and the machine manufacturer and the colliery owner and so on. For they sell him commodities which he only intends to transform into money, whereas he pays them "in advance" the *value* of the component parts entering into his commodity net only before the commodity is sold, but before it is even produced. The worker provides him with linen, a commodity in a marketable form, in contrast to other sellers whose commodities, machinery, raw materials, etc., have to go through a process before they acquire a saleable form. It is a pretty kettle of fish for such an inveterate Ricardian as Mill, according to whom purchase and sale, supply and demand are identical terms, and money a mere formality, if the transformation of the commodity into money—and nothing else takes place when the 2 yards of linen are sold to the capitalist—includes the fact that the seller has to sell the commodity below its value, and the buyer, with his money, has to buy it above its value.

[Mill's argument] therefore amounts to the absurdity that, in this transaction, the buyer buys the commodity in order to resell it at a profit and that, consequently, the seller must sell the commodity *below* its value—and with this the whole theory of value falls to the ground. This second attempt by Mill to resolve a Ricardian contradiction, in fact destroys the whole basis of the system, especially its great merit that it defines the relationship between capital and wage-labour as a direct exchange between hoarded and immediate labour, that is, that it grasps its specific features.

In order to extricate himself, Mill would have to go further and to say that it is not merely a question of the simple transaction of the purchase and sale of commodities; that, on the contrary, insofar as it involves payment or the turning into money of the worker's product, which is equal to his share of the total product, the relationship between worker and capitalist is similar to that prevailing between the lending capitalist or discounting capitalist (the moneyed capitalist) and the industrial capitalist. It would be a pretty state of affairs to presuppose interest-bearing capital—a special form of capital—in order to deduce the general form of capital, capital which produces profit; that is, to present a derived form of surplus-value (which already presupposes capital) as the cause of the appearance of surplus value. In that case, moreover, Mill would have to be consistent and in place of all the definite laws concerning wages and the rate of wages elaborated by Ricardo, he would have to derive them from the rate of interest, and if he did that it would indeed be impossible to explain what determines the rate of interest, since, according to the Ricardians and all other economists worth naming, the rate of interest is determined by the rate of profit.

The proposition concerning the *"share"* of the worker in his own product is in fact based on this: If one considers not simply the isolated transaction between capitalist and worker, but the exchange which takes place between both in the course of reproduction, and if one considers the real content of this process instead of the form in which it appears, then it is in fact evident that what the capitalist pays the worker (as well as the part of capital which confronts the worker as constant capital) is nothing but a part of the worker's product itself and, indeed, a part which does not have to be transformed into money, but which has already been sold, has already been transformed into money, since wages are paid in money, not in kind. Under slavery, etc., the false appearance brought about by the previous transformation of the product into money—insofar as it is expended on wages—does not arise; it is therefore obvious that what the slave receives as wages is, in fact, nothing that the slave-owner "advances" him, but simply the portion of the realised labour of the slave that returns to him in the form of means of subsistence. The same applies to the capitalist. He "advances" something only in appearance. Since he pays for the work only after it has been done, he advances or rather ||796| *pays* the worker as wages a part of the product produced by the worker and already transformed into money. A part of the worker's product which the capitalist appropriates, which is *deducted beforehand*, returns to the worker in the form of wages—as an advance on the new product, if you like.

It is quite unworthy of Mill to cling to this *appearance* of the transaction in order to explain the transaction itself (this sort of thing might suit McCulloch, Say or Bastiat). The capitalist can advance the worker nothing except what he has taken previously from the worker, i.e., what has been advanced to him by other people's labour. Malthus himself says that what the capitalist advances consists not "of cloth" and "other commodities", but *"of labour"*,[34] that is, precisely of that which he himself does not perform. He advances the worker's own labour to the worker.

However, the whole paraphrase is of no use to Mill, for it does not help him to avoid resolving the question: how can the exchange between hoarded and immediate labour (and this is the way the exchange process between capital and labour is perceived by Ricardo and by Mill and others after him) correspond to the law of value, which it contradicts directly? One can see from the following passage that it is of no help to Mill:

"What *determines* the share of the labourer, or the portion in which the commodity, or commodity's worth, is divided between him and the capitalist. Whatever the share of the labourer, such is the rate of wages.... It is very evident, that the share of the two parties is the subject of a *bargain* between them [....] All bargains, when left in freedom, are determined by competition, and the terms alter according to the *state of supply and demand*" ([Mill, *Elements*, pp. 41-42; Parisot,] pp. 34-35).

The worker is paid for his "share" of the product. This is said in order to transform him into an ordinary seller of a *commodity* (a product) vis-à-vis the capitalist and to eliminate the specific feature of this relationship. [According to Mill] the worker's share of the product is *his* product, that is, the share of the product in which his newly applied labour is realised. But this is not the case. On the contrary, we now ask which is his "share" of the product, that is, *which* is *his* product? For the part of the product which belongs to him is *his* product, which he sells. We are now told that *his* product and his *product* are two quite different things. We must establish, first of all, what his product (in other words, his share of the product, that is, the part of the product that belongs to him) is. His product is thus a mere phrase, since the quantity of value which he receives from the capitalist is not determined by his own production. Mill has thus merely removed the difficulty one step. He has got no farther than he was at the beginning.

There is a *quid pro quo* here. Supposing that the exchange between capital and wage-labour is a continuous activity—as it is if one does not isolate and consider one individual act or element of capitalist production—then the worker receives a part of the value of his product which he has replaced, plus that part of the value which he has given the capitalist for nothing. This is repeated continuously. Thus he receives in fact continuously a portion of the value of his own product, a part of, or a share in, the value he has produced. Whether his wages are high or low is not determined by his share of the product but, on the contrary, his share of the product is determined by the amount of his wages. He actually receives a share of the value of the product. But the share he receives is determined by the value of labour, not conversely, the value of labour-by his share in the product. The value of labour, that is, the labour-time required by the worker for his own reproduction, is a definite magnitude; it is determined by the sale of his labour power to the capitalist. This virtually determines his share of the product as well. It does not happen the other way round, that his share of the product is determined first, and as a result, the amount or value of his wages. This is precisely one of Ricardo's most important and most emphasised propositions, for otherwise the price of labour would determine the prices of the commodities it produces, whereas, according to Ricardo, the price of labour determines nothing but *the rate of profit.*

And how does Mill determine the "share" of the product which the worker receives? By demand and supply, competition between workers and capitalists. What Mill says applies to all commodities:

"... It is very evident, that the share" (read: in the value of commodities) "of the two parties" (seller and buyer) "is the subject of a bargain between ||797| them [....] All bargains, when left in freedom, are determined by competition, and the terms alter according to the state of supply and demand" [Mill, *Elements*, pp. 41-42; Parisot, pp. 34-35].

Here we have the gist of the matter. [This is said by] Mill who, as a zealous Ricardian, proves that although demand and supply can, to be sure, determine the vacillations of the market price either above or below the *value* of the commodity, they cannot determine that value itself, that these are meaningless words when applied to the determination of value, for the determination of demand and supply presupposes the determination of value. In order to determine the value of labour, i.e., the *value* of a commodity, Mill now resorts to something for which Say had already reproached Ricardo:determination by demand and supply.

But even more.

Mill does not say which of the two parties represents supply and which demand—which is of no importance to the matter here. Still, since the capitalist offers money and the worker offers something for the money, we will assume that demand is on the side of the capitalist and supply on that of the worker. But what then does the worker "sell"? What does he supply? His "share" of the product which does not [yet] exist? But it is just his share in the future product which has to be determined by competition between him and the capitalist, by the "demand and supply" relationship. One of the sides of this relationship—supply—cannot be something which is itself the result of the struggle between demand and supply. What then does the worker offer for sale? His *labour*? If this is so, then Mill is back again at the original difficulty he sought to evade, the *exchange between hoarded and immediate labour*. And when he says that what is happening here is not the exchange of equivalents, or that the value of labour, the commodity sold, is not measured by "the labour-time" itself, but by competition, by demand and supply, then he admits that Ricardo's theory breaks down, that his opponents are right, that the determination of the value of commodities by labour-time is false, because the value of the most important commodity, labour itself, contradicts this law of value of commodities. As we shall see later, *Wakefield* says this quite explicitly.

Mill can turn and twist as he will, he cannot extricate himself from the dilemma. At best, to use his own mode of expression, competition causes the workers to offer a *definite quantity of la-*

bour for a price which, according to the relation of demand and supply, is equal to a larger or smaller part of the product which they will produce with this quantity of labour. That this *price*, this *sum of money*, which they receive in this way, is equal to a larger or smaller part of the value of the product to be manufactured, does not, however, as a matter of course, in any way prevent a *definite amount of living labour* (immediate labour) from being exchanged for a greater or lesser amount of *money* (accumulated labour, existing moreover in the form of exchange-value). It does not therefore prevent the exchange of unequal quantities of labour, that is, of less hoarded labour for more immediate labour. This was precisely the phenomenon that Mill had to explain and he wished to clear the problem up without violating the law of value. The phenomenon is not changed in the slightest, much less explained, by declaring that the proportion in which the worker exchanges his immediate labour for money *is expressed* at the end of the production process in the ratio of the value paid him to the value of the product he has produced. The original *unequal* exchange between capital and labour thus only *appears* in a different form.

How Mill boggles at direct exchange between labour and capital--which Ricardo takes as his point of departure without any embarrassment at all—is also shown by the way he proceeds. Thus he says:

||798| "Let us begin by supposing that there is a certain number of capitalists [...] that there is also a certain number of labourers; and that *the proportion*, in *which the commodities produced are divided between them, has fixed itself at some particular point.*

"Let us next suppose that the labourers have increased in number [...] without any increase in the *quantity of capital*.... To prevent their being left out of employment" the additional labourers "have but one resource; they must endeavour to supplant those who have forestalled the employment; that is, they must *offer to work* for *a smaller reward*. Wages, therefore, decline. If we suppose ... that the quantity of capital has increased, while the number of labourers remains the same, the effect will be reversed. ... if the ratio which capital and population bear to one another remains the same; wages will remain the same" ([Mill, *Elements*, pp. 42-44 passim; Parisot,] p. 35 et seq. passim).

What has to be determined is "the proportion in which they" (capitalists and workers) "divide the product". In order to establish this by competition, Mill *assumes* that this proportion *"has fixed itself"* at some particular point". In order to establish the "share" of the worker by means of competition, he *assumes* that it is determined *before* competition "at some particular point". Moreover, in order to demonstrate how competition alters the division of the product which is *determined* "at some particular point", he assumes that workers "*offer to work for a smaller reward*" when their number grows more rapidly than the quantity of capital. Thus he says here outright that what the workers supply consists of "*l a b o u r*" and that they offer this labour for a "*reward*", i.e., money, a definite quantity of "hoarded labour". In order to avoid direct exchange between labour and capital, direct *sale of labour*, he has recourse to the theory of the "division of the product". And in order to explain the proportion in which the product is divided, he presupposes *direct sale* of labour for money, so that this original exchange between capital and labour is later *expressed* in the proportion of [the share] the worker receives of his product, and not that the original exchange is determined by his share of the product. And finally, if the number of workers and the amount of capital remain the same, then the "wage rate" will remain *the same*. But what is the wage rate when demand and supply balance? That is the point which has to be explained. It is not explained by declaring that this rate is altered when the equilibrium between demand and supply is upset. Mill's tautological circumlocutions only demonstrate that he feels there is a snag here in the Ricardian theory which he can only overcome by abandoning the theory altogether.

* * *

Against Malthus, Torrens, and others, against the determination of the value of commodities by the value of capital, Mill remarks correctly:

"Capital *is* commodities. If the value of commodities, then, depends upon the value of capital, it depends upon the value of commodities; the value of commodities depends upon itself" ([James Mill,] *Elements of Political Economy*, London, 1821, p. 74).

* * *

(Mill does not gloss over the contradiction between capital and labour. The *rate of profit* must be high so that the social class which is free from immediate labour may be important; and for that purpose wages must be relatively low. It is necessary that the mass of the labourers should not be masters of their own time and slaves of their own needs, so that human (social) capacities can develop freely in the classes for which the working class serves merely as a basis. The working class represents lack of development in order that other classes can represent human development. This in fact is the contradiction in which bourgeois ||799| society develops, as has every hitherto existing society, and this is declared to be a *necessary law*, i.e., the existing state of affairs is declared to be absolutely reasonable.

"All the blessings which flow from that grand and distinguishing attribute of our nature, its *progressiveness*, the power of advancing continually from one degree of knowledge, one degree of command over the means of happiness, to another, seem, in a great measure, to depend upon the existence of a class of men which have *their time at their command*; that is, who are rich enough to be freed from all solicitude with respect to the means of living in a certain state of enjoyment. It is by this class of men that knowledge is cultivated and enlarged; it is also by this class that it is diffused; it is this class of men whose children receive the best education, and are prepared for all the higher and more delicate functions of society, as legislators, judges, administrators, teachers, inventors in all the arts, and superintendents in all the more important works, by which the dominion of the human species is extended over the powers of nature. ... to enable a considerable proportion of the community to enjoy the advantages of *leisure*, the *return to capital* must *evidently be large* ([James Mill, *Elements*, pp. 64-65, 65-66; Parisot,] pp. 65, 67).⟩

* * *

In addition to the above.

Mill, as a Ricardian, defines labour and capital simply as *different forms* of labour.

"... Labour and Capital [...] the one, *immediate labour*, ... the other, *hoarded* labour" ([James Mill, *Elements*,] first Engl. ed., London, 1821, p. 75).

In another passage he says:

"... of these two *species of labour*, two things are to be observed ... they are *not always paid according to the same rate*" ([James Mill, *Elements*, p. 100;] Parisot, p. 100).

Here he comes to the point. Since what pays for immediate labour is always hoarded labour, capital, the fact that it is not paid at *the same rate* means nothing more than that more immediate labour is exchanged for less hoarded labour, and that this is "*always*" the case, since otherwise hoarded labour would not be exchanged as "capital" for immediate labour and would not only fail to yield the *very high interest* desired by Mill, but would yield none at all. The passage quoted thus contains the admission (since Mill along with Ricardo regards the exchange between capital and labour as a direct exchange of hoarded and immediate labour), that they are exchanged in *unequal proportions*, and that in respect of them the law of value—according to which equal quantities of labour are exchanged for one another—breaks down.

[c] **Mill's Lack of Understanding of the Regulating Role of Industrial Profit]**

Mill advances as a basic law what Ricardo actually assumes in order to develop his theory of rent.[35]

"All other profits ... must sink to the level of agricultural profits" ([*Elements,*] second ed., London, 1824, p. 78).

This is fundamentally wrong, since capitalist production develops first of all in industry, not in agriculture, and only embraces the latter by degrees, so that it is only as a result of the advance of capitalist production that agricultural profits become equalised to industrial profits and only as a result of this equalisation do the former influence the latter. Hence it is in the first place wrong historically. But secondly, once this equalisation is an accomplished fact—that is, presupposing a level of development of agriculture in which capital, in accordance with the rate of profit, flows from industry to agriculture and vice versa —it is equally wrong to state that from this point on *agricultural profits* become the regulating force, instead of the influence being reciprocal. Incidentally, in order to develop the concept of rent, Ricardo himself assumes the opposite. The price of corn rises; as a result agricultural *profits* do not *fall* (as long as there are no new supplies either from inferior land or from additional, less productive investments of capital)—for the rise in the price of corn more than compensates the farmer for the loss he incurs by the rise in wages following on the rise in the price of corn— but *profits fall* in industry, where no such compensation or over-compensation takes place. Consequently the *industrial profit rate* falls and capital which yields this lower rate of profit can therefore be employed on inferior lands. This would not be the case if the old profit rate prevailed. Only because the decline of industrial profits thus reacts on the agricultural profit yielded by the worse land, does agricultural profit generally fall, ||800|

and a part of it is detached in the form of rent from the profit the better land yields. This is the way Ricardo describes the process, according to which, therefore, industrial profit regulates profit in agriculture.

If agricultural profits were to rise again as a result of improvements in agriculture, then industrial profits would also rise. But this does not by any means exclude the fact that—as originally the *decline in industrial profit* causes a decline in agricultural profit—*a rise* in industrial profit may bring about a rise in agricultural profit. This is always the case when industrial profit rises *independently of the price of corn* and of other agricultural necessaries which enter into the wages of the workers, that is, when it rises as a result of the fall in the value of commodities which constitute constant capital, etc. Rent moreover cannot possibly be explained if industrial profit does *not* regulate agricultural profit. The *average rate of profit* in industry is established as a result of equalisation of the profits of the different capitals and the consequent transformation of the values into *cost-prices*. These cost-prices—the value of the capital advances plus average profit—are the *prerequisite* received by agriculture from industry, since the equalisation of profits cannot take place in agriculture owing to landownership. If then the value of agricultural produce is higher than the cost-price determined by the *industrial average profit* would be, the excess of this value over the cost-price constitutes the absolute rent. But in order that this excess of value over cost-price can be measured, the *cost-price* must be the primary factor; it must therefore be imposed on agriculture as a law by industry.

* * *

A passage from Mill must be noted:

"That which is *productively* consumed is always capital. This is a property of productive consumption which deserves to be particularly marked.... Whatever is consumed productively *becomes* capital" ([James Mill, *Elements*, p. 217;] Parisot, pp. 241-42).

[d)] Demand, Supply. Over-Production

"A demand means, the *will to purchase*, and the *means of purchasing*.... The equivalent" (means of purchasing) "which a man brings is the *instrument* of demand. The extent of his demand is measured by the extent of his equivalent. The demand and the equivalent are convertible terms, and one may be substituted for the other.... His" (a man's) "will, therefore, to *purchase*, and his *means of purchasing*, in other words his demand, is exactly equal to the amount of what he has produced and does not mean to consume" ([James Mill, *Elements*, pp. 224-25;] Parisot, pp. 252-53).

One sees here how the direct identity of demand and supply (hence the impossibility of a general glut) is proved. The product constitutes demand and the extent of this demand, moreover, is measured by the value of the product. The same abstract "reasoning" with which Mill demonstrates that buying and selling are but identical and do not differ; the same tautological phrases with which he shows that prices depend on the amount of money in circulation; the same methods used to prove that supply and demand (which are only more developed forms of buyer and seller) must balance each other. The logic is always the same. If a relationship includes opposites, it comprises not only opposites but also the *unity* of opposites. It is therefore a *unity without opposites*. This is Mill's logic, by which he eliminates the "contradictions".

Let us begin with *supply*. What I supply is *commodities*, a unity of use-value and exchange-value, for example, a definite quantity of iron worth £3 (which is equal to a definite quantity of labour-time). According to the assumption I am a manufacturer of iron. I supply a use-value—iron—and I supply a value, namely, the value expressed in the price of the iron, that is, in £3. But there is the following little difference. A definite quantity of iron is *in reality* placed on the market by me. The *value* of the iron, on the other hand, exists only as its *price* which must first be realised by the buyer of the iron, who represents, as far as I am concerned, the *demand* for iron. The demand of the seller of iron consists in the demand for the *exchange-value* of the iron, which, although it is embodied in the iron, is not realised. It is possible for the same *exchange-value* to be represented by very different quantities of iron. The supply of use-value and the supply of value to be realised are thus by no means identical, since quite different quantities of use-value ||801| can represent the same quantity of exchange-value.

The same value—£3—can be represented by one, three or ten tons of iron. The quantity of iron (use-value) which I supply and the quantity of value I supply, are by no means proportionate to one another, since the latter quantity can remain unchanged no matter how much the former changes. No matter how large or small the quantity of iron I supply may be, it is assumed that

I always want to realise the value of the iron, which is *independent* of the actual quantity of iron and in general of its existence as a use-value. The value supplied (but not yet realised) and the quantity of iron which is realised, do not correspond to each other. No grounds exist therefore for assuming that the possibility of selling a commodity at its value corresponds in any way to the quantity of the commodity I bring to market. For the buyer, my commodity exists, above all, as use-value. He buys it as such. But what he needs is a definite quantity of iron. His need for iron is just as little determined by the quantity produced by me as the value of my iron is commensurate with this quantity.

It is true that the man who buys has in his possession merely the *converted form* of a commodity — money — i.e., the commodity in the form of exchange-value, and he can act as a buyer only because he or others have earlier acted as sellers of commodities which now exist in the form of money. This, however, is no reason why he should reconvert his money into my commodity or why his need for my commodity should be determined by the quantity of it that I have produced. Insofar as he wants to buy my commodity, he may want either a smaller quantity than I supply, or the entire quantity, but *below* its value. His demand does not have to correspond to my supply any more than the quantity I supply and the value at which I supply it are identical.

However, the inquiry into demand and supply does not belong here.

Insofar as I supply iron, I do not demand iron, but money. I supply a particular use-value and demand its value. My supply and demand are therefore as different as use-value and exchange-value. Insofar as I supply a *value* in the iron itself, I demand the *realisation of this value*. My supply and demand are thus as different as something conceptual is from something real. Further, the quantity I supply and its value stand in no proportion to each other. The demand for the quantity of use-value I supply is however measured not by the value I wish to realise, but by the quantity which the buyer requires at a definite price.

Yet another passage from Mill:

> "But it is evident, that each man contributes to the general supply the whole of what he has produced and does not mean to consume. In whatever shape any part of the annual produce has come into his hands, if he proposes to consume no part of it himself, he wishes to dispose of the whole; and the whole, therefore, becomes matter of supply: if he consumes a part, he wishes to dispose of all the rest, and all the rest becomes matter of supply" ([James Mill, *Elements*, p. 225;] Parisot, p. 253).

In other words, this means nothing else but that all commodities placed on the market constitute supply.

"As every man's demand, therefore, is equal to that part of the annual produce, or of the property generally, which he has to dispose of"

⟨Stop! His demand is equal to the *value* (when it is realised) of the portion of products which he wants to dispose of. What he wants to dispose of is a certain quantity of use-value; what he wishes to have is the *value* of this use-value. Both things are anything but identical⟩

"and each man's supply is exactly the same thing"

⟨by no means; his demand does not consist in what he wishes to dispose of, i.e., the product, but in the demand for the value of this product; on the other hand, his supply really consists of this product, whereas the value is only conceptually supplied⟩

"the supply and demand of every individual are of necessity equal" ([James Mill, *Elements*, pp. 225-26;]Parisot, pp. 253-54).

(That is, the *value* of the commodity supplied by him and the *value* which he asks for it but does not possess are equal; *provided* he sells the commodity at its value, the value supplied (in the form of commodity) and the value received (in the form of money) are equal. But it does not follow that, because he wants to sell the commodity at its value, he actually does so. A quantity of commodities is supplied by him, and is on the market. He tries to get the value for it.)

"Demand and supply are terms ||802| related in a peculiar manner. A commodity which is supplied, is always, at the same time, a commodity which is the *instrument* of demand. A commodity which is the instrument of demand, is always, at the same time, a commodity added to the stock of supply. Every commodity is always *at one and the same time* matter of demand and matter of supply. Of two men who perform an exchange, the one does not come with only a supply, the other with only a demand; each of them comes with both a demand and a supply. The *supply which he brings* is the instrument of his demand; and his demand and supply are of course exactly equal to one another.

But if the demand and supply of every individual are always equal to one another, and demand and supply of all the individuals in the nation, taken aggregately, must be equal. Whatever, therefore, be the amount of the annual produce, it never can exceed the amount of the annual demand. The whole of the annual produce is divided into a number of shares equal to that of the people to whom it is distributed. The whole of the demand is equal to as much of the whole of the shares as the owners do not keep for their own consumption. But the whole of the shares is equal to the whole of the produce" ([James Mill, *Elements*, pp. 226-27;] Parisot, pp. 254-55).

Once Mill has *assumed* that supply and demand are equal for each individual, then the whole long-winded excursus to the effect that supply and demand are also equal for *all* individuals, is quite superfluous.

* * *

How Mill was regarded by contemporary Ricardians can be seen, for instance, from the following:

"There is thus at least one case" ⟨writes Prévost with regard to Mill's definition of the value of labour⟩ "in which the price" (i.e., the price of labour) "is permanently determined by supply and demand relations" (Prévost, *Réflexions sur le système de Ricardo* [p. 187] appended to *Discours sur l'économie politique*. Par McCulloch, traduit par G-me Prévost, Genève-Paris, 1825).

In the work cited, *McCulloch* says that Mill's object is:

"... to give a strictly *logical deduction* of the principles of Political Economy.... Mr. Mill touches on almost every topic of discussion: He has disentangled and simplified the most complex and difficult questions; has placed the various principles which compose the science in their natural order" (op. cit., p. 88a).

One can conclude from his logic that he takes over the quite illogical Ricardian structure, which we analysed earlier,[36] and naïvely regards it on the whole as a "natural order".

[e)] Prévost [Rejection of Some of the Conclusions of Ricardo and James Mill. Attempts to Prove That a Constant Decrease of Profit Is Not Inevitable]

As far as the above-mentioned *Prévost* is concerned, who made Mill's exposition of the Ricardian system the basis of his *Réflexions*, a number of his objections are founded on sheer, callow misunderstanding of Ricardo.

But the following remark about rent is noteworthy:

"One may entertain a doubt about the influence of *inferior land* on the determination of prices, if one bears in mind, as one should, its *relative area*" (Prévost, op. cit., p. 177).

Prévost cites the following from *Mill*, which is also important for my argument, since Mill himself here thinks of one exam-

---

a This passage taken by Marx from Prévost's translation of McCulloch's book *A Discourse on the Rise, Progress, Peculiar Objects, and Importance of Political Economy*, is quoted here from the English original, p. 71.— *Ed.*

ple where *differential rent* arises because the new demand, the additional demand, is supplied by a better, not a worse soil, consequently, the ascending line.

"*Mr. Mill* uses this comparison: Suppose that all the land cultivated in the country were of one uniform quality, and yielded the same return to every portion of the capital employed upon it, with the exception of one acre: that acre, we shall suppose, yields six times as much as any other acre (Mill, *Elements*, second ed., p. 71). It is certain—as Mr. Mill demonstrates —that the farmer who rents this last acre, cannot increase his rent" (that is, cannot make a higher profit than the other farmers; it is very badly expressed[37]) "and that five-sixths of the product will go to the landowner."

(Thus there is here differential rent without the lowering of the rate of profit and without any increase in the price of agricultural products) (this must happen all the more frequently, since the *situation* ||803| must *improve* continuously with the industrial development of the country, the growth of its means of communication and the increase in population, irrespective of the natural fertility, and the relatively better location has the same effect as [greater] natural fertility.)

"But had the ingenious author thought of making a similar supposition in the opposite case, he would have realised that the result would be different. Let us suppose that all the land was of equal quality with the exception of one acre of inferior land. The profit on the capital on this single acre amounted to one-sixth of the profit yielded by every other acre. Does he believe that the profit on several million acres would be reduced to one-sixth of their accustomed level? It is probable that this solitary acre would have no effect at all, because the various products (particularly corn), when they come onto the market, would not be markedly affected by such a *minute* amount. That is why we say that the assertions of Ricardo's supporters about the effect of inferior soil should be modified by taking the *relative areas* of land of different quality into account" (Prévost, loc. cit., pp. 177-78).

* * *

⟨*Say*, in his notes to Ricardo's book translated by Constancio, makes only *one* correct remark about *foreign trade*.[38] Profit can also be made by cheating, one person gaining what the other loses. Loss and gain within a *single* country cancel each other out. But not so with trade between different countries. And even according to Ricardo's theory, three days of labour of one country can be exchanged against one of another country—a point *not* noted by Say. Here the law of value undergoes essential modification. The relationship between labour days of different countries may be similar to that existing between skilled, complex labour and unskilled, simple labour within a country. In this case, the richer country exploits the poorer one, even where the latter gains by the exchange, as John Stuart Mill explains in his *Some Unsettled Questions*.[39]⟩

* * *

[Prévost says the following about the relationship between agricultural and industrial profit:]

"We admit that, in general, the rate of agricultural profit determines that of industrial profit. But at the same time we must point out that the latter also reacts of necessity on the former. If the price of corn rises to a certain point, industrial capitals turn to agriculture, and necessarily depress agricultural profits" (loc. cit., p. 179).

The point is correct, but is conceived in a much too limited sense. See above.[a]

The Ricardians insist that profit can fall only as a result of a rise in wages, because necessaries rise in price with [the growth of] population, this, however, is a consequence of the accumulation of capital, since inferior soils are cultivated as a result of this accumulation. But Ricardo himself admits that profits can also fall when capitals increase faster than population, when the competition of capitals causes wages to rise. This [corresponds to] Adam Smith's theory. Prévost says:

"When the growing demand of the capitals increases the price of the labourer, that is, *wages*, does it not then appear that there are no grounds for asserting that the growing supply of these selfsame capitals never causes the price of capitals, in other words, *profit*, to fall?" (op. cit., p. 188.)

Prévost builds on the false Ricardian foundation which can only explain falling profits as a result of decreasing surplus-value, and therefore decreasing surplus labour, and consequently as a result of greater value or *rising cost of the necessaries consumed by the worker*, that is, increasing value of labour, although the real wages of the labourer may not rise but decline; on this basis he seeks to prove that a continual decline in profits is not inevitable.

He says *first*:

"To begin with, the state of prosperity increases profits"

(namely, agricultural profits, for the population increases with the state of prosperity, the demand for agricultural produce

---

[a] See this volume, pp. 99-100.—*Ed.*

therefore grows and consequently the farmer makes additional profits)

"and this happens long before new land is taken into cultivation. The increased area under cultivation does indeed affect rent and decreases profits. But although profit is thus directly decreased, it still remains as high as before the advance.... Why is the cultivation of land of inferior quality undertaken at certain times? It is undertaken in the expectation of a profit which is *at least equal to the customary profit*. And what circumstance can lead to the realisation of such a profit on this kind of land? Increase ||804| of population. It presses on ... the existing means of subsistence, thereby raising the prices of food (especially of corn) so that agricultural capitals obtain high profits. The other capitals pour into agriculture, but since the soil is limited in area, this competition has its limits and the point is reached when *even higher profits can be made than in trade or manufacture* through the cultivation of inferior soils. If there is a sufficient area of inferior land available, then agricultural profit must be adjusted to the last capitals applied to the land. If one proceeds from the rate of' profit prevailing at the beginning of the increasing prosperity" (division of profit into profit and rent), "then it will be found that profit has no tendency to decline. It rises with the increase in the population until agricultural profit rises to such a degree that it can suffer a considerable reduction as a result of the cultivation [of new land] without ever sinking below its original rate, or, to be more precise, below the average rate determined by various circumstances" (op. cit., pp. 190-92).

Prévost obviously misunderstands the Ricardian view. As a result of prosperity, the population increases, thus raising the price of agricultural products and hence agricultural profits. (Although it is not easy to see why, if this rise is constant, rents should not be increased after the leases run out and why these additional agricultural profits should not be collected in the form of rent even before the inferior land is cultivated.) But the same rise in [the price of] agricultural produce which causes agricultural profits to go up, increases wages in all industries and consequently brings about a fall in industrial profits. Thus a new rate of profit arises in industry. If at the existing market prices the inferior lands even pay only this *lower rate of profit*, capitals can be transferred to the inferior land. They will be attracted to it by the high agricultural profits and the high market price of corn. As Prévost says, they may, before a sufficient amount of capital has been transferred, even yield higher profits than the industrial profits, which have declined. But as soon as the additional supply is adequate, the market price falls, so that the inferior soils only yield the ordinary industrial profit. The additional amount yielded by the product of the better [soils] is converted into rent. This is the Ricardian conception, whose basic premises are accepted by *Prévost* and from which he reasons. Corn is now dearer than it was before the rise in agricultural profit. But the additional profit which it brought the farmer is transformed into rent. In this way, therefore, profit also declines on the better land to the lower rate of industrial profit brought about by the rise in the price of agricultural produce. There is no reason for assuming that as a consequence profits do not have to fall below their "original rate" if no other modifying circumstances intervene. Other circumstances *may*, of course, intervene. According to the assumption, after the increase in the price of necessaries, agricultural profit is in any case higher than industrial profit. If, however, as a result of the development of productive power, the part of the workers' necessaries supplied by industry has fallen to such a degree that wages (even though they are paid at their average value) do not rise as much as they would have done without the intervention of these paralysing circumstances, proportionally to the increased [price of] agricultural produce; if, furthermore, the same development of productive power has reduced the prices of the products of the extractive industries, and also of agricultural raw materials which are not used as food (although the supposition is not very likely), industrial profit need not fall, though it would be lower than agricultural profit. A decline of the latter as a result of a transfer of capital to agriculture and the building-up of rent, ||805| would only restore the old rate of profit.

[*Secondly*,] Prévost tries a different approach.

"Soils of inferior quality ... are only put into cultivation if they yield profits as high as—or even higher than—the profit yielded by industrial capitals. Under these conditions, the price of corn or of other agricultural products often remains very high despite the newly cultivated land. These high prices press on the working population, since rises in wages do not correspond exactly to rises in the prices of the goods used by workers. They are more or less a burden to the whole population, since nearly all commodities are affected by the rise in wages and in the prices of essential goods. This general pressure, linked with the increasing mortality brought about by too large a population, results in a decline in the number of wage-workers and, consequently, in a rise in wages and a decline in agricultural profits. Further development now proceeds in the opposite direction to that taken previously. Capitals are withdrawn from the inferior soils and reinvested in industry. But the population principle soon begins to operate once again. As soon as poverty has been ended, the number of workers increases, their wages decline, and profits rise as a consequence. Such fluctuations follow one another repeatedly without bringing about a change in the average rate of profit. Profit may decline or rise for other reasons or as a result of these causes; it may alternately go up and down, and yet it may not be possible to attribute the average rise or fall to the necessity for cultivating new soils. The population is the regulator which establishes the natural order and keeps profit within certain limits" (op. cit., pp. 194-96).

Although confused, this is correct according to the "population principle". It is however not in line with the assumption that agricultural profits rise until the additional supply required by the population has been produced. If this presupposes a constant increase in the prices of agricultural produce, then it leads not to a decrease in population, but to a general lowering of the rate of profit, hence of accumulation, and, consequently, to a decrease of population. According to the Ricardian-Malthusian view, the population would grow more slowly. But Prévost's basis is: that the process would depress wages below their average level, this fall in wages and the poverty of the workers causes the price of corn to fall and hence profits to rise again.

This latter argument, however, does not belong here, for here it is assumed that the value of labour is always paid; that is, that the workers receive the means of subsistence necessary for their reproduction.

This [exposition] of Prévost is important, because it demonstrates that the Ricardian view—along with the view he adopted from Malthus—can indeed explain fluctuations in the rate of profit, but cannot explain (constant) falls in the same without repercussions, for upon reaching a certain level the rise in corn prices and the drop in profit would force wages below their level, bringing about a violent decrease in the population, and therefore a fall in the prices of corn and other necessaries, and this would lead again to a rise in profit.

3. Polemical Writings

||806| The period between 1820 and 1830 is metaphysically speaking the most important period in the history of English political economy—theoretical tilting for and against the Ricardian theory, a whole series of anonymous polemical works, the most important of which are quoted here, especially in relation to those matters which concern our subject. At the same time, however, it is a characteristic of these polemical writings that all of them, in actual fact, merely revolve around the definition of the concept of value and its relation to capital.

a) ["Observations on certain Verbal Disputes". Scepticism in Political Economy]

Observations on certain Verbal Disputes in Political Economy, particularly relating to Value, and to Demand and Supply, London, 1821.

This is not without a certain acuteness. The title *Verbal Disputes* is characteristic.

Directed in part against Smith and Malthus, but also against Ricardo.

The real sense of this work lies in the following:

"... disputes ... are entirely owing to the use of words in different senses by different persons; to the disputants looking, like the knights in the story, at different sides of the shield" (*Observations etc.*, London, 1821, pp. 59-60).

This kind of scepticism always heralds the dissolution of a theory, it is the harbinger of a frivolous and unprincipled eclecticism designed for domestic use.

First of all in relation to Ricardo's theory of value:

"There is an obvious difficulty in supposing that *labour* is what we mentally allude to, when we talk of value or of real price, as opposed to nominal price; for we often want to speak of the *value or price of labour itself*. Where by labour, as the real price of a thing, we mean the labour which *produced* the thing, there is another difficulty besides; for we often want to speak of the *value or price of land*; but land is not produced by labour. This definition, then, will only apply to *commodities*" (op. cit., p. 8).

As far as labour is concerned, the objection to Ricardo is correct insofar as he presents capital as the purchaser of immediate labour and consequently speaks directly of the value of labour, while what is bought and sold is the temporary use of labour-power, itself a product. Instead of the problem being resolved, it is only emphasised here that a problem remains unsolved.

It is also quite correct that "the *value* or *price of land*", which is not produced by labour, appears directly to contradict the concept of value and cannot be derived directly from it. This proposition is [all the more] insignificant when used against Ricardo, since its author does not attack Ricardo's theory of rent in which precisely Ricardo sets forth how the nominal value of land is evolved on the basis of capitalist production and does not contradict the definition of value. The value of land is nothing but the price which is paid for capitalised ground-rent. Much more far-reaching developments have therefore to be presumed here than can be deduced *prima facie* from the simple consideration of the commodity and its value, just as from the simple concept of productive capital one cannot evolve fictitious capital,[40] the object of gambling on the stock exchange, which is actually nothing but the selling and buying of entitlement to a certain part of the annual tax revenue.

The second objection—that Ricardo transforms value, which is a *relative* concept, into an *absolute* concept—is made the chief point of the attack on the whole Ricardian system in another polemical work (written by Bailey), which appeared later. In considering this latter work, we will also cite relevant passages from the *Observations*.

A very pertinent observation about the source from which capital, which pays labour, arises, is contained in an incidental remark unconsciously made by the author, who on the contrary wants to use it to prove what is said in the following sentence not underlined [by me], namely, that the supply of labour itself constitutes a check on the tendency of labour to sink to its natural price.

"⟨*An increased supply of labour is an increased supply of that which is to purchase labour.*⟩ If we say, then, with Mr. Ricardo, that labour is at every moment *tending* to what he calls its natural price, we must only recollect, that the increase made in its supply, in order to *tend* to that, is itself one cause of the counteracting power, which prevents the tendency from being *effectual*" (op. cit., pp. 72-73).

No analysis is possible unless the average price of labour, i.e., the value of labour, is made the point of departure; just as little would it be possible if óne failed to take the *value* of commodities in general as the point of departure. Only on this basis is it possible to understand the real phenomena of price fluctuations.

||807| "... it is not meant to be asserted by him" (Ricardo), "that two particular lots of two different articles, as a hat and a pair of shoes, exchange with one another when *those two particular lots* were produced by equal quantities of labour. By '*commodity*', we must here understand '*description of commodity*', not a particular individual hat, pair of shoes, etc. The whole labour which produces all the hats in England is to be considered, to this purpose, as divided among all the hats. This seems to me not to have been expressed at first, and in the general statements of his doctrine" (op. cit., pp. 53-54).

... for example, Ricardo says that "a portion of the labour of the engineer" who makes the machines (Ricardo, *On the Principles of Political Economy, and Taxation*, third ed., London, 1821, quoted from the *Observations*) is contained, for instance, in a pair of stockings. "Yet the 'total labour' that produced each single pair of stockings, if it is of a single pair we are speaking, includes the *whole* labour of the engineer; not a 'portion'; for one machine makes many pairs, and none of those pairs could have been done without any part of the machine..." (*Observations etc.*, London, 1821, p. 54).

The last passage is based on a misunderstanding. The whole machine enters into the labour process, but only a part of it enters the formation of value.

Apart from this, some things in the remark are correct.

We start with the *commodity*, this specific social form of the product, as the foundation and prerequisite of capitalist production. We take individual products and analyse those distinctions of form which they have as commodities, which stamp them as commodities. In earlier modes of production—*preceding* the capitalist mode of production—a large part of the output never enters into circulation, is never placed on the market, is not produced as commodities, and does not become commodities. On the other hand, at that time a large part of the products which enter into production are not commodities and do not enter into the process as commodities. The transformation of products into commodities only occurs in individual cases, is limited only to the surplus of products, etc., or only to individual spheres of production (manufactured products), etc. A whole range of products neither enter into the process as articles to be sold, nor arise from it as such. Nevertheless, the *prerequisite*, the *starting-point*, of the formation of capital and of capitalist production is the development of the product into a commodity, commodity circulation and consequently money circulation within certain limits, and consequently trade developed to a certain degree. It is as such a prerequisite that we treat the commodity, since we proceed from it as the simplest element in capitalist production. On the other hand, the product, the result of capitalist production, is the commodity. What appears as its element is later revealed to be its own product. Only on the basis of capitalist production does the commodity become the general form of the product and the more this production develops, the more do the products in the form of commodities enter into the process as ingredients. The commodity, as it emerges in capitalist production, is different from the commodity taken as the element, the starting-point of capitalist production. We are no longer faced with the individual commodity, the individual product. The individual commodity, the individual product, manifests itself not only as a real product but also as a commodity, as a *part* both really and conceptually of production as a whole. Each individual commodity represents a definite portion of capital and of the surplus-value created by it.

The value of the capital advanced plus the surplus labour appropriated, for example, a value of £120 (if it is assumed that £100 is the value of the capital and £20 that of surplus labour), is, as far as its value is concerned, contained in the total product, let us say, in 1,200 yards of cotton. Each yard, therefore, equals $£^{120}/_{1,200}$ or $^1/_{10}$ of £1 or 2s. It is not the individual commodity which appears as the result of the process, but the mass of the commodities in which the value of the total capital has been reproduced plus a surplus-value. The total value produced divided by the number of products determines the value of the individual product and it becomes a commodity only as such an aliquot part. It is no longer the labour expended on the individual particular commodity (in most cases, it can no longer be calculated, and may be greater in the case of one commodity than in that of another) but a proportional part of the total labour—i.e., the average of the total value [divided] by the number of products—which determines the value of the individual product and establishes it as a commodity. Consequently, the total mass of commodities must also be sold, each commodity at its value, determined in this way, in order to replace the total capital together with a surplus-value. If only 800 out of the 1,200 yards were sold, then the capital would not be replaced, still less would there be a profit. But each yard would *also* have been sold below its value, for its value is determined not in isolation but as an aliquot part of the total product.

||808| "If you call labour a commodity, it is not like a commodity which is first produced in order to exchange, and then brought to market where it must exchange with other commodities according to the respective quantities of each which there may be in the market at the time; labour is *created* at the moment it is brought to market; nay, it is brought to market, before it is created" (op. cit., pp. 75-76).

What is in fact brought to market is not labour, but the labourer. What he sells to the capitalist is not his labour but the temporary use of himself as a working power. This is the immediate object of the contract which the capitalist and the worker conclude, the purchase and sale which they transact.

Where payment is for piece-work, task-work, instead of according to the time for which the labour-power is placed at the disposal of the employer, this is only another method of determining the time. It is measured by the product, a definite quantity of products being considered as a standard representing the socially necessary labour-time. In many branches of industry in London where piece-work is the rule, payment is thus made by the hour, but disputes often arise as to whether this or that piece of work constitutes "an hour" or not.

Irrespective of the individual form, it is the case not only with regard to piece-work, but in general, that, although labour-power is sold on definite terms before its use, it is only *paid for* after the work is completed, whether it is paid daily, weekly, and so on. Here money becomes the *means of payment* after it has served previously as an abstract means of purchase, because the nominal transfer of the commodity to the buyer is distinct from the actual transfer. The sale of the commodity—labour-power—the legal transfer of the use-value and its actual alienation, do not occur at the same time. The realisation of the price therefore takes place later than the sale of the commodity (see *the first part* of my book, p. 122).[41] It can also be seen that here it is the worker, not the capitalist, who does the advancing, just as in the case of the renting of a house, it is not the tenant but the landlord who advances use-value. The worker will indeed be paid (or at least he may be, if the goods have not been ordered beforehand and so on) before the commodities produced by him have been sold. But *his* commodity, his labour-power, has been consumed industrially, i.e., has been transferred into the hands of the buyer, the capitalist, before he, the worker, has been paid. And it is not a question of what the buyer of a commodity wants to do with it, whether he buys it in order to retain it as a use-value or in order to sell it again. It is a question of the *direct* transaction between the first buyer and seller.

[Ricardo says in the *Principles*:]

"In different stages of society, the accumulation of c a p i t a l, or of the m e a n s   o f   e m p l o y i n g   l a b o u r, is more or less rapid, and must in all cases depend on the productive powers of labour. The productive powers of labour are generally greatest where there is an abundance of fertile land" (David Ricardo, *Principles of Political Economy*, third ed., London, 1821, p. 92). [Quoted from *Observations on certain Verbal Disputes in Political Economy etc.*, London, 1821, p. 74.]

[The author of the *Observations* makes] the following remark on this passage of Ricardo's:

"If, in the first sentence, *the productive powers of labour mean the smallness of that aliquot part of any produce that goes to those whose manual la-*

bour produced it, the sentence is nearly identical, because the *remaining aliquot part is the fund whence capital can*, if the owner pleases, *be accumulated*" [*Observations*, London, 1821, p. 74].

(This is a tacit admission that from the standpoint of the capitalist *"productive powers of labour* mean the smallness of that aliquot part of any produce that goes to those whose manual labour produced it". This sentence is very nice.)

"But then this does not generally happen where there is most fertile land" [loc. cit., p. 74].

(This is silly. Ricardo presupposes capitalist production. He does not investigate whether it develops more freely with fertile or relatively unfertile land. Where it exists, it is most productive where land is most fertile.) Just as the social productive forces, the natural productive forces of labour, that is, those labour finds in inorganic nature, appear as the productive power of capital. (Ricardo himself, in the passage cited above, rightly identifies productive power of labour with labour productive of capital, productive of the wealth that commands labour, not of the wealth that belongs to labour. *His expression "c a p i t a l, o r t h e m e a n s o f e m p l o y i n g l a b o u r "* is, in fact, the only one in which he grasps the real nature of capital. He himself is so much the prisoner of a ||809| capitalist standpoint that this conversion, this *quid pro quo*, is for him a matter of course. The objective conditions of labour—created, moreover, by labour itself—raw materials and working instruments, are not *means employed by labour as its means*, but, on the contrary, they are *the means of employing labour*. They are not employed by labour; they employ labour. For them labour is a means by which they are accumulated as capital, not a means to provide products, wealth for the worker.)

"It does in North America, but that is an artificial state of things" (that is, a capitalistic state of things).

"It does not in Mexico. It does not in New Holland. The productive powers of labour are, indeed, in *another* sense, greatest where there is much fertile land, viz. the power of man, if he chooses it, to raise much *raw produce* in proportion to the whole labour he performs. It is, indeed, *a gift of nature, that men can raise more food than the lowest quantity that they could maintain and keep up the existing population on...*" [loc. cit., pp. 74-75].

(This is the basis of the doctrine of the *Physiocrats*. The physical basis of surplus-value is this "gift of nature", most obvious in agricultural labour, which originally satisfied nearly all human needs. It is not so in manufacturing labour, because the product must first be sold as a commodity. The Physiocrats, the first to analyse surplus-value, understand it in its natural form.)

"... but *'surplus produce'* (the term used by Mr. Ricardo, page 93), generally means the excess of the whole price of a thing above that part of it which goes to the labourers who made it..."

(the fool does not see that where the land is fertile, the part of the price of the produce that goes to the labourer, although it may be small, buys a sufficient quantity of necessaries; the part that goes to the capitalist is great)

"a point, which is settled by human arrangement, and not fixed by nature" (loc. cit., pp. 74-75).

If the last, concluding passage has any meaning at all, it is that "surplus produce" in the capitalist sense must be strictly distinguished from the productivity of industry as such. The latter is of interest to the capitalist only insofar as it realises profit for him. Therein lies the narrowness and limitation of capitalist production.

"When the demand for an article exceeds [...] that which is, with reference to the present rate[a] of supply, the effectual demand; and when, consequently, the price has risen, either additions can be made to the rate of supply at the same rate of cost of production as before; in which case they will be made till the article is brought to exchange at the same rate as before with other articles [...]: or, 2ndly, *no* possible additions can be made to the former rate of supply: and then the price, which has risen, will not be brought down [...], but continue to afford, as Smith says, a greater rent, or profits, or wages (or all three), to the particular land, capital, or labour, employed in producing the article, [...] or, 3rdly, the additions which can be made will require proportionally *more* land, or capital, or labour, or all three, than were required *for the periodical production*" (*note these words*) "of the amount previously supplied. Then the addition will not be made till the demand is strong enough, 1st, to pay this increased price for the addition; 2ndly, to pay the same increased price upon the old amount of supply. For the person who has produced the additional quantity will be no more able to get a high price for it, than those who produced the former quantity.... There will then be *surplus profits* in this trade.... The *surplus profits* will be either in the hands of some particular producers only'... or, if the *additional* produce cannot be *distinguished* from the rest, will be a surplus shared by all.... People will give something to belong to a trade in which *surplus profit* can be made.... What they so give, is *rent*" (op. cit., pp. 79-81).

Here, one need only say that in this book rent is for the first time regarded as the general form of consolidated *surplus profit*.

---

[a] The manuscript has "state".—*Ed.*

||810| "'Conversion of revenue into capital' is another of these *verbal sources of controversy*. One man means by it, that the capitalist lays out part of the profits he has made by his capital, in making additions to his capital, instead of spending it for his private use, as he might else have done: another man means by it, that a person lays out as capital something which he never got as profits, or any capital of his own, but received as rent, wages, salary" op. cit., pp. 83-84).

This last passage—"another of these *verbal sources* of controversy. One man means by it ... another man means by it..." —testifies to the method used by this smart alec.

b) "An Inquiry into those Principles..."
[The Lack of Understanding of the Contradictions of the Capitalist Mode of Production Which Cause Crises]

An Inquiry into those Principles, respecting the Nature of Demand and the Necessity of Consumption, lately advocated by Mr. Malthus etc., London, 1821.
A Ricardian work. Good against Malthus. Demonstrates the infinite narrow-mindedness to which the perspicacity of these fellows is reduced as soon as they examine not landed property, but capital. Nevertheless, it is one of the best of the polemical works of the decade mentioned.

"If the capital employed in cutlery is increased as 100:101, and can only produce an increase of cutlery in the same proportion, the degree in which it will increase the command which its producers have over things in general, no increased production of *them* having by the supposition taken place, *will be in a less proportion*; and this, and not the increase of the quantity of cutlery, constitutes the employers' profits, or the increase of their wealth. But if the like addition of one per cent had been *making at the same time to the capitals of all other trades* [...] and *with the like result as to produce*, this [...] would not follow: for the rate at which each article would exchange with the rest would remain unaltered, and therefore a given portion of each would give the same command as before over the rest" ([*An Inquiry into those Principles*, London, 1821,] p. 9).

First of all, if there has been no increase of production (and of the capital devoted to production) except in the cutlery trade, as is assumed, then the return will not be "*in a less proportion*", but an absolute loss. There are then only three courses open to the cutlery producer. Either he must exchange his increased product as he would have done his smaller product, and his increased production would thus result in a positive loss. Or he must try to get new consumers; if amongst the old circle, this could only be done by withdrawing customers from another trade and shifting his loss upon other shoulders; or he must enlarge his market beyond his former limits; but neither the one nor the other operation depends on his good will; nor on the mere existence of an increased quantity of knives. Or, in the last instance, he must carry over his production to another year and diminish his new supply for that year, which, if his addition of capital did exist not only in additional wages, but in additional fixed capital, will equally result in a loss.[a]

Furthermore: If all other capitals have accumulated at the same rate, it does not follow at all that their production has increased at the same rate. But if it has, it does not follow that they want one per cent more of cutlery, as their demand for cutlery is not at all connected, either with the increase of their own produce, or with their increased power of buying cutlery. What follows is merely the tautology: If the increased capital used in each particular branch of production is proportionate to the rate in which the wants of society increase the demand for each particular commodity, then the increase of one commodity secures a market for the increased supply of other commodities.

Here, therefore, is presupposed 1. *capitalist production*, in which the production of each particular industry and its increase are not *directly* regulated and ||811| *controlled* by the wants of society, but by the productive forces at the disposal of each individual capitalist, independent of the wants of society. 2. It is assumed that nevertheless production is *proportional* [to the requirements] as though capital were employed in the different spheres of production directly by society in accordance with its needs.

On this assumption—if capitalist production were entirely socialist production—a contradiction in terms—no over-production could, in fact, occur.

By the way, in the various branches of industry in which *the same accumulation* of capital takes place (and this too is an unfortunate assumption that capital is accumulated at an *equal rate* in different spheres), the amount of products corresponding to the increased capital employed may vary greatly, since the productive forces in the different industries or the total use-values produced in relation to the labour employed differ considerably. The same value is produced in both cases, but the quantity of commodities in which it is represented is very different. It is

---

[a] Marx wrote most of this and of the two following paragraphs in English.—*Ed.*

quite incomprehensible, therefore, why industry A, because the value of its output has increased by 1 per cent while the mass of its products has grown by 20 per cent, must find a market in B where the value has likewise increased by 1 per cent, but the quantity of its output only by 5 per cent. Here, the author has failed to take into consideration the difference between use-value and exchange-value.

Say's earth-shaking discovery that "commodities can only be bought with commodities"[42] simply means that money is itself the converted form of the commodity. It does not prove by any means that because I can buy only with commodities, I can buy with *my* commodity, or that my purchasing power is related to the *quantity* of commodities I produce. The same *value* can be embodied in very different quantities [of commodities]. But the use-value—consumption—depends not on value, but on the quantity. It is quite unintelligible why I should buy six knives because I can get them for the same price that I previously paid for one. Apart from the fact that the workers do not sell commodities, but labour, a great number of people who do not produce commodities at all buy things with money. Buyers and sellers of commodities are not identical. The landlord, the moneyed capitalist and others obtain in the form of *money* commodities produced by other people. They are buyers without being sellers of "commodities". Buying and selling occurs not only between industrial capitalists, but they also sell to workers; and likewise to owners of revenue who are not commodity producers. Finally, the purchases and sales transacted by them as capitalists are very different from the purchases they make as revenue-spenders.

"Mr. Ricardo (p. 359, second ed.), after quoting the doctrine of Smith about the cause of the fall of profits, adds, 'M. Say has, however, most satisfactorily shown, that there is no amount of capital which may not be employed in a country, because demand is only *limited* by production'" [*An Inquiry into those Principles*, London, 1821, p. 18].

(This is very wise. *Limited*, indeed. Nothing can be demanded which *cannot* be produced upon demand, or which the demand does not find ready made in the market. Hence, because demand is *limited* by production, it by no means follows that *production is, or was, limited by demand*, and can never exceed the demand, particularly the demand at the market price. This is Say-like acumen.)

"'There cannot be accumulated (p. 360) in a country any amount of capital which cannot be employed *productively*' (meaning, I presume,"—says the äuthor in brackets—"'with profit to the owner) 'until wages rise so high *in consequence* of the rise of necessaries, and so little consequently remains for the profits of stock, that the motive for accumulation ceases'" [loc. cit., pp. 18-19].

(Ricardo here equates "productively" and "profitably", whereas it is precisely the fact that in capitalist production "profitably" alone is "productively", that constitutes the difference between it and absolute production, as well as its limitations. In order to produce "productively", production must be carried on in such a way that the mass of producers are excluded from the demand for a part of the product. Production has to be carried on in opposition to a class ||812| whose consumption stands in no relation to its production—since it is precisely in the excess of its production over its consumption that the profit of capital consists. On the other hand, production must be carried on for classes who consume without producing. It is not enough merely to give the surplus product a form in which it becomes an object of demand for these classes. On the other hand, the capitalist himself, if he wishes to accumulate, must not himself consume as much of his own products, insofar as they are consumer goods, as he produces. Otherwise he cannot accumulate. That is why Malthus opposes to the capitalist classes whose task is not accumulation but expenditure. And while on the one hand all these contradictions are assumed, it is assumed on the other that production proceeds without any friction just as if these contradictions did not exist at all. Purchase is divorced from sale, commodity from money, use-value from exchange-value. It is assumed however that this separation does not exist, but that there is barter. Consumption and production are separated; [there are] producers who do not consume and consumers who do not produce. It is assumed that consumption and production are identical. The capitalist directly produces exchange-value in order to increase his profit, and not for the sake of consumption. It is assumed that he produces directly for the sake of consumption and only for it. [If it is] assumed that the contradictions existing in bourgeois production—which, in fact, are reconciled by a process of adjustment which, at the same time, however, manifests itself as crises, violent fusion of disconnected factors operating independently of one another and yet correlated—if it is assumed that the contradictions existing in bourgeois production do not exist, then these contradictions obviously cannot come into play. In every industry each individual capitalist produces in proportion to *his* capital irrespective of the needs of society and especially irrespective of the supply of competing capitalists in the same industry. It is assumed that he produces as if he were fulfilling orders placed by society. If there were no foreign trade, then luxuries could be produced at home, whatever their cost. In that case, labour, with the exception of [the branches producing] necessaries, would, in actual fact, be very unproductive. Hence accumulation of capital [would proceed at a low rate]. Thus every country would be able to employ all the capital accumulated there, since according to the assumption very little capital would have been accumulated.)

"The latter sentence limits (not to say contradicts) the former, if 'which may not be employed', in the former, means 'employed productively', or rather, 'profitably'. And if it means simply 'employed', the proposition is useless; because neither Adam Smith nor any body else, I presume, denied that it might 'be employed' if you did not care what profit is brought" (loc. cit., p. 19).

Ricardo says indeed that all capital in a given country, at whatever rate accumulated, may be employed profitably; on the other hand he says that the very fact of the accumulation of capital checks its "profitable" employment, because it must result in lessening profits, that is, the rate of accumulation.

"... the very meaning of an increased demand by them" (the labourers) "is a disposition to take less themselves, and leave a larger share for their employers; and if it be said that this, by diminishing consumption, increases glut, I can only answer, that glut [...] is synonymous with high profits..." (op. cit., p. 59).

This is indeed the secret basis of glut.

"... the labourers do not, considered as consumers, derive any benefit from machines, while flourishing" (as Mr. Say says in his *Traité d'économie politique*, fourth ed., Vol. I, p. 60) "unless the article, which the machines cheapen, is one that can be brought, by cheapening, within their use. Threshing-machines, windmills, may be a great thing for them in this view; but the invention of a veneering machine, or a block machine, or a lace frame, does not mend *their* condition much" (op. cit., pp. 74-75).

"The habits of the labourers, where division of labour has been carried very far, are applicable only to the particular line they have been used to; *they are a sort of machines*. Then, there is a long period of idleness, that is, of labour lost; of wealth cut off at its root. It is quite useless to repeat, like a parrot, that things have a tendency to find their level. We must look about us, and see they ||813| *cannot* for a long time find a level; that when they do, it will be a far lower level than they set out from" (op.cit., p.72).

This Ricardian, following Ricardo's example, recognises correctly crises resulting from sudden changes in the channels of trade.[43] This was the case in England after the war of 1815. And consequently, whenever a crisis occurred, all later economists declared that the *most obvious cause* of the particular crisis was the only possible cause of all crises.

The author also admits that the credit system may be a cause of crises (p. 81 et seq.) (as if the credit system itself did not arise out of the difficulty of employing capital "productively", i.e., "profitably"). The English, for example, are forced to lend their capital to other countries in order to create a market for their commodities. Over-production, the credit system, etc., are means by which capitalist production seeks to break through its own barriers and to produce over and above its own *limits*. Capitalist production, on the one hand, has this driving force; on the other hand, it only tolerates production commensurate with the profitable employment of existing capital. Hence crises arise, which simultaneously drive it onward and beyond [its own limits] and force it to put on seven-league boots, in order to reach a development of the productive forces which could only be achieved very slowly within its own limits.

What the author writes about Say is very true. This should be dealt with in connection with Say (see p. 134, *notebook VII*[44]).

"He" (the worker) "will agree *to work part of his time for the capitalist,* or, what comes to the same thing, to consider part of the whole produce, when raised and exchanged, as belonging to the capitalist. He must do so, or the capitalist would not have afforded him this[a] assistance" [op. cit., p. 102].

(Namely capital. Very fine that it comes to the same thing whether the capitalist owns the whole produce and pays part of it as wages to the labourer, or whether the labourer leaves, makes over to the capitalist part of his (the labourer's) produce.)

"But as the capitalist's *motive was gain*, and as these advantages always depend, in a certain degree, on the *will* to save, as well as on the *power*, the capitalist will be disposed to afford an additional portion of these assistances; and as he will find fewer people in want of this additional portion, than were in want of the original portion, he must expect to have a less share of the benefit to himself; he must be content to make a *present*" (!!!) "(as it were) to the labourer, of part of the benefit his assistance occasions, or else he would not get the other part: the profit is reduced, then, by competition" (loc. cit., pp. 102-03).

---

[a] The manuscript has "his".—*Ed.*

This is very fine. If, as a consequence of the development of labour productivity, capital accumulates so quickly that the demand for labour increases wages and the worker works for a shorter time gratis for the capitalist and shares to some degree in the benefits of his more productive labour—the capitalist makes him a *"present"*.

The same author demonstrates in great detail that high wages are bad, a discouragement for workers, although, speaking of the landlords, he considers that low profit is a discouragement for the capitalists (see p. 13, notebook XII[45]).

"Adam Smith thought [...] that accumulation or increase of stock in general lowered the rate of profit in general, on the same principle which makes the increase of stock in any particular trade lower the profits of that trade. But such increase of stock in a particular trade means an increase more *in proportion* than stock is at the same time increased in other trades" (op. cit., p. 9).

Against Say. (Notebook XII, p. 12.[46])

"The immediate market for capital, or *field* for capital may be said to be labour. The amount of capital which can be invested at a given moment, in a given country, or the world, so as to return not less than a given rate of profits, seems principally to depend on the *quantity of labour*, which it is possible, by laying out that capital, to induce the then existing number of human beings to perform" (op. cit., p. 20).

||814| *"Profits* do not depend on *price,* they depend on price compared with outgoings" (op. cit., p. 28).

"The proposition of M. Say does not at all prove that *capital* opens a market for itself, but only that capital and labour open a market for one another" (op. cit., p. 111).

c) **Thomas De Quincey**
[Failure to Overcome the Real Flaws in the Ricardian Standpoint]

Dialogues of Three Templars on Political Economy, chiefly in relation to the Principles of Mr. Ricardo (*London Magazine,* Vol. IX, 1824) (author: Thomas De Quincey).

Attempt at a refutation of all the attacks made on Ricardo. That he is aware of what is at issue is to be seen from this sentence:

"... all [...] difficulties" of political economy "will be found reducible" [to] "this: What is the ground of exchangeable value?" ([De Quincey, *Dialogues of Three Templars,* 1824,] p. 347.)

In this work, the inadequacies of the Ricardian view are often pointedly set forth, although the dialectical depth is more affected than real. The real difficulties, which arise not out of the determination of value, but from Ricardo's inadequate elaboration of his ideas on this basis, and from his arbitrary attempt to make concrete relations directly fit the simple relation of value, are in no way resolved or even grasped. But the work is characteristic of the period in which it appeared. It shows that in political economy consistency and thinking were still taken seriously at that time.

(A later work by the same author: *The Logic of Political Economy*, Edinburgh, 1844, is weaker.)

De Quincey very clearly outlines the differences between the Ricardian view and those which preceded it, and does not seek to mitigate them by re-interpretation or to abandon the essential features of the problems in actual fact while retaining them in a purely formal, verbal way as happened later on, thus opening the door wide to easy-going, unprincipled eclecticism.

One point in the Ricardian doctrine which is especially emphasised by De Quincey and which should be mentioned here because it plays a role in the polemic against Ricardo to which we shall refer below, is that the command which one commodity has over other commodities (its purchasing power; in fact, its value expressed in terms of another commodity) is altogether different from its *real value*.

It is quite wrong to conclude "that the real value is great because the quantity it buys is great, or small because the quantity it buys is small.... If A double its value, it will not therefore command double the former quantity of B. It may do so: and it may also command five hundred times more, or five hundred times less.... No man has ever denied that A by doubling its own value will command a double quantity of all things which have been stationary in value. [...] But the question is whether universally, from doubling its value, A will command a double quantity..." ([*Dialogues of Three Templars*,] pp. 552-54 passim).

d) Samuel Bailey

[α) Superficial Relativism on the Part of the Author
of "Observations on certain Verbal Disputes"
and on the Part of Bailey in Treating the Category
of Value. The Problem of the Equivalent. Rejection
of the Labour Theory of Value as the Foundation
of Political Economy]

A Critical Dissertation on the Nature, Measures, and Causes of Value; chiefly in Reference to the Writings of Mr. Ricardo and his Followers. By the Author of Essays on the Formation and Publication of Opinions (Samuel Bailey), London, 1825.

This is the main work directed against Ricardo., (Also aimed against Malthus.) It seeks to overturn the foundation of the doctrine—*value*. It is definitely worthless except for the definition of the *"measure of value"*, or rather, of money in this function. Compare also the same author's: *A Letter to a Political Economist; occasioned by an Article in the Westminster Review on the Subject of Value etc.*, London, 1826.

Since, as has been mentioned,[a] this work basically agrees with *Observations on certain Verbal Disputes in Political Economy*, it is here necessary to add the relevant passages from these *Observations*.

The author of the *Observations* accuses Ricardo of having transformed *value* from a relative attribute of commodities in their relationship to one another, into something absolute.

The only thing that Ricardo can be accused of in this context is that, in elaborating the concept of value, he does not clearly distinguish between the various aspects, between the exchange-value of the commodity, as it *manifests itself, appears* in the process of commodity exchange, and the existence of the commodity as *value* as distinct from its existence as an object, product, use-value.

||815| It is said in the *Observations*:

"If the absolute quantity of labour, which produces the greater part of commodities, or all except one, is increased, would you say that the value of that one is unaltered? In what sense? since it will exchange for less of every commodity besides. If, indeed, it is meant to be asserted that the *meaning* of increase or diminution of value is increase or diminution in the quantity of labour that produced the commodity spoken of, the conclusions I have just been objecting to might be true enough. But to say, as Mr. Ricardo does, that the comparative quantities of labour that produce two commodities are the cause of the rate at which these two commodities will exchange with each other, i.e., of the exchangeable value of each, understood in relation to the other, is very different from saying that the *exchangeable value of either means* the quantity of labour which produced it, understood without any reference to the other, or to the existence of any other" (*Observations etc.*, p. 13).

"Mr. Ricardo tells us indeed [...] that 'the inquiry to which he wishes to draw the reader's attention relates to the effect of the variations in the *relative* value of commodities, and not in their *absolute* value'; as if he there considered that there *is* such a thing as exchangeable value which is not relative" (op. cit., pp. 9-10).

"That Mr. Ricardo has departed from his original use of the term value, and *has made of it something absolute, instead of relative*, is still more evi-

---

[a] See this volume, p. 111.—*Ed.*

dent in his chapter entitled 'Value and Riches, their distinctive Properties'. The question there discussed, has been discussed also by others, and is purely verbal and useless..." (op. cit., pp. 15-16).

Before dealing with this author, we shall add the following about Ricardo. In his chapter on "Value and Riches", he argues that social wealth does not depend on the value of the commodities produced, although this latter point is decisive for every individual producer. It should have been all the more clear to him that a mode of production whose exclusive aim is surplus-value, in other words, which is based on the relative poverty of the mass of the producers, cannot possibly be the absolute form of the production of wealth, as he constantly asserts.

Now to the *Observations* of the "verbal" wiseacre.

If all commodities except one increase in value because they cost more labour-time than they did before, smaller amounts of these commodities will be exchanged for the single commodity whose labour-time remains unchanged. Its *exchange-value*, insofar as it is realised in other commodities—that is, its exchange-value expressed in the *use-values* of all other commodities—has been reduced. "Would you then say that the value of that one is *unaltered*?" This is merely a formulation of the point at issue, and it calls neither for a positive nor for a negative reply. The same result would occur if the labour-time required for the production of the one commodity were reduced and that of all the others remained unchanged. A given quantity of this particular commodity would exchange for a reduced quantity of all the other commodities. The same phenomenon occurs in both cases although from directly opposite causes. Conversely, if the labour-time required for the production of commodity A remained unchanged, while that of all others were reduced, then it would exchange for larger amounts of all the other commodities. The same would happen for the opposite reason, if the labour-time required for the production of commodity A increased and that required for all other commodities remained unchanged. Thus, sometimes commodity A exchanges for smaller quantities of all the other commodities, and this for either of two different and opposite reasons. At other times it exchanges for larger quantities of all the other commodities, again for two different and opposite reasons. But it should be noted that it is assumed that it always exchanges at *its value*, consequently for an *equivalent*. It always realises its value in the quantity of use-values of the other commodities for which it exchanges, no matter how much the quantity of these use-values varies.

From this it obviously follows: that the rate at which commodities exchange for one another as use-values, although it is an *expression* of their value, their *realised* value, is not their value itself, since the same proportion of value can be represented by quite different quantities of use-values. Value as an aspect of the commodity is not expressed in its own use-value, or in its existence as use-value. Value *manifests* itself when commodities are expressed in other use-values, that is, it manifests itself in the rate at which these other use-values are exchanged for them. If one ounce of gold equals a ton of iron, that is, if a small quantity of gold exchanges for a large quantity of iron, is therefore the value of the gold expressed in iron greater than the value of the iron expressed in gold? That commodities exchange for one another in proportion to the labour embodied in them, means that they are equal, alike, insofar as they constitute the same quantity of labour. Consequently it means likewise that every commodity, considered in itself, is something *different* from its own use-value, ||816| from its own existence as use-value.

The *value* of the same commodity can, without changing, be expressed in infinitely *different* quantities of use-values, always according to whether I express it in the use-value of this or of that commodity. This does not alter the value, although it does alter the way it is expressed. In the same way, all the various quantities of different use-values in which the value of commodity A can be expressed, are equivalents and are related to one another not only as values, but as equal values, so that when these very unequal quantities of use-value replace one another, the value remains completely unchanged, as if it had not found expression in quite different use-values.

When commodities are exchanged in the proportion in which they represent equal amounts of labour-time, then it is their aspect as materialised labour-time, as embodied labour-time, which manifests their *substance*, the *identical element* they contain. As such, they are *qualitatively* the same, and differ only *quantitatively*, according to whether they represent smaller or larger quantities of the *same* substance, i.e., labour-time. They are *values* as expressions of the same element; and they are equal values, *equivalents*, insofar as they represent an equal amount of labour-time. They can only be compared as magnitudes, because they are already homogeneous magnitudes, qualitatively identical.

It is as manifestations of this substance that these different things constitute *values* and are related to one another as values; their different *magnitudes of value*, their immanent measure of value are thus also given. And only *because of this* can the value of a commodity be represented, expressed, in the use-values of other commodities as its equivalents. Hence the *individual commodity* as *value*, as the *embodiment of this substance*, is different from itself as use-value, as an object, quite apart from the expression of its value in other commodities. As the embodiment of labour-time, it is *value* in general, as the embodiment of a definite quantity of labour-time, it is a definite *magnitude of value*.

It is therefore typical of our wiseacre when he says: If we *mean* that, we do n o t *mean* that and vice versa. Our "meaning" has nothing at all to do with the essential character of the thing we consider. If we speak of the *value in exchange* of a thing, we *mean* in the first instance of course the *relative quantities* of all other commodities that can be exchanged for the first commodity. But, on further consideration, we shall find that for the proportion, in which one thing exchanges for an infinite mass of other things which have nothing in common with it—and even if there are natural or other similarities between those things, they are not considered in the exchange—for the proportion to be a *fixed proportion*, all those various heterogeneous things must be considered as proportionate representations, expressions of the *same common unity*, [of] an element quite different from their natural existence or appearance. We shall furthermore find, that if our views have any sense, the value of a commodity is something which not only distinguishes it from or relates it to other commodities, but is a quality differentiating it from its own existence as a thing, a value in use.[a]

"The rise of value of article A, only meant *value estimated* in articles B, C, etc., i.e., value in exchange for articles B, C, etc." ([*Observations*, London, 1821,] p. 16).

To *estimate* the value of A, a book for instance, in B, coals, and C, wine, A, B and C must be as *value* something different from their existence as books, coals or wine. To estimate the value

---

[a] Marx wrote this paragraph and the one following the passage quoted almost entirely in English.—*Ed.*

of A in B, A must have a value independent of the estimation of that value in B, and both must be equal to a third thing expressed in both of them.

It is quite wrong to say that the value of a commodity is thereby transformed from something *relative* into something *absolute*. On the contrary, as a use-value, the commodity appears as something independent. On the other hand, as value it appears as something merely *contingent*, something merely determined by its relation to socially necessary, equal, simple labour-time. It is to such an extent relative that when the labour-time required for its reproduction changes, its value changes, although the labour-time really contained in the commodity has remained unaltered.

||817| How deeply our wiseacre has sunk into *fetishism* and how he transforms what is relative into something positive, is demonstrated most strikingly in the following passage:

"*Value* is a *property of things, riches of men*. Value, in this sense, necessarily implies exchange, riches do not" (loc. cit., p. 16).

Riches here are use-values. These, as far as men are concerned, are, of course, riches, but it is through its *own properties*, its own qualities, that a thing is a use-value and therefore an element of wealth for men. Take away from grapes the qualities that make them grapes, and their use-value as grapes disappears for men and they cease to be an element of wealth for men. Riches which are identical with use-values are *properties of things* that are made use of by men and which express a relation to their wants. But "value" is supposed to be a "*property of things*".

As values, commodities are *social* magnitudes, that is to say, something absolutely different from their "properties" as "things". As values, they constitute only relations of men in their productive activity. Value indeed "implies exchanges", but exchanges are exchanges of things between men, exchanges which in no way affect the things as such. A thing retains the same "properties" whether it be owned by A or by B. In actual fact, the concept "value" presupposes "exchanges" of the products. Where labour is communal, the relations of men in their social production do not manifest themselves as "values" of "things". Exchange of products as commodities is a method of exchanging labour, [it demonstrates] the dependence of the labour of each upon the labour of the others [and corresponds to] a certain mode of social labour or social production.

In the first part of my book,[47] I mentioned that it is characteristic of labour based on private exchange that the social character of labour "manifests" itself in a perverted form—as the "property" of things; that a social relation appears as a relation between things (between products, values in use, commodities). This *appearance* is accepted as something real by our fetish-worshipper, and he actually believes that the exchange-value of things is determined by their properties as things, and is altogether a natural property of things. No scientist to date has yet discovered what natural qualities make definite proportions of snuff tobacco and paintings "equivalents" for one another.

Thus he, the wiseacre, transforms value into something absolute, "a property of things", instead of seeing in it only something relative, the relation of things to social labour, social labour based on private exchange, in which things are defined not as independent entities, but as mere expressions of social production.

But to say that "value" is not an absolute, is not conceived as an entity, is quite different from saying that commodities must impart to their exchange-value a *separate* expression which is *different* from and *independent* of their use-value and of their existence as real products, in other words, that commodity circulation is bound to evolve money. Commodities express their exchange-value in money, first of all in the *price*, in which they all present themselves as materialised forms of *the same* labour, as only quantitatively different expressions of *the same* substance. The fact that the *exchange-value* of the commodity *assumes an independent existence* in money is itself the result of the process of exchange, the development of the contradiction of use-value and exchange-value embodied in the commodity, and of another no less important contradiction embodied in it, namely, that the definite, particular labour of the private individual must manifest itself as its opposite, as equal, necessary, general labour and, in this form, social labour. The representation of the commodity as money implies not only that the different magnitudes of commodity values are measured by expressing the values in the use-value of one exclusive commodity, but at the same time that they are all expressed in a form in which they exist as the embodiment of *social labour* and are therefore exchangeable for every other commodity, that they are translatable at will into any use-value desired. Their representation as money—in the price—therefore appears first only as something nominal, a representation which is realised only through actual sale. *Ricardo's mistake is that he is concerned only with the magnitude of value.* Consequently his attention is concentrated on ||818| the *relative quantities of labour* which the different commodities represent, or which the commodities as values embody. But the labour embodied in them must be represented as *social* labour, as alienated individual labour. In the price this representation is nominal; it becomes reality only in the sale. This transformation of the labour of private individuals contained in the commodities into *uniform social labour*, consequently into labour which can be expressed in all use-values and can be exchanged for them, this *qualitative* aspect of the matter which is contained in the representation of exchange-value as money, is not elaborated by Ricardo. This circumstance—the necessity of *presenting* the labour contained in commodities as *uniform social labour*, i.e., as money—is overlooked by Ricardo.

For its part, the development of capital already *presupposes* the full development of the exchange-value of commodities and consequently its independent existence as money. The point of departure in the process of the production and circulation of capital, is the independent form of value which maintains itself, increases, measures the increase against the original amount, whatever changes the commodities in which it manifests itself may undergo, and quite irrespective of whether it presents itself in the most varied use-values and moves from commodity to commodity. The relation between the value antecedent to production and the value which results from it—capital as antecedent value is capital in contrast to profit—constitutes the all-embracing and decisive factor in the whole process of capitalist production. It is not only an independent expression of value as in money, but dynamic value, value which maintains itself in a process in which use-values pass through the most varied forms. Thus in capital the independent existence of value is raised to a higher power than in money.

From this we can judge the wisdom of our "verbal" wiseacre, who treats the independent existence of exchange-value as a figure of speech, a manner of talking, a scholastic invention.

"Value, or valeur in French, is not only used absolutely instead of relatively as a quality of things, but is even used by some [...] as [...] a measurable commodity, 'Possessing a value', 'transferring a portion of value'" (a very important factor with regard to fixed capital), "'the sum, or totality of values' (valeurs), etc. I do not know what this means" (op. cit., p. 57).

The fact that the value which has become independent acquires only a relative expression in money, because money itself is a commodity, and hence has a changeable value, makes no difference but is a shortcoming which arises from the nature of the commodity and the necessity of expressing its exchange-value, as distinct from its use-value. Our author has made it abundantly clear that he does "not know" this. This is shown by the kind of criticism which would like to talk out of existence the difficulties innate in the contradictory functions of things themselves, by declaring them to be the result of reflexions or of conflicting definitions.

"'The *relative* value of two things' [...] is open to two meanings: the rate at which two things exchange or would exchange with *each other*, or the comparative portions of *a third* for which each exchanges or would exchange" (op. cit., p. 53).

To begin with, this is a fine definition. If 3 lbs. of coffee exchange for 1 lb. of tea today or would do so tomorrow, it does not at all mean that equivalents have been exchanged for each other. According to this, a commodity could always be exchanged only at its value, for its value would constitute any quantity of some other commodity for which it had been accidentally exchanged. This, however, is not what people generally *mean*, when they say that 3 lbs. of coffee have been exchanged for their equivalent in tea. They assume that after, as before, the exchange, a *commodity of the same value* is in the hands of either of the exchangers. The rate at which two commodities exchange does not determine their value, but their value determines the rate at which they exchange. If value were nothing more than the quantity of commodities for which commodity A is accidentally exchanged, how is it possible to express the value of A in terms of commodity B, or C, etc.? Because ||819| then, since there is no *immanent* measure common to the two commodities, the value of A could not be expressed in terms of B before it had been exchanged against B.

Relative value means first of all *magnitude of value* in contradistinction to the quality of having *value* at all. For this reason, the latter is not something absolute. It means, secondly, the value of one commodity expressed in the use-value of another commodity. This is *only* a *relative* expression of its value, namely, in relation to the commodity in which it is expressed. The value of a pound of coffee is only relatively expressed in tea; to express it absolutely—even in a relative way, that is to say, not in regard to labour-time, but to other commodities— it ought to be expressed in an infinite series of equations *with all other commodities*. This would be an *absolute* expression of its *relative value*; its absolute expression would be its expression *in terms of labour-time* and this absolute expression would express it as something relative, but in the absolute relation, by which it *is* value.

* * *

Let us now turn to Bailey.

His book has only one positive merit—that he was the first to give a more accurate definition of the *measure of value*, that is, in fact, of one of the functions of money, or money in a particular, determinate form. In order to measure the *value* of commodities—to establish an *external* measure of value—it is not necessary that the value of the commodity in terms of which the other commodities are measured, should be invariable. (It must on the contrary be variable, as I have shown in the first part,[48] because the measure of value is, and must be, a commodity since otherwise it would have no *immanent* measure in common with other commodities.) If, for example, the value of money changes, it changes to an equal degree in relation to all other commodities. Their relative values are therefore expressed in it just as correctly as if the value of money had remained unchanged.

The problem of finding an "invariable measure of value" is thereby eliminated. But this problem itself (the interest in comparing the value of commodities in different historical periods, is, indeed, not an *economic* interest as such, [but] an academic interest) arose out of a misunderstanding and conceals a much more profound and important question. "Invariable measure of value" signifies primarily a measure of value which is itself of invariable value, and consequently, since value itself is a predicate of the commodity, a commodity of invariable value. For example, if gold and silver or corn, or labour, were such commodities, then it would be possible to establish, by comparison with them, the rate at which other commodities are exchanged for them, that is, to measure exactly the variations in the values of these other commodities by their prices in gold, silver, or corn, or their relation to wages. Stated in this way, the problem therefore presupposes from the outset that in the "measure of value" we are dealing simply with the commodity in which the values of all other commodities are expressed, whether it be the commodity by which they are really represented—i.e., money, the commodity which functions as money—or a commodity which, because its value remains invariable, would function as the money in terms of which the theoretician makes his calculations. It thus becomes evident that in this context it is in any case a question only of a kind of money which as the measure of value—either theoretically or practically—would itself not be subject to changes in value.

But for commodities to express their exchange-value independently in money, in a third commodity, the exclusive commodity, the *values of commodities* must already be presupposed. Now the point is merely to compare them quantitatively. A *homogeneity* which makes them the same—makes them values—which as values makes them qualitatively equal, is already presupposed in order that their value and their differences in value can be represented in this way. For example, if all commodities express their value in gold, then this expression in gold, their gold price, their equation with gold, is an equation on the basis of which it is possible to elucidate and compute their value relation to one another, for they are now expressed as *different quantities of gold* and in this way the commodities are represented in their *prices*, ||820| as comparable magnitudes of the same common denominator.

But in order to be represented in this way, the commodities must *already* be *identical* as *values*. Otherwise it would be impossible to solve the problem of expressing the value of each commodity in gold, if commodity and gold or any two commodities as values were not representations of the same substance, capable of being expressed in one another. In other words, this presupposition is already implicit in the problem itself. Commodities are already presumed as values, as *values* distinct from their use-values, before the question of representing this value in a special commodity can arise. In order that two quantities of different use-values can be equated as equivalents, it is already presumed that they are *equal* to a third, that they are *qualitatively* equal and only constitute different quantitative expressions of this qualitative equality.

The problem of an "invariable measure of value" was simply a spurious name for the quest for the concept, the nature, of *value* itself, the definition of which could not be another value, and consequently could not be subject to variations as value. This was *labour-time, social labour*, as it presents itself specifically in commodity production. A quantity of labour has no value, is not a commodity, but is that which transforms commodities into values, it is their *common substance*; as manifestations of it commodities are *qualitatively equal* and only *quantitatively different*. They [appear] as expressions of definite quantities of social labour-time.

Let us assume that gold has an invariable value. If the value of all commodities were then expressed in gold one could measure variations in the values of commodities by their gold prices. But in order to express the value of commodities in gold, commodities and gold must be identical as *values*. Gold and commodities can only be considered to be identical as definite quantitative expressions of this value, as definite magnitudes of value. The invariable value of gold and the variable value of the other commodities would not prevent them, as *value*, from being the same, [consisting of] the same substance. Before the invariable value of gold can help us to make a step forward, the value of commodities must first be expressed, assessed, in gold—that is, gold and commodities must be represented as equivalents, as expressions of *the same substance*.

{In order that the commodities may be measured according to the quantity of labour embodied in them—and the measure of the quantity of labour is time—the different kinds of labour contained in the different commodities must be reduced to uniform, simple labour, average labour, ordinary, unskilled labour. Only then can the amount of labour embodied in them be measured according to a common measure, according to time. The labour must be qualitatively equal so that its differences become merely quantitative, merely differences of magnitude. This reduction to simple, average labour is not, however, the only determinant of the *quality* of this labour to which as a unity the values of the commodities are reduced. That the quantity of labour embodied in a commodity is the quantity *socially necessary* for its production—the labour-time being thus *necessary labour-time*— is a definition which concerns only the *magnitude of value*. But the labour which constitutes the substance of value is not only uniform, simple, average labour; it is the labour of a private individual represented in a definite product. However, the product as value must be the embodiment of *social* labour and, as such, be directly convertible from one use-value into all others.

(The particular use-value in which labour is directly represented is irrelevant so that it can be converted from one form into another.) Thus the *labour of individuals* has to be directly represented as its opposite, *social* labour; this transformed labour is, as its immediate opposite, *abstract, general labour*, which is therefore represented in a general equivalent. Only by its alienation does individual labour manifest itself as its opposite. The commodity, however, must have this general expression before it is alienated. This necessity to express individual labour as general labour is equivalent to the necessity of expressing a commodity as money. The commodity receives this expression insofar as the money serves as a measure and expresses the value of the commodity in its *price*. It is only through sale, through its real transformation into money, that the commodity acquires its adequate expression as exchange-value. The first transformation is merely a theoretical process, the second is a real one.

||821| Thus, in considering the existence of the commodity as *money*, it is not only necessary to emphasise that in money commodities acquire a definite *measure* of their value—since all commodities express their value in the use-value of *the same* commodity—but that they all become manifestations of social, abstract, general labour; and as such they all possess the same form, they all appear as the direct incarnation of social labour and as such they all act as social labour, that is to say, they can be *directly exchanged* for all other commodities in proportion to the size of their value; whereas in the hands of· the people whose commodities have been transformed into money, they exist not as exchange-value in the form of a particular use-value, but as use-value (gold, for example) which merely represents exchange-value. A commodity may be sold either below or above its value. This is purely a matter of the *magnitude of its value*. But whenever a commodity is sold, transformed into money, its exchange-value acquires an independent existence, separate from its use-value. The commodity now exists only as a certain quantity of social labour-time, and it proves that it is such by being *directly* exchangeable for any commodity whatsoever and convertible (in proportion to its magnitude) into any use-value whatsoever. This point must not be overlooked in relation to money any more than the formal transformation undergone by the labour a commodity contains as its element of value. But an examination of money—of that absolute exchangeability which the commodity possesses as money, of its absolute effectiveness as *exchange-value*

which has nothing to do with the magnitude of value—shows that it is *not quantitatively, but qualitatively determined* and that as a result of the very process through which the commodity itself passes, its *exchange-value* becomes independent, and is really represented as a separate aspect alongside its use-value as it is already nominally in its price.

This shows, therefore, that the "verbal observer" understands as little of the value and the nature of money as Bailey, since both regard the independent existence of value as a scholastic invention of economists. This independent existence becomes even more evident in capital, which, in one of its aspects, can be called *value in process*—and since value only exists independently in money, it can accordingly be called *money in process*, as it goes through a series of processes in which it preserves itself, departs from itself, and returns to itself increased in volume. It goes without saying that the paradox of reality is also reflected in paradoxes of speech which are at variance with common sense and with what vulgarians mean and believe they are talking of. The contradictions which arise from the fact that on the basis of commodity production the labour of the individual presents itself as general social labour, and the relations of people as relations between things and as things—these contradictions are innate in the subject-matter, not in its verbal expressions.}

Ricardo often gives the impression, and sometimes indeed writes, as if the quantity of labour is the solution to the false, or falsely conceived problem of an "invariable measure of value" in the same way as corn, money, wages, etc., were previously considered and advanced as panaceas of this kind. In Ricardo's work this false impression arises because for him the decisive task is the definition of the magnitude of value. Because of this he does not understand the specific form in which labour is an element of value, and fails in particular to grasp that the labour of the individual must present itself as abstract general labour and, in this form, as *social* labour. Therefore he has not understood that the development of money is connected with the nature of value and with the determination of this value by labour-time.

Bailey's book has rendered a good service insofar as the objections he raises help to clear up the confusion between "measure of value" expressed in money as a commodity along with other commodities, and the immanent measure and substance of value. But if he had analysed money as a "measure of value", not only as a quantitative measure but as a qualitative transformation of commodities, he would have arrived at a correct analysis of value. Instead of this, he contents himself with a mere superficial consideration of the external "measure of value"—which already presupposes value—and remains rooted in a purely frivolous approach to the question.

||822| There are, however, occasional passages in Ricardo in which he directly emphasises that the quantity of labour embodied in a commodity constitutes the immanent measure of the *magnitude* of its value, of the *differences in the amount* of its value, only because labour is the factor the different commodities have in *common*, which constitutes their uniformity, their substance, the intrinsic foundation of their value. The thing however he failed to investigate is the specific form in which labour plays that role.

"In making *labour* the *foundation of the value* of commodities, *and* the *comparative quantity of labour* which is necessary to their production, *the rule which determines the respective quantities of goods* which shall be given in exchange for each other, we must not be supposed to deny the accidental and temporary deviations of the actual or market price of commodities from this, their primary and natural price" ([David Ricardo, *The Principles of Political Economy, and Taxation,*] third ed., 1821, p. 80). Destutt de Tracy says that "To measure ... is to find how many times they" (the things measured) "contain [...] *unities of the same description.*" A franc is not a measure of value for any thing, but for a quantity of *the same metal* of which francs are made, unless francs, and the thing to be measured, can be referred to *some other measure which is c o m m o n to both*. This, I think, they can be, for they are both the *result of labour*; and, therefore" (because labour is their effective cause) "labour is a *common measure*, by which their *real* as well as their *relative value* may be estimated" (op. cit., pp. 333-34).

All commodities can be reduced to labour as their common element. What Ricardo does not investigate is the *specific* form in which labour manifests itself as the common element of commodities. That is why he does not understand money. That is why in his work the transformation of commodities into money appears to be something merely formal, which does not penetrate deeply into the very essence of capitalist production. He says however: only because labour is the common factor of commodities, only because they are all mere manifestations of the same common element, of labour, is labour their measure. It is their measure only because it forms their *substance* as values. Ricardo does not sufficiently differentiate between labour insofar as it is represented in use-values or in exchange-value. Labour as the foundation of value is not any particular labour, with particular qualities. Ricardo continuously confuses the labour which is represented in use-value and that which is represented in exchange-value. It is true that the latter species of labour is only the former species expressed in an abstract form.

By *real value*, Ricardo, in the passage cited above, understands the commodity as the embodiment of a definite amount of labour-time. By *relative value*, he understands the labour-time the commodity contains expressed in the use-values of other commodities.

Now to *Bailey*.

Bailey clings to the form in which the exchange-value of the commodity—as commodity—appears, manifests itself. It manifests itself in a *general form* when it is expressed in the use-value of a third commodity, in which all other commodities likewise express their value—a commodity which serves as money—that is, in the *money price* of the commodity. It manifests itself in a *particular form* when the exchange-value of any particular commodity is expressed in the use-value of any other, that is, as the *corn price*, *cotton price*, etc. In actual fact, the exchange-value of the commodity always appears, manifests itself with regard to other commodities, only in the *quantitative relationship* in which they exchange. The individual commodity as such cannot express general labour-time, or it can only express it in its equation with the commodity which constitutes money, in its *money price*. But then the value of commodity A is always expressed in a certain quantity of the use-value of the commodity which functions as money.

This is how matters *appear directly*. And Bailey clings to this. The most superficial form of exchange-value, that is the *quantitative relationship* in which commodities exchange with one another, *constitutes*, according to Bailey, their value. The advance from the surface to the core of the problem is not permitted. He even forgets the simple consideration that if y yards of linen equal x lbs. of straw, this [implies] a parity between two unequal things—linen and straw—making them equal magnitudes. This existence of theirs as things that are equal must surely be different ||823| from their existence as straw and linen. It is not as straw and linen that they are equated, but as equivalents. The one side of the equation must, therefore, express the same value as the other. The value of straw and linen must, therefore, be neither straw nor linen, but something common to both and different from both commodities considered as straw and linen. What is it? He does not answer this question. Instead, he wanders off into all the categories of political economy in order to repeat the same monotonous litany over and over again, namely, that value is the exchange relation of commodities and consequently is not anything different from this relation.

> *"If* the *value* of an object *is its power of purchasing*, there must be something to purchase. Value denotes *consequently* nothing positive or intrinsic, but merely the *relation* in which two objects stand to each other as *exchangeable commodities*" ([Samuel Bailey, *A Critical Dissertation on the Nature, Measures, and Causes of Value*, London, 1825,] pp. 4-5).

His entire wisdom is, in fact, contained in this passage. "If *value* is *nothing* but *power of purchasing*" (a very fine definition since "purchasing" presupposes not only value, but the representation of value as "money"), "it denotes", etc. However let us first clear away from Bailey's proposition the absurdities which have been smuggled in. "Purchasing" means transforming money into commodities. Money already presupposes value and the development of value. Consequently, out with the expression "purchasing" first of all. Otherwise we are explaining value by value. Instead of purchasing we must say "exchanging against other objects". It is quite superfluous to say that "there must be something to purchase". If the "object" was to be consumed by its producers as a use-value, if it was not merely a means of appropriating other objects, not a "commodity", then obviously there could be no question of value.

First, it is a matter of objects. But then the relation "in which two objects stand to each other" is transformed into "the relation in which two objects stand to each other as exchangeable commodities". After all, the objects stand only in relation of exchange or as exchangeable objects to each other. That is why they are *"commodities"*, which is something different from "objects". On the other hand, the "relation of exchangeable commodities" is either nonsense, since "not exchangeable objects" are not commodities, or Mr. Bailey has beaten himself. The objects are not to be exchanged in any arbitrary proportion, but are to be exchanged as commodities, that is, they are to stand to one another as exchangeable commodities, that is, as objects each of which has a value, and which are to be exchanged with one another in *proportion to their equivalence*. Bailey thereby admits that the rate at which they are exchanged, that is, the power of each of the commodities to purchase the other, is determined by its *value*, but this value however is not determined by this power, which is merely a corollary.

If we strip the passage of everything that is wrong, nonsensical or smuggled in, then it will read like this.

But wait: we must dispose of yet another snare and piece of nonsense. We have two sorts of expression. An object's "power" of exchanging, etc. (since the term "purchasing" is unjustified and makes no sense without the concept of money), and the *"relation in which"* an object exchanges with others. If "power" is to be regarded as something different from "relation", then one ought not to say that "power of exchanging" is *"merely the relation"*, etc. If it is meant to be *the same thing*, then it is confusing to describe the same thing with two different expressions which have nothing in common with each other. The *relation* of a thing to another is a relation of the two things and cannot be said to belong to either. *Power of a thing*, on the contrary, is something intrinsic to the thing, although this, its intrinsic quality, may only ||824| manifest itself in its relation to other things. For instance, power of attraction is a power of the thing itself although that power is "latent" so long as there are no things to attract. Here an attempt is made to represent the value of the "object" as something intrinsic to it, and yet as something merely existing as a "relation". That is why Bailey uses first the word "power" and then the word "relation".

Accurately expressed it would read as follows:

"*If* the value of an object is the relation in which it exchanges with other objects, value denotes, *consequently*" (viz., in consequence of the "if"), "nothing but the relation in which two objects stand to each other as exchangeable objects."

Nobody will contest this tautology. What follows from it, by the way, is that the "value" of an object "denotes *nothing*". For example, 1 lb. of coffee=4 lbs. of cotton. What then is the value of 1 lb. of coffee? 4 lbs. of cotton. And of 4 lbs. of cotton? 1 lb. of coffee. Since the value of 1 lb. of coffee is 4 lbs. of cotton, and, on the other hand, the value of 4 lbs. of cotton is 1 lb. of coffee, then it is clear that the value of 1 lb. of coffee is 1 lb. of coffee (since 4 lbs. of cotton=1 lb. of coffee), $a=b$, $b=a$, hence $a=a$. What arises from this explanation is, therefore, that the value of a use-value is equal to a [certain] quantity of the same use-value. Consequently, the value of 1 lb. of coffee is nothing else than 1 lb. of coffee. If 1 lb. of coffee=4 lbs. of cotton, then it is clear that 1 lb. of coffee > 3 lbs. of cotton and 1 lb. of coffee < 5 lbs. of cotton. To say that 1 lb. of coffee > 3 lbs. of cotton and < 5 lbs. of cotton, expresses a *relation* between coffee and cotton just as well as saying that 1 lb. of coffee=4 lbs. of cotton. The symbol = does not express any more of a relation than does the symbol > or the symbol <, but simply a *different* relation. Why is it then precisely the relation represented by the sign of equality, by =, which expresses the value of the coffee in cotton and that of the cotton in coffee? Or is this sign of equality the result of the fact that these two amounts exchange for one another at all? Does this sign = merely express the fact of exchange? It cannot be denied that if coffee exchanges for cotton in any proportion whatever, they are exchanged for one another, and if the mere fact of their exchange constitutes the *relation* between the commodities, then the value of the coffee is equally well expressed in cotton whether it exchanges for 2, 3, 4 or 5 lbs. of cotton. But what is then the word *"relation"* supposed to mean? Coffee in itself has no "intrinsic, positive" quality which determines the *rate at which* it exchanges for cotton. It is not a relation which is determined by any kind of determinant intrinsic to coffee and separate from real exchange. What is then the purpose of the word "relation"? What is the relation? The quantity of cotton against which a quantity of coffee is exchanged. Then one could not speak of a relation in which it exchanges but only of a relation in which it *is* or *has been* exchanged. For if the relation were determined before the exchange, then the exchange would be determined by "the relation" and not the relation by the exchange. We must therefore drop the *relation* as signifying something which *stands over and above* the coffee and the cotton and is distinct from them.

[Thus the passage from Bailey cited above takes the following form:]

"*If* the value of an object is the quantity of another object exchanged with it, value denotes, consequently, nothing but the quantity of the other object exchanged with it."

As a commodity, a commodity can only express its value in other commodities, since general labour-time does not exist for it as a commodity. [Bailey believes that] if the value of one commodity is expressed in another commodity, the value of one commodity is nothing apart from this equation with another commodity. Bailey flaunts this piece of wisdom tirelessly—

and all the more tiresomely. As he conceives it, it is a *tautology*, for he says [in essence]: If the value of any commodity is nothing but its exchange relation with another commodity, it is nothing apart from this relation.

He reveals his philosophical profundity in the following passage:

"As we cannot speak of *the distance of any object without* implying some other object, *between which and the former this relation exists*, so we cannot speak of the value of a commodity but in reference to *another commodity* ||825| compared with it. A thing cannot be valuable in itself without reference to another thing" (Is social labour, to which the value of a commodity is related, not another thing?) "any more than a thing can be *distant in itself* without reference to another thing" (loc. cit., p. 5).

If[a] a thing is distant from another, the distance is in fact a relation between the one thing and the other; but at the same time, the distance is something different from this relation between the two things. It is a dimension of space, it is a certain length which may as well express the distance of two other things besides those compared. But this is not all. If we speak of the distance as a relation between two things, we presuppose something "intrinsic", some "property" of the things themselves, which enables them to be distant from each other. What is the distance between the syllable A and a table? The question would be nonsensical. In speaking of the distance of two things, we speak of their difference in space. Thus we suppose both of them to be contained in space, to be points of space. Thus we equalise them as being both existences of space, and only after having them equalised *sub specie spatii*[b] we distinguish them as different points of space. To belong to space is their unity.*

---

* ||XV-887| ⟨The following has to be added with regard to Bailey's insipidity.

When he says that A is distant from B, he does not thereby compare them with one another, equalise them, but *separates* them in space. They do *not* occupy *the same* space. Nevertheless he still declares that both are *spatial* things and are differentiated in virtue of being things which belong in space. He therefore makes them equal in advance, gives them the same unity. However, here it is a question of equation.

If I say that the area of the triangle A is equal to that of the parallelogram B, this means not only that the area of the triangle is expressed in the parallelogram and that of the parallelogram in the triangle, but it means that if the height of the triangle is equal to h and the base equal to b, then

---

[a] Marx wrote this paragraph in English.—*Ed.*
[b] Under the aspect of space.—*Ed.*

But what is this unity of objects exchanged against each other? This exchange is not a relation which exists between them as natural things It is likewise not a relation which they bear as natural things to human needs, for it is not the degree of their utility that determines the quantities in which they exchange. What is therefore their identity, which enables them to be exchanged in certain proportions for one another? As what do they become *exchangeable*?

In fact, in all this Bailey merely follows the author of the *Verbal Observations*.

"... it" (value) "cannot alter as to one of the objects compared, without altering as to the other..." (loc. cit., p. 5).

This again simply means that the expression of the value of one commodity in another commodity can only change as *such an expression*. And the expression as such presupposes not one but two commodities.

Mr. Bailey is of the opinion that if one were to consider *only two commodities*—in exchange with one another—one would automatically discover the mere relativity of *value*, in his sense. The fool. As if it were not just as necessary to say, in connection with [two] commodities which exchange with one another— two products which are related to one another as *commodities*— *in what* they are identical, as it would be in the case of a thousand. For that matter, if only two products existed, the products would never become commodities, and consequently the exchange-value of commodities would never evolve either. The necessity for the labour in product I to manifest itself as social labour would not arise. Because the product is not produced as an immediate object of consumption for the producers, but only as a *bearer of value*, as a claim, so to speak, to a certain quantity

---

$A = \frac{h \times b}{2}$, a property which belongs to it itself just as it is a property of the parallelogram that it is likewise equal to $\frac{h \times b}{2}$. As areas, the triangle and the parallelogram are here declared to be equal, to be equivalents, although as a triangle and a parallelogram they are different. In order to equate these different things with one another, each must represent *the same common element* regardless of the other. If geometry, like the political economy of Mr. Bailey, contented itself with saying that the equality of the triangle and of the parallelogram means that the triangle is expressed in the parallelogram, and the parallelogram in the triangle, it would be of little value.⟩ |XV-887||

of all materialised social labour, all products as *values* are compelled to assume a form of existence distinct from their existence as use-values. And it is this development of the labour embodied in them as social labour, it is the development of their *value*, which determines the formation of money, the necessity for commodities to represent themselves in respect of one another as *money*—which means merely as independent forms of existence of exchange-value—and they can only do this by setting apart one commodity from the mass of commodities, and all of them measuring their values in the use-value of this excluded commodity, thereby directly transforming the labour embodied in this exclusive commodity into *general, social* labour.

Mr. Bailey, with his queer way of thinking which only grasps the surface appearance of things, concludes on the contrary: Only *because*, besides commodities, *money* exists, and we are so used to regarding the value of *commodities* not in their relation to one another but as a relation to a *third*, as ||826| a third relation distinct from the *direct* relation, is the *concept of value* evolved—and consequently value is transformed from the merely quantitative relation in which commodities are exchanged for one another into something independent of this relation (and this, he thinks, transforms the value of commodities into something absolute, into a scholastic entity existing in isolation from the commodities). According to Bailey, it is not the determination of the product as value which leads to the establishment of money and which expresses itself in *money*, but it is the existence of money which leads to the fiction of the concept of value. Historically it is quite correct that the search for value is at first based on money, the *visible* expression of commodities as value, and that consequently the search for the definition of value is (wrongly) represented as a search for a commodity of "invariable value", or for a commodity which is an "invariable measure of value". Since Mr. Bailey now demonstrates that money as an external measure of value—and expression of value — has fulfilled its purpose, even though it has a *variable* value, he thinks he has done away with the question of the concept of value—which is not affected by the variability of the magnitudes of value of commodities—and that in fact it is no longer necessary to attribute any meaning at all to value. Because the representation of the value of a commodity in money—in a third, exclusive commodity—does not exclude variation in the value of this third commodity, because the problem of an "invariable measure of value" disappears, the problem of the determination of value itself disappears. Bailey carries on this insipid rigmarole for hundreds of pages, with great self-satisfaction.

The following passages, in which he constantly repeats the same thing, are, in part, illicitly copied from the *"Verbal Disputes"*.

Supposing that only two commodities existed, both exchangeable in proportion to the amount of labour [they contained], "If [...] A should, at a subsequent period, require double the quantity of labour for its production, while B continued to require only the same, A would become of double value to B.... But although B continued to be produced by the same labour, it would not continue of the same value, for it would exchange for only half the quantity of A, the only *commodity*, by the supposition, with which it could be compared" (loc. cit., p. 6).

"It is from this circumstance of constant reference to other commodities" (instead of regarding value *merely as a relation between two commodities*) "or to *money*, when we are *speaking of the relation between any two commodities*, that the *notion of value*, as *something intrinsic and absolute*, has arisen" (op. cit., p. 8).

What I assert is, that if all commodities were produced under exactly the same circumstances, as for instance, by labour alone, any commodity, which always required the same quantity of labour, could not be *invariable in value*" (that is, invariable when its value is *expressed* in other commodities—a tautology) "while every other commodity underwent alteration" (op. cit., pp. 20-21).

Value is nothing intrinsic and absolute... (op. cit., p. 23).[a]

"It is impossible to *d e s i g n a t e*, or *e x p r e s s* the value of a commodity, except by *a quantity of some other commodity*" (op. cit., p. 26).

(As impossible as it is to *"designate"* or *"express"* a thought except by a quantity of syllables. Hence Bailey concludes that a thought is—syllables.)

"Instead of regarding value as a *relation between two objects*, they" (Ricardo and his followers) "seem to consider it as a positive result produced by a definite quantity of labour" (op. cit., p. 30).

"Because the values of A and B, according to their doctrine, are to each other as the quantities of producing labour, or ... are determined by the quantities of producing labour, they appear to have concluded, that the value of A alone, without reference to any thing else, is as the quantity of its producing labour. There is no meaning certainly in this last proposition..." (op. cit., pp. 31-32).

They speak of "value as a sort of general and independent property" (op. cit., p. 35).

"The value of a commodity must be its value in something" (loc. cit.).

---

[a] Marx here sums up Bailey's argument in his own words.—*Ed.*

We can see why it is so important for Bailey to limit value to *two commodities*, to understand it as the relation between *two commodities*. But a difficulty now arises:

"The *value of a commodity* denoting its *relation of exchange* to some other commodity"

(what is in this context the purpose of the "relation ||827| of exchange"? Why not its *"exchange"*? But at the same time exchange is intended to express a *definite* relation, not *merely the fact of exchange*. Hence value is equal to relation in exchange)

"... we may speak of it as money-value, corn-value, cloth-value, according to the commodity with which it is compared; and hence there are *a thousand different kinds of value, as many kinds of value as there are commodities in existence*, and all are equally *real* and equally *nominal*" (op. cit., p. 39).

Here we have it. *Value* equals *price*. There is no difference between them. And there is no "intrinsic" difference between *money price* and any other expression of price, although it is the *money price* and not the cloth price, etc., which expresses the *nominal value*, the general value of the commodity.

But although the commodity has a thousand different kinds of value, or a thousand different prices, as many kinds of value as there are commodities in existence, all these thousand expressions always express *the same value*. The best proof of this is that all these different expressions are *equivalents* which not only can replace one another in this expression, but do replace one another in exchange itself. This *relation* of the commodity, with the price of which we are concerned, is expressed in a thousand different "relations in exchange" to all the different commodities and yet always expresses *the same* relation. Thus this relation, which remains the same, is distinct from its thousand different expressions, or value is different from price, and the *prices* are only expressions of value: money price is its *general* expression, other prices are *particular* expressions. It is not even this simple conclusion that Bailey arrives at. In this context Ricardo is not a fictionist but Bailey is a fetishist in that he conceives value, though not as a property of the individual object (considered in isolation), but as a *relation of objects to one another*, while it is only a representation in objects, an objective expression, of a relation between men, a social relation, the relationship of men to their reciprocal productive activity.

[β) Confusion with Regard to Profit
and the Value of Labour]

[Bailey says the following about the value of labour.]

"Hence Mr. Ricardo, ingeniously enough, avoids a difficulty, which, on a first view, threatens to encumber his doctrine, that value depends on the quantity of labour employed in production. If this principle is rigidly adhered to, it follows, that the *value of labour depends on the quantity of labour employed in producing it*—which is evidently absurd. By a dexterous turn, therefore, Mr. Ricardo makes the *value of labour* depend on *the quantity of labour required to produce wages*, or, to give him the benefit of his own language, he maintains, that the value of labour is *to be estimated* by the quantity of labour required to produce wages, by which he means, the quantity of labour required to produce the money or commodities given to the labourer. This is similar to saying, that the value of cloth is to be estimated, not by the quantity of labour bestowed on its production, but by the quantity of labour bestowed on the production of the silver for which the cloth is exchanged" (op. cit., pp. 50-51).

This is a justified criticism of Ricardo's mistake of making capital exchange directly with labour instead of with labour-power. It is the same objection which we have already come across in another form.[a] Nothing else. Bailey's comparison cannot be applied to labour-power. It is not cloth, but an organic product such as mutton, that he ought to compare with living labour-power. Apart from the labour involved in tending live-stock and that required for the production of their food, the labour required for their production is not to be understood as meaning the labour which they themselves perform in the act of consumption, the act of eating, drinking, in short, the appropriation of those products or means of subsistence. It is just the same with labour-power. [What does] the labour required for its production consist of? Apart from the labour involved in developing a person's labour-power, his *education*, his apprenticeship—and this hardly arises in relation to unskilled labour—its reproduction costs no labour apart from that involved in the reproduction of the means of subsistence which the labourer consumes. The appropriation of these means of subsistence is not "*labour*". ||828| Any more than the labour contained in the cloth, in addition to the labour of the weaver and the labour which is contained in the wool, the dye-stuff, etc., comprises the chemical or physical action of the wool in absorbing the dye-

---

[a] See this volume, pp. 110-11.—*Ed.*

stuff, etc., an action which corresponds to the appropriation of the means of subsistence by the worker or the cattle.

Bailey then seeks to invalidate Ricardo's law that the value of labour and profit stand in *inverse* proportion to one another. He seeks, moreover, to invalidate that part of it which is correct. Like Ricardo, he identifies surplus-value with profit. He does not mention the one possible exception to this law, namely, when the working-day is lengthened and workers and capitalists share equally in that prolongation, but even then, since the value of the working power will be consumed more quickly—in fewer years—the surplus-value rises at the expense of the workingman's life, and his working power depreciates in comparison with the surplus-value it yields to the capitalist.

Bailey's reasoning is most superficial. Its starting-point is his conception of value. The value of the commodity is the expression of its value in a certain quantity of other values in use (the use-value of other commodities). The value of labour is thus equal to the quantity of other commodities (use-values) for which it is exchanged. ⟨The real problem, how it is possible to express the value in exchange of A in the value in use of B—does not even occur to him.⟩ So long, therefore, as the worker receives the same quantity of commodities, the value of labour remains unchanged, because, as before, it is expressed in the same quantity of other useful things. Profit, on the other hand, expresses a relation to capital, or else to the total product. The *portion* received by the worker can, however, remain the same although the *proportion* received by the capitalist rises if the productivity of labour increases. It is not clear why, in dealing with capital, we suddenly come to a proportion and of what use this *proportion* is supposed to be to the capitalist, since the value of what he receives is determined not by the proportion, but by its "expression in other commodities".

The point he makes here has, in fact, already been mentioned by Malthus.[a] Wages are equal to a quantity of *use-values*. Profit, on the other hand, is (but Bailey must avoid saying so) a relation of *value*. If I measure wages according to use-value and profit according to exchange-value, it is quite evident that neither an inverse nor any other kind of relation exists between them, because I should then be comparing incommensurable magnitudes, things which have nothing in common.

---

[a] See this volume, p. 34.—*Ed.*

[CHAPTER XX]

But what Bailey says here about the *value of labour* applies—according to his principle—to the *value of every other commodity* as well. It is nothing but a certain quantity of other things exchanged against it. If I receive 20 lbs. of twist for £1, then [according to this theory] the value of the £1 always remains the same, and will therefore be always paid, although the labour required to produce 1 lb. of twist can on one occasion be double that required on another. The most ordinary merchant does not believe that he is getting the same value for his £1 when he receives 1 quarter of wheat for it in a period of famine and the same amount in a period of glut. But the concept of value ends here. And there remains only the unexplained and inexplicable fact that a quantity of A is exchanged against a quantity of B in an arbitrary proportion. And whatever that proportion may be it is an equivalent. Even Bailey's formula, the value of A expressed in B, thus becomes quite meaningless. If the value of A is expressed in B, the same value is supposed to be expressed, at one time in A, and at another time in B, so that, when it is expressed in B, the value of A remains the same as it was before. But according to Bailey there is no value of A that could be expressed in B, because neither A nor B have a value apart from that expression. The value of A expressed in B must be something quite different from the value of A in C, as different as B and C are. It is not the same value, identical in both expressions, but there are two relations of A which have nothing in common with each other, and of which it would be nonsense to say that they are equivalent expressions.[a]

||829| "... a rise or fall of labour implies an increase or decrease in the quantity of the commodity given in exchange for it" (op. cit., p. 62).

Nonsense! [From Bailey's standpoint] there can be no rise or fall in the value of labour, nor in the value of any other thing. For one A I get today 3 Bs, tomorrow 6 Bs and the day after tomorrow 2 Bs. But [according to Bailey] in all these cases the value of A is nothing but the quantity of B for which it has been exchanged. It was 3 Bs, it is now 6 Bs. How can its value be said to have risen or fallen? The A expressed in 3 Bs had a different value from that expressed in 6 Bs or 2 Bs. But then it is not the identical A which at the identical time has been exchanged for

---

[a] Marx wrote most of this paragraph and the one following the quotation in English.—*Ed.*

3 or 2 or 6 Bs. The identical A at the identical time has always been expressed in the same quantity of B. It is only with regard to different moments of time that it could be said the value of A had changed. But it is only with "contemporaneous" commodities that A can be exchanged, and it is only the fact (not even the mere possibility of exchange) of exchange with other commodities which makes [according to Bailey] A a value. It is only the actual "relation in exchange" which constitutes its value; and the actual "relation in exchange" can of course only take place for the same A at the identical time. Bailey therefore declares the comparison of commodity values at different periods to be nonsense. But at the same time he should also have declared the rise or fall of value—which is impossible if there is no comparison between the value of a commodity at one time and its value at another time—to be nonsense and consequently, also, the *"rise or fall in the value of labour"*.

"Labour is an exchangeable thing, or one which commands other things in exchange; but the term profits denotes only a share or *proportion of commodities, not an article which can be exchanged against other articles*. When we ask whether wages have risen, we mean, whether a definite portion of labour exchanges for a greater quantity of other things than before" (loc. cit., pp. 62-63).

(Thus when corn becomes dearer, the value of labour falls because less corn is exchanged for it. On the other hand, if cloth becomes cheaper at the same time, the value of labour *rises* simultaneously, because more cloth can be exchanged for it. Thus the value of labour both rises and falls at the same time and the two expressions of its value—in corn and in cloth—are not identical, not equivalent, because its *increased* value cannot be equal to its *reduced value*.)

"... but when we ask whether profits have risen, we ... mean ... whether the gain of the capitalist bears a higher ratio to the capital employed..." (loc. cit., p. 63).

"... the value of labour does not entirely depend on the proportion of the whole produce which is given to the labourers in exchange for their labour, but also on the productiveness of [...] labour" (loc. cit., pp. 63-64).

"The proposition, that when labour rises profits must fall, is true only when its rise is not owing to an increase in its productive powers" (loc. cit., p. 64).

"... if this productive power be augmented, that is, if the same labour produce more commodities in the same time, labour may rise in value without a fall, nay even with a rise of profits" (loc. cit., p. 66).

(Accordingly it can also be said of every other commodity that a rise in its value does not imply a fall in the value of the other commodity with which it exchanges, nay, may even imply a rise in value on the other side. For instance, supposing the same labour which produced 1 quarter of corn, now produces 3 quarters. The 3 quarters cost £1, as the one quarter did before. If 2 quarters are now exchanged for £1, the value of money has risen, because it is expressed in 2 quarters instead of one. Thus the purchaser of corn gets a greater value for his money. But the seller who sells for £1 what has cost him only $2/3$ [of £1] gains $1/3$. And thus the value of his corn has risen at the same time that the money price of corn has fallen.)

||830| "Whatever the produce of the labour of six men might be, whether 100 or 200 or 300 quarters of corn, yet so long as the proportion of the capitalist was one-fourth of the produce, that fourth part estimated in labour would be invariably the same."

(And so would the $3/4$ of the produce accruing to the labourer, if estimated in labour.)

"Were the produce 100 quarters, then, as 75 quarters would be given to 6 men, the 25 accruing to the capitalist would command the labour of 2 men;"

(and that given to the labourers would command the labour of 6 men)

"if the produce were 300 quarters, the 6 men would obtain 225 quarters, and the 75 falling to the capitalist would still command 2 men and no more."

(Likewise the 225 quarters falling to the 6 men would still command 6 men and no more.) (Why does the almighty Bailey then forbid Ricardo to estimate the portion of the men, as well as that of the capitalist, in labour, and compare their mutual value as expressed in labour?)

"Thus a rise in the proportion which went to the capitalist would be the same as an increase of the *value of profits estimated in labour*,"

(How can he speak of the *value of profits* and an increase in their value, if "profit ... does not denote an article which can be exchanged against other articles" (see above) and, consequently, denotes no "value"? And, on the other hand, is a rise in the *proportion* which went to the capitalist possible without a fall *in the proportion* that goes to the labourer?)

"or, in other words, an increase in their power of commanding labour" (op. cit., p. 69).

(And is this *increase* in the power of the capitalist to appropriate the labour of others not exactly identical with the *decrease* in the power of the labourer to appropriate his own labour?)

"Should it be objected to the doctrine of profits and the value of labour rising at the same time, that as *the commodity produced is the only source whence the capitalist and the labourer can obtain their remuneration*, it necessarily follows that what one gains the other loses, the reply is obvious. So long as the product continues the same, this is undeniably true; but it is equally undeniable, that if the product be doubled *the portion of both may be increased*, although *the proportion of one is lessened and that of the other augmented*" (loc. cit., p. 70).

(This is just what Ricardo says. The *proportion* of both cannot increase, and if the *portion* of both increases, it cannot increase in the same proportion, as otherwise portion and proportion would be identical. The proportion of the one cannot increase without that of the other decreasing. However, that Mr. Bailey calls the *portion* of the labourer *"value"* of "wages", and the *proportion* [of the capitalist] value of "profits", in other words, that the same commodity has two values for him, one in the hands of the labourer, and the other in the hands of the capitalist, is nonsense of his own.)

"So long as the product continues the same, this is undeniably true; but it is equally undeniable, that if the product be doubled the *portion* of both may be increased, although the *proportion* of one is lessened and that of the other augmented. Now it is an increase in the *portion* of the product assigned to the labourer which constitutes a rise in the *value* of his labour..."

(because here we understand by *value* a certain quantity of articles)

"... but it is an increase in the *proportion* assigned to the capitalist which constitutes a rise in [...] profits,"

(because here we understand by *value* the same articles not estimated by their quantity, but by the labour worked up in them)

"whence"

(that is, because of the absurd use of two measures, in the one case articles, in the other case the value of the same articles)

"it clearly follows, that there is nothing inconsistent in the supposition of a *simultaneous rise in both*" (loc. cit., p. 70).

This absurd argument against Ricardo is quite ||831| futile since he merely declares that the *value* of the two portions must rise and fall in inverse proportion to one another. It merely amounts to a repetition by Bailey of his proposition that *value* is the quantity of articles exchanged for an article. In dealing with *profit* he was bound to find himself in an embarrassing position. For here, the value of capital is compared with the value of the product. Here he seeks refuge in taking *value* to mean the value of an article estimated in labour (in the Malthusian manner).

"Value is a relation between *contemporary* commodities, because such only admit of being exchanged for each other; and if we compare the value of a commodity at one time with its value at another, it is only a comparison of the relation in which it stood at these different times to some other commodity" (op. cit., p. 72).

Consequently, as has been stated, value can neither rise nor fall, for this always involves comparing the value of a commodity at one time with its value at another. A commodity cannot be sold below its value any more than above it, for its value is what it is sold for. Value and market price are identical. In fact one cannot speak either of *"contemporary"* commodities, or of *present* values, but only of *past* ones. What is the value of 1 quarter of wheat? The £1 for which it was sold yesterday. For its value is only what one gets in exchange for it, and as long as it is not exchanged, its "relation to money" is only imaginary. But as soon as the exchange has been transacted, we have £1 instead of the quarter of wheat and we can no longer speak of the value of the quarter of wheat. In comparing values at different periods, Bailey has in mind merely academic researches into the different values of commodities, for example in the eighteenth and the sixteenth centuries. There the difficulty arises from the fact that the same monetary expression of value—owing to the vicissitudes of the value of money itself—denotes different values [at different times]. The difficulty here lies in reducing the money price to value. But what a fool he is! Is it not a fact that, in the process of circulation or the process of reproduction of capital, the value of one period is constantly compared with that of another period, an operation upon which production itself is based?

Mr. Bailey does not understand at all what the expressions—to determine the value of commodities by labour-time or by the value of labour—mean. He simply does not understand the difference.

"... I beg not to be understood as contending, either that the values of commodities are to each other as the *quantities of labour* necessary for their production, or that the values of commodities are to each other as the *val-*

ues of the labour: all that I intend to insist upon is, that if the former is true, the latter cannot be false..." (op. cit., p. 92).

The determination of the value of commodities by the value of another commodity (and insofar as they are determined by the "value of labour", they are determined by another commodity; for *value of labour* presupposes labour as a commodity) and its determination by a third entity, which has neither value nor is itself a commodity, but is the substance of value, and that which turns products into commodities, are for Bailey identical. In the first case, it is a question of a *measure of the value of commodities*, that is, in fact, of *money*, of a commodity in which the other commodities *express* their value. In order that this can happen, the *values* of the commodities must already be *presupposed*. The commodity which measures as well as that to be measured must have a *third* element in common. In the second case, this *identity* itself is first established; later it is expressed in the price, either money price or any other price.

Bailey identifies the "invariable measure of value" with the search for an immanent measure of value, that is, the concept of value itself. So long as the two are confused it is even a reasonable instinct which leads to the search for an "invariable measure of value". Variability is precisely the characteristic of value. The term "invariable" expresses the fact that the immanent measure of value must not itself be a commodity, a value, but rather something which constitutes value and which is *therefore* also the immanent *measure* of value. Bailey demonstrates ||832| that commodity values can find a monetary expression and that, if the *value relation of commodities is given*, all commodities can express their value in *one* commodity, although the value of this commodity may change. But it nevertheless always remains the same for the other commodities at a given time, since it changes simultaneously in relation to all of them. From this *he* concludes that no value relation between commodities is necessary nor is there any need to look for one. Because he finds it reflected in the *monetary expression*, he does not need to "understand" how this expression becomes possible, how it is determined, and *what* in fact it expresses.

These remarks, in general, apply to Bailey as they do to Malthus, since he believes that one is concerned with *the same* question, on the same plane, whether one makes quantity of labour or value of labour the measure of value. In the latter case, one presupposes the *values* whose measure is being sought, that is to say, their external measure, their representation as value. In the first case one investigates the genesis and immanent nature of value itself. In the second, the development of the commodity into money or the form which exchange-value acquires in the process of the exchange of commodities. In the first, we are concerned with *value*, independent of this representation, or rather *antecedent* to this representation. Bailey has this in common with the other fools: to determine the value of commodities means to find their *monetary expression*, an external measure of their value. They say, however, impelled by an instinctive thought, that this measure then must have invariable value, and must itself therefore stand *outside the category* of value, whereas Bailey says that one does not need to understand it, since one does in fact find the *expression of value* in practice, and this expression itself has and can have variable value without prejudice to its function.

In particular, he himself has informed us that 100, 200 or 300 quarters can be the product of the labour of 6 men, that is, of the same quantity of labour, whereas "value of labour" only means for him the portion of the 100, 200 or 300 quarters which the 6 men receive. This could be 50, 60 or 70 quarters per man.[49] The quantity of labour and the value of the same quantity of labour are therefore, according to Bailey himself, very different expressions. And how can it be the same if the value is expressed first in one thing and then in something essentially different? If the same labour which formerly produced 3 quarters of corn now produces 1 quarter, while the same labour which formerly produced 20 yards of cloth (or 3 quarters of corn) still produces 20 yards, then, reckoned according to labour-time, 1 quarter of corn is now equal to 20 yards of cloth, or 20 yards of cloth to 1 quarter of corn, and 3 quarters of corn equal 60 yards of cloth instead of 20. Thus the values of the quarter of corn and the yard of linen have been altered relatively. But they have by no means been altered according to the "value of labour", for 1 quarter of corn and 20 yards of cloth remain the same usevalues as before. And it is possible that 1 quarter of corn does not command a larger quantity of labour than before.

If we take a single commodity, then Bailey's assertion makes no sense whatever. If the labour-time required for the production of shoes decreases and now only one-tenth of the labour-time formerly required is necessary, then the value of shoes drops to one-tenth of the former value; and this also holds true when the shoes are *compared* with, or expressed in, other commodities, provided the labour required for their production has remained the same or has not decreased at the same rate. Nevertheless, the value of labour—for example the daily wage in shoemaking as well as in all other industries—may have remained the same; or it may even have increased. Less labour is contained in the individual shoe, hence also less paid labour. But when one speaks of the *value of labour*, one does not mean that for one hour's labour, i.e., for a smaller quantity of labour, less is paid than for a greater quantity. Bailey's proposition could have meaning only in relation to the total product of capital. Suppose 200 pairs of shoes are the product of the same capital (and the same labour) which formerly produced 100 pairs. In this case, the value of the 200 pairs is the same as [previously] that of 100 pairs. And it could be said that the 200 pairs of shoes are to 1,000 yards of linen (say the product of £200 of capital) as the *value* of the labour set in motion by the two amounts of capital. In what sense? In the sense in which it would *also* apply ||833¦ to the relation of the individual shoe to the single yard of linen?

The *value* of labour is the part of the labour-time contained in a commodity which the worker himself appropriates; it is the part of the product in which the *labour-time which belongs to the worker himself is embodied*. If the entire value of a commodity is reduced to paid and unpaid labour-time—and if the rate of unpaid to paid labour is the same, that is, if surplus-value constitutes the same proportion of total value in all commodities —then it is clear that if the ratio of one commodity to another is proportional to the total quantity of labour they contain, they must also represent *equal proportionate parts* of these total quantities of labour, and their ratio must therefore also be as that of the paid labour-time in one commodity to the paid labour-time in the other.

C [commodity]: C′ = TLT (total labour-time [embodied in C]) to TLT′ (total labour-time [embodied in C′]).
$\frac{TLT}{x}$ = the paid labour-time in C, and $\frac{TLT'}{x}$ = the paid labour-time in C′, since it is presupposed that the paid labour-time in both commodities constitutes the same *proportional part* of the total labour-time.
C : C′ = TLT : TLT′

$$\text{TLT} : \text{TLT}' = \frac{\text{TLT}}{x} : \frac{\text{TLT}'}{x}$$
$$\text{therefore } \text{C} : \text{C}' = \frac{\text{TLT}}{x} : \frac{\text{TLT}'}{x}$$

or the commodities are to one another as *the quantities of paid labour-time contained in them*, that is, as the values of the labour contained in them.

The *value of labour* is then, however, not determined in the way Bailey would like, but by the labour-time [contained in the commodity].

Further, disregarding the conversion of values into prices of production and considering only the values themselves, capitals consist of different proportions of variable and constant capital. Hence, as far as values are concerned, the surplus-values are not equal, or the paid labour does not form the same proportion of the total labour advanced.

In general, wages—or values of labour—would here be indices of the values of commodities, not as values, not insofar as wages rise or fall, but insofar as the *quantity of paid labour*—represented by wages—contained in a commodity would be an index of the *total quantity* of the labour contained in the corresponding commodities.

In a word, the point is that, if the values of commodities are to one another as LT to LT' (the amounts of labour-time contained in them), then their ratio is likewise as $\frac{\text{LT}}{x}$ to $\frac{\text{LT}'}{x}$, i.e., the amounts of paid labour-time embodied in them, *if* the proportion of the paid labour-time to the unpaid is the same in all commodities, that is, *if* the paid labour-time is always equal to the total labour-time, whatever this may be, divided by x. But the "if" does not correspond to the real state of affairs. Supposing that the workers in different industries work the same amount of surplus labour-time, the relation of paid to actually employed labour-time is nevertheless different in different industries, because the ratio of *immediate labour* employed to *accumulated labour* employed is different. [Let us take two capitals consisting] for example, the one of $50v$ [variable] and $50c$ [constant] and the other of $10v$ and $90c$. In both cases, let the unpaid labour amount to one-tenth. [The value of] the first commodity would accordingly be 105, [of] the second 101. The paid labour-time would be equal to one-half of the labour advanced in the first case, and only to one-tenth in the second.

||834| Bailey says:

"... if commodities are to each other as the quantities, they must also be to each other as the values of the producing labour; for the contrary would necessarily imply, that the two commodities A and B might be equal in value, although the value of the labour employed in one was greater or less than the value of the labour employed in the other; or that A and B might be unequal in value, if the labour employed in each was equal in value. But this *difference in the value of two commodities*, which were *produced by labour of equal value*, would be inconsistent with *the acknowledged equality of profits*, which Mr. *Ricardo maintains in common with other writers*" (op. cit., pp. 79-80).

In this last phrase, Bailey stumbles unconsciously on a real objection to Ricardo, who directly identifies profit with surplus-value and values with cost-prices. Correctly stated, it is— if the commodities are sold at their *value*, they yield *unequal profits*, for then profit is equal to the surplus-value embodied in them. And this is correct. But this objection does not refer to the theory of value, but to a blunder of Ricardo's in applying this theory.

How little Bailey himself, in the above passage, can have correctly understood the problem, is shown in the following statement:

Ricardo on the other hand maintains "that labour may rise and fall in value without affecting the value of the commodity. This is obviously a very different proposition from the other, and depends in fact on the falsity of the other, or on the contrary proposition" (loc. cit., p. 81).

The fool himself previously asserted that the result of the same labour may be 100, 200 or 300 quarters [of corn]. This determines the relation of a quarter to other commodities irrespective of the changing value of labour, that is, irrespective of how much of the 100, 200 or 300 quarters falls to the labourer himself. The fool would have shown some consistency if he had said: the values of labour may rise or fall, nevertheless the values of commodities are as the values of labour, because—according to a false assumption—the rise or fall of wages is general, and the value of wages always forms the same *proportionate part* of the total quantity of labour employed.

[γ) Confusion of Value and Price.
Bailey's Subjective Standpoint]

[Bailey says:]

"... the capability of *expressing* the values of commodities has nothing to do with the *constancy of their values*...."

⟨Indeed not! but it has much to do with first finding the value, before expressing it; finding in what way the values in use, so different from each other, fall under the common category and denomination of *value*, so that the value of one commodity may be expressed in the other⟩

"... either to each other or to the medium employed; neither has the capability of comparing these *expressions of value* anything to do with it."

⟨If the values of different commodities are expressed in the same third commodity, however variable its value may be, it is of course very easy to compare these *expressions*, which already have a common denomination.⟩

"Whether A is worth 4 B or 6 B"

⟨the difficulty consists in equating A with a portion of B; and this is only possible if there exists a common element for A and B, or if A and B are different representations of the same element. If all commodities are to be expressed in gold, or money, the difficulty remains the same. There must be an element common to gold and to each of the other commodities⟩

"... and whether C is worth 8 B or 12 B, are circumstances which make no difference *in the power of expressing* the value of A and C in B, and certainly no difference in the power of comparing the value of A and C when expressed" (op. cit., pp. 104-05).

But how [is it possible] to *express* A in B or C? In order to *express* "them" in each other, or, what amounts to the same thing, to treat them as equivalent expressions of the same unity, A, B, C must all be considered as something different from what they are as things, as products, as values in use. A=4 B. Then the value of A is *expressed* in 4 B, and the value of 4 B in A, so that both sides express the same. They are equivalents. They are both *equal* expressions of value. It would be the same if they were unequal ones or A greater than 4 B, A smaller than 4 B. In all these cases they are, insofar ||835| as they are values, only different or equal in quantity, but they are always quantities of the same quality. The difficulty is to find this quality.

"The requisite condition in the process is, that the commodities to be measured should be reduced to a *common denomination*"

⟨for example, in order to compare a triangle with any of the other polygons it is only necessary to transform the latter into triangles, to express them in triangles. But to do this the triangle and the polygon are in fact supposed to be something *identical*, different figures of the same thing—space)

"... which may be done at all times with equal facility; or rather it *is* ready done to our hands, since it is the *prices* of commodities which are recorded, or their relations in value to money" (op. cit., p. 112).

"*Estimating* value is the same thing as *expressing* it..." (op. cit., p. 152).

We have the fellow here. We find the values measured, expressed in the *prices*. We can therefore [asserts Bailey] content ourselves with *not* knowing what value is. He confuses the development of the measure of value into money and further the development of money as the standard of price with the discovery of the *concept of value* itself in its development as the immanent measure of commodities in exchange. He is right in thinking that this money need not be a commodity of invariable value; from this he concludes that no separate determination of value independent of the commodity itself is necessary.

As soon as the value of commodities, as the element they have in common, is given, the measurement of their relative value and the expression of this value coincide. But we can never arrive at the *expression* so long as we do not find the common factor, which is different from the immediate existence of the commodities.

This is shown by the very example he gives, the distance between A and B.[a] When one speaks of their distance one already presupposes that they are points (or lines) in space. Having been reduced to points, and points of the same line, their distance may be expressed in inches, or feet, etc. The element the two commodities A and B have in common is, at first sight, their exchangeability. They are "exchangeable" objects. As "exchangeable" objects they are magnitudes of the same denomination. But this "their" existence as "exchangeable" objects must be different from their existence as values in use. What is it?

Money is already a *representation* of value, and presupposes it. As the *standard* of price money, for its part, already presupposes the (hypothetical) transformation of the commodity into money. If the values of all commodities are represented in money prices, then one can compare them, they are in fact already compared. But for the value to be represented as price, the value of commodities must have been expressed previously as money. Money is merely the form in which the value of commodities

---

[a] See this volume, p. 143.—*Ed*.

appears in the process of circulation. But how can one express x cotton in y money? This question resolves itself into this—how is it at all possible to express one commodity in another, or how to present commodities as equivalents? Only the elaboration of value, independent of the representation of one commodity in another, provides the answer.

> It is a "... mistake ... that the relation of value can exist between commodities at different periods, which is in the nature of the case impossible; and if no relation exists there can be no measurement of it" (op. cit., p. 113).

We have already had the same nonsense before.[a] "The relation of value between commodities at different periods" already exists when money acts as means of payment. The whole circulation process is a perpetual comparison of values of commodities at different periods.

> "... if [...] it" (money) "is not a good medium of comparison between commodities at different periods [it asserts] its incapability of performing a function in a case where there is no function for it to perform"[b] (op. cit., p. 118).

Money has this function to perform as means of payment and as treasure.

All this is simply copied from the "*verbal observer*" and in fact the secret of the whole nonsense oozes out in the following phrase which has also convinced me that the *Verbal Observations*,[c] which were very carefully concealed by Bailey, were used by him in the manner of a plagiarist.

> ||836| "Riches are the attribute of men, value is the attribute of commodities. A man or a community is rich; a pearl or a diamond is valuable" (op. cit., p. 165).

A pearl or a diamond is valuable *as* a pearl or a diamond, that is, by their qualities, as values in use for men, that is, as *riches*. But there is nothing in a pearl or a diamond by which a relation of exchange between them is given, etc.

Bailey now becomes a profound philosopher:

> Difference between labour as *cause* and *measure*, and in general between *cause* and *measure* of value (op. cit., p. 170 et seq.).[d]

---

[a] See this volume, pp. 150 and 153-54.—*Ed.*
[b] In the manuscript, this reads: "there is for it no function to perform".—*Ed.*
[c] See this volume, p. 129.—*Ed.*
[d] Marx here summarises the ideas developed by Bailey in Chapter X of his bool .—*Ed.*

There is, in actual fact, a very significant difference (which Bailey does not notice) between "measure" (in the sense of money) and "cause of value". The "cause" of value transforms use-values into *value*. The external measure of value already presupposes the existence of *value*. For example, gold can only measure the value of cotton if gold and cotton—as values—possess a *common factor* which is different from both. The "cause" of value is the substance of value and hence also its immanent measure.

"Whatever circumstances ... act with assignable influence, whether mediately or immediately, on the *mind* in the interchange of commodities, may be considered as causes of value" (op. cit., pp. 182-83).

This in fact means nothing more than: the *cause* of the value of a commodity or of the fact that two commodities are equivalent are the circumstances which cause the seller, or perhaps both the buyer and the seller, to consider something to be the value or the equivalent of a commodity. The "circumstances" which determine the value of a commodity are by no means further elucidated by being described as circumstances which influence the "mind" of those engaging in exchange, as circumstances which, as such, likewise exist (or perhaps they do not, or perhaps they are incorrectly conceived) in the consciousness of those engaging in exchange.

These same circumstances (independent of the mind, but influencing it), which compel the producers to sell their products as *commodities*—circumstances which differentiate one form of social production from another—provide their products with an exchange-value which (also in their mind) is independent of their use-value. Their "mind", their consciousness, may be completely ignorant of, unaware of the existence of, what in fact determines the value of their products or their products as values. They are placed in relationships which determine their thinking but they may not know it. Anyone can use money as money without necessarily understanding what money is. Economic categories are reflected in the mind in a very distorted fashion. He [Bailey] transfers the problem into the sphere of consciousness, because his theory has got stuck.

Instead of explaining what he himself understands by "value" (or "cause of value") Bailey tells us that it is something which buyers and sellers imagine in the act of exchange.

In fact, however, the following considerations are the basis of the would-be philosophical proposition.

1) The market price is determined by various circumstances which express themselves in the relation of demand and supply and which, as such, influence "the mind" of the operators on the market. This is a very important discovery!

2) In connection with the *conversion of commodity values into cost-prices*, "various circumstances" are taken into account which as "reasons for compensation" influence the mind or are reflected in the mind. All these reasons for compensation, however, affect only the mind of the capitalist as capitalist and stem from the nature of capitalist production itself, and not from the subjective notions of buyers and sellers. In their mind they exist rather as self-evident "eternal truths".

Like his predecessors, Bailey catches hold of Ricardo's confusion of values and cost-prices in order to prove that |value is not determined by labour, because cost-prices are deviations from values. Although this is quite correct in relation to Ricardo's identification [of values with cost-prices], it is incorrect as far as the question itself is concerned.

In this context, Bailey quotes first from Ricardo himself about the change in the relative values of ||837| commodities in consequence of a rise in the value of labour. He quotes further the "effect of time" (different times of production though the labour-time remains unchanged), the same case which aroused scruples in Mill.[a] He does not notice the real *general* contradiction— the very existence of *an average rate* of profit, despite the different composition of capital [in different industries], its different times of circulation, etc. He simply repeats the particular forms in which the contradiction appears, and which Ricardo himself— and his followers—had *already* noticed. Here he merely echoes what has been previously said but does not advance criticism a step forward.

He emphasises further that the costs of production are the main cause of "value", and therefore the main element in value. However, he stresses correctly—as was done [by other writers] after Ricardo—that the concept of *production costs* itself varies. He himself in the last analysis expresses his agreement with Torrens that value is determined by the capital advanced, which is correct in relation to cost-prices but meaningless if it is not evolved on the basis of value itself,| that is, if the *value of a commodity*

---

[a] See this volume, pp. 85-88.—*Ed.*

is to be derived from a more developed relationship, the *value of capital*, and not the other way round.

His last objection is this: The value of commodities cannot be measured by labour-time if the labour-time in one trade is not the same as in the others, so that the commodity in which, for example, 12 hours of an engineer's labour is embodied has perhaps twice the value of the commodity in which 12 hours of the labour of an agricultural labourer is embodied. What this amounts to is the following: A simple working-day, for example, is not a measure of value if there are other working-days which, compared with days of simple labour, have the effect of composite working-days. Ricardo showed that this fact does not prevent the measurement of commodities by labour-time if the relation between unskilled and skilled labour is given.[50] He has indeed not described how this relation develops and is determined. This belongs to the definition of *wages*, and, in the last analysis, can be reduced to the *different values of labour power itself*, that is, its varying production costs (determined by labour-time).

The passages in which Bailey expresses what has been summarised above are:

"It is not, indeed, disputed, that the main circumstance, which determines the quantities in which articles of this class" (that is, where no monopoly exists and where it is possible to increase output by expanding industry) "are exchanged, is the *cost of production*; but our best economists do not exactly agree on the meaning to be attached to this term; some contending that the *quantity of labour* expended on the production of an article constitutes its cost; others, that the *capital employed upon it* is entitled to that appellation" (op. cit., p. 200).

"What the labourer produces without capital, costs him his labour; what the capitalist produces costs him his capital" (p. 201).

(This is the factor which determines Torrens's views. The labour which the capitalist employs, costs him nothing apart from the capital he lays out in wages.)

"... the mass of commodities are determined in value by the capital expended upon them" (p. 206).

[Bailey raises the following objections] to the determination of the value of commodities simply by the quantity of labour contained in them:

"Now this cannot be true if we can find any instances of the following nature: 1) Cases in which two commodities have been produced by an equal quantity of labour, and yet sell for different quantities of money. 2) Cases in which two commodities, once equal in value, have become unequal in value, without any change in the quantity of labour respectively employed in each" (p. 209).

"It is no answer" (with regard to cases of the first kind) "to say, with Mr. Ricardo, that 'the estimation in which different qualities of labour are held, comes soon to be adjusted in the market with sufficient precision for all practical purposes'; or with Mr. Mill, that 'in estimating equal quantities of labour, an allowance would, of course, be included for different degrees of hardness and skill'. Instances of this kind entirely destroy the integrity of the rule" (p. 210).

"There are only two possible methods of comparing one quantity of labour with another; one is to compare them *by the time expended*, the other *by the results produced*" (the latter is done in the piece-rate system). "The former is applicable to all kinds of labour; the latter can be used only in comparing labour bestowed on similar articles. If therefore, in estimating two different sorts of work, the time spent will not determine the proportion between the ||839|[51] quantities of labour, it must remain undetermined and undeterminable" (p. 215).

With reference to 2: "Take any two commodities of equal value, A and B, one produced by fixed capital and the other by labour, without the intervention of machinery; and suppose, that without any change whatever in the fixed capital or the quantity of labour, there should happen to be a rise in the value of labour; according to Mr. Ricardo's own showing, A and B would be instantly altered in their relation to each other; that is, they would become unequal in value" (pp. 215-16).

"To these cases we may add the *effect of time* on value. If a commodity take more time than another for its production, *although no more capital and labour*, its value will be greater. The influence of this cause is admitted by Mr. Ricardo, but Mr. Mill contends..." and so on (loc. cit. [p. 217]).

Finally Mr. Bailey remarks, and this is the only new contribution he makes in this respect:

"... although we have arranged commodities under three divisions,"[a] ⟨this, i.e., the three divisions, is again taken from the author of the *Verbal Observations*⟩ (these three divisions depend on the existence of absolute monopoly, limited monopoly, as is the case with corn, or completely free competition) "yet they are all, not only promiscuously exchanged for each other, but *blended in production*. A commodity, therefore, may owe part of its value to monopoly, and part to those causes which determine the value of unmonopolised products. An article, for instance, may be manufactured amidst the freest competition out of a raw material, which a complete monopoly enables its producer to sell at six times the actual cost" (p. 223).

"In this case it is obvious, that although the value of the article might be correctly said to be determined by the quantity of capital expended upon it by the manufacturer, yet no analysis could possibly resolve the value of the capital into quantity of labour" (pp. 223-24).

This remark is correct. But monopoly does not concern us here, where we are dealing with two things only, *value* and

---

[a] Instead of this part of the sentence Marx wrote in the manuscript: "The three types of commodities cannot be entirely distinguished from one another."—*Ed.*

cost-price. It is clear that the conversion of value into cost-price works in two ways. First, the profit which is added to the capital advanced may be either above or below the *surplus-value* which is contained in the commodity itself, that is, it may represent more or less *unpaid* labour than the commodity itself contains. This applies to the variable part of capital and its reproduction in the commodity. But apart from this, the cost-price of constant capital—or of the commodities which enter into the value of the newly produced commodity as raw materials, auxiliary materials and machinery [or] labour conditions—may likewise be either above or below its value. Thus the commodity comprises a portion of the price which differs from value, and this portion is independent of the quantity of labour newly added, or of the labour whereby these conditions of production with given cost-prices are transformed into a new product. It is clear that what applies to the difference between the cost-price and the value of the *commodity* as such—as a result of the production process—likewise applies to the *commodity* insofar as, in the form of constant capital, it becomes an ingredient, a pre-condition, of the production process. Variable capital, whatever difference between value and cost-price it may contain, is replaced by a certain quantity of labour which forms a constituent part of the value of the new commodity, irrespective of whether its price expresses its value correctly or stands above or below the value. On the other hand, the difference between cost-price and value, insofar as it enters into the price of the new commodity independently of its own production process, is incorporated into the value of the new commodity as an antecedent element.

The difference between the cost-price and the value of the commodity is thus brought about in two ways: by the difference between the cost-price and the values of commodities which constitute the pre-conditions of the process of production of the new commodity; by the difference between the surplus-value which is really added to the conditions of production and the profit which is calculated [on the capital advanced]. But every commodity which enters into another commodity as constant capital, itself emerges as the result, the product, of another production process. And so the commodity appears alternately as a pre-condition for the production of other commodities and as the result of a process in which the existence of other commodities is the pre-condition for its own production. In agriculture (cattle-breeding), the same commodity appears at one point of time as a product and at another as a condition of production.

This important deviation of cost-prices from values brought about by capitalist production does not alter the fact that cost-prices continue to be determined by values.

4. McCulloch

[a) Vulgarisation and Complete Decline of the Ricardian System under the Guise of Its Logical Completion. Cynical Apologia for Capitalist Production. Unprincipled Eclecticism]

||840| McCulloch, the vulgariser of Ricardian political economy and simultaneously the most pitiful embodiment of its decline.

He vulgarises not only Ricardo but also James Mill.

He is moreover a vulgar economist in everything and an apologist for the existing state of affairs. His only fear, driven to ridiculous extremes, is the tendency of profit to fall; he is perfectly contented with the position of the workers, and in general, with all the contradictions of bourgeois economy which weigh heavily upon the working class. Here everything is green. He even knows that

> "the introduction of machines into any employment necessarily occasions an equal or greater demand *for the disengaged labourers* in some other employment" [J. R. McCulloch, *The Principles of Political Economy*, Edinburgh, 1825, pp. 181-82; quoted by Cazenove in *Outlines of Political Economy*, London, 1832, pp. 119-20].

In this question he deviates from Ricardo, and in his later writings, he also becomes very mealy-mouthed about the landowners. But his whole tender anxiety is reserved for the poor capitalists, in view of the tendency of the rate of profit to fall.

Mr. McCulloch, unlike other exponents of science, seems to look not for *characteristic differences*, but only "for *resemblances*; and proceeding upon this principle, he is led to confound material with immaterial objects; productive with unproductive labour; capital with revenue; the food of the labourer with the labourer himself; production with consumption; and labour with profits"[a] (T. R. Malthus, *Definitions in Political Economy*, London, 1827, pp. 69-70).

---

[a] The beginning of this paragraph up to "for *resemblances*" is Marx's summary of Malthus's views on McCulloch. The rest is a direct quotation.—*Ed.*

"Mr. McCulloch, in his *Principles of Political Economy*, divides *value* into *real* and *exchangeable*[a]; the former, he says, (page 225)[b] is dependent on the quantity of labour required for the production of any commodity,[c] and the latter on the *quantity of labour, or of any other commodity*, for which it will *exchange*; and these two values are, he says, (page 215), *identical*, in the ordinary state of things, that is, when the supply of commodities in the market is exactly proportioned to the effectual demand for them. Now, if they be identical, the two quantities of labour which he refers to must be identical also; but, at page 221, he tells us that they are not, for that the one includes profits, while the other excludes them" ([John Cazenove,] *Outlines of Political Economy*, London, 1832, p. 25).

McCulloch says [in a note] on page 221 of his *Principles of Political Economy*:

"In point of fact, it" (the commodity) "will always exchange for more" ⟨labour than has been required for its production⟩ "*and it is this excess that constitutes profits.*"

This is a brilliant example of the methods used by this archhumbug of a Scotsman.

The arguments of Malthus, Bailey, etc., compel him to differentiate between *real value* and *exchangeable* or *relative value*. But he does so, basically, in the way he finds the difference dealt with by Ricardo. *Real* value means the commodity examined with regard to the labour required for *its* production; *relative* value implies the consideration of the proportions of *different commodities* which can be produced in the same amount of time, which are *consequently* equivalents, and the value of one of which can therefore be *expressed* in the quantity of usevalue of the other which costs the same amount of labour-time. The *relative value* of commodities, in this Ricardian sense, is only another expression for their *real value* and means nothing more than that the commodities exchange with one another in proportion to the labour-time embodied in them, in other words, that the *labour-time embodied in both is equal*. If, therefore, the market price of a commodity is equal to its exchange-value (as is the case when supply and demand are in equilibrium), then the commodity bought contains as much labour as that

---

[a] Instead of *"real* and *exchangeable"*, the manuscript has *"real* and *relative* or *exchangeable value"*.—*Ed.*
[b] Marx mentions p. 211 and p. 225.—*Ed.*
[c] Instead of "required for the production of any commodity", the manuscript has "expended in its appropriation or production".—*Ed.*

which is sold. It merely realises its exchange-value, or it is only sold at its *exchange-value* when one receives *the same amount of labour* in exchange for it as one hands over.

McCulloch relates all this, correctly repeating what has already been said. But he goes too far here since the Malthusian definition of exchange-value—the quantity of wage-labour which a commodity commands—already sticks in his throat. He therefore defines relative value as the "quantity of labour, *or* of any other commodity, for which it" (a commodity) "will exchange". Ricardo, in dealing with relative value, always speaks only of commodities and does not include labour, since in the exchange of commodities a profit is only realised because in the exchange between commodity and labour *unequal* quantities of labour are exchanged. By putting the main emphasis right at the beginning of his book on the fact that the determination of the value ||841| of a commodity by the labour-time embodied in it differs immensely from the determination of this value by the quantity of labour which it can buy,[52] Ricardo, on the one hand, establishes the difference between the quantity of labour contained in a commodity and the quantity of labour which it commands. On the other hand, he excludes the exchange of commodity and labour from the relative value of a commodity. For if a commodity is exchanged for a commodity, equal quantities of labour are exchanged; but if a commodity is exchanged for labour, unequal quantities of labour are exchanged, and capitalist production rests on the inequality of this exchange. Ricardo does not explain how this *exception* fits in with the concept of value. This is the reason for the arguments amongst his followers. But his instinct is sound when he makes the *exception*. (In actual fact, there is no exception; it exists only in *his* formulation.) Thus McCulloch goes farther than Ricardo and is apparently more consistent than he.

There is no flaw in his system; it is all of a piece. Whether a commodity is exchanged for a commodity or for labour, this ratio of exchange is the *relative value* of the commodity. And if the commodities exchanged are sold at their value (i.e., if demand and supply coincide), this relative value is always the expression of *the real value*. That is, there are equal quantities of labour at both poles of the exchange. Thus "in the ordinary state of things" a commodity only exchanges for a quantity of wage-labour equal to the quantity of labour contained in it. The workman receives in wages just as much materialised labour as he gives back to capital in the form of immediate labour. With this the source of surplus-value disappears and the whole Ricardian theory collapses.

Thus Mr. McCulloch first destroys it under the appearance of making it more consistent.

And what next? He then flits shamelessly from Ricardo to Malthus, according to whom the value of a commodity is determined by the quantity of labour which it buys and which must always be greater than that which the commodity itself contains. The only difference is that in Malthus this is plainly stated to be what it is, *opposition* to Ricardo, and Mr. McCulloch adopts this opposite viewpoint after he has adopted the Ricardian formula with an apparent consistency (that is, with the consistency of incogitancy) which destroys the whole sense of the Ricardian theory. McCulloch therefore does not understand the essential kernel of Ricardo's teaching—how profit is realised because commodities exchange *at their value*—and abandons it. Since exchangeable value—which "in the ordinary state of [...] the market" is, according to McCulloch, equal to the real value but *"in point of fact"* is always greater, since profit is based on this surplus (a fine contradiction and a fine discourse based on a "point of fact")—is "the quantity of labour, *or* of any other commodity", for which the commodity is exchanged, hence what applies to "labour" applies to "any other commodity". This means that the commodity is not only exchanged for a greater amount of immediate labour than it itself contains, but for more materialised labour in the other commodities than it itself contains; in other words, profit is "profit upon expropriation" and with this we are back again amongst the Mercantilists. Malthus draws this conclusion. With McCulloch this conclusion follows naturally but with the pretence that this constitutes an elaboration of the Ricardian system.

And this total decline of the Ricardian system into twaddle—a decline which prides itself on being its most consistent exposition—has been accepted by the mob, especially by the mob on the Continent (with Herr Roscher naturally amongst them), as the conclusion of the Ricardian system *carried too far*, to its extreme limit; they thus believe Mr. McCulloch that the Ricardian mode of "coughing and spitting",[53] which he uses to conceal his helpless, thoughtless and unprincipled eclecticism, is in fact a scientific attempt to set forth Ricardo's system consistently.

McCulloch is simply a man who wanted to turn Ricardian

economics to his own advantage—an aim in which he succeeded in a most remarkable degree. In the same way *Say* used Smith, but Say at least made a contribution by bringing Smith's theories into a certain formal order and, apart from misconceptions, he occasionally also ventured to advance theoretical objections. Since McCulloch first obtained a professorial chair in London on account of Ricardian economics, in the beginning he had to come forward as a Ricardian and especially to participate in the struggle against the landlords. As soon as he had obtained a foothold and climbed to a position on Ricardo's shoulders, ||842| his main effort was directed to expounding political economy, especially Ricardian economics, within the framework of Whiggism and to eliminate all conclusions which were distasteful to the Whigs. His last works on money, taxes, etc., are mere pleas on behalf of the Whig Cabinet of the day. In this way the man secured lucrative jobs. His statistical writings are merely catch-penny efforts. The incogitant decline and vulgarisation of the theory likewise reveal the fellow himself as a vulgarian, a matter to which we shall have to return before we have done with that speculating Scotsman.

In *1828* McCulloch published Smith's *Wealth of Nations*, and the fourth volume of this edition contains his own "notes" and "dissertations" in which, to pad out the volume, he reprints in part some mediocre essays which he had published previously, e.g., on "entail", and which have absolutely nothing to do with the matter, and in part, his lectures on the history of political economy repeated almost verbatim; he himself says that he "largely draws upon them"; in part, however, he tries in his own way to assimilate the new ideas advanced in the interim by Mill and by Ricardo's opponents.

In his *Principles of Political Economy*,[54] Mr. McCulloch presents us with nothing more than a copy of his "notes" and "dissertations" which he had already copied from his earlier "scattered manuscripts". But things turned out slightly worse in the *Principles*, for inconsistencies are of less importance in notes than in an allegedly methodical treatment. Thus the passages quoted above, though they are, in part, taken verbatim from the "notes", look rather less inconsistent in these "notes" than they do in the *Principles*. ⟨In addition the *Principles* contain plagiarisms of Mill amplified by absurd illustrations, and reprints of articles on corn trade, etc., which he has repeatedly published, maybe verbatim, under twenty different titles in different periodicals, often even in *the same* periodical at different periods.⟩

In the above-mentioned *Volume IV* of his edition of Adam Smith (London, 1828), Mac says (he repeats the same thing word for word in his *Principles of Political Economy* but without making the distinctions which he still felt to be necessary in the "notes"):

"... it is necessary to distinguish between the *exchangeable value*, and the *real* or *cost value* of commodities or products. By the *first*, or the exchangeable value of a commodity or product, is meant its power or capacity of exchanging either for other commodities *or* for labour; and by the *second*, or its real or cost value, is meant the quantity of labour which it required for its production or appropriation, or rather the quantity which would be required for the production or appropriation of a similar commodity at the time when the investigation is made" ([J. R. McCulloch in: Adam Smith, *An Inquiry into the Nature and Causes of the Wealth of Nations*, Vol. IV, London, 1828,] pp. 85-86 [Note II]).

"A *commodity* produced by a certain quantity of labour will" ⟨when the supply of commodities is equal to the effectual demand⟩ "uniformly exchange for, or buy any other commodity produced by the same quantity of labour. It will never, however, exchange for, or buy exactly the same quantity of labour that produced it; but though it will not do this, it will *always* exchange for, or buy the same quantity of labour as any other commodity produced under the same circumstances, or by means of the same quantity of labour, as itself" (op. cit., pp. 96-97).

"*In point of fact*" (this phrase is repeated literally in the *Principles*, since, in point of fact, this "in point of fact" constitutes the whole of his deduction), "it" (the commodity) "will always exchange for more" ⟨viz., for more labour than that by which it was produced⟩ "*and it is this excess that constitutes profits.* No capitalist could have *any motive*" (as if the "motive" of the buyer was the point in question when dealing with the exchange of commodities and the investigation of their value) "to exchange the produce of a given quantity of labour already performed ||843| for the produce of the same *quantity of labour to be performed.* This would be *to lend*" ("to exchange" would be "to lend") "without receiving any interest on the loan" (loc. cit., p. 96 [note to Note II]).

Let us start at the end.

If the capitalist did not get back more labour than the amount he advances in wages, he would "lend" without receiving a "profit". What has to be explained is how profit is possible if commodities (labour or other commodities) are exchanged at their value. And the answer is that no profit would be possible if equivalents were exchanged. It is assumed, first of all, that capitalist and worker "exchange". And then, in order to explain profit, it is assumed that they do "not" exchange, but that one of the parties lends (i.e., gives commodities) and the other borrows, that is, pays only after he has received the commodities.

In other words, in order to explain profit, it is said that the capitalist secures "no interest" if he makes no profit. This is [putting] the thing wrongly. The commodities in which the capitalist pays wages and the commodities which he gets back as a result of the labour, are different *use-values*. He does not therefore receive back what he advanced, any more than he does when he exchanges one commodity for another. Whether he buys another commodity, or whether he buys the specific [commodity] labour which produces the other commodity for him, amounts to the same. For the use-value he advances he receives back another use-value, as happens in all exchanges of commodities. If, on the other hand, one pays attention only to the value of the commodity, then it is no longer a contradiction to exchange "a given quantity of labour already performed" for "the same quantity of labour to be performed" (although the capitalist in fact pays only after the labour *has been* performed), nor is it a contradiction to exchange a quantity of labour performed for the same quantity of labour performed. This latter is an insipid tautology. The first part of the passage implies that "the labour to be performed" will be embodied in a use-value different from that in which the labour performed is embodied. In this case there is thus a difference [between the objects to be exchanged] and, consequently, a motive for exchange arising out of the relationship itself, but this is not so in the other case, since A only exchanges for A insofar as in this exchange it is a matter of the quantity of labour. This is why Mr. Mac has recourse to the *motive*. The motive of the capitalist is to receive back a greater "quantity of labour" than he advances. Profit is here explained by the fact that the capitalist has the *motive* to make "profit". But the same thing can be said about the sale of goods by the merchant and about every sale of commodities not for consumption but for gain. The seller has no motive to exchange a quantity of performed labour for the same quantity of performed labour. His motive is to get in return more performed labour than he gives away. Hence he *must* get more performed labour in the form of money or commodities than he gives away in the form of a commodity or of money. He must, therefore, buy cheaper than he sells, and sell dearer than he has bought. Profit *upon alienation* is thus explained, not by the fact that it corresponds to the law of value, but by declaring that buyers and sellers have no "motive" for buying and selling in accordance with the law of value. This is Mac's first "sublime" discovery, it fits beautifully into the Ricardian system, which seeks to show how the law of value asserts itself despite the "motives" of seller and buyer.

||844| For the rest, Mac's presentation in the "notes" differs from the one in the *Principles* only in the following:

In the *Principles* he makes a distinction between "real value" and "relative value" and says that both are equal "under ordinary circumstances" but "in point of fact" they cannot be equal if there is to be a profit. He therefore says merely that the "fact" contradicts the "principle".

In the "notes" he distinguishes three sorts of value: "real value", the "relative value" of a commodity in its exchange with other commodities, and the relative value of a commodity exchanged with labour. The "relative value" of a commodity in its exchange with another commodity is its *real* value *expressed* in another commodity, or in an "equivalent". On the other hand, its relative value in exchange with labour is its real value expressed in another real value that is greater than itself. That means, its value is the exchange with a greater value, with a non-equivalent. If it were exchanged for an equivalent in labour, then there would be no profit. The value of a commodity in its exchange with labour is a greater value.

Problem: The Ricardian definition of value conflicts with the exchange of commodities with labour.

Mac's solution: In the exchange of a commodity with labour the law of value does not exist, but its contrary. Otherwise profit could not be explained. Profit for him, the Ricardian, is to be explained by the law of value.

Solution: The law of value (in this case) is profit. "In point of fact" Mac only reiterates what the opponents of the Ricardian theory say, namely, that there would be *no profit* if the law of value applied to exchange between capital and labour. Consequently, they say, the Ricardian theory of value is invalid. He [McCulloch] says that *in this case*, which he must explain by the Ricardian law, the law does not exist and that in this case "value" "means" something else.

From this it is obvious how little he understands of the Ricardian law. Otherwise he would have had to say that profit arising in exchange between commodities which are exchanged in proportion to the labour-time [embodied in them], is due to the fact that "unpaid" labour is contained in the commodities. In other words, the unequal exchange between capital and labour explains the exchange of commodities at their value and the profit which is realised in the course of this exchange. Instead of this he says: Commodities which contain the same amount of labour-time command the same amount of surplus labour, which is not contained in them. He believes that in this way he has reconciled Ricardo's propositions with those of Malthus, by establishing an identity between the determination of the value of commodities by labour-time and the determination of the value of commodities by their command over labour. But what does it mean when he says that commodities which contain the same amount of labour-time command the same amount of *surplus* labour in addition to the labour contained in them? It means nothing more than that a commodity in which a *definite* amount of labour-time is embodied commands a definite quantity of surplus labour [that is, more labour] than it itself contains. That this applies not only to commodity A, in which x hours of labour-time are embodied, but also to commodity B, in which x hours of labour-time are likewise embodied, follows by definition from the Malthusian formula itself.

The contradiction is therefore solved by Mac in this way: If the Ricardian theory of value were really a valid one, then profit, and consequently capital and capitalist production, would be impossible. This is exactly what Ricardo's opponents assert. And this is what Mac answers them, how he refutes them. And in so doing, he does not notice the beauty of an explanation of exchangeable value in [exchange with] labour which amounts to saying that *value is exchange for something which has no value.*

[b) Distortion of the Concept of Labour Through Its Extension to Processes of Nature. Confusion of Exchange-Value and Use-Value]

||845| After Mr. Mac has thus abandoned the basis of Ricardian political economy, he proceeds even further and destroys the basis of this basis.

The first difficulty in the Ricardian system was [to present] the exchange of capital and labour so that it corresponded to the "*law of value*".

The second difficulty was that *capitals of equal magnitude*, no matter what their organic composition, yield *equal profits* or the *general rate of profit*. This is indeed the unrecognised problem of how values are converted into cost-prices.

The difficulty arose because *capitals of equal magnitude*, but of unequal composition—it is immaterial whether the unequal composition is due to the capitals containing unequal proportions of constant and variable capital, or of fixed and circulating capital, or to the unequal period of circulation of the capitals—set in motion *unequal* quantities of immediate labour, and therefore unequal quantities of unpaid labour; consequently they cannot appropriate equal quantities of surplus-value or surplus product in the process of production. Hence they cannot yield equal profit if profit is nothing but the surplus-value calculated on the value of the whole capital advanced. *If, however, the surplus-value were something different from (unpaid) labour, then labour could after all not be the "foundation and measure" of the value of commodities.*

The difficulties arising in this context were discovered by Ricardo himself (although not in their general form) and set forth by him as *exceptions* to the law of value. Malthus used these exceptions to throw the whole law overboard on the grounds that the exceptions constituted the rule. Torrens, who also criticised Ricardo, indicated the problem at any rate when he said that *capitals of equal size set unequal quantities of labour in motion, and nevertheless produce commodities of equal "values", hence value cannot be determined by labour. Ditto Bailey*, etc. *Mill* for his part accepted the exceptions noted by Ricardo as exceptions, and he had no scruples about them except with regard to one single form. One particular *cause of the equalisation* of the profits of the capitalists he found *incompatible* with the law. It was the following. Certain commodities remain in the process of production (for example, wine in the cellar) without any labour being applied to them; there is a period during which they are subject to certain natural processes (for example, prolonged breaks in labour occur in agriculture and in tanning before certain new chemicals are applied—these cases are not mentioned by Mill). These periods are nevertheless considered as profit-yielding. The period of time during which the commodity is not being worked on by labour [is regarded] as labour-time (the same thing in general applies where a *longer period of circulation time is involved*). *Mill "lied" his way—so to speak—out of the difficulty by saying that one can consider the time in which the wine,* for example, is in the cellar as a period when it is soaking up labour, *although* according to the assumption this is, in point of fact, not the case. Otherwise one would have to say that "time" creates profit and [according to Mill][55] time as such is "sound and fury". McCulloch uses this balderdash of Mill as a starting-point, or rather he reproduces it in his customary affected, plagiarist manner in a general form in which the latent nonsense becomes apparent and the last vestiges of the Ricardian system, as of all economic thinking whatsoever, are happily discarded.

On closer consideration, all the difficulties mentioned above resolve themselves into the following difficulty.

That part of capital which enters into the production process in the form of commodities, i.e., as raw materials or tools, does not add more value to the product than it possessed before production. For it only has value insofar as it is embodied labour and the labour contained in it is in no way altered by its entry into the production process. It is to such an extent independent of the production process into which it enters and dependent on the socially determined labour required for its own production that its own value changes when more labour or less labour than it itself contains is required for its reproduction. As value, this part of capital therefore enters unchanged into the production process and emerges from it unchanged. Insofar as it really enters into the production process and is changed, this change affects only its *use-value*, i.e., it undergoes a change as *use-value*. And all operations undergone by the raw material or carried out by the instrument of labour are merely processes to which they are submitted as specific kinds of raw material, etc., and particular tools (spindles, etc.), processes which affect their use-value, but which, as processes, have nothing to do with their exchange-value. Exchange-value is maintained in this ||846| change. That is all.

It is different with that part of capital which is exchanged against labour-power. The use-value of labour-power is *labour*, the element which produces exchange-value. Since the labour provided by labour-power in industrial consumption is greater than the labour which is required for the reproduction of the labour-power, i.e., it provides more than an equivalent of the wages the worker receives, the value which the capitalist receives from the worker in exchange is greater than the price he pays for this labour. It follows from this that, if equal rates of exploitation are assumed, of two capitals of equal size, that which sets less living labour in motion— whether this is due to the fact that the proportion of variable capital is less from the start, or to the fact that it has a [longer] period of circulation or period of production during which it is not exchanged against labour, does not come into contact with it, does not absorb it—will produce less surplus-value, and, in general, commodities of less value. How then can the *values* created be *equal* and the surplus-values proportional to the capital advanced? Ricardo was unable to answer this question because, put in this way, it is *absurd* since, in fact, neither equal values nor [equal] surplus-values are produced. Ricardo, however, did not understand the genesis of the general rate of profit nor, consequently, the transformation of values into costprices which differ specifically from them.

Mac, however, eliminates the difficulty by basing himself on Mill's insipid "evasion". One gets round the inconvenience by talking out of existence by means of a phrase the characteristic difference out of which it arose. This is the characteristic difference: The use-value of labour-power is labour; it consequently produces exchange-value. The use-value of the other commodities is use-value as distinct from exchange-value, therefore no change which this use-value undergoes can change the predetermined exchange-value. McCulloch gets round the difficulty by calling the use-values of commodities—exchange-value, and the operations in which they are involved as use-values, the services they render as use-values in production—*labour*. For after all, in ordinary life we speak of labouring animals, working machines, and even say poetically that the iron works in the furnace, or works under the blows of the hammer. It even screams. *And nothing is easier than to prove that every "operation" is labour, for labour is—an operation. In the same way one can prove that everything material experiences sensation, for everything which experiences sensation is—material.*

"... labour may *properly* be defined to be any sort of action or operation, whether performed by man, the lower animals, machinery, or natural agents, that tends to bring about any[a] desirable result" (op. cit., p. 75, Note I).

And this does not by any means apply [solely] to instruments of labour. It is in the nature of things that this applies equally to raw materials. Wool undergoes a physical action or operation when it is dyed. In general, nothing can be acted upon physically, mechanically, chemically, etc., in order "to bring about

---

[a] The manuscript has "a".—*Ed.*

any desirable result" without the thing itself reacting. It cannot therefore be worked upon without itself working. Thus all commodities which enter into the production process bring about an increase in value not only by retaining their own value, but by creating new value, because they "work" and are not merely materialised labour. In this way, all the difficulties are naturally eliminated. In reality, this is merely a paraphrase, a new name for Say's "productive services of capital", "productive services of land", etc., which Ricardo attacked continuously and against which Mac—strange to say—himself polemises in the same "dissertation" or "note" where he pompously presents his discovery, borrowed from Mill and embellished still further. In criticising Say, McCulloch makes lavish use of recollected passages from Ricardo and remembers that these "productive services" are in fact only the attributes displayed by things as *use-values* in the production process. But naturally, all this is changed when he calls these "productive services" by the sacramental name of *"labour"*.

||847| *After Mac has happily transformed commodities into workers*, it goes without saying that these workers also draw wages and that, in addition to the value they possess as "accumulated labour", they must be paid wages for their "operations" or "action". These wages of the commodities are pocketed by the capitalists *per procurationem*; they are *"wages of accumulated labour"—*alias *profit*. And this [according to McCulloch] is proof that equal profit on equal capitals, whether they set large or small amounts of labour in motion, follows directly from the determination of value by *labour-time*.

The most extraordinary thing about all this, as we have already noted, is the way Mac, at the very moment when he is basing himself on Mill and appropriating Say, hurls Ricardian phrases against Say. How literally he copies Say—except that where Say speaks of *action*, he [McCulloch] calls this action *l a b o u r*—can best be seen ·from the following passages from Ricardo where the latter is criticising Say.

"M. Say ... imputes to him" (Adam Smith) "as an error, that 'he attributes to the *labour of man alone*, the power of producing value. A more correct analysis shews us that value is owing to the action of labour, or rather the industry of man, combined with the *action of those agents* which nature supplies, and with *that of capital*. His ignorance of this principle prevented him from establishing the true theory of the influence of machinery in the production of riches.'[56] In contradiction to the opinion of Adam Smith, M. Say ... speaks of the value which is given to commodities by natural agents.... But these natural agents, though they add greatly to *value in use*, never *add exchangeable value*, of which M. Say is speaking..." (David Ricardo, *Principles of Political Economy, and Taxation*, third ed., London, 1821, pp. 334-36).

"... *machines* and natural agents might very greatly add to the riches of a country," but they do "not ... add any thing to the value of those riches" (loc. cit., p. 335 [note]).

Like all economists worth naming, [including] Adam Smith (although in a fit of humour he once called the ox a productive labourer[57]), Ricardo emphasises that labour as *human activity*, even more, as socially determined *human activity*, is the sole source of value. It is precisely through the consistency with which he treats the value of commodities as merely "representing" socially determined labour, that Ricardo differs from the other economists. All these economists understand more or less clearly, but Ricardo more clearly than the others, that the exchange-value of *things* is a mere expression, a specific social form, of the productive activity of men, something entirely different from things and their use as things, whether in industrial or in non-industrial consumption. For them, value is, in fact, simply an objectively expressed relation of the productive activity of men, of the different types of labour to one another. When he argues against Say, Ricardo explicitly quotes the words of Destutt de Tracy, as expressing his own views.

"As it is certain that our physical and moral faculties are alone our original riches, the *employment of those faculties*" (the faculties of men), "*labour of some kind*" (that is, labour as the realisation of the faculties of men), "is our only original treasure, and that it is always from this employment, that all those things are created which we call riches.... It is certain too, that all *those t h i n g s only represent the labour which has created them*, and if they have *a value*, or even two distinct values, they can only derive them from that of the labour from which they emanate" ([Destutt de Tracy, *Elémens d'idéologie*, IV-e et V-e parties. "Traité de la volonté et de ses effets", Paris, 1826, pp. 35-36; quoted by Ricardo in his *Principles of Political Economy, and Taxation*, third ed., London, 1821,] p. 334).

Thus commodities, things in general, have value only because they *represent* human ||848| labour, not insofar as they are things in themselves, but insofar as they are incarnations of social labour.

And yet some persons have had the temerity to say that the miserable Mac has taken Ricardo to extremes, he who, in his incogitant efforts to "utilise" the Ricardian theory eclectically along with those opposed to it, *identifies* its *basic principle* and that of all political economy—*labour itself* as human activity and as socially determined human activity—with the physical action, etc., which commodities possess as *use-values*, as things. He who abandons the very concept of labour itself!

Rendered insolent by Mill's "evasion", he plagiarises Say while arguing against him with Ricardian phrases and copies precisely those phrases of Say which Ricardo in Chapter 20 of his book, entitled "Value and Riches", attacks as being fundamentally opposed to his own ideas and those of Smith. (Roscher naturally repeats that Mac has carried Ricardo to extremes.[58]) Mac, however, is sillier than Say, who does not call the "action" of fire, machinery, etc., *labour*. And more inconsistent.

While Say attributes the creation of "value" to wind, fire, etc., Mac considers that only those use-values, things, which can be monopolised create value, as if it were possible to utilise the wind, or steam, or water as motive power without the possession of windmills, steam-driven machinery or waterwheels! As if those who own, monopolise, the things, whose possession alone enables them to employ the natural agents, did not also monopolise the natural agents. I can have as much air, water, etc., as I like. But I possess them as productive agents only if I have the commodities, the things, by the use of which these agents will operate as such. Thus Mac is even lower than Say.

This vulgarisation of Ricardo represents the most complete and most frivolous decline of Ricardo's theory.

"In so far, however, as that result" (i.e., the result produced by the action or operation of any thing) "is effected by the labour *or* operation of natural agents, that can neither be monopolised nor appropriated by a greater or smaller number of individuals to the exclusion of others, it has *no value*. What is done by these agents is done *gratuitously*" (J. R. McCulloch [in: Adam Smith, *An Inquiry into the Nature and Causes of the Wealth of Nations*, Vol. IV, London, 1828], p. 75 [Note I]).

As if what is done by cotton, wool, iron or machinery, were not also done "gratuitously". The machine costs money, but the operation of the machine is not paid for. No use-value of any kind of commodity costs anything after its exchange-value has been paid.

"The man who sells oil makes no charge for its natural qualities. In estimating its cost he puts down the value of the labour employed in its pursuit, and such is its value" (H. C. Carey, *Principles of Political Economy...*, Part I, Philadelphia, 1837, p. 47).

In arguing against Say, Ricardo emphasises precisely that

the action of the machine, for example, costs just as little as that of wind and water.

"... the services which ... natural agents *and m a c h i n e r y* perform for us ... are serviceable to us ... by adding to value in use; but as *they* perform their work *gratuitously* ... the assistance which they afford us, adds nothing to *value in exchange*" (David Ricardo, [*Principles of Political Economy, and Taxation*, third ed., London, 1821,] pp. 336-37).

Thus Mac has not understood the most elementary propositions of Ricardo. But the sly dog thinks: if the use-value of cotton, machinery, etc., costs *nothing*, is not paid for apart from its exchange-value, then, on the other hand, this use-value is *sold* by those who use cotton, machinery, etc. They sell what costs them nothing.

|849| The brutal thoughtlessness of this fellow is evident, for after accepting Say's "principle", he sets forth rent with great emphasis, plagiarising extensively from Ricardo.

Land is a

"natural agent" that can be "monopolised or appropriated by a greater or smaller number of individuals to the exclusion of others" [J. R. McCulloch, loc. cit., p. 75, Note I],

and its natural, vegetative action *or* "labour", its productive power, consequently has *value*, and rent is thus ascribed to the "productive power" of land, as is done by the Physiocrats. This is an outstanding example of Mac's way of vulgarising Ricardo. On the one hand, he copies Ricardo's arguments, which only make sense if they are based on the Ricardian assumptions, and on the other hand, he takes from others the direct negation of these assumptions (with the reservation that he uses his "nomenclature" or makes some small changes in the propositions). He should have said: "Rent is the wages of land" pocketed by the landowner.

"If a capitalist expends the same sum in paying the wages of labourers, in maintaining horses, or in hiring a machine, and if the men, the horses, and the machine can all perform *the same piece of work*, *its* value will obviously be the same by whichever of them it may have been performed" (op. cit., p. 77 [Note I]).

In other words: the value of the product depends on the value of the capital laid out. This is the problem to be solved. The formulation of the problem is, according to Mac, *"obviously"* the solution of it. But since the machine, for example, performs a greater piece of work than the men displaced by it, it is even more "obvious" that the product of the machine will not fall but rise in value compared with the value of the product of the men who "perform the same work". Since the machine can produce 10,000 units of work where a man can only produce one, and every unit has *the same value*, the product of the machine should be 10,000 times as dear as that "of man".

Moreover, in his anxiety to distinguish himself from Say by stating that *value* is produced not by the action of natural agents but only by the action of monopolised agents, or agents produced by labour, Mac gets into difficulties and falls back on Ricardian phrases. For example, the *labour* of the wind produces the desired effect on the ship (produces a change in it).

"... but the *value* of that change is not increased by, and is in no degree dependent on, the operation or labour of the natural agents concerned, but on the *amount of capital*, or the *produce of previous labour*, that co-operated in the production of the effect; just as *the cost of grinding* corn does not depend on the action of the wind or water that turns the mill, but on the amount of capital *wasted* in the operation" (op. cit., p. 79 [Note I]).

Here, all of a sudden, grinding is viewed as adding value to the corn insofar only as capital—"the produce of previous labour"—is "wasted" in the act of grinding. That is, it is not due to the millstone "working", but to the fact that along with the "waste" of the millstone, the value contained in it, the labour embodied in it, is also *"wasted"*.

After these pretty arguments, Mac sums up the wisdom (borrowed from Mill and Say) in which he brings the concept of value into harmony with all kinds of contradictory phenomena, in the following way:

"... the word *labour* means ... in all discussions respecting *value* ... either the immediate labour of man, or the *labour of the capital* produced by man, or both" (op. cit., p. 84 [note to Note II]).

Hence labour ||850| is to be understood as meaning the labour of man, then his accumulated labour, and finally, the *practical application*, that is, the physical, etc., properties of use-values evolved in (industrial) consumption. Apart from these properties, use-value means nothing at all. Use-value operates only in consumption. Consequently, by the exchange-value of the products of labour, we [are to] understand the use-value of these products, for this use-value consists only in its *action*, or, as Mac calls it, *"labour"*, in consumption, regardless of whether this is industrial consumption or not. However, the types of "operation", "action", or "labour" of use-values, as well as their physical measures, are as varied as the use-values themselves. But what is the unity, the measure by means of which we compare them? This is established by the general word "labour" which is substituted for these quite different applications of use-values, after labour itself has been reduced to the words "operation" or "action".

Thus, with the identification of use-value and exchange-value ends this vulgarisation of Ricardo, which we must therefore consider as the last and most sordid expression of the decline of the Ricardian school as such.

"The *profits of capital* are only another name for the *wages of accumulated labour*" (J. R. McCulloch, *The Principles of Political Economy*, London, 1825, p. 291),

that is, for the wages paid to commodities for the services they render as *use-values* in production.

In addition, these wages of accumulated labour have their own mysterious connotation as far as Mr. McCulloch is concerned. We have already mentioned that, apart from his plagiarism of Ricardo, Mill, Malthus and Say, which constitutes the real basis of his writings, he himself continually reprints and sells his "accumulated labour" under various titles, always "largely drawing" upon writings for which he has been paid before. This method of drawing "the wages of accumulated labour" was discussed at great length as early as *1826* in a special work, and what has not McCulloch done since then—from 1826 to 1862—with regard to drawing wages for accumulated labour![59] (This miserable phrase has also been adopted by Roscher in his role of Thucydides.[60])

The book referred to is called: *Some Illustrations of Mr. McCulloch's Principles of Political Economy*, Edinburgh, 1826, by Mordecai Mullion.[61] It traces how our *chevalier d'industrie* made a name for himself. Nine-tenths of his work is copied from Adam Smith, Ricardo and others, the remaining tenth being culled repeatedly from his own accumulated labour which he repeats most shamelessly and contemptibly. Mullion shows, for example, not only that McCulloch sold *the same articles* to *The Edinburgh Review*[62] and *The Scotsman*[63] and the *Encyclopaedia Britannica*[64] as his own "dissertations" and as new works, but also that he published *the same* articles *word for word* and with only a few transpositions and under new titles in different issues of *The Edinburgh Review* over the years.

In this respect Mullion says the following about "this most incredible cobbler", "this most Economical of all Economists":

"Mr. McCulloch's articles are as unlike as may be to the heavenly bodies [...] but, in one respect, they resemble such luminaries—they have stated times of return" ([Mordecai Mullion,] (op. cit., p. 21).

No wonder he believes in "the wages of accumulated labour". Mr. McCulloch's fame illustrates the power of fraudulent baseness.

||850a| In order to perceive how McCulloch exploits some of Ricardo's propositions to give himself airs, see, *inter alia*, *The Edinburgh Review* for March 1824, where this friend of the wages of accumulated labour gives vent to a veritable jeremiad about the fall in the rate of profit. (This claptrap is called "Considerations on the Accumulation of Capital".)

"The author ... expresses the fears in him by *the decline in profit* as follows:

"'... the condition of' (England) 'however prosperous in appearance, is bad and unsound at bottom; [...] the plague of poverty is secretly creeping on the mass of her citizens; [...] the foundations of her power and greatness have been shaken....

... where [...] the rate of interest is low, as in [Holland and] England, [...] the profits of stock are also low [...], those are countries [...] that [...] are approaching the termination of their career.'

"These observations must surprise everybody acquainted with England's splendid situation" ([McCulloch, *Discours sur l'économie*, traduit par] Prévost, p. 197ᵃ).

There was no need for Mr. Mac to distress himself over the fact that "land" gets better "wages" than "iron, bricks, etc." The cause must be that it "labours" harder. |XIV-850a||

* * *

||XV-925| ⟨Even a blind sow sometimes finds an acorn and so does McCulloch in the following passages. But even this, as he presents it, is only an inconsistency, since he does not distinguish surplus-value from profit. Secondly, it is again one of his thoughtless, eclectic acts of plagiarism. According to fellows like Torrens, for whom value is determined by capital—and the same applies to Bailey—profit is proportionate to the capital advanced. Unlike Ricardo, they do not consider that profit and surplus-value are identical concepts, but only

---

ᵃ This passage from McCulloch which Marx quotes from Prévost's translation is quoted here from *The Edinburgh Review*, Vol. XL, *March-July 1824.—Ed.*

because they have no need whatsoever to explain profit on the basis of value, since they regard the visible form of surplus-value—*profit* as the relation of surplus-value to the capital advanced—as the original form and, in fact, they merely translate the apparent form into words.

The passages in Mac's work, who is (1) a Ricardian and (2) plagiarises Ricardo's opponents—without attempting to reconcile [the conflicting ideas]—read:

> Ricardo's law [that a rise in profits can be brought about in no other way than by a fall in wages, and a fall in profits only by a rise in wages] is only true "in those cases in which the *productiveness of industry* [...] remains constant"a (J. R. McCulloch, *The Principles of Political Economy*, London, 1825, p. 373), that is, the productiveness of the industry which produces constant capital.
>
> "... profits depend on the proportion which they bear to the capital by which they are produced, and not on the proportion [...] to wages"b (loc. cit., pp. 373-74). If the productivity of industry *in general* is doubled and the additional product thus obtained is divided between capitalists and workers, then the proportion of the share of the capitalists to that of the workers remains unchanged, although the *rate of profit* calculated on the capital advanced has risen.c

Even in this case, as Mac also notes, one can say that *wages* have fallen relatively as compared with the product, because *profits* have risen. (But in this case it is the rise in profits which is the cause of the fall in wages.) This calculation, however, rests on the incorrect method of calculating wages as a share in the product, and, as we saw previously,[65] Mr. John Stuart Mill seeks to generalise the Ricardian law in this sophistical manner.) |XV-925||

5. Wakefield [Some Objections to Ricardo's Theory Regarding the "Value of Labour" and Rent]

||XIV-850a| Wakefield's real contribution to the understanding of capital has already been dealt with in the previous section on the *Conversion of Surplus-Value into Capital*.[66] Here we shall only deal with what is directly relevant to the "topic".

> "Treating labour as a commodity, and capital, the produce of labour, as another, then, if the value of these two commodities were regulated by equal quantities of labour, a given amount of labour would, under all cir-

---

a The manuscript has "stationary" instead of "constant".—*Ed.*
b The manuscript has "to the wages".—*Ed.*
c In this sentence, which is written in German, Marx summarises the ideas set forth by McCulloch on pp. 373-74.—*Ed.*

cumstances, exchange for that quantity of capital which had been produced by the same amount of labour; *antecedent labour* [...] would always exchange for the same amount of *present labour* [....] the[a] value of labour in relation to other commodities, in so far, at least, as wages depend upon share, is determined, not by equal quantities of labour, but by the proportion between supply and demand" (Wakefield's edition of Adam Smith, *An Inquiry into the Nature and Causes of the Wealth of Nations*, Vol. I, London, 1835, pp. 230-31, note).

Thus, according to Wakefield, profit would be inexplicable if wages corresponded to the *value* of labour.

In Vol. II of his edition of Adam Smith's work Wakefield remarks:

"Surplus produce[67] [...] always constitutes rent: *still rent may be paid, which does not consist of surplus produce*" (p. 216).

"If" (as in Ireland) "the bulk of a people be brought to live upon potatoes, and in hovels and rags, and to pay, for permission so to live, all that they can produce beyond hovels, rags, and potatoes, then, in proportion as they put up with less, the owner of the land on which they live, obtains more, even though the return to capital or labour should remain unaltered. *What the miserable tenants give up, the landlord gathers.* [...] *A*[b] *fall in the standard of living amongst the cultivators of the earth is another cause of surplus produce*.... When wages fall, the effect upon surplus produce is the same as a fall in the standard of living: the whole produce remaining the same, the surplus part is greater; the producers have less, and the landlord more" (pp. 220-21).

In this case, profit is called *rent*, just as it is called *interest* when, for example, as in India, the worker (although nominally independent) works with advances he receives from the capitalist and has to hand over all the surplus produce to the capitalist.

6. Stirling [Vulgarised Explanation of Profit by the Interrelation of Supply and Demand]

Patrick James Stirling, *The Philosophy of Trade etc.*, Edinburgh, 1846.

"... the quantity of every commodity [...] must be so regulated that the supply of each commodity shall bear a less proportion to the demand for it than the supply of labour bears to the demand for labour. The difference between the price or value of the commodity, and the price or value of the labour worked up in it [...] constitutes the [...] *profits*"[c] (op. cit., pp. 72-73).

---

[a] The manuscript has "But the". —*Ed*.
[b] The manuscript has "So a". —*Ed*.
[c] Instead of "constitutes the [...] *profits*", the manuscript has "constitutes the *profit* or *surplus* which Ricardo cannot explain on the basis of his theory". —*Ed*.

||851|| The same author informs us:

When the values of commodities are exchanged with one another according to their production costs, "the value of these commodities may be said to be *at par*" (p. 18).[a]

Thus if demand and supply of labour correspond with one another, then labour would be sold at its *value* (whatever Stirling may understand by value). And if demand and supply of the commodities in which the labour is worked up do correspond, then the commodities would be sold at their *production costs*, by which Stirling understands the *value of labour*. The price of the commodity would then be equal to the value of the labour worked up in it. And the price of labour would be on a par with its own *value*. The price of the commodity would therefore be equal to the price of the labour worked up in it. Consequently there would be no profit or surplus.

Stirling explains profit, or the surplus, in this way.

The supply of labour in relation to the demand for it must be greater than the supply of commodities in which the labour is worked up is in relation to the demand for them. The matter must be so arranged that the commodity is sold at a higher price than that paid for the labour contained in it.

This is what Mr. Stirling calls explaining the phenomenon of the surplus, whereas it is, in fact, nothing but a paraphrase of what is supposed to be explained. If we go into it further, then there are only three possibilities. [1] The price of labour is on a par with value, that is, the demand for and supply of labour balance, the price of labour is equal to the value of labour. In these circumstances, the commodities must be sold *above* their value, or things must be arranged in such a way that the supply is *below* the demand. This is pure *"profit upon alienation"*, except that the condition is stated under which it is possible. [2] Or the demand for labour is greater than the supply and the price [of labour] is higher than its value. In these circumstances, the capitalist has paid the worker more than the value of the commodity, and the buyer must then pay the capitalist a twofold surplus—first to replace the amount he [the capitalist] has already paid to the worker and then his profit. [3] Or the price of labour is *below* its value and the supply of labour above the demand for it. The surplus would then arise from

---

[a] Marx here is summarising a paragraph printed on p. 18 of Stirling's book.—*Ed.*

the fact that labour is paid *below its* value and is sold [embodied in commodities] at its *value* or, at least, above its *price*.

If one strips this of all nonsense, then Stirling's surplus is [here] due to the fact that labour is bought by the capitalist *below* its value and is sold again *above* its price in the form of commodities.

The other cases, divested of their ridiculous form—according to which the producer has to "arrange" matters in such a way that he is able to sell his commodity above its value, or above "the par of value"—mean nothing but that the *market price* of a commodity rises *a b o v e* its value, if the demand for it is greater than the supply. This is certainly not a new discovery and explains one sort of "surplus" which never caused Ricardo or anyone else the slightest difficulty. |XIV-851||

7. John Stuart Mill
[Unsuccessful Attempts to Deduce the Ricardian Theory of the Inverse Proportionality Between the Rate of Profit and the Level of Wages Directly from the Law of Value]

[a) Confusion of the Rate of Surplus-Value with the Rate of Profit. Elements of the Conception of "Profit upon Alienation". Confused Conception of the "Profits Advanced" by the Capitalist]

||VII-319| In the booklet mentioned above,[68] which, in fact, contains all that is original in Mr. John Stuart Mill's writings about political economy (in contrast to his bulky compendium[69]), he says in *Essay IV—"On Profits, and Interest"*:

"Tools and materials, like other things, have originally cost nothing but labour.... The labour employed in making the tools and materials being added to the labour afterwards employed in working up the materials by the aid of tools, the sum total gives the whole of the labour employed in the production of the completed commodity.... *To replace capital, is to replace nothing but the wages of the labour employed*" ([John Stuart Mill, *Essays on some Unsettled Questions of Political Economy*, London, 1844,] p. 94).

This in itself is quite wrong, because the employed labour and the wages paid are by no means identical. On the contrary, the employed labour is equal to the sum of wages and profit. To replace capital means to replace the labour for which the capitalist pays (wages) and the labour for which he does not pay but which he nevertheless sells (profit). Mr. Mill is here confusing "employed labour" and that portion of the employed labour which is paid for by the capitalist who employs it. This confusion is itself no recommendation for his understanding of the Ricardian theory, which he claims to teach.

Incidentally, it should be noted in relation to constant capital that though each part of it can be reduced to previous labour and therefore one can imagine that at some time it represented profit or wages or both, but once it exists as constant capital, one part of it—for example, seeds, etc.—can no longer be transformed into profit or wages.

Mill does not distinguish surplus-value from profit. He therefore declares that the *rate of profit* (and this is correct for the surplus-value which has already been transformed into profit) is equal to the ratio of the price of the product to the price of its means of production (labour included). (See pp. 92-93.) At the same time he seeks to deduce the laws governing the *rate of profit* directly from the Ricardian law, in which Ricardo confuses surplus-value and profit, [and to prove] that "profits depend upon wages; rising as wages fall, and falling as wages rise" [p. 94].

Mr. Mill himself is not quite clear about the *question* which he seeks to answer. We will therefore formulate *his* question briefly before we hear his answer. The rate of profit is the ratio of surplus-value to the *total amount* of the capital advanced (constant and variable capital taken together) while surplus-value itself is the excess of the quantity of labour performed by the labourer over the quantity of labour which is advanced him as wages; that is, surplus-value is considered only in relation to the variable capital, or to the capital which is laid out in wages, not in relation to the whole capital. Thus the rate of surplus-value and the rate of profit are two different rates, although profit is only surplus-value considered from a particular point of view. It is correct to say with regard to the rate of surplus-value that it exclusively depends "upon wages; rising as wages fall, and falling as wages rise". (But it would be wrong with regard to the total amount of surplus-value, for this depends not only on the rate at which the surplus labour of the individual worker is appropriated but likewise on the number of workers exploited at the same time.) Since the rate of profit is the ratio of surplus-value to the total amount of capital advanced, it is naturally affected and determined by the fall or rise of surplus-value, and hence, by the rise or fall of wages, but in addition to this, the rate of profit includes factors ||320| which are independent of it and not directly reducible to it.

Mr. John Stuart Mill, who, on the one hand, *directly* identifies profit and surplus-value, like Ricardo, and, on the other hand (moved by considerations concerning the polemic against the anti-Ricardians), does not conceive the *rate of profit* in the Ricardian sense, but in its real sense, as the *ratio* of surplus-value to the total value of the capital advanced (variable capital plus constant capital), goes to great lengths to prove that the rate of profit is determined *directly* by the law which determines surplus-value and can be simply reduced to the fact that the smaller the portion of the working-day in which the worker works for himself, the greater the portion going to the capitalist, and vice versa. We will now observe his torment, the worst part of which is that he is not sure which problem he really wants to solve. If he had formulated the problem correctly, it would have been impossible for him to solve it wrongly in *this* way.

He says, then:

"Though [...] tools, materials, and buildings [...] are themselves the produce of labour [...] yet the *whole* of their value is not resolvable into the wages of the labourers by whom they were produced." ⟨He says above that the replacement of capital is the replacement of wages.⟩ The profits which the capitalists make on these wages, need to be added. The last capitalist has to replace from his product "not only *the wages* paid both by himself and by the tool-maker, but also the profit of the tool-maker, advanced by him himself out of his own capital" (op. cit., p. 98).[a] Hence "... *profits* do not compose merely the *surplus* after replacing the outlay; they also enter into the outlay itself. Capital is expended partly in paying or reimbursing wages, and partly in paying the profits of other capitalists, whose concurrence was necessary in order to bring together the means of production" (loc. cit., pp. 98-99). "An article, therefore, may be *the produce of the same quantity of labour as before*, and yet, if any *portion of the profits* which the last producer has to make good to previous producers can be economised, *the cost of production of the article is diminished*.... It is, therefore, strictly true, that the rate of profit varies inversely as the cost of production of wages" (op. cit., pp. 102-03).

We are naturally always working on the assumption here that the price of a commodity is equal to its value. It is on this basis that Mr. Mill himself carries on the investigation.

Profit, in the passages quoted, appears first of all to bear a very strong resemblance to profit upon alienation, but let us proceed. Nothing is more wrong than to say that (if it is sold at its *value*) an article is "the produce of the same quantity of labour as before" and at the same time that by some circumstance

---

[a] This sentence and the one preceding it are a summary by Marx of Mill's arguments on this page.—*Ed.*

or other "the cost of production of the article" can be diminished. ⟨Unless it is in the sense I first advanced, i. e., when I distinguished between the [real] production cost of the article and the production cost to the capitalist, since he does not pay a part of the production costs.[70] In this case, it is indeed true that the capitalist makes his profit out of the unpaid surplus labour of his own workers just as he may also make it by *underpaying* the capitalist who supplies him with his constant capital, that is, by not paying this capitalist for a part of the surplus labour embodied in the commodity and not paid for by this capitalist (and which precisely for that reason constitutes his profit). This amounts to the fact that he always pays for the commodity *less* than its value. The rate of profit (that is, the ratio of surplus-value to the total value of the capital advanced) can increase either because the quantity of capital [goods] advanced by the capitalist becomes objectively cheaper (due to the increased productivity of labour in those spheres of production which produce constant capital) or because it becomes subjectively cheaper for the buyer, since he pays for the goods at *less* than their value. *For him*, it is then always the result of a smaller quantity of labour.⟩

||321| What Mill says first of all, is that the *constant capital* of the capitalist who manufactures the last commodity resolves not into wages alone, but also into profit. His line of reasoning is as follows:

If it were resolvable into wages alone, then profit would be the surplus accruing to the last capitalist after he has reimbursed himself for all wages paid ⟨and the whole (paid) costs of the product could be reduced to wages⟩, which would constitute the whole of the capital advanced. The total value of the capital advanced would be equal to the total value of the wages embodied in the product. Profit would be the surplus over this. And since the rate of profit is equal to the ratio of this surplus to the total value of the capital advanced, then the rate of profit would obviously rise and fall in proportion to the total value of the capital advanced, that is, in proportion to the *value of wages*, the aggregate of which constitutes the capital advanced. ⟨This objection is, in fact, silly, if we consider the *general* relation of profits and wages. Mr. Mill needed only to put on one side that part of the whole product which is resolvable into profit (irrespective of whether it is paid to *the last* or to the previous capitalists, the co-functionaries in the production of the commodity) and then put that part which resolves into wages on the other, and the amount of profit would still be equal to the surplus over the total amount of wages, and it could be asserted that the Ricardian "inverse ratio" applied directly to the rate of profit. It is not true, however, that the whole of the capital advanced can be resolved into profit and wages.⟩ But the capital advanced does not resolve itself into wages alone, but also into profits advanced. Profit therefore is a surplus not only over and above the wages advanced, but also over the profits advanced. The *rate of profit* is therefore determined not only by the surplus over wages, but by the last capitalist's surplus over the total sum of wages plus profits, the sum of which, according to this assumption, constitutes the whole of the capital advanced. Hence this rate can obviously be altered not only as a result of a rise or fall in wages, but also as a result of a rise or fall in profit. And if we disregarded the changes in the rate of profit arising from the rise or fall in wages, that is, if we assumed—as is done innumerable times in practice—that the value of the wages, in other words, the costs of their production, the labour-time embodied in them, remained the same, remained unchanged, then, following the path outlined by Mr. Mill, we would arrive at the pretty law that the rise or fall in the rate of profit depends on the rise or fall of profit.

"... if any portion of the profits which the last producer has to make good to previous producers can be economised, the cost of production of the article is diminished" [loc. cit., p. 102].

This is in fact very true. If we assume that no portion of the previous producers' profit was a mere surcharge—"profit upon alienation" as James Stuart says, then every economy in one "portion of profit" ⟨so long as it is not achieved by the latter producer swindling the previous one, that is, by not paying him for the whole of the value contained in his commodity⟩ is an economy in the quantity of labour required for the production of the commodity. ⟨Here we disregard the profit paid, for instance, for that time during the period of production, etc., when the capital lies idle.⟩ For example, if two days were required to bring raw materials—coal, for instance—from the pit to the factory, and now only one day is required, then there is an "economy" of one day's work, but this applies as much to that part of it which resolves into wages as to that which resolves into profit.

After Mr. Mill has made it clear to himself that the rate of *surplus* of the last capitalist, or the rate of profit in general, depends not only on the direct ratio of wages to profits, but on the ratio of the last profit, or the profit on every particular capital, to the whole value of the capital advanced, which is equal to the variable capital (that laid out in wages) plus the constant capital—that, in other words, ||322| the rate of profit is determined not only by the ratio of profit to the part of capital laid out in wages, that is, not only by the cost of production or the value of wages, he continues:

"It is, therefore [...] true, that the rate of profits varies inversely as the cost of production of wages" [loc. cit., p. 103].

Although it is false, it is nevertheless true.

The illustration which he now gives can serve as a classical example of the way in which economists use illustrations, and it is all the more astonishing since its author has also written a book about the science of logic.[71] ¹

"Suppose, for example, that 60 agricultural labourers, receiving 60 quarters of corn for their wages, consume fixed capital and seed amounting to the value of 60 quarters more, and that the result of their operations is a produce of 180 quarters. When we analyse the price of the seed and tools into its elements, we find that they must have been the produce of the labour of 40 men: for the wages of those 40, together with profit at the rate previously supposed (50 per cent) make up 60 quarters. *The produce, therefore, consisting of 180 quarters, is the result of the labour altogether of 100 men.*"

Now:ᵃ supposing that the amount of labour required remained the same, but as a *result of some discovery no fixed capital and seed were needed.* Whereas previously the outlay of 120 quarters was required to obtain a product of 180 quarters, now an outlay of only 100 quarters is necessary to achieve this result.

"The produce (180 quarters) is still the result of the same quantity of labour as before [...], the labour of 100 men. A quarter of corn, therefore, is still, as before, the produce of ¹⁰/₁₈ of a man's labour. [...] Aᵇ *quarter of corn*, which is the remuneration of a single labourer, is indeed the *produce of the same quantity of labour as before*; but its cost of production is nevertheless diminished. It is now the produce of ¹⁰/₁₈ of a man's labour, and nothing else; whereas formerly it required for its production the conjunction of that quantity of labour withᶜ an expenditure, in the form of reimbursement of profit, amounting to one-fifth more. If the cost of production of wages had remained the same as before, profits could not have risen. Each labourer received one quarter of corn; but one quarter of corn at that time was the result of the same cost of production, as 1¹/₅ quarter now. In order,

---

ᵃ This and the following sentence are a compression by Marx of Mill's ideas, which are spread over several paragraphs in his book.—*Ed.*
ᵇ The manuscript has "For a".—*Ed.*
ᶜ The manuscript has "plus".—*Ed.*

[CHAPTER XX]

therefore, that each labourer should receive the same cost of production, each must now receive one quarter of corn, plus one-fifth" (op. cit., pp. 99-103 passim).
"Assuming, therefore, that the labourer is paid in the very article he produces, it is evident that, when any saving of expense takes place in the production of that article, if the labourer still receives the same cost of production as before, he must receive an increased quantity, in the very same ratio in which the productive power of capital has been increased. But, if so, the outlay of the capitalist will bear exactly the same proportion to the return as it did before; and profits will not rise. The variations, therefore, in the rate of profits, and those in the cost of production of wages, go hand in hand, and are inseparable. Mr. Ricardo's principle [...] is strictly true,[a] if by low wages be *meant not merely wages which are the produce of a smaller quantity of labour, but wages which are produced at less cost, reckoning labour and previous profits together*" (loc. cit., p. 104).

With regard to this wonderful illustration, we note first of all that, as a result of a discovery, corn is supposed to be produced without seeds (raw materials) and without fixed capital; that is, without raw materials and without tools, by means of mere manual labour, out of air, water and earth. This ||323| absurd presupposition contains nothing but the assumption that a product can be produced *without constant capital*, that is, simply by means of newly applied labour. In this case, what he set out to prove has of course been proved, namely, that profit and surplus-value are identical, and consequently that the rate of profit depends *solely* on the ratio of surplus labour to necessary labour. The difficulty arose precisely from the fact that the rate of surplus-value and the rate of profit are two different things because there exists a ratio of surplus-value to the constant part of capital—and this ratio we call the rate of profit. Thus if we assume constant capital to be zero, we solve the difficulty arising from the existence of constant capital by abstracting from the existence of this constant capital. Or we solve the difficulty by *assuming* that it does not exist. *Probatum est.*[b]

Let us now arrange the problem, or Mill's illustration of the problem, correctly.

According to the first assumption we have:

Constant capital (fixed capital and seed)	Variable capital (capital laid out in wages)	Total product	Profit
60 quarters	60 quarters (60 workmen)	180 quarters	60 quarters

[a] The manuscript has "is therefore strictly true".—*Ed.*
[b] It is proved.—*Ed.*

It is assumed in this example that the labour which is added to the constant capital amounts to 120 quarters and that, since every quarter represents the wages of a working-day (or of a year's labour, which is merely a working-day of 365 working-days), the 180 quarters contain only 60 working-days, 30 of which account for the wages of the workers and 30 constitute profit. We thus assume in fact that one working-day is embodied in 2 quarters and that consequently the 60 working-days of the 60 workmen are embodied in 120 quarters, 60 of which constitute their wages and 60 constitute the profit. In other words, the worker works one half of the working-day for himself, to make up his wages, and one half for the capitalist, thus producing the capitalist's surplus-value. The rate of surplus-value is therefore 100 per cent and not 50 per cent. On the other hand, since the variable capital constitutes only half of the total capital advanced, the rate of profit is not 60 quarters to 60 quarters, that is, not 100 per cent, but 60 quarters to 120 quarters and therefore only 50 per cent. If the constant part of the capital had equalled zero, then the whole of the capital advanced would have consisted of only 60 quarters, i.e., only of the capital advanced in wages, equalling 30 working-days; in this case, profit and surplus-value, and therefore also their rates, would be identical. Profit would then amount to 100 per cent and not 50 per cent; 2 quarters of corn would be the product of one working-day, and 120 quarters the product of 60 working-days, even though one quarter of corn would only be the wages of one working-day and 60 quarters the wages of 60 working-days. In other words, the worker would only receive half, 50 per cent, of his product, while the capitalist would receive twice as much—100% calculated on his outlay.

What is the position with regard to the *constant capital*, the 60 quarters? These were likewise the product of 30 working-days, and if it is assumed with regard to this constant capital that the elements which went into its production are so made up that one-third consists of constant capital and two-thirds of newly added labour, and that the [rate of] surplus-value and the rate of profit are also the same as before, we get the following calculation:

Constant capital	Variable capital	Total product	Profit
20 quarters	20 quarters (wages for 20 workers)	60 quarters	20 quarters

[CHAPTER XX]

Here again the rate of profit would be 50 per cent and the rate of surplus-value 100 per cent. The total product would be ||324| the product of 30 working-days, 10 of which however (equalling 20 quarters) would represent the pre-existing labour (the constant capital) and 20 working-days the newly added labour of 20 workers, each of whom would only receive half his product as wages. Two quarters would be the product of one man's labour as in the previous case, although, again as previously, one quarter would represent the wages of one man's labour and one quarter the capitalist's profit, the capitalist thus appropriating half of the man's labour.

The 60 quarters which the last capitalist producer makes as surplus-value mean a rate of profit of 50 per cent, because these 60 quarters of surplus-value are calculated not only on the 60 quarters advanced in wages but also on the 60 quarters expended in seed and fixed capital, which together amount to 120 quarters.

If Mill calculates that the capitalist who produces the seed and the fixed capital—a total of 60 quarters—makes a profit of 50 per cent, if he assumes further that the constant and variable capital enter into the product in the same proportion as in the case of the production of the 180 quarters, then it will be correct to say that the profit equals 20 quarters, wages 20 quarters and the constant capital 20 quarters. Since wages equal one quarter [a day], then 60 quarters contain 30 working-days in the same way as 120 quarters contain 60 working-days.

But what does Mill say?

"When we analyse the price of the seed and tools into its elements, we find that they must have been the produce of the labour of 40 men: for the wages of those 40, together with profit at the rate previously supposed (50 per cent) make up 60 quarters" [op. cit., p. 99].

In the case of the first capitalist, who employed 60 workers, each of whom he paid one quarter per day as wages (so that he paid out 60 quarters in wages), and laid out 60 quarters in constant capital, the 60 working-days resulted in 120 quarters, of which, however, the workers only received 60 in wages; in other words, wages amounted to only half the product of the labour of 60 men. Thus the 60 quarters of constant capital were only equal to the product of the labour of 30 men; if they consisted only of profit and wages, then wages would amount to 30 quarters and profit to 30 quarters, thus wages would equal the labour of 15 men and profit as well. But the profit amounted to only 50 per cent, since it is assumed that of the 30 days embodied in the 60 quarters, 10 represent pre-existing labour (constant capital) and only 10 are allocated to wages. Thus, 10 days are embodied in constant capital, 20 are newly added working-days, of which, however, the workers only work 10 for themselves, the other 10 being for the capitalist. But Mr. Mill asserts that these 60 quarters are the product of 40 men, while just previously he said that 120 quarters were the product of 60 men. In the latter case, one quarter contains half a working-day (although it is the wages paid for a whole working-day); in the former, $3/4$ of a quarter would equal half a working-day, whereas the one-third of the product (i.e., the 60 quarters) which is laid out in constant capital has just as much value, that is, it contains just as much labour-time, as any other third part of the product. If Mr. Mill desired to convert the constant capital of 60 quarters wholly into wages and profit, then this would not make the *slightest* difference as far as the quantity of labour-time embodied in it is concerned. It would still be 30 working-days as before, but now, since there would be no constant capital to replace, profit and surplus-value would coincide. Thus, profit would amount to 100 per cent, not to 50 per cent as previously. Surplus-value also amounted to 100 per cent in the previous case, but the profit was only 50 per cent precisely because constant capital entered into the calculation.

We have here, therefore, a doubly false manoeuvre on the part of Mr. Mill.

In the case of the first 180 quarters, the difficulty consisted in the fact that surplus-value and profit did not coincide, because the 60 quarters surplus-value had to be calculated not only on 60 quarters (that part of the total product which represented wages) but ||325| on 120 quarters, i.e., 60 quarters constant capital plus 60 quarters wages. Surplus-value therefore amounted to 100 per cent, and profit only to 50 per cent. With regard to the 60 quarters which constituted constant capital, Mr. Mill disposes of this difficulty by assuming that, in this case, the whole product is divided between capitalist and worker, i.e., that no constant capital is required to produce the constant capital, that is, the 60 quarters consisting of seed and tools. The circumstance which had to be explained in the case of capital I, *is assumed* to have disappeared in the case of capital II, and in this way the problem ceases to exist.

[CHAPTER XX]

But secondly, after he has assumed that the value of the 60 quarters which constitute the constant capital of capital I contains only [immediate] labour, but no *pre-existing labour*, no constant capital, that profit and surplus-value therefore coincide, and consequently also the rate of profit and the rate of surplus-value, that no difference exists between them, he then assumes, on the contrary, that just as in the case of capital I, *a difference between them does exist*, and that therefore the profit is only 50 per cent as in the case of capital I. If a third of the product of capital I had not consisted of constant capital, then profit would have been the same as surplus-value; the whole product consisted of only 120 quarters, equal to 60 working-days, 30 of which (equal to 60 quarters) are appropriated by the workers and 30 (equal to 60 quarters) by the capitalist. The rate of profit was the same as the rate of surplus-value, that is, 100 per cent. It was 50 per cent because the 60 quarters of surplus-value were not calculated on 60 quarters (wages) but on 120 quarters (wages, seed and fixed capital). In the case of capital II, he assumes that it contains no constant capital. He also assumes that wages remain the same in both cases—a quarter [of corn]. But he nevertheless assumes that profit and surplus-value are different, that profit amounts only to 50 per cent, although surplus-value amounts to 100 per cent. In actual fact he assumes that the 60 quarters, one-third of the total product, contain more labour-time than another third of the total product; he assumes that these 60 quarters are the product of 40 working-days while the other 120 quarters were the product of only 60.

In actual fact, however, there peeps out the old delusion of profit upon alienation, which has nothing whatever to do with the labour-time contained in the product and likewise nothing to do with the Ricardian definition of value. For he [Mill] assumes that the wages a man receives for working for a day are equal to what he produces in a working-day, i.e., that they contain as much labour-time as he works. If 40 quarters are paid out in wages, and if the profit amounts to 20 quarters, then the 40 quarters embody 40 working-days. The payment for the 40 working-days is equal to the product of the 40 working-days. If 50 per cent profit, or 20 quarters, is made on 60 quarters, it follows that 40 quarters are the product of the labour of 40 men, for, according to the assumption, 40 quarters constitute wages and each man receives one quarter per day. But in that case where do the other 20 quarters come from? The 40 men work 40 working-days because they receive 40 quarters. A quarter is therefore the product of one working-day. The product of 40 working-days is consequently 40 quarters, and not a bushel more. Where, then, do the 20 quarters which make up the profit come from? The old delusion of profit upon alienation, of a merely nominal price increase on the product over and above its value, is behind all this. But here it is *quite absurd* and impossible, because the value is not represented in money but in a part of the product itself. Nothing is easier than to imagine that—if 40 quarters of grain are the product of 40 workers, each one of whom receives one quarter per day or per year, they therefore receive *the whole of their product* as wages, and if one quarter of grain in terms of money is £3, 40 quarters are therefore £120—the capitalist sells these 40 quarters for £180 and makes £60, i.e., 50 per cent profit, equal to 20 quarters. But this notion is reduced to absurdity if out of 40 quarters—which have been produced in 40 working-days and for which he pays 40 quarters—the capitalist sells 60 quarters. He has in his possession only 40 quarters, but he *sells* 60 quarters, 20 quarters more than he has to sell.

||326| Thus first of all Mill proves the Ricardian law, that is, the false Ricardian law, which confuses surplus-value and profit, by means of the following convenient assumptions:

1) he assumes that the capitalist who produces constant capital does not himself in his turn need constant capital, and thus he *assumes out of existence* the whole difficulty which is posed by constant capital;

2) he assumes that, although the capitalist does not [need] constant capital, the difference between surplus-value and profit caused by constant capital nevertheless continues to exist although no constant capital exists;

3) he assumes that a capitalist who produces 40 quarters of wheat can sell 60 quarters, because his total product is sold as constant capital to another capitalist, whose constant capital equals 60 quarters, and because capitalist No. II makes a profit of 50 per cent on these 60 quarters.

This latter absurdity resolves itself into the notion of profit upon alienation, which appears here so absurd only because the profit is supposed to stem not from the nominal value expressed in money, but from a part of the product which has been sold. Thus, Mr. Mill, in seeking to defend Ricardo, has abandoned his basic concepts and fallen far behind Ricardo, Adam Smith and the Physiocrats.

His first defence of Ricardo's teachings therefore consists in his abandoning them from the outset, namely, abandoning the basic principle that profit is only a part of the value of the commodity, i.e., merely that part of the labour-time embodied in the commodity which the capitalist sells in his product although he has *not paid* the worker for it. Mill makes the capitalist pay the worker for the whole of his working-day and still derive a profit.

Let us see how he proceeds.

He does away with the need for seed and agricultural implements in the production of corn by means of an invention, that is, he does away with the need for constant capital in the case of the last capitalist in the same way as he abandoned seed and fixed capital in the case of the producer of the first 60 quarters. Now he ought to have argued as follows:

Capitalist No. I does not now need to lay out 60 quarters in seed and fixed capital, for we have stated that his constant capital equals zero. He therefore has to lay out only 60 quarters for the wages of 60 workers who work 60 working-days. The product of these 60 working-days amounts to 120 quarters. The workers receive only 60 quarters. The capitalist therefore makes 60 quarters profit, i.e., 100 per cent. His rate of profit is exactly equal to the rate of surplus-value, that is, it is exactly equal [to the ratio] of the labour-time the workers [worked for themselves to the labour-time they] worked not for themselves, but for the capitalist. They worked 60 days. They produced 120 quarters, they received 60 quarters in wages. They thus received the product of 30 working-days as wages, although they worked 60 days. The quantity of labour-time which 2 quarters cost is still equal to one working-day. The working-day for which the capitalist *pays* is still equal to one quarter, i.e., it is equal to half the working-day worked. The product has fallen by a third, from 180 quarters to 120 quarters, but the profit has nevertheless risen by 50 per cent, namely, from 50 per cent to 100 per cent. Why? Of the total of 180 quarters, a third merely replaced constant capital, it did not therefore constitute a part of either profit or wages. On the other hand, the 60 quarters, or the 30 working-days during which the workers produced or worked for the capitalist, were *calculated* not on the 60 quarters spent on wages, that is, the 30 days during which they worked for themselves, but on the 120 quarters, i.e., the 60 working-days, which were expended on wages, seed and fixed capital. Thus, although out of the total of 60 days they worked 30 days for themselves and 30 for the capitalist, and although a capital outlay of 60 quarters on wages yielded 120 quarters to the capitalist, his rate of profit was not 100 per cent, but only 50 per cent, because it was calculated *differently*, in the one case on 2×60 and in the other on 60. The surplus-value ||327| was the same, but the rate of profit was different.

But how does Mill tackle the problem?

He does not assume that the capitalist [who, as a result of an invention, spends nothing on constant capital] with an outlay of 60 quarters obtains 120 quarters (30 out of 60 working-days), but that he now employs 100 men who produce 180 quarters for him, always on the supposition that the wage for one working-day is one quarter of wheat. The calculation is therefore as follows:

Capital expended (only variable, only on wages)	Total product	Profit
100 quarters (wages for 100 working-days)	180 quarters	80 quarters

This means that the capitalist makes a profit of 80 per cent. Profit is here equal to surplus-value. Therefore the rate of surplus-value is likewise only 80 per cent. Previously it was 100 per cent, i.e., 20 per cent higher. Thus we have the phenomenon that the rate of profit has risen by 30 per cent while the rate of surplus-value has fallen by 20 per cent.

If the capitalist had only expended 60 quarters on wages as he did previously, we would have the following calculation:

100 quarters yield 80 quarters surplus-value
10   "   "   8   "   "   "
60   "   " 48   "   "   "

But 60 quarters previously yielded 60 quarters [of surplus-value] (that means it has fallen by 20 per cent). Or to put it another way, previously:

[Capital expended]	Total product	Surplus-value
60 quarters	120 quarters	60 quarters
10 "	20 "	10 "
100 "	200 "	100 "

Thus the surplus-value has fallen by 20 per cent, from 100 to 80 (we must take 100 as the basis of the calculation in both [cases]).

(60 : 48=100 : 80; 60 · 48=10 : 8; 60 : 48=5 : 4; 4×60=240 and 48×5=240.)

Further, let us consider the labour-time or the value of a quarter. Previously, 2 quarters were equal to one working-day, or one quarter was equal to half a working-day or $9/18$ of a man's labour. As against this, 180 quarters are now the product of 100 working-days, one quarter is therefore the product of $100/180$ or $10/18$ of a working-day. That is, the product has become dearer by $1/18$ of a working-day, or the labour has become less productive, since previously a man required $9/18$ of a working-day to produce a quarter, whereas now he requires $10/18$ of a working-day. The rate of profit has risen although the surplus-value has fallen and, consequently, the productivity of labour has fallen or the real value, the cost of production, of wages has risen by $1/18$ or by $5^5/9$ per cent. 180 quarters were previously the product of 90 working-days (1 quarter, $90/180$, equals half a working-day or $9/18$ of a working-day). Now they are the product of 100 working-days (1 quarter$=\frac{100}{180}=\frac{10}{18}$ of a working-day).

Let us assume that the working-day lasts 12 hours, i.e., 60×12 or 720 minutes. ||328| One-eighteenth part of a working-day, that is, $\frac{720}{18}$, therefore amounts to 40 minutes. In the first case, the worker gives the capitalist $9/18$ or half of these 720 minutes, that is, 360 minutes. 60 workers will therefore give him 360×60 minutes. In the second case, the worker gives the capitalist only $8/18$, that is, 320 minutes out of the 720. But the first capitalist employs 60 men and therefore obtains 360×60 minutes. The second employs 100 men and therefore obtains 100×320, 32,000 minutes. The first gets 360×60, 21,600 minutes. Thus the second capitalist makes a larger profit than the first because 100 workers at 320 minutes a day amounts to more than 60 [workers] at 360 minutes. His profit is bigger only because he employs 40 more men, but he obtains relatively less from each worker. He has a higher profit, although the rate of surplus-value has declined, that is, the productivity of labour has declined, the production costs of real wages have therefore risen, in other words, the quantity of labour embodied in them has risen. *But Mr. Mill wanted to prove the exact opposite.*

Assuming that capitalist No. I, who has not "discovered" how to produce corn without seed or fixed capital, likewise uses 100 working-days (like capitalist No. II), whereas he only uses 90 days in the above calculation. He must therefore use 10 more working-days, $3^1/_3$ of which are accounted for by his constant capital (seed and fixed capital) and $3^1/_3$ by wages. The product of these 10 working-days on the basis of the old level of production would be 20 quarters, $6^2/_3$ quarters of which, however, would replace constant capital,[a] while $12^4/_3$ quarters would be the product of $6^2/_3$ working-days. Of this, wages would take $6^2/_3$ quarters and surplus-value $6^2/_3$ quarters.

We would thus arrive at the following calculation:

Constant capital	Wages	Total product	Surplus-value	Rate of surplus-value
$66^2/_3$ quarters ($33^1/_3$ working-days)	$66^2/_3$ quarters (wages for $66^2/_3$ working-days)	200 quarters (100 working-days)	$66^2/_3$ quarters ($33^1/_3$ working-days)	100 per cent

He makes a profit of $33^1/_3$ working-days on the total product of 100 working-days. Or $66^2/_3$ quarters on 200 quarters. Or, if we calculate the capital he lays out in quarters, he makes a profit of $66^2/_3$ quarters on $133^1/_3$ quarters (the product of $66^2/_3$ working-days), whereas capitalist No. II makes a profit of 80 quarters on an outlay of 100 quarters. Thus, the profit of the second capitalist is greater than that of the first. Since the first capitalist produces 200 quarters in the same labour-time that it takes the second to produce 180, for the first capitalist one quarter is equal to half a working-day and for the second capitalist one quarter is equal to $^{10}/_{18}$ or $^5/_9$ of a working-day, that is, it contains $^1/_{18}$ more labour-time and would consequently be dearer, and the first capitalist would drive the second out of business. The latter would have to give up his discovery and accommodate himself to using seed and fixed capital in corn production, as before.

---

[a] The manuscript has "fixed capital".—*Ed.*

[CHAPTER XX]

Let us assume that the profit of capitalist I amounted to 60 quarters on an outlay of 120 quarters, or to 50 per cent (the same as $66^2/_3$ quarters on $133^1/_3$ quarters).

The profit of capitalist II amounted to 80 quarters on 100 quarters, or to 80 per cent.

The profit of the second capitalist compared to that of the first is $80:50$, or $8:5$, or $1:^5/_8$.

As against this, the surplus-value of the second capitalist compared to that of the first is: $80:100$, or $8:10$, or $1:^{10}/_8$, or $1:1^2/_8$, or $1:1^1/_4$.

The rate of profit of the second capitalist is 30 per cent higher than that of the first.

The surplus-value of the second capitalist is 20 per cent smaller than that of the first.

The second capitalist employs $66^2/_3$ per cent more workers, while the first one appropriates only $^1/_8$, or $12^1/_2$ per cent, more labour in a single day.

||329| Mr. Mill has therefore proved that capitalist No. I—who uses a total of 90 days, $^1/_3$ of which [is embodied] in constant capital (seed, machinery, etc.), and employs 60 workers whom, however, he pays only [the product of] 30 days—produces one quarter of corn in half a day or in $^9/_{18}$ of a day; so that in 90 working-days he produces 180 quarters, 60 quarters of which represent the 30 working-days contained in the constant capital, 60 quarters the wages for 60 working-days or the product of 30 working-days, and 60 quarters the surplus-value (or the product of 30 working-days). The [rate of] surplus-value of this capitalist is 100 per cent, his [rate of] profit is 50 per cent, for the 60 quarters of surplus-value are not calculated on the 60 quarters of the capital laid out in wages, but on 120 quarters, i.e., both parts of capital (that is, variable capital plus constant capital).

He has proved further that capitalist No. II, who uses 100 working-days and lays out nothing in constant capital (by virtue of his discovery), produces 180 quarters, one quarter is therefore equal to $^{10}/_{18}$ of a day, i.e., it is $^1/_{18}$ of a day (40 minutes) dearer than that of No. I. His labour is $^1/_{18}$ less productive. Since the worker receives a daily wage of one quarter, as he did previously, his wages have risen by $^1/_{18}$ in real value, that is, in the labour-time required for their production. Although the production cost of wages has now risen by $^1/_{18}$ and the total product is smaller in relation to labour-time, and the surplus-value produced by him amounts only to 80 per cent, whereas that of No. I was 100 per cent, his rate of profit is 80 per cent, while that of the first was 50. Why? Because, although the cost of wages has risen for capitalist No. II, he employs more labour, and because the rate of surplus-value is equal to the rate of profit in the case of No. II, since his surplus-value is calculated only on the capital laid out in wages, the constant capital amounting to zero. But Mill wanted on the contrary to prove that the rise in the rate of profit was due to a *reduction in the production cost of wages* according to the Ricardian law. We have seen that this rise took place *despite the increase in the production cost of wages*, that, consequently, the Ricardian law is false if profit and surplus-value are *directly* identified with one another, and the rate of profit is understood as the ratio of surplus-value or gross profit (which is equal to the surplus-value) to the total value of the capital advanced.

Mr. Mill continues:

"A return of 180 quarters could not before be obtained but by an outlay of 120 quarters; it can now be obtained by an outlay of not more than 100..." [loc. cit., p. 100].

Mr. Mill forgets that in the first case, the outlay of 120 quarters represents an outlay of 60 working-days. And that in the second case, the outlay of 100 quarters represents an outlay of $55^5/_9$ working-days (that is, a quarter equals $^9/_{18}$ of a working-day in the first case and $^{10}/_{18}$ in the second).

"The produce (180 quarters) is still the result of the [same] quantity of labour as before, [namely] the labour of 100 men" [loc. cit., p. 100].

(Pardon me! The 180 quarters were previously the result of 90 working-days. Now they are the result of 100.)

"A quarter of corn, therefore, is still [...] the produce of $^{10}/_{18}$ of a man's labour" [loc. cit., p. 100].

(Pardon me! It was previously the produce of $^9/_{18}$ of a man's labour.)

"A[a] *quarter of corn*, which is the *remuneration* of a single labourer, is indeed the produce of the same [...] *labour* as before..." [loc. cit., p. 102].

(Pardon me! Firstly, now a quarter of corn is "indeed the produce" of $^{10}/_{18}$ of a working-day, whereas previously it was the produce of $^9/_{18}$; it therefore costs $^1/_{18}$ of a day more labour;

---

[a] The manuscript has "For a".—*Ed.*

and secondly, whether the quarter costs $^9/_{18}$ or $^{10}/_{18}$ of his working-day, the *remuneration* of an individual worker should never be confused with the *product of his labour*; since it is always only a part of that product.)

"It is now the produce of $^{10}/_{18}$ of a man's labour, and *nothing else*" (this is correct); "whereas formerly it required for its production the conjunction of that quantity of labour with[a] an expenditure, in the form of reimbursement of profit, amounting to one-fifth more" [loc. cit., pp. 102-03].

Stop! First of all it is wrong, as has been ||330| emphasised repeatedly, to say that one quarter previously cost $^{10}/_{18}$ of the working-day. It only cost $^9/_{18}$. It would be even more wrong (if a gradation in absolute falsehood were possible) if there were added to these $^9/_{18}$ of a working-day "the conjunction [...] of reimbursement of profit, amounting to one-fifth more". In 90 working-days (taking constant and variable capital together) 180 quarters are produced. 180 quarters are equal to 90 working-days. One quarter equals $^{90}/_{180}$, which equals $^9/_{18}$, which equals one half of a working-day. Consequently, no "conjunction" whatsoever is added to these $^9/_{18}$ of a working-day, or to the half of a working-day which a quarter costs in case No. I.

We here discover the real delusion which is the centre around which the whole of this nonsense revolves. Mill first of all made a fool of himself by supposing that, if 120 quarters are the product of 60 days of labour, and this product is equally divided between the 60 labourers and the capitalist, the 60 quarters which represent the constant capital could be the product of 40 days of labour. They could only be the product of 30 days, in whatever proportion the capitalist and the labourers producing the 60 quarters might happen to share in them. But let us proceed. In order to make the delusion quite clear, let us assume that not one-third, i.e., 20 quarters of the 60 quarters of constant capital, would be converted into profit, but the whole amount of the 60 quarters. We can make this assumption all the more readily since it is not in our interest, but in Mill's, and simplifies the problem. Moreover it is easier to believe that the capitalist who produces 60 quarters of constant capital, *discovers* that 30 workers, who produce 60 quarters or an equivalent value in 30 days, can be made to work for *nothing*, without being paid any wages at all (as happens in the case of stat-

---

[a] The manuscript has "plus".—*Ed.*

ute labour), than to believe in the ability of Mill's capitalist to produce 180 quarters of corn without seed or fixed capital, simply by means of a "discovery". Let us therefore assume that the 60 quarters contain only the profit of capitalist II, the producer of constant capital for capitalist I, since capitalist II has the product of 30 working-days to sell without having paid a single farthing to the 30 workers, each of whom worked one day. Would it then be correct to say that these 60 quarters, which can be entirely resolved into profit, enter into the *production cost of wages* on the part of capitalist I, in "conjunction" with the labour-time worked by these workers?

Of course, the capitalist and the workers in case No. I could not produce 120 quarters or even one single quarter without the 60 quarters which constitute constant capital and which are resolvable into profit only. These are conditions of production necessary for them, and conditions of production, moreover, which have to be paid for. Thus the 60 quarters were necessary to produce 180. 60 of these 180 quarters replace the 60 quarters [constant capital]. Their 120 quarters—the product of 60 working-days—are not affected by this. If they had been able to produce the 120 quarters without the 60, then *their* product, the product of the 60 working-days, would have been the same, but the total product would have been smaller, precisely because the 60 pre-existing quarters would not have been reproduced. The capitalist's rate of profit would have been greater because his production costs would not have included the expenditure on, or the cost of, the means of production which enable him to make a surplus-value of 60 quarters. The absolute amount of profit would have been the same—60 quarters. These 60 quarters, however, would have required an outlay of only 60 quarters. Now they require an outlay of 120. This outlay on constant capital therefore enters into the production costs of the capitalist, but not into the production costs of wages.

Let us assume that capitalist III, also without paying his workers, can produce 60 quarters in 15 working-days [instead of 30] by means of some "discovery", partly because he uses better machines, and so on. This capitalist III would drive capitalist II out of the market and secure the custom of capitalist I. The capitalist's outlay would now have fallen ||331| from 60 to 45 working-days. The workers would still require 60 working-days to transform the 60 quarters into 180. And they would need 30 working-days in order to produce their wages. For them one quarter would be equal to half a working-day. But the 180 quarters would only cost the capitalist an outlay of 45 working-days instead of 60. Since however it would be absurd to suggest that corn under the name of seed costs less labour-time than it does under the name of corn pure and simple, we would have to assume that in the case of the first 60 quarters, seed corn costs just as much as it did previously, but that less seed is necessary, or that the fixed capital which forms part of the value of the 60 quarters has become cheaper.

* * *

Let us write down the results so far obtained from the analysis of Mill's "illustration".

First, it has emerged that:

Supposing that the 120 quarters were produced without any constant capital and were the product of 60 working-days as they were previously, whereas formerly, the 180 quarters, 60 quarters of which were constant capital, were the product of 90 working-days. In this case, the capital of 60 quarters laid out in wages, equal to 30 working-days but commanding 60 working-days, would produce the same product as formerly, namely, 120 quarters. The value of the product would likewise remain unchanged, that is, one quarter would be equal to half a working-day. Previously the product was equal to 180 instead of 120 as at present; but the 60 additional quarters represented only the labour-time embodied in the constant capital. The cost of production of wages has thus remained unchanged, and the wages themselves—in terms of both use-value and exchange-value—have also remained unchanged—one quarter being equal to half a working-day. Surplus-value would similarly remain unchanged, namely, 60 quarters for 60 quarters, or half a working-day for half a working-day. The rate of surplus-value in both cases was 100 per cent. Nevertheless the rate of profit was only 50 per cent in the first case, while it is now 100 per cent. Simply because $60:60=100$ per cent, while $60:120=50$ per cent. The increase in the rate of profit, in this case, is not [due] to any change in the production cost of wages, but merely to the fact that constant capital has been assumed to be zero. The position is similar when the value of constant capital diminishes, and with it the value of the capital advanced; that is, the proportion of surplus-value to capital increases, and this proportion *is* the rate of profit.

To obtain the rate of profit surplus-value is not only calculated on that part of capital which really increases and creates surplus-value, namely, the part laid out in wages, but also on the value of the raw materials and machinery whose value only reappears in the product. It is calculated moreover on the value of the whole of the machinery, not only on the part which really enters into the process of creating value, i.e., the part whose wear and tear has to be replaced, but also on that part which enters only into the labour process.

Secondly, in the second example it was assumed that capital I yields 180 quarters, equal to 90 working-days, so that 60 quarters (30 working-days) represent constant capital; 60 quarters are variable capital (representing 60 working-days, for 30 of which the workers are paid); thus wages amount to 60 quarters (30 working-days) and surplus-value to 60 quarters (30 working-days); on the other hand, the product of capital II represents 100 working-days although it likewise comes to 180 quarters, 100 quarters of which are wages, and 80 surplus-value. In this case, the whole of the capital advanced is laid out in wages. Here constant capital is at zero; the real value of wages has risen although the use-value the workers receive has remained the same—one quarter; but a quarter is now equal to $^{10}/_{18}$ of a working-day whereas previously it was only worth $^{9}/_{18}$. The [rate of] surplus-value has declined from 100 per cent to 80 per cent, that is, by $^{1}/_{5}$ or by 20 per cent. The rate of profit has increased from 50 per cent to 80 per cent, that is, by $^{3}/_{5}$ or by 60 per cent. In this case, therefore, the real production cost of wages has not simply remained unchanged, but has risen. Labour has become less productive and consequently the surplus labour has diminished. And yet the rate of profit has risen. Why? First of all, because in this case there is no constant capital and the rate of profit is consequently equal to the rate of surplus-value. In all cases where capital is not exclusively laid out on wages—an almost impossible contingency in capitalist production—the rate of profit must be smaller than the rate of surplus-value and it must be smaller in the same proportion as the total value of the capital advanced is greater than the value of the part of the capital laid out in wages. Secondly, [the rate of profit has risen because] capitalist II employs a considerably greater number of workers than capitalist I, thus more than counterbalancing the difference in the productivity of the labour they respectively employ.

Thirdly, from one point of view, the cases outlined under the headings "*firstly*" and "*secondly*" are a conclusive proof that variations in the rate of profit can take place quite independently of the cost of production of wages. For under the heading "*firstly*" it was demonstrated that the rate of profit can rise although the cost of production of labour remains the same. Under "*secondly*" it was demonstrated that the rate of profit for capital II compared with that for capital I rises although the productivity of labour declines, in other words, although the production cost of wages rises. This case therefore proves ||VIII-332| that if, on the other hand, we compare capital I with capital II, the rate of profit falls although the rate of surplus-value rises, the productivity of labour increases and consequently the production costs of wages fall. They amount to only $9/_{18}$ of a working-day [per quarter] for capital I, whereas for capital II they amount to $10/_{18}$ of a working-day; but despite this, the rate of profit is 60 per cent higher in the case of capital II than in the case of capital I. *In all these cases, not only are variations in the rates of profit not determined by variations in the production costs of wages, but they take place in the same proportions.* Here it must be noted that it does not follow from this that the movement of one is the *cause* of movement of the other (for example, that the rate of profit does not fall because the production costs of wages fall, or that it does not rise because the production costs of wages rise), but only that different circumstances paralyse the opposite movements. Nevertheless, the Ricardian law that variations in the rate of profit take place in the opposite direction to variations in wages, that one rises because the other falls, and vice versa, is false. This law applies only to the *rate of surplus-value*. At the same time, there exists however a necessary connection (although not always) in the fact that the rate of profit and the value of wages rise and fall not in the opposite but in the same direction. More manual labour is employed where the labour is less productive. More constant capital is applied where the labour is more productive. Thus in this context the same circumstances which bring about an increase or a decline in the rate of surplus-value, must as a consequence bring about a decline or an increase in the rate of profit [i.e., a movement] in the opposite direction.

[b) Apparent Variation in the Rate of Profit Where the Production of Constant Capital Is Combined with Its Working Up by a Single Capitalist]

But we shall now outline the case as Mill himself conceived it, although he did not formulate it correctly. This will at the same time clarify the real meaning of his talk about the profits advanced by the capitalist.

Despite any kind of "discovery" and any possible "conjunction", the example cannot be left in the form in which Mill puts it forward, because it contains absolute contradictions and absurdities and the various presuppositions he makes cancel one another out.

Of the 180 quarters, 60 quarters (seed and fixed capital) are supposed to consist of 20 quarters for profit and 40 quarters [wages] for 40 working-days, so that if the 20 quarters profit are omitted, the 40 working-days still remain. According to this presupposition, the workers therefore receive the whole product for their labour, and consequently it is absolutely impossible to see where the 20 quarters profit and their value come from. If it is assumed that they are merely nominal additions to the price, if they do not constitute labour-time appropriated by the capitalist, their omission would be just as profitable as if 20 quarters wages for workers who had not done any work were included in the 60 quarters. Furthermore, the 60 quarters here simply express the value of the constant capital. They are however supposed to be the product of 40 working-days. On the other hand, it is assumed that the remaining 120 quarters are the product of 60 working-days. But here working-days must be understood as equal average labour. The assumption is therefore absurd.

Thus one must assume, firstly, that in the 180 quarters only 90 working-days are embodied and in the 60 quarters, that is, the value of the constant capital, only 30 working-days. The assumption that the profit—amounting to 20 quarters or to 10 working-days—can be omitted, is once again absurd. For it must then be assumed that the 30 workers employed in the production of constant capital, although not working for a capitalist, are nevertheless so obliging that they are content to pay themselves wages which only amount to half their labour-time, and not to reckon the other half in their commodity. In a word, that they sell their working-day 50 per cent below its value. Hence this assumption too is absurd.

But let us assume that capitalist I, instead of buying his constant capital from capitalist II and then working it up, combines both the production and the working up of constant capital in his own undertaking. He thus supplies seed, agricultural implements, etc., to himself. Let us likewise ignore the discovery which makes seed and fixed capital unnecessary. Supposing that he expends 20 quarters (equal to 10 working-days) on constant capital (for the production of his constant capital) and 10 quarters on wages for 10 working-days, of which the workers work 5 days for nothing, the calculation would then be as follows:
||333|

Constant capital	Variable capital for 80 workers	Surplus-value	Total product
20 quarters (10 working-days)	60 + 20 = 80 qrs. (wages for 80 working-days) (=40 working-days)	60 + 20 = 80 qrs. (= 40 working-days)	180 qrs. (=90 working-days)

The actual production costs of wages have remained the same, and consequently the productivity of labour too. The total product has remained the same, that is, 180 quarters, and the value of the 180 quarters has also remained unchanged. The rate of surplus-value has remained the same—80 quarters over 80 quarters. The total amount or quantity of surplus-value has risen from 60 quarters to 80 quarters, that is, by 20 quarters. The capital advanced has fallen from 120 to 100 quarters. Previously, 60 quarters were made on 120 quarters, or a rate of profit of 50 per cent. Now 80 quarters are made on 100 quarters, or a rate of profit of 80 per cent. The total value of the capital advanced has fallen from 120 quarters by 20 quarters and the rate of profit has risen from 50 per cent to 80 per cent. The profit itself, irrespective of its rate, now amounts to 80 quarters, whereas previously it was 60 quarters, that is, it has risen by 20 quarters, or as much as the amount (not the rate) of the surplus-value.

Thus there has been no change here, no variation in the production costs of real wages. The rise in the rate of profit is due:

Firstly, to the fact that although the rate of surplus-value has not risen, the total amount has increased from 60 quarters to 80 quarters, that is, by a third; and it has risen by a third, by $33^1/_3$ per cent, because the capitalist now employs 80 workers and not 60 as previously, that is, he exploits a third or $33^1/_3$ per cent more living labour; and obtains the same rate of surplus-value from the 80 workers he now employs as previously when he employed only 60 workers.

Secondly. While the absolute magnitude of surplus-value (that is, the total profit) has risen by $33^1/_3$ per cent, i.e., from 60 to 80 quarters, the rate of profit has risen from 50 per cent to 80 per cent, by 30, that is, by $^3/_5$ (since $^1/_5$ of 50 is 10, and $^3/_5$ 30), i.e., by 60 per cent. That is to say, the value of the capital laid out has fallen from 120 [quarters] to 100, although the value of the part of capital laid out in wages has risen from 60 to 80 quarters (from 30 to 40 working-days). This part of the capital has increased by 10 working-days (20 quarters). On the other hand, the constant portion of capital has decreased from 60 to 20 quarters (from 30 working-days to 10), that is, by 20 working-days. If we subtract the 10 working-days by which the part of capital laid out in wages has increased, then the total capital expended decreases by 10 working-days (20 quarters). Previously, it amounted to 120 quarters (60 working-days). Now it amounts to only 100 quarters (50 working-days). It has therefore decreased by a sixth, that is, by $16^2/_3$ per cent.

Incidentally, this whole variation in the rate of profit is only an illusion, only a transfer from one account book to another. Capitalist I has 80 quarters profit instead of 60 quarters, that is, an additional profit of 20 quarters. This, however, is the exact amount of profit that the producer of constant capital made previously and which he has now lost because capitalist I, instead of buying his constant capital, now produces it himself, that is, instead of ||334| paying capitalist II the surplus-value of 20 quarters (10 working-days) which the producer [of constant capital] obtained from the 20 workers employed by him, capitalist I now keeps it for himself.

80 quarters profit is made on 180 quarters as previously, the only difference being that previously it was divided between two people. The rate of profit appears to be bigger, because previously capitalist I regarded the 60 quarters as constant capital only, which in fact they were for him; he therefore disregarded the profit accruing to the producer of constant capital. The rate of profit has not altered, any more than the

surplus-value or any factor of production, including the productivity of labour. Previously, the capital laid out by the producer [of constant capital] amounted to 40 quarters (20 working-days); that [variable capital] laid out by *capitalist I* amounted to 60 quarters (30 working-days), making a total of 100 quarters (50 working-days), and the profit of the first capitalist came to 20 quarters, that of the other to 60, together 80 quarters (40 working-days). The whole product amounting to 90 working-days (180 quarters) yielded 80 quarters profit on 100 laid out in wages and constant capital. For society, the revenue deriving from the profit has remained the same as before, and so has the ratio of surplus-value to wages.

The difference arises from the fact that, when the capitalist enters the commodity market as a buyer, he is simply a commodity owner. He has to pay the full value of a commodity, the whole of the labour-time embodied in it, irrespective of the proportions in which the fruits of the labour-time were divided or are divided between the capitalist and the worker. If, on the other hand, he enters the labour market as a buyer, he buys in actual fact more labour than he pays for. If, therefore, he produces his raw materials and machinery himself instead of buying them, he himself appropriates the surplus labour he would otherwise have had to pay out to the seller of the raw materials and machinery.

It certainly makes a difference to the individual capitalist although not to the rate of profit, whether he himself derives a profit or pays it out to someone else. (In calculating the reduction in the rate of profit as a result of the growth of constant capital, the social average is always taken as the basis, that is, the aggregate amount of constant capital employed by society at a particular moment and the proportion of this amount to the amount of capital laid out directly in wages.) But this point of view is seldom decisive and can seldom be decisive even for the individual capitalist with regard to such complex enterprises which do occur, for example, when the capitalist is at the same time engaged in spinning and weaving, making his own bricks, etc. What is decisive here is the real saving in production costs, through saving of time on transport, savings on buildings, on heating, on power, etc., greater control over the quality of the raw materials, etc. If he himself decided to manufacture the machines he required, he would then produce them on a small scale like a small producer who works to supply his own needs or the individual needs of a few customers, and the machines would cost him more than they would if he bought them from a machine manufacturer who produced them for the market. Or if he wished at the same time to spin and to weave and to make machines not only for himself, but also for the market, he would require a greater amount of capital, which he could probably invest to greater advantage (division of labour) in his own enterprise. This point of view can only apply when he provides for himself a market sufficient to enable him to produce his constant capital himself on an advantageous scale. His own demand must be large enough to achieve this. In this case, even if his work is less productive than that of the proper producers of constant capital, he appropriates a share of the surplus labour for which he would otherwise have to pay another capitalist.

It can be seen that this has nothing to do with the rate of profit. If—as in the example cited by Mill—90 working-days and 80 workers were involved previously, then nothing is saved from the production costs by the fact that the surplus labour of 40 days (or 80 quarters) contained in the product is now pocketed by one capitalist instead of by two, as was the case previously. The 20 quarters profit (10 working-days) simply disappears from one account book in order to appear again in another.

This saving on previous profit, if it does not coincide with a saving in labour-time and thus with a saving in wages, is therefore a pure delusion.[72]

[c) On the Influence a Change in the Value of Constant Capital Exerts on Surplus-Value, Profit and Wages]

||335| *Fourthly*, there remains the case in which the value of constant capital decreases as a result of the increased productivity of labour, and it remains for us to investigate whether or not, and to what extent, this case is related to the real production cost of wages or to the value of labour. The question is, therefore, to what extent a real change in the value of constant capital causes at the same time a variation in the ratio of profit to wages. The value of constant capital, its production costs, can remain constant, yet more or less of it can be embodied in the product. Even if its value is assumed to be constant, the constant capital will increase in the measure that the productivity of labour and production on a large scale develop.

Variations in the *relative amount of constant capital employed while the production costs of the constant capital remain stable or rise*—variations which all affect the rate of profit—are excluded in advance from this investigation.

Furthermore, all branches of production whose products do not enter directly or indirectly into the consumption of the workers are likewise excluded. But variations in the real rate of profit (that is, the ratio of the surplus-value really produced in these branches of industry to the capital expended) in these branches of industry affect the general rate of profit, which arises as a result of the levelling of profits, just as much as variations in the rate of profit in branches of industry whose products enter directly or indirectly into the consumption of the workers.

The question moreover must be reduced to the following: How can a change in the value of constant capital retrospectively affect the surplus-value? For once surplus-value is assumed as given, the ratio of surplus to necessary labour is given, and therefore also the value of wages, i.e., their production cost. In these circumstances, no change in the value of constant capital can have any effect on the value of wages, any more than on the ratio of surplus labour to necessary labour, although it must always affect the rate of profit, the cost of production of the surplus-value for the capitalist, and in certain circumstances, namely, when the product enters into the consumption of the worker, it affects the quantity of use-values into which wages are resolved, although it does not affect the exchange-value of wages.

Let us assume that wages are given, and that, for example, in a cotton factory they come to 10 working hours and surplus-value to 2 working hours. The price of raw cotton falls by half as a result of a good harvest. The same quantity of cotton which previously cost the manufacturer £100, now costs him only £50. The same amount of cotton requires just the same amount of spinning and weaving as it did before. With an expenditure of £50 for cotton, the capitalist can now acquire as much surplus labour as he did previously with an expenditure of £100, or, should he continue to spend £100 on cotton, he will now receive, for the same amount of money as he spent before, a quantity of cotton from which he will be able to acquire twice the amount of surplus labour. In both cases, the rate of surplus-value, that is, the ratio of surplus-value to wages, will be the same, but in the second case the amount of surplus-value will rise, since twice as much labour will be employed at the same rate of surplus labour. The rate of profit will rise in both cases, although there has been no change in the production cost of wages. It will rise because, to obtain the rate of profit, the surplus-value is calculated on the *production costs* of the capitalist, that is, on the *total value* of the capital he expends, and this has fallen. He now needs a smaller outlay in order to produce the same amount of surplus-value. In the second case, not only the rate but also the amount of profit will rise, because surplus-value itself has risen as a consequence of the increased employment of labour, without this increase resulting in an additional cost for raw material. Here again, increases in the rate and the amount of profit will take place without any kind of change in the value of labour.

Suppose on the other hand that cotton doubles in value as a result of a bad harvest so that the same amount of cotton ||336| which formerly cost £100 now costs £200. In this case, the rate of profit will fall at all events, but in certain circumstances, the amount or absolute magnitude of profit may fall as well. If the capitalist employs the same number of workers, who do the same amount of work as they did before, under exactly the same conditions as before, the rate of profit will fall, although the ratio of surplus labour to necessary labour, and therefore the rate and the yield of surplus-value, will remain *the same*. The rate of profit falls because the production costs of surplus-value have risen, i.e., the capitalist has to spend £100 more on raw material in order to appropriate the same amount of other people's labour-time as before. However, if the capitalist is now forced to allocate a part of the money which he formerly spent on wages to buying cotton, e.g., to spend £150 on cotton, of which sum £50 formerly went on wages, then the rate and the amount of profit fall, the amount decreases because less labour is being employed, even though the rate of surplus-value remains the same. The result would be the same if, owing to a bad harvest, there were not enough cotton available to absorb the same amount of living labour as formerly. In both cases, the amount and the rate of profit would fall, although the value of labour would remain the same; in other words, the rate of surplus-value or the quantity of unpaid labour which the capitalist receives in relation to the labour for which he pays wages, remains unchanged.

Thus, when the *rate of surplus-value*, that is, when the *value of labour*, remains unchanged, a change in the value of constant capital must produce a change in the rate of profit and may be accompanied by a change in the total amount of profit.

On the other hand, as far as the worker is concerned:

If the value of cotton, and therefore the value of the product into which it enters, falls, he still receives the same amount of wages, equal to 10 hours of labour. But he can now buy the cotton goods which he himself uses more cheaply, and can therefore spend part of the money he previously spent on cotton goods on other things. It is only in this proportion that the necessities of life available to him increase in quantity, that is, in the proportion in which he saves money on the price of cotton goods. For apart from this, he now receives no more for a greater quantity of cotton goods than he did previously for a smaller quantity. Other goods have risen in the same proportion as cotton goods have fallen. In short, a greater quantity of cotton goods now has no more value than the smaller quantity had previously. *In this case, therefore, the value of wages would remain the same, but it would represent a greater quantity of other commodities* (use-values). *Nevertheless, the rate of profit would rise although, given the same circumstances, the rate of surplus-value could not rise.*

The opposite is the case when cotton becomes dearer. If the worker is employed for the same amount of time and still receives a wage equal to 10 hours as he did previously, the value of his labour would remain the same, but its use-value would fall insofar as the worker himself is a consumer of cotton goods. In this case, the *use-value of wages would fall*, its *value*, however, would remain *unchanged*, although the rate of profit would also fall. Thus, whereas surplus-value and (real) wages always fall and rise in inverse ratio (with the exception of the case where the worker participates in the [yield of the] absolute lengthening of his working-day; but when this happens, the worker uses up his labour-power all the more quickly), it is possible for the rate of profit to rise or fall in the first case although the value of wages remains the same and their use-value increases, in the second case although the *value of wages* remains the same, while their use-value falls.

Consequently, a rise in the rate of profit resulting from a fall in the *value* of constant capital, has no direct connection whatever with any kind of variation in the real value of wages (that is, in the labour-time contained in the wages).

If we assume, as in the above case, that cotton falls in value by 50 per cent, then nothing could be more incorrect than to say either that the production costs of wages have fallen or that, if the worker is paid in cotton goods and receives the same value as he did previously, that is, if he receives a greater *amount* of cotton goods than he did previously (since although 10 hours, for example, still equals 10sh., I can buy more cotton goods for 10 sh. than I could before, because the value of raw cotton has fallen), the rate of profit would remain the same. The rate of surplus-value remains the same, but the ||337| rate of profit rises. The *production costs of the product* fall, because an element of the product—its raw material—now costs less labour-time than previously. The production costs of wages remain the same as before, since the worker works the same amount of labour-time *for himself* and the same *for the capitalist* as he did before. (The production costs of wages do not depend however on the labour-time which the means of production used by the worker cost, but on the time he works in order to reproduce his wages. According to Mr. Mill, the production costs of a worker's wages would be greater if, for example, he worked up copper instead of iron, or flax instead of cotton; and they would be greater if he sowed flax seed rather than cotton seed, or if he worked with an expensive machine rather than with no machine at all, but simply with tools.) The *production costs of profit* would fall because the aggregate value, the total amount of the capital advanced in order to produce the surplus-value would fall. The cost of surplus-value is never greater than the cost of the part of capital spent on wages. On the other hand, the cost of profit is equal to the total cost of the capital advanced in order to create this surplus-value. It is therefore determined not only by the value of the portion of capital which is spent on wages and which creates the surplus-value, but also by the value of the elements of capital necessary to bring into action the one part of capital which is exchanged against living labour. Mr. Mill confuses the production costs of profit with the production costs of surplus-value, that is, he confuses profit and surplus-value.

This analysis shows the importance of the cheapness or dearness of raw materials for the industry which works them up (not to speak of the relative cheapening of machinery*), even

---

* By *relative* cheapening of machinery, I mean that the absolute value of the amount of machinery employed increases, but that it does not increase in the same proportion as the mass and efficiency of the machinery.

assuming that the market price is equal to the value of the commodity, that is, that the market price of the commodity falls in exactly the same ratio as do the raw materials embodied in it.

Colonel Torrens is therefore correct when he says with regard to England:

> In relation "... to a country in the condition of England, the importance of a foreign market must be measured not by the quantity of finished goods which it receives, but by the quantity of the elements of reproduction which it returns" (R. Torrens, *A Letter to [the Right Honourable] Sir Robert Peel* [...] *on the Condition of England etc.*, second ed., London, 1843, p. 275).

⟨The way Torrens seeks to prove this, however, is bad. The usual talk about supply and demand. According to him it would appear that if, for example, English capital which manufactures cotton goods grows more rapidly than capital which grows cotton, in the United States for instance, then the price of cotton rises and then, he says:

> "... the value of cotton fabrics will decline in relation to the elementary cost of their production" [op. cit., p. 240].

That is to say, while the price of the raw material is rising due to the growing demand from England, the price of cotton fabrics, raised by the rising price of the raw material, will fall; we can indeed observe at the present time (spring 1862), for instance, that cotton twist is scarcely more expensive than raw cotton and woven cotton hardly any dearer than yarn. Torrens, however, assumes that there is an adequate supply of cotton, though at a rather high price, available for consumption by English industry. The price of cotton rises above its value. Consequently, if cotton fabrics are sold at their value, this is only possible provided the cotton-grower secures more surplus-value from the total product than is his due, by actually taking part of the surplus-value due to the cotton manufacturer. The latter cannot replace this portion by raising the price, because demand would fall if prices rose. On the contrary, his profit may decline even more as a consequence of falling demand than it does as a consequence of the cotton-grower's surcharge.

The demand for raw materials—raw cotton, for example—is regulated annually not only by the effective demand existing at a given moment, but by the average demand throughout the year, that is, not only by the demand from the mills that are working at the time, but by this demand increased by the number of mills which, experience shows, will start operating during the course of the coming year, that is, by the *relative increase in the number of mills taking place during the year*, or by the surplus demand ||338| corresponding to this relative increase.

Conversely, if the price of cotton, etc., should fall, e.g., as a result of an especially good harvest, then in most cases the price falls below its value, again through the law of demand and supply. The rate of profit—and possibly, as we saw above, the total amount of profit—increases, consequently, not only in the proportion in which it would have increased had the cotton which has become cheaper been sold at its value; but it increases because the finished article has not become cheaper in the *total* proportion in which the cotton-grower sold his raw cotton below its value, that is, because the manufacturer has pocketed part of the surplus-value due to the cotton-grower. This does not diminish the demand for his product, since its price falls in any case due to the decrease in the value of cotton. However, its price does not fall as much as the price of raw cotton falls below its own value.

In addition, demand increases at such times because the workers are fully employed and receive full wages, so that they themselves act as consumers on a significant scale, consumers of their own product. In cases in which the price of the raw material declines, not as a result of a permanent or continuous fall in its average production costs but because of either an especially good or an especially bad year (weather conditions), the workers' wages do not fall, the demand for labour, however, grows. The effect produced by *this* demand is not merely proportionate to its growth. On the contrary, when the product suddenly becomes dearer, on the one hand many workers are dismissed, and on the other hand the manufacturer seeks to recoup· his loss by reducing wages below their normal level. Thus the normal demand on the part of the workers declines, intensifying the now general decline in demand, and worsening the effect this has on the market price of the product.⟩

It was mainly his (Ricardian) conception of the division of the product between worker and capitalist which led Mill to the idea that changes in the value of constant capital alter the value of labour or the production costs of labour; for example, that a fall in the value of the constant capital advanced results in a decline in the value of labour, in its production costs, and therefore also in wages. The value of yarn falls as a result of a decrease in the value of the raw material—raw cotton, for example. *Its* costs of production decline: the amount of labour-time embodied in it is reduced. If, for example, a pound of cotton twist were the product of one man working a twelve-hour day, and if the value of the cotton contained in this twist fell, then the value of the pound of twist would fall in the precise degree that the cotton required for spinning fell. For example, [the price of] one pound of No. 40 Mule yarn 2nd quality was 1s. on May 22nd, 1861. It was 11d. on May 22nd, 1858 ($11^6/_8$d. in actual fact, since its price did not fall to the same extent as that of raw cotton). But in the first case a pound of fair raw cotton cost 8d. ($8^1/_8$d. in actual fact) and 7d. ($7^3/_8$d. in actual fact) in the second. In these cases, the value of the yarn fell in exactly the same degree as the value of cotton, its raw material. Consequently, says Mill, the amount of labour remains the same as it was previously; if it was 12 hours, the product is the result of the same 12 hours of labour. But there was 1d. less worth of the pre-existing labour in the second case than in the first. The labour[-time] is the same, but the production costs of labour have been reduced (by 1d.). Now although one pound of cotton twist as twist, as a use-value, remains the product of 12 hours labour as it was previously, the *value* of the pound of twist is neither now, nor was it previously, the product of 12 hours work by the spinner. The value of the raw cotton, which in the first case amounted to two-thirds of 1s., i.e., 8d., was not the product of the spinner; in the second case, two-thirds of 11d., that is, 7d., was not his product. In the first case the remaining 4d. is the product of 12 working hours, and just the same amount—4d.—is the product in the second. In both cases, his labour adds only a third to the value of the twist. Thus, in the first case, only $1/_3$ lb. of twist out of 1 lb. of yarn was the product of the spinner (disregarding machinery) and it was the same in the second case. The worker and the capitalist have only 4d. to divide between them, the same as previously, that is, $1/_3$ lb. of twist. If the worker buys cotton twist with the 4d., he will receive a greater quantity of it in the second case than in the first, now however a bigger quantity of twist is worth the same as a smaller quantity of twist was previously. But the division of the 4d. between worker and capitalist remains the same. If the time worked by the worker to reproduce or produce his wages is 10 hours, his surplus labour amounts to 2 hours, as it did previously. He receives $5/_6$ of 4d. or of $1/_3$ lb. of cotton twist—as he did previously—and the capitalist receives $^1/_6$. Therefore no change ||339| has taken place in respect of the division of the product, of the cotton twist. None the less, the rate of profit has risen, because the value of the raw material has fallen and, consequently, the ratio of surplus-value to the total capital advanced, that is, to the production costs of the capitalist, has increased.

If, for the sake of simplification, we abstract from the machines, etc., then the two cases stand as follows:

	Price of 1 lb. of twist	Constant capital	Labour added	Wages	Total expenditure	Surplus-value	Rate of profit
1st case	12d.	8d.	4d.	$13^1/_3$ farthings	$11d. \ ^4/_3$ farthings	$2^2/_3$ farthings	$5^{15}/_{17}$ per cent
2nd case	11d.	7d.	4d.	$13^1/_3$ farthings	$10d. \ ^4/_3$ farthings	$2^2/_3$ farthings	$6^{14}/_{31}$ per cent

Thus the rate of profit has risen although the *value* of labour has remained the same and the use-value of the labour as expressed in cotton twist has risen. The rate of profit has risen without any kind of variation in the labour-time which the worker appropriates for himself, *solely* because the value of the cotton, and consequently the total value of the production costs of the capitalist, has fallen. $2^2/_3$ farthings on 11d. $^4/_3$ farthings expenditure is naturally less than $2^2/_3$ farthings on 10d. $^4/_3$ farthings expenditure.

* * *

In the light of what has been said above, the fallaciousness of the following passages with which Mill concludes his illustration becomes clear.

"If the cost of production of wages had remained the same as before, profits could not have risen. Each labourer received one quarter of corn; but one quarter of corn at that time was the result of the same cost of production as $1^1/_5$ quarter now. In order, therefore, that each labourer should receive the same cost of production, each must [...] receive one quarter of corn, plus one-fifth" ([John Stuart Mill, *Essays on some unsettled Questions of Political Economy*, London, 1844,] p. 103).

"Assuming, therefore, that the labourer is paid in the very article he produces, it is evident that, when any saving of expense takes place in the production of that article, if the labourer still receives the same cost of production as before, he must receive an increased quantity, in the very same ratio in which the productive power of capital has been increased. But, if so, the outlay of the capitalist will bear exactly the same proportion to the return as it did before; and profits will not rise." (This is wrong.) "The variations, therefore, in the rate of profits, and those in the cost of production of wages, go hand in hand, and are inseparable. Mr. Ricardo's principle [...] is strictly true, if by low wages be meant not merely wages which are the produce of a smaller quantity of labour, but wages which are produced at less cost, reckoning labour and previous profits together" (loc. cit., p. 104).

Thus according to Mill's illustration, Ricardo's view is strictly true if low wages (or the production costs of wages in general) are taken to mean not only the opposite of what he said they mean, but if they are taken to mean absolute nonsense, namely, that the production costs of wages are taken to mean not that portion of the working-day which the worker works to replace his wages, but also the production costs of the raw material he works up and the machinery he uses, that is, labour-time which he has *not* expended at all—neither for himself nor for the capitalist.

* * *

Fifthly. Now comes the real question: How far can a change in the value of constant capital affect the surplus-value?

If we say that the value of the average daily wage is equal to 10 hours or, what amounts to the same thing, that from the working-day of, let us say, 12 hours which the worker labours, 10 hours are required in order to produce and replace his wages, and that only the time he works over and above this is unpaid labour-time in which he produces values which the capitalist ||340| receives without having paid for them; this means nothing more than that 10 hours of labour are embodied in the total quantity of means of subsistence which the worker consumes. These 10 hours of labour are expressed in a certain sum of money with which he buys the food.

The value of commodities however is determined by the labour-time embodied in them, irrespective of whether this labour-time is embodied in the raw material, the machinery used up, or the labour newly added by the worker to the raw material by means of the machinery. Thus, if there were to be a constant (not temporary) change in the value of the raw material or of the machinery which enter into this commodity—a change brought about by a change in the productivity of labour which produces this raw material and this machinery, in short, the constant capital embodied in this commodity—and if, as a result, more or less labour-time were required in order to produce this part of the commodity, the commodity itself would consequently be dearer or cheaper (provided both the productivity of the labour which transforms the raw material into the commodity and the length of the working-day remained unchanged). This would lead either to a rise or to a fall in the production costs, i.e., the value, of labour-power; in other words, if previously out of the 12 hours the worker worked 10 hours for himself, he must now work 11 hours, or, in the opposite case, only 9 hours for himself. In the first case, his labour for the capitalist, i.e., the surplus-value, would have declined by half, from two hours to one; in the second case it would have risen by half, from two hours to three. In this latter case, the rate of profit and the total profit of the capitalist would rise, the former because the value of constant capital would have fallen, and both because the rate of surplus-value (and its amount in absolute figures) would have increased.

This is the only way in which a change in the value of constant capital can affect the value of labour, the production cost of wages, or the division of the working-day between capitalist and worker, hence also the surplus-value.

However, this simply means that for the capitalist who, for example, spins cotton, the necessary labour-time of his own workers is determined not only by the productivity of labour in the spinning industry, but likewise by the productivity of labour in the production of cotton, of machinery, etc., just as it is also determined by the productivity in all branches of industry whose products—although they do not enter as constant capital, that is, either as raw material or as machinery, etc., into his product (a product which, it is assumed, enters into the consumption of the worker), into the yarn—constitute a part of the circulating capital which is expended in wages, that is, by the productivity in the industries producing food, etc. What appears as the product in one industry appears as raw material or instrument of labour in another; the constant capital of one industry thus consists of the products of another industry; in the latter it does not constitute constant capital, but is the result of the production process within this branch. To the individual capitalist it makes a great deal of difference whether the increased productivity of labour (and therefore also the fall in the value of labour-power) takes place within his own branch of industry or amongst those which supply his industry with constant capital. For the capitalist class, for capital as a whole, it is all the same.

Thus this case ⟨in which a fall (or a rise) in the value of constant capital is not due to the fact that the industry employing this constant capital produces on a large scale, but to the fact that the production costs of constant capital itself have changed⟩ concurs with the laws elaborated for surplus-value.

When in general we speak about profit or rate of profit, then *surplus-value* is supposed to be *given*. The influences therefore which determine surplus-value *have* all operated. This is the presupposition.

* * *

Sixthly. In addition, one could have set forth how the ratio of constant capital to variable capital and *hence* the rate of profit is altered by a particular form of surplus-value. Namely, by the lengthening of the working-day beyond its normal limits. ||341| This results in the diminution of the relative value of the constant capital or of the proportionate part of value which it constitutes in the total value of the product. But we will leave this till Chapter III[73] where the greater part of what has been dealt with here really belongs.

* * *

Mr. Mill, basing himself on his brilliant illustration, advances the general (Ricardian) proposition:

"The *only* expression of the law of profits ... is, that they depend on the cost of production of wages" (loc. cit., pp. 104-05).

On the contrary, one should say: The rate of profit ⟨and this is what Mr. Mill is talking about⟩ depends *exclusively* on the cost of production of wages only in one *single* case. And this is when the rate of surplus-value and the rate of profit are *identical*. But this can only occur if the whole of the capital advanced is laid out directly in wages, so that no constant capital, be it raw material, machinery, factory buildings, etc., enters into the product, or that the raw material, etc., insofar as it does enter, is not the product of labour and costs nothing—a case which is virtually impossible in capitalist production. *Only* in this case are the variations in the rate of profit identical with the variations in the rate of surplus-value, or, what amounts to the same thing, with the variations in the production costs of wages.

In general however (and this also includes the exceptional case mentioned above) the rate of profit is equal to the ratio of surplus-value to the total value of the capital advanced.

If we call the surplus-value S, and the value of the capital advanced C, then profit works out at $S:C$ or $\frac{S}{C}$. This ratio is determined not only by the size of S ⟨and all the factors which determine the production cost of wages enter into the determination of S⟩ but also by the size of C. But C, the total value of the capital advanced, consists of the constant capital, c, and the variable capital, v (laid out in wages). The rate of profit is therefore $S:(v+c)=S:C$. But S itself, the surplus-value, is determined not only by its own rate, i.e., by the ratio of surplus labour to necessary labour, in other words, by the division of the working-day between capital and labour, that is, its division into paid and unpaid labour-time. The quantity of surplus-value, i.e., the total amount of surplus-value, is likewise determined by the number of working-days which capital exploits simultaneously. And, for a particular capital, the amount of labour-time employed at a definite rate of unpaid labour depends on the time in which the product remains in the actual *production process* without labour being applied or without the same amount of labour as was required formerly (for example, wine before it has matured, corn once it has been sown, skins and other materials which are subjected to chemical treatment for a certain period, etc.), as well as on the length of time involved in the circulation of the commodity, the length of time required for the metamorphosis of the commodity, that is, the interval between its completion as a product and its reproduction as a commodity. How many days can be worked simultaneously ⟨if the value of wages, and therefore the rate of surplus-value, is given⟩ depends in general on the *amount of capital* expended on wages. But on the whole, the factors mentioned above modify the total amount of living labour-time which a capital of a given size can employ during a definite *period*—during a year, for example. These circumstances determine the absolute amount of labour-time which a given capital can employ. This does not, however, alter the fact that surplus-value is determined exclusively by its own rate multiplied by the number of days worked simultaneously. These circumstances only determine the operation of the last factor, the amount of labour-time employed.

The rate of surplus-value is equal to the ratio of surplus labour in *one* working-day, that is, it is equal to the surplus-value yielded by a single working-day. For example, if the working-day is 12 hours and the surplus labour 2 hours, then these 2 hours constitute $^1/_6$ of the total labour-time of 12 hours; but we must calculate them on the necessary labour (or on the wages paid for it, they represent *the same* quantity of labour-time in materialised form); [therefore it is] $^1/_5$ ($^1/_5$ of 10 hours=2 hours) ($^1/_5$=20 per cent). In this case the amount of surplus-value (yielded in a single day) is determined entirely by the rate. If the capitalist operates on the scale of 100 such ||342| days, then the surplus-value (its total amount) will be 200 labour hours. The rate has remained the same—200 hours for 1,000 hours of necessary labour will give $^1/_5$, or 20 per cent. If the rate of surplus-value is given, its amount depends entirely on the number of workers employed, that is, on the total amount of capital expended on wages, variable capital. If the number of workers employed is given, that is, the *amount* of capital laid out in wages, the variable capital, then the amount of surplus-value depends entirely on its rate, that is, on the ratio of surplus labour to necessary labour, on the production costs of wages, on the division of the working-day between capitalist and worker. If 100 workers (working 12 hours a day) provide me with 200 labour hours, then the total amount of surplus-value will be 200, the rate $^1/_5$ of a [paid] working-day, or 2 hours. And the surplus-value comes to 2 hours multiplied by 100 [=200]. If 50 workers provide me with 200 labour hours, then the total amount of the surplus-value is 200 hours; the rate is $^2/_5$ of a (paid) working-day, that is, 4 hours. And the surplus-value amounts to 4 hours multiplied by 50 =200. Since the total amount of surplus-value is equal to the product of its rate and the number of working-days, it can remain the same although the factors change in an inverse ratio.

The rate of surplus-value is always expressed in the ratio of surplus-value to variable capital. For variable capital is equal to the total amount of the paid labour-time; surplus-value is equal to the total amount of unpaid labour-time. Thus the ratio of surplus-value to variable capital always expresses the ratio of the unpaid part of the working-day to the paid part. For example, in the case mentioned previously, let the wage for 10 hours be 1 thaler, where 1 thaler represents a quantity of silver which contains 10 hours of labour. 100 working-days are consequently paid for with 100 thaler. Now if the surplus-value amounts to 20 thaler, the rate is $^{20}/_{100}$, or $^{1}/_{5}$, or 20 per cent. Or what amounts to the same thing, the capitalist receives 2 hours for every 10 working hours (equal to 1 thaler); for 100×10 working hours, that is, 1,000 hours, he receives 200 hours or 20 thaler.

Thus, although the rate of surplus-value is determined exclusively by the ratio of surplus labour-time to necessary time, in other words, by the corresponding part of the working day which the worker requires to produce his wages, that is, by the production cost of wages, the amount of surplus-value is moreover determined by the number of working-days, by the total quantity of labour-time which is employed at this definite rate of surplus-value, that is, by the total amount of capital expended on wages (if the rate of surplus-value is given). But since profit is the ratio, not of the rate of surplus-value, but of the total amount of surplus-value to the total value of the capital advanced, then clearly its rate is determined not only by the rate, but also by the total amount of surplus-value, an amount which depends on the compound ratio of the rate and the number of working-days, on the amount of capital expended on wages and the production costs of wages.

If the rate of surplus-value is given, then its amount depends exclusively on the amount of capital advanced (laid out in wages). Now the average wage is the same, in other words, it is assumed that workers in all branches of industry receive a wage of 10 hours, for example. (In those branches of industry where wages are higher than the average, this, from our point of view and for the matter under consideration, would amount to the capitalist employing a *greater number* of unskilled workers.) Thus, if it is assumed that the surplus labour is equal, and this means that the entire normal working-day is equal (the inequalities cancel one another out in part since one hour of skilled labour, for example, is equal to two hours of unskilled labour), ||343| then the amount of the surplus-value depends entirely on the amount of capital expended [on wages]. It can therefore be said that the amounts of surplus-value are proportional to the amounts of capital laid out (in wages). This does not, however, apply to profit, since profit [expresses] the ratio of surplus-value to the total value of the capital expended, and the portion which capitals of equal size lay out in wages, or the ratio of variable capital to the total capital, can be and is very different. The amount of profit—as regards the different capitals—here depends on the ratio between the variable capital and the total capital, that is, on $\frac{v}{c+v}$. Thus, if the rate of surplus-value is given, and it is always expressed by $\frac{s}{v}$, by the ratio of surplus-value to variable capital, then the rate of profit is determined entirely by the ratio of variable capital to the total capital.

The rate of profit is thus *determined, firstly, by the rate of surplus-value*, that is, by the ratio of unpaid labour to paid labour; and it changes, rises or falls (insofar as this action is not rendered ineffectual by movements of the other determining factors), with changes in the rate of surplus-value. This, however, rises or falls in *direct* proportion to the productivity of labour and in *inverse* proportion to the value of labour, that is, to the production costs of wages or the quantity of necessary labour.

Secondly, however, the rate of profit is determined by the ratio of variable capital to the total capital, by $\frac{v}{c+v}$. The total amount of surplus-value, where its rate is given, depends of course only on the size of the variable capital, which, on the assumption made, is determined by, or simply expresses, the number of working-days worked simultaneously, that is, the total amount of labour-time employed. But the rate of profit depends on the ratio of this absolute magnitude of surplus-value, which is determined by the variable capital, to the total capital, that is, on the ratio between variable capital and total capital, on $\frac{v}{c+v}$. Since S, surplus-value, has been assumed as given in calculating the rate of profit, and therefore v is likewise assumed as given, any variations occurring in $\frac{v}{c+v}$ can be due only to variations in c, that is, in constant capital. For if v is given, the sum $c+v$, equal to C, can only change if c changes and the ratio $\frac{v}{c+v}$ or $\frac{v}{C}$ changes with changes in the sum.

If $v=100$, $c=400$, then $v+c=500$ and $\frac{v}{v+c}=\frac{100}{500}=\frac{1}{5}=20$ per cent. Therefore, if the rate of surplus-value came to $^5/_{10}$ or $^1/_2$, [the amount of surplus-value] would be 50. But since the variable capital is only equal to $^1/_5$ the total capital, the profit is therefore a half of a fifth, that is, one-tenth [of the total capital] and, in fact, $^1/_{10}$ of 500, which is 50, that is, 10 per cent. The ratio $\frac{v}{v+c}$ changes with every change in c, but naturally not by the same numerical quantity. If we assume that v and c amount originally to 10 each, that is to say, that the total capital consists of half variable and half constant capital, then $\frac{v}{v+c}=\frac{10}{10+10}=\frac{10}{20}=\frac{1}{2}$. If the rate of surplus-value is $1/2$ of v, then it is equal to $1/4$ of C. In other words, if the surplus-value is 50 per cent, then in this case, where the variable capital is $\frac{C}{2}$, the rate of profit comes to 25 per cent. If we now assume that the constant capital is doubled, i.e., it increases from 10 to 20, then $\frac{v}{c+v}=\frac{10}{20+10}=\frac{10}{30}=\frac{1}{3}$. (The rate of surplus-value, $1/2$ of 10, would now be $1/2$ of $1/3$ of C, that is, $1/6$ of 30, that is, 5. Thus $1/2$ of $10=5$, 5 calculated on 10 is 50 per cent, 5 calculated on 30 is $16^2/_3$ per cent. On the other hand, 5 calculated on 20 was $1/4$, that is, 25 per cent.) The constant capital has doubled, that is, it has increased from 10 to 20. But the sum $c+v$ has only increased by half, namely, from 20 to 30. The constant capital has increased by 100 per cent, the sum $c+v$ only by 50 per cent. The ratio $\frac{v}{c+v}$, originally $10/_{20}$, has fallen to $10/_{30}$, that is, from a half to a third, that is, from $3/_6$ to $2/_6$. Thus it has fallen by only $1/_6$, whereas the constant capital has been doubled. How the growth or decline in the constant capital affects the ratio $\frac{v}{c+v}$ depends evidently on the proportion in which c and v originally constitute parts of the whole capital C (consisting of $c+v$).

||344| The *constant* capital (that is, its value) can *firstly* rise (or fall) although the amounts of raw material, machinery, etc., employed, remain the same. In this case therefore, the variations in constant capital are not determined by the conditions of production prevailing in the industrial process into which it enters as constant capital, but are independent of them. Whatever the *causes* bringing about the change in value may be, they always influence the rate of profit. In this case, the same amount of raw material, machinery, etc., has more or less value than it did previously, because more or less labour-time was required to produce them. The variations, then, are determined by the conditions of production of the processes from which the component parts of constant capital emerge as products. We have already[a] examined how this affects the rate of profit.

---

[a] See this volume, pp. 218-25.—*Ed.*

As far as the rate of profit is concerned, whether in a particular industry constant capital, raw material, for example, rises or falls in value because its own production has become dearer, etc., amounts to the same thing as if in some branch of industry (or even in the same branch) more expensive raw material were used for the production of one type of commodity than for that of another type, while the outlay on wages remained unchanged.

When there is equal expenditure on wage-labour, but the raw material worked up by one kind of capital (corn, for example) is dearer than the raw material worked up by another (oats, for example) (or, for that matter, silver and copper, etc., or wool and cotton, etc.), the rate of profit for the two capitals must be in inverse proportion to the dearness of the raw material. Thus, if on the average the same profit is made in both branches of industry, then this is only possible because the surplus-value is shared between the capitalists, not in accordance with the ratio of surplus-value which each capitalist produces in his own particular sphere of production but in relation to the size of the capital they employ. This can happen in two ways. A, who works up the cheaper material, sells his commodity at its real value; he thereby also pockets the surplus-value he himself has produced. The price of his commodity is equal to its value. B, who works up dearer material, sells his commodity above its value and charges as much in his price [in order that his commodity should yield a corresponding profit] as if he had been working up a cheaper material. If A and B exchange their products, then it is the same for A as if he had included a smaller amount of surplus-value in the price of his commodity than it actually contains. Or as if both A and B had from the very beginning charged a rate of profit commensurate with the size of the capital invested, that is, had divided the joint surplus-value between them on the basis of the amount of the capital they had invested. And this is what the term general rate of profit denotes.

Naturally this equalisation does not take place when the constant element in a particular capital such as raw materials, for example, falls or rises temporarily under the influence of the seasons, etc. Although the extraordinary profits made by the cotton-spinners, for example, in years of especially good cotton crops, undoubtedly lead to an influx of new capital into this branch of industry and give rise to the building of a large number of new factories and of textile machinery. If a bad year for cotton ensues, then the loss [because of the sudden rise in the price of cotton] will be all the greater.

Secondly, the production costs of machinery, raw materials, in short of constant capital, remain the same, but larger amounts of them may be required; their value therefore grows in proportion to the growing amount used as a result of the changed conditions of production in the processes in which those elements enter as means of production. In this case, as in the previous example, the increase in the value of constant capital results of course in a fall in the rate of profit. On the other hand however, these variations in the conditions of production themselves indicate that labour has become more productive and thus that the rate of surplus-value has risen. For more raw material is now being consumed by the same amount of living labour only because it can now work up the same amount in less time, and more machinery is now being used only because the cost of machinery is smaller than the cost of the labour it replaces. Thus it is a question here of making up to a certain extent the fall in the rate of profit by increasing the rate of surplus-value and therefore also the total amount of surplus-value.

Finally, the two factors responsible for the change in value can operate together in very different combinations. For example, ||345| the average value of raw cotton has fallen, but simultaneously the value of the amount of cotton which can be worked up in a certain time, has increased even more. [Or] the value of cotton has risen, and so has the value of the total amount of it which can be worked up in a given time. Machinery with increased productive capacity has become dearer in absolute terms, but has become cheaper in relation to its efficiency, and so forth.

It has been assumed hitherto that the variable capital remains unchanged. Variable capital, however, can also decline not only relatively but absolutely, as for example in agriculture; that is, it can decline not only relative to the size of the constant capital. Alternatively, variable capital can increase absolutely. In this case, however, it is the same as if it remained unchanged, insofar as the constant capital grows in a greater or in the same ratio for the reasons mentioned above.

If the constant capital remains unchanged, then any rise or fall of it in relation to the variable capital is accounted for only by a relative rise or fall of the constant capital due to an absolute fall or rise of the amount of variable capital.

If the variable capital remains unchanged, then every rise or fall in the constant capital can be explained only by its own absolute rise or fall.

If variations take place in both variable and constant capital simultaneously, then after deducting the variations which are identical in both, the result is the same as if one had remained unchanged while the other had risen or fallen.

Once the *rate of profit* is given, the amount of profit depends on the size of the capital employed. A large capital with a low rate of profit yields a larger profit than a small capital with a high rate of profit.

* * *

So much for this digression.

Apart from this, only the two following passages from John Stuart Mill require comment:

"*Capital*, strictly speaking, has no *productive power*. The only productive power is that of labour; assisted, no doubt, by tools, and acting upon raw materials[a]" (op. cit., p. 90).

Strictly speaking, he here confuses capital with the material elements of which it is constituted. However, the passage is valuable for those who do the same thing and who nevertheless assert that capital has productive power. Of course, here too the matter is only stated correctly insofar as the production of value is considered. After all, nature also produces insofar as it is only a question of use-values.

"... *productive power of capital* [...] can only mean[b] the quantity of real productive power which the capitalist, by means of his capital, can command" (loc. cit., p. 91).

Here capital is conceived correctly as a production relation. |VIII-345||

* * *

||XIV-851| •In a previous notebook[74] I have traced in detail how Mill violently attempts to derive Ricardo's law of the *rate of profit* (in inverse proportion to wages) directly from the law of value without distinguishing between *surplus-value* and *profit*.

---

[a] The manuscript has "machinery".—*Ed.*
[b] The manuscript has "is nothing but" instead of "can only mean".—*Ed.*

[8. Conclusion]

This whole account of the Ricardian school shows that it declines at two points.

1) Exchange between capital and labour corresponding to the law of value.

2) Elaboration of the general rate of profit. Identification of surplus-value and profit. Failure to understand the relation between values and cost-prices.

[CHAPTER XXI]

OPPOSITION TO THE ECONOMISTS
(BASED ON THE RICARDIAN THEORY)

||852| During the Ricardian period of political economy its antithesis, communism (Owen) and socialism (Fourier, St. Simon, the latter only in his first beginnings), [comes] also [into being]. According to our plan we are here concerned only with that opposition, which takes as its starting-point the premises of the economists.

It will be seen from the works which we quote that in fact they all derive from the Ricardian form.

1. [The Pamphlet] "The Source and Remedy of the National Difficulties"

[a) Profit, Rent and Interest Regarded as Surplus Labour of the Workers. The Interrelation Between the Accumulation of Capital and the So-called "Labour Fund"]

The Source and Remedy of the National Difficulties, [deduced from Principles of Political Economy, in] a Letter to Lord John Russell, London, 1821 (anonymous).

This scarcely known pamphlet (about 40 pages) [which appeared] at a time when McCulloch, "this incredible cobbler",[75] began to make a stir, contains an important advance on Ricardo. It bluntly describes surplus-value—or "profit", as Ricardo calls it (often also "surplus produce"), or *"interest"*, as the author of the pamphlet terms it—as *"surplus labour"*, the labour which the worker performs gratis, the labour he performs over and above the quantity of labour by which the value of his labour-power is replaced, i.e., by which he produces an equivalent for his wages. Important as it was to reduce *value* to labour, it was equally important [to present] *surplus-value*, which manifests itself in *surplus product*, as *surplus labour*. This was in fact already stated by Adam Smith and constitutes one of the main elements in Ricardo's argumentation. But nowhere did he clearly express it and record it in an *absolute form*.

Whereas the only concern of Ricardo and others is to understand the conditions of capitalist production, and to assert them as the absolute forms of production, the pamphlet and the other works of this kind to be mentioned seize on the mysteries of capitalist production which have been brought to light in order to combat the latter from the standpoint of the industrial proletariat.

[We read in the pamphlet:]

"... whatever may be *due* to the capitalist" (from the viewpoint of the capitalist) "he *can only receive the surplus labour* of the labourer; for the labourer *must live*..." (*The Source and Remedy of the National Difficulties*, p. 23).

To be sure, these conditions of life, the minimum on which the worker can live, and consequently also the quantity of surplus labour which can be squeezed out of him, are relative magnitudes.

"... if capital does not decrease in value[76] as it increases in amount, the capitalists will exact from the labourers the produce of every hour's labour beyond what it is *possible* for the labourer to subsist on: and however horrid and disgusting it may seem, the capitalist may eventually speculate on the food that requires the least labour to produce it, and eventually say to the labourers, 'You sha'n't eat bread, because barley meal is cheaper; you sha'n't eat meat, because it is possible to subsist on beet root and potatoes'. And to this point have we come!" (loc. cit., pp. 23-24).

"... if the labourer can be brought to feed on potatoes instead of bread, it is indisputably true that more can be exacted from his labour; that is to say,[a] if when he fed on bread he was obliged *to retain for the maintenance of himself and family the labour of Monday and Tuesday*, he will, on potatoes, require only the half of Monday; and *the remaining half of Monday and the whole of Tuesday* are available either *for the service of the state or the capitalist*" (loc. cit., p. 26).

Here profit, etc., is reduced directly to appropriation of the labour-time for which the worker receives no equivalent.

"It is admitted that the interest paid to the capitalists, whether in the nature of rents, interests of money, or profits of trade, is paid out of *the labour of others*" (loc. cit., p. 23).

Rent, money interest, industrial profit, are thus merely different forms of "*interest* of capital", which again is reduced

---

[a] In the manuscript "i.e." instead of "that is to say".—*Ed.*

to the "*surplus labour* of the labourer". This surplus labour takes the form of surplus produce. The capitalist is the owner of the surplus labour or of the surplus produce. The surplus produce is capital.

"Suppose ... there is no *surplus labour*, consequently, nothing that can be allowed to accumulate as capital" (op. cit., p. 4).

And, immediately after this he says:

"... the possessors of the surplus produce, *or* capital..." (loc. cit., p. 4).

The author says, in a quite different sense from the whining Ricardians:

"... the natural and necessary consequence of an increased capital, [is] its decreasing value..." (op. cit., pp. 21-22).

And in reference to Ricardo:

"Why set out by telling us that no accumulation of capital will lower profits, because nothing will lower profits but increased wages, when it appears that if population does not increase with capital, wages would increase from the disproportion between capital and labour; and if population does increase, wages would increase from the difficulty of producing food" (loc. cit., p. 23, note).

||853| If the value of capital, that is, the interest of capital, i.e., the surplus labour which it commands, which it appropriates, did not decrease when the amount of capital increases, the [accumulation of] interest from interest would follow in geometrical progression, and just as, calculated in money (see *Price*), this presupposes an *impossible* accumulation (rate of accumulation), so, reduced to its real element—labour, it would swallow up not only the surplus labour, but also the necessary labour as "being due" to capital. (We shall return to Price's fantasy in the section on Revenue and its Sources.[77])

"... if it were possible to continue to increase capital and keep up the value of capital, which is proved by the interest of money continuing the same, the interest to be paid for capital would soon exceed the whole produce of labour. ... capital tends in more than arithmetical progression to increase capital. It is admitted that the *interest* paid to the capitalists, whether in the nature of rents, *interests* of money, or *profits* of trade, is paid out of the labour of others. If then[a] capital go on accumulating [...] the labour to be given for the use of capital must go on increasing, interest paid for capital continuing the same, till all the labour of all the labourers of the society is engrossed by the capitalist. [...] that it is[b] [...] impossible to happen;

---

[a] In the manuscript "Consequently, if" instead of "If then".—*Ed.*
[b] In the manuscript "But this is" instead of "that it is".—*Ed.*

for whatever may be *due* to the capitalist, he can *only receive the surplus labour* of the labourer; for the labourer must live..." (loc. cit., p. 23).

But it is not clear to him how the value of capital decreases. He himself says, when dealing with Ricardo, that this recurs because wages rise when capital accumulates more rapidly than the population grows, or because the *value* of wages (not the quantity) increases when the population grows more rapidly than capital accumulates (or even if population *increases simultaneously*) as a result of decreasing productivity of agriculture. But how does he explain it? He does not accept the latter alternative; he assumes that wages are reduced more and more to the minimum possible. [A reduction of "interest" on capital] can only take place, he says, because the portion of capital which is exchanged for living labour declines relatively, although the worker is exploited more than, or just as much as, before.

In any case, it is a step forward that the nonsense about the geometrical progression of interest is reduced to its true sense, that is, nonsense.*

There are, by the way, according to the pamphleteer, two methods which, in spite of the growth of surplus product or surplus labour, prevent capital from being forced to give a greater share of its plunder back to the workers.

The first is the conversion of surplus product into fixed capital, which prevents the labour fund—or the part of the product consumed by the worker—from necessarily increasing with the accumulation of capital.

The second is foreign trade, which enables the capitalist to exchange the surplus product for foreign luxury articles and thus to consume it himself. In this way, even that part of the product which exists as *necessaries* may quite well increase without the need for it to be returned to the worker in the form of a proportionate increase in wages.

---

* ||XV-862a| Because surplus-value and surplus labour are identical, a *qualitative* limit is set to the accumulation of capital, [it is determined by] the *total working-day* (the period in the 24 hours during which labour-power can be active), the given stage of development of the productive forces and the *population*, which limits the total *number* of working-days that can be utilised simultaneously at a given time. If, on the contrary, surplus yield is understood in the abstract form of *interest*, that is, as the proportion in which capital increases itself by means of a mythical "sleight of hand", then the limit is purely *quantitative* and it is absolutely impossible to see why capital does not daily add to itself interest as capital every morning, thus creating interest on interest in infinite progression. |XV-862a†|

It should be noted that the first method—which is only effective for a time and then neutralises its own effect (at least as regards the fixed capital consisting of machinery, etc., which itself is used in the production of necessaries)—implies the transformation of surplus product into capital, whereas the second method implies consumption of an ever-increasing portion of the surplus product by the capitalists—increasing consumption on the part of the capitalists and not the *reconversion* of surplus product into capital. If the same surplus product were to remain in the form in which it immediately exists, a greater part of it would have to be exchanged with the workers as variable capital. The result would be an increase in wages and a reduction in the amount of absolute or relative surplus-value. Here is the real secret of the necessity for increasing consumption by "the rich", advocated by Malthus, *in order that the part of the product which is exchanged for labour and converted into capital, should have great value, yield large profits, absorb a large amount of surplus labour*. He does not however propose that the industrial capitalists themselves should increase their consumption, but [allots] this *function* to *landlords*, sinecurists, etc., because the urge for accumulation and the urge for expenditure, if united in the same person, would play tricks on each other. It is here also that the erroneousness of the view of Barton, Ricardo, and others stands out. Wages are not determined by that portion of the total product that is either consumed as, or can be converted into, *variable* capital, but by that part of it which is actually converted into variable capital. A part can be consumed by retainers even in its natural form, another can be consumed in the shape of luxury products by means of foreign trade, etc.

Our pamphleteer overlooks two things:

As a result of the introduction of machinery, a mass of workers is constantly being thrown out of employment, a section of the population is thus made redundant; the surplus product therefore finds fresh labour for which it can be exchanged without any increase in population and without any need to extend the absolute working-time. Let us assume that 500 workers were employed previously, whereas now there are 300 workers, who perform relatively more surplus labour. The other 200 can be employed by the surplus product as soon as it has increased sufficiently. One portion of the old [variable] capital is converted into fixed capital, the other gives employment to fewer workers but extracts from them more surplus-value in relation to their number and in particular also more surplus product. The remaining 200 are material created for the purpose of capitalising additional surplus product.

||853a| The transformation of *necessaries* into *luxuries* by means of foreign trade, as interpreted in the pamphlet, is important in itself:

1) because it puts an end to the nonsensical idea that wages depend on the amount of necessaries produced, as if these necessaries had to be consumed in this form by the producers or even by the whole body of people engaged in production, in other words that they must be transformed again into variable capital or "circulating capital", as it is termed by Barton and Ricardo;

2) because it determines the whole social pattern of backward nations—for example, the slave-holding states in the United States of North America (see *Cairnes*[78]) or *Poland*, etc. (as was already understood by old *Büsch*, unless he stole the idea from Steuart)—which are associated with a world market based on capitalist production. No matter how large the surplus product they extract from the surplus labour of their slaves in the simple form of cotton or corn, they can adhere to this simple, undifferentiated labour because foreign trade enables them [to convert] these simple products into any kind of use-value.

The assertion that the portion of the annual product which must be expended as wages depends on the size of the circulating capital, is equal to the assertion that, when a large part of the product consists of "buildings", houses for workers are built in large numbers relative to the size of the working population, and that consequently the workers must live in cheap and well-built houses because the supply of houses increases more quickly than the demand for them.

It is correct, on the other hand, that, if the surplus product is large and the greater part of it is to be employed as capital, then there must be an increase in the demand for labour and therefore also in that part of the surplus product which is exchanged for wages (provided large numbers of workers did not have to be thrown out of work in order to obtain a surplus product of this size). At all events, it is not the *absolute size* of the surplus product (in whatever form it may exist, even that of necessaries) which necessarily requires it to be expended as variable capital and which consequently causes an increase in wages, but it is the desire to capitalise which results in a large part of the surplus product being laid out in variable capital and this would *consequent-*

ly make wages grow with the accumulation of capital if machinery did not constantly make [a section of] the population redundant and if an ever greater portion of capital (in particular as a result of foreign trade) were not exchanged for capital, not for labour. *The portion of surplus product which is already produced directly in a form in which it can only serve as capital, and that portion of it which acquires this form as a result of foreign trade, grow more rapidly than the portion which must be exchanged against immediate labour.*

The proposition that wages depend on existing capital and that therefore a rapid accumulation of capital is the sole means by which wages are made to rise, amounts to this:

On the one hand, to a *tautology*, if we disregard the form in which the conditions of labour exist as capital. How rapidly the number of workers can be increased without worsening their living conditions depends on the *productivity of labour* which a given number of workers perform. The more raw materials, tools and means of subsistence they produce, the greater the means at their disposal not only to bring up their children so long as these cannot work themselves, but to realise the labour of the new, growing generation, and consequently to make the growth of production keep up with, and even outdo, the growth of population, since with the growth of the population, the [workers'] skill increases, division of labour grows, the possibility [for using] machinery grows, constant capital grows, in short, the productivity of labour grows.

While the growth of population depends on the productivity of labour, the productivity of labour depends on the growth of population. It is a case of reciprocity. But this, expressed in capitalist terms, signifies that the means of subsistence of the working population depend on the productivity of capital, on the largest possible portion of their product confronting them as a force which commands their labour. Ricardo himself expresses the matter *correctly*—I mean the tautology—when he makes wages depend on the productivity of capital, and the latter dependent on the productivity of labour.[a]

That labour depends on the growth of capital signifies nothing more than, on the one hand, the tautology ||854| that the increase in the means of subsistence and the means of employment of the

---

[a] See *Theories of Surplus-Value*, Part II, pp. 541-42 and this volume, pp. 114-15.—*Ed.*

population depends on the productivity of the population's own labour and, secondly, expressed in capitalist terms, that *it depends on the fact* that the population's own product confronts them as *alien property* and that as a consequence, their own productivity confronts them as the *productivity* of the things which they create.

In practice this means that the worker must appropriate the smallest possible part of his product in order that the largest possible part of it may confront him as *capital*; he must surrender as much as possible to the capitalist *gratis*, in order that the latter's means for purchasing his labour—with what has been taken away from the worker without compensation—may increase as much as possible. In this case it can happen that, if the capitalist has made the worker work a great deal for nothing, he may then, in exchange for what he has received for nothing, allow the worker to do a little less work for nothing. However, since this prevents the achievement of what is aimed at, namely, *accumulation of capital as rapidly as possible*, the worker must live in such circumstances that this reduction in the amount of labour he performs for nothing is in turn counteracted by a growth of the working population, either relatively as a result of the use of machinery, or absolutely as a result of early marriage. (It is the same relationship which is derided by the Ricardians when the Malthusians preach it between landlords and capitalists.) The workers must relinquish the largest possible part of their product to the capitalist without receiving anything in return, so as, when conditions are *more favourable*, to buy back with new labour a part of the product so relinquished. However, since the conditions for the favourable change are at the same time counteracted by this favourable change, it can only be temporary and must turn again into its own opposite.

3) What applies to the transformation of necessaries into luxuries by means of foreign trade, applies in general to luxury production, whose unlimited diversification and expansion depends, however, on foreign trade. Although the workers engaged in luxury production produce capital for their employers, their product, in the form in which it exists, cannot be transformed into capital, either constant or variable capital.

Luxury products, apart from those which are sent abroad to be exchanged for necessaries which enter into variable capital either in whole or in part, simply constitute *surplus labour* and [moreover] surplus labour which is immediately *in the shape of surplus products* which the rich consume as revenue. But they do not represent only the surplus labour of the workers who produce them. On the average, these perform the same surplus labour as the workers in other branches of industry. But in the same way as one-third of the product, which contains a third of the surplus labour, can be considered as the embodiment of this surplus labour, and the remaining two-thirds as reproduction of the capital advanced, so the surplus labour of the producers of those necessaries which constitute the wages of the producers of luxuries can also be considered as the necessary labour of the working class as a whole. Their surplus labour consists 1) of that part of the necessaries which is consumed by the capitalists and their retainers; and 2) of the total amount of luxuries. With regard to the individual capitalist or a particular branch of industry the matter appears quite different. For the capitalist, one part of the luxuries created by him represents merely an equivalent for the capital laid out.

If too large a part of surplus labour is embodied directly in luxuries, then clearly, accumulation and the rate of reproduction will stagnate, because too small a part is reconverted into capital. If too small a part [of surplus labour] is embodied in luxuries, then the accumulation of capital (that is, of that part of the surplus product which can in kind serve as capital again) will proceed more rapidly than increase in population, and the rate of profit will fall, unless a foreign market for necessaries exists.

[b) On the Exchange Between Capital and Revenue in the Case of Simple Reproduction and of the Accumulation of Capital]

In the exchange between capital and revenue I have regarded wages, too, as revenue and have merely examined the relationship of constant capital to revenue.[79] The fact that the revenue of the worker is at the same time variable capital is important only insofar as in the accumulation of capital—the formation of new capital—the surplus consisting of means of subsistence (necessaries) in the possession of the capitalist producing them can be exchanged directly for the surplus consisting of raw materials or machinery in the possession of the capitalist producing constant capital. Here one form of revenue is exchanged for the other, ||855| and, once the exchange is effected, the revenue of A is converted into the constant capital of B and the revenue of B into the variable capital of A.

In considering this circulation, reproduction and manner of replacement of the different capitals, etc., one must first of all disregard foreign trade.

Secondly, it is necessary to distinguish between the two aspects of the phenomenon:

1) Reproduction on the existing scale,
2) Reproduction on an extended scale, or accumulation; transformation of revenue into capital.

With regard to 1.

I have shown:

That what the *producers of necessaries* have to replace is 1) their constant capital, 2) their variable capital. The part of their product in excess of these two constitutes the *surplus product*, the material existence of *surplus-value*, which in its turn only represents *surplus labour*.

Variable capital, that part of their product which represents it, is made up of wages, the revenue of the workers. This part already exists here in the *natural form* in which it serves as variable capital once again. With this part, the equivalent reproduced by the worker, the labour of the worker is bought once again. This is the exchange of capital for immediate labour. The worker receives this part in the form of money with which he buys back his own product, or other products of the same category. This is the exchange *of the different portions of the variable part of capital for one another* after the worker has in the form of money received an assignment to his quota. This is exchange of one part of newly added labour for another part within the same category (necessaries).

The part of the surplus product (newly added labour) consumed by the capitalists (who produce necessaries) themselves, is either consumed by them in kind or they exchange one type of surplus product existing in consumable form against another type. This is exchange of revenue for revenue, both of them consisting of newly added labour.

We cannot really speak of exchange between revenue and capital in the above transaction. Capital (necessaries) is exchanged against labour (labour-power). This is therefore not an exchange of revenue for capital. It is true that as soon as the worker receives his wages, he consumes them. But what he exchanges for capital is not his revenue, but his labour.

The third part [of the product of the producer of necessaries which constitutes] constant capital is exchanged for a part of the product of those manufacturers who produce constant capital; namely, for that part which represents newly added labour. This consists of an equivalent for the wages (that is, of variable capital) and of the surplus product, the surplus-value, the revenue of the capitalists which exists in a form in which it can only be consumed industrially and not individually. On the one hand, this is therefore exchange of the *variable capital of these producers* for a part of the necessaries which constitute the constant capital [of the producers of necessaries]. In fact they exchange a part of their product which constitutes variable capital but exists in the form of constant capital, for a part of the product of those manufacturers who produce necessaries, a part which constitutes constant capital but exists in the form of variable capital. Here newly added labour is exchanged for constant capital.

On the other hand, that part of the product which represents surplus product but exists in the form of constant capital is exchanged for a portion of necessaries which represents constant capital for its producers. Here revenue is exchanged for capital. The revenue of the capitalists who produce constant capital is exchanged for necessaries and replaces the constant capital of the capitalists who produce necessaries.

Finally, a part of the product of the capitalists who produce constant capital, namely, that part which itself represents constant capital, is replaced partly in kind, partly through barter (concealed by money) between the producers of constant capital.

It is assumed in all this that the scale of reproduction is the same as the original scale of production.

If we enquire what part of the total annual product is made up of newly added labour, then the calculation is quite simple.

A. *Consumable articles* [for individual consumption. These] consist of three parts. [Firstly,] the revenue of the capitalist which equals the surplus labour added during the year.

Secondly, wages, i.e., variable capital, which is equal to the newly added labour by which the workers have reproduced their wages.

Finally, the third part, raw materials, machinery, etc. This is constant capital, that part of the value of the product which is only retained, not produced. That is, it is not labour newly added during the course of the year.

||856| If we call constant capital [in this category] c', variable capital v', and surplus product, the revenue r', then this category consists of $[c'$ and $v'+r']$:

c' (which constitutes a part of the product) is merely retained value and does not consist of newly added labour; on the other hand, $v'+r'$ consist of labour newly added during the course of the year.

The total product [of the category A] (or its value) P^a after deduction of c', therefore, consists of newly added labour.

Thus the product of category A, namely: P^a-c', is equal to the labour newly added during the course of the year.

B. *Articles for industrial consumption.*

Here also $v''+r''$ are made up of newly added labour. But not c'', the constant capital which operates in this sphere.

But $v''+r''=c'$ for which they are exchanged. c' is transformed into variable capital and revenue for B. On the other hand, v'' and r'' are transformed into c', into constant capital for A.

The product of the category [B, that is] P^b. P^b-c'' is equal to the labour newly added during the course of the year.

But $P^b-c''=c'$, for the whole product of P^b after deduction of c'', the constant capital employed in this category, is exchanged for c'.

After $v''+r''$ have been exchanged for c', the matter can be presented as follows:

P^a consists solely of newly added labour, the product of which is divided between profits and wages, that is, it constitutes the equivalent of necessary labour and the equivalent of surplus labour. For the $v''+r''$ which now replace c' are equal to the newly added labour in category B.

Thus the whole product P^a—not only its surplus product, but also its variable capital and its constant capital—consists of the products of labour newly added during the course of the year.

On the other hand, P^b can be regarded in such a way that it does not represent any part of the newly added labour, but merely old labour which is retained. For its part c'' does not represent newly added labour. Neither does the part c' which it has received in exchange for $v''+r''$, for this c' represents the constant capital laid out in A, and not newly added labour.

The whole part of the annual product which, as variable capital, constitutes the revenue of the workers and as surplus product constitutes the consumption fund of the capitalist, therefore consists of newly added labour, whereas the remaining part of the product, which represents constant capital, consists merely of old labour which has been retained and simply replaces constant capital.

Consequently, just as it is correct to say that the whole portion of the annual product which is consumed as revenue, wages and profits (together with the branches of profit, rent, interest, etc., as well as the wages of the unproductive labourers) consists of newly added labour, so it is false to assert that the total annual product resolves itself into revenue, wages and profits and thus merely into portions of newly added labour. A part of the annual product resolves itself into constant capital, which regarded as value does *not* comprise newly added labour and, as regards use does not form part of either wages or profits. Its value represents accumulated labour in the real sense of the word, and its use-value, the utilisation of this accumulated past labour.

On the other hand, it is equally correct that the *labour added during the year* is not represented entirely by that part of the product which constitutes wages and profits. For these wages and profits also buy services, that is, labour which does not enter into the product of which wages and profit form [a part]. These services are labour which is used up in the consumption of the product and does not enter into its immediate production.

||857|| With regard to 2.

It is a different matter with regard to accumulation, transformation of revenue into capital, *reproduction on an extended scale*, insofar as this latter does not simply result from *more productive employment* of the old capital. Here the whole new capital consists of newly added labour, that is, of surplus labour in the form of profit, etc. But although it is correct that here the entire element in new production arises from and consists of newly added labour—which is a part of the surplus labour of the labourers—it is wrong to assume, as the economists do, that, when it is converted into capital, it constitutes only variable capital, that is, wages. Let us suppose for example that a part of the surplus product of the farmer is exchanged for a part of the surplus product of the machine manufacturer. It is then possible that the latter will convert the corn into variable capital and employ more workers, directly or indirectly. On the other hand, the farmer has converted a part of his surplus product into constant capital, and it is possible that, as a result of this conversion, he will discharge some of his old workers instead of taking on new ones. The farmer may cultivate more land. In this case, a part of his corn will be converted not into wages, but into constant capital, etc.

It is precisely accumulation which reveals clearly that everything—i.e., revenue, variable capital and constant capital—is nothing but *appropriated alien* labour; and that both the means of labour with which the worker works, and the equivalent he receives for his labour, consist of labour performed by the worker and appropriated by the capitalist, who has *not given any equivalent for it*.

[The same applies] even to original accumulation. Let us assume that I have saved £500 from my *wages*. In fact, therefore, this sum represents not only *accumulated labour* but, in contrast to the "accumulated labour" of the capitalist, *my* own labour accumulated by me and for me. I convert the £500 into capital, buy raw material, etc., and take on workers. Profit is, say, 20 per cent, that is, £100 a year. In five years I shall have "eaten up" my capital in the form of revenue (provided new accumulation does not continuously take place and the £100 [profit] is consumed). In the sixth year, my capital of £500 itself consists of other people's labour appropriated without any equivalent. If, on the other hand, I had always accumulated half of the profit made, the process [of eating up my original capital] would have been slower, for I would not have consumed so much, and [the process of appropriating other people's labour] more rapid.

	Capital	Profit	Consumed
First year	500	100	50
Second year	550	110	55
Third year	605	121	60
Fourth year	665	133	66
Fifth year	731	146	73
Sixth year	804	160	80
Seventh year	884	176	88
Eighth year	972	194	97
			569

My capital will have been almost doubled in eight years although I have consumed more than my original capital. The capital of £972 does not contain a single farthing of paid labour or of labour for which I have returned any kind of equivalent. I have consumed my entire original capital in the form of revenue, that is, I have received an equivalent for it, which I have consumed. The new capital consists solely of the appropriated labour of other people.

In considering surplus-value as such, the original form of the product, hence of the surplus product, is of no consequence. It becomes important when considering the actual process of reproduction, partly in order to understand its forms, and partly in order to grasp the influence of luxury production, etc., on reproduction. Here is another example of how *use-value* as such acquires economic significance.

[c) The Merits of the Author of the Pamphlet and the Theoretical Confusion of His Views. The Importance of the Questions He Raises about the Role of Foreign Trade in Capitalist Society and of "Free Time" as Real Wealth]

||858| Now to return to our pamphlet.

"Suppose the whole labour of the country to raise just sufficient for the support of the whole population; it is evident there is no surplus labour, consequently, nothing that can be allowed to accumulate as capital. Suppose the whole labour of the country to raise as much in *one* year as would maintain it two years, it is evident one year's consumption must perish, or for one year men must cease from productive labour. But the *possessors of the surplus produce, or capital*, will neither maintain the population the following year in idleness, nor allow the produce to perish; they will employ them upon something not directly and immediately productive, for instance, in the erection of machinery, etc., etc., etc. But the third year, the whole population may again return to productive labour, and the machinery erected in the last year coming now into operation, it is evident the produce [...] will be greater than the first year's produce [...] and[a] the produce of the machinery in addition. [...] this surplus labour must[b] perish, or be put to use as before; and this usance again adds to the productive power [...] of the society [...] till men *must* cease from productive labour for a time, or the produce of their labour must perish. This is the palpable consequence in the simplest state of society" (op. cit., pp. 4-5).

"The demand of other countries is limited, not only by *our* power to produce, but by *their* power to produce...."

(This is the answer to Say's assertion that we do not produce too much, but they produce too little. Their power to produce is not necessarily equal to our power to produce.)

"For do what you will, in a series of years the whole world can take little more of us, than we take of the world [...] so that all your foreign trade, of which there is so much talking, never did, never could, nor ever can, add one shilling, or one doit to the wealth of the country, as for every bale of silk, chest of tea, pipe of wine that ever was imported, something of equal value was exported; and even the profits made by our merchants in their foreign trade are paid by the consumer of the return goods here" (op. cit., pp. 17-18).

---

[a] In the manuscript "for".—*Ed.*
[b] Instead of "this surplus labour must", the manuscript has "This surplus labour, that is an even larger amount, must".—*Ed.*

"... foreign trade is mere barter and exchange for the convenience and enjoyment of the capitalist: he has not a hundred bodies, nor a hundred legs: he cannot consume, in cloth and cotton stockings, all the cloth and cotton stockings that are manufactured; therefore they are exchanged for wines and silks; but those *wines and silks represent the surplus labour of our own population*, as much as the cloths and cottons, and in this way *the destructive power of the capitalist is increased beyond all bounds*: —by foreign trade the capitalists contrive to outwit nature, who had put a thousand natural limits to their exactions, and to their wishes to exact; there is no limit now, either to their power, or [...] desires..." (loc. cit., p. 18).

One sees that he accepts Ricardo's teaching on foreign trade. In Ricardo's work its only purpose is to support his *theory of value* or to demonstrate that his views on foreign trade are not at variance with it. But the pamphlet stresses that it is not only national labour, but *also national surplus labour which is embodied in the outcome of foreign trade.*

If surplus labour or surplus-value were represented only in the national surplus product, then the increase of value for the sake of value and therefore the exaction of surplus labour would be restricted by the limited, narrow circle of use-values in which the value of the [national] labour would be represented. But it is foreign trade which develops its [the surplus product's] real nature as value by developing the labour embodied in it as social labour which manifests itself in an unlimited range of different use-values, and this in fact gives meaning to abstract wealth.

"... It is *the infinite variety of wants*, and of the *kinds* of commodities" ⟨and therefore also the infinite variety of real labour, which produces those different kinds of commodities⟩ "*necessary to their gratification*, which alone renders the passion for wealth" ⟨and hence the passion for appropriating other people's labour⟩ "indefinite and insatiable" (Wakefield's edition of Adam Smith, *An Inquiry into the Nature and Source of the Wealth of Nations*, Vol. 1, London, 1835, p. 64, note).

But it is only foreign trade, the development of the market to a world market, which causes money to develop into world money and *abstract labour* into social labour. Abstract wealth, value, money, hence *abstract labour*, develop in the measure that concrete labour becomes a totality of different modes of labour embracing the world market. Capitalist production rests on the *value* or the transformation of the labour embodied in the product into social labour. But this is only [possible] on the basis of foreign trade and of the world market. This is at once the pre-condition **and** the result of capitalist production.

||859| The pamphlet is no theoretical treatise. [It is a] protest against the false reasons given by the economists for the distress and the "national difficulties" of the times. It does not, consequently, make the claim that its conception of surplus-value as *surplus labour* carries with it a general criticism of the entire system of economic categories, nor can this be expected of it. The author stands rather on Ricardian ground and is only consistent in stating one of the consequences inherent in the system itself and he advances it in the interests of the working class against capital.

For the rest, the author remains a captive of the economic categories as he finds them. Just as in the case of Ricardo the confusion of surplus-value with profit leads to undesirable contradictions, so in his case the fact that he christens surplus-value the *interest of capital*.

To be sure, he is in advance of Ricardo in that he first of all reduces all surplus-value to surplus labour, and when he calls surplus-value *interest of capital*, he at the same time emphasises that by this he understands the general form of surplus labour in contrast to its special forms—rent, interest of money and industrial profit.

"... *interest* paid to the capitalists, whether in the *nature*" (it should be shape, form) "*of rents, interests of money,* or *profits of trade*..." ([*The Source and Remedy of the National Difficulties*, London, 1821,] p. 23).

He thus distinguishes the general form of surplus labour or surplus-value from their particular forms, something which neither Ricardo nor Adam Smith [does], at least not consciously or consistently. But on the other hand, he applies the name of one of these particular forms—interest—to the general form. And this suffices to make him relapse into economic slang.

"The progress of [...] increasing capital would, in established societies, be marked by the decreasing interest of money, or, which is the same thing,[a] the decreasing quantity of the labour of others that would be given for its use..." (op. cit., p. 6).

This passage reminds one of Carey. But with him it is not the labourer who uses capital, but capital which uses the labourer. Since by *interest* he understands surplus labour in any form, the matter of the remedy of our "national difficulties" amounts to an increase in *wages*; for the reduction of interest means a reduc-

---

[a] Instead of "which is the same thing", the manuscript has "which comes to the same thing".—*Ed.*

tion of surplus labour. However, what he really means is that in the exchange of capital for labour the appropriation of alien labour should be reduced or that the worker should appropriate more of his own labour and capital less.

Reduction of surplus labour can mean two things:

Less work should be performed over and above the time which is necessary to reproduce the labour-power, that is, to create an equivalent for wages;

or, less of the *total quantity of labour* should assume the *form of surplus labour*, that is, the form of time worked gratis for the capitalist; therefore less of the product in which labour manifests itself should take the form of *surplus product*; in other words, the worker should receive more of his own product and less of it should go to the capitalist.

The author is not quite clear about this himself, as can be seen from the following passage which is really the last word in this matter as far as the pamphlet is concerned:

"A[a] nation is really rich only if no interest is paid for the use of capital; when only six hours instead of twelve hours are worked.... "Wealth [...] is *disposable time*, and nothing more" (loc. cit., p. 6).

Since what is understood by interest here is profit, rent, interest—in short, all the forms of surplus-value—and since, according to the author himself, capital is nothing but the produce of labour, i.e., accumulated labour which is able to exact in exchange for itself not only an equal quantity of labour, but surplus labour, according to him the phrase: capital bears no interest, therefore means that capital ||860| does not exist. The product is not transformed into capital. No *surplus product* and no *surplus labour* exist. Only then is a nation really rich.

This can mean however: There is no product and no labour *over and above* the product and the labour required for the reproduction of the workers. Or, they [the workers] *themselves* appropriate this surplus either of the product or of the labour.

That the author does *not simply mean* the latter is, however, clear from the fact that the words "no interest is paid for the use of capital" are juxtaposed to the proposition that a nation is really rich when only six hours not twelve hours are worked[b]; "*wealth* [...] *is disposable time, and nothing more*".

---

[a] The following sentence is Marx's paraphrase (written in German) of the ideas the author sets forth in the pamphlet.—*Ed.*

[b] The first part of the sentence up to the words: "are worked" is not a quotation but a paraphrase by Marx (in German).—*Ed.*

This can now mean:

If everybody has to work, if the contradiction between those who have to work too much and those who are idlers disappears—and this would in any case be the result of capital ceasing to exist, of the product ceasing to provide a title to alien *surplus labour*—and if, in addition, the development of the productive forces brought about by capitalism is taken into account, society will produce the necessary abundance in six hours, [producing] more than it does now in twelve, and, moreover, all will have six hours of "disposable time", that is, real wealth; time which will not be absorbed in direct productive labour, but will be available for enjoyment, for leisure, thus giving scope for free activity and development. Time is *scope* for the development of man's faculties, etc. The economists themselves justify the slave-labour of the wage-labourers by saying that it creates leisure, free time for *others*, for another section of society—and thereby also for the society of wage-labourers.

Or it can also mean:

The workers now work six hours more than the time (*now*) required for their own reproduction. (This can hardly be the author's view, since he describes what they use *now* as an inhuman minimum.) If capital ceases to exist, then the workers will work for six hours only and the idlers will have to work the same amount of time. The material wealth of all would thus be depressed to the level of the workers. But all would have *disposable time*, that is, free time for their development.

The author himself is obviously not clear about this. Nevertheless, there remains the fine statement:

A nation is really rich when six hours instead of twelve hours are worked. "Wealth [...] is disposable time, and nothing more."

Ricardo himself, in the chapter entitled *"Value and Riches, Their Distinctive Properties"*, also says that real wealth consists in producing the greatest possible amount of values in use having the least possible [exchange-] value. This means, in other words, that the greatest possible abundance of material wealth is created in the shortest possible labour-time. Here also, the "disposable time" and the enjoyment of that which is produced in the labour-time of others, appear as the real wealth, but like everything in capitalist production—and consequently in its interpreters—it appears in the form of a contradiction. In Ricardo's work the contradiction between riches and value later appears in the form that the net product should be as large as possible in relation to the gross product, which again, in this contradictory form, amounts to saying that those classes in society whose time is only partly or not at all absorbed in material production although they enjoy its fruits, should be as numerous as possible in comparison with those classes whose time is totally absorbed in material production and whose consumption is, as a consequence, a mere item in production costs, a mere condition for their existence as beasts of burden. There is always the wish that the smallest possible portion of society should be doomed to the slavery of labour, to forced labour. This is the utmost that can be accomplished from the capitalist standpoint.

The author puts an end to this. *Labour-time*, even if exchange-value is eliminated, always remains the creative substance of wealth and the measure of the *cost* of its production. But free time, *disposable time*, is wealth itself, partly for the enjoyment of the product, partly for free activity which—unlike labour—is not dominated by the pressure of an extraneous purpose which must be fulfilled, and the fulfilment of which is regarded as a natural necessity or a social duty, according to one's inclination.

It is self-evident that if labour-time is reduced to a normal length and, furthermore, labour is no longer performed for someone else, but for myself, and, at the same time, the social contradictions between master and men, etc., being abolished, it acquires a quite different, a free character, it becomes real social labour, and finally the basis of *disposable time*—the *labour* of a man who has also disposable time, must be of a much higher quality than that of the beast of burden.

2. Ravenstone. [The View of Capital as the Surplus Product of the Worker. Confusion of the Antagonistic Form of Capitalist Development with Its Content. This Leads to a Negative Attitude Towards the Results of the Capitalist Development of the Productive Forces]

||861| Piercy Ravenstone, M. A., *Thoughts on the Funding System, and its Effects*, London, 1824.

A most remarkable work.

The author of *The Source and Remedy of the National Difficulties* discussed above understands surplus-value in its original form, i.e., that of *surplus labour*. Consequently his attention is mainly centred on the extent of labour-time. In particular, the conception of *surplus labour* or [surplus-] value in its absolute form; the extension of labour-time beyond that required for the reproduction of the labourer himself, not the reduction of necessary labour as a result of the development of the productive power of labour.

The reduction of this necessary labour is the principal aspect examined by Ricardo, but in the way it is carried out in capitalist production, namely, as a means for extending the amount of labour-time accruing to capital. This pamphlet, on the contrary, declares that the final aim is the *reduction of* the producers' *labour-time* and the cessation of labour for the *possessor of surplus produce*.

Ravenstone seems to assume the working-day as given. Hence, what he is particularly interested in—just as was also the author of the pamphlet previously discussed, so that the theoretical questions only crop up incidentally—is relative surplus-value or the surplus product (which accrues to capital) as a result of the development of the productive power of labour. As is usual with those who adopt this standpoint, surplus labour is conceived here more in the form of surplus product, whereas in the previous [pamphlet], surplus product is conceived more in the form of surplus labour.

"To teach that the wealth and power of a nation depend on its *capital* is to make industry ancillary to riches, to make men subservient to property" ([Ravenstone, *Thoughts on the Funding System, and its Effects*, London, 1824,] p. 7).

The opposition evoked by the Ricardian theory—on the basis of its own assumptions—has the following characteristic feature.

To the same extent as political economy developed—and this development finds its most trenchant expression in Ricardo, as far as fundamental principles are concerned—it presented labour as the sole element of value and the only creator of use-values, and the development of the productive forces as the only real means for increasing wealth; the greatest possible development of the productive power of labour as the economic basis of society. This is, in fact, the foundation of *capitalist production*. Ricardo's work, in particular, which demonstrates that the law of value is not invalidated either by landed property or by capitalist accumulation, etc., is, in reality, only concerned with eliminating all contradictions or phenomena which appear to run counter to this conception. But in the same measure as it is understood that labour is the *sole* source of exchange-value and the active source of use-value, *"capital"* is likewise conceived by the same economists, in particular by Ricardo (and even more by Torrens, Malthus, Bailey, and others after him), as the regulator of production, the source of wealth and the aim of production, whereas labour is regarded as wage-labour, whose representative and real instrument is inevitably a pauper (to which Malthus's theory of population contributed), a mere production cost and instrument of production dependent on a minimum wage and forced to drop even below this minimum as soon as the existing quantity of labour is "superfluous" for capital. In this contradiction, political economy merely expressed the essence of capitalist production or, if you like, of wage-labour, of labour alienated from itself, which stands confronted by the wealth it has created as alien wealth, by its own productive power as the productive power of its product, by its enrichment as its own impoverishment and by its social power as the power of society. But this definite, *specific*, historical form of social labour which is exemplified in capitalist production is proclaimed by these economists as the general, eternal form, as a natural phenomenon, and *these* relations of production as the absolutely (not historically) necessary, natural and reasonable relations of social labour. Their thoughts being entirely confined within the bounds of capitalist production, they assert that the *contradictory* form in which social labour manifests itself there, is just as necessary as labour itself freed from this contradiction. Since in the selfsame breath they proclaim on the one hand, *labour* as such (for them, labour is synonymous with wage-labour) and on the other, *capital* as such—that is the poverty of the workers and the wealth of the idlers—to be the sole source of wealth, they are perpetually involved in absolute contradictions without being in the slightest degree aware of them. (*Sismondi* was epoch-making in political economy because he had an inkling of this contradiction.) Ricardo's phrase "labour *or* capital"[80] reveals in a most striking fashion both the contradiction inherent in the terms and the naïvety with which they are stated to be identical.

Since the same real development which provided bourgeois political economy with this striking theoretical expression, unfolded the real contradictions contained in it, especially the contradiction between the growing wealth of the English "nation" and the growing misery of the workers, and since moreover these contradictions are given a *theoretically* compelling if unconscious expression in the Ricardian theory, etc., it was natural for those thinkers ||XV-862| who rallied to the side of the proletariat to seize on this contradiction, for which they found the theoretical ground already prepared. Labour is the sole source of exchange-value and the only active creator of use-value. This is what you say. On the other hand, you say that *capital* is everything, and the worker is nothing or a mere production cost of capital. You have refuted yourselves. Capital is *nothing* but defrauding of the worker. *Labour* is *everything*.

This, in fact, is the ultimate meaning of all the writings which defend the interests of the proletariat from the Ricardian standpoint basing themselves on his assumptions. Just as little as he [Ricardo] understands the identity of *capital* and *labour* in his own system, do they *understand* the contradiction they describe. That is why the most important among them—Hodgskin, for example—accept all the economic pre-conditions of capitalist production as eternal forms and only desire to eliminate capital, which is both the basis and necessary consequence [of these pre-conditions].

Ravenstone's main idea is as follows:

The development of the productive power of labour creates *capital* or *property*, in other words a surplus product for "idlers", non-workers; and indeed the more the productive power of labour develops, the more it produces this, its parasitical excrescence which sucks it dry. Whether the title to this surplus product, or the power to appropriate the product of other people's labour, accrues to the non-worker because he already possesses wealth, or because he possesses land, landed property, does not affect the case. Both are *capital*, that is, mastery over the product of other people's labour. For Ravenstone property is merely *appropriation* of the products of other people's labour and this is only possible insofar as and in the degree that *productive industry* develops. By productive industry Ravenstone understands industry which produces necessaries. Unproductive industry, the *industry of consumption*,[81] is a consequence of the development of capital, or property. Ravenstone appears ascetic like the author of the pamphlet discussed above.[a] In this respect he himself remains a captive of the notions set forth by the economists.

---

[a] *The Source and Remedy of the National Difficulties, deduced from Principles of Political Economy, etc.*—Ed.

Without *capital*, without *property*, the necessaries of the workers would be produced in abundance, but there would be no luxury industry. Or it can also be said that Ravenstone, like the author of the pamphlet discussed above, understands or at least in fact admits the *historical necessity* of capital; since capital, according to the author of the pamphlet, produces *surplus labour* over and above the labour strictly necessary for the maintenance [of the worker] and at the same time leads to the creation of machinery (what he calls fixed capital) and gives rise to foreign trade, the world market, in order to utilise the surplus product filched from the workers partly to increase productive power, partly to give this surplus product the most diverse forms of use-value far removed from those required by necessity. Similarly, according to Ravenstone, no conveniences, no machinery, no luxury products would be produced without *capital and property*, neither would the development of the natural sciences have taken place, nor the literary and artistic productions which owe their existence to leisure, nor the urge of the wealthy to receive an equivalent for their "surplus product" from the non-workers.

Ravenstone and the pamphleteer do not say this in justification of capital, but simply seize on it as a point of attack because all this is done in *opposition* to [the interest of] the workers and not *for* them. But in fact they thus admit that this is a result of capitalist production, which is therefore a historical form of social development, even though it stands in contradiction to that part of the population which constitutes the basis of that whole development. In this respect they share the narrow-mindedness of the economists (although from a diametrically opposite position) for they confuse the *contradictory form* of this development with its content. The latter wish to perpetuate the contradiction on account of its results. The former are determined to sacrifice the fruits which have developed within the antagonistic form, in order to get rid of the contradiction. This distinguishes their opposition to [bourgeois] political economy from that of contemporary people like Owen; likewise from that of Sismondi, who harks back to antiquated forms of the contradiction in order to be rid of it in its acute form.

[Ravenstone writes:]

It is the "wants" of the poor which "constitute his" (the rich man's) "wealth.... When all were equal, none would labour for another. The necessaries of life would be overabundant whilst its comforts were entirely wanting" (op. cit., p. 10).

"The industry which produces is the parent of property; that which aids consumption is its child" (loc. cit., p. 12).

"It is this[a] growth of property, this greater ability to maintain idle men, and unproductive industry, that in political economy is called capital" (loc. cit., p. 13).

"As the destination of property is expense, as without that it is wholly useless to its owner, its existence is intimately connected with that ||863| of the industry of consumption" (loc. cit.).

"If each man's *labour were but enough ·to procure his own food*, there *could be no property*, and no part of a people's industry could be turned away to work for the wants of the imagination" (loc. cit., pp. 14-15).

"In every [subsequent] stage of society, as increased numbers and better contrivances add to each man's power of production, the *number of those who labour is gradually diminished*.... Property grows from the improvement of the means of production; its sole business is the encouragement of idleness. When each man's labour is barely sufficient for his own subsistence, as there can be no property, there will be no idle man. When one man's labour can maintain five, there will be four idle men for one employed in production: in no other way can the produce be consumed. ... the object of society is to magnify the idle at the expense of·the industrious, to create power out of plenty" (loc. cit., p. 11).

⟨With regard to rent he says (not quite correctly, for it is precisely here that it is necessary to explain why rent accrues to the landlord and not to the farmer, the industrial capitalist) what applies to surplus-value in general, insofar as it develops as a result of the increase in the productivity of labour.

"In the early stages of society, when men have no artificial assistance to their powers of industry, the proportion of their earnings which can be afforded to rent is exceedingly small: for land [...] has no natural value, it owes all its produce to industry. But every increase of skill adds to the proportion which can be reserved for rent. Where the labour of nine is required for the maintenance of ten, only one-tenth of the gross produce can be given to rent. Where one man's labour is sufficient for the maintenance of five, four-fifths will go to rent, or the other charges of the state, which can only be provided for out of the surplus produce of industry. The first proportion seems to have prevailed in England at the time of the Conquest, the last is that which actually takes place" now since "only one-fifth part of the people are [...] employed in the cultivation of the land"... (op. cit., pp. 45-46).

"... so true it is that society turns every improvement but to the increase of idleness"... (loc. cit., p. 48).⟩

Note. An original piece of work. Its real subject is the modern system of national debt, as its title indicates.

Amongst other things he says:

---

[a] In the manuscript "The". —*Ed.*

"... the history of the last thirty years[a] [...] has achieved no higher adventure than the turning of a few Jews into gentlemen, and a few blockheads into political economists" (op. cit., pp. 66-67).

The funding system has one beneficial consequence although "the ancient gentry of the land" are robbed "of a large portion of their property" in order "to transfer it to these new fangled hidalgos as a reward for their skill in the arts of fraud and peculation.... If it encourage fraud and meanness; if it clothe quackery and pretension in the garb of wisdom; if it turn a whole people into a nation of jobbers ... if it break down all the prejudices of rank and birth to render money the only distinction among men ... it destroys the perpetuity of property..." (op. cit., pp. 51-52).

3. Hodgskin

Labour Defended against the Claims of Capital; or, the Unproductiveness of Capital Proved. By a Labourer, London, 1825. (*With reference to the Present Combinations amongst Journeymen.*)

Thomas Hodgskin, *Popular Political Economy. Four Lectures delivered at the London Mechanics' Institution*, London, 1827.

The anonymous first work is also by Hodgskin. Whereas the pamphlets mentioned previously and a series of similar ones have disappeared without trace, these writings, especially the first one, made a considerable stir and are still regarded as belonging to the most important works of English political economy (see John Lalor, *Money and Morals*, London, 1852). We shall consider each of these works in turn.

[a) The Thesis of the Unproductiveness of Capital as a Necessary Conclusion from Ricardo's Theory]

Labour Defended etc. As the title indicates, the author wishes to prove the *"unproductiveness of capital"*.

Ricardo does not assert that capital is *productive of value*. It only adds its own value to the product, and its own value depends on the labour-time required for its reproduction. It only has value as accumulated labour (or rather ||864|, materialised labour) and it only adds this—its value—to the product in which it is embodied. It is true that he is inconsistent when discussing

---

[a] In the manuscript "The entire war against the French Revolution" instead of "the history of the last thirty years".—*Ed.*

the general rate of profit. But this is precisely the contradiction which his opponents attacked.

As far as the productivity of capital in relation to *use-value* is concerned, this is construed by Smith, Ricardo and others, and by political economists in general, as meaning nothing else than that products of previous useful work serve anew as means of production, as objects of labour, instruments of labour and means of subsistence for the workers. The objective conditions of labour do not face the worker, as in the primitive stages, as mere natural objects (as such, they are never capital), but as natural objects already transformed by human activity. But in this sense the word "capital" is quite superfluous and meaningless. Wheat is nourishing not because it is capital but because it is wheat. The use-value of wool derives from the fact that it is wool, not capital. In the same way, the action of steam-powered machinery has nothing in common with its existence as capital. It would do the same work if it were not "capital" and if it belonged, not to the factory owner, but to the workers. All these things serve in the real labour process because of the relationship which exists between them as *use-values*—not as exchange-values and still less as capital—and the labour which sets them in motion. Their productivity in the real labour process, or rather the productivity of the labour materialised in them, is due to their nature as objective conditions of real labour and not to their *social existence* as *alienated, independent conditions* which confront the worker and are embodied in the capitalist, the *master* over living labour. It is as *wealth*, as *Hopkins* (not our Hodgskin) rightly says,[82] and not as *"net"* wealth, as product and not as "net" product, that they are here consumed and used. It is true that the particular social form of these things in relation to labour and their real determinateness as factors of the labour process are as confused and inseparably interwoven with one another in the minds of the economists as they are in the mind of the capitalist. Nevertheless, as soon as they analyse the labour process, they are compelled to abandon the term capital completely and to speak of *material of labour, means of labour, and means of subsistence*. But the determinate form of the product as material, instrument and means of subsistence of the worker expresses nothing but the relationship of these *objective* conditions to labour; labour itself appears as the activity which dominates them. It says however nothing at all about [the relationship of] labour and capital, only about the relationship of the purposeful activity of men to their own products in the process of reproduction. They neither cease to be products of labour nor mere objects which are at the disposal of labour. They merely express the relationship in which labour appropriates the objective world which it has created itself, at any rate in this form; but they do not by any means express *any other domination of these things over labour*, apart from the fact that activity must be appropriate to the material, otherwise it would not be purposeful activity, labour.

One can only speak of the *productivity* of capital if one regards it as the embodiment of definite social relations of production. But if it is conceived in this way, then the historically transitory character of this relationship becomes at once evident, and the general recognition of this fact is incompatible with the continued existence of this relationship, which itself creates the means for its abolition.

But the economists do not regard it [capital] as such a relationship because they cannot admit its *relative* character, and do not understand it either. They simply express in theoretical terms the notions of the practical men who are engrossed in capitalist production, dominated by it and interested in it.

In his polemic [with the bourgeois economists], Hodgskin himself starts out from a standpoint which is economically narrow-minded. Insofar as they [the economists] define capital as an eternal production relation, they reduce it to the general relations of labour to its material conditions, relations which are common to all modes of production and do not express the specific nature of capital. Insofar as they hold that capital produces "value", the best of them and [especially] Ricardo, admit that it does not produce any value which it has not received and constantly continues to receive from labour, since the value of a product is determined by the labour-time necessary to reproduce it, that is, its value is the result of living, present labour and not of past labour. And as Ricardo emphasises, increase in the productivity of labour is marked by the continuous devaluation of the products of past labour. On the other hand, the economists continually mix up the definite, specific form in which these things constitute capital with their nature as things and as simple elements of every labour process. The mystification contained in capital—as *employer of labour*—is not explained by them, but it is constantly expressed by them unconsciously, for it is inseparable from the material aspect of capital.

||867|[83] The first pamphlet[a] draws the correct conclusions from Ricardo and reduces surplus-value to *surplus labour*. This is in contrast to Ricardo's opponents and followers who continue to adhere to his confusion of surplus-value with profit.

In opposition to them, the second pamhlet[b] defines relative surplus-value more exactly as being dependent on the level of development of the productive power of labour. Ricardo says the same thing, but he avoids the conclusion drawn by the second pamphlet [that by Ravenstone], namely, that the increase in the productive power of labour only increases capital, the wealth of others which dominates labour.

Finally, the third pamphlet[c] bursts forth with the general statement, which is the inevitable consequence of Ricardo's presentation—that *capital is unproductive*. This is in contrast to Torrens, Malthus and others, who, taking one aspect of the Ricardian theory as their point of departure, turn Ricardo's statement that labour is the creator of value into the opposite— that capital is the creator of value. The pamphlet, moreover, disputes the statement—which recurs in all of them, from Smith to Malthus, especially in the latter where it is elevated into an absolute dogma (ditto in the case of James Mill)—that labour is absolutely dependent on the *amount of capital available*, as this is the condition of its existence.

Pamphlet No. 1 ends with the statement:

"Wealth is disposable time, and nothing more".[d]

[b) Polemic against the Ricardian Definition of Capital as Accumulated Labour. The Concept of Coexisting Labour. Underestimation of the Importance of Materialised Past Labour. Available Wealth in Relation to the Movement of Production]

According to Hodgskin, circulating capital is nothing but the *juxtaposition* of the different kinds of social labour (coexisting labour) and accumulation is nothing but the amassing of the productive powers of social labour, so that the accumulation of the skill and knowledge (scientific power) of the workers themselves is the chief form of accumulation, and infinitely more

---

[a] *The Source and Remedy of the National Difficulties*, published anonymously.—*Ed.*

[b] Ravenstone, *Thoughts on the Funding System, and its Effects.*—*Ed.*

[c] *Labour Defended against the Claims of Capital*; or, the *Unproductiveness of Capital Proved*, which Hodgskin published anonymously.—*Ed.*

[d] In the manuscript "Wealth is nothing but disposable time".—*Ed.*

important than the accumulation—which goes hand in hand with it and merely represents it—of the *existing objective* conditions of this accumulated activity. These objective conditions are only nominally accumulated and must be constantly produced anew and consumed anew.

"... productive capital and skilled labour are [...] one." "Capital and a labouring population are precisely synonymous" ([Hodgskin, *Labour Defended against the Claims of Capital*, London, 1825,] p. 33).

These are simply further elaborations of Galiani's thesis:

"... The real wealth ... is man" (*Della Moneta*, Custodi. Parte Moderna, t. III, p. 229).

The whole objective world, the "world of commodities", vanishes here as a mere aspect, as the merely passing activity, constantly performed anew, of socially producing men. Compare this "idealism" with the crude, material fetishism into which the Ricardian theory develops in the writings "of this incredible cobbler", McCulloch, where not only the difference between man and animal disappears but even the difference between a living organism and an inanimate object. And then let them say that as against the lofty idealism of bourgeois political economy, the proletarian opposition has been preaching a crude materialism directed exclusively towards the satisfaction of coarse appetites.

In his investigations into the productivity of capital, Hodgskin is remiss in that he does not distinguish between how far it is a question of producing use-values or exchange-values.

Further—but this has historical justification—he takes capital as it is defined by the economists. On the one hand (insofar as it operates in the real process of production) as a merely physical condition of labour, and therefore of importance only as a material element of labour, and (in the process of the production of value) nothing more than the quantity of labour measured by time, that is, nothing different from this quantity of labour itself. On the other hand, although in fact, insofar as it appears in the real process of production, it is a mere *name for, and rechristening of*, labour itself, it is represented as the power dominating and engendering labour, as the basis of the productivity of labour and as wealth alien to labour. And this without any intermediate links. This is how he found it. And he counterposes the real aspect of economic development to this bourgeois humbug.

[CHAPTER XXI]

"... capital is a sort of *cabalistic word*, like church or state, or any other of those *general terms* which are invented by those who fleece the rest of mankind to conceal the hand that shears them" (*Labour Defended etc.*, p. 17).

In accordance with the tradition he found prevailing among the economists, he distinguishes between circulating and fixed capital; circulating capital moreover is described as that part which mainly consists of, or is used as, means of subsistence for the workers.

It is maintained "that *division of labour* is a consequence of *previous accumulation of capital*". But "the effects attributed to *a stock of commodities*, under *the name of circulating capital*, are caused by *coexisting labour*" (op. cit., pp. 8, 9).

Faced with the crude conception of the economists, it is quite correct to say that "circulating capital" is only "the name" for "a stock of" certain "commodities". Since the economists have not analysed the specific social relationship which is represented in the *metamorphosis of commodities*, they can understand *only* the material aspect of circulating capital. All the differentiations in capital arising from the circulation process ||868|—in fact the circulation process itself—are actually nothing but the metamorphosis of commodities (determined by their relationship to wage-labour as capital) as an aspect of the reproduction process.

Division of labour is, in one sense, nothing but *coexisting labour*, that is, the coexistence of *different* kinds of labour which are represented in *different kinds* of products or rather commodities. The *division of labour* in the capitalist sense, as the breaking down of the particular labour which produces a definite commodity into a series of simple and co-ordinated operations divided up amongst different workers, presupposes the division of labour within society outside the workshop, as *separation of occupations*. On the other hand, it [division of labour] increases it [separation of occupations]. The product is increasingly produced as a commodity in the strict sense of the word, its exchange-value becomes the more independent of its immediate existence as use-value—in other words its production becomes more and more independent of its consumption by the producers and of its existence as use-value for the producers—the more one-sided it itself becomes, and the greater the variety of commodities for which it is exchanged, the greater the kinds of use-values in which its exchange-value is expressed, and the larger the market for it becomes. The more this happens, the more the product can be produced as a commodity; therefore also on an increasingly *large scale*. The producer's indifference to the use-value of his product is expressed *quantitatively* in the amounts in which he produces it, which bear no relation to his own consumption needs, even when he is at the same time a consumer of his own product. The *division of labour* within the workshop is one of the methods used in this *mass production* and consequently in the production of the product [as a commodity]. Thus the division of labour within the workshop is based on the division of occupations in society.

The size of the market has two aspects. First, the mass of consumers, their numbers. But secondly, also, the number of occupations which are independent of one another. The latter is possible without the former. For example, when spinning and weaving become divorced from "domestic" industry and agriculture, all those engaged in agriculture become a market for spinners and weavers. They likewise [form markets] for one another as a consequence of the separation of their occupations. What the division of labour in society presupposes above all, is that the different kinds of labour have become independent of one another in such a way that their products confront one another as commodities and must be exchanged, that is, undergo the metamorphosis of commodities and stand in relation to one another as *commodities*. (This is why in the Middle Ages, the towns prohibited the spread of as many professions as possible to the countryside, not merely for the purpose of preventing competition—the only aspect seen by Adam Smith—but in order to create markets for themselves.) On the other hand, the proper development of the division of labour presupposes a certain density of population. The development of the division of labour in the workshop depends even more on this density of population. This latter division is, to a certain extent, a pre-condition for the former and in turn intensifies it still further. It does this by splitting formerly correlated occupations into separate and independent ones, also by differentiating and increasing the indirect preliminary work they require; and as a result of the increase in both production and the population and the freeing of capital and labour it creates new wants and new modes of satisfying them.

Therefore when Hodgskin says "division of labour" is the effect not of *a stock of commodities* called circulating capital but of *"coexisting labour"*, it would be tautologous if in this context he understood by division of labour the separation of trades. It would only mean that division of labour is the cause or the effect of the division of labour. He can therefore only mean that division of labour within the workshop depends on the separation of occupations, the social division of labour, and is, in a certain sense, its effect.

It is not a stock of commodities which gives rise to this separation of occupations and with it the division of labour in the workshop, but it is the *separation of occupations* (and division of labour) that is manifested in the stock of commodities, or rather in the fact that a *stock of products* becomes a *stock of commodities*. ⟨The properties, the characteristic features of the *capitalist mode of production* and therefore of capital itself insofar as it expresses a definite relation of the producers to one another and to their products, are inevitably always described by the economists as the properties of the objects.⟩

||869| If, however, "previous accumulation of capital" is being discussed from an economic standpoint (see Turgot, Smith, etc.) as a condition for the division of labour, then what is understood by this is the previous concentration of a *stock of commodities* as *capital* in the possession of the buyer of labour, since the kind of co-operation characteristic of the division of labour presupposes a *conglomeration of workers*—consequently, accumulation of the means of subsistence necessary for them while they are working—increased productivity of labour—consequently, increase in the amount of raw materials, tools and auxiliary materials which must be available in order that labour proceeds continuously, since it constantly requires large amounts of these things—in short, of the objective conditions of production on a large scale.

Here, *accumulation of capital* cannot mean increase in the amount of means of subsistence, raw materials and instruments of labour as a *condition for the division of labour*, for insofar as the accumulation of capital is taken to mean this, it is a consequence of the division of labour, not its pre-condition.

Similarly, *accumulation of capital* cannot here mean that means of subsistence for the workers must be available in general before new necessaries are reproduced, or that products of their labour must constitute the raw material and means of labour for the new production which they carry out. For this is the pre-condition of labour in general and was just as true *before the development* of the division of labour as it is after it. *On the one hand*: if we consider the material element of *accumulation*, it means nothing more than that the division of labour requires the concentration of means of subsistence and means of labour at particular points, whereas formerly these were scattered and dispersed as long as the workers in individual trades— which could not have been very numerous under these conditions—themselves carried out all the manifold and consecutive operations required for the production of one or more products. Not an increase in *absolute* terms is presupposed, but *concentration*, the gathering together of more at a given point, and of *relatively* more [means of labour] compared with the numbers of workers brought together there. More flax, for example, [is used] by the workers in manufacture (in proportion to their numbers) than the relative amount of flax required in proportion to all the peasants—both men and women—who used to spin flax as a sideline. Hence, *conglomeration* of workers, *concentration* of raw materials, instruments, and means of subsistence.

On the other hand: if we consider the historical foundation on which this process develops, from which manufacture arises, the industrial mode of production whose characteristic feature is the division of labour, then this concentration can only take place in the form that these workers are assembled together as wage-workers, that is, as workers who must sell their labour-power because their conditions of labour confront them as alien property, as an independent, alien force. This implies that these conditions of labour confront them as *capital*; in other words, these means of subsistence and means of labour (or, what amounts to the same thing, the disposal of them through the intermediary of money) are in the hands of individual owners of money or of commodities, who, as a result, become *capitalists*. The loss of the conditions of labour by the workers is expressed in the fact that these conditions become independent as capital or as things at the disposal of the capitalists.

Thus primitive accumulation, as I have already shown, means nothing but the separation of labour and the worker from the conditions of labour, which confront him as independent forces.[84] The course of history shows that this separation is a factor in social development. Once capital exists, the capitalist mode of production itself evolves in such a way that it maintains and reproduces this separation on a constantly increasing scale until the historical reversal takes place.

It is not the ownership of money which makes the capitalist a capitalist. For money to be transformed into capital, the prerequisites for capitalist production must exist, whose first historical presupposition is that separation. The separation, and therefore the existence of the means of labour as capital, is given in capitalist production; this separation which constantly reproduces itself and expands, is the foundation of production.

Accumulation by means of the reconversion of profit, or surplus product, into capital now becomes a continuous process as a result of which the increased products of labour which are at the same time its objective conditions, conditions of reproduction, continuously confront labour as *capital*, i.e., as forces—personified in the capitalist—which are alienated from labour and dominate it. Consequently, it becomes a specific function of the capitalist to accumulate, that is, to reconvert a part of the surplus product into conditions of labour. And the stupid economist concludes from this that if this operation did not proceed in this contradictory, specific way, it could not take place at all. Reproduction on an extended scale is inseparably connected in his mind with *accumulation*, the capitalist form of this reproduction.

||870| Accumulation merely presents as a *continuous process* what in *primitive accumulation* appears as a distinct historical process, as the process of the emergence of capital and as a transition from one mode of production to another.

The economists, caught as they are in the toils of the notions proper to the agents of the capitalist mode of production, advance a double *quid pro quo*, each side of which depends on the other.

On the one hand, they transform capital from a relationship into a thing, a stock of commodities (already forgetting that commodities themselves are *not* things) which, insofar as they serve as conditions of production for new labour, are called capital and, with regard to their mode of reproduction, are called circulating capital.

On the other hand, they transform things into capital, that is, they consider the social relationship which is represented in them and through them as an attribute which belongs to the thing as such as soon as it enters as an element into the labour process or the technological process.

[*On the one hand,*] *the concentration* in the hands of non-workers *of raw materials and of the disposition over the means of subsistence*, i.e., the powers dominating labour, the *preliminary* condition for the division of labour (later on, the division of labour increases not only concentration, but also the amount [available for] concentration by increasing the productivity of labour), in other words the *preliminary accumulation of capital* as the condition for the division of labour therefore means for them the augmentation or concentration (they do not differentiate between the two) of means of subsistence and means of labour.

On the other hand, these necessaries and means of labour would not operate as objective conditions of production if these things did not possess the attribute of being capital, if the product of labour, the condition of labour, did not absorb labour itself; [if] past labour did not absorb living labour, and if these things did not belong to themselves or by proxy to the capitalist instead of to the worker.

As if the division of labour was not just as possible if its conditions belonged to the associated workers (although historically it could not at first appear in this form, but can only achieve it as a result of capitalist production) and were regarded by the latter as their own products and the material elements of their own activity, which they are by their very nature.

Furthermore, because in the capitalist mode of production capital appropriates the surplus product of the worker, consequently, because it *has appropriated* the products of labour and these now confront the worker in the form of capital, it is clear that the conversion of the surplus product into conditions of labour can only be initiated by the capitalist and only in the form that he turns the products of labour—which he has appropriated without any equivalent—into means of production of new labour performed without receiving an equivalent. Consequently, the extension of reproduction appears as the transformation of profit into capital and as a *saving* by the capitalist who, instead of consuming the surplus product which he has acquired gratis, converts it anew into a means of exploitation, but is able to do this only insofar as he converts the surplus product again into productive capital; this entails the conversion of surplus product into means of labour. As a result, the economists conclude that the surplus product cannot serve as an element of new production if it has not been transformed previously from the product of the worker into the property of his employer in order to serve as capital once again and to repeat the old process of exploitation. The more inferior economists add to this the idea of hoarding and the accumulation of treasure. Even the better ones—Ricardo, for example—transfer the notion of renunciation from the hoarder to the capitalist.

The economists do not conceive capital as a relation. They cannot do so without at the same time conceiving it as a historically transitory, i.e., a relative—not an absolute—form of production. Hodgskin himself does not share this concept. Insofar as it justifies capital it does not justify its justification by the economists, but on the contrary refutes it. Thus Hodgskin is not concerned in all this.

As far as matters stood between him and the economists, the kind of polemic he had to wage seemed to be mapped out beforehand and quite simple. To put it simply, he had to vindicate the one aspect which the economists elaborate "scientifically" against the fetishistic conception they accept without thinking, naïvely and unconsciously from the capitalist way of looking at things.

The utilisation of the products of previous labour, of labour in general, as materials, tools, means of subsistence, is necessary if the worker wants to use his products for new production. This particular mode of consumption of his products is productive. But what on earth has this kind of utilisation, this mode of consumption of his product, to do with the domination of his product over him, with its existence as capital, with the concentration ||870a| in the hands of individual capitalists of the right to dispose of raw materials and means of subsistence and the exclusion of the workers from ownership of their products? What has it to do with the fact that first of all they have to hand over their product gratis to a third party in order to buy it back again with their own labour and, what is more, they have to give him more labour in exchange than is contained in the product and thus have to create more surplus product for him?

Past labour exists here in two forms. [In one] as *product, use-value*. The process of production requires that the workers consume one portion of this product [as means of subsistence, and use] another portion as raw materials and instruments of labour. This applies also to the technological process and merely demonstrates the relations that have to exist *in industrial production* between the workers and the products of their own labour, their own products, in order to turn them into means of production.

Or, [past labour exists as] *value*. This only shows that the value of their new product represents not only their present, but also their past labour, and that by increasing it they retain the old value, because they increase it.

The claim put forward by the capitalist has nothing to do with this process as such. It is true that he has appropriated the products of labour, of past labour, and that he therefore possesses a means for acquiring new products and living labour. This, however, is precisely the kind of procedure against which protests are made. The preliminary concentration and accumulation necessary for the "division of labour" must not take the form of *accumulation of capital*. It does not follow that because this [concentration'] is necessary, the capitalist must inevitably have the disposal of the conditions of labour of today created by the labour of yesterday. If accumulation of capital is supposed to be nothing but accumulated labour, it by no means implies that accumulation of other people's labour has **to** take place.

Hodgskin however does not follow this simple path, and at first this seems strange. In his polemic against the productivity of capital, to begin with, against circulating and then even more, against fixed capital, he seems to oppose or to reject the importance of *past labour*, or of its *product* for the reproduction process as a condition of new labour. From this follows the importance of past labour embodied in products for labour as present ἐνέργεια.[a] Why this change?

Since the economists identify past labour with *capital*—past labour being understood in this case not only in the sense of concrete labour embodied in the product, but also in the sense of social labour, materialised labour-time—it is understandable that they, the Pindars of capital, emphasise the *objective* elements of production and overestimate their importance as against the *subjective element*, living, immediate labour. For them, labour only becomes efficacious when it becomes *capital* and confronts itself, the passive element confronting its active counterpart. The producer is therefore controlled by the product, the subject by the object, labour which is being embodied by labour embodied in an object, etc. In all these conceptions, past labour appears not merely as an objective factor of living labour, subsumed

---

[a] Activity.—*Ed.*

by it, but vice versa; not as an element of the power of living labour, but as a power over this labour. The economists ascribe a false importance to the material factors of labour compared with labour itself in order to have also a *technological* justification for the *specific social form*, i.e., the *capitalist form*, in which the relationship of labour to the conditions of labour is turned upside-down, so that it is not the worker who makes use of the conditions of labour, but the conditions of labour which make use of the worker. *It is for this reason* that Hodgskin asserts on the contrary that this physical factor, that is, the entire material wealth, is quite unimportant compared with the living process of production and that, in fact, this wealth has no value in itself, but only insofar as it is a factor in the living production process. In doing so, he underestimates somewhat the value which the labour of the past has for the labour of the present, but in opposing economic fetishism this is quite all right.

If in capitalist production—hence in political economy, its theoretical expression—past labour were met with only as a pedestal etc. created by labour itself, then such a controversial issue would not have arisen. It only exists because in the real life of capitalist production, as well as in its theory, *materialised labour* appears as a contradiction to itself, to *living labour*. In exactly the same way in religious reasoning, the product of thought not only claims but exercises domination over thought itself. |870a||

||865| The proposition

"... the effects attributed to a *stock of commodities*, under the name of circulating capital, are caused by *coexisting labour*" (op. cit., p. 9),

means first of all:

the simultaneous coexistence of living labour brings about a large part of the effects which are attributed to the product of previous labour called circulating capital.

For example, a part of circulating capital consists of the stock of means of subsistence which the capitalist is supposed to have stored up to support the labourer while working.

The *formation* of a *reserve stock* is by no means a feature peculiar to capitalist production although, since under it production and consumption are greater than ever before, the amount of commodities on the market—the amount of commodities in the sphere of circulation—is likewise greater than ever before. Here memories of hoarding, of *accumulation of treasure by hoarders* are still discernible.

The consumption fund must be disregarded first of all because we are speaking here of capital and of industrial production. What has reached the sphere of individual consumption, whether it is consumed more quickly or more slowly, has ceased to be capital. ⟨Although it can be partly reconverted into capital, for instance, houses, parks, crockery.⟩

"Do all the capitalists of Europe possess at this moment one week's food and clothing for all the labourers they employ? Let us first examine the question as to food. One portion of the food of the people is *bread*, which is never prepared till within a few hours of the time when it is eaten.... The produce [...] of the baker, cannot be stored up. In no case can the material of bread, whether it exist as corn or flour, be *preserved without continual labour*. [...] His conviction[a] that he will obtain bread when he requires it, and his master's conviction that the money he pays him will enable him to obtain it, arise simply from the fact that the bread has always been obtained when required" (loc. cit., p. 10).

"Another article of the labourer's food is milk, and milk is manufactured ... twice a day. If it be said that the cattle to supply it are already there;— why the answer is, they require *constant attention and constant labour, and their food, through the greater part of the year, is of daily growth*. The fields in which they pasture, require the hand of man. [...] The meat, also [...] it cannot be stored up, for it begins instantly to deteriorate after it is brought to market" (loc. cit., p. 10).

Because of moths, even of clothing "... only *a very small stock is ever prepared*, compared to the general consumption" (loc. cit., p. 11).

"Mr. Mill says, and says justly, 'what is annually produced is annually consumed', so that, in fact, *to enable men to carry on all those operations which extend beyond a year*, there cannot be *any stock of commodities stored up*. Those who undertake them must rely, therefore, not on *any commodities already created*, but that other men will labour and produce what they are to subsist on till their own products are completed. Thus, should the labourer admit that some accumulation of circulating capital is necessary for operations terminated within the year [...] it is plain, that in all operations which extend beyond a year, the labourer does not, and he cannot, rely on *accumulated* capital" (loc. cit., p. 12).

"If we duly consider the number and importance of those wealth-producing operations which are not completed within the year, and the numberless products of daily labour, necessary to subsistence, which are consumed as soon as produced, we shall [...] be sensible that *the success and productive power of every d i f f e r e n t s p e c i e s o f l a b o u r is at all times m o r e dependent on the coexisting productive labour of other men than on any* accumulation of circulating capital" (loc. cit., p. 13).

"... it is by the *command* the capitalist possesses *over the labour of some men*, not by his possessing a *stock of commodities*, that he is *enabled* to support and consequently employ *other labourers*" (loc. cit., p. 14).

"... the only thing which can be said to be stored up or previously prepared, is the *skill of the labourer*" (loc. cit., p. 12).

---

[a] In the manuscript this reads: "The conviction of the worker employed by the cotton spinner...."—*Ed.*

"... all the effects usually attributed to accumulation of circulating capital are derived from the *accumulation and storing up of skilled labour*; and [...] this most important operation is performed, as far as the great mass of the labourers is concerned without any *circulating capital* whatever" (loc. cit., p. 13).

"... the number of labourers must at all times depend on the *quantity of circulating capital*; o r, as I should say, on the quantity of the *products of coexisting labour*, which labourers are allowed to consume..." (op. cit., p. 20).

||866| "Circulating capital [...] is created only for consumption; while fixed capital [...] is made, not to be consumed, but to aid the labourer in producing those things which are to be consumed" (loc. cit., p. 19).

Thus first of all:

"... the success and productive power of every different species of labour is at all times more dependent on the *coexisting* productive labour of other men than on any accumulation of circulating capital" [op. cit., p. 13], that is, of "commodities already created". These "already created commodities" confront "the products of coexisting labour".

{The part of capital which consists of instruments and materials of labour is as "commodities already created" always a pre-condition in each *particular* branch of production. It is impossible to spin cotton which has not yet been produced, to operate spindles which have yet to be manufactured, or to burn coal which has not yet been brought up from the mine. These always enter the [production] process as forms of existence of *previous labour*. Existing labour thus depends on antecedent labour and not only on coexisting labour, although this antecedent labour, whether in the form of means of labour or materials of labour, can only be of any use (productive use) when it is in contact with living labour as a material element of it. Only as an element of industrial consumption, i.e., consumption by labour.

But when considering circulation and the reproduction process, we have seen that it is only possible to reproduce the commodity after it is finished and converted into money, because *simultaneously* all its elements have been produced and reproduced by means of coexisting labour.[85]

A twofold progression takes place in production. Cotton, for example, advances from one phase of production to another. It is produced first of all as raw material, then it is subjected to a number of operations until it is fit to be exported or, if it is further worked up in the same country, it is handed over to a spinner. It then goes on from the spinner to the weaver and from the weaver to the bleacher, dyer, finisher, and thence to various workshops where it is worked up for definite uses, i.e., articles of clothing, bed-linen, etc. Finally it leaves the last producer for the consumer and enters into individual consumption if it does not enter into industrial consumption as means (not material) of labour. But whether it is to be consumed industrially or individually, it has acquired its final form as use-value. What emerges from one sphere of production as a product enters another as a condition of production, and in this way, goes through many successive phases until it receives its last finish as use-value. Here previous labour appears continually as the condition for existing labour.

Simultaneously, however, while the product is advancing in this way from one phase to another, while it is undergoing this real metamorphosis, production is being carried on at every stage. While the weaver spins the yarn, the spinner is simultaneously spinning cotton, and fresh quantities of raw cotton are in the process of production.

Since the continuous, constantly repeated process of production is, at the same time, a process of reproduction, it is therefore equally dependent on the *coexisting labour* which produces the various phases of the product simultaneously, while the product is passing through metamorphosis from one phase to another. [Raw] cotton, yarn, fabric, are not only produced one after the other and from one another, but they are produced and reproduced *simultaneously*, alongside one another. What appears as the effect of antecedent labour, if one considers the production process of the individual commodity, presents itself at the same time as the effect of coexisting labour, if one considers the *reproduction process* of the commodity, that is, if one considers this production process in its continuous motion and in the entirety of its conditions, and not merely an isolated action or a limited part of it. There exists not only a cycle comprising various phases, but all the phases of the commodity are simultaneously produced in the various spheres and branches of production. If the same peasant just plants flax, then spins it, then weaves it, these operations are performed in succession, but not simultaneously as the mode of production based on the division of labour within society presupposes.

No matter what phase of the production process of an individual commodity is considered, the antecedent labour only acquires significance as a result of the living labour which it provides with the necessary conditions of production. On the other hand, however, these conditions of production without which living labour cannot realise itself always appear as the result of antecedent labour. Thus the co-operating labour of the contributing branches of labour always appears as a passive factor and, as such a passive factor, it is a pre-condition. The economists emphasise this aspect. In production and circulation, on the other hand, the mediating social labour on which the [production] process of the commodity in each particular phase depends and by which it is determined, appears as present, co-existing, contemporaneous labour. The early forms of the commodity and its successive or completed forms are produced simultaneously. Unless this happened it would not be possible, after it has undergone its real metamorphosis, to reconvert it from money into its conditions of existence. ||870b| A commodity is thus the product of antecedent labour only insofar as it is the product of contemporaneous living labour. From the capitalist point of view, therefore, all material wealth appears only as a fleeting aspect of the flow of production as a whole, which includes the process of circulation.}

[c)] **So-called Accumulation as a Mere Phenomenon of Circulation. (Stock, etc.—Circulation Reservoirs)**

Hodgskin examines only one of the constituent parts of circulating capital. One part of circulating capital is however continuously converted into fixed capital and auxiliary materials and only the other part is converted into articles of consumption. Moreover, even that part of circulating capital which is ultimately transformed into commodities intended for individual consumption always exists, alongside the final form in which it emerges from the finishing phase as end product, simultaneously in the earlier phases of production in its rudimentary forms—as raw material or semi-manufactured goods, removed in various degrees from the final form of the product—in which it cannot as yet enter into consumption.

The problem Hodgskin is concerned with is: what is the relation of the present labour performed by the worker for the capitalist to the labour embodied in his articles of consumption, the labour contained in those articles on which his wages are spent, which, in actual fact, are the use-values of which variable capital consists? It is admitted that the worker cannot labour without finding these articles ready for consumption. And that is why the economists say that circulating capital—the previous labour, commodities already created which the capitalist has stored up—is the condition for labour and, amongst other things, also the condition for the division of labour.

When the conditions of production, and especially circulating capital in Hodgskin's sense of the term, are being discussed, it is usual to declare that the capitalist must have accumulated the food which the worker has to consume before his new commodity is finished, that is, while he works, while the commodity he produces is only *in statu nascendi*.[a] This is shot through with the notion that the capitalist either gathers things like a hoarder or that *he* stores up a supply of food like the bees their honey.

This however is merely a *modus loquendi*.[b]

First of all, we are not speaking here of the shopkeepers who sell means of subsistence. These must naturally have a full stock in trade. Their stores, shops, etc. are simply reservoirs in which the various commodities are stored once they are ready for circulation. This kind of storing is merely an *interim period* in which the commodity remains until it leaves the sphere of circulation and enters that of consumption. It is its mode of existence as a *commodity* on the market. Strictly speaking, as a commodity it exists only in this form. It does not affect the matter whether, instead of being in the possession of the first seller (the producer), the commodity is in the possession of the third or fourth and finally passes into the possession of the seller who sells it to the real consumer. It merely means that, in the intermediate stage, exchange of capital (really of capital plus profit, for the producer sells not only the capital in the commodity but also the profit made on the capital) for capital is taking place, and in the last stage exchange of capital for revenue (provided the commodity is intended not for industrial but for individual consumption, as is assumed here).

The commodity which is a finished use-value and marketable, enters the market as a commodity, in the phase of circulation; all commodities enter this phase when they undergo their first metamorphosis, the transformation into money. If this is called "storing up" then it means nothing more than "circulation" or the existence of commodities as commodities. This kind of "storing" is exactly the opposite of treasure-hoarding, the aim of

---

[a] In the nascent state.—*Ed.*
[b] A mode of expression, a figure of speech.—*Ed.*

which is to retain commodities permanently in the form in which they are capable of entering into circulation, and it achieves this only by withdrawing commodities in the form of money from circulation. If production, and therefore also consumption, is varied and on a mass scale, then a greater quantity of the most diverse commodities will be found continually at this *stopping place*, at this *intermediate station*, in a word, in circulation or on the market. Regarded from the standpoint of *quantity*, storing on a large scale in this context means nothing more than production and consumption on a large scale.

The *stop* made by the *commodities*, their sojourn at this stage of the process, their presence on the market instead of in the mill or in a private house (as articles of consumption) or in the shop or the store of the shopkeeper, is only ||871| a tiny fraction of time in their life-process. The immobile, independent existence of this world of commodities, of things, is only illusory. The station is always full, but always full of different travellers. The same commodities (commodities of the same kind) are constantly produced anew in the sphere of production, available on the market and absorbed in consumption. Not the identical commodities, but commodities of the same type, can always be found in these three stages *simultaneously*. If the intermediate stage is prolonged so that the commodities which emerge anew from the sphere of production find the market still occupied by the old ones, then it becomes overcrowded, a stoppage occurs, the market is glutted, the commodities decline in value, there is *over-production*. Where, therefore, the intermediate stage of circulation acquires independent existence so that the flow of the stream is not merely slowed down, where the existence of the commodities in the circulation phase appears as *storing up*, then this is not brought about by a free act on the part of the producer, it is not an aim or an immanent aspect of production, any more than the flow of blood to the head leading to apoplexy is an immanent aspect of the circulation of the blood. Capital as *commodity capital* (and this is the form in which it appears in the circulation phase, on the market) must not become stationary, it must only constitute a pause in the movement. Otherwise the reproduction process is interrupted and the whole mechanism is thrown into confusion. This materialised wealth which is concentrated at a few points is—and can only be—very small in comparison to the continuous stream of production and consumption. Wealth, therefore, according to Smith, is *"the annual"* reproduction. It is not, that is to say, something out of the dim past. It is always something which emerges from yesterday. If, on the other hand, reproduction were to stagnate due to some disturbances or others, then the stores etc. would soon empty, there would be shortages and it would soon be evident that the permanency which the existing wealth appears to possess, is only the permanency of its being replaced, of its reproduction, that it is a continuous materialisation of social labour.

The movement C—M—C also takes place in the transactions of the shopkeeper. Insofar as he makes a "profit", it is a matter which does not concern us here. He sells goods and buys the same goods (the same type of goods) over again. He sells them to the consumer and buys them again from the producer. Here the same (type of) commodity is converted perpetually into money and money back again continuously into the same commodity. This movement, however, simply represents continuous reproduction, continuous production and consumption, for reproduction includes consumption. (The commodity must be sold, must reach the sphere of consumption in order that it can be reproduced.) It must be accepted as a use-value. (For C—M for the seller is M—C for the buyer, that is, the conversion of money into a commodity as use-value.) The reproduction process, since it is a unity of circulation and production, includes consumption, which is itself an aspect of circulation. Consumption is itself both an aspect and a condition of the reproduction process. If one considers the process in its entirety, the shopkeeper, in fact, pays the producer of the commodities with the same sum of money as the consumer pays him when he buys from him. He represents the consumer in his dealings with the producer and the producer in his dealings with the consumer. He is both seller and buyer of the same commodity. The money with which he pays is, in fact, considered from a purely formal standpoint, the final metamorphosis of the consumer's commodity. The latter transforms his money into the commodity as a use-value. The passing of the money into the shopkeeper's hands thus signifies the consumption of the commodity or, considered formally, the transition of the commodity from circulation into consumption. Insofar as he buys again from the producer with the money, this constitutes the first metamorphosis of the producer's commodity and signifies the transition of the commodity into the *intermediate stage*, where it remains as a *commodity* in the sphere of circulation. C—M—C, insofar as it concerns the transformation of the commodity into the consumer's money and the transformation back again of the money, whose owner is now the shopkeeper, into the same commodity (a commodity of the same kind), expresses merely the *constant* passing over of commodities into consumption, for the vacuum left by the commodity reaching the sphere of consumption must be filled by the commodity emerging from the production process and now entering this stage.

||872| The *period during which the commodity stays* in circulation and is replaced by new commodities naturally depends also on the length of time in which the commodities remain in the production sphere, that is, on the duration of their reproduction time, and varies in accordance with their different length. For example, the reproduction of corn requires a year. The corn harvested in the autumn, for example, of 1862 (insofar as it is not used again for seed) must suffice for the whole coming year—until autumn 1863. It is thrown all at once into circulation (it is already in circulation when it is placed in the farmers' granaries) and absorbed in the various reservoirs of circulation—storehouses, corn merchants, millers, etc. These reservoirs serve as channels both for the commodities issuing from production and those going to the consumer. As long as the commodities remain in one of them, they are *commodities* and are therefore on the market, in circulation. They are withdrawn only piecemeal, in small quantities, by the annual consumption. The replacement, the stream of new commodities which are to displace them, arrives only in the following year. Thus these reservoirs are only depleted gradually, in the measure that their replacements move forward. If there is a surplus and if the new harvest is above the average, then a stoppage takes place. The space which these particular commodities were to have occupied in the market is overstocked. In order to permit the whole quantity to find a place on the market, the price of the commodities is reduced, and this causes them to move again. If the total quantity of use-values is too large, they accommodate themselves to the space they have to occupy by a reduction of their *prices*. If the quantity is too small, it is expanded by an increase of their *prices*.

On the other hand, commodities which quickly deteriorate as use-values remain only for a very short time in the reservoirs of circulation. The period of time during which they have to be converted into money and reproduced, is prescribed by the nature of their use-value which, if it is not consumed daily or almost daily, is spoilt and consequently ceases to be a commodity.

For exchange-value along with its basis, use-value, disappears provided the disappearance of use-value is not itself an act of production.

In general, it is clear that although in *absolute* terms the *quantity* of the commodities which have been stored up in the reservoirs of circulation increases as a result of the development of industry, because production and consumption increase, this same quantity represents a decrease in comparison with the total annual production and consumption. The *transition* of commodities from circulation to consumption takes place more rapidly. And for the following reasons. The speed of reproduction increases:

1) When the commodity passes rapidly through its various production phases, that is, when each production phase of the production process is reduced in length; this is due to the fact that the labour-time necessary to produce the commodity in each one of its forms is reduced, this is a result, therefore, of the development of the division of labour, use of machinery, application of chemical processes, etc. ⟨The development of chemistry makes it possible to speed up the transition of commodities from one state of aggregation to another, their combination with other material which, for instance, occurs in dyeing, their separation from [other] substances as in bleaching; in short, both [modifications in] the form of the same substance (its state of aggregation) as well as changes to be brought about in the substance, are artificially accelerated quite apart from the fact, that for vegetative and organic reproduction, plants, animals, etc., are supplied with cheaper substances, that is, substances which cost less labour-time.⟩

2) Partly as a result of the combination of various branches of industry, that is, the establishment of centres of production for particular industrial branches, [partly] through the *development of means of communication*, the commodity proceeds rapidly from one phase to another; in other words, the interim period, the interval during which the commodity remains in the intermediate station between one production phase and another is reduced, that is, the *transition* from one phase of production to another is shortened.

3) This whole development—the shortening both of the various phases of the production process and of the transition from one phase to another—presupposes production on a large scale, mass production and, at the same time, production based on

a large amount of constant capital, especially fixed capital; [it requires] therefore a continuous flow of production. But not in the sense in which we have earlier considered the flow, that is, not as the closing of and overlapping of the separate production phases, but in the sense that there are no *deliberate* breaks in production. These occur as long as work is done to order, as in ||873| the handicrafts, and continue even in manufacture properly so-called (insofar as this has not been reshaped by large-scale industry). In modern industry, however, work is carried out on the scale allowed by the capital. This process does not wait on demand, but is a function of capital. Capital works on the same scale continuously (if one disregards accumulation or expansion) and constantly develops and extends the productive forces. Production is therefore not only *rapid*, so that the commodity quickly acquires the form in which it is suitable for circulation, but it is continuous. Production here appears only as constant reproduction and at the same time it takes place on a mass scale.

Thus if the commodities remain in the circulation reservoirs for a long time—if they accumulate there—then they will soon glut them as a result of the speed with which the waves of production follow one another and the huge amount of goods which they deposit continuously in the reservoirs. It is in this sense that *Corbet*, for example, says the market is *always* overstocked. [86] But the same circumstances which produce this speed and mass scale of reproduction likewise reduce the necessity for the accumulation of commodities in the reservoirs. In part—insofar as it is concerned with *industrial consumption*—this is already implied by the close succession of the production phases which the commodity itself or its ingredients have to undergo. If coal is produced daily on a mass scale and brought to the manufacturer's door by railways, steamships, etc., he does not need to have a stock of coal, or at most only a very small one; or, what amounts to the same thing, if a merchant acts as an intermediary, he only needs to keep a small amount of stock over and above the amount he sells daily and which is daily delivered to him. The same applies to yarn, iron, etc. But apart from *industrial consumption*, in which the stock of commodities (that is, the stock of the ingredients of commodities) must decline in this way, the shopkeeper likewise enjoys the benefits of the speed of communications first of all, and secondly, the certainty of a continuous and rapid renewal and delivery. Although his stock of commodities may grow in size, each element of it will remain in his reservoir, in a state of transition, for a shorter period of time. In relation to the total amount of commodities which he sells, that is, in relation to the scale of both production and consumption, the stock of commodities which he *accumulates* and *keeps* in store, will be small. It is different in the less developed stages of production where reproduction proceeds slowly—where therefore more commodities must remain in the circulation reservoirs— the means of transport are slow, the communications difficult and, as a consequence, the *renewal of stock* can be interrupted and a great deal of time elapses as a result between the emptying and the refilling of the reservoir—that is, the *renewal* of the stock in hand. The position is then similar to that of products whose reproduction takes place yearly or half-yearly, in short in more or less prolonged periods of time, owing to the nature of their use-values.

⟨For example, cotton is an illustration of how transport and communications affect the emptying of the reservoir. Since ships continually ply between Liverpool and the United States— speed of communications is one factor, continuity another—all the cotton supply is not shipped at once. It comes on to the market gradually (the producer likewise does not want to flood the market all at once). It lies at the docks in Liverpool, that is, already in a kind of circulation reservoir, but not in such quantities—in relation to the total consumption of the article—as would be required if the ship from America arrived only once or twice a year, after a journey of six months. The cotton manufacturer in Manchester and other places stocks his warehouse roughly in accordance with his immediate consumption needs, since the electric telegraph and the railway make the transfer from Liverpool to Manchester possible at a moment's notice.⟩

Special filling of the reservoirs—insofar as this is not due to the overstocking of the market, which can happen much more easily in these circumstances than under archaically slow conditions—occurs only for speculative reasons and merely in exceptional cases because of a real or suspected fall or rise of prices. Regarding this *relative decline* in stock, that is, the commodities which are in circulation, compared with the amount of production and consumption, see *Lalor, The Economist*,[87] *Corbet* (give the corresponding quotations ||874| after Hodgskin). *Sismondi* wrongly saw something lamentable in all this[88] (his writings to be looked up as well).

(On the other hand, there is indeed a continuous *extension of the market* and in the degree that the *interval of time* decreases in which the commodity remains on the market, its *flow in space* increases, that is, the market expands spatially, and the periphery in relation to the centre, the production sphere of the commodity, is circumscribed by a constantly extending radius.)

The fact that consumption lives from hand to mouth, changes its linen and its coat as rapidly as it does its opinions and does not wear the same coat ten years running, etc. is connected with the speed of reproduction, or is another expression of it. To an increasing extent consumption—even of articles where this is not demanded by the nature of their use-value—takes place almost simultaneously with production and becomes therefore more and more dependent on the present, coexisting labour (since it is, in fact, exchange of coexisting labour). This takes place in the same degree in which past labour becomes an ever more important factor of production, even though this past itself is after all a very recent and only relative one.

(The following example demonstrates how closely the keeping of a stock is linked with deficiencies of production. As long as it is difficult to keep cattle throughout the winter, there is no fresh meat in winter. As soon as stock-farming is able to overcome this difficulty, the *stock* previously made up of substitutes for fresh meat—pickled or smoked varieties—ceases of itself.)

The product only becomes a commodity where it enters into circulation. The production of goods as commodities, hence circulation, expands enormously as a result of capitalist production for the following reasons:

1. *Production* takes place on a large scale, the *quantity*, the *huge amounts produced*, therefore, do not stand in any kind of quantitative relationship to the producer's needs [of his own product]; in fact it is *pure chance* whether he consumes any, even a small part of his own product. He only consumes his own product on a mass scale where he produces some of the ingredients of his own capital. On the other hand, in the earlier stages [of economic development] only those products which exceed the amount required by the producer himself become commodities or, at any rate, this is mainly the case.

2. The *narrow range* of goods produced [stands] in inverse ratio to the increased variety of needs. This is due to previously combined branches of production becoming increasingly separated and independent—in short, to increasing division of labour

within society—a contributing factor is the establishment of new branches of production and the increasing variety of commodities produced. ([To be inserted] at the end, after Hodgskin, also *Wakefield* about this.) This increased variety and differentiation of commodities arises in two ways. The different *phases of one and the same product*, as well as the auxiliary operations (that is, the labour connected with various constituent parts, etc.) are separated and become different branches of production, independent of one another; or various phases *of one product* become *different commodities*. But secondly, owing to labour and capital (or labour and surplus product) becoming free; on the other hand, to the discovery of new practical applications of the same use-value, either because new needs arise as a result of the modification of No. 1 (for example, the need for more rapid and universal means of transport and communication arising with the application of steam in industry) and therefore new means of satisfying them, or new possibilities of utilising the same use-value are discovered, or new substances or new methods (plastic-galvanisation, for instance) for treating well-known substance in different ways.

All this amounts to the following: *successive phases* or *states* of *one product* are converted into *separate commodities*. *New products* or *new values in use* are created and become commodities.

3. *Transformation of the majority of the population* who formerly consumed a mass of products *in naturalibus*[a] into *wageworkers*.

4. *Transformation of the tenant farmer into an industrial capitalist* (and with it the conversion of rent into money rent and generally of all payments in kind (taxes, etc., rent) into money payments). In general—industrial exploitation of the land with the result that it is no longer confined to its own muckheap as previously, but that both its chemical and mechanical conditions of production—even seeds, fertilisers, cattle, etc.—are subjected to the process of exchange.

5. *Mobilisation of a mass of previously "inalienable" possessions by conversion into commodities* and the creation of forms of property which only exist in negotiable papers. On the one hand, alienation of landed property (the lack of property of the

---

[a] In kind, in this context it means: within the framework of a natural economy.—*Ed.*

masses causes them, for example, to regard the dwelling in which they live as a commodity). [On the other hand,] railway shares, in short, all kinds of shares.

[d) Hodgskin's Polemic Against the Conception that the Capitalists "Store Up" Means of Subsistence for the Workers. His Failure to Understand the Real Causes of the Fetishism of Capital]

||875| Back again to Hodgskin now.

It is obvious that by *"storing up"* [means of subsistence] *for* the workers by the capitalists one cannot understand that commodities which are passing from production into consumption are in the circulation reservoirs, in the circulation system, on the market. This would mean that the products circulate for the benefit of the worker and become *commodities* for his sake; and that in general, the production of products as commodities is undertaken for his sake.

The worker shares with every other [commodity owner the need] to transform the commodity he sells—which in actual fact, though not in form, is his labour—at first into money in order to convert the money back again into commodities which he can consume. It is perfectly obvious that [no] division of labour (insofar as it is based on commodity production), [no] wage-labour and, in general, no capitalist production can take place without *commodities*—whether they be means of consumption or means of production—being available on the market; that this kind of production is impossible *without* commodity circulation, without the commodities spending a period of time in the circulation reservoir. For the product is a commodity in the strict sense of the word only within the framework of circulation. It is as true for the worker as for anybody else that he must find his means of subsistence in the form of *commodities*.

The worker, moreover, does not confront the shopkeeper as a worker confronts a capitalist, but as money confronts the commodity, as a buyer faces the seller. There is no relationship of wage-labour to capital here, except of course, where the shopkeeper is dealing with his *own* workers. But even they, insofar as they buy things from him, do not confront him as workers. They confront him as workers only insofar as he buys from them. Let us therefore leave this *circulation agent*.

But as far as the industrial capitalist is concerned, his *stock*, his accumulation, consists of:

[*First*] his fixed capital, i.e., buildings, machinery, etc., which the worker does not consume or, insofar as he does consume them, does so through labour, and thus consumes them industrially *for* the capitalist, and although they are means of labour they are not means of subsistence for him.

Secondly, his raw materials and auxiliary materials, the stock of which, insofar as it does not enter directly into production, declines, as we have seen. This likewise does not consist of means of subsistence for the workers. This *accumulation* by the capitalist for the workers means nothing more than that he does the worker the favour of depriving the latter of his conditions of labour and converting the means of his labour (which are themselves merely the transformed product of his labour) into means for the exploitation of labour. In any case, the worker, while he uses the machines and the raw materials, does not live on them.

Thirdly, the commodities, which he keeps in the storehouse or warehouse before they enter into circulation. These are products of labour, not means of subsistence stored in order to maintain labour during the course of production.

Thus the "accumulation" of means of subsistence by the capitalist for the worker means merely that he must possess enough money in order to pay wages with which the worker withdraws the articles of consumption he needs from the circulation reservoir (and, if we consider the [working] class as a whole, with which he buys back part of his own product). This money, however, is simply the transformed form of the commodity which the worker has sold and handed over. In this sense, the means of subsistence are "stored up" for him in the same way as they are stored up for his capitalist, who likewise buys consumption goods etc. with money (the transformed form of the same commodity). This money may be a mere token of value, it therefore does not have to be a representation "of previous labour" but, in the hands of whoever possesses it, simply expresses the realised price not of past labour (or previously [sold] commodities) but of the contemporaneous labour or commodities which he sells. [Money has] merely a formal existence.[89] Or—since in previous modes of production the worker also had to eat and consume during the course of production irrespective of the period of time required for the production of his product—"storing up" may mean that the worker must first of all transform the product of his labour into the product of the capitalist, into capital, in order to receive back a portion of it in the form of money, in lieu of payment.

||876| What interests Hodgskin about this whole process (with regard to the process as such it is indeed a matter of indifference whether the worker receives the product of contemporaneous or previous labour, just as it does not matter whether he receives the product of his own previous labour or the product of labour performed simultaneously in a different branch) is this:

A great part, [or] the greatest part of the products consumed daily by the worker—which he must consume whether his own product is finished or not—represent by no means *stored up labour* of bygone time. On the contrary he uses to a large extent products of labour performed the same day or during the same week in which the worker produces his own commodity. For example, bread, meat, beer, milk, newspapers, etc. Hodgskin could also have added that they are partly the products of *future* labour, for the worker who buys an overcoat with what he has saved out of six months' wages buys one which has only been made at the end of the six months, etc. (We have seen that the whole of production presupposes *simultaneous* reproduction of the required constituent parts and products in their different forms as raw materials, semi-manufactured goods, etc. But all fixed capital presupposes *future* labour for its reproduction and for the reproduction of its equivalent, without which it cannot be reproduced.) Hodgskin says that during the course of the year the worker must rely to some degree on previous labour (because of the nature of the production of corn, vegetable raw materials, etc.). ⟨This does not apply to a house, for example. As regards use-values which, by their nature, only wear out slowly, are not consumed at once, but gradually used up, it is not due to any action specially devised for the benefit of the workers that these products of previous labour are available on "the market". The worker also used to have a "dwelling" before the capitalist "piled up" deadly stink-holes for him. (See *Laing* on this.[90])⟩ (Apart from the enormous mass of day-to-day needs which are of decisive importance especially to the *worker*, who, at best, can only satisfy his everyday needs, we have seen that, in general, *consumption* becomes more and more contemporaneous with *production*, and therefore, if one considers society as a whole, consumption depends more and more on *simultaneous* production, or rather on the products of *simultaneous* production.) But when operations extend over several years, the worker must "depend" on his own production, on the simultaneous and future producers of other commodities.

The worker always has to find his means of subsistence in the form of commodities on the market (the "services" he buys are *ipso facto* only brought into being at the moment they are bought); as far as he is concerned they must therefore be the products of antecedent labour, that is of labour which is antecedent to their existence as products but which is by no means antecedent to his own labour with whose price he buys these products. They can be—and mostly are—contemporaneous products, especially for those who live from hand to mouth.

Taking it all in all the "storing up" of means of subsistence for the workers by the capitalists comes to this.

1) Commodity production presupposes that articles of consumption which one does not produce oneself are available on the market as commodities, or that *in general, commodities* are produced *as commodities*.

2) The majority of the commodities consumed by the worker in the final form in which they confront him as commodities, are in fact products of *simultaneous* labour (they are therefore by no means stored up by the capitalist).

3) In capitalist production, the means of labour and the means of subsistence produced by the worker himself confront him as capital, the one as constant, the other as variable capital; these, the worker's conditions of production, appear as the property of the capitalist; their transfer from the worker to the capitalist and the partial return of the worker's product to the worker, or of the value of his product to the worker, is called the "storing up" of circulating capital for the worker. These means of subsistence which the worker must always consume before his product is finished, become "circulating capital" because he [the worker], instead of *buying* them direct or *paying* for them with the value either of his past or of his future product ||877|, must first of all receive a *draft* (money) on it; a draft moreover which the capitalist is entitled to issue only thanks to the worker's past, present or future product.

Hodgskin is concerned here with demonstrating the dependence of the worker on the coexisting labour of other workers as against his dependence on previous labour,

1) in order to do away with the phrase about "storing up";

2) because "present labour" confronts capital, whereas the economists always consider previous labour as such to be capital, that is, an *alienated* and independent form of labour which is hostile to labour itself.

To grasp the all-round significance of *contemporaneous labour* as against previous labour is however in itself a very important achievement.

Hodgskin thus arrives at the following:

Capital is either a mere name and pretext or it does not express a thing; the social relation of the labour of one person to the *coexisting labour* of another, and the consequences, the *effects* of this relationship, are ascribed to the things which make up so-called circulating capital. Despite the fact that the commodity exists as money, its realisation in use-values depends on contemporaneous labour. ([The labour performed in] the course of a year is itself contemporaneous [labour].) Only a small portion of the commodities entering into direct consumption are the product of more than one year's labour and when they are— such as cattle etc., they require renewed labour every year. All operations requiring more than a year depend on continuous annual production.

"... it is by the command the capitalist possesses over the *labour of some men*, not by his possessing a stock of commodities, that he is enabled to *support* and consequently employ *other* labourers" (*Labour Defended etc.*, p. 14).

Money however gives everyone "command" over "the labour of some men", over the labour contained in their commodities as well as over the reproduction of this labour, and to that extent therefore over labour itself.

What is really "stored up", not however as a dead mass but as something living, is the *skill* of the worker, the level of development of labour. ⟨It is true, however, that the stage of the development of the productivity of labour which exists at any particular time and serves as the starting-point, comprises not only the skill and capacity of the worker, but likewise the material means which this labour has created and which it daily renews. (Hodgskin does not emphasise this because, in opposing the crude views of the economists, it is important for him to lay the stress on the *subject*—so to speak, on the subjective in the subject—in contrast to the object.)⟩ This is really the primary factor, the point of departure and it is the result of a process of development. *Accumulation* in this context means *assimilation*, continual preservation and at the same time transformation of what has already been handed over and realised. In this way Darwin makes "accumulation" through inheritance the driving principle in the formation of all organic things, of plants and animals; thus the various organisms themselves are formed as a result of "accumulation" and are only "inventions", gradually accumulated inventions of living beings. But this is not the only prerequisite of production. Such a prerequisite in the case of animals and plants is external nature, that is both inorganic nature and their relationship with other animals and plants. Man, who produces in society, likewise faces an already modified nature (and in particular natural factors which have been transformed into means of his own activity) and definite relations existing between the producers. This accumulation is in part the result of the historical process, in part, as far as the individual worker is concerned, transmission of skill. Hodgskin says that as far as the majority of the workers are concerned, circulating capital plays no part in this accumulation.

He has demonstrated that "the stock of commodities" (means of subsistence) "prepared" is always small in comparison with the total amount of consumption and production. On the other hand, the degree of skill of the existing population is always the pre-condition of production as a whole; it is therefore the principal accumulation of wealth and the most important result of antecedent labour; its form of existence, however, is living labour itself.

||878| "... all the effects usually attributed to accumulation of circulating capital are derived from the *accumulation and storing up of skilled labour*; and, [...] this most important operation is performed, as far as the great mass of labourers is concerned without any circulating capital whatever" (op. cit., p. 13).

With regard to the assertion of the economists that the number of workers (and therefore the well-being or poverty of the existing working population) depends on the amount of circulating capital available, Hodgskin comments correctly, as follows:

"... the number of labourers must at all times depend on the *quantity of circulating capital*; o r, as I should say, on the *quantity of the products of coexisting labour*, which labourers are *allowed* to consume" (op. cit., p. 20).

What is attributed to *circulating capital*, to a stock of commodities, is the effect of "coexisting labour".

In other words, Hodgskin says that the effects of a certain social form of labour are ascribed to objects, to the products of labour; the relationship itself is imagined to exist in *material* form. We have already seen that this is a characteristic of labour based on commodity production, on exchange-value, and this *quid pro quo* is revealed in the commodity, in money (Hodgskin does not see this), and to a still higher degree in capital.[91] The effects of things as materialised aspects of the labour process are attributed to them in capital, in their personification, their independence in respect of labour. They would cease to have these effects if they were to cease to confront labour in this *alienated form*. The *capitalist*, as capitalist, is simply the personification of capital, that creation of labour endowed with its own will and personality which stands in opposition to labour. Hodgskin regards this as a pure subjective illusion which conceals the deceit and the interests of the exploiting classes. He does not see that the way of looking at things arises out of the actual relationship itself; the latter is not an expression of the former, but vice versa. In the same way, English socialists say "We need capital, but not the capitalists". But if one eliminates the capitalists, the means of production cease to be *capital*.

* * *

⟨The "Verbal Observer", Bailey, and others remark that "value", "valeur" express a property of things. In fact the terms originally express nothing but the use-value of things for people, those qualities which make them useful or agreeable etc. to people. It is in the nature of things that "value", "valeur", "Wert" can have no other etymological origin. Use-value expresses the natural relationship between things and men, in fact the existence of things for men. *Exchange-value*, as the result of the social development which created it, was later superimposed on the word value, which was synonymous with use-value. It [exchange-value] is the *social existence* of things.

The *Sanskrit*—Wer [means] cover, protect, consequently respect, honour and love, cherish. From these the adjective *Wertas* (excellent, respectable) is derived; *Gothic*, wairths; *Old German*, *Old Frankish*, wert; *Anglo-Saxon*, weorth, vordh, wurth; *English*, worth, worthy; *Dutch*, waard, waardig; *Alemanic*, werth; *Lithuanian*, wertas (respectable, precious, dear, estimable).
The *Sanskrit*, wertis; *Latin*, virtus; *Gothic*, wairthi; *German*, Werth[a] [Chavée, *Essai d'étymologie philosophique*, Brussels, 1844, p. 176].

---

[a] This is not a quotation from Chavee but a free summary of some of his ideas.—*Ed.*

The value of a thing is, in fact, its own *virtus*[a], while its exchange-value is quite independent of its material qualities.

The *Sanskrit* "*Wal* [means] to cover, to fortify; [*Latin*] *vallo*,[b] *valeo*,[c] *vallus*[d]: that which protects and defends, *valor* is the power itself." Hence *valeur, value*. "Compare Wal with the German *walle*, *walte*[e] and English *wall, wield*"[92] [op. cit., p. 70].⟩

* * *

Hodgskin now turns to *fixed capital*. It is productive power which has been produced and, in its development in large-scale industry, it is an instrument which *social* labour has created. As far as fixed capital is concerned:

"... all instruments and machines are the produce of labour. [...] As long as they are merely the result of *previous* labour, and are not applied to their respective uses by labourers, they do not repay the expense of making them. [...] most of them diminish in value from being kept. [...] *Fixed capital does not derive its utility from previous, but present labour*; and does not *bring its owner a profit* because it has been stored up, but because it is a *means of obtaining command over labour*" ([Thomas Hodgskin,] *Labour Defended* etc., pp. 14-15).

Here at last, the nature of capital is understood correctly.

||879| "After any instruments have been made, what do *they* effect? Nothing. On the contrary, they begin to rust or decay unless used or applied by labour." "Whether an instrument shall be regarded as productive capital or not, depends entirely on its *being used*, or not, by some productive labourer" (loc. cit., pp. 15-16).

"One easily comprehends why [...] the road-maker should receive some of the benefits, accruing only to the road-user; but I do not comprehend *why all these benefits should go to the road itself*, and be *appropriated* by a set of persons who neither make nor use it, under the name of profit for their capital" (loc. cit., p. 16).

"Its vast utility does[f] not depend on stored up iron and wood, but on that *practical and living knowledge of the powers of nature* which enables some men to construct it, and others to guide it" (loc. cit., p. 17).

"Without knowledge they" (the machines) "could not be invented, without manual skill and dexterity they could not be made, and without skill and labour they could not be productively used. But there is nothing more than knowledge, skill, and labour requisite, on which the capitalist can found a claim to any share of the produce" (loc. cit., p. 18).

---

[a] Virtue.—*Ed.*
[b] To surround with a wall, to fortify, to defend.—*Ed.*
[c] To be strong, vigorous.—*Ed.*
[d] Wall.—*Ed.*
[e] Rule, govern, control.—*Ed.*
[f] In the manuscript "the vast utility of the steam-engine does".—*Ed.*

"After he" (man) "has *inherited the knowledge of several generations, and when he lives congregated in great masses*, he is enabled by his mental faculties to complete [...] the work of nature..." (loc. cit., p. 18).

"... it is not [...] the *quantity* but the *quality* of the fixed capital on which the productive industry of a country depends. [...] fixed capital as a means of nourishing and supporting men, depends for its efficiency, altogether on the skill of the labourers, and consequently the productive industry of a country, as far as fixed capital is concerned, is in *proportion* to the *knowledge and skill of the people*" (loc. cit., pp. 19-20).

[e)] **Compound Interest: Fall in the Rate of Profit Based on This**

"A mere glance must satisfy every mind that *simple profit* does not decrease but increase in the progress of society—that is, the same quantity of labour which at any former period produced 100 quarters of wheat, and 100 steam-engines, will now produce somewhat more [....] In fact, also, we find that a much greater number of persons now live in opulence on profit in this country than formerly. It is clear, however, that *no labour, no productive power*, no ingenuity, and no art *can answer the overwhelming demands of compound interest*. But all saving *is made from the revenue*" (that is from simple profit) "*of the capitalist*, so that actually these demands are constantly made, and as constantly the productive power of labour refuses to satisfy them. A sort of balance is, therefore, constantly struck"[93] (loc. cit., p. 23).

For example, if the profit were always accumulated, a capital of 100 at 10 per cent would amount to something like 673, or—since a little more or less makes no difference here—say 700, in 20 years. Thus the capital will have multiplied itself sevenfold over a period of 20 years. According to this yardstick, if only simple interest were paid, it would have to be 30 per cent per annum instead of 10 per cent, that is, three times as much profit, and the more we increase the number of years that elapse, the more the rate of interest or the rate of profit calculated at simple interest per annum will increase, and this increase is the more rapid, the larger the capital becomes.

In fact, however, capitalist accumulation is nothing but the reconversion of interest into capital (since interest and profit for our purpose, i.e., for the purpose of our calculation, are identical). Thus it is compound interest. First there is a capital of 100; it yields 10 per cent profit (or interest). This is added to the capital which is now 110. This now becomes the capital. The interest on this amount is therefore not simply interest on a capital of 100 but interest on 100 capital plus 10 interest. That is compound interest. Thus, at the end of the second year, we have (100 capital+10 interest)+10 interest+1 interest=(100 capital+10 interest)+11 interest=121. This is the *capital* at the beginning of the third year. In the third year we get (100 capital+10 interest)+11 interest+$12^1/_{10}$ interest, so that at the end of it the capital is 133 $^1/_{10}$.

||880| We have:

Capital	Interest	Total
First year 100	10	110
Second year 100 + 10 = 110	10 + 1'*	121
Third year 100 + 20 + 1 = 121	10 + 2' + $^1/_{10}$'	133 $^1/_{10}$
Fourth year 100 + 30 + 3 $^1/_{10}$ = 133 $^1/_{10}$	10 + $3^{31}/_{100}$'	$146^{41}/_{100}$
Fifth year 100 + 40 + $6^{41}/_{100}$ = $146^{41}/_{100}$	10 + $4^{641}/_{1,000}$'	$161^{51}/_{1,000}$

etc.

In the second year the capital comprises 10 interest (simple)
" " third " " " " 21 interest
" " fourth " " " " 31 $^1/_{10}$ interest
" " fifth " " " " $46^{41}/_{100}$ interest
" " sixth " " " " $61^{51}/_{1,000}$ "
" " seventh " " " " $77^{1,561}/_{10,000}$ "
" " eighth " " " " $94^{87,171}/_{100,000}$ "
[In the ninth year the capital comprises $114^{358,881}/_{1,000,000}$ interest]

* The sign ' indicates interest on interest.

In other words, more than half the capital is made up of interest in the ninth year and the portion of capital consisting of interest thus increases in geometrical progression.

We have seen that over 20 years, capital increased sevenfold, whereas, even according to the "most extreme" assumption of Malthus, the population can only double itself every twenty-five years. But let us assume that it doubles itself in twenty years, and therefore the working population as well. Taking one year with another, the interest would have to be 30 per cent— three times greater than it is. If one assumes, however, that the rate of exploitation remained unchanged, in 20 years the doubled population would only be able to produce twice as much labour as it did previously (and [the new generation] would be unfit for work during a considerable part of these 20 years, scarcely during half this period would it be able to work, in spite of the employment of children); it would therefore produce only twice as much surplus labour, but not three times as much.

The rate of profit (and consequently the rate of interest) is determined:

1) If the rate of exploitation is assumed to be constant—by the number of workers in employment, by the absolute mass of workers employed, that is, by the growth of the population. Although this number increases, its ratio to the total amount of capital employed declines with the accumulation of capital and with industrial development (consequently the rate of profit declines if the rate of exploitation remains the same). Likewise the population does not by any means [increase] in the same geometrical progression as the computed compound interest. The growth of the population at a given stage of industrial development is the explanation for the increase in the amount of surplus-value and of profit, but also for the fall in the rate of profit.

2) [By] the absolute length of the "normal" working-day, that is, by increasing the rate of surplus-value. Thus the rate of profit can increase as a result of the extension of labour-time beyond the normal working-day. However, this has its *physical* and—by and large—its social limits. That in the same measure as workers set more capital in motion, the same capital commands more absolute labour-time ||881| is out of the question.

3)' If the normal working-day remains the same, surplus labour can be increased relatively by reducing the necessary labour-time and reducing the prices of the necessaries which the worker consumes, in comparison with the development of the productive power of labour. But this very development of productive power reduces variable capital relative to constant. It is physically impossible that the surplus labour-time of, say, two men who displace twenty, can, by any conceivable increase of the absolute or relative [surplus] labour-time, equal that of the twenty. If each of the twenty men only work 2 hours of surplus labour a day, the total will be 40 hours of surplus labour, whereas the total life span of the two men amounts only to 48 hours in one day.

The value of labour-power does not fall in the same degree as the productivity of labour or of capital increases. This increase in productive power likewise increases the ratio between constant and variable capital in all branches of industry which do not produce necessaries (either directly or indirectly) without giving rise to any kind of alteration in the value of labour. The development of productive power is not even. It is in the nature of capitalist production that it develops industry more rapidly than agriculture. This is not due to the nature of the land, but to the fact that, in order to be exploited really in accordance with its nature, land requires different social relations. Capitalist production turns towards the land only after its influence has exhausted it and after it has devastated its natural qualities. An additional factor is that, as a consequence of landownership, agricultural products are expensive compared with other commodities, because they are sold at *their* value and are not reduced to their cost-price. They form, however, the principal constituent of the necessaries. Furthermore, if one-tenth of the land is dearer to exploit than the other nine-tenths, these latter are likewise hit "artificially" by this relative barrenness, as a result of the law of competition.

The rate of profit would in fact have to grow if it is to remain constant while accumulation of capital is taking place. *The same worker* as long as capital yields 10 of surplus labour must, as soon as interest accumulates on interest and thus increases the capital employed, produce threefold, fourfold, fivefold in progression of compound interest, which is nonsense.

The *amount of capital* which the worker sets in motion, and whose value is maintained and reproduced by his labour, is something quite different from the *value* which he adds, and therefore from the surplus-value. If the amount of capital is 1,000 and the labour added equals 100, then the capital reproduced amounts to 1,100. If the capital is 100 and the labour added is 20, then the capital reproduced is 120. The rate of profit in the first case is 10 per cent and in the second, it is 20 per cent. Nevertheless, more can be accumulated from 100 than from 20. Thus the flow of capital or its "accumulation" continues (apart from the reduction in its value as a result of the increase in productive power) in proportion to the force it already possesses, but not in proportion to the size of the rate of profit. This explains that accumulation—its amount—may increase in spite of a falling rate of profit, apart from the fact that, while productivity rises, a larger portion of the revenue can be accumulated, even when the rate of profit declines, than when there is a higher rate of profit together with lower productivity. A high rate of profit— insofar as it is based on a high rate of surplus-value—is possible if very long hours are worked, although the labour is unproductive. It is possible because the workers' needs, and *therefore* the minimum wage, are small, although the labour is unproductive. The lack of energy with which the labour is performed will correspond to the low level of the minimum wage. Capital is accumulated slowly in both cases despite the high rate of profit. The population is stagnant and the labour-time which the product costs is high, although the wages received by the workers are small.

||882| I have explained the decline in the rate of profit in spite of the fact that the rate of surplus-value remains the same or even rises, by the decrease of the variable capital in relation to the constant, that is, of the living; present labour in relation to the past labour which is employed and reproduced.[94] Hodgskin and the man who wrote *The Source and Remedy of the National Difficulties* explain it by the fact that it is impossible for the worker to fulfil the demands of capital which accumulates like *compound interest*.

"... no labour, no productive power, no ingenuity, and no art can answer the overwhelming demands of compound interest. But all saving is made from the revenue of the capitalist" (that is from simple profit) "so that actually these demands are constantly made, and as constantly the productive power of labour refuses to satisfy them. A sort of balance is, therefore, constantly struck" (op. cit., p. 23).

In its general sense, this amounts to the same thing. If I say that, as capital accumulates, the rate of profit declines because constant capital increases in relation to variable capital, it means that, disregarding the specific form of the different portions of capital, the capital employed increases in relation to the labour employed. [The rate of] profit falls not because the worker is exploited less, but because altogether less labour is employed in relation to the capital employed.

For example, let us assume that the ratio of variable to constant capital is 1:1. Then, if the total capital amounts to 1,000, c [constant capital] will be 500, and v [variable capital] likewise 500. If the rate of surplus-value is 50 per cent, then 50 per cent of 500 is 50×5, or 250. Thus the rate of profit on 1,000 yields a profit of 250, or $\frac{250}{1,000}$, or $\frac{25}{100}$, or $\frac{1}{4}$ which is 25 per cent.

If the total capital is 1,000 and if c equals 750 and v 250, then at 50 per cent [the rate of surplus-value] 250 will yield 125. But $\frac{125}{1,000}$ comes to $1/8$, or 12 $1/2$ per cent.

But in comparison with the first case [less] living labour is employed in the second case. If we assume that the annual wage of the worker is £25, then in the first case £500 [wages] will employ 20 workers; in the second case £250 wages will employ 10 workers. The same capital [£1,000] employs 20 workers in one case and only 10 in the other. In the first case, the ratio of total capital to the number of working-days is as 1,000:20; in the second as 1,000:10. In the first case, for each of the 20 workers £50 capital (constant and variable) is used (for 20×50= =500×2=1,000). In the second case, the capital employed per individual worker is £100 (for 100×10=1,000). Nevertheless, in both cases, the capital which is allocated to wages is, pro rata, the same.

The formula I have given provides a new ground for explaining why, with accumulation, less workers are employed by the same amount of capital or, what amounts to the same thing, why a greater amount of capital has to be used for *the same amount of labour*. It comes to the same thing if I say that one worker is employed for a capital outlay of 50 in the one case, and one worker for a capital outlay of 100 in the other, that therefore only half the number of workers is employed by a capital of 50; in other words, if I say that in one case there is one worker for 50 capital and only half a worker for 50 capital in the other, or if I say that in one case 50 capital is used by one worker and in the other case 50×2 capital is used by one worker.

This latter formula is the one used by Hodgskin and others. According to them, accumulation means in general the demand for compound interest; in other words, that more capital is expended on *one* worker and that he has therefore to produce more surplus labour proportionally to the amount of capital expended on him. Since the capital expended on him increases at the same rate as compound interest, but on the other hand, his labour-time has very definite limits which even relatively no [development of the] productive powers can reduce in accordance with the demands of this compound interest "a sort of balance is constantly struck". "Simple profit" remains the same, or rather it grows. (This is in fact the surplus labour or surplus-value.) But as the result of the accumulation of capital it is compound interest which is disguised in the form of simple interest.

||883| It is clear furthermore that if compound interest equals accumulation, then, apart from the absolute limits of accumulation, the growth of this interest depends on the extent, the intensity, etc., of the accumulation process itself, that is, on the *mode of production*. Otherwise compound interest is nothing

but appropriation of the *capital* (property) of *others* in the form of interest as was the case in Rome and in general with usurers.

Hodgskin's view is as follows: Originally £50 capital, for example, falls to the share of one worker, on which he produces, let us say, a profit of [£]25. Later, as a result of the conversion of a part of the interest into capital and of the fact that this process repeats itself again and again, a capital of £200 is allocated to the worker. If the entire interest of 50 per cent received per annum was always capitalised, the process would be complete in less than four years. Just as the worker produced [a profit of] 25 on [a capital of] 50, he is now expected to produce [a profit of] 100 on a capital of 200, or four times as much. But that is impossible. To do that either the worker would have to work four times as long, that is, 48 hours a day if he worked 12 hours previously, or the value of labour would have to fall by 75 per cent as a result of increased productivity of labour.

If the working-day is 12 hours, £25 the [annual] wage, and the worker produces £25 profit [per annum], then he has to work as much for the capitalist as he does for himself. That is for 6 hours or half the working-day. In order to produce 100, he would have to work 4×6 hours for the capitalist in a 12-hour working-day—which is nonsense. Let us assume that the working-day is lengthened to 15 hours, then the worker still cannot produce 24 hours work in 15 hours. And still less can he work for 30 hours, which is what would be necessary, since [he would have to work] 24 hours for the capitalist and 6 for himself. If he worked the whole of his working-time for the capitalist, he would be able to produce only £50; he would only double the amount of interest, that is, he would produce 50 profit on a capital of 200, whereas he produced £25 for £50 capital. The rate of profit is 50 per cent in the second case and 25 per cent in the first. But even this is impossible, since the worker must live. No matter how much productive power increases, if, as in the above example, the value of 12 hours is 75, then that of 24 hours adds up to 2×75, or 150. And since the worker must live, he can never produce 150 profit, still less 200. His surplus labour is always a *part* of his working-day, from which it does not at all follow, as Mr. Rodbertus thinks, that profit can never reach 100 per cent. It can never be 100 per cent if it is calculated on the working-day as a whole (for it is *itself* included in it). But it can most certainly be 100 per cent in relation to that part of the working-day which is paid for.

Let us take the above example of 50 per cent.

Capital constant	variable	Surplus-value	Rate of surplus-value	Rate of profit
25	25	25	100 per cent	50 per cent

Here the profit, half a working-day, is equal to a third of the whole [product].

|884| If the worker worked three-quarters of the working-day for the capitalist then:

Capital constant	variable	Surplus-value	Rate of surplus-value	Rate of profit
25	$12^{1}/_{2}$			
Total capital $37^{1}/_{2}$		$37^{1}/_{2}$	300 per cent	100 per cent

[calculated on a capital] of 100

Capital constant	variable	Surplus-value	Rate of surplus-value	Rate of profit
$66^{2}/_{3}$	$33^{1}/_{3}$			
Total capital 100		100	300 per cent	100 per cent

Let us examine this a little more closely and see what is implied by the view that [the rate of] *profit falls* because, in consequence of progressive accumulation, it does not constitute *simple profit* (consequently the rate of exploitation of the worker does not decline but, as Hodgskin says, increases) but *compound profit* and it is impossible for labour to keep pace with the demands of compound interest.

It has to be noted first of all that this has to be defined in more detail if it is to make any sense at all. Regarded as a product of accumulation (that is, of the appropriation of surplus labour) —and this approach is necessary if one considers reproduction as a whole—all capital is made up of profit (or of interest, if this word is considered to be synonymous with profit and not with interest in the strict sense). If the rate of profit is 10 per cent, then this is "compound interest", compound profit. And it would be impossible to see how 10 to 100 could—in economic terms— differ from 11 to 110. So what emerges is that "simple profit" too is impossible, or at least that simple profit must also decline, because, in fact, simple profit is made up in exactly the same way as compound profit. If one narrow the problem, that is, considers solely interest-bearing capital, then compound interest would swallow up profit and more than profit; and the fact that the producer (capitalist or not) has to pay the lender compound interest means that sooner or later, in addition to profit he has to pay him part of his capital as well.

Thus it should be noted first of all that Hodgskin's view only has meaning if it is assumed that capital grows more rapidly than population, that is, than the working population. (Even this latter is a relative growth. It is in the nature of capitalism to overwork one section of the working population while it turns another into paupers.) If the population grows at the same rate as capital, then there is no reason whatsoever why I should not be able to extract from 8 x workers with £800 the [same rate of] surplus labour that I can extract from x workers with £100. ||885| Eight times 100 C makes no greater demand on 8 times x workers than 100 C on x workers. Thus "Hodgskin's" *argument* becomes groundless. (In reality, things turn out differently. Even if the population grows at the same rate as capital, capitalist development nevertheless results in one part of the population being made redundant, because constant capital develops at the expense of variable capital.)

⟨"... it is very material, with reference to *labour*, whether you distribute them" (*goods*) "so as to induce a *greater supply of labour* or a less: whether you distribute them where they will be conditions for labour, or where they will be opportunities for idleness" (*An Inquiry into those Principles, respecting the Nature of Demand and the Necessity of Consumption, lately advocated by Mr. Malthus* etc., London, 1821, p. 57).

"... that increased supply of labour is promoted by the increased *numbers of mankind*..." (loc. cit., p. 58).

"The not being able to *command so much labour* as before, too, is only important where that[a] labour would produce no more than before. If labour has been rendered more productive, production will not be checked, though the *existing mass of commodities should command less labour than before*" (loc. cit., p. 60).

(This is directed against Malthus. True, production would not be checked, but the rate of profit would. These cynical propositions stating that a "mass of commodities *commands* labour", reflect the same cynicism which finds expression in Malthus's explanation of value[b]; *command of the commodity over labour* is very good and is absolutely characteristic of the nature of capital.)

The same author makes the following correct observation directed against West:

---

[a] In the manuscript "the".—*Ed.*
[b] See this volume, pp. 16-17 and 31-32—*Ed.*

"The author of the *Essay* [...] observes[a] [...] that more will be given for labour when there is most increase of stock, and *that* [...] will be when profits on stock are highest. 'The greater the profits of stock', he adds, 'the higher will be the wages of labour'. The fault of this is, that a word or two is left out. 'The greater *have been* the profits of stock' ... 'the higher *will be* the wages of labour'.... The high profits and the high wages are not *simultaneous*; they do not occur in the same *bargain*; the one counteracts the other, and reduces it to a level. It might as well be argued, 'the supply of a commodity is most rapid when the price is highest, therefore, large supply and high price go together'. It is a mixing up of cause and effect" (op. cit., pp. 100-01).⟩

Hodgskin's proposition, therefore, has meaning only if, as a result of the process of accumulation, *more capital* is set in motion by the same workers, or if the capital grows in relation to labour. That is, if, for example, the capital was 100 and becomes 110 by accumulation, and if the same worker who produced a surplus-value of 10, is to produce a surplus-value of 11, corresponding to the growth of capital, i.e., compound interest. So that it is not simply the same capital he set in motion previously which, after its reproduction, is to yield the same profit (simple profit) but this capital has been increased by his surplus labour [so that] he has to provide surplus labour for the original capital (or its value) and also for his own accumulated (i.e. capitalised) surplus labour. And since this capital increases every year, the same worker would constantly have to furnish more labour.

It is however only [under the following conditions] possible for more capital to be applied per worker:

First. If the productive power of labour remains the same, then this is only possible if the worker prolongs his working-time absolutely, i.e., for example, if he works 15 hours instead of 12 hours, or if he works more intensively and performs 15 hours' labour in 12 hours, does 5 hours' labour in 4 hours or 1 hour's labour in $4/5$ of an hour. Since he reproduces his means of subsistence in a definite number of hours, then, in this case, three hours of labour are won for the capitalist in the same way as if the productive power of labour had been increased, while, in fact, it is labour which has been increased, not its productive power. If the intensification of labour were to become general, then the value of commodities would fall in proportion to the reduced labour-time which they cost. The degree of intensity would become the average [intensity of labour], its natural quality. If,

---

[a] In the manuscript "The Author of *An Essay on the Application of Capital to Land* says".—*Ed.*

however ||886|, this only occurs in particular spheres, then it amounts to more complex labour, simple labour raised to a higher power. Less than an hour of more intensive labour then counts as much—and creates as much value—[as an hour of] the more extensive labour. For example, in the above case, $^4/_5$ of an hour [produces] as much as $^5/_5$, or an hour.

Both the extension of labour-time and the increase of labour through its greater intensification by means of the compression of the pores of labour as it were, have their limits (although the London bakers, for example, regularly work 17 hours [a day] if not more), very definite, physical, limitations, and it is when encountering these that compound interest—composite profit— ceases.

Within these limitations the following applies:

If the capitalist pays nothing for the extension or intensification of labour, then his *surplus-value* (his profit as well, provided there is no change in the *value* of the constant capital, for we assume that the mode of production remains the same)— and, in accordance with the proviso, his profit—increases more rapidly than his capital. He pays no necessary labour for the capital which has been added.

If he pays for the surplus labour at the same rate as previously, then the growth of the surplus-value is proportionate to the increase in capital. The profit grows more rapidly. For there is a more rapid turnover of fixed capital, while the more intensive use of the machinery does not cause the wear and tear to increase at the same rate. There is a reduction of expenditure on fixed capital, for less machinery, workshops etc. are required for 100 workers who work longer hours than for 200 workers employed simultaneously. Likewise fewer overseers, etc. (This gives rise to a most satisfactory situation. for the capitalist, who is able to expand or contract his production without hindrance, in accordance with the market conditions. In addition, his power grows, since that portion of labour which is over-employed, has its counterpart in an unemployed or semi-employed reserve army, so that competition amongst the workers increases.)

Although there is in this case no change in the purely numerical ratio between necessary labour and surplus labour—this is however the only case where both can simultaneously increase in the same proportion—the exploitation of labour has nevertheless grown, both by means of an extension of the working-day and by its intensification (condensation) provided the working-day is not shortened at the same time (as with the 10 Hours Bill). The period for which the worker is fit to work is reduced and his labour-power is exhausted in a much greater measure than his wages increase and he becomes even more of a work machine. But disregarding the latter aspect, if he lives for 20 years working a normal working-day and only 15 years when his working-day is extended and intensified, then he sells the value of his labour-power in 15 years in the latter case and in 20 years in the former. In one case it has to be replaced in 15 years, in the other, in 20 years.

A value of 100 which lasts for 20 years is replaced if 5 per cent is paid on it annually, for $5 \times 20 = 100$. A value of 100 which lasts 15 years is replaced if $6^{10}/_{15}$ or $6^2/_3$ per cent is paid on it annually. But in the given case, the worker receives for 3 hours of additional labour only an amount equivalent to the daily value of his labour calculated over 20 years. Assuming that he works 8 hours necessary labour and 4 hours surplus labour, then he receives two-thirds of each hour, for $\frac{12 \times 2}{3} = 8$. And in the same way he receives 2 out of the 3 hours over-time that he works. Or two-thirds of each hour. But this is only the value of his hourly labour-power on the assumption that it will last for 20 years. If he uses it up in 15 years, its value [per hour] increases.

Anticipation of the future—real anticipation—occurs in the production of wealth only in relation to the worker and to the land. The future can indeed be anticipated and ruined in both cases by premature over-exertion and exhaustion, and by the disturbance of the balance between expenditure and income. In capitalist production this happens to both the worker and the land. As far as so-called anticipation is concerned, in relation to the national debt for example, Ravenstone remarks with justice:

||887| "In pretending to stave off the expenses of the present hour to a future day, in contending that you can burthen posterity to supply the wants of the existing generation, they in reality assert the monstrous proposition[a] that you can consume what does not yet exist, that you can feed on provisions before their seeds have been sown in the earth" (Piercy Ravenstone, [*Thoughts on the Funding System, and Its Effects*, London, 1824], p. 8.)

"All the wisdom of our statesmen will have ended in a great transfer of property from one class of persons to another, in creating an enormous fund for the reward of jobs and peculation" (loc. cit., p. 9)."

---

[a] Instead of the phrase: "they in reality assert the monstrous proposition" Marx wrote in the manuscript in German: they assert the absurd proposition.—*Ed.*

It is different in the case of the worker and the land. What is expended here exists as δίναμις[a] and the life span of this δίναμις is shortened as a result of accelerated expenditure.

Finally, if the capitalist is forced to pay more for over-time than for normal working-time, then, according to the facts outlined above, this is by no means an increase in wages, but only compensation for the increased value of over-time—and in reality over-time pay is rarely sufficient to cover this. In fact, in order to pay for the increased wear and tear of the labour-power, when over-time is worked, a higher rate ought to be paid for every working hour not merely for the additional hours.

Thus there is in any case an increased exploitation of labour. At the same time, as a result of the accumulation of capital, a reduction in surplus-value takes place at all events and also a decline in the rate of profit, insofar as this is not counteracted by saving on constant capital. ||887||

||887| This is therefore a situation where, in consequence of the accumulation of capital—of the appearance of compound profit—the rate of profit must decline. If on a capital of [£] 300 (the original amount) the rate of profit was 10 per cent (that is profit came to [£] 30), and if for an additional [£] 100 it is 6 per cent, then profit is [£] 36 for [£] 400. Thus on the whole it is 9 for 100. And the rate of profit has fallen from 10 per cent to 9 per cent.

But, as has been stated, on this basis (if the productivity of labour remains the same) not only must the profit on additional capital fall, but at a certain point it must cease altogether, thus the whole accumulation based on this compound profit would be stopped. In this case, the decline in profit is linked with increased exploitation of labour and the cessation of profit at a certain point is not due to the worker or someone else receiving the whole product of his labour, but to the fact that it is physically impossible to work over and above a certain amount of labour-time or to increase the intensity of labour beyond a certain degree.

Secondly. The only other case, where, with the number of workers remaining constant, more capital is applied per worker, and therefore the additional capital can be laid out and used for the increased exploitation of the same number ||888| of workers, *occurs when the productivity of labour increases, i.e. the method*

---

[a] Power.—*Ed.*

of production is changed. This presupposes a change in the organic ratio between constant and variable capital. In other words, the increase in the capital in relation to labour is here identical with the increase of constant capital as compared with variable capital and, in general, with the amount of living labour employed.

This is where Hodgskin's view merges with the general law which I have outlined.

The surplus-value, i.e. the exploitation of the worker, increases, but, at the same time, the rate of profit falls because the variable capital declines as against the constant capital, because in general, the amount of living labour falls relatively in comparison with the amount of capital which sets it in motion. A larger portion of the annual product of labour is appropriated by the capitalist under the signboard of capital, and a smaller portion under the signboard of profit.

⟨Hence the phantasy of the *Rev. Thomas Chalmers* to the effect that the smaller the amount of the annual product laid out by the capitalists as capital, the larger the profit they pocket.[95] The Established Church then comes to their assistance and sees to it that a large part of the surplus product is consumed instead of being capitalised. The miserable priest confuses cause with effect. Moreover, with a smaller rate [of profit] the amount of profit increases as the size of the capital laid out grows. In addition, the quantity of use-value which this smaller proportion represents, increases. At the same time, however, this leads to the centralisation of capital, since the conditions of production now demand the application of capital on a mass scale. It brings about the swallowing up of the smaller capitalists by the bigger ones and the "decapitalisation" of the former. This is once again, only in a different form, the separation of the conditions of labour from labour (for there is still a great deal of self-employment amongst the smaller capitalists; in general the labour done by the capitalist stands in inverse proportion to the size of his capital, that is, to the degree in which he is a capitalist. This process would soon bring capitalist production to a head if it were not for the fact that, alongside the centripetal forces, counteracting tendencies exist, which continuously exert a decentralising influence; this need not be described here, for it belongs to the chapter dealing with the competition of capitals⟩. It is this separation which constitutes the concept of capital and of *primitive* accumulation, which then appears as a continual process in the accumulation of capital and here finally takes the form of the centralisation of already existing capitals in a few hands and of many being divested of capital.)

The fact that the (proportionally) declining quantity of labour is not fully offset by increased productivity, or that the ratio of surplus labour to the capital expended does not increase *at the same* rate as the relative *amount of labour employed* declines, is due partly to the fact that the development of the productive power of labour reduces the value of labour, the necessary labour, only in certain capital investment spheres, and that, even in these spheres, it does not develop uniformly, and that factors exist which nullify this effect; for example, the workers themselves, although they cannot prevent reductions in (real) wages, will not permit them to be reduced to the absolute minimum; on the contrary, they achieve a certain quantitative participation in the general growth of wealth.

But this growth of surplus labour too is relative, [and is only possible] within certain limits. In order to make this growth correspond to the demands of compound interest, the necessary labour-time in this case would have to be reduced to zero in the same way as [the surplus labour-time] had to be extended endlessly in the case considered previously.

The rise and fall in the rate of profit—insofar as it is determined by the rise or fall of wages resulting from the conditions of demand and supply [in the labour market], or caused by the temporary rise or fall in the prices of necessaries compared with those of luxuries, as a result of the changes in demand and supply and the rise or fall in wages to which this leads—has as little to do with the general law of ||889| the rise or fall in the profit rate as the rise or fall in the market prices of commodities has to do with the determination of value in general. This has to be analysed in the chapter on the real movement of wages. If the conditions of demand and supply are favourable to the workers and wages rise, then it is *possible* (but by no means certain) that the prices of certain necessaries, especially food, will rise correspondingly for a time. The author of the *Inquiry into Those Principles etc.* rightly remarks in this connection:

In this case there will be "... an increase of demand for necessaries, in proportion to that for superfluities, as compared with what would have been the proportion between these two sorts of demand, if he had exerted that command" (i.e., the capitalist, his command over commodities) "to procure things for his own consumption. Necessaries will thereby exchange for more of things in general.... And, in part, at least, these necessaries will be food" (op. cit., p. 22).

He then correctly expresses the Ricardian view as follows:

"At all events, then, the increased price of corn was not the *original* cause of that rise of wages which made profits fall, but, on the contrary, the rise of wages was the cause of the increased price of corn at first, and the nature of land, yielding less and less proportional returns to increased tillage, made part of that increase of price *permanent*, prevented a complete *reaction* from taking place through the principle of population" (loc. cit., p. 23).

Hodgskin and the author of *The Source and Remedy etc.* since they explain the fall of profits by the impossibility of living labour to fulfil the demands of compound interest, and although they do not analyse this, are much nearer the truth than Smith and Ricardo, who explain the fall of profits by the rise in wages, one of them, [by the rise in] real and nominal wages, the other [by the rise in] nominal wages, with rather a decrease of real wages. Hodgskin and all the other proletarian opponents have enough common sense to emphasise the fact that the proportional number of those who live on profit has increased with the development of capital.

[f) Hodgskin on the Social Character of Labour and on the Relation of Capital to Labour]

Now a few concluding passages from Hodgskin's *Labour Defended etc.*

The treatment of the exchange-value of the product, hence of the labour embodied in the commodity, as social labour.

"Almost every product of art and skill is the *result of joint and combined labour*...."

(This is the result of capitalist production.)

"... So dependent is man on man, and so much does this dependence *increase* as society advances, that hardly any labour of any single individual ... is of the least value but as forming part of the great social task...."

(This passage has to be quoted, and in doing so [it is necessary to emphasise] that it is only on the basis of capitalism that *commodity* production or the production of products as commodities becomes all-embracing and affects the nature of the products themselves.)

"Wherever the division of labour is introduced [...] the judgement of other men intervenes before the labourer can realise his earnings, and there is no longer any thing which we can call natural reward of individual labour. Each labourer produces only some part of a whole, and each part, having no value or utility of itself, there is nothing on which the labourer can seize and say, 'this is my product, this I will keep to myself'. Between the commencement of any joint operation, such as that of making cloth, and the division of its product among the different persons whose combined exertions have produced it, the judgement of men must intervene several times, and the question is, how much of this joint product should go to each of the individuals whose united labour produced it?" ([Thomas Hodgskin, *Labour Defended etc.*, London, 1825,] p. 25.)

"... I know no way ||890| of deciding this but by leaving it to be settled by the unfettered judgements of the labourers themselves" (loc. cit., p. 25).

"I must [...] add that it is doubtful whether one species of labour is more valuable than another; certainly it is not more necessary" (loc. cit., p. 26).

Finally Hodgskin writes about the *relation of capital* [and labour]:

"Masters [...] are labourers as well as their journeymen. In this character their interest is precisely the same as that of their men. But they are also either capitalists or the agents of the capitalist, and in this respect their interest is decidedly opposed to the interest of their workmen" (loc. cit., p. 27).

"The wide spread of education among the journeymen mechanics of this country, diminishes daily the value of the labour and skill of almost all masters and employers, by increasing the numbers of persons who possess their peculiar knowledge" (loc. cit., p. 30).

"But put the capitalist, the oppressive middleman out of view"[a] then "... it is plain that *capital*, or the *power to employ labour*, and *coexisting labour*, are one; and [...] *productive capital* and *skilled labour* are also *one*; consequently capital and a labouring population are precisely synonymous. In the system of nature, mouths are united with hands and with intelligence" (loc. cit., p. 33).

The capitalist mode of production disappears with the form of alienation which the various aspects of social labour bear to one another and which is represented in *capital*. This is the conclusion arrived at by Hodgskin.

* * *

The primitive accumulation of capital. Includes the centralisation of the conditions of labour. It means that the conditions of labour acquire an independent existence in relation to the

---

[a] In the manuscript "The *capitalist* is the *oppressive middleman* between the different labourers. If he is put out of view...".—*Ed.*

worker and to labour itself. This historical act is the historical genesis of capital, the *historical* process of separation which transforms the conditions of labour into capital and labour into wage-labour. This provides the basis for capitalist production. *Accumulation of capital* on the basis of capital itself, and therefore also on the basis of the relationship of capital and wage-labour, reproduces the separation and the independent existence of material wealth as against labour on an ever increasing scale. *Concentration of capital.* Accumulation of large amounts of capital by the destruction of the smaller capitals. Attraction. Decapitalisation of the intermediate links between capital and labour. This is only the last degree and the final form of the process which transforms the conditions of labour into capital, then reproduces capital and the separate capitals on a larger scale and finally separates from their owners the various capitals which have come into existence at many points of society, and centralises them in the hands of big capitalists. It is in this extreme form of the contradiction and conflict that production—even though in alienated form—is transformed into social production. There is social labour, and in the real labour process the instruments of production are used in common. As *functionaries* of the process which at the same time accelerates this *social* production and thereby also the development of the productive forces, the capitalists become superfluous in the measure that they, on behalf of society, enjoy the usufruct and that they become overbearing as *owners* of this social wealth and *commanders* of social labour. Their position is similar to that of the feudal lords whose exactions in the measure that their *services* became superfluous with the rise of bourgeois society, became mere outdated and inappropriate privileges and who therefore rushed headlong to destruction. |XV-890||

[g) **Hodgskin's Basic Propositions as Formulated in His Book—"Popular Political Economy"**]

||XVIII-1084| Thomas Hodgskin, *Popular Political Economy. Four Lectures delivered at the London Mechanics' Institution,* London, 1827.

"Easy labour is only *transmitted skill*" (p. 48).
"But as all the advantages derived from the division of labour naturally centre in, and [...] belong to the labourers, if they are deprived of them, and in the progress of society those only are enriched by their

improved skill who never labour,—this must arise from unjust appropriation; from usurpation and plunder in the party enriched, and from consenting submission in the party impoverished" (op. cit., pp. 108-09).

||1085| "The labourers, to be sure, multiply too rapidly when that multiplication is only compared with the want of the capitalist for their services..."[a] (op. cit., p. 120).

"Mr. Malthus points out the effects which an increase in the *number of labourers* has in lessening the share which each one receives of the annual produce—the portion of that *distributed* amongst them being a definite and determinate quantity, not regulated in any degree by what they annually create" (op. cit., p. 126).

"... labour [...] the exclusive standard of value," but "labour, the creator of all wealth" [is] *"not a commodity"* (op. cit., p. 186, note).

Regarding the influence of money on the expansion of wealth, Hodgskin remarks correctly:

"As a man can dispose of small portions of produce that is corruptible, for what is incorruptible, he is under no temptation to throw it away; and thus the use of money adds to wealth, by preventing waste" (op. cit., p. 197).

The chief advantage of retail trade derives from the fact that the quantity in which commodities are best produced is not that in which they are best distributed[b] (op. cit., p. 146).

"Both the theory relative to capital, and the practice of stopping labour at that point where it can produce, in addition to the subsistence of the labourer, a profit for the capitalist, seem opposed to the natural laws which regulate production" (op. cit., p. 238).

With regard to the *accumulation of capital*, Hodgskin advances roughly the same ideas as those contained in his first book. Nevertheless—for the sake of completeness—we will reproduce the main passages.

"Taking only fixed capital into consideration [...] the subject most favourable to the idea of capital aiding production [....] For this purpose we may distinguish three classes of circumstances under which the effects of an accumulation of capital will be very different. First, if it is made and used by the same persons [...][c] every accumulation in his possession of

---

[a] The words up to "rapidly" represent Marx's own synopsis of Hodgskin's argument and have been translated here from the German. The rest of the sentence is quoted directly from Hodgskin.—*Ed.*

[b] Marx paraphrases this proposition of Hodgskin in German (apart from the words "retail trade" and "quantity") and his rendering has been translated here.—*Ed.*

[c] This part of the quotation is slightly condensed and partly translated into German in the manuscript; rendered in English it reads: "If one considers for example fixed capital, the most favourable position for the idea of capital aiding production, three classes of circumstances are to be distinguished under which [the results of] accumulation of capital are very different.
1. When it is made and used by the same person. It is obvious [that]".—*Ed.*

the instruments he makes and uses, facilitates his labour. The *limit to such an accumulation* is [...] *the power of the labourer to make and use the instruments in question.*

"... second, if it be^a made and used by different [...] persons, who share between them in just proportion the produce of their combined labour [....] Capital may be made by one labourer and used by another [...] both may^b divide the commodity [...] in proportion as each has contributed by his labour to produce it.... I should rather express this fact, however, by saying that a part of the society employed in making instruments, while another part uses them, is a *branch of division of labour* which aids productive power and adds to the general wealth. As long as the produce of the two [...] classes of labourers—be^c divided between them, the accumulation or^d increase of such instruments as they can make and use, is as beneficial as if they were made and used by one person."

Third, "if it be owned by a class of persons who neither make nor use it [....] The capitalist being the mere *owner* of the instruments, is not, as such, a labourer. He in no manner assists production."

⟨In other words, production is assisted by the *instrument*, but not by the title which A holds to the instrument, i.e. not by the circumstance that the instrument is owned by a non-labourer.⟩

"He *acquires possession of the produce of*one labourer, which he makes over to another*, either for a time—as is the case with most kinds of fixed capital, or for ever, as is the case with wages—whenever he thinks it can be used or consumed for *his* advantage. He never does allow the produce of one labourer, when it comes into his possession, to be either used or consumed by another, unless it is for his benefit. He employs or lends his property *to share the produce*, or natural revenue, *of labourers*; and every *accumulation of such property* in his hands is a *mere extension of his power over the produce of labour*, and retards the progress of national wealth. [...] this [is] at present the case.... When the capitalist, being the owner of all the produce, will allow labourers neither to make nor use instruments, unless *he* obtains a profit over and above the subsistence of the labourer, it is plain that bounds are set to productive labour much within what Nature prescribes. In *proportion as capital in the hands of a third party is accumulated, so the whole amount of profit required by the capitalist increases,* and so there arises an artificial check to production and population.... In the present state of society, the labourers being in no case the owners of capital, *every accumulation of it adds to the amount of profit demanded from them,* and extinguishes all that labour which would only procure the labourer his comfortable subsistence. ...when it is admitted that labour produces all things, even capital, it *is nonsense to attribute productive power to the instruments labour makes and uses*...."

---

^a In the manuscript "when" instead of "if it be".—*Ed.*
^b In the manuscript "they" instead of "both may".—*Ed.*
^c In the manuscript "is".—*Ed.*
^d In the manuscript "and".—*Ed.*

"*... wages do not*, like instruments, facilitate *production*.[a] [...] *labour, not capital, pays all wages*" (op. cit., pp. 243-47).

||1086| "... the greater part of [...] the *advances of capitalists* consists of such *promises*.[b]

"... the invention and employment of paper-money had done nothing else but show [the incorrectness of the notion] that capital is *something saved*[c] [....] As long as the capitalist, to realise his wealth, or command over other people's labour, was obliged to have in his possession an actual accumulation of the precious metals or of commodities, we might have continued to suppose,[d] that accumulation of capital was the result of an actual saving, and that on it depended the progress of society. But when paper-money and parchment securities were invented—when the possessor of nothing but such a piece of parchment received an annual revenue in pieces of paper with which he obtained whatever was necessary for his own use and consumption, and not giving away all the pieces of paper, was richer at the end of the year than at the beginning, or was entitled next year to receive a still greater number of pieces of paper, obtaining a still greater command over the produce of labour, it became evident [...] that capital was not any thing saved; and that the individual capitalist did not grow rich by an actual and material saving, but by doing something which enabled him ... to obtain more of the produce of other men's[e] labour" (loc. cit., p. 248, note).

"The master manufacturer has either money or paper with which he pays wages; those wages his labourer exchanges for the produce of other labourers, who will not keep the wages, whether money or paper; and it is returned to the manufacturer, who gives in exchange for it the cloth which his own labourers have made. With it he again pays wages, and the money or paper again goes the same round...

"It ascribes to his" (the capitalist's) "*property* merely, whether he employ it to *pay wages*, or whether it consist in useful instruments, all that vast assistance, which *knowledge and skill, when realised in machinery*, give to labour. [...] the united labours of the miner, the smelter, the smith, the engineer, the stoker, and of numberless other persons, and not the lifeless machines, perform whatever is done by steam engines.... *By the common mode of speaking, the productive power of this skill is attributed to its visible products*, the instruments, *the mere owners of which*, who neither make nor use them, imagine themselves to be very productive persons..." (loc. cit., pp. 248-51).

With regard to his polemic against "*the danger of forcing* [...] *capital out of the country*" [loc. cit., p. 253], and against the interest of capital as a necessary stimulus for [the development

---

[a] In the manuscript "*wages do not facilitate production, like instruments*".—*Ed.*

[b] In the manuscript "consists of promises to pay".—*Ed.*

[c] In the manuscript "The invention and employment of paper-money has revealed that capital is by no means something saved".—*Ed.*

[d] In the manuscript "one could suppose".—*Ed.*

[e] In the manuscript "people".—*Ed.*

of] industry, or concerning the savings theory, see IX, 47.[96] To be included in the chapter on the vulgar economists.

"As their numbers are increased,[a] both increased production and consumption take place, which is all that is ever meant by the terms accumulation or increase of national wealth" (op. cit., p. 257). |XVIII-1086||

[h) Hodgskin on the Power of Capital and on the Upheaval in the Right of Property]

||XIII-670a| [Hodgskin,] *The Natural and Artificial Right of Property Contrasted*, London, 1832.

"At present, all the wealth of society goes first into the possession of the *capitalist*, and even most of the land has been purchased by him; *he pays* the landowner his rent, the labourer his wages, the tax and tithe gatherer their claims, and *keeps a large, indeed the largest and continually augmenting share, of the annual produce of labour for himself*. The capitalist may now be said to be the *first owner* of all the wealth of the community; though no law has conferred on him the right to this property" (p. 98).

"... this change has been effected *by the taking of interest on capital*, and by the process of compound interest; and it is not a little curious, that all the lawgivers of Europe endeavoured *to prevent this by statutes*, viz., statutes against usury" (loc. cit., p. 98, note).

"... the power of the capitalist over all the wealth of the country, is a *complete change in the right of property*, and by what law, or series of laws, was it effected?" (loc. cit., p. 99). |XIII-670a||

[4.] Bray as an Opponent of the Economists[97]

||X-441| J. F. Bray, *Labour's Wrongs and Labour's Remedy*, etc., Leeds, 1839.

Since human existence is determined by labour, and labour presupposes instruments of labour ... "the great field for all exertion and the *raw material* of all wealth—the earth—is[b] the common property of all its inhabitants" (p. 28).

"... life is dependent upon food, [...] food [...] upon labour [...], those dependencies are absolute [...] therefore, if labour be evaded by any human being, it can be thus evaded by individuals only on the condition of increased labour by the mass" (loc. cit., p. 31).

"... all the wrongs and the woes which man has ever committed or endured, may be traced to the assumption of a right in the soil, by certain individuals and classes, to the exclusion of other individuals and classes.... The next step which man has ever taken, after having claimed property in land, has been to claim property in man..." (loc. cit., p. 34).

Bray declares that his purpose is:

---

[a] In the manuscript "As the population increases."—*Ed.*
[b] In the manuscript "must be".—*Ed.*

"... fighting them" (the economists) "upon their own ground, and with their own weapons" (loc. cit., p. 41) (in order to prove that poverty need not be the lot of the workers under every social system). "Before the conclusions arrived at by such a course of proceeding can be overthrown, the economists must unsay or disprove those established truths and principles on which their arguments are founded" (loc. cit., p. 41).

According to the economists the production of wealth requires: 1) labour, 2) accumulation of previous labour, or capital, and 3) exchange.[a] These are, according to the economists themselves, the *universal conditions of production.*

"They are applied to society at large, and, from their nature, cannot exempt any individual or any class from their operation" (loc. cit., p. 42).

"The ban—'Thou shalt labour'—rests alike on all created beings.... Man only can escape this law; and, from its nature, it can be evaded by one man only at the expense of another" (loc. cit., p. 43).

"From the very nature of labour and exchange, strict justice not only requires" (in this context, Bray refers to the economic definitions of the exchange-value of commodities) "that all exchangers should be *mutually*, but that they should *likewise be equally*, benefited.... If a just system of exchanges were acted upon, the value of all articles would be determined by the entire cost of production; and equal values should always exchange for equal values. ... the workmen have given the capitalist the labour of a whole year, in exchange for the value of only half a year—and from this [...] has arisen the inequality of wealth and power which at present exists around us. It is an inevitable condition of inequality of exchanges—of buying at one price and selling at another—that capitalists shall continue to be capitalists, and working men be working men—the one a class of tyrants and the other a class of slaves—to eternity" (op. cit., pp. 48-49).

"By the present [...] system, exchanges are not only not mutually beneficial to all parties, as the political economists have asserted, but it is plain [...] that there is, in most transactions between the capitalist and the producer, [...] no exchange whatever ... what is it that the capitalist, whether he be manufacturer or landed proprietor gives [...] for the labour of the working man? The capitalist gives no labour, for he does not work—he gives no capital, for his store of wealth is being perpetually augmented. ...the capitalist [...] *cannot* [...] make an exchange with anything that belongs to himself. The whole transaction, therefore, plainly shews that the capitalists and proprietors do no more than give the working man, for his labour of one week, a part of the wealth which they obtained from him the week before!—which just amounts to giving him nothing for something.... The wealth which the capitalist appears to give in exchange for the workmen's labour was generated neither by the labour nor the riches of the capitalist, but it was originally obtained by the labour of the workman; and it is still daily taken from him, by a fraudulent system of unequal exchanges" (loc. cit., pp. 49-50). "The whole transaction [...] between the producer and the capitalist, is a palpable deception, a mere farce" (loc. cit., p. 50).

---

[a] Marx here summarises Bray's ideas and presents them in German.—*Ed.*

"... the law which says 'There shall be accumulation', is only half fulfilled, and is made to subserve the interests of a particular class, to the detriment of all the rest of the community..." (loc. cit., p. 50).

"Under the present social system, the whole of the working class are dependent upon the capitalist or employer for the means of labour; and where one class, by its position in society, is thus dependent upon another class for the *means of labour*, it is dependent, likewise, for the *means of life*; and this is a condition so contrary to the very intention of society—so revolting to reason ∴ that it cannot for one moment be palliated or defended. It confers on man a power which ought to be vested in nothing mortal" (loc. cit., p. 52).

"Our daily experience teaches us, that if we take a slice from a loaf, the slice never grows on again: the loaf is but an accumulation of slices, and the more we eat of it, the less will there remain to be eaten. Such is the ||442| case with the loaf of the working man; but that of the capitalist follows not this rule. His loaf continually increases instead of diminishing: with him, it is cut and come again, for ever. ... if exchanges were equal, would the wealth of the present capitalists gradually go from them to the working classes: every shilling that the rich man spent, would leave him a shilling less rich" (loc. cit., pp. 54-55).

Bray also shows in his work that:

"... it is [...] impossible that any capitalist can have derived even one thousand pounds sterling from the actual hoarded labour of his workingclass progenitors" (loc. cit., p. 55).

It follows from the teachings of the economists themselves that "... there can be no exchanges without accumulations—no accumulations without labour" (loc. cit., p. 55).

"... under the present system, every working man gives to an employer at least six days' labour for an equivalent worth only four or five days' labour, the gains of the last man are necessarily the losses of the first man" (loc. cit., p. 56).

"Thus, in whatever light" [the genesis of wealth is] "examined—whether as a gift, [...] individual accumulation, [...] exchange, [...] inheritance—there is proof upon proof that there is a flaw in the rich man's title which takes away at once its very show of justice, and its value" (loc. cit., pp. 56-57).

"... this wealth has all been derived from the bones and sinews of the working classes during successive ages, and it has been taken from them by the fraudulent and slavery-creating system of unequal exchanges" (loc. cit., p. 57).

If "a working man under the present system [...] would become wealthy, he [...] instead of exchanging his own labour, must become a capitalist, or exchanger of the labour of other people; and thus, by plundering others in the same manner as he was plundered, through the medium of unequal exchanges, he will be enabled to acquire great gains from the small losses of other people" (loc. cit., p. 57).

"The political economists and capitalists have written and printed many books to impress upon the working man the fallacy that 'the gain of the capitalist *is not* the loss of the producer'. We are told that Labour cannot move one step without Capital—that Capital is as a shovel to the man who digs—that Capital is just as necessary to production as Labour itself is. ... this mutual dependency between Capital and Labour has nothing to do with the relative position of the capitalist and the working man; nor does it show that the former should be maintained by the latter.... It is the capital, and not the capitalist, that is essential to the operations of the producer; and there is as much difference between the two, as there is between the actual cargo and the bill of lading" (loc. cit., p. 59).

"From the relation which capital and labour bear to each other, it is evident that the more capital or accumulated produce there is in a country, the greater will be the facilities for production, and the less labour will it require to obtain a given result. Thus the people of Great Britain, with the aid of their present vast accumulations of capital—their buildings, machinery, ships, canals and railways—can produce more manufactured wealth in one week, than their ancestors of a thousand years since could have created in half a century. It is not our superior physical powers,[a] but our capital, which enables us to do this; for, wherever there is a deficiency of capital, production will progress slowly and laboriously, and vice versa. From these considerations, then, it is apparent, that whatever is gained to Capital, is likewise gained to Labour—that every increase of the former tends to diminish the toil of the latter—and that, therefore, every loss to Capital must also be a loss to Labour. This truth, though long since observed by the political economists, has never yet been fairly stated by them" [loc. cit., pp. 59-60].

⟨In fact, the fellows argue in the following way:

Accumulated products of labour, i.e., products not consumed, lighten labour and make it more productive. As a consequence, the fruits of this lightening and so on must go not to labour itself but to accumulation. Consequently, it is not accumulation which must be the property of labour but labour must be the property of accumulation—[that is, it must be the property] of its own products. Consequently, the worker must not accumulate for himself but for someone else, and the accumulation must confront him as capital.

For the economists, the material element of capital is so integrated with its social form as capital—with its antagonistic character as the product of labour dominating labour—that they cannot write a single sentence without contradicting themselves.⟩

"They *have even identified Capital with one class of the community, and Labour with another class*—although the two powers have naturally, and should have artificially, no such connection. The economists always attempt to make the prosperity, if not the very existence, of the working man dependent upon the condition of maintaining the capitalist in luxury and idleness. They would not have the working man to eat a meal until he has produced two—one for himself and the other for his master—the latter receiving his portion indirectly, by unequal exchanges" (ibid., p. 60).

---

[a] In the manuscript "forces".—*Ed.*

"When the workman has produced a thing, it is his no longer—it belongs to the capitalist—it has been conveyed from the one to the other by the unseen magic of unequal exchanges" (loc. cit., p. 61).

"Under the present social system, Capital and Labour—the shovel and the digger—are two separate and antagonistic powers" (loc. cit., p. 60).

||443| "But even if all the land and the machinery and the houses did belong to the capitalists, and the working class were not in being, the former would not thereby be enabled to evade the great condition 'that there shall be labour'. Their wealth would leave them in the choice only of working or starving. They cannot eat the land and the houses; and the land will not yield sustenance, nor the machinery make clothing, without the application of human labour. Therefore, when the capitalists and proprietors say that the working class must support them, they likewise say, in effect, that the producers belong to them as well as the houses and lands do—that the working man was created only for the rich man's use!" (op. cit., p. 68).

"... the producer [...] receives, in exchange for what he gives to the capitalist—not the labour nor the produce of the labour of the capitalist, but—work! Through the instrumentality of money, the working class are not only compelled to perform the labour which the preservation of existence naturally imposes upon them, but they are likewise saddled with the labour of other classes. It matters not whether the producers now receive gold, or silver, or other commodities from a non-producing class: it all amounts to this—that the working class perform their own labour, and support themselves, and likewise perform the labour of the capitalist, and maintain him into the bargain! Whatever may be the *nominal* recéipts which the producers receive from the capitalists, their actual receipts are—*the transfer of that labour which ought to be rendered by the capitalists*" (op. cit., pp. 153-54).

"... we will suppose the population of the United Kingdom [...] to be [...] 25,000,000 of human beings. [...] we may [...] estimate the entire maintenance of the twenty-five millions of people to be worth,[a] on the average, at least £15 per head annually. This gives £375,000,000 as the yearly value of the maintenance of the whole people of the United Kingdom. We do not, however, employ ourselves merely in producing articles of subsistence, for our labour creates, likewise, many unconsumable articles. We every year add to our stock of accumulations, or capital, by increasing the number of our houses, ships, implements, machines, roads, and other assistants to further production, beside making good all wear and tear. Thus, although our subsistence may be worth but three hundred and seventy-five millions sterling a year, the total annual value of the wealth created by the people [...] will not be less than five hundred millions sterling" (op. cit., p. 81).

"... we cannot calculate upon having above one-fourth of our population, or about six millions of men—that is, those between the ages of fourteen and fifty.—as effective producers. Of this number [...] scarcely five millions can be said, under the present arrangements '[...] to assist in production;" (Bray writes later on that only four millions are directly employed

---

[a] Instead of "we may estimate the entire maintenance of the 25 millions of people to be worth", in the manuscript "We assume that their maintenance is".—*Ed.*

in actual production) "for thousands of able-bodied men [...] are compelled to stand idle while the work which they ought to do is being performed by women and children; and hundreds of thousands of men in Ireland can obtain no employment whatever. Thus less than five millions of men, assisted by a few thousands of women and children, have [...] to create produce for [...] twenty-five millions..." (loc. cit., pp. 81-82).

"... the present number of working men, if unassisted by machinery, could not support themselves and the present number of idlers and unprofitable labourers [....] The agricultural and manufacturing machinery of every kind which we bring to our aid in the business of productions, has been computed to perform the labour of about one hundred millions of effective men. ... this machinery—and its application under the present system, which has generated the hundreds of thousands of idlers and livers on profit who now press the working class into the earth" (loc. cit., p. 82).

"The present constitution of society has been fertilised by machinery, and by machinery will it be destroyed.... The machinery itself is good—is indispensable; it is the application of it—the circumstance of its being possessed by individuals instead of by the nation—that is bad" (loc. cit., pp. 82-83).

"The five millions of men already enumerated as assisting in production will include all who labour little or much. Some [...] do not work five hours a day, while others again toil on fifteen hours;[a] and when to this is added the time lost by the compulsory idleness of great numbers in times of depression in trade, it will be found that our annual production is created and distributed by less than one-fifth of the community, working, on the average, ten hours a day" (loc. cit., p. 83).

"... we suppose that the wealthy non-producers of every description, with their families, and dependents, amount only to two millions of persons, yet this number alone would cost the working classes £30,000,000 annually, if their maintenance were averaged, like that of the latter, at £15 per head. ...therefore,[b] upon the most moderate computation their maintenance will cost not less than £50 per head. This gives a total of £100,000,000 as the annual cost of the mere drones of society—the utterly unproductive..." (loc. cit., pp. 83-84).

"... likewise[c] the double and quadruple allowance received by the various classes of small proprietors, manufacturers, and tradesmen, in the shape of profit and interest. ||444| Upon the most moderate computation, the share of wealth enjoyed by this extensive portion of the community will amount to not less than £140,000,000 annually, *above* the average of what is received by an equal number of the best paid of the working class. Thus, along with their government, the two classes of idlers and livers on profit—comprising perhaps one-fourth of the entire population—absorb about £300,000,000 annually, or above one half of the entire wealth produced [...] an average loss of above £50 per head to every working man in the empire! — This leaves no more than an average of £11 per head per

---

[a] In the manuscript the two sentences, which are translated into German, are condensed to read as follows: "Of the five million men who at present assist in production some work only five hours a day, others fifteen."—*Ed.*
[b] In the manuscript "But".—*Ed.*
[c] In the manuscript "Add to this".—*Ed.*

annum, to be divided amongst the remaining three-fourths of the nation. From calculations made in 1815, it appears that the annual income of the whole people of the United Kingdom amounted to about £430,000,000; of which the working class received £99,742,547, and the rent, pension, and profit class £330,778,825! The whole property of the country was at the same time calculated to be worth nearly three thousand millions of pounds sterling" (loc. cit., pp. 84-85).

Cf. the list of Gregory King etc.[98]

England, 1844. Population: Nobility and gentry—1,181,000. *Trades men, farmers*, etc.—4,221,000 (combined total—5,402,000). Labourers, paupers, etc.—9,567,000. Banfield (T.C.), *The Organisation of Industry*, second ed., London, 1848. |X-444||

[CHAPTER XXII]

RAMSAY

[1. The Attempt to Distinguish Between Constant and Variable Capital. The View that Capital Is Not an Essential Social Form]

||XVIII-1086| Ramsay, George (of Trinity College, Cambridge), *An Essay on the Distribution of Wealth*, Edinburgh, 1836.

With Ramsay we return again to the political economists. ⟨In order to find a place for commercial capital, he calls it "the transport of commodities from one place to another" (op. cit., p. 19). He thus confuses trade with the carrying industry.⟩

Ramsay's chief contribution:

First: That he does in fact make the distinction between *constant and variable capital*. True, this occurs in such a manner, that the distinction between fixed and circulating capital which he takes from the circulation process is the only one which he *nominally* retains, but he defines fixed capital in such a way that it includes all the elements of constant capital. He therefore regards as *fixed* capital not only machinery and instruments, buildings in which labour is carried on or in which the results of labour are stored, draught and breeding animals, but also all raw materials (semi-manufactures, etc.) "the seed of the agriculturist, and the raw material of the manufacturer" (op. cit., p. 22). Moreover "manure of all kinds, fences [...] for agriculture, and the fuel consumed in manufactories" (loc. cit., p. 23) are fixed capital.

"*Circulating capital* consists exclusively of subsistence and other necessaries advanced to the workmen, previous to the completion of the produce of their labour" (loc. cit., p. 23).

It can be seen therefore that by "circulating capital" he understands nothing ||1087| but that part of capital which constitutes wages, and by fixed capital, that part which constitutes the objective conditions—means and materials—of labour.

The mistake here, however, is the identification of this division of capital, which is directly derived from the production process, with the distinction which arises from the circulation process. This is due to his adherence to the economic tradition.

On the other hand, Ramsay again confuses the purely material element of the fixed capital thus defined with its existence as "capital". Circulating capital (i.e., variable capital) does not enter into the real labour process, but what does enter, is living labour, which is bought with circulating capital, and which replaces it. What enters in addition into the labour process is constant capital, that is, labour embodied in the objective conditions of labour, in the materials and means of labour. Ramsay therefore writes:

"... fixed capital alone, not circulating, is properly speaking a source of national wealth" (loc. cit., p. 23). "...labour and fixed capital are the only elements of expense of production" (op. cit., p. 28).

What is really expended in the production of a commodity are raw materials, machinery, etc., and the living labour which sets them in motion.

"Circulating" capital is superfluous, extraneous to the process of production.

"... were we to suppose the labourers not to be paid until the completion of the product, there would be no occasion whatever for circulating capital. [...] industry would be carried on on a scale quite as great[a] [....] Nothing can prove more strongly[b] that circulating capital is not an *immediate* agent in[c] production, *nor even essential to it at all*, but merely a *convenience rendered necessary by the deplorable poverty of the mass of the people*" (op. cit., p. 24).

"... fixed capital [...] alone constitutes an element of cost of production in a national point of view"... (loc. cit., p. 26).

In other words: the labour materialised in the conditions of labour—materials and means of labour—which we call "fixed capital", and the living labour, in short, embodied, materialised labour and living labour, are necessary conditions of production, elements of the national wealth. On the other hand, [according to Ramsay], it is a mere "convenience" due to the "deplorable poverty of the mass of the people" that the means of subsistence of the workers at all assume the form of "circulating capital". Labour is a condition of production, but wage-

---

[a] The manuscript has "Production would be just as great."—*Ed.*
[b] The manuscript has "This proves".—*Ed.*
[c] The manuscript has "of".—*Ed.*

labour is not, and neither, therefore, is it necessary that the workers' means of subsistence confront them as "capital", as an "advance by the capitalist". What Ramsay overlooks is that if the means of subsistence of the workers did not confront them as "capital" (as "circulating capital", as he calls it), neither would the objective conditions of labour confront them as "capital", as "fixed capital", as he calls it. Ramsay attempts in earnest, and not merely in words as the other economists do, to reduce capital to "a portion of the national wealth, employed, or meant to be employed, in favouring reproduction" (op. cit., p. 21); he therefore declares wage-labour and consequently capital—that is the *social form which the means of reproduction assume on the basis of wage-labour*—to be unimportant and due merely to the poverty of the mass of the people.

Thus we have arrived at the point where political economy itself—on the basis of its analysis—declares the *capitalist form* of production, and consequently *capital*, to be not an absolute, but merely an "accidental", historical condition of production.

Ramsay's analysis, however, does not go far enough to draw the correct conclusions from his premises, from the new definition which he has given to capital in the immediate production process.

[2. Ramsay's Views on Surplus-Value and on Value. Reduction of Surplus-Value to Profit. The Influence Which Changes in the Value of Constant and Variable Capital Exert on the Rate and Amount of Profit]

Ramsay comes indeed close to the correct definition of surplus-value.

"... a circulating capital will always maintain more labour than that formerly bestowed upon itself. Because, could it employ no more than had been previously bestowed upon itself, what advantage could arise to the owner from the use of it as such?" (op. cit., p. 49). "There is no possible way of escaping this conclusion, except by asserting[a] that the *quantity of labour* which any circulating capital will employ is no more than equal to that previously bestowed upon it. [...] This would be [...] to say, that the value of the capital expended is[b] equal to that of the product" (loc. cit., p. 52).

---

[a] Marx translated the first part of this passage and condensed it to: "or will people assert".—*Ed.*

[b] The manuscript has "was".—*Ed.*

This means, therefore, that the capitalist exchanges less materialised labour for more living labour and that this surplus of unpaid living labour constitutes the excess of the value of the product over the value of the capital consumed in its production, in other words, the *surplus-value* (profit, etc.). If the amount of labour for which the capitalist pays wages were equal to the amount which he receives back from the worker in the product, then the value of the product would be no greater than that of the capital and there would be no profit. Although Ramsay is very close here to the real origin of surplus-value, he is nevertheless too bound up in the tradition of the economists not to begin immediately straying again along false paths. First of all, the way he explains this exchange between variable capital ||1088| and labour is ambiguous. If he had been quite clear about this, then further misunderstanding would have been impossible. He says:

"... circulating capital", for instance, "raised by the labour of 100 men, will [...] employ a greater number, say 150.[a] Therefore the product at the end of the [...] year, will, in this case, be the result of the labour of 150 men" (loc. cit., p. 50).

Under what circumstances can the product of 100 men buy [the labour of] 150 men?

If the wages received by a worker for 12 hours' labour were equal to the value of 12 hours' labour, then only one working-day could be bought back with the product of his labour and only 100 working-days with the product of 100 working-days. But if the value of the daily product of his labour is equal to 12 labour hours and the value of the daily wage he receives is equal to 8 labour hours, then $1^1/_2$ working-days or the labour of $1^1/_2$ men can be paid for, bought back, for the value of his daily product. And $100 \, (1+^1/_2$ men or working-days$)=100+50$ or 150 men can be employed with the product of 100 working-days. Thus, the condition in which the product of 100 men sets 150 in motion is that each of the 100 men and, in general, every worker, spends half as much time working gratis for the capitalist as he works for himself, or that he spends a third of the working-day working gratis. Ramsay does not make this clear. The ambiguity appears in the conclusion: "Therefore the product at the end of the ... year, will, in this case, be the result of the labour of 150 men" [loc. cit., p. 50]. It will indeed be

---

[a] In the manuscript "will employ 150 men".—*Ed.*

the result of the labour of 150 men in the same way as the product of 100 men was the result of the labour of 100 men. The ambiguity (and certainly the lack of clarity, more or less derived from Malthus) is to be found in this: It appears as if the profit arises merely from the fact that 150 men are now employed instead of 100. Just as if the profit derived from the 150 workers arose from the fact that 225 workers can now be set in motion by the product of the 150 [in the ratio of] $100:150 = 150:225$ [or] $20:30 = 30:45$ [or] $4:6 = 6:9$. But that is not the point.

The labour which the 100 men supply amounts to x, if x equals their total working-day. The wages they receive will then equal $2/3 x$. Hence the value of their product equals x, the value of their wages equals $x - 1/3 x$, and the surplus-value made on them is $1/3 x$.

If the entire product of the labour of 100 men is again laid out in wages, then 150 men can be employed with it and their product will be equal to the wages of 225 men. The labour-time of 100 men is the labour-time of 100 men. But the labour they are *paid for* is the product of $66^2/_3$ men, that is, only $2/_3$ of the value embodied in their product. The ambiguity [arises] because it appears as if the 100 men or the 100 working-days (it makes no difference whether they are days calculated over a year or separate days) produce 150 working-days—a product embodying the value of 150 working-days; while, conversely, the value of 100 working-days suffices to *pay for* 150 working-days. If the capitalist continues to employ 100 men as he did previously, then his profit remains the same. He will continue to pay the 100 men a product equal to the labour-time of $66^2/_3$ men and pocket the rest as he did before. If, on the other hand, he lays out the whole product of the 100 men in wages once again, then he *accumulates* and appropriates a new amount of surplus labour equal to 50 working-days instead of only $33^1/_3$ as he did previously.

It is immediately apparent that Ramsay is not clear on the point, since he once again advances against the determination of value by labour-time the otherwise "inexplicable" phenomenon that the *rates of profit* are equal for capitals which exploit different masses of labour-power.

"The use of fixed capital modifies to a considerable extent the principle that value depends upon quantity of labour. For some commodities on which the same quantity of labour has been expended, require very different periods before they are fit for consumption. But as during this time the capital brings no return, *in order that the employment in question should not be less lucrative than others* in which the product is sooner ready for use, it is necessary that the commodity, when at last brought to market, *should be increased in value by all the amount of the profit withheld.* This shews [...] how capital may regulate value independently of labour" (op. cit., p. 43).

It shows rather that capital regulates average prices[99] independently *of the value* of the particular product and that it exchanges commodities not according to their value, but in such a way that one employment of capital "should not be less ||1089| lucrative than others". Since empty tradition is more powerful in political economy than in any other science, Ramsay does not fail either to reproduce the "wine in the cellar"[a] argument which has been notorious since the time of [James] Mill. And he therefore concludes that "capital is a source of value independent of labour" (op. cit., p. 55), whereas the most he would have been justified in concluding was that the surplus-value realised by capital in a particular branch of production does not depend on the quantity of labour employed by that particular capital. |1089||

||1090| This false conception of Ramsay's in this case is all the more surprising since, on the one hand, he grasps *the natural basis*, so to speak, of surplus-value, and, on the other hand, he affirms with regard to one instance that the *distribution of surplus-value*—its equalisation to the general rate of profit—does not increase the surplus-value itself.

[Ramsay says *firstly*:]

"... profits owe their existence to a[b] law of the material world, whereby the beneficence of nature when aided and directed by the labour and skill of man, gives so ample a return to national industry as to leave a *surplus* of products over and above what is absolutely necessary for replacing in kind the fixed capital consumed, and *for perpetuating the race of labourers employed*" [op. cit., p. 205].

⟨*"Perpetuating* the race of labourers" ||1091| is a fine result of capitalist production. Of course, if labour only sufficed to reproduce the conditions of labour and to keep the workers alive, no *surplus* would be possible, hence no profit and no capital. But that nature has nothing whatever to do with it and

---

[a] See this volume, pp. 86-87, 177, 229.—*Ed.*
[b] Instead of "profits owe their existence to a", the manuscript has: "The source of profits is the".—*Ed.*

that the race of labourers perpetuates itself despite this *surplus* and that the surplus assumes the form of profit and on this basis, the race of capitalists perpetuates itself has been admitted by Ramsay himself since he declares that "circulating capital", by which he means wages, wage-labour, is not an essential condition of production, but is due merely to the "deplorable poverty of the mass of the people". He does not draw the conclusion that it is capitalist production which "perpetuates" this "deplorable poverty", although he admits it when he says that it "perpetuates the race of labourers" and leaves them only as much as is necessary for that perpetuation. In the sense indicated above it can be said that surplus-value etc. rests on a *natural law*, that is, on the productivity of human labour in its exchange with nature. But Ramsay himself states that a source of surplus-value is the *absolute lengthening of labour-time* (p. 102) as well as the increased productivity of labour brought about by industry.)

"... let the gross produce be ever so little more than is strictly essential for the above purposes, and the separation of a distinct revenue from the general mass, under the appellation of profit, and belonging to another class of men, becomes possible" (loc. cit., p. 205). "... *the very existence of the former*[a] *as a distinct class is dependent on the productiveness of industry*" (loc. cit., p. 206).

Secondly, with regard to the equalisation of the rate of profit as a result of the rise in prices in some branches caused by increases in wages, Ramsay observes:

The rise in prices in some branches of industry resulting from increases in wages "... by no means exempted the master-capitalists from suffering in their profits, nor even *at all diminished their total loss*, but only served *to distribute it more equally among the different orders composing that body*" (op. cit., p. 163).

And if the capitalist whose wine is the product of 100 men (Ramsay's example) sells it for the same price as a capitalist whose commodity is the product of 150 men, in order that "... the employment [of capital] in question should not be less lucrative than others" [p. 43], then it is clear that thereby the surplus-value embodied in the wine and in the other commodity is not increased, but only distributed equally between different orders of capitalists |1091||.

||1089| He also brings up again Ricardo's exceptions [to the

---

[a] In the manuscript "master-capitalists".—*Ed.*

determination of value by labour-time]. These latter will have to be discussed in that part of *our* text where we speak of the conversion of value into *price of production*.[100] That is, very briefly, as follows. Provided that in the different branches of production the length of the working-day (insofar as this is not compensated by the intensity of labour, the unpleasantness of the work, etc.) is the same, or rather the surplus labour is the same [as well as] the rate of exploitation, the rate of surplus-value can change only if wages rise or fall. Such variations in the rate of surplus-value, like the rise or fall in wages, will affect the production prices of commodities in different ways according to the organic composition of capital. Capital in which the variable part is large compared to the constant part, would acquire more surplus labour as a result of a fall in wages and would appropriate less surplus labour as a result of a rise in wages than capital with a larger proportion of the constant part to the variable part. A rise or fall in wages would therefore have opposite effects on the rate of profit in the two branches or on the general rate of profit. In order to maintain the general rate of profit, if wages rise, the prices of the first kind of commodities will rise, and those of the second kind will fall. (Either type of capital will of course be *directly* affected by variations in wages only in proportion to the greater or less quantity of living labour it employs in comparison with the total capital expended.) Conversely, if wages fall, the prices of the first kind of commodities will fall and those of the second kind will rise.

Strictly speaking, all this hardly belongs to the discussion of the original conversion of values into production prices and the original establishment of the general rate of profit, since it is much more a question of how a *general rise or fall in wages* will affect production prices regulated by the general rate of profit.

This problem has even less to do with the difference between fixed and circulating capital. Bankers and merchants employ almost exclusively circulating capital and hardly any variable capital; that is, they lay out relatively small amounts of capital on living labour. Contrariwise, a mine-owner employs incomparably more fixed capital than a capitalist engaged in tailoring. But it is very questionable whether he employs relatively as much living labour. It is merely because Ricardo advanced this special, relatively insignificant case as the *only instance of a divergence* between production price and value (or, as he incorrectly put it, [as] an exception to the determination of value by labour-time) and presented it in the form of a difference between fixed and circulating capital, that this blunder—and in an incorrect form at that—has survived as an important dogma in all subsequent political economy. (The mine-owner should be counterposed not to the tailor but to the banker and the merchant.)

[Ramsay writes:]

"... the rise of wages [...] is limited by the productiveness of industry. In other words, ... a man can never receive more for the labour of a day or year than with the aid of all the other sources of wealth, he can produce in the same time. ... his pay must be less than this, for a *portion of the gross produce* always goes to replace fixed capital" (i.e., *constant capital*, raw materials and machinery, according to Ramsay) "with its profit" (op. cit., p. 119).

Here Ramsay confuses two things. The amount of "fixed capital" embodied in the daily product is not the product of the day's labour of the worker; in other words, this portion of the *value* of the product represented by a portion of the product in kind is not the product of this day's labour. On the other hand, profit is indeed a deduction from the daily product of the worker or from the value of this daily product.

Although Ramsay has not clearly elaborated the nature of surplus-value and although in particular he remains firmly rooted in the old prejudices with regard to the relation of value and production price and the conversion of surplus-value into average profit, he has on the other hand drawn another, correct ||1090| conclusion from his conception of fixed and circulating capital.

Before coming to this, [here is another passage about "value"]:

"... *value* must be in proportion not merely to the capital truly consumed, but to that also which continues unaltered, in a word,[a] to the total capital employed" (op. cit., p. 74).

By this he means that profit, and therefore also the production price, must be in proportion [to the total capital employed] whereas the value obviously cannot be altered by that part of the capital which does not enter into the value of the product.

[Ramsay drew the following conclusion from his conception of fixed and circulating capital.]

---

[a] The manuscript has "viz."—*Ed.*

With the advance of society (i.e., of capitalist production) the fixed portion of capital increases at the expense of the circulating capital, i.e., that laid out in labour. Therefore the demand for labour declines *relatively* as wealth increases or capital is accumulated. In manufacture, the "evils" which the development of the productive forces generate for the workers are temporary, but reappear constantly. In agriculture, they are continuous, especially in connection with the conversion of arable land into pasture. The general result is: with the advance of society, i.e., with the development of capital, here with that of national wealth, the condition of the workers is affected less and less by this development, in other words, it *worsens* relatively in the same ratio as the general wealth increases, i.e., as capital is accumulated, or, what amounts to the same thing, as the scale of reproduction increases. One can see that it is a far cry from this conclusion to the naive conceptions of Adam Smith or the apologetics of vulgar political economy. For Adam Smith, the accumulation of capital is identical with growing demand for labour, continual rise of wages, and *consequently* with a fall of profits. In his time, the demand for labour did in fact grow at least in the same proportion in which capital was accumulated, because manufacture still predominated at that time and large-scale industry was only in its infancy.

[Ramsay says:]

"... that demand[a] must depend" (directly, immediately) "upon the amount of the latter species of capital alone"[b] (op. cit., p. 87). (This is tautology on Ramsay's part, since he equates circulating capital with capital laid out in wages.) "At every change of this kind,[c] the fixed capital of the country is increased at the expense of the circulating" (loc. cit., p. 89). "... the demand for labour will generally increase as capital augments, still it by no means follows that it will do so in the same proportion"[d] (loc. cit., p. 88). "It is not, until, in the progress of industry, favoured by the new inventions, circulating capital shall have become increased beyond what it formerly was,"

⟨here again the wrong assumption creeps in that an increase of necessaries in general and increase of that portion of necessaries intended for the workers are the same thing⟩

---

[a] The manuscript has "The demand for labour".—*Ed.*
[b] The manuscript has "amount of circulating capital alone".—*Ed.*
[c] The manuscript has "With the progress of civilisation".—*Ed.*
[d] The manuscript has "The demand for labour will not therefore generally increase as capital augments, at least not in the same proportion."—*Ed.*

"that a greater demand for labour will spring up. Demand will then rise, but not in proportion to the accumulation of the general capital. In countries where industry has much advanced, fixed capital comes gradually to bear a greater and greater proportion to circulating. *Every augmentation, therefore, in the national stock destined for reproduction, comes, in the progress of society, to have a less and less influence upon the condition of the labourer*" (loc. cit., pp. 90-91). "Every addition to fixed capital, is made [...] at the expense of the circulating", i.e., at the expense of the demand for labour (loc. cit., p. 91).

"The evils resulting from the invention of machinery, to the labouring population employed in the latter,[a] will probably be but temporary, *liable to be perpetually renewed however*, as fresh improvements are constantly making for economising labour" [loc. cit., p. 91].

And for the following reasons. [*Firstly*:] The capitalists who use the *new machinery* obtain extraordinary profits; consequently their capacity to save and to increase their capital grows. A portion of this is also used as circulating capital. Secondly, the price of the manufactured commodities falls in proportion to the diminished cost of production; thus the consumers save, and this facilitates the accumulation of capital, a portion of which may find its way to the manufacturing industry in question. Thirdly: the fall in the price of these products increases the demand for them.

"Thus [...] though [...] it[b] may throw out of employment a considerable body of persons, "this" will yet probably be followed, after a longer or shorter period, by the re-engagement of the same, or even a much greater number of labourers" (loc. cit., pp. 92-93).

"... in agriculture the case is widely different. The demand for raw produce cannot increase in that rapid way in which it may for manufactured goods.... But the change of all others most fatal[c] to the country people is the conversion of arable land into pasture.... Almost all the funds which formerly supported men, are now vested in cattle, sheep and other elements of fixed capital" (loc. cit., p. 93). |1090||

||1091| Ramsay remarks correctly:

"*Wages* ... as well as *profits*, are to be considered each of them as really a *portion of the finished product*, totally distinct in the national point of view from the cost of raising it" (op. cit., p. 142).

"Independent of its results, it" (fixed capital) "is a pure loss.... But, besides this, labour ... not what is paid for it, ought to be reckoned as[d]

---

[a] The manuscript has "manufactures".—*Ed.*
[b] The manuscript has "the machinery".—*Ed.*
[c] Instead of "But the change of all others most fatal", the manuscript has "the most fatal".—*Ed.*
[d] Instead of "labour [...] not what is paid for it, ought to be reckoned as", the manuscript has "Only labour, not wages, not what is paid for it is".—*Ed.*

another element of cost of production. Labour is [...] a sacrifice [....] The more of it is expended in one employment, the less ... for another, and therefore if[a] applied to unprofitable undertakings ... the nation suffers from the waste of the principal source of wealth. ... the *reward of labour* ought not to be considered as[b] an element of cost" ... (loc. cit., pp. 142-43).

(This is quite right: *labour*, and not *paid* labour or wages, must be considered as an element of value.)

Ramsay describes the *real* reproduction process correctly:

"In what manner is a comparison to be instituted between[c] the product and the stock expended upon it?... With regard to a whole nation.... It is evident that *all the various elements of the stock expended* must be reproduced in some employment or another, otherwise the industry of the country could not go on as formerly. The raw material of manufactures, the implements used in them, as also in agriculture, the extensive machinery engaged in the former, the buildings necessary for fabricating or storing the produce, must all be parts of the total return of a country, as well as of the advances of all its master-capitalists. Therefore, the quantity of the former may be compared with that of the latter, each article being supposed placed as it were beside that of a similar kind" (loc. cit., pp. 137-39).

As regards the individual capitalist

(this is a false abstraction. The nation does not exist, or exists only as the capitalist class, and the whole class operates in exactly the same way as the individual capitalist. The two methods of approach differ from one another only in that one clings to and isolates use-value, the other exchange-value)

since the stock expended by him is not *replaced* in kind, because "the greater number [of its elements] must be obtained by exchange, a certain portion of the product being necessary for this purpose. Hence each individual master-capitalist comes to look much more to the exchangeable value of his product than to its quantity" (loc. cit., pp. 145-46).[d]

||1092| "... the more the *value of the*[e] *product exceeds the value of the capital advanced, the greater will be his profit*. Thus, then, will he estimate it, by comparing value with value, not quantity with quantity. This is the first difference to be remarked in the mode of reckoning profits between nations and individuals" (loc. cit., p. 146).

(The nation too—if it is not supposed to be identical with the body of capitalists—can so far compare value with value. It can calculate the total labour-time which it has to expend to replace the used-up part of its constant capital and the part

---

[a] The manuscript has "when".—*Ed.*
[b] The manuscript has "does not constitute".—*Ed.*
[c] The manuscript has "How is it possible to compare".—*Ed.*
[d] The first part of the passage starting with "As regards" and ending with "because" is a free summary (mainly in German), not a quotation.—*Ed.*
[e] The manuscript has "his".—*Ed.*

of the product consumed individually, and the time of labour spent in producing a surplus designed to enlarge the scale of reproduction.⟩

"The second is, that, since the master-capitalist always makes an *advance of wages* to the labourers, *instead of paying them out of the finished commodity*, he considers this as well as the fixed capital consumed, a part of his expenses, though [...] nationally speaking, it is not[a] an element of cost" (loc. cit., p. 146).

⟨This difference too disappears in fact in the process of reproduction as a whole. The capitalist always pays *out of the finished commodity*, that is to say, out of the commodity finished by the labourer yesterday he pays his wages tomorrow, or in point of fact, he gives him, in the form of wages, only an assignation of products *to be finished in future* or *almost produced*, i.e., finally produced by the time they are bought. The *advance* disappears as a mere illusion in reproduction, i.e., in the continuity of the process of production.⟩

"Hence his rate of profit will depend upon the excess in the value of his product over and above the value of the capital advanced, both fixed and circulating" (loc. cit., p. 146).

⟨This is likewise true in a "national point of view". His profit always depends on what he himself pays for the product, whether finished or not, when he pays wages.⟩

Ramsay has the merit, firstly, that he contradicts the false notion—current since Adam Smith—of the value of the whole product dissolving into revenue under different names; secondly, that he defines the rate of profit in two-ways, [once] by the rate of wages, i.e., the rate of surplus-value, and a second time, by the value of the constant capital. But he transgresses in the opposite direction to Ricardo. Ricardo arbitrarily seeks to equalise the rate of profit and the rate of surplus-value. On the other hand, the twofold determination of the rate of profit—1) by the rate of surplus-value (hence by the rate of wages) and 2) by the ratio of this surplus-value to the total capital advanced, that is, in fact determined by the ratio of the constant capital to the total capital—is irrationally presented by Ramsay as two parallel circumstances which determine the rate of profit. He does not grasp the transformation which surplus-value undergoes before it becomes profit. Whereas therefore Ricardo arbitrarily

---

[a] The manuscript has "though they, nationally speaking, are not".—*Ed.*

seeks to reduce the rate of profit to the rate of surplus-value in order to work out the theory of value consistently, Ramsay seeks to reduce surplus-value to profit. We shall see later that the way he describes the influence of the value of constant capital on the rate of profit is very inadequate, and even incorrect.

[Ramsay writes:]

"Profit [...] must rise or fall exactly as the *proportion* of the gross produce, or of *its value*, required to replace necessary advances, falls or rises.... Therefore, the rate of profit must depend [...] upon two circumstances; first, the proportion of the whole produce which goes to the labourers; secondly, the proportion which must be set apart for replacing, *either in kind or by exchange*, the fixed capital" (loc. cit., pp. 147-48).

In other words, therefore, the rate of profit depends on the excess of the value of the product over the sum of circulating and fixed capital; hence on the proportion which, firstly, the circulating capital, and, secondly, the fixed capital bear to the value of the whole produce. If we know where this *surplus* comes from, then the whole matter is very simple. But if we only know that the profit depends on the *ratio* of the surplus to these outlays, then we can acquire the most inaccurate notions about the origin of this surplus, for example we can, like Ramsay, imagine that it originates in part in fixed (constant) capital.

||1093| "To me it seems certain,[a] that an increased facility of raising the various objects which enter into the composition of fixed capital, tends, by diminishing this proportion,[b] to raise the rate of profit, just as in the former case of an augmented return of the elements of circulating capital, which serves to maintain labour" (op. cit., p. 164).

With regard to the tenant farmer, for example:

"... be the [amount of gross] return small or great, the quantity of it required for replacing what has been consumed in these different forms, can undergo no alteration whatsoever. This quantity must be considered as *constant, so long as production is carried on on the same scale*. Consequently, *the larger the total return*, the less must be the proportion of the whole which the farmer must set aside for the above purposes" (loc. cit., p. 166).

The more easily the farmer who produces food and raw materials such as flax, hemp, wood, can reproduce them, [the more] his profit will increase.[c]

The farmer's profit [increases] as a result of the *increase in the quantity* of his produce, *the total value of which remains the same*, but "a smaller

---

[a] The manuscript has "It is certain".—*Ed.*

[b] That is, diminishing the part of the gross product which is required to replace the fixed capital.—*Ed.*

[c] This paragraph and part of the next are summaries (in German) by Marx of the ideas developed by Ramsay.—*Ed.*

proportion of this sum total, and consequently of its value, is required for restoring the various elements of fixed capital, with which *the farmer can supply himself;*" while the manufacturer would benefit because his product would have a greater purchasing power (loc. cit., pp. 166-67).

Let us assume that the harvest amounts to 100 quarters and the seed corn to 20, that is, a fifth of the harvest. Let us assume further that the harvest is doubled the following year (with the expenditure of the same amount of labour) and now comes to 200 quarters. If the scale of production remains the same, then the amount of seed corn remains 20 quarters as previously, but this is now only one-tenth of the harvest. One has to take into account however that the value of the 100 quarters [previously harvested] is equal to that of the 200 quarters [now obtained], therefore one quarter of the first harvest is equal to two quarters of the second. 80 quarters remain over in the first case, 180 in the second. Since wages are irrelevant to the present problem, which concerns the influence that a change in the value of constant capital exerts on the rate of profit, let us assume that the value of wages remains unchanged. Then, if wages were 20 quarters in the first case, they are 40 in the second. Finally, let us assume that the value of the other ingredients of constant capital which the farmer does not reproduce in kind amounted to 20 quarters in the first case and therefore to 40 in the second.

We now have the following calculation:

1) *The product* amounts to 100 quarters. *The seed corn* to 20 quarters. *The other elements of constant capital* come to 20 quarters, *wages* to 20 quarters, *profit* to 40 quarters.

2) *The product* amounts to 200 quarters. The *seed corn* to 20 quarters. *The other elements of constant capital* come to 40 quarters, *wages* to 40 quarters and *profit* to 100 quarters; i.e., its value is equal to 50 quarters in the first case. There would therefore be a surplus profit of 10 quarters [in the second case].

Thus not [only] the rate of profit, but also the amount of profit, would have increased here, as a result of a change in the value of constant capital. Although wages remained the same in both 1 and 2, the ratio of profit to wages, that is, the rate of surplus-value, would have risen. But this is only an illusion. The profit would consist firstly of 80 quarters, equal to 40 quarters in case 1, and the ratio to wages would remain the same; secondly, [in case] 2, of 20 quarters, equal only to 10 quarters in the first case, which would have been converted into revenue from constant capital.

But is this calculation correct? We must assume that the result in the second case was due to a successful harvest which came about although work was carried on in the same conditions as prevailed in the first case. In order to clarify the matter, let us assume that 1 quarter equals £2 in the first case. This means that for the harvest which has yielded him 200 quarters, the farmer has laid out: 20 quarters for seed corn (or £40), 20 quarters for other elements of constant capital (or £40), 20 quarters for wages (or £40). *A total* of £120, and the product amounts to 200 quarters. In the first case he likewise laid out only £120 (60 quarters) and the product amounting to 100 quarters was worth £200. The profit remaining was £80, or 40 quarters. Since the 200 quarters [in case 2] are the product of the same amount of labour [as the 100 quarters in case 1], then once again they are likewise equal to only £200. Thus, only £80 profit remains, which is now, however, equal to 140 quarters. Consequently, a quarter now [costs the farmer] only £$4/_7$ and not £1. In other words, the value of a quarter has fallen from £2 to £$4/_7$, that is, by £$1^3/_7$, and not from [£2] to [£1], that is, by a half as we assumed above in [case] 2 as opposed to [case] 1.

The farmer's total product amounts to 200 quarters, that is, £200. But £120 out of this £200 replaces the 60 quarters which he has expended, each one of which cost him £2. There thus remains a profit of £80 which is equal to the remaining 140 quarters. How does this happen? The quarter is now worth £1, but each of the 60 quarters expended in production cost £2. They cost the farmer as much as if he had expended 120 of the new quarters. The remaining 140 quarters are worth £80, or no more than the remaining 40 were worth previously. It is true that he sells each of the 200 quarters for £1 (if he sells his total product) and receives £200 for them. But of the 200 quarters, 60 have cost him £2 each, the remaining quarters therefore only yield him £$4/_7$ each.

If he now again lays out 20 quarters [for seed] (equal to £10 [if one reckons 10s. for a quarter]), 40 quarters for wages (equal to £20), and 40 quarters for the other elements of constant capital (equal to £20), that is, a total of 100 quarters instead of 60 as previously and he harvests 180 quarters, then these 180 quarters have not the same value as did the 100 previously [if one reckons £1 for a quarter]. True, he has employed as much living labour as he did previously, and consequently the ||1094| value of the variable capital has remained the same and so has

the value of the surplus product. But he has laid out less materialised labour, since the 20 quarters, which were worth £20 previously, are now worth only £10.
The account will therefore work out as follows:

Constant capital	Variable capital	Surplus-value
1) 20 qrs. seed corn = £20 20 qrs. implements, etc. = £20	20 qrs. (£20)	40 qrs. (£40)
2) 20 qrs. [seed corn] = £10 40 qrs. [implements, etc.] = £20	40 qrs. (£20)	80 qrs. (£40)

In the first case the product comes to 100 qrs., or £100. In the second case the product comes to 180 qrs., or £90.

Nevertheless the rate of profit would have risen [despite the fall in the value of the product], for in the first case the return on an outlay of £60 was £40 and in the second it was £40 for an outlay of £50. In the first case it amounted to $66^2/_3$ per cent, in the second to 80 per cent.

Anyhow, the rise in the *rate of profit* is not due to the *value* remaining unchanged, as Ramsay supposes. Since one part of the labour expended, i.e., the part contained in the constant capital (in seeds in this case), has diminished, the value of the product falls if *production* continues *on the same scale*, just as the value of 100 lbs. of twist falls if the cotton it is made of becomes cheaper. But the ratio of variable to constant capital increases (without the *value* of the variable capital increasing). In other words, the ratio of the total capital outlay declines in relation to the surplus. Hence the rate of profit rises.

If what Ramsay says were correct, if the value remained the same, then the *profit*, the amount of profit, and consequently also the rate of profit, would rise. There can be no question of a rise merely in the rate of profit.

The question [of the influence of a change in the value of constant capital on the rate of profit] is not however disposed of for the special case [where a part of the constant capital is replaced in kind]. In agriculture this special case takes the following form.

A certain amount of seed corn at the *old price of the product* figures in the harvest, this part is incorporated in the harvest in kind. The other expenses are defrayed by the sale of the corn at its old price. The old outlay yields a product which is twice as big as before. Thus, in the above-mentioned case, for example, where 20 quarters are used as seed corn (equal to £40) and the other outlays amount to 40 quarters, equalling £80, the harvest yields 200 quarters and not, as the previous harvest, 100 quarters (worth £200), of which 40 quarters, equalling £80, were profit on an outlay of 60 quarters costing £120. The outlay in connection with this second harvest is absolutely the same as it was in the first—60 quarters, the value of which is £120, but instead of a surplus of 40 quarters, the surplus is now 140 quarters. The surplus in kind has in this case increased considerably. But because the labour expended is the same in both cases, the 200 quarters have no greater value than did the 100, that is, £200. In other words the value of the quarter has fallen from £2 to £1. But since there was a surplus of 140 quarters, it seemed that it had to come to £140, for one quarter is worth just as much as any other.

The matter would be simplified if we considered it first of all without regard to the reproduction process, that is if we assumed that the tenant farmer was withdrawing from the business and selling his whole product. Then he would indeed have to sell 120 quarters to recover his outlay of £120 (to reimburse himself). In this way he would recover his capital outlay. Thus a surplus of 80 quarters would remain, and not of 140, and since these 80 quarters are equal to £80, they are worth in absolute terms as much as the surplus in the first case.

In the course of the *reproduction* process, however, the matter is altered to a certain extent. For the farmer replaces the 20 quarters of seed corn in kind out of his own product. [As far as their value is concerned] they are replaced by 40 quarters in the [new] product. But in the reproduction process he only needs to replace them with 20 quarters in kind, as was the case previously. The rest of his expenditure [expressed in quarters] increases in the same ratio as the quarter is devalued (provided wages do not fall).'To replace the remaining portion of constant capital, the farmer now needs 40 quarters and not 20 as previously, and to replace wages he also needs 40 quarters instead of 20. Altogether he must now lay out 100 quarters, compared to 60 quarters previously; but he need not lay out 120 quarters, the amount corresponding to the depreciation of the corn, because the 20 quarters used [as seed] which were worth £40, are replaced by 20 [quarters] (since in this context only their use-value matters) which are worth [£] 20. So evidently he has made a gain ||1095| of these 20 qrs., now worth £20. His surplus is therefore not £80 but £100, not 80 qrs., but 100. (Expressed in quarters of the old value, not 40 quarters but 50.) This is an unquestionable fact, and if the market price does not fall as a result of abundance, the farmer can sell 20 quarters more at the new value, thus gaining £20.

In the course of *reproduction*, moreover, the farmer obtains this surplus of £20 on the same outlay, because labour has become more productive without the rate of surplus-value having risen or the workers having performed more surplus labour than previously or having received a smaller portion of the *reproduced part* of the product (which represents living labour). On the contrary, it is assumed that in the reproduction process the worker receives 40 quarters, whereas he received only 20 previously. This then is a rather peculiar phenomenon. It does not occur without reproduction, but it takes place in connection with it and it takes place [moreover] because the farmer replaces a part of his advances in kind. Not only the rate of profit could increase in this case, but the amount of profit as well. (With regard to the reproduction process itself, the farmer can either carry on on the old scale, in which case the price of the product will fall if he again obtains as good a harvest, because a portion of the constant capital has cost less, but the rate of profit will rise; or the farmer can increase the scale of production, sow more with the same outlay, and then both the rate of profit and the amount of profit will rise.)

Let us [now] consider the manufacturer. Let us assume that he has laid out £100 in cotton twist and made a profit of £20. The product therefore amounts to £120. It is assumed that £80 out of the outlay of £100 has been paid for cotton. If the price of cotton falls by half, he will now need to spend only £40 on the cotton and £20 on the rest, that is £60 in all (instead of £100) and the profit will be £20 as previously, the total product will amount to £80 (if he does not increase the scale of his production). £40 thus remains in his pocket. He can either spend it or invest it as additional capital. If he invests it, he will lay out [an additional] £$26^2/_3$ on cotton and £$13^1/_2$ on labour, etc., on the new scale. The profit [will amount to] £$13^1/_3$. The total product will now be $60+40+33^1/_3$, or £$133^1/_3$.

Thus it is not the fact that the farmer replaces his seed corn in kind which is the key, for the manufacturer buys his cotton and does not replace it out of his own product. What this phenomenon amounts to is this: release of a portion of the capital previously tied up in constant capital, or the conversion of a portion of the capital into revenue. If exactly the same amount of capital is laid out in the reproduction process as previously, then it is the same as if additional capital had been employed on the old scale of production. This is therefore a kind of accumulation which arises from the increased productivity of those branches of industry which supply the productive ingredients of capital. However, such a fall in the [price of] raw materials, if due to the seasons, is counteracted by unfavourable seasons, in which the prices of raw materials rise. The capital released in this way in one or several seasons is, therefore, to a certain extent, reserve capital for the other seasons. For instance, the manufacturer whose [fixed capital] turns over once every twelve years, must arrange things in such a way that he can continue to produce—at least *on the same scale* throughout the twelve years. One has therefore to take into account that the *prices* [of the raw materials] he has *to replace* fluctuate and even themselves out to a certain extent over a long period of years.

A rise in prices of the ingredients [of constant capital] has the opposite effect to a fall of the prices. (We are leaving variable capital out of account here, although if wages fall, less variable capital—in terms of value—will need to be laid out, and if they rise more.) If production is to be continued on the old scale, then a greater outlay of capital is necessary. Therefore, apart from a fall in the rate of profit, extra capital must be employed or a part of the revenue must be converted into capital, although it will not have the effect of additional capital.

Accumulation has taken place in the one case although the value of the capital advanced has remained the same (but its material elements have been increased). The rate of creating surplus-value increases, and the absolute magnitude of profit increases, because the effect is the same as if additional capital had been advanced on the old scale. *Accumulation* has taken place in the other case insofar as the value of the capital advanced, i.e., that part of the value of the total output which functions as capital, has increased. But the material elements *have not been* increased. The rate of profit falls. (The amount of profit only falls if either a different number of workers is employed or if their wages rise as well.)

This phenomenon of the conversion of capital into revenue should be noted, because it creates the *illusion* that the amount of profit grows (or in the opposite case decreases) independently of the amount of surplus-value. We have seen that, under ||1096|

certain circumstances, a part of rent can be explained[101] by this phenomenon.

In the way mentioned above (that is, if the remaining 20 quarters worth £20 are not used immediately to extend the scale of production, i.e., if they are not accumulated), a money capital of £20 is set free. This is an example of how *redundant money capital* can be extracted from the reproduction process although the aggregate value of commodities remains the same, namely, by a portion of the capital which existed previously in the form of fixed (constant) capital being converted into money capital.

How little the above phenomenon [conversion of a portion of the capital into revenue] has to do with Ramsay's determination of the *rate of profit*, becomes clear if one considers the case of a farmer (or manufacturer) who enters business under the new conditions of production. Formerly he needed £120 to enter the business: £40 to buy 20 quarters of seeds, £40 to buy the other ingredients of constant capital, and £40 to pay wages. And his profit was £80. 80 on 120 is equal to 8 on 12, or 2 on 3, or $66^2/_3$ per cent.

He now has to advance £20 to buy 20 quarters of seed, £40 as previously [to buy the other elements of constant capital], £40 to pay wages, so that his outlay of capital amounts to £100. His profit is [£]80, that is, 80 per cent. The amount of profit has remained *the same*, but the *rate* of profit has increased by 20 per cent. Thus one can see that the fall in the value of seed (or of the price which has to be paid to *replace* the seed) has in itself nothing to do with the increase in [the amount of] profit, but implies merely an increase in the rate of profit.

Moreover, the farmer in the one case—or the manufacturer in the other—will not consider that he has obtained a larger profit, but that a portion of the capital previously tied up in production has been freed. And his view will be based on the following simple calculation. Previously, the amount of capital advanced in production was £120; now it is £100, and £20 is now in the hands of the farmer as free capital, money which can be invested in any way he likes. But in either case the capital amounts to £120 only, its size has therefore not been increased. The fact, however, that a sixth of the capital has been divested of the form in which it is inseparable from the production process does indeed have the same *effect* as an additional investment of capital.

Ramsay has not got to the bottom of this matter because he has not at all clearly worked out the relationship between value, surplus-value and profit.

* * *

Ramsay correctly expounds to what extent machinery, etc., insofar as it affects variable capital, influences profit and the rate of profit. That is to say, he shows that this influence results from the depreciation of labour-power, the increase of relative surplus labour or, if the production process is considered as a whole, also the reduction of the part of the gross return which goes to replace wages.

"... an increased or diminished productiveness of the industry employed in raising commodities which do not enter into the composition of fixed capital, can have no influence on the rate of profit, except by affecting the proportion of the gross amount which goes to maintain labour" (op. cit., p. 168).

If[a] the manufacturer has doubled his output as a result of improvements in machinery, the value of his goods must, in the end, fall in the same proportion as their quantity has increased.

⟨It is assumed that in fact, taking the wear and tear of the machinery into account, twice the quantity costs no more than half did previously. If this is not the case, the value of the commodity falls, but not *in proportion* to its quantity. Its quantity may double and, whereas the value of the aggregate product rises, the value of a unit of the commodity, may drop only from 2 to $1^1/_4$, etc., instead of from 2 to 1.⟩

... the manufacturer benefits only insofar as he is able to clothe the worker more cheaply so that a smaller portion of the gross return goes to the worker.... The farmer too benefits ⟨as a result of the increased industrial productivity⟩ only insofar as a portion of his outlay is expended on clothing for the labourers and he can buy this more cheaply now; that is, [he benefits] in the same way as the manufacturer (loc. cit., pp. 168-69).

A fall [or rise] in the value of the elements of constant capital affects the rate of profit by altering the *ratio of surplus-value*

---

[a] This paragraph and the one after the next beginning with the words: "the manufacturer benefits..." are not a quotation, but a paraphrase by Marx of the ideas expressed by Ramsay on pp. 168-69 of his book. They are written in German but interspersed with many English words and phrases.—*Ed.*

to the total capital outlay. A fall (or rise) in wages, on the other hand, affects the rate of profit by influencing the *rate of surplus-value* directly.

Supposing for example, that, in the above-mentioned case, the price of the seed (assuming the farmer grows flax) remains the same, that is, £40 (20 quarters) and the rest of the constant capital costs £40 (20 quarters) as before, but that wages—that is, wages for *the same* number of workers—fall from £40 to £20 (from 20 quarters to 10 quarters). In this case, the total *value*, which is equal to the wages plus surplus-value, remains unchanged. Since the number of workers remains the same, their labour is embodied in a value of £40+£80, i.e., £120, as it was previously. But from this £120, £20 now goes to the workers and the surplus-value now amounts to £100. ⟨It is assumed that no improvements have taken place which affect the number of labourers employed in this branch.⟩

The capital advanced is now £100 instead of £120 just as in the case where the value of the seed fell by half. But the profit is now £100, i.e., 100 per cent, whereas in the other case, where the capital advanced was likewise reduced from £120 to £100, it was 80 per cent. And as in that other case £20, or a sixth of the capital ||1097|, is set free. But in the former case, the surplus-value remained unchanged—£80—(and since £40 was paid as wages, [the rate of surplus-value] was 200 per cent). In the latter case, the surplus-value rises to £100 (and, since wages now come to £20, [the rate of surplus-value increases] to 500 per cent).

In this case, not only has the rate of profit risen but the *profit* itself, because the rate of surplus-value has risen and consequently the surplus-value itself. This differentiates this case from the other, something which Ramsay does not grasp. This always takes place when the increase in profit is not nullified by a corresponding reduction in the rate of profit resulting from a simultaneous change in the value of constant capital. In the above-mentioned case for example, the capital outlay is £120 and the profit £80, that is, $66^2/_3$ per cent. In the present case, the capital outlay is £100 and the profit £100, which works out at 100 per cent. If, however, the capital outlay had risen from £100 to £150 as a result of a change in the price of constant capital, then the profit—which has increased from £80 to £100—would only give a rate of $66^2/_3$ per cent.

[Ramsay continues] .

Because these commodities "help to make up neither fixed capital nor circulating, it follows that profit can in no way be affected by any alteration in the facilities for raising these. Such are luxuries of all kinds" (loc. cit., pp. 169-70).

"Master-capitalists gain by the abundance" (of luxuries) "because their profits will command a greater quantity for their private consumption; but the rate of this profit is in no degree affected either by their plenty or scarcity" (loc. cit., p. 171).

First of all, a portion of the luxuries can be used as one of the elements of constant capital. Grapes, for example, in [the production of] wine, gold in luxury articles, diamonds in glass cutting, etc. But Ramsay excludes this case insofar as he says: commodities which do not enter into fixed capital. In that case, however, the concluding sentence—"Such are luxuries of all kinds", is incorrect.

However, productivity in the luxury industries can only increase in the same way as it does in all others—either because natural resources such as the land, mines, etc., from which the raw materials for the luxury industries are procured, become more productive, or new, more productive sources are discovered; or again by application of the division of labour, or, especially, by the use of machinery (or of better tools) and of natural forces. ⟨The improvement of tools, as well as the production of more specialised ones, belongs to the *division of labour*.⟩ (One should not forget *chemical processes*.)

Let us now assume that the production time for luxuries is reduced due to machinery (or chemical processes), that less labour is required to produce them. This cannot have the slightest influence on wages, on the *value* of labour-power, since these articles do not enter into the consumption of the workers (at least never into that part of their consumption which determines the value of their labour-power). ⟨It can influence the *market price* of labour, if workers are thrown onto the streets as a result of these developments and the supply of labour-power is thereby increased.⟩ Increased productivity in the luxury industries, therefore, has no influence on the rate of surplus-value nor, consequently, on the rate of profit insofar as this is determined by the rate of surplus-value. Nevertheless, it can influence the rate of profit insofar as it affects either the *amount* of surplus-value or the ratio of variable capital to constant capital and to the total capital.

If for example, [in the production of luxury articles] machinery makes it possible to employ 10 workers where 20 were previously employed, then, indeed the rate of surplus-value is not modified in any way. The cheapening of luxury articles does not enable the worker to live more cheaply. He requires the same amount of labour-time to reproduce his labour-power as he did previously.

⟨In practice, therefore, the manufacturer of luxury articles seeks to depress the wages of labour below its value, [below] its minimum. This he is able to do because of the *relative surplus population* engendered by increasing productivity in other branches of industry, for example among knitters. Or—as likewise happens in these branches—he seeks to extend the *absolute labour-time*, thus, in fact, producing *absolute surplus-value*. It is correct, however, that *productivity* in the luxury industries cannot reduce the *value* of labour-power, it cannot produce any relative surplus-value and, in general, cannot produce *that form* of surplus-value which results from the *growing productivity* of industry *as such*.⟩

The amount of surplus-value is determined in two ways. [First,] by the rate of surplus-value, that is, the surplus labour (absolute or relative) of the individual workers. Secondly, by the number of workers simultaneously employed. Insofar therefore as increasing productivity in the luxury industry reduces the *number of workers* which a certain quantity of capital employs, it reduced the *amount of surplus-value*, hence all other circumstances remaining unchanged, it reduces also the *rate of profit*. The same thing occurs if the number of workers is reduced, or remains the *same*, but the capital laid out on machinery and raw materials is increased; in other words, it occurs wherever there is any diminution in the ratio of variable capital to the total capital which [according to our assumption] is not balanced or partially offset by a reduction in wages. But since the rate of profit in this sphere ||1098| enters into the equalisation process of the general rate of profit just as much as that in any other sphere, increased productivity in the luxury industry would, in the case under consideration, bring about a fall in the general rate of profit.

Conversely: If the increased productivity in the luxury industry was [due to improvements carried out not in that industry itself, but] in those branches of industry which provide it with constant capital, then the rate of profit would rise in the luxury industry.

⟨*Surplus-value* (that is, its size, its quantity, its total amount⟩

is determined by the rate of surplus-value multiplied by the number of workers employed. Certain circumstances may affect both factors simultaneously either in the same direction or in opposite directions, or they may affect only one of the factors. Apart from the absolute lengthening of the working-day, increased productivity in the luxury industry can affect only the number [of workers employed]. The inevitable consequence therefore is a reduction in the amount of surplus-value and hence in the rate of profit, even if no increase in constant capital takes place. If the constant capital increases, however, a reduced amount of surplus-value is calculated on an increased total capital.⟩

* * *

Ramsay comes closer to a correct understanding of the rate of profit than the others. The shortcomings too are therefore more conspicuous in his exposition. He brings out all the factors involved, but he does it one-sidedly and therefore incorrectly.

Ramsay sums up his view of profit in the following passage:

"... the causes which regulate the rate of profit in individual cases [...] we have found to be,[a] 1) The Productiveness of the Industry engaged in raising those articles of primary[b] necessity which are required by the Labourer for Food, Clothing, etc. 2) The Productiveness of the Industry employed in raising those[c] objects which enter into the composition of Fixed Capital. 3) *The rate of Real Wages*"

⟨here this must mean the quantity of necessaries, etc., which the worker receives, irrespective of the price of the commodities which that quantity comprises⟩.

"A variation in the first and third of these causes, acts upon profit by altering the proportion of the gross produce which goes to the labourer: a change in the *second* affects the same, by modifying the proportion necessary for replacing, either *directly* or *by means of exchange*, the fixed capital consumed in production; for [...] profit is essentially a question of proportion" (loc. cit., p. 172).

He rightly reproaches Ricardo (although Ramsay's own presentation is also inadequate):

---

[a] The manuscript has "The rate of profit in individual cases is therefore determined by the following causes".—*Ed.*
[b] The manuscript has "the articles of first".—*Ed.*
[c] The manuscript has "the".—*Ed.*

"Mr. *Ricardo* [...] seems always to consider the whole produce as divided between wages and profits, forgetting the part necessary for replacing fixed capital"[a] (loc. cit., p. 174, note).

* * *

⟨It can already be noted in the first description of accumulation, i.e., of the conversion of surplus-value into capital, that the entire surplus labour takes the form of *capital* (constant and variable) and of *surplus labour* (profit, interest, rent). For this conversion reveals that surplus labour itself assumes the form of capital and that the unpaid labour of the worker confronts him as the *totality of the objective conditions of labour*. In this form it confronts him as alien property with the result that the capital which is antecedent to his labour, appears to be independent of it. [It appears] as a ready-made value of a given magnitude, whose value the worker merely has to augment. It is never the product of his past labour (nor any circumstances which, *independently of the particular labour process* into which the past labour of his enters, affect or increase its value) which, or the replacement of which, appears as exploitation, but it is always merely the manner and the rate in which his present labour is exploited. As long as the individual capitalist continues to operate on the same scale of production (or on an expanding one), the replacement of capital appears as an operation which does not affect the worker, since, if the means of production belonged to the worker, he would likewise have to replace them out of the gross product in order to continue reproduction on the same scale or on an expanded scale (and the latter too is necessary because of the natural increase of population). But this affects the worker in three respects. 1) The perpetuation of the means of production as property alien to him, as capital, perpetuates his condition as wage-worker and hence his fate of always having to work part of his labour-time for a third person for nothing. 2) The extension of these means of production, alias accumulation of capital, increases the extent and the size of the classes who live on the surplus labour of the worker; it worsens his position *relatively* by augmenting the relative wealth of the capitalist and his co-partners, by fur-

---

[a] The manuscript has "Ricardo forgets that the whole product is divided not only between wages and profits, but that a part of it is also necessary for replacing fixed capital."—*Ed.*

ther increasing his relative surplus labour through the division of labour, etc., and reduces that part of the gross product which is used to pay wages; finally, since the conditions of labour confront the individual worker in an ever more gigantic form and increasingly as social forces, the chance of his taking possession of them himself as is the case in small-scale industry, disappears.⟩

[3. Ramsay on the Division of "Gross Profit" into "Net Profit" (Interest) and "Profit of Enterprise". Apologetic Elements in His Views on the "Labour of Superintendence", "Insurance Covering the Risk Involved" and "Excess Profit"]

||1099| Ramsay uses the term *gross profit* for what I call simply profit. He divides this *gross profit* into *net profit* (interest) and *profit of enterprise* (industrial profit).*

Ramsay, like Ricardo, takes issue with Adam Smith on the question of the *fall in the general rate of profit*. Refuting Smith, he writes:

"Competition of the master-capitalists" can indeed even out profits which rise considerably above "the ordinary level" ⟨this levelling is by no means a sufficient explanation for the formation of a general rate of profit⟩ but it is wrong to say that *this ordinary level itself is lowered*.[a]

"... could we suppose it[b] possible that the Price of every commodity, both raw and fabricated, should fall in consequence of the competition among the producers, yet this could not in any way affect profit. Each mastercapitalist would sell his produce for less money, but on the other hand, every article of his expenses, whether belonging to fixed capital or to circulating, would cost him a proportionally smaller sum" (op. cit., pp. 180-81).

The following passage is directed *against Malthus*:

"The idea of profits being paid by the consumers, is, assuredly, very absurd. Who are the consumers? They must be either landlords, capitalists, masters, labourers, or else people who receive a salary..." (loc. cit., p. 183).

---

* ||1130| ⟨The reason Mr. Senior—whose *Outline* appeared at approximately the same time as Ramsay's *Essay on the Distribution of Wealth*, in which latter work the division of profit into profit of enterprise and into "net profits of capital or interest" (Chapter IV) is dealt with at length—is supposed to have discovered this division, which was already known in 1821 and 1822[102], can be explained only by the fact that Senior—a mere apologist of the existing order and consequently a vulgar economist—is very congenial to Herr Roscher.⟩ |1130||

---

[a] This is not a quotation but Marx's rendering (mainly in German) of the ideas developed by Ramsay on pp. 179-80 of his book.—*Ed.*
[b] Instead of "Could we suppose it", the manuscript has "If it were".—*Ed.*

"*The only competition* which can *affect the general rate of gross profits*, is that between master-capitalists and labourers..." (op. cit., p. 206).

The last sentence expresses the true gist of Ricardo's proposition. The rate of profit can fall independently of the competition between capital and labour, but *this* is the *only kind of competition* which can bring about its decrease. Ramsay himself, however, does *not* advance *any* reasons why the general rate of profit has a tendency to fall. The only thing he says—and which is correct—is that the *rate of interest* can fall quite independently of the rate of gross profits in a given country, namely:

"But were we even to suppose, that capital was never borrowed with any view but to productive employment [I think] it very possible that interest might vary without any change in the rate of gross profits. For, as a nation advances in the career of wealth, a class of men springs up and increases more and more, who by the labours" ⟨exploitation, robbery⟩ "of their ancestors find themselves in the possession of funds sufficiently ample to afford a handsome maintenance from the interest alone. Very many also who during youth and middle age were actively engaged in business, retire in their latter days to live quietly on the interest of the sums they have themselves accumulated. This class[a] [...] has a tendency to increase with the increasing riches of the country, for those who begin with a tolerable stock are likely to make an independence sooner than they who commence with little. Thus it comes to pass, that[b] in old and rich countries, the amount of national capital belonging to those who are unwilling to take the trouble of employing it themselves, bears a larger proportion to the whole productive stock of the society, than in newly settled and poorer districts.[c] How [...] numerous [is] the class of rentiers [...] in England [....] As the class of *rentiers* increases, so also does that of lenders of capital, for they are one and the same. Therefore, from this cause interest must have a tendency to fall in old countries..." (loc. cit., pp. 201-02).

Ramsay says the following about the *rate of net profit* (interest):

"The rate of these" [profits] "must depend,[d] partly upon the rate of gross profits [...] partly on the proportion in which these are separated into profits of capital and those of enterprise.[e] This proportion [...] depends upon the competition between the lenders of capital and [...] borrowers [...], which competition[f] is influenced, though by no means entire-

---

[a] The manuscript has "These two classes".—*Ed.*
[b] Instead of "Thus it comes to pass, that", the manuscript has "Therefore".—*Ed.*
[c] The manuscript has "poor countries".—*Ed.*
[d] The manuscript has "it depends".—*Ed.*
[e] The manuscript has "separated into interest and industrial profit".—*Ed.*
[f] The manuscript has "borrowers of capital. This competition is influenced, but not entirely".—*Ed.*

ly *regulated*, by the rate of gross profit expected to be realised. And the [...] competition is not exclusively regulated by this cause [...] because on the one hand many borrow without any view to productive employment; and [...] because *the proportion of the whole national capital to be lent, varies with the riches of the country independently of any change in gross profits*" (loc. cit., pp. 206-07). *"The profits of enterprise depend upon the net profits of capital,* not the latter upon the former" (loc. cit., p. 214).

||1100| Apart from the circumstance mentioned earlier, Ramsay says—rightly:

Interest is only a measure of net profits where the level of civilisation is such that the "want of certainty" of repayment is not a factor which enters into the calculation.[a] "In England, for instance, at the present day, we cannot, I think, consider[b] compensation for risk as at all entering into the interest received from funds lent on what would be called good security" (op. cit., p. 199, note).

Speaking of the *industrial capitalist*, whom he calls the master-capitalist, Ramsay remarks:

"He is the general distributor of the national revenue; the person who undertakes to pay[c] [...] to the labourers, the wages, [...]—to the capitalist, the interest [...]—to the proprietor, the rent [....] On the one hand are masters, on the other, labourers, capitalists and landlords [....] The interests of these two grand classes are diametrically opposed to each other. It is the master who *hires* labour, capital, and land, and of course tries to get the use of them on as low terms as possible; while the owners of these sources of wealth do their best to *let* them as high as they can" (op. cit., pp. 218-19).

Industrial profit. (*Labour of superintendence.*)

What Ramsay writes about *industrial profit* (and especially, about the labour of superintendence) is on the whole the most reasonable part of his book, although part of his demonstration is borrowed from *Storch*.[103]

The exploitation of labour costs labour. Insofar as the labour performed by the industrial capitalist is rendered necessary only because of the contradiction between capital and labour, it enters into the cost of his overseers (the industrial non-commissioned officers) and is already included in the category of wages in the same way as costs caused by the slave overseer and his whip are included in the production costs of the slave-owner. These costs, like the greater part of the trading expenses, belong to the

---

[a] This sentence is a paraphrase of Ramsay by Marx.—*Ed.*
[b] The manuscript has "We cannot consider."—*Ed.*
[c] The manuscript has "The industrial capitalist is the general distributor of the revenue; he pays".—*Ed.*

incidental expenses of capitalist production. As far as the general *rate of profit* is concerned, the labour of the capitalists arising from their competition with one another and their attempts to ruin one another counts just as little as the greater or lesser skill of one industrial capitalist compared to another in extracting the largest amount of surplus labour from his workers for the smallest expenditure and making the best use of this extracted surplus labour in the process of circulation. These matters should be dealt with in the analysis of the competition of capitals. Such an analysis deals in general with the struggle of the capitalists and their effort to acquire the greatest possible amount of surplus labour and it is concerned only with the division of the surplus labour amongst the different individual capitalists, and not with the origin of surplus labour or its general extent.

All that remains for the labour of superintendence is the general function of organising the division of labour and the co-operation of certain individuals. This labour is fully taken into account in the wages of the general manager in the larger capitalist enterprises. It has already been deducted from the general rate of profit. The best practical proof of this is provided by the co-operative factories set up by the English workers,[104] for these, despite the higher rate of interest they have to pay, yield profits higher than average, although the wages of the general manager, which are naturally determined by the market price for this kind of labour, are deducted. The industrial capitalists who are their own general managers save one item of the production costs, pay wages to themselves, and consequently receive a rate of profit above the average. If this assertion of the apologists [that profit of enterprise constitutes wages for the labour of superintendence] were taken literally tomorrow, and the profit of the industrial capitalist limited to the *wages of management and direction*, then capitalist production, the appropriation of the surplus labour of others and its transformation into capital would come to an end the day after tomorrow.

However, if we consider this [payment of the] labour of superintendence as wages concealed in the *general rate of profit*, then the law established by Ramsay and others applies, namely, that while profit (industrial profit as well as gross profit [including interest]) is proportional to the amount of capital invested, this portion of the profit stands in *inverse ratio* to the size of the capital, it is infinitesimally small in the case of large capital and enormously large where the capital is small, i.e., where the capitalist production is purely nominal. Whereas the small capitalist, who does almost all the work himself, seems to obtain a very high rate of profit in proportion to his capital, what happens in fact is that, if he does not employ a few workers whose surplus labour he appropriates, he actually makes *no profit* at all and his enterprise is only *nominally* a capitalist one (whether he is engaged in industry or in commerce). What distinguishes him from the wage-worker is that, because of his nominal capital he is indeed the master and owner of his own conditions of labour and consequently has no master over him; ||1101| and hence he appropriates his whole labour-time himself instead of it being appropriated by someone else. What appears to be profit here, is merely the excess [of his income] over ordinary wages, an excess which results from the fact that he appropriates his own surplus labour. However, this phenomenon belongs exclusively to those spheres which have not as yet been really conquered by the capitalist mode of production.

[Ramsay says:]

"The profits of enterprise may ... be considered as made up of 3 parts: one... the salary of ... the master; another an insurance for risk; the remainder ... his *surplus gains*" (op. cit., p. 226).

As regards point 2, it is quite irrelevant here. Corbet (and Ramsay himself) has stated[105] that the *insurance* which covers the risk only distributes the losses of the capitalists uniformly or distributes them more generally amongst the whole class. The profits of the insurance companies—that is, of the capitals which are employed in the business of insurance, and take over this distribution—must be deducted from these uniformly distributed losses. These companies receive a part of the surplus-value in the same way as mercantile or moneyed capitalists do, without participating in its direct production. This is a question of the distribution of the surplus-value amongst the different sorts of capitalists and of the deductions which are consequently made from [the surplus-value accruing to] the individual capitalists. It has nothing to do either with the nature or with the magnitude of the surplus. The worker obviously cannot provide any more than his surplus labour. He cannot make an additional payment to the capitalist so that the latter may insure the fruits of this surplus labour against loss. At most one could say that, even apart from capitalist production, the producers themselves might have certain expenses, that is, they would have to spend a part of their labour, or of the products of their labour in order to insure their products, their wealth, or the elements of their wealth, against accidents, etc. Instead of each capitalist insuring himself, it is safer as well as cheaper for him if one section of capital is entrusted with this job. Insurance is paid out of a portion of surplus-value, its protection and distribution between the capitalists has nothing to do with its origin and magnitude.

What is left is 1) the salary and 2) the surplus gains, as Ramsay calls that part of surplus-value which falls to the industrial capitalist as opposed to the interest-grabber and which, consequently, is determined by the ratio of interest to industrial profit; the two parts into which the surplus-value accruing to capital (in contrast to landed property) is divided.

As far as 1), the salary, is concerned, it is first of all self-evident that in capitalist production, the function of capital as lord over labour falls to the capitalist, or a clerk or a representative paid by him. Even this function would disappear together with the capitalist mode of production, insofar as it does not arise from the nature of co-operative labour but from the domination of the conditions of labour over labour itself. Ramsay himself however sweeps away this element or reduces it to such an extent that it is not worth speaking of.

The salary [of the employer], like the work [of superintendence], remains roughly the same, be the concern large or small (loc. cit., pp. 227-29). A worker will never be able to say that he can do the same amount of work as two, three or more of his workmates. But one industrial capitalist or farmer can take the place of ten or more[a] (p. 255).

The third part [of the profits of enterprise], the *surplus gains*, includes [compensation for] risks—which are only *possible* risks, nothing but the possibility of losing the gains and the capital—it in fact however takes the form of insurance and therefore of a share which certain capitals in a particular branch receive in the total surplus-value.

"These surplus gains," Ramsay writes, "do truly represent [...] the revenue derived *from the power of commanding the use of capital*" (in other words from the power of commanding other people's labour) "whether belonging to the person himself or borrowed from others.... these[b] net profits" (interest) "vary exactly as the amount of capital [...] on the contrary [...] the larger the capital, the greater the proportion they bear[c] to the stock employed" (loc. cit., p. 230).

---

[a] This is Marx's summing up of the arguments advanced by Ramsay.—*Ed.*
[b] The manuscript has "the".—*Ed.*
[c] The manuscript has "the larger the capital, the larger the proportion of the surplus gains".—*Ed.*

In other words, this means nothing more than that the salaries of masters stand in inverse ratio to the size of the capital. The larger the scale on which the capital operates, the more *capitalist* the mode of production, the more negligible is the element of industrial profit which is reducible to salary, and the more clearly appears the real character of industrial profit, namely, that it is a part of the surplus gains, i.e., of surplus-value, i.e., of unpaid surplus labour.

The whole contradiction between industrial profit and interest only has meaning as a contradiction between the rentier and the industrial capitalist, but it has not the slightest bearing on the relationship of the worker to capital, the nature of capital, or the origin of the profit capital yields.

With regard to *rent not derived from corn*, Ramsay says:

"In this manner the rent paid for one species of produce becomes the cause of the *high value of others*" (op. cit., p. 279).

"*Revenue*," says Ramsay in the final chapter, "differs from the annual gross produce, simply by the absence of all those objects which go to keep up *fixed capital*" (by which he means *constant capital*, raw materials in all stages of production, auxiliary materials and machinery, etc.) (op. cit., p. 471).

||1102| Ramsay has already said[a] and repeats in the final chapter that

"circulating capital"—that is his term for capital laid out in wages—is superfluous, it is "... not[b] an *immediate* agent in production, nor even *essential* to it at all..." (loc. cit., p. 468).

But he does not draw the obvious conclusion that by denying that wage-labour and capital laid out in wages are essential, the *necessity* for capitalist production in general is denied and the conditions of labour consequently cease to confront the workers as "capital" or, to use Ramsay's term, as "fixed capital". One part of the conditions of labour appears as fixed *capital* only because the other part appears as circulating *capital*. But once capitalist production is presupposed as a fact, Ramsay declares that *wages* and *gross profits of capital* (industrial profit or, as he calls it, profit of enterprise included) are necessary forms of revenue (loc. cit., pp. 478, 475).

These are naturally the two forms of revenue which, in their simplicity and generality, indeed epitomise the essence of the

---

[a] See this volume, p. 327.—*Ed.*
[b] The manuscript has "neither".—*Ed.*

capitalist mode of production and of the two classes on which it is based. On the other hand, Ramsay declares that *rent*, in other words landed property, is a superfluous form of capitalist production (l.c., p. 472), but forgets that it is a necessary product of this mode of production. The same applies to his statement that the "net profit of capital", that is, interest, is not a necessary form.

[In case of a sharp reduction in gross profits] it would only be necessary for the rentiers to become industrial capitalists. As regards national wealth this makes no difference.... The gross profit need certainly not be so high as to afford separate incomes to the owner and the employer[a] (pp. 476-77).

Here Ramsay again forgets what he has said himself, namely that, as a necessary consequence of the development of capital, a constantly growing class of rentiers comes into being.[b]

"... gross profit [of capital and enterprise] is [...] essential in order that production should go on at all..." (loc. cit., p. 475).

Naturally. Without profit, no capital and without capital, no capitalist production.

* * *

Thus, the conclusion at which Ramsay arrives is, on the one hand, that the capitalist mode of production based on wage-labour is not really a necessary, i.e., not an absolute form of social production (which Ramsay himself expresses only in a rather limited form by stating that "circulating capital", and "wages" [would be] superfluous if the mass of the people were not so poor that they had to receive their share of the product in advance, before it was completed). On the other hand, he concludes that interest (in contrast to industrial profit) and rent (that is the form of landed property created by capitalist production itself) are superfetations which are not essential to capitalist production and of which it can rid itself. If this bourgeois ideal were actually realisable, the only result would be that the whole of the surplus-value would go to the industrial capitalist directly, and society would be reduced (economically) to the simple contradiction between capital and wage-labour, a simplification which would indeed accelerate the dissolution of this mode of production. |1102||

---

[a] This is in part Marx's paraphrase of Ramsay's argument.—*Ed.*
[b] See this volume, p. 354.—*Ed.*

* * *

||1102| ⟨In the *Morning Star*[106] (December 1, 1862), a manufacturer moans:

"*Deduct* from the *gross produce* the wages of labour, the rent of land, the interest on capital, the cost of raw material, and the *gains of the agent, merchant, or dealer*, and what remained was the *profit of the manufacturer*, the Lancashire resident, the occupier, on whom the *burden of maintaining the workmen for so many partakers in the distribution of the gross produce is thrown.*"

If one disregards the value and considers the gross produce in kind, it is clear that after the replacement of the constant capital and the capital laid out in wages, that portion of the product which remains constitutes the surplus-value. From this however has to be deducted a portion for rent and the gains of the agents, merchants or dealers, all of whom, whether they use capital of their own or not, also share in that part of the gross product which constitutes surplus-value. All these therefore are *deductions* for the manufacturer. His profit itself is subdivided into industrial profit and interest—if he has borrowed capital.⟩

⟨With regard to *differential rent*: The work of the labourer working on more fertile soil is more productive than that of a man working on less fertile soil. If, therefore, he were to be paid in kind, he would receive a smaller share of the gross product than the labourer working on less fertile soil. Or, what amounts to the same thing, his relative surplus labour would be greater than that of the other labourer, although he worked the same number of hours per day. But the value of the wage of the one is equal to that of the other. Hence the profit of his employer is no greater [than that of the other employer]. The surplus-value contained in the additional amount of his product, the greater relative productivity of his labour, or the differential surplus labour performed by him, is pocketed by the landlord.⟩ |1102||

[CHAPTER XXIII]

CHERBULIEZ

||1102| Cherbuliez, *Richesse au pauvreté*, Paris, 1841 (Reprint of the Geneva edition) [published under the title *Riche ou pauvre*].

(It is questionable whether we should specially include this fellow in this group [of economists] since most of what he writes is based on Sismondi, or whether we should on occasion insert his pertinent remarks in the form of quotations.[107] |1102||

[1. Distinction Between Two Parts of Capital—the Part Consisting of Machinery and Raw Materials and the Part Consisting of "Means of Subsistence" for the Workers]

||1103| Capital, says Cherbuliez, consists of "the raw materials, the tools, the means of subsistence" (op. cit., p. 16). "There is no difference between a capital and any other part of wealth. It is only the way in which it is employed which determines whether a thing becomes capital, that is. if it is employed in a *production* as raw material, as tools, or as means of subsistence" (loc. cit., p. 18).

This is the standard way of reducing capital to the material elements in which it presents itself in the labour process, i.e., means of production and means of subsistence. The latter category, moreover, is not accurate since, though means of subsistence are indeed a condition for the producer, a prerequisite enabling him to exist during production, they themselves do not enter into the labour process, into which nothing enters but the object of labour, the means of production and labour itself. Thus the objective factors of the labour process—which are common to all forms of production—are here called *capital*, although the *means of subsistence* (in which wages are already included) tacitly implies the *capitalist* form of these conditions of production.

Cherbuliez, like Ramsay, [assumes] that the *means of subsistence*—which Ramsay calls circulating capital—diminish (relatively, at any rate, to the total amount of capital and absolutely insofar as machinery continually throws workers out of employment). But both he and Ramsay appear to think that there is an inevitable reduction in the amount of means of subsistence, of necessaries, which can be employed as productive capital. But this is by no means the case. In this context, people always confuse that part of the gross product which replaces capital and is employed as capital, with that part which represents the surplus product. The means of subsistence decrease because a large portion of capital, that is, the part of the gross product employed as capital, is reproduced as constant capital instead of as variable capital. A larger portion of the surplus product, consisting of means of subsistence, is consumed by unproductive workers or idlers or exchanged for luxuries. That's all.

True, the fact that a constantly smaller part of the total capital is converted into variable capital can also be expressed in other ways. The part of capital which consists of variable capital is equal to that part of the total product which the worker himself appropriates, produces for himself. Therefore, the smaller this part is the smaller accordingly is the portion of the total number of workers which is required to reproduce it (just as in the case of the individual worker, who works correspondingly less labour-time for himself). The total product, like the total labour of the workers, falls into two parts. One part the workers produce for themselves; the other part they produce for the capitalist. Just as the [labour-] time of the individual worker can be divided into two parts, so can the [labour-] time of the whole working class. If the surplus labour is equal to half a day, it is the same as if half the working class produces means of subsistence for the working class and the other half produces raw materials, machinery and finished products for the capitalists, partly as producers and partly as consumers.

It is ridiculous that Cherbuliez and Ramsay believe that the part of the gross product which can be consumed by the workers and can enter into their consumption in kind has been reduced of necessity or reduced at all. Only that part has been reduced which is consumed in this form and therefore as *variable capital*. On the other hand, a larger portion is eaten up by servants, soldiers, etc., or exported and exchanged for more sumptuous means of subsistence.

The only important thing in both Ramsay and Cherbuliez is that they counterpose *constant* and *variable capital* and do not confine themselves to the distinction between fixed and circulating capital derived from circulation. For Cherbuliez counterposes that part of capital which goes on means of subsistence to that which consists of raw materials, auxiliary materials and means of labour, i.e., instruments, machines. Although two constituent elements of constant capital—raw material and auxiliary material—belong to circulating capital as far as the mode of circulation is concerned.

The important thing in variations in the constituent elements of capital is not that relatively more workers are occupied in the production of raw materials and machinery than in that of direct means of subsistence—this concerns only the division of labour—but the proportion of the product which has to be used to replace past labour (i.e., to replace constant capital) to that which has to be used to pay living labour. The larger the scale of capitalist production, and hence the greater the accumulation of capital—the greater is the share in the value of the product falling to the machinery and raw material of which the capital employed in the production of machinery and raw material consists. A correspondingly larger portion of the product must therefore be returned to production either in kind or by the producers of constant capital exchanging some of their products amongst themselves. The part of the product which belongs to production becomes larger, and the part which represents living, newly added labour becomes relatively smaller. Although, this part grows in terms of commodities—use-values—the development described is synonymous with increased productivity of labour. But the portion of this part which the worker receives falls relatively all the more. And the same process gives rise to a continuous relative redundancy of the working population.

[2. On the Progressive Decline in the Number of Workers in Relation to the Amount of Constant Capital]

||1104| ⟨It is an incontrovertible fact that, as capitalist production develops, the portion of capital invested in machinery and raw materials grows, and the portion laid out in wages declines. This is the only question with which both Ramsay and Cherbuliez are concerned. For us, however, the main thing is:

does this fact explain the decline in the rate of profit? (A decline, incidentally, which is far smaller than it is said to be.) Here it is not simply a question of the quantitative ratio but of the *value ratio*.

If one worker can spin as much cotton as 100 [workers spun previously], then the supply of raw material must be increased a hundredfold, and this is moreover brought about only by the spinning-machine which enables one worker to control 100 spindles. But if simultaneously, one worker produces as much cotton as 100 workers did previously and one worker produces a spinning-machine whereas previously he produced only a spindle, then the ratio of value remains the same, that is, the labour expended in the spinning, [in the production of] the cotton and the spinning-machine remains the same as that expended previously in spinning, the cotton and the spindle.

As far as the *machinery* is concerned, its cost is not as great as that of the labour it displaces, although the spinning-machine is much more expensive than the spindle. The individual capitalist who owns a spinning-machine must possess a greater amount of capital than the individual spinner who buys a spinning-wheel. But the spinning-machine is cheaper than the spinning-wheel in relation to the number of workers it employs. Otherwise it would not have displaced the spinning-wheel. The place of the spinner is taken by a capitalist. But the capital which the former laid out on the spinning-wheel was *larger* relative to the size of the product, than that which the capitalist lays out on the spinning-machine.)

The increasing productivity of labour (insofar as it is connected with machinery) is identical with the decreasing number of workers relatively to the number and extent of the machinery employed. Instead of a simple and cheap instrument a collection of such instruments (even though they are modified) is used, and to that collection has to be added the whole part of the machinery which consists of the moving and transmitting parts; and also the materials used (like coal, etc.) to produce the motive power (such as steam). Finally, the buildings. If one worker is in charge of 1,800 spindles instead of driving a spinning-wheel, it would be quite ridiculous to ask why these 1,800 spindles are not as cheap as the single spinning-wheel. The productivity in this case is brought about precisely by the amount of capital employed as machinery. The ratio of the wear and tear of the machinery affects only the commodity; the worker confronts the total amount of machinery and similarly the value of the capital laid out in labour confronts the value of the capital laid out in machinery.

There can be no doubt that machinery becomes cheaper, and this for two reasons: [1] The application of machinery to the production of raw materials from which the machinery is made. [2] The application of machinery in the transformation of these materials into machinery. In saying this, we already say two things. *Firstly*, that in both these branches, compared with the instruments required in the manufacturing industry, the value of the capital laid out in machinery also grows as compared with that laid out in wages. *Secondly*, what becomes cheaper is the individual machine and its component parts, but a system of machinery develops; the tool is not simply replaced by a single machine, but by a whole system, and the tools which perhaps played the major part previously, the needle for example (in the case of a stocking-loom or a similar machine), are now assembled in thousands. Each individual machine confronting the worker is in itself a colossal assembly of instruments which he formerly used singly, e.g. 1,800 spindles instead of one. But in addition, the machine contains elements which the old instrument did not have. Despite the cheapening of individual elements, the price of the whole aggregate increases enormously and the [increase in] productivity consists in the continuous expansion of the machinery.

Further, one factor in the cheapening of machinery apart from that of its elements, is the cheapening of the source of the motive power (the steam-boiler, for example) and of the transmission mechanism. Economy of power. But this results precisely from the fact that to an increasing extent the same motor can drive a larger system of machines. The motor becomes relatively cheaper (or its cost does not grow in the same ratio as the increase in the size of the system in which it is employed; the motor becomes more expensive as its power grows, but not in the same degree in which it grows); even when its cost increases absolutely, it declines relatively. This is therefore a new and important motive, quite apart from the price of the individual machine, for increasing the capital that is laid out in machinery and confronts labour. One element—the increasing speed of machinery—increases productivity enormously but it does not affect the value of the machinery itself in any way.

It is therefore self-evident or a tautological proposition that the increasing productivity of labour caused by machinery corresponds to increased value of the machinery relative to the amount of labour employed (consequently to the value of labour, the variable capital).

||1105| All circumstances which result in the use of machinery leading to a reduction in the price of commodities can be attributed, firstly, to a decrease in the amount of labour embodied in each individual commodity, secondly, however, to a decrease in the wear and tear of the machinery whose value enters into the individual commodity. The less rapid the wear and tear of the machinery, the less labour is required for its reproduction. This therefore increases the amount and the value of the capital existing as machinery as compared with that existing in labour.

Only the question of raw material therefore remains to be dealt with. It is obvious that the quantity of raw material must increase proportionally with the productivity of labour; that is, the amount of raw material must be proportionate to that of labour. This relationship is closer than it appears.

Let us assume, for example, that 10,000 lbs. of cotton are consumed weekly. Calculating 50 weeks to the year, this would amount to 10,000 ×50, that is, 500,000 lbs. Let us also assume that the amount paid out in wages is £5,000 over the year. And if a pound of cotton is assumed to cost 6d. this comes to 250,000 shillings or £12,500. Let us assume that the capital turns over 5 times during the year. This means that in the course of a fifth of a year, 100,000 pounds of raw material—cotton—is used, equal to a value of £2,500. And £1,000 goes on wages in the same fifth of a year. This is more than a third of the value of the capital laid out on the cotton. This does not alter the ratio. If the value of the cotton amounts to £10,000 every fifth of a year and that of the labour to £1,000, then it amounts to one-tenth. (If one considers the product of the whole year, £50,000 on one side and £5,000 on the other—it is also one-tenth.)

⟨The value of a commodity, as far as machinery is concerned, is determined by the wear and tear of the machinery, that is, solely by the value of the machinery insofar as it enters into the process of the formation of value, in other words, insofar as it is used up in the labour process. Profit, on the contrary, is determined (leaving raw materials out of account) by the value of the whole of the machinery which enters into the labour process irrespective of the degree to which it is used up. Profit must therefore decline as the total amount of labour employed declines compared with the part of capital laid out in machinery. It does not decline in the same proportion because surplus labour increases.⟩

One may ask with regard to raw material: If, for example, productivity in spinning increases tenfold, that is, a single worker spins as much as ten did previously, why should not one Negro produce ten times as much cotton as ten did previously, that is, why should the *value ratio* not remain the same? The spinner uses ten times as much cotton in the same time, but the Negro produces ten times as much cotton in the same time. The ten times larger amount of cotton therefore costs no more than a tenth of this amount cost previously. This means that despite the increase in the amount of the raw material, its value ratio to variable capital remains the same. In fact it was only the large fall in the price of cotton which enabled the cotton industry to develop in the way it did.* The dearer the material (gold and silver, for example) the less are machinery and the division of labour applied in transforming it into articles of luxury. This is because too much capital has been advanced for the raw materials and the demand for these products is limited owing to the expensive raw materials.

To this it is quite easy to answer that some kinds of raw materials, such as wool, silk, leather, are produced by animal *organic* processes, while *cotton*, *linen*, etc., are produced by vegetable organic processes and capitalist production has not yet succeeded, and never will succeed in mastering these processes in the same way as it has mastered purely mechanical or inorganic chemical processes. Raw materials such as skins, etc., and other animal products become dearer partly because the insipid law of rent increases the value of these products as civilisation advances. As far as coal and metal (wood) are concerned, they become much cheaper with the advance of production; this will however become more difficult as mines are exhausted, etc.

⟨While it can be said with regard to corn-rent and mine-rent that they do not increase the value of the product (only its market price) but are rather the expression of the value of the product (the excess of its value *over* the production price), there is, on the other hand, no doubt that animal rent, house rent, etc., are not consequences but *causes* of the increasing values of these things.⟩

---

* ||1105|⟨ If tomorrow the price of cotton were to drop by 90 per cent, the spinning industry would develop even more rapidly the day after tomorrow.⟩ |1105||

The cheapening of raw materials, and of auxiliary materials, etc., checks but does not cancel the growth in the value of this part of capital. It checks it to the degree that it brings about a fall in profit.

This rubbish is herewith disposed of |1105||.

||1105| ⟨In considering profit, surplus-value is assumed as given. And only the variations in constant capital and their influence on the rate of profit are considered. There is only one way in which surplus-value directly affects constant capital, namely through *absolute surplus labour*, lengthening of the working-day, as a result of which the relative value of constant capital is reduced. Relative surplus labour—where the working-day remains unaltered (apart from the greater intensification of labour)—increases the value ratio of profit to total capital by increasing the surplus itself. Absolute surplus labour-time reduces the cost of constant capital relatively.⟩

[3. Cherbuliez's Inkling that the Organic Composition of Capital Is Decisive for the Rate of Profit. His Confusion on This Question. Cherbuliez on the "Law of Appropriation" in Capitalist Economy]

||1106| Let us return to Cherbuliez.

The formulas he uses for the rate of profit are either mathematical expressions for profit as it is commonly understood, without involving any kind of law, or they are quite wrong, although he has an *inkling* of the matter, approaches close to it.

"... commercial profit[108] is determined by the *value of the products* compared with the value of the *different elements* of productive capital" [op. cit., p. 70].

⟨In point of fact, profit is the relationship of the surplus-value of the product to the value of the total capital outlay regardless of the differences in its elements. But the surplus-value is itself determined by the size of the variable capital and the rate at which it produces surplus-value, and the *ratio* of this surplus-value to the total capital is again determined by the ratio of the variable to the constant capital and also by changes in the value of constant capital.⟩

"Evidently the two chief elements in this determination are the price of the raw materials and amount of means of subsistence required to work them up [...] the economic progress of society affects these two elements in an *opposite* way [...] it tends to make raw materials dearer by increasing the value of all the products of the extractive industries,[109] which are carried out on land that is privately owned and limited in extent" (loc. cit., p. 70). On the other hand, the means of subsistence decrease (relatively), a matter to which we shall return presently.

"The total amount of products, less the total amount of capital expended in producing them, provides us with the total amount of profit gained during a definite period of time. The *growth* in the total amount of products *is proportionate to the capital advanced* and not the capital used up. The *rate of profit*, or the ratio of profit to capital, is therefore the result of the combination of two other ratios, namely, the *ratio between the capital laid out and that used up*, and the *ratio between the capital used up and the product*" (loc. cit., p. 70).

Cherbuliez first states correctly that profit is determined by the *value* of the product in relation to the "different elements" of productive capital. Then he flies off suddenly to the product itself, to the total amount of products. But the amount of products may increase without its value increasing. Secondly, a comparison between the amount of the product and the quantity of products of which the capital—used up and not used up—consisted, can at best only be made in the way Ramsay does, by comparing the aggregate national product with the constituent elements expended in kind during its production.^a But as regards capital, the form taken by the product is different from its ingredients in every sphere of production (even in those branches of industry in which, as in agriculture, one part of the product is used in kind as a production element of the product). Why does Cherbuliez stray on to this false path? Because, despite his vague idea that the organic composition of capital is decisive for the rate of profit, he in no way uses the contradiction between variable capital and the other part of capital in order to explain surplus-value—which, like value itself, he does not explain at all. He has not shown how surplus-value arises and therefore has recourse to *surplus product*, i.e., to *use-value*.

Although all surplus-value takes the form of surplus product, surplus product as such does not represent surplus-value. ⟨A product may contain no surplus-value, as, for example, in the case of a peasant who owns his own implements as well as his own land and only works exactly the same amount of time as any wage-worker does to reproduce his own wages, say six hours. In a good year, he might produce twice as much [as usual]. But the value would remain the same, There would be no surplus-value, although there would be surplus product.⟩

---

^a See this volume, p. 337.—*Ed.*

In itself it was already a mistake on the part of Cherbuliez to represent variable capital in the "passive" and purely material form of means of subsistence, that is, as use-value, a form which it obtains in the hands of the workers. If, on the other hand, he had considered it in the form in which it actually appears, namely, as money (as the form in which exchange-value, i.e., a certain amount of social labour-time as such, exists), then [he would have seen that] for the *capitalist* it represents the labour which he exchanges for it (and, as a result of this exchange of materialised labour for living labour, the variable capital would be set in motion and would grow); variable capital in the shape of labour—but not if it is regarded as means of subsistence—becomes an element of productive capital. Means of subsistence, on the other hand, are the use-value, the material existence of the variable capital when it becomes the revenue of the worker. Variable capital regarded as *means of subsistence* is, therefore, just as *"passive"* an element as both the other parts of capital which Cherbuliez describes as "passive".*

The same distortion of views prevents him from elaborating the rate of profit out of the *relationship* of this active element to the passive element, and from showing that it declines as society advances. Cherbuliez in fact reaches no other conclusion but that the means of subsistence ||1107| decline as a consequence of the development of productivity while the working population grows, that is, as a result of the redundant population, wages are consequently pushed down below their value. None of his explanations are based on the exchange of [equal] values—or the payment of labour-power at its value—and profit thus *actually* appears to be a *deduction from wages* (although he doesn't say so). This deduction may indeed occasionally constitute a part of real profits, but it can never serve as the foundation for the elaboration of the category of profit.

Let us first of all reduce the first proposition to its correct formulation.

"The *value* of the total amount of products, less the *value* of the total amount of capital used up in its production, provides us with the total amount of profit gained during a definite period of time."

This is the primary (usual) form in which profit appears and

---

* ||1110| On page 59, Cherbuliez calls raw materials and machinery, etc., "the two *passive elements of capital*" in contrast to the means of subsistence. |1110||

it is likewise the form in which it appears in the consciousness of capitalists. In other words, [profit is] the excess of the value of the product gained during a definite period of time over the value of the capital expended. Or the excess of the value of the product over the cost-price of the product. Even the "definite period of time" in Cherbuliez's statement appears like a bolt from the blue, since he has not dealt with the circulation process of capital. The first proposition, therefore, is nothing but the usual definition of profit, of the immediate form in which it appears.

The second proposition:

"*The growth in the total amount of products* is proportionate to the capital employed and not to the capital used up."

Paraphrased again, it would read thus:

"the *growth* in the *value* of the total amount of products is proportionate to the capital advanced" (whether used up or not).

The only purpose of this is the *surreptitious introduction* of the completely unproven and, in the way it is formulated, quite false proposition (for it already presupposes equalisation to the general rate of profit) that the amount of profit depends on the amount of capital employed. But an apparent causal nexus is to be introduced because "the *growth in the total amount of products* is proportionate to the capital *employed* and not to the capital used up".

Let us take this sentence in both its formulations—that in which it is written and that in which it ought to have been written. In this context—and in accordance with the conclusion which it is intended to serve as intermediate clause—it should be written as follows:

"The *growth* in the *value* of the total amount of products is proportionate to the capital employed and not to the capital used up."

Here, evidently, surplus-value is to be evolved on the basis of the fact that the excess of the capital employed over that used up creates the *excess value of the products*. But the capital which is not used up (machinery, etc.) retains its value (for the fact that it is not used up means precisely that its value has not been used up); it retains the same value after the conclusion of the production process as it had before this process started. If *any change in value* has taken place, it can only have happened in that part of the capital which has been used up, and which therefore entered into the process of the formation of value. In point of fact it is also wrong to say that, for example, a capital of which a third is not used up and two-thirds are used up in production, would inevitably yield a higher profit than one in which two-thirds are not used up and one-third is used up, provided the *rate of exploitation is the same* (and disregarding the equalisation of the rate of profit). For obviously, the second capital contains more machinery, etc., and other elements of constant capital, while the first capital contains less of these elements and sets more living labour in motion, and therefore produces more surplus labour as well.

If we take the proposition as formulated by Cherbuliez himself, then it must be said first that it is of no use to him, because the amount of products or the amount of use-values as such by no means determines either the value or the surplus-value or the profit. But what is behind all this? A part of constant capital consisting of machinery, etc., enters into the labour process without entering into the formation of value, it helps to increase the volume of products without adding anything to its value. (For insofar as its wear and tear adds value to the product, it belongs to the capital *used up* and not to the capital *employed* as opposed to that used up.) But, by itself, this unconsumed part of constant capital does not bring about a *growth in the amount of products*. It helps to produce a greater output in a given labour-time. Therefore, if only the same amount of labour-time were expended as is contained in the means of subsistence, the same amount of products would be produced. The excess of products is therefore due to a change which takes place in this part of the *capital used up* and not to the excess of the capital employed over that consumed (assuming that it is not a matter of branches of industry in which—as in agriculture—the *volume* of products is, or can be, independent of the amount of capital laid out, [because] the productivity of labour is, in part, dependent on uncontrollable natural conditions).

If however he considers constant capital—used up or otherwise—as independent of the labour-time, independent of the change in the variable capital which takes place in the realisation process, then he might just as well say:

"The growth in the total amount ||1108| of products" (at least in manufacturing industry) "is proportionate to the growth of the part of capital consisting of raw materials which is used up."

For the increase of products is physically identical with the growth of this part of capital. In agriculture on the other hand

(and likewise in the extractive industries), where only a small proportion of the capital invested is not [annually] used up (i.e., constant capital) and a relatively large proportion of capital is used up (as wages for example), the amount of products, provided the land is fairly fertile, can be much larger than in the advanced countries where the ratio of capital invested to capital used up is infinitely greater.

The second proposition thus amounts to an attempt to bring in surreptitiously surplus-value (the indispensable basis of profit). [Cherbuliez's conclusion:]

"The rate of profit or the *ratio* of the profit to capital is therefore the result of the combination of two other ratios, namely the *ratio* between the *capital laid out* and that *used up*, and the *ratio between the capital used up and the product"* (op. cit., p. 70).

Previously, *profit* ought to have been explained. But nothing emerged except a definition of it which merely states the form in which it appears, i.e., the fact that profit is equal to the excess of the value of the total product over the cost-price of the product or over the value of the capital used up, which is the vulgar definition of profit.

Now the *rate of profit* ought to be explained. But once again nothing emerges except the vulgar definition. The rate of profit is equal to the ratio of profit to the total capital, or, what amounts to the same thing, it is equal to the ratio of the excess of the value of the product over its cost-price to the total capital advanced for production. The distorted conception and bungling application of the approximately correct distinction between the elements of capital, and the vague idea that profit and rate of profit are directly connected with the ratio of these elements to one another, only lead to a repetition of the generally known phrases in a rather doctrinaire fashion, in fact merely to a statement that profit and rate of profit exist without, however, anything being said about their nature.

The matter is not improved by the fact that Cherbuliez expresses his doctrinaire formulae in algebraic language:

"Let P be the aggregate product of a given period of time, C the capital invested, π the profit, r the *ratio* of profit to capital (rate), c the capital used up, then $P-c=\pi$, $r=\frac{\pi}{C}$, therefore $Cr=\pi$. Therefore $P-c=Cr$; therefore $r=\frac{P-c}{C}$" (loc. cit., p. 70, Note 1).

Which means nothing more than that the rate of profit equals the ratio of profit to capital and that profit equals the excess of the value of the product over its cost-price.

In general, when Cherbuliez speaks about consumed and unconsumed capital he has at the back of his mind the difference between fixed and circulating capital, and not the distinction which he himself has drawn, namely, that between the different types of capital based on the production process. Surplus-value is antecedent to circulation and no matter how much the differences arising out of circulation affect the rate of profit, they have nothing to do with the origin of profit.

"Productive capital [...] is composed of a consumable part [...] and a non-consumable part [....] The more wealth and population increase, the more the consumable part tends to increase, because the extractive industries demand an ever greater supply of labour. On the other hand, this same progress [...] causes the *amount* of capital invested to increase at a much faster rate than the amount of capital *consumed*. Thus although the total mass of capital consumed tends to increase [...] the effect is neutralised, because the mass of products grows in more rapid progression and the *total amount of profit* must be considered as growing at a rate at least as high as that at which the *total amount of capital invested* grows" (loc. cit., p. 71).

"The amount of profit grows, not the rate, which is the ratio of this amount to the capital invested, $r = \frac{P-c}{C}$. It is clear that $P-c$ or the profit, since $P-c=\pi$, *can* grow although r declines, if C grows more rapidly than $P-c$" (p. 71, note).

Here the reason for the decline in the rate of profit is touched on, but in view of the preceding distortions, it can only lead to confusion and contradictions which cancel each other out. First the amount of capital consumed grows but the amount of products grows even more rapidly (i.e., the excess of the value of the products over their cost-price in this case), for it grows in proportion to the capital invested and this grows more rapidly than the capital consumed. *Why* the fixed capital grows more rapidly than the mass of raw materials, for example, is not explained anywhere. But never mind, the amount of profit grows *in proportion to* the capital *invested*, to the total capital, but ||1109|| the *rate of profit* is nevertheless supposed to fall, because the total capital grows more rapidly than the mass of products or rather than the amount of profit.

First the *amount of profit grows* at a rate at least as great as that at which "the total amount of the capital invested" grows, and then the rate of profit *falls*, because the total amount of capital invested grows more rapidly than the amount of profit.

First $P-c$ grows "at least" proportionally to C, and then $\frac{P-c}{C}$ falls, because C increases even more rapidly than $P-c$, which increases at least as rapidly as C. If we throw aside all this confusion, then all that remains is the tautology that $\frac{P-c}{C}$ can fall again although $P-c$ increases, that is, that the rate of profit can fall although profit increases when the rate falls. The rate of profit simply signifies the ratio of $P-c$ to C, [and this ratio declines] when capital increases more rapidly than the amount of profit.

Thus the final pearl of wisdom is that the rate of profit can fall, that is, the ratio of an increasing amount of profit to capital can fall when the capital increases more rapidly than the amount of profit, or if the amount of profit, despite the absolute growth, declines relatively in comparison with the capital. This is nothing but a different expression for the decline in the rate of profit. But that this phenomenon is within the bounds of possibility, and even its existence, has never been called to question. The sole point at issue was precisely to explain the cause of this phenomenon, and Cherbuliez explains the decline in the rate of profit, the decline in the amount of profit in relation to the total capital, by the relative increase in the amount of profit which is at least proportionate to the growth of the capital. He obviously surmises that the mass of living labour employed declines relatively to past labour, although it increases absolutely, and that *therefore* the rate of profit must decline. But he never arrives at a clear understanding. The closer one comes to the threshold of understanding, the more distorted the statements become, unless the threshold is actually crossed and [the greater is] the illusion of having crossed it.

On the other hand, what he says about the *equalisation of the general rate of profit* is very much to the point.[110] ||1109||

||1109| "After the deduction of rent, what remains of the *amount of profit*, that is, of the excess of products over the capital consumed, is divided between the capitalist producers *in proportion to the capital each has invested*, whereas the portion of the product which corresponds to the capital used up and is intended to replace it, is divided in proportion with the capital actually used up. This *dual law of division* comes about *as a result of competition*, which tends to equalise the advantages of the different investments of capital. Finally, this dual law of division determines the respective *values* and *prices* of the different kinds of products" (loc. cit., pp. 71-72).

This is very good. Only the concluding words are wrong, namely, that the formation of the general rate of profit determines the *values* and *prices* (it should be prices of production) of commodities. On the contrary, the determination of the value is the primary factor, antecedent to the rate of profit and to the establishment of production prices. How can any kind of *division* of the "amount of profit", i.e., of the surplus-value ||1110|—which is itself only a part of the total value of commodities—determine the "*amount* of profit", that is, the surplus-value, that is, the value of the commodities? This is only correct if, by relative values of commodities, one means their production prices. The whole lopsidedness of Cherbuliez's presentation arises from the fact that he does not examine the origin and the laws of value and surplus-value independently.

In other respects, he describes the relation between wage-labour and capital more or less correctly.

People who neither receive anything by devolution (legal transfer, inheritance, etc.), nor have any possessions they can exchange, can[a] "obtain what they need only by offering their *labour* to the capitalist. They only acquire the right to the things which are allocated to them as the *price of labour*, but they have no right to the *product* of their labour, nor to the *value* which they have added" (op. cit., pp. 55-56). "By *exchanging* his labour for a certain volume of means of subsistence, [...] the worker completely renounces all right to the other portions of capital [....] The distribution of these products remains the same as it was previously; it is not modified in any way by the above-mentioned convention. The products continue to belong exclusively to the capitalist who has provided the raw materials and the means of subsistence. *This is an inescapable sequence of the law of appropriation, the fundamental principle of* which was, conversely, *the exclusive right of every worker to the product of his labour*" (p. 58).

This fundamental principle, according to Cherbuliez, is as follows:

"The worker has an exclusive right to the value resulting from his labour" (p. 48).

Cherbuliez does not understand nor does he explain how the law of commodities, according to which commodities are equivalents and exchange with one another in proportion to their value, i.e., to the labour-time embodied in them, unexpectedly leads to the result that on the contrary capitalist production—and only on the basis of capitalist production is it essential for the product to be produced as a commodity—depends on the fact that

---

[a] In this phrase Marx summarises (in German) a lengthy paragraph from *Riche ou pauvre* and then quotes from the book.—*Ed.*

one portion of labour is appropriated without exchange. He only senses that a *transformation* has suddenly taken place.

This fundamental principle is a pure fiction. It arises from the surface appearance of *commodity circulation*. Commodities are exchanged with one another according to their value, that is, according to the labour embodied in them. Individuals confront one another only as commodity owners and can therefore only acquire other individuals' commodities by alienating their own. It therefore *appears* as if they exchanged only their own labour since the exchange of commodities which contain *other people's* labour, insofar as they themselves were not acquired by the individuals in exchange for their own commodities, presupposes different relations between people than those of [simple] commodity owners, of buyers and of sellers. In capitalist production this appearance, which its surface displays, disappears. What does not disappear, however, is the illusion that originally men confront one another only as commodity owners and that, consequently, a person is only a property owner insofar as he is a worker. As has been stated, this "originally" is a delusion arising from the surface appearance of capitalist production and has never existed historically. In general, man (isolated or social) always comes on to the stage as a property owner before he appears as a worker, even if the property is only what he procures for himself from nature (or what he as a member of the family, tribe, communal organisation, procures partly from nature, partly from the means of production which have already been produced in common). And as soon as the first animal state is left behind, man's property in nature is mediated by his existence as a member of a communal body, family, tribe, etc., by his relationship to other men, which determines his relationship to nature. The "propertyless labourer" as a "fundamental principle" is rather a creature of civilisation and, on the historical scale, of "capitalist production". This is a law of "expropriation" not of "appropriation", at least not simply of appropriation in the way Cherbuliez imagines it, but a kind of appropriation which corresponds to a definite, specific mode of production. |1110||

||1111| Cherbuliez says:

"The products are appropriated before they are converted into capital; and this conversion does not eliminate such appropriation" (op. cit., p. 54).

But this applies not only to the products, but also to labour. Raw materials, etc., and instruments belong to the capitalist.

They are the *converted* form of his money. On the other hand, when he has bought labour-power or the daily (say 12 hours) use of labour-power, with a sum of money equal to the product of six hours of labour, then the labour of 12 hours belongs to him; it is *appropriated* by him before it is carried out. The process of production itself turns labour into capital. But this transformation is an act which takes place later than its appropriation.

The "products" are converted into capital, *physically* converted insofar as in the process of production they function as conditions of labour, conditions of production, objects and instruments of labour, and *formally* converted insofar as not only their *value* is perpetuated but as they become means for absorbing *labour and surplus labour*, insofar as they actually function as absorbers of labour. ||1112| On the other hand: the labour-power *appropriated before* the [production] process is turned directly into capital *in* the course of the process by being converted into the conditions of labour and into surplus-value, [since] as a result of its embodiment in the product, it not only preserves the constant capital but replaces the variable capital and adds surplus-value. |1112||

[4. On Accumulation as Extended Reproduction]

[Cherbuliez writes:]

||1110| "Every accumulation of wealth provides the means for accelerating further accumulation" (op. cit., p. 29).

{Ricardo's view (derived from Smith) that all accumulation can be reduced to expenditure on wages, would be incorrect even if no accumulation in kind took place—which is the case, for example, when the farmer sows more seed, the stock-breeder increases his stock of cattle for breeding or for fattening, the owner of engineering works uses part of his surplus-value in the form of machine tools—and even if all producers who produce the elements of some part of capital did not over-produce regularly, counting on the fact of annual accumulation, i.e., the expansion of the general scale of production. Moreover, the peasant can exchange part of his surplus corn with the stock-breeder, who may convert this corn into variable capital while the peasant converts his corn into constant capital [by means of this exchange]. The flax-grower ||1111| sells part of his surplus product to the spinner, who converts it into constant capital. With this money the flax-grower can buy tools and the tool-maker can then buy iron, etc., so that all these elements are turned directly into constant capital.

But disregarding all this, let us assume that a manufacturer of machines wants to convert an additional capital of £1,000 into elements of production. He will of course lay out part of it on wages, say £200. But he buys iron, coal, etc., with the remaining £800. Let us assume that this iron, coal, etc., has first to be produced. Then, if the iron or coal producers either have no excess (accumulated) stocks of their commodities, and likewise have no additional machinery and are unable to buy it immediately (for in this case too constant capital would be exchanged for constant capital), they can only produce the required iron and coal if they work their old machinery longer. As a result, they would have to replace it more rapidly, but a part of its value would enter into the new product. Irrespective of this, however, the iron manufacturer needs more coal in any case and must therefore transform at least part of his share in the £800 into constant capital. Both coal and iron producers sell their wares in such a way that they contain unpaid surplus labour. And if this amounts to a quarter, then this alone means that £200 out of the £800 is not converted into wages, not to mention the part which has to make good the wear and tear of the old machinery.

The surplus consists always of the articles produced by the particular capital, i.e., coal, iron, etc. Part of the surplus is converted directly into constant capital when the producers whose commodities serve as elements of production for other producers exchange these commodities with one another. That part of the surplus value, however, which is exchanged against the products of those who produce means of subsistence and replaces the constant capital in these branches, provides the necessary variable capital. The producers of means of subsistence that can no longer enter as elements into their production (except as variable capital) acquire additional constant capital through the same process which provides the other producers with additional variable capital.

The following features distinguish reproduction—insofar as it constitutes accumulation—from simple reproduction.

Firstly: Both the constant and variable elements of production which are accumulated consist of newly added labour. They are not used as revenue, although they arise from profit. They consist of profit or surplus labour, whereas in the case of simple reproduction part of the product represents past labour (i.e., in this context, labour which has not been performed in the current year).

Secondly: If the labour-time in certain branches is lengthened, that is, if no additional instruments or machines are employed, the new product must indeed, to a certain extent, pay for the more rapid wear and tear of the old [tools or machines], and this accelerated consumption of the old constant capital is likewise an aspect of accumulation.

Thirdly: As a result of the additional money capital which arises in the process of [extended] reproduction—partly through the freeing of capital, partly through the conversion of part of the product into money, partly because, as a result of the money collected by the producer, the demand for other [commodities], e.g., [those offered by the] sellers of luxury goods, is reduced—the systematic replacement of the elements [of production] is by no means a necessity, as it is in the case of simple reproduction.

With the additional money anyone can buy or command products, although the producer from whom the purchase is made may neither expend his revenue on the product of the purchaser nor replace his capital with it}. ⟨Additional capital (constant or variable) must appear in the form of money capital on one side, even if this only exists in the form of outstanding claims, whenever it is not balanced by a corresponding addition on the other side.⟩

[5. Elements of Sismondism in Cherbuliez. On the Organic Composition of Capital. Fixed and Circulating Capital]

For the rest, Cherbuliez presents a remarkable amalgam of Sismondian and Ricardian contradictory views. |1111||
||1112| *Sismondian*.

"The hypothesis [...] that an *invariable ratio exists* between the different elements of capital is not substantiated at any stage of the development of society. The relationship is essentially *variable* and for two reasons: a) the division of labour, and b) the replacement of human labour by natural agents. These two factors tend to reduce the *ratio* of the means of subsistence to the other two elements of capital" (op. cit., pp. 61-62).

In this situation, "the *increase in productive capital* does not necessarily lead to an increase in the amount of means of subsistence intended to constitute the price of labour; it can be accompanied—at least for a time—by an absolute diminution of this element of capital, and consequently by a *reduction in the price of labour*" (loc. cit, p. 63).

⟨This is Sismondian; the effect on the *wage level* is the only aspect considered by Cherbuliez. This problem does not arise at all in an investigation where labour is always supposed to be paid at its value and the fluctuations of the *market price* of labour above or below that point (the value [of labour]) are not taken into consideration.⟩

"The producer who wishes to introduce a new division of labour in his enterprise or to exploit some natural force, will not wait until he has accumulated sufficient capital to be able to employ in this new way *all* the workers he needed previously. In the case of division of labour, he will perhaps be satisfied to produce with five workers what he previously produced with ten. In the case of the exploitation of a natural force, he will perhaps use only one machine and two workers. The means of subsistence will, in consequence, be reduced to 1,500 in the first case and to 600 in the second. But since the number of workers remains the same, *their competition* will soon force the price of labour below its original level" (loc. cit., pp. 63-64). "This is one of the most astonishing results of the *law of appropriation*. The absolute increase in wealth, that is, in the products of labour, does not give rise to a proportional increase and may lead to a diminution in the means of subsistence for the workers, in the portion they receive of all kinds of products" (p. 64). "The factors determining the *price of labour*" ⟨in this context it is always a question only of the *market price* of labour⟩ "are the absolute amount of productive capital and the ratio between the different elements of capital, two social facts on which the will of the workers can exercise no influence" (p. 64). "Nearly all the odds are against the worker" (loc. cit.).

The ratio between the different elements of productive capital is determined in two ways:
First: By the organic composition of productive capital. By this we mean the technological composition. With a *given productivity* of labour, which can be taken as constant so long as no change occurs, the amount of raw material and means of labour, that is, the amount of constant capital—in terms of its *material elements*—which corresponds to a definite *quantity of living labour* (paid or unpaid), that is, to the *material elements* of *variable* capital, is determined in every sphere of production.

If the proportion of the materialised labour to the living labour employed is small, then the portion of the product that represents living labour will be large regardless of how this portion is divided between capitalist and worker. If the reverse is the case, the portion will be small. With a given rate of exploitation of labour, the surplus labour too will be large in the former case and small in the latter. This can only change as a result of a change in the mode of production which alters the technological relationship between the two parts of capital. Even in this case, the absolute amount of living labour employed by the capital which uses a greater proportion of constant capital may be equal or even larger if capitals of different *size* are compared. But it must be smaller *relatively*. For capitals of the same size, or calculated in proportion to the total capital—100 for example—it must be smaller both relatively and absolutely. All changes arising from the development (not the decline) of the productive power of labour, reduce that part of the product which represents living labour, that is, they reduce variable capital. Regarding capital invested in different branches of production ||1113|, one can say [that these changes] reduce the *variable* capital absolutely in those branches which have reached a higher level of production, since wages are assumed to be equal.

So much with regard to the changes arising from changes in the mode of production.

Secondly, however, if one assumes that the organic composition of capitals is given and likewise the differences which arise from the differences in their organic composition, then the *value* ratio can change although the technological composition remains the same. What can happen is: a) a change in the value of constant capital; b) a change in the value of the variable capital; c) a *change in both*, in equal or unequal proportions.

a) If the technological composition remains the same and a change in the value of constant capital takes place, its value will either fall or rise. If it falls, and only the same amount of living labour is employed as previously, i.e., if the *scale* or *level of production* remains the same, if, for example, 100 men are employed as previously, then in physical terms, the same amount of raw material and means of labour is required as previously. But the surplus labour bears a greater proportion to the total capital advanced. The rate of profit rises. In the opposite case it declines. In the former case, for the capitals already employed in that sphere (not those newly invested in it after the change of value in the elements of constant capital has taken place), the total sum of the capital employed diminishes, that is, some portion of the capital is set free, although production continues to be carried on on the same scale; or the capital thus liberated is again employed in the same sphere of production and has then the same effect as an accumulation of capital. The scale of production is enlarged, and the absolute amount of surplus labour is increased proportionally. With a given *method of production*, every accumulation of capital results in an increase in the total amount of surplus-value whatever the rate of surplus-value may be.

Conversely, if the value of the elements of constant capital increases, then *either the scale of production* (hence the mass of the total capital advanced) must increase to employ the *same quantity* of labour (the same variable capital the value of which has remained unchanged) as before; and then although the absolute amount of surplus-value—and the rate of surplus-value—remains the same, its proportion to the total capital advanced decreases, and hence the rate of profit falls. Or the scale of production and the total capital advanced is not enlarged, then in all circumstances, the variable capital must decrease.

If the same sum as previously is laid out in constant capital, it now represents a smaller amount of material elements and since the *technological conditions* remain the same, less labour will be employed. The total capital advanced therefore decreases by [an amount corresponding to] the labour dismissed; the total value of the capital advanced thus decreases, but a greater proportion of the diminished capital is laid out in constant capital (in terms of value). The surplus-value decreases absolutely, because less labour is employed, and the ratio of the remaining surplus-value to the total capital advanced falls, because variable capital bears a smaller proportion to constant capital.

On the other hand, if the same total capital is employed as before—the reduced value of the variable capital (representing a smaller quantity of labour, living labour, employed), being counterbalanced by the increased value of the constant capital; the one being diminished in the same proportion as the other is augmented, then the absolute quantity of surplus-value falls; because less labour is employed, and at the same time, the proportion of this surplus-value to the total capital advanced falls. Thus the rate of profit falls for two reasons, the diminution in the amount of surplus labour, and the decreasing proportion of that surplus labour to the total capital advanced.

In the first case where (with decreasing value of the elements of constant capital) the *rate of profit rises* in all circumstances, the *s c a l e o f p r o d u c t i o n* must be extended if the *amount of profit* is to increase. Let us assume that the capital is 600—half constant, half variable. If the constant capital were to lose half its value, it would only amount to 150, although the variable capital would remain 300. The total capital employed would be only 450, 150 being freed. If the 150 are added to the capital again, then 100 of the 150 will now be laid out in variable capital. ||1114| Thus the *scale of production* is expanded and more labour employed, if the same capital continues to be used in the production process.

In the opposite case, where with rising value of the elements of constant capital the *rate of profit* falls in all circumstances, the *scale of production*, and therefore the capital advanced, must be increased if the amount of profit *is not to decrease* and the *amount* of labour employed (and therefore surplus-value) is to remain the same. If this is not done, if only the old or less than the old capital is employed, then not only does the rate of profit decline, but also the amount of profit.

The rate of surplus-value remains unchanged in both cases; it changes, however, if any change in the *technological* composition of capital takes place: it increases if the constant capital increases (because labour is then more productive) and declines when it falls (because labour is then less productive).

b) If there is any change in the value of variable capital independent of the *organic composition*, it can only occur because of a fall or a rise in the price of means of subsistence that are not produced in the sphere of production under consideration but enter into it as commodities from outside.

If the *value of variable* capital falls, it nevertheless represents the same amount of living labour as before. The same quantity of labour merely costs less. If therefore the *scale of production* remains the same (since the value of constant capital is unchanged), then the part of the total capital used for the purchase of labour is diminished. Less capital needs to be laid out in order to pay the same number of workers. Thus, in this case, if the *scale of production remains the same*, the amount of capital laid out diminishes. The rate of profit increases, and this for two reasons. The [*amount of*] *surplus-value has increased*; the ratio of living labour to materialised labour has remained the same, but the increased surplus-value correlates with a smaller total capital. If, on the other hand, the capital freed is again invested, then this amounts to *accumulation*.

If the *value of the variable capital* increases, then a greater total capital must also be laid out in order to employ the same number of workers as before, because the value of the constant capital remains the same and that of the variable capital has risen. The amount of labour remains the same, but a smaller part of it is surplus labour, and this smaller part corresponds to a larger capital. This takes place when the *scale of production remains the same*, while the value of the total capital increases. If the value of the total capital does not increase, the *scale of production* must be reduced. The amount of labour declines and a smaller portion of this reduced amount constitutes surplus labour, which, too, bears a smaller proportion to the total capital advanced.

The organic changes and those brought about by changes of value can have a similar effect on the rate of profit in certain circumstances. They differ however in the following way. If the latter are not due simply to fluctuations of market prices and are therefore not temporary, they are invariably caused by an organic change in the spheres that provide the elements of constant or of variable capital.

[c)] It is not necessary here to examine *case 3* in detail.

In the case of capitals of equal size—or if the calculation is based on equal amounts of the total capital, 100, for example—the *organic composition* may be *the same* in *different spheres of production*, but the *value ratio* of the primary component parts of constant and variable capital may be *different* according to the different values of the amount of instruments and raw materials used. For example, copper instead of iron, iron instead of lead, wool instead of cotton, etc.

On the other hand, is it possible for the organic composition to be different if the *value ratio* remains the same? If the organic composition is the same, the relative amounts which constitute constant capital and living labour are *the same* per 100. The quantitative proportions are the same. The value of the constant capital may be the same, although the relative amounts of labour set in motion are different. If the machinery or raw materials are dearer (or cheaper), less labour, for example, may be required, but in this case the value of the variable capital is also relatively smaller or vice versa.

||1115| Let us take A and B. c' and v' are the component parts (in terms of value) of A, and c and v those of B (again in terms of value). If $c':v'$ is equal to $c:v$ then $c'v$ equals $v'c$. Consequently likewise $\frac{c'}{c}$ equals $\frac{v'}{v}$.

Since the *value ratios* [of constant to variable capital] are equal, only the following variations are possible. If in one sphere *more surplus labour is carried out* than in another sphere, ⟨for example, night work is impossible in agriculture, and although the individual agricultural labourer can be over-worked, nevertheless the total amount of labour which can be expended on a given area of land is limited by the object being produced (corn), whereas in a factory of a given size the amount produced depends (δυνάμει[a]) on the hours of labour worked—that is to say, it is due to the different kinds of production that more surplus labour can be employed in one sphere at a given level of production than in another⟩ then, even if the value ratio of constant and variable capital is the same, the amount of labour employed in proportion to the total capital will nevertheless be different.

Or, let us assume that the raw material is dearer and labour (of greater *skill*) is dearer, in the same proportion. In this case [capitalist] A employs 5 workers, where [capitalist] B employs 25, and they cost him £100—as much as the 25 workers, because their labour is dearer (their surplus labour is therefore also worth more). These 5 workers work up 100 lbs. of raw material, y, worth [£] 500 and B's workers work up 1,000 lbs. of raw material, x, worth [£] 500, because the raw material is dearer and the productive power of the workers is less highly developed in the case of A. The value ratio here—£100 v to [£] 500 c is the same in both cases, but the *organic composition* is different.

The *value ratio* is the same: The value of constant capital in A is the same as in B, and proportionately A lays out the same amount of capital in wages as B. But the quantity of his products will be smaller. Although he employs the same absolute quantity of labour as B, he uses more relatively, because his constant capital is dearer. He processes less raw material, etc., in the same time, but this smaller quantity costs him as much as the larger quantity processed by B. The *value ratio* in this case is the same, the organic composition is different. In the other case the value ratio being assumed to be the same, this can occur only if the amounts of the surplus labour are different or if the value of the different kinds of labour are different.

The organic composition can be taken to mean the following: Different ratios in which it is necessary to expend constant capital in the different spheres of production in order to absorb the same amount of labour. The *combination of the same amount of labour* with the object of labour requires either that both

---

[a] Potentially.—*Ed.*

more raw material and more machinery are used in one case than in the other, or that more of only one of these is used.

{Where the ratios between fixed and circulating capital are very different, those between *constant and variable* capital can be *the same*, consequently the surplus-value can be the same although the *values* produced annually must be different. Let us assume that in the coal industry—where no raw materials are used (apart from auxiliary materials), the fixed capital constitutes half the total capital and variable capital the other half. Let us assume that in tailoring the fixed capital is zero (as in the previous case we disregard auxiliary materials), that the raw materials constitute half and the variable capital the other half of the total capital. Given the same degree of exploitation of labour, both will realise the same amount of *surplus-value*, since both employ the same amount of labour in proportion to capital, i.e., per 100. But let us assume that fixed capital in the coal industry turns over once every 10 years while there is no difference in the rate of turnover of circulating capital in both cases. At the end of the year (we will assume that the variable capital turns over once a year in both cases) the tailor's capital will have produced values amounting to 150 if the surplus-value is 50. The coal producer, on the other hand, will have produced values amounting to 105 at the end of the first year (consisting of 5 for fixed capital, 50 for variable and 50 for surplus labour). As in the case of the tailor, the total value of his product plus the fixed capital will amount to 150, that is, the product, 105, plus 45 for the remaining fixed capital. The production of different magnitudes of value therefore does not preclude the production of *the same* amount of surplus-value.

In the second year, the fixed capital of the coal producer would amount to 45, variable capital to 50 and surplus-value to 50, that is, the capital advanced would be 95 and the profit would be 50. The rate of profit would have *risen*, because the value of the fixed ||1116| capital would have declined by one tenth as a result of wear and tear during the first year. Thus there can be no doubt that in the case of all capitals employing a great deal of fixed capital—provided the scale of production remains unchanged—the rate of profit must *rise* in proportion as the value of the machinery, the fixed capital, declines annually, because wear and tear has already been taken into account. If the coal producer sells his coal at the same price throughout the ten years, then his rate of profit must be higher in the second year than it was in the first and so forth. Or one would have to assume that the maintenance work, etc., stands in direct proportion to the depreciation, so that the total sum advanced annually under the heading of fixed capital remains the same. This extra profit may be equalised also as a result of the fact that—apart from wear and tear—the value of fixed capital falls in the course of time, because it has to compete with new, more recently invented, better machinery. On the other hand, this rising rate of profit, which results naturally from wear and tear, makes it possible for the declining value of the fixed capital to compete with newer, better machinery, the full value of which has still to be taken into account. Finally, the coal producer sold his coal more cheaply [at the end of the second year], on the basis of the following calculation: 50 on 100 means 50 per cent profit, 50 per cent on 95 comes to $47^1/_2$; if therefore he sold the same quantity of coal [not for 105 but] for $102^1/_2$—then he would have sold it more cheaply than the man whose machinery, for example, began to operate only in the current year. Large installations of fixed capital presuppose possession of large amounts of capital. And since these big owners of capital dominate the market, it appears that only for this reason their enterprises yield surplus profit (rent). In the case of agriculture, this rent derives from working relatively fertile land, but here we are dealing with a case where relatively cheaper machinery is utilised.}

⟨A large number of instances which are adduced in connection with the relation of fixed to circulating capital, refer to the difference between variable and constant capital. First of all, the proportion of constant to variable capital can be the same although the proportion of fixed to circulating capital is different. Secondly, in the case of constant and variable capital it is a question of the primary division of capital between living and *materialised* labour, *not* of the modification of this relationship by the circulation process or the influence of this latter on reproduction.

It is clear first of all that the difference between fixed and circulating capital can affect surplus-value (apart from the differences in the mass of living labour employed, i.e., differences which are related to the ratio of variable to constant capital) only insofar as it affects the *turnover* of the total capital. It is therefore necessary to investigate how the *turnover* affects surplus-value. Two factors are obviously closely connected with it:

1) surplus-value cannot be accumulated, reconverted into capital, so rapidly (so often); 2) the *capital advanced* must increase both to continue to employ the same number of workers, etc., and because the advances of money which the capitalist makes to himself to cover his own consumption costs must extend over a longer period. These factors are important in connection with *profit*. Here, however, it is, to begin with, only necessary to examine how they affect surplus-value. One must moreover always clearly distinguish between these two factors.⟩

⟨Everything which increases the *capital outlay* without proportionally increasing the surplus-value, reduces the rate of profit even if the surplus-value remains the same; the opposite is the case with everything which reduces the outlay. Insofar, therefore, as a large amount of fixed capital in proportion to circulating capital—or different turnover periods of capital—affects the size of the capital outlay, it affects the rate of profit even if it does not at all affect the surplus-value.⟩

⟨The rate of profit is not simply the surplus-value calculated on the capital advanced, but the mass of surplus-value realised within a given period, that is, in a definite period of circulation. Insofar as the difference between fixed and circulating capital affects the mass of surplus-value which a particular capital yields *within a given period*, it affects the rate of profit. Two aspects must be taken into consideration: firstly, the difference in the size of the *capital advanced* (relative to the surplus-value realised) and secondly, the difference in the *length of time* for which these advances have to be made before they are returned with a surplus.⟩

||1117| {The reproduction time, or rather, the number of reproductions taking place in a definite period of time, is substantially affected by two circumstances.

1) *The product remains longer in the sphere of production, in the strict sense of the term.*

It is possible firstly that, in order to be produced, one product requires a longer period of time than another; it may require a larger part of a year, a whole year or even more than a year. (The latter is the case for example with buildings, in stockbreeding and the production of certain luxuries.) In this case, the product continually absorbs labour—often a great deal of labour is absorbed (for instance by luxury articles and buildings) in relation to the constant capital—the amount depending on the composition of the productive capital, its division into constant and variable capital. Thus in the measure as the time required for the production of the commodity increases and the labour process continues uniformly, a continuous absorption of labour and of surplus labour takes place. This happens for example with cattle or buildings if the latter require more than a year's work. The product can enter the sphere of circulation, that is, it can be sold, be thrown on the market, only when the work is completed. The surplus labour expended in the first year is embodied with the rest of the labour in the unfinished product of the first year. It is neither greater nor smaller than in other branches of production where constant and variable capital are used in the same proportions. But the value of the product cannot be *realised*, that is, in the sense that it cannot be converted into money, and neither can the surplus-value. The latter cannot therefore be accumulated as capital nor used for consumption. The capital advanced, and also the surplus-value, serve, so to speak, as foundations for further production. They are a pre-condition for it and enter, to some extent, as semi-finished products, or, in one way or another, as raw material into the production process of the second year.

Let us assume that the capital is [£] 500, labour [£] 100 and surplus-value [£] 50, so that the capital advanced in production amounts to [£] 550 plus [£] 500 which is advanced in the second year. The surplus-value is again [£] 50. The value of the product is therefore [£] 1,100, of which [£] 100 is surplus-value. In this case, the surplus-value is the same as if the capital had been reproduced in the first year and [£] 500 had been invested again in the second year. In each year the variable capital employed is [£] 100 and the surplus-value [£] 50. But the *rate of profit* is different. In the first year it is $\frac{50}{500}$, or 10 per cent. But in the second year the capital outlay amounts to [£] 550 plus [£] 500, that is, [£] 1,050, and a tenth of this is [£] 105. If one adds the same rate of profit, then the value of the product comes to: [£] 550 in the first year; [£] 550+ [£] 500+ [£] 55 + [£] 50= [£] 1,155 in the second year. At the end of the second year, the value of the product is [£] 1,155. Otherwise it would have been only [£] 1,100. In this case, the profit is greater than the surplus-value produced, for this only amounts to [£] 100. If one includes the consumption costs which the capitalist has to advance over two years, then the capital laid out is even greater in proportion to the surplus-value. On the other hand, it is true that the *entire* surplus-value gained in the first year has been converted into capital in the second. Furthermore, the capital laid out in wages is greater, because the £100 is not reproduced at the end of the first year, so that in the second year £200 must be advanced for the same labour for which £100 would have been sufficient if it had been reproduced in the first year.

Secondly. After the labour process has been completed, the product must continue to remain in the production sphere in order to undergo natural processes which require either no labour or relatively quite insignificant amounts of it, like wine in the cellar. Only when this period has elapsed can the capital be reproduced. It is obvious that in this case quite irrespective of what the ratio of variable to constant capital may have been, the effect is the same as if more constant and less variable capital had been laid out. The surplus labour, as well as the total amount of labour employed during a definite period of time, is smaller. If the *rate of profit* is the same, this is due to equalisation, not to the amount of surplus-value produced in this sphere. More capital must be advanced beforehand to maintain the reproduction process—the continuity of production. And for this very reason the surplus-value declines *in proportion* to the capital advanced.

Thirdly. *Interruptions in the labour process* while the product is in the production process, as in agriculture or in processes such as tanning, etc., where chemical processes involve intervals before the product can proceed from one stage to the next, higher one. If in such cases, the interval is reduced by chemical discoveries, the productivity of labour rises, the surplus-value is increased and materialised labour has to be advanced for a shorter period of time. In all these cases, the surplus-value is smaller and the capital outlay larger.

2) The same thing happens if the rate of turnover of the circulating capital is lower than the average because of distant markets. In this case, too, the capital outlay is greater, the surplus-value smaller ·and its *proportion* to the capital advanced is also smaller.} ⟨In the latter case [the capital] is retained longer in the circulation sphere, in the former case, in the production sphere.⟩

||1118| {Let us assume that the capital advanced in some branch or other of the transport industry is [£] 1,000—fixed

capital [£] 500, which will be worn out in five years. The variable capital, which amounts to [£] 500, turns over four times during the year. The annual value of the product will thus be [£] 100+ [£] 2,000+ [£] 100, if the [annual] rate of surplus-value is 20 per cent, a total of [£] 2,200. On the other hand, let us assume that in a branch of tailoring the constant capital, which consists only of circulating capital since fixed capital is assumed to be zero, amounts to 500 and the variable capital to 500, surplus-value is 100. [The capital] turns over four times a year. Then the (annual) value of the product will be 4(500+500)+100, that is, 4,100. The surplus-value is the same in both cases. In the last-mentioned case, the entire capital turns over four times a year or once a quarter. Of the other capital [£] 600 turn over in the course of a year [of which £ 500 turn over four times], therefore [£] $500+\frac{100}{4}=$ [£] 525 in a quarter of a year. That is, 175 in a month, [£] 350 in two months, and [£] 1,400 in eight months. The whole capital requires $5^5/_7$ months in order to turn over. It turns over only $2^1/_{10}$ times a year.

Now it will be said that in order to make a profit of 10 per cent, less is added per quarter on a value of [£]1,000 in the case of the first capital than in that of the other. But here it is not a question of addition. One makes more surplus-value on the capital used up but not on the capital employed. The difference here arises from the surplus-value, not from the addition of profit. The difference here lies in the value not in the surplus-value. In both cases the variable capital amounting to 500 turns over four times in a year. Both capitals yield a surplus-value of [£]100 in a year, the [annual] rate of surplus-value amounts to 20 per cent. But £25 in a quarter, therefore a higher percentage? [£]25 on [£]500 each quarter is 5 per cent a quarter, that is, 20 per cent per annum.

The first [capitalist] turns over half his capital 4 times a year and only a fifth of the remaining half once during the year. A half of four times is *twice*. Thus he turns his capital over $2^1/_{10}$ times during the year. The entire capital of the second capitalist turns over four times a year. But this makes absolutely no difference to the surplus-value. If the second capitalist continues the reproduction process uninterruptedly, then he must constantly convert [£] 500 into raw materials, etc., and must always use [£] 500 for labour, while the other capitalist likewise uses [£] 500 for labour and has invested the remaining [£]500 once and for all (that is, for five years) in such a form that he does not need to reconvert it again. This applies however only when the ratio of variable to constant capital is the same [in both capitals] despite the difference between fixed and circulating capital.

If in both cases, one half consists of constant and the other half of variable capital, then it is only possible for one half [in one case] to consist of fixed capital if the circulating constant capital amounts to zero, and [in the other case], one half can consist of circulating constant capital only if the fixed capital amounts to zero. Although the circulating constant capital can amount to zero, as in the extractive and transport industries where, however, the auxiliary materials rather than the raw materials constitute the circulating constant capital, the fixed capital can never be zero (except in banking, etc.). This is however immaterial so long as the ratio of constant capital to variable capital is the same in both cases, even though in one case there may be more fixed and less circulating constant capital than in the other, or vice versa. The only difference here is the time of reproduction required by one half of the capital and by the total capital. One capitalist must invest a capital of £500 for five years before it is returned to him, the other, for a quarter of a year or a whole year. The ability to dispose of the capital is different. The amount advanced is the same but the time for which it is advanced is different. This difference does not concern us here. When one considers the total capital outlay, surplus-value and profit are the same—£100 in the first year on the £1,000 advanced. In the second year, it is rather the fixed capital that has a higher rate of profit, since the variable capital has remained the same, whereas the value of the fixed capital has declined. The capitalist only advances [£] 400 fixed and [£] 500 variable capital in the second year and receives a profit of [£] 100 as he did before. But 100 on 900 amounts to $11^1/_9$ per cent, while the other capitalist, if he continues to reproduce his capital, advances [£] 1,000 as he did previously and makes a profit of [£]100, that is, 10 per cent.

The position is different, of course, if, along with the fixed capital, the constant capital as a whole increases as compared with the variable, or if altogether more capital must be advanced in order to set the same amount of labour in motion. In the case discussed above, the question is not how often the total capital is returned or how large the advance is, but how often that portion is returned which is sufficient to set the same amount of productive labour in motion as that used in the other instance, in order to renew the process of production. However, if in the case cited above, the fixed capital were [not £500 but £] 1,000 and the circulating capital only [£] 500 [as previously], then matters would be different. This, however, would not be due to the fact that it is fixed capital. For if the circulating part of the constant capital in the second case were to amount to [£]1,000 instead of [£] 500 (because of the dearness of raw materials, for example), then the result would be the same. Because in the first examples [of the two cases] the larger the fixed capital, the greater the relative size of the capital outlay as a whole to the variable capital, these two factors are often confused. Moreover, the whole business of the turnover was in fact originally derived from merchant capital, where it is determined by different laws. In the case of merchant capital, as I have demonstrated,[111] the rate of profit is indeed determined by the average number of turnovers, regardless of the composition of this type of capital which, incidentally, consists mainly of circulating capital. For in the case of merchant capital, profit is determined by the general rate of profit.}

||1119| ⟨The point is this. If the fixed capital equals x, and it turns over only once every 15 years, then $1/_{15}$ of it is turned over in a single year, but likewise only $1/_{15}$ needs to be replaced each year. It would make no difference at all if it were replaced 15 times in a year. Its mass would still be the same as before. The product would only become dearer as a result. But it is more difficult to dispose of it and the risk of depreciation is greater than if the same amount of capital were advanced in the form of circulating capital. But this does not affect the *surplus* [-value] in any way, although it does enter into the capitalists' calculation of the *rate of profit* since this risk is included in the calculation of the depreciation.

As far as the other part of capital is concerned, let us assume that the circulating part of constant capital—raw materials and auxiliary materials—amounts to [£] 25,000 a year and wages to [£] 5,000. If it were returned only once during the year £30,000 would have to be advanced during the whole year, and if the surplus-value were at the rate of 100 per cent it would amount to £5,000, and profit at the end of the year would be 5,000 on 30,000, or $16^2/_3$ per cent.

If, on the other hand, [the capital turns over] five times during the year, then a capital outlay of only [£] 5,000 for constant circulating capital and [£] 1,000 for wages will be sufficient. Profit will be [£] 1,000, and for five-fifths of a year [£] 5,000. But this surplus-value is made on a capital of £6,000, because more than this amount is never advanced. Profit would therefore be 5,000 on 6,000, or $^5/_6$, five times as much [as previously], that is, $83^1/_3$ per cent. (Disregarding fixed capital.) There is thus a very considerable difference in the rate of profit because, in fact, labour worth [£] 5,000 is bought with a capital of [£] 1,000 and raw materials, etc., worth [£] 25,000 with a capital of [£] 5,000. If the amounts of capital were equal in these cases of different rates of turnover, then only [£] 6,000 need have been advanced in the first case, that is only [£] 500 a month, five-sixths of which would have consisted of constant capital and one-sixth of variable capital. This sixth would amount to [£] $83^1/_3$, on which surplus-value at 100 per cent would be £$83^1/_3$, and this would amount in a year to $(83+\frac{1}{3})12=\frac{12}{3}$(or 4)+ 996= [£]1,000. But 1,000 on 6,000=$16^2/_3$ per cent.)

[6. Cherbuliez Eclectically Combines Mutually Exclusive Propositions of Ricardo and Sismondi]

To return to ***Cherbuliez.***
[The following is] *Sismondian*:

"Insofar as the economic progress of society is characterised by an absolute growth of productive capital and by a *change in the proportions* between the different elements of capital, it offers the workers some advantages [....] First, productivity[a] of labour [...], resulting especially from the use of machinery, brings about such a rapid growth of productive capital that despite the change that takes place in the proportion of the *means of subsistence* to the other elements of capital, this element nevertheless increases absolutely, which makes it possible not only to employ the same number of workers as before, but also an additional number, so that for the workers the result of progress [...] *apart from some interruptions* means an increase in productive capital and in the demand for labour. Secondly, the[b] greater productivity of capital tends to diminish the value of the whole mass of products considerably, thus *placing them within reach of the workers*, thereby increasing the range of enjoyments they are able to obtain" (op. cit., p. 65).
On the other hand:

---

[a] The manuscript has "1). the greater productivity".—*Ed.*
[b] The manuscript has "2). the".—*Ed.*

"First, however impermanent, however partial the temporary diminution of the means of subsistence which constitute the price of labour may be, it produces harmful effects nevertheless.... Second, the factors tending to promote the economic advance of society are for the most part accidental, independent of the will of the producing capitalist. The effects of these causes are therefore not permanent..." etc. (p. 66). "Third, it is not so much the *absolute* as the *relative* amount consumed by the worker which makes his lot happy or unhappy. What does it matter to the worker if he is able to obtain a few more products which formerly were inaccessible to him if the *number of products inaccessible to him has grown in even greater proportion, if the distance which separates him from the capitalist* has only increased, if his social position has deteriorated and become more disadvantageous? Apart from the consumption strictly necessary for the maintenance of our strength, the *value of our enjoyments is essentially relative*" (loc. cit., p. 67).

"People frequently forget [...] that the wage-labourer is a thinking man, endowed with the same capacities, impelled by the same motives as the working capitalist" (p. 67).

||1120| "Whatever advantages a rapid growth in social wealth may bring to the wage-workers, *it does not cure the causes of their poverty*.... They continue *to be deprived of all rights to capital and are consequently obliged to sell their labour and to renounce all claims to the products of their labour*" (loc. cit., p. 68). "This is the principal error of the law of appropriation.... *The evil lies in this absolute lack of any bond* between the wage-worker and the capital which is set in motion by his industry" (p. 69).

This last phrase about *"bond"* is written in the typical Sismondian manner and is quite silly to boot.

About the *normal man [who is] equated with capitalist*, etc., see op. cit., pp. 74 to 76.

About the *concentration of capitals* and the elimination of the smaller capitalists (l.c., pp. 85-88).

"If in present circumstances real profit derives from the thrift of the capitalists, it could derive just as well from that of the wage earners" (loc. cit., p. 89).

[On the other hand] *Cherbuliez* shares:

1). [James] Mill's view that all taxes should be imposed only on rent[112] (p. 128), but since it is impossible "to impose a tax which is levied only on rent and affects nothing but rent", since it is difficult to separate profit from rent and impossible when the landowner is himself the cultivator, Cherbuliez proceeds to

2). the real conclusion of the Ricardian theory:

"Why do people not take a step further and *abolish private ownership of land?*" (p. 129) "The landowners are idlers who are maintained at the public expense without any kind of benefit to industry or to the general welfare of society" (p. 129). "What makes land productive is the capital employed in agriculture. The landowner contributes nothing to it. He only exists to pocket rent, which does not constitute a part of the profit on his capital, neither is it the product of labour nor that of the productive power of the soil, but the effect of the price of the agricultural products, which is increased by the competition of the consumers..." etc. (p. 129). "Since the elimination of the private ownership of land would in no way change the causes responsible for rent, rent would continue to exist, but the state would receive it, for all the land would belong to it and it would lease out arable sections of the land to private persons owning sufficient capital to exploit them" (p. 130). Rent would replace all state revenues. "Finally industry, liberated, released from all fetters, would take an unprecedented leap forward..." (p. 130).

But how does this Ricardian conclusion agree with the pious Sismondian wish to place "bonds" on capital and capitalist production? How does it agree with the lamentation:

"Capital will ultimately rule the world if an upheaval does not halt the course which the development of our society is taking under the domination of the law of appropriation" (op. cit., p. 152). "Capital will eliminate the old social distinctions everywhere in order to replace them by this simple classification of men into rich and poor, the rich, who enjoy themselves and rule, and the poor who work and obey" (p. 153). "The general appropriation of *productive wealth and of the products* has always reduced the numerous class of proletarians to a position of subjugation and political impotence, but this appropriation was once combined with a system of restrictive laws which, by *impeding the development of industry and the accumulation of capital* ||1121|, placed limits on the growth of the class of the disinherited, restricted their civil rights within narrow bounds and thus in different ways rendered this class harmless. Today, capital has broken part of these fetters. It is preparing to break all of them" (pp. 155-56).

"The demoralisation of the proletarians is the second result of the distribution of wealth"[113] (p. 156).

[CHAPTER XXIV]

RICHARD JONES

1. Reverend Richard Jones, "An Essay on the Distribution of Wealth, and on the Sources of Taxation," London, 1831, Part I, Rent [Elements of a Historical Interpretation of Rent. Jones's Superiority over Ricardo in Particular Questions of the Theory of Rent and His Mistakes in This Field]

Even this first work on *rent* is distinguished by what has been lacking in all English economists since Sir James Steuart, namely, a sense of the *historical* differences in modes of production. (Such a correct distinction of historical forms generally speaking is not contradicted by the very important archaeological, philological and historical blunders attributed to Jones. See, for example, *The Edinburgh Review*, Vol. LIV, Article IV.[114]

He found that the modern economists after Ricardo define rent as *surplus profit*, a definition which presupposes that the farmer is a capitalist (or a farming capitalist who exploits the land), who expects average profit on the capital which he invests in this particular sphere, and that agriculture itself has been subordinated to the capitalist mode of production. In short, landed property is conceived only in its modern bourgeois form, that is, in the modified form which it has been given by capital, the dominant relation of production in society. Jones by no means shares the illusion that capital has been in existence since the beginning of the world.

His views on the origin of rent in general are summarised in the following passages:

"The power of the earth to yield, even to the rudest labours of mankind, more than is necessary for the subsistence of the cultivator himself, enables him to pay [...] a tribute: hence the origin of rent" ([Richard Jones, *An Essay on the Distribution of Wealth,*] p. 4).

"... rent has usually originated in the *appropriation of the soil*, at a time when the bulk of the people must cultivate it on such terms as they can obtain, or starve; and when their scanty capital of implements, seeds, etc., being utterly insufficient to secure their maintenance in any other occupation than that of agriculture, is chained with themselves to the land by an overpowering necessity" (op. cit., p. 11).

Jones traces rent throughout all its changes, from its crudest form, performance of labour services, to modern farmer's rent. He finds that everywhere a specific form of rent, i.e., of landed property, corresponds to a definite form of labour and of the conditions of labour. Thus, labour rents or serf rents, the change from labour rent to produce rent, metayer rents, ryot[115] rents, etc., are examined in turn, a development the details of which do not concern us here. In all previous forms, it is the landed proprietor, not the capitalist, who directly appropriates the *surplus labour* of other people. *Rent* (as the Physiocrats conceive it by *reminiscence* [of feudal conditions]) appears historically (and still on the largest scale among the Asiatic peoples) as the general form of *surplus labour*, of labour performed without payment in return. The appropriation of this surplus labour is here not mediated by exchange, as is the case in capitalist society, but its basis is the forcible domination of one section of society over the other. (There is, accordingly, direct slavery, serfdom or political dependence.)

Since we are only considering landed property here insofar as an understanding of it contributes to an understanding of capital, we shall leave Jones's analysis and proceed directly to his result—which distinguishes him from, and shows his superiority over, all his predecessors.

But first a few incidental remarks.

In discussing *forced labour* and the forms of serfdom (or slavery) which correspond to it more or less ||1122|, Jones *unconsciously* emphasises the two forms to which all surplus-value (surplus labour) can be reduced. It is characteristic that, in general, real forced labour *displays in the most brutal form, most clearly the essential features of wage-labour.*

Under these conditions ⟨where there is serf labour⟩ *rent* can only be increased either by the more skilful and effective utilisation of the labour of the tenantry ⟨relative surplus labour⟩, this however is hampered by the inability of the proprietors to advance the science of agriculture, *or* by an increase in the *total quantity* of the labour exacted, and in this case, while the lands of the proprietors will be better tilled, those of the serfs, from which labour has been withdrawn, all the worse.[a] (Op. cit., Chapter II.)

What distinguishes this book on *rent* by Jones from his *Syllabus* to be mentioned in *section 2*—is this: in the first work

---

[a] Marx is not quoting here but paraphrasing—mainly in German—a paragraph from p. 61 of Jones's book.—*Ed.*

he proceeds from the various forms of landed property as a given fact; in the second, from the various forms of labour to which they correspond.

Jones also shows how different stages in the development of the productive power of social labour correspond to these different production relations.

Serf-labour (just as slave-labour) has this in common with wage-labour, in respect of rent, that the latter is paid in *labour* not in *products*, still less in *money*.

As far as metayer rent is concerned "... *the advance of stock* by the proprietor, and the *abandonment of the management of cultivation to the actual laborers*, indicate[a] the continued absence of an intermediate class of capitalists..." (op. cit., p. 74).

"Ryot rents are [...] *produce rents paid by a laborer, raising his own wages from the soil, to the sovereign as its proprietor*" (op. cit., Chapter IV, [p. 109]). (In Asia especially) "... Ryot rents [...] are sometimes mixed up with [...] labor rents and metayer rents" (p. 136 et seq.). [Under this system] the sovereign is the chief landlord. "... the prosperity, or rather the *existence, of the towns* of Asia, proceeds from[b] the *local expenditure of the government*" (p. 138).

"Under *cottier rents* we may include all rents *contracted to be paid in money*, by peasant tenants, extracting their own maintenance from the soil" (p. 143). (*Ireland*.) Over the greater part of the globe, no money rents are paid[c] [loc. cit.].

"All the forms"[d] (serf, ryot, metayer, cottier, etc., in short, peasant rents) prevent "the full development of the productive powers of the earth" [p. 157].

"... *the difference which exists in the productiveness of the industry*" [depends] "*first*, on the *quantity* of contrivance used in applying manual labour: *secondly*, to the extent to which the mere *physical exertions* [...] *are assisted by the accumulated results of past labour*: in other words, on the different quantities of skill, knowledge, and capital, brought to the task of production...." [pp. 157-58].

"*Small Numbers of the Non-Agricultural Classes.* It is obvious, that the relative numbers of those persons who can be maintained without agricultural labor, *must be measured wholly by the productive powers of the cultivators*" (Chapter VI [pp. 159-60]).

"In England, the tenants who on the disuse of the labor of the serf tenantry, took charge of the cultivation of the domains of the proprietors, were found on the land; they were *yeomen*" (loc. cit. [p. 166]).

We now come finally to the point which is of decisive interest to us here—*farmers' rents*. It is here that Jones's superiority

---

[a] The manuscript has "shows".—*Ed.*
[b] The manuscript has "proceeds entirely from".—*Ed.*
[c] Marx here paraphrases (in German) the idea developed by Jones on p. 143 of his book.—*Ed.*
[d] The manuscript has "All these forms".—*Ed.*

is most striking, for he shows that what Ricardo and others regard as the eternal form of landed property, is its bourgeois form, which, after all, only develops, firstly, when landed property has ceased to be the dominant relation in production and, consequently, in society; secondly, when agriculture itself is carried on in a capitalist way, which presupposes the development of large-scale industry (at least of manufacture) in the towns. Jones shows that rent in the Ricardian sense only exists in a ||1123| society the basis of which is the capitalist mode of production. As a consequence of the transformation of rent into surplus profit, the *direct* influence of landed property on wages ceases, which, in other words, merely means that the landed proprietor ceases to be the *direct appropriator of surplus labour*, this role being now assumed by the capitalist. The relative size of the rent affects only the division of *surplus-value* between capitalist and proprietor, not the exaction of that surplus labour itself. This conclusion in fact emerges from Jones's analysis, though it is not explicitly stated.

Jones marks a substantial advance on Ricardo, in his historical explanation as well as in the economic details. We shall follow his theory step by step. Blunders, of course, occur.

In the following passages, Jones correctly explains the historical and economic conditions under which rent is equivalent to surplus profit, that is the expression of *modern* landed property.

"Farmers' Rents [...] can only exist when the *most important relations of the different classes of society have ceased to originate in the ownership and occupation of the soil"* (op. cit., p. 185).

The capitalist mode of production begins with manufacture and only later subjugates agriculture.

"... it is the artizans and the handicraftsmen who first range themselves under the *management of capitalists*..." (p. 187).

"One of the immediate consequences of this change[a] is the *power of moving at pleasure* the labor and capital employed in agriculture, to other occupations."

⟨And only with this power can there be any question of equalisation of agricultural and industrial profit.⟩

"While the tenant was himself a laboring peasant, forced, in the absence of other funds for his maintenance, to extract it himself from the soil, he was chained to that soil by necessity; [...] the little stock he might possess, since it was not sufficient to procure him a maintenance unless used for the

---

[a] The manuscript has "system".—*Ed.*

single purposes of cultivation, was virtually chained to the soil with its master." [With the capitalist master] "this dependance on the soil is broken: and unless as much *can be gained by employing the working class on the land, as from their exertions in various other employments*, which in such a state of society abound, the business of cultivation will be abandoned. Rent, in such a case, necessarily consists merely of *surplus profits*..." (loc. cit., p. 188). Rent ceases to have any influence on wages. "When the engagement of the laborer is with a capitalist, this *dependance on the landlord is dissolved*..." (p. 189).

As we shall see later, Jones does not really explain how *surplus profit* arises, or rather, he explains it only in Ricardian fashion, i.e., by the difference in the degrees of natural fertility of different soils.

"When rents *consist of surplus profits*, there are three causes from which the rent of a particular spot of ground may increase:

"First, an increase of the produce from the accumulation of larger quantities of capital in its cultivation;

"Secondly, the more efficient application of capital already employed;

"Thirdly, (the capital and produce remaining the same) the diminution of the share of the producing classes in that produce, and a corresponding increase of the share of the landlord.

"These causes may combine in different proportions..." (p. 189).

We shall see what is involved by these different causes. First of all they all presuppose that rent consists of surplus profit; and then there is not the slightest doubt that the first cause to which Ricardo alludes only once and then only incidentally, is correct. When the capital employed in agriculture increases, the amount of rent increases as well, even though the *price of corn*, etc., does not rise and no other change whatever takes place. It is clear that, in this case, the *price of land rises*, although corn prices do not and no change whatever takes place in them.

Jones declares rent on the *worst soil* to be *monopoly price*. He therefore restricts the real source of rent either to *monopoly price* (in the same way as Buchanan, Sismondi, Hopkins, and others) if it is *absolute rent* (not arising from differences in the fertility of the different kinds of soil) or to *differential rent* (in the Ricardian sense).

⟨As regards *absolute rent*, let us take a *gold mine*. We assume that the capital employed is £100, the average profit £10, rent £10, and that half the capital consists of constant capital (in this case, machinery and auxiliary materials) and half of variable capital. The £50 of constant capital means nothing more than that it contains the same amount of labour-time as ||1124|

is embodied in £50 worth of gold. That part of the product which is worth £50 therefore replaces this constant capital. If the rest of the product is worth £70 and if 50 workers are set to work with the £50 of variable capital (assuming a working-day of 12 hours), then the labour of these 50 workers must be expressed in £70 worth of gold, of which £50 goes to pay wages and £20 represents unpaid labour. The value of the products of all capitals of the same composition will then be 120; the product will then consist of 50c and 70, [the 70] corresponding to 50 working-days, that is, 50v plus 20s. A capital of 100, utilising more constant capital and a smaller number of workers, would produce a product of less value. However, all ordinary industrial capitals, although the value of their products would, in these circumstances, amount to 120, would only sell them at their production price of 110. But in the case of the gold mine, this is impossible quite apart from the ownership of land, because in this case the value is expressed in the product in kind. A rent of £10 would therefore of necessity arise.⟩

"Corn may be selling [...] at a *monopoly price*, that is, at a price which more than pays the *costs and profits of those who grow it under the least favourable circumstances*; or at such a price as will only *repay* their[a] *common profits*." In the first case "abstracting from all difference of fertility in the soils cultivated", (the) "*increased produce obtained by increased capital* (prices remaining the same) may increase the rents, in proportion to the increased capital laid out." "Let[b] 10 per cent be the ordinary rate of profit. If the corn produced [...] by ₤100 sold for ₤115, the rent would be ₤5. If in the progress of improvement the capital employed on the same land were doubled, and the produce doubled, then ₤200 would yield ₤230 and [...] ₤10 would be rent and the rent will be doubled" (op. cit., p. 191).

⟨This applies to absolute rent as well as to differential rent.⟩

"In small communities corn may be constantly at a *monopoly price*.... In larger countries too [...] corn may [...] be at a monopoly price,[c] provided the increase of population keeps steadily ahead of the increase of tillage [....] however [...] monopoly price of corn is [...] unusual in countries of considerable extent and great variety of soil. In such countries, if the produce of the soils in cultivation sells for more than will realise the usual rate of profit on the capital employed, other[d] lands are cultivated; or more capital laid out on the old lands, till the cultivator finds he can barely get the ordinary profit on his outlay. Then [...] tillage will stop, and in such coun-

---

[a] The manuscript has "the".—*Ed.*
[b] The manuscript has "For example".—*Ed.*
[c] The manuscript has "This is possible in larger countries too".—*Ed.*
[d] In the manuscript this part of the sentenc is condensed and reads: "When prices rise steeply more."—*Ed.*

tries [...] corn is usually sold at a price not more than sufficient to replace the capital employed under the least favorable circumstances, and the ordinary rate of profit on it: and the rent paid on the better soils is then measured by the excess of their produce over that of the poorest soil cultivated by similar capitals" (loc. cit., pp. 191-92).

"All [...] that is necessary to effect a rise of rents over the surface of a country possessing soils of unequal goodness, is this: that the better soils should yield to the additional capital employed upon them in the progress of cultivation, something more than the soils confessedly inferior to them; for then while the means can be found of employing fresh capital on any soil between the extremes A and Z, at the ordinary rate of profit, rents will rise on all the soils superior to that particular soil" (p. 195).

"Let A have been [...] cultivated with £100 yielding annually £110, £10 being the ordinary profits [...] and B with £100 yielding £115: and C with £100 yielding £120: and so on to Z [....] the rent of B would be £5, and that of C £10 [....] each of these qualities of soil be cultivated with a capital of £200 [...] A will produce £220, B £230, C £240.... The rent of B, therefore, will have become £10, that of C £20" (p. 193).

"... the *general accumulation* of the capital employed in cultivation, while it augments the produce of all gradations of soil, somewhat in proportion to their original goodness, *must of itself raise rents*; *without reference to any progressive diminution in the return to the labor and capital employed*, and, indeed, *quite independently of any other cause whatever*" (p. 195).

It is one of Jones's merits, that he is the first who clearly brings out the fact that once rent has come into being, its growth will on the whole ⟨provided no revolution in the mode of production takes place⟩ result from the increase of agricultural capital, that is, of capital employed on land. This may be the case not only if prices remain the same but even when they *fall* below their former level.

||1125| In opposition to the view that productivity [in agriculture] gradually diminishes, Jones remarks:

"The average corn produce of England at one time did not exceed 12 bushels per acre; it is now about double" (p. 199).

"... every successive portion of capital and labor concentrated on the land, may be more economically and efficiently applied than the last" (pp. 199-200).

Rent will double, triple and quadruple, and so on, if the capital invested in the old land is doubled, tripled, quadrupled,[a] "without a diminished return, and without altering the relative fertility of the soils cultivated" p. 204).

This is therefore the first point on which Jones is in advance of Ricardo. Once rent exists, it may increase as a result of the mere increase in the amount of capital employed on the land,

---

[a] The first part of the sentence up to "quadrupled" is not a quotation but Marx's paraphrase of the passage.—*Ed.*

irrespective of any change either in the relative fertility of the soils, or in the returns yielded by the successive doses of capital employed, or any alteration whatever in the *price* of agricultural produce.

Jones's next point is this:

"... it is not essential to the rise that the *proportion between the fertility of the soils* should be exactly *stationary*" (p. 205).

⟨Here Jones overlooks the fact that conversely, an *increasing disparity*, even when the whole agricultural capital is more productively employed, must and will increase the amount of the differential rent. On the other hand, a *diminution* in the differences of the fertility of the various soils must diminish differential rent, i.e., rent arising from *those differences*. By taking away the cause you take away the effect. Nevertheless, rent (apart from absolute rent) may increase, but in that case only in consequence of an increase of the agricultural capital employed.⟩

"... Mr. Ricardo [...] had [...] overlooked the necessarily *unequal effects of additional capital on soils of unequal fertility*" (l. c., [p. 205]).

(This means nothing more than that the employment of additional capital adds to the differences of relative fertility, and, in that way, to differential rent.)

"If [...] numbers, bearing a certain proportion to each other, are multiplied by the same number [...] the proportion [...] will be the same as those of the original numbers; yet the *difference between*[a] *the amounts* of the several products, will increase at each step of the process. If 10, 15, 20, be multiplied by 2 or 4, and become 20, 30, 40, or 40, 60, 80, their relative proportions will not be disturbed: 80 and 60 bear the same proportion to 40, as 20 and 15 to 10: but the *differences between the amounts of their products* will have increased at each operation, and from being 5 and 10, become 10 and 20, and then 20 and 40" (pp. 206-07).

This law works out simply as follows:

1. $10,^5$ $15,^{10}$ 20. The difference 5 [and 10]. Sum of the differences 15.
2. $20,^{10}$ $30,^{20}$ 40.   "   "   10 [and 20].   "   "   30.
3. $40,^{20}$ $60,^{40}$ 80.   "   "   20 [and 40].   "   "   60.
4. $80,^{[40]}$ $120,^{[80]}$ 160. ["   "   40 and 80.   "   "   120.]

The difference between the terms is doubled in 2 and quadrupled in 3. The sum of the differences is likewise doubled in 2 and quadrupled in 3.

---

[a] In the manuscript, "of".—*Ed.*

This therefore is the second law.

The *first law* (applied by Jones only to differential rent) is that the amount of rent increases with the increase of the amount of capital employed. If rent is 5 for 100, then it is 10 for 200.
||1126| The *second law*. All other circumstances remaining the same, and the proportional difference between the capitals employed on different soils remaining the same, the *amount of that difference*, and hence the amount of the aggregate rent or the sum of those differences increases, as the absolute quantity of that difference—resulting from the increase of the capitals employed—increases. Hence the *second law* is: the amount of differential rent increases in proportion as the differences of the products increase when the relative fertility remains the same, but capital employed on the different soils is increased uniformly.

Further: "If £100 be employed on classes A, B and C, with a produce of £110, £115, £120, and subsequently £200, with returns of £220, £228 and £235, the relative differences of the products will have diminished, and the soils will have *approximated in fertility*; still the *difference of the amounts of their products* will be increased from £5 and £10 to £8 and £15, and rents will have risen accordingly. Improvements, therefore, which tend to approximate the degrees of fertility of the cultivated soils, may very well raise rents, and that without the co-operation of any other cause" (loc. cit., p. 208).

"The turnip and sheep husbandry, and the fresh capital employed to carry it on, produced a greater alteration in the fertility of the poor soils than in that of the better; still it increased the *absolute produce of each*, and, therefore, it raised rents, while it diminished the differences in the fertility of the soils cultivated" (loc. cit.).

With regard to Ricardo's view that improvements may cause rents to fall, "it is only necessary to remember the slowly progressive manner in which agricultural improvements are practically discovered, completed, and spread..." (p. 211).

(This last passage is only of practical interest and does not affect the problem as such, but refers only to the fact that improvements do not proceed so rapidly as to considerably augment supply in regard to demand and thus to reduce market prices.)

Originally we have:

	a	b	c
1.	10	15	20

The capital employed in each class amounts to 100; the product to 110, 115, 120. The *difference* amounts to $5+10=15$.

As a result of improvements made, twice as much capital is

employed, that is, [£]200 instead of [£]100 in each of the classes a, b and c. But the capital has a different effect in the different classes and the products yielded are 220 (that is, double that of a), 228 and 235. Thus:

	a	b	c
2.	20	28	35

£200 capital is employed in each class. The products amount to [£]220, [£] 228 and [£]235. The *difference* amounts to [£] 8+ [£]15=[£]23. But the rate of difference has been reduced. 5:10 (i.e., [the ratio of the differences] b—a [to a] in the first case)=$^1/_2$ and 10:10=1, whereas 8:20 is only $^8/_{20}$ or $^2/_5$ and 15:20= $^{15}/_{20}$ or $^3/_4$. The rate of difference has declined but its amount has increased. This does not, however, constitute a new law, but only shows that the increase of capital employed leads to an increase in rent as in the first law, although the increase in a, b and c is not proportional to their original differences of fertility. If prices were to fall as a consequence of this increased fertility (which is however [relatively] diminished fertility for b and c, for otherwise their product would have to be 230 and 240 respectively), it would by no means be necessary for the rent to rise or even to remain stationary.

||1127| As a consequence, a sequel, of the second law, a further application of it can be considered:

The *third law*—if "improvements in the efficiency of the capital employed in cultivation" increase the *surplus profits* realised on particular spots of land, they increase rent.

The following passages (together with the earlier ones) refer to this.

"... the[a] first source [...] of a rise of farmers' rents, namely,[b] the *progressive accumulation* and *unequal effects of capital on all gradations of soils*" (p. 234).

⟨This, however, can only refer to improvements which relate directly to the fertility of the soil as, for instance, manures, rotation of crops, etc.⟩

"Improvements [...] in the efficiency of the capital employed in cultivation, raise rents by increasing the *surplus profits realised on particular spots of land*. They invariably produce this increase of surplus profits, *unless they augment the mass of raw produce so rapidly as to outstrip the progress of demand* [....] Such improvements in the efficiency of the capital

---

[a] The manuscript has "Thus the".—*Ed.*
[b] The manuscript has "are".—*Ed.*

employed, do usually occur in the progress of agricultural skill, and of the accumulation of *greater masses of auxiliary capital*" (constant capital). "A rise of rents from this cause, is generally followed *by the spread of tillage to inferior soils*, without any diminution[a] in the returns to agricultural capital on the worst spots reclaimed" (p. 244).

⟨Jones very correctly declares that a fall in profits *does not prove* decreasing efficiency of agricultural industry. But he himself explains most inadequately how such a fall can come about. [According to him] either the amount produced or its division between labourers and capitalists may change. Jones has as yet not the faintest notion of the real law of declining rate of profit.

"A fall of Profits is no Proof of the decreasing Efficiency of agricultural Industry" (p. 257).

"... profits depend partly on the *amount* of the produce of labor, partly on the *division* of that produce between the laborers and capitalists; and [...] their amount, therefore, might vary from a change in either of these particulars" (p. 260).

This is the reason for the incorrect law which he elaborates:

"When, abstracting from the effects of taxation, an apparent diminution takes place in the revenues of the producing classes considered jointly" (what revenue means is not explained here, [whether] value in use or value in exchange, amount of profit or rate [of profit]), "when there is a *fall in the rate of profits, not compensated by a rise of wages*, or a fall of wages not compensated by a rise in the rate of profits",[b] (that is precisely what Ricardo's law says, and it is wrong) "there has been, it may be argued, some decrease in the productive power of labor and capital" ... (p. 273).⟩

Jones correctly grasps that a *relative increase* [in the value] of agricultural produce as compared to [that of] industrial produce may take place in the progress of society although in point of fact, agriculture is progressing absolutely.

"In the progress of nations, an increase of manufacturing power and skill usually occurs, *greater* than that which can be expected in the agriculture of an increasing people. This is an unquestionable [...] truth. *A rise in the relative value of raw produce* may, therefore, be expected in the advance of nations, and this from a cause quite distinct from[c] *any positive decrease* in the efficiency of agriculture" (p. 265).

But this does not explain the *positive* rise in the *money prices*

---

[a] The manuscript has "decrease".—*Ed.*
[b] The manuscript has "and vice versa" instead of "or a fall of wages not compensated by a rise in the rate of profits".—*Ed.*
[c] The manuscript has "*without*" instead of "and this from a cause quite distinct from".—*Ed.*

of raw produce, unless a fall in the value of gold takes place which in manufacture is balanced and more than balanced by a still greater fall in the [value of] commodities produced, while in agriculture it is not balanced in this way. This may happen, even ||1128| if no general fall in the value of gold (money) takes place, but when a particular nation, for instance, buys more money with a day's work than the competing nations do.

Jones explains his reasons for *not* believing that in England the Ricardian law operates, the abstract possibility of which he does admit however.

"If rents [...] should ever rise from that cause alone, which has been so confidently stated by Mr. Ricardo [...] 'the employment of an additional quantity of labor with a proportionally less return', and a consequent transfer to the landlords of a part of the produce [...] obtained on the better soils; then the *average proportion of the gross produce* taken by the landlords as rent, will necessarily increase." Secondly, "the industry of a larger proportion of the population must be devoted to agriculture" (pp. 280 and 281).

(This last statement is not quite correct. It is possible that a greater portion of indirect labour is employed—i.e., more commodities provided by industry and commerce enter the agricultural process, without increasing the gross product proportionally, and without the employment of more immediate labour. There may be even less employed.)

"The statistical history of England presents to us [...] three facts [...] a spread of tillage accompanied by a rise in the general rental of the country [...] a diminution of the proportion of people employed in agriculture [...] a decrease in the landlord's proportion of the produce" (p. 282).

(This last development, just as the decline in the rate of profit, is due to the increase in that part of the product which replaces constant capital. At the same time, rent can increase in both amount and value.)

"Adam Smith [...] goes on to say [...] 'In the progress of improvement, rent, though it increases in proportion to the extent, diminishes in proportion to the produce of the land'"[116] (p. 284).

Jones calls constant capital "auxiliary capital".

"It appears from various returns made at different times to the Board of Agriculture, that the whole capital agriculturally employed in England, is to that applied to the support of labourers, as 5 to 1; that is, there are four times as much auxiliary capital used, as there is of capital applied to the maintenance of the labor used directly in tillage. In France, [...] more than twice" (p. 223).

"... when a given quantity of additional capital is applied *in the shape of the results of past labor*, to assist the laborers actually employed, *a less annual return* will suffice to make the employment of such capital profitable, and, therefore, permanently practicable, than if the same quantity of fresh capital were expended in the support of additional laborers..." (p. 224).

"Let us suppose £100 employed upon the soil[a] in the maintenance of three men, producing their own wages, and 10 per cent profit on them, or £110. Let the capital employed [...] be doubled. And first let the fresh capital support three additional laborers. In that case, the increased produce must consist of the full amount of their wages, and the ordinary rate of profit on them. It must consist, therefore, of the whole £100, and the profit on it; or of £110. Next let the same additional capital of £100 be applied in the shape of implements, manures, or any results of past labor, while the number of actual laborers remains the same [...] this auxiliary capital to last on the average for five years: the annual return to repay the capitalist must now consist of £10 his profit, and of £20 the annual wear and tear of his capital: or £30 will be the annual return, necessary to make the continuous employment of the second £100 profitable, instead of £110, the amount necessary when direct labor was employed by it. It will be obvious, therefore, that the accumulation of auxiliary capital in cultivation, will be practicable when the employment of the same amount of capital in the support of additional labor has ceased to be so: and that the accumulation of such capital [...] may go on for an indefinite period..." (pp. 224-25).

"... the progress[b] of auxiliary capital both increases the command of man over the powers of the soil, relatively to the ||1129| amount of labor directly or indirectly employed upon it; and *diminishes the annual return* necessary to make the progressive employment of given quantities of fresh capital profitable..." (p. 227).

"If we suppose any capital (£100 for instance) employed upon the soil, wholly in paying the wages of labor, and yielding 10 per cent profit, the revenue of the farmer will [...] be one-tenth that of the laborers. If the capital be doubled[c] [...] then the revenue of the farmers will continue to bear the same proportion to that of the laborers. But if the number of laborers remaining the same, the amount of capital is doubled, profits [...] become £20, or one-fifth of the revenue [....] If the capital be quadrupled, profits become £40, or two-fifths of the revenue of the laborers: if the capital be increased to £500, profits would become £50, or half the revenue of the laborers. And the wealth, the influence, and probably to some extent, the numbers of the capitalists in the community, would be *proportionably* increased.... A *great increase* of capital [...] usually makes the *employment of some additional direct labor* necessary. This circumstance, however, will not prevent the *steady progress of the relative increase of the auxiliary capital*" (pp. 231-32).

The first important point in this passage is that, with the increase in capital, the auxiliary capital increases in comparison to the variable capital, in other words, that the latter declines *relatively* in comparison with the constant capital.

---

[a] In the manuscript, "land".—*Ed.*
[b] In the manuscript, "thus the increase".—*Ed.*
[c] In the manuscript, "trebled and so on."—*Ed.*

The fact that the *annual returns* decline in proportion to the capital advanced if there is an increase in that part of the auxiliary capital which consists of fixed capital, that is, if its turnover period extends over several years—its value only entering into the product annually in the form of depreciation—is not a phenomenon peculiar to agriculture, but a general one. Although, in industry, the raw material worked up during the year increases even more rapidly than the size of the fixed capital. Compare, for example, the amount of raw cotton which a spinning-jenny consumes weekly or annually with that used up by a spinning-wheel. But suppose, for example, that in (large-scale) tailoring the same amount of raw material in terms of *value* is worked up (although not the same physical amount, the raw material being dearer than that used in spinning), then the annual return in tailoring will be considerably larger than in spinning, because a greater part of the (fixed) capital laid out in the latter only enters into the product as annual depreciation.

The *value* of the annual return in agriculture (where what one can regard as the raw material, the seed, does not increase in the same proportion as the other elements of constant capital, especially fixed capital) is naturally smaller if the capital increases as a result of an increase in the constant capital only and not in the variable. For the variable capital must be entirely replaced in the product, the other [constant capital] only insofar as it is consumed annually. If it is assumed that the *price of grain* is given, when a quarter is equal to 10s., 220 quarters are required to replace a capital of £100 at a profit of 10 per cent, whereas only 60 quarters (£30) are required to replace a wear and tear amounting to £20 and a profit of £10. A smaller absolute return yields the same profit (as is the case in industry in similar circumstances). Jones's reasoning, however, contains several fallacies.

First of all, it cannot be asserted (on the assumptions *made*) that the productive powers of the soil have increased. They have increased in comparison with the labour employed directly, but not compared with the total capital employed. All that can be said is that less *gross produce* is necessary in order to yield the same *net produce*, i.e., the same profit as before.

||1130| Further, the increase in the farmer's revenue in comparison to *that of the labourers*, is important in this *special* sphere insofar as here the part of the total product which consti-

tutes profit increases, and goes on increasing, relatively to that part which goes to the labourers. As a result, the wealth and influence of the farming capitalist as compared to his labourers undoubtedly grow and expand. But Jones seems to make the following calculation: [£]10 on [£]100 is $1/_{10}$. £20 on £120 (i.e., £100 expended in labour and £20 depreciation) is $1/_6$ and the £20 is $1/_5$ of the sum paid out to the workers, etc. But nothing is more fallacious than that, generally speaking, the rate of profit can increase while the amount of capital laid out on labour declines. Exactly the opposite takes place. Proportionally less surplus-value is produced, and the rate of profit therefore falls. As regards the farmer specifically (and also each particular enterprise taken in isolation) the rate of profit may remain the same whether he employs three workers or six workers with a capital of £200.

The fact that rent is equal to surplus profit, i.e., to the excess over and above the average profit, presupposes not only that agriculture is *formally* subordinated to capitalist production, but also that equalisation of rates of profit takes place in the various spheres of production, specifically also between agriculture and industry. If this is not the case rent (like profit) may be equal to the *surplus over wages*. It may even represent a part of profit or be a deduction from wages.

2. Richard Jones, "An Introductory Lecture on Political Economy etc." [The Concept of the "Economical Structure of Nations". Jones's Confusion with regard to the "Labor Fund"]

Richard Jones, *An Introductory Lecture on Political Economy, delivered at King's College, London, 27th February, 1833*. To which is added a Syllabus of a Course of Lectures on the Wages of Labor, London, 1833.

[In the *Introductory Lecture*, Jones says:]

"... property in the soil almost universally rests, at one time of a people's career, either in the general government, or in persons deriving their interest from it" (p. 14).

"... by economical structure of nations, I mean those relations between the different classes which are established in the first instance by the institution of property in the soil, and by the distribution of its surplus produce; afterwards modified and changed (to a greater or less extent) by the *introduction of capitalists* as agents in producing and exchanging wealth, and in feeding and employing the labouring population" (pp. 21-22)[117]. ||1130||

||1130| By "labour fund" Jones understands:

"... the aggregate amount of the revenues consumed by the laborers, whatever be the source of those revenues" ([*Syllabus,*] p. 44).

The main point (the term "labor fund" probably comes from Malthus?)[118] in Jones's work is that the whole economic structure of society revolves around the *form of labour,* in other words, the form in which the worker appropriates his means of subsistence, or that part of his product upon which he lives. This labour fund has various forms and *capital* is merely one of them, it is a form which arises rather late in the historical development. It is only in Richard Jones's work that the important differentiation—between labour that is paid out of capital and labour paid directly out of revenue—made by Adam Smith receives the full elaboration of which it is capable and becomes a major key for understanding the various economic formations of society. And with it disappears the absurd notion that, because in capital the worker's revenue first takes the form of something appropriated, alias *saved,* by the capitalist, this signifies more than a formal difference.

"Even when we travel westward and observe the more advanced European nations [...] we can [...] trace[a] the effects of [...] the social conformation which results from the peculiar mode of distributing the produce of their land and labor, established in the early period ||1131| of the existence of agricultural nations" (p. 16) (namely a class of agricultural labourers, secondly landlords, thirdly menials, retainers and artisans who participate in the consumption of the revenue of the landlords either directly or indirectly).

Capital, that is, *accumulated wealth employed for the purpose of obtaining profit* is the great agent, the motive power which causes the *changes* that take place in this economic conformation.[b]

"Let me assure you [...] that ... in analysing the respective productive powers of different nations,[c] you will find the distinct division of wealth here pointed out, acting a most important part in modifying the ties which connect the different classes of the community, and in determining their productive power" [p. 17].

"In Asia, and in part of Europe, (it was formerly the case throughout Europe,) the *non-agricultural* classes are almost wholly maintained from the incomes of the other classes; principally from the incomes of the landholders. If you want the labour of an artisan, you provide him with materials; he comes to your house, you feed and pay him his wages. After a time, the

---

[a] In the manuscript, "Even among the Western European nations we still find."—*Ed.*

[b] This is a summary by Marx, in his own words (mostly in English), of a much longer passage on pages 16-17 of Jones's book.—*Ed.*

[c] Instead of the first part of the sentence, in the manuscript "Among all nations".—*Ed.*

capitalist steps in, *he provides the materials, he advances the wages of the workman, he becomes his employer,* and he is *the owner of the article produced,* which he exchanges for your money.... An intermediate class appears between the landowners and a portion of the *non-agriculturists,* upon which intermediate class, those non-agriculturists are dependent for employment and subsistence. The ties which formerly bound the community together are worn out and fall to pieces; other bonds, other principles of cohesion, connect its different classes: *new economical relations* spring into being.... Not only is the[a] great body of non-agriculturists almost wholly in[b] the pay of capitalists, but even the labouring cultivators of the soil [...] are their servants too" (loc. cit., pp. 18-19).

The *Syllabus of a Course of Lectures on the Wages of Labor* differs from the book on rent in this: the book examines the different forms of landed property to which different social forms of labour correspond. In the *Syllabus,* these different forms of labour are the point of departure and both the different forms of landed property and capital are regarded as their offspring. The determinate social form of the worker's labour corresponds to the form which the conditions of labour—that is, in particular, the land, nature, since this relationship embraces all others —assume in respect of the worker. But the former is in fact merely the objective expression of the latter.

We shall see, therefore, that the different forms of the labour fund correspond to the different ways in which the worker confronts his own conditions of production. The manner in which he appropriates his product (or part of it) depends on his relations to his conditions of production.

The "Labor Fund," says Jones, "may be divided [...] into three [...] classes.

"1st.—Revenues which are produced by the laborers who consume them, and never belong to any other persons." ⟨In this case, quite irrespective of the *particular* form, the worker must in fact be the owner of his instruments of production.⟩

"2nd.—Revenues belonging to classes distinct from the laborers, and expended by those classes in the direct maintenance of labor.

"3rd.—*Capital* in its [...] proper sense [....]

"These distinct branches of the Labor Fund may all be observed in our own country; but when we look abroad, we see those parts of that Fund, which are the most limited here, constituting elsewhere the main sources of subsistence to the population [...] and determining the character and position of the majority of the people..." (pp. 45-46).

To point 1. "... the wages of *laboring cultivators, or occupying peasants....*

[a] In the manuscript, "Here in England not only the".—*Ed.*
[b] In the manuscript, "depend on".—*Ed.*

[CHAPTER XXIV]

Laboring[a] cultivators, or peasants, may be divided into three groups[b]—*hereditary occupiers, proprietors, tenants*. The [...] tenants may be subdivided into[c] *serfs, metayers, cottiers*; the last [...] peculiar to Ireland. Something which may be called rent, or something which may be called profit, is often[d] mixed up with the revenues of peasant cultivators of all classes; but *when 'their subsistence is essentially dependent on the reward of their manual labor',* they come within the limits of our present inquiry"[e] (p. 46).

"Thus, among the labouring peasants there are:

α) *"Hereditary occupiers, who are laboring cultivators*; ||1132| [...] ancient Greece, modern Asia, more especially India" (p. 46).

β) [peasant] *"... proprietors* [...] France, Germany, America, Australia [...] state of Ancient Palestine".

γ) "cottiers" (pp. 46-48).

The characteristic feature of these groups is that the worker reproduces the labour fund for himself. It *is not transformed into capital*. Just as the worker directly produces the labour fund, so he appropriates it directly, although his surplus labour may be appropriated either wholly or in part by him himself or may be appropriated entirely by other classes, depending on the particular form which his relation to his conditions of production assumes. It is entirely due to economic prejudice that Jones describes this category as wage-labourers. Nothing which characterises wage-labourers exists amongst them. It is a pretty bourgeois economic fancy that, because that part of the product which the worker appropriates to himself under capitalism appears as *wages*, the part of his product which the worker himself consumes must be *wages*.

With regard to point 2. "The laborers so maintained are now limited in England to[f] menial servants, soldiers [...] sailors, and a *few artizans working on their own account*, and paid *out of the incomes of their employers*. Over a considerable portion of the earth this branch of the General Labor Fund maintains nearly the whole of the *non-agricultural laborers* [....] Former prevalence of this Fund in England. Warwick the king-maker[119]. The English gentry. Present prevalence in the East. Mechanics, menials. Large bodies of troops so maintained. Consequences of the concentration of this Fund throughout Asia in the hands of the sovereign. Sudden rise of cities; sudden desertion. Samarcand; Candahar, and others" (pp. 48-49).

---

[a] In the manuscript, "these laboring".—*Ed.*
[b] Instead of "may be divided into three groups", in the manuscript "are".—*Ed.*
[c] Instead of "may be subdivided into", in the manuscript "are".—*Ed.*
[d] The first part of this sentence is shortened by Marx and reads in the manuscript "Something resembling rent or profit is often."—*Ed.*
[e] In the manuscript, "they may be regarded as wage-labourers".—*Ed.*
[f] In the manuscript the first part of the sentence reads "In England limited to".—*Ed.*

Jones overlooks two main forms: the Asiatic communal system with its unity of agriculture and industry. And secondly, the urban craft guild system of the Middle Ages, [which] also [existed] partially in the Ancient World.

With regard to point 3. *Capital* "should never be confounded with the *General Labor Fund* of the world—of which a large proportion consists of [...] revenues [....] All branches of a nation's revenues ... contribute to the accumulations by which capital is formed. They contribute in different proportions in different countries and different stages of society. When wages and rents contribute the most" (p. 50).

Because surplus labour is converted into capital (instead of being exchanged directly as revenue for labour), capital seems to appear as something *saved* out of revenue. Jones considers it mainly from this point of view. And in the progress of society the great mass of capital does, in fact, consist of revenue reconverted in this way. But in the capitalist mode of production the original labour fund itself likewise appears as something *saved* by the capitalist. The reproduced labour fund does not remain in the possession of the worker as in case 1), but appears as the property of the capitalist and confronts the worker as the property of *someone else*. And this point is not elaborated by Jones.

What Jones has to say about the rate of profits and its influence on accumulation in the *Course [of Lectures]* is rather inadequate:

"*All other things being equal*, the power of a nation to save from its profits varies with the *rate of profits*: is great when they are high, less when low; but as the rate of profits decline, *all other things do not remain equal*. The *quantities of capital employed relatively to the numbers of the population may increase*" [p. 50].

⟨What Jones does not understand is how, as a result of the "*may*" increase, the rate of profits *s i n k s* because "the *quantities of capital* employed *relatively to the numbers of the population have increased*". But he approaches close to the correct view.⟩

"Inducements and facilities to accumulate may increase.... a *low rate of profits* is ordinarily accompanied by a *rapid rate of accumulation*, relatively to the numbers of the people, as in England, and a *high rate of profit* by a slower rate of accumulation, relatively to the numbers of [...] people, ||1133| as in Poland, Russia, India, etc. ..." (pp. 50-51).

Where the rate of profit is high (apart from cases where, as in North America, there is capitalist production on the one hand and, on the other hand, the value of all agricultural produce is low) it is *generally* due to the fact that capital consists mainly of variable capital, that is, direct labour predominates Assume a capital of 100, of which $^1/_5$ is variable capital. And assume further that the surplus labour amounts to a third of a working-day. In this case, profit would amount to 10 per cent. Assume [on the other hand] that $^4/_5$ of the capital consists of variable capital and that surplus labour amounts to $^1/_6$ of the working-day. In this case, profit would amount to 16 per cent.

"Error of the doctrine, that whenever, in the progress of nations, the *rate of profit* declines, the means of providing subsistence for an increasing population must be becoming less. Foundations of this error: 1st. A mistaken notion, that accumulation from profits must be slow where the rate of profits is low, and rapid where it is high. 2d. A mistaken belief that profits are the only source of accumulation. 3d. A mistaken belief that all the laborers of the earth subsist on accumulations and *savings from revenue*, and never *on revenue itself"* (p. 51).

[Jones speaks of]

"Alterations which take place in the economical structure of nations when *capital assumes the task of advancing the wages of labour".* |1133||

||1157| Richard Jones sums up correctly in the following passage: |1157||

||1133| *"The amount of capital devoted to the maintenance of labour may vary, independently of any changes in the whole amount of capital."* (This proposition is important.) "Great fluctuations in the amount of employment and great suffering [...] may sometimes be observed to become more frequent *as capital itself becomes more plentiful"* (p. 52).[120] |1133||

||1157| The total amount of capital may remain *the same* and a *change* (decline especially) may take place in the variable capital. A change in the proportion between the two constituent parts of capital does not necessarily involve a change in the size of the total [capital].

An increase in the total capital, on the other hand, may be accompanied not only by a relative, but by an absolute diminution of variable capital and is always connected with violent fluctuations in the variable capital and consequently with "fluctuations in the amount of employment". |1157||

[Later on in the *Syllabus,* Jones writes:]

||1133| *"Periods of gradual transition of the laborers from dependence on one fund to dependence on another.... Transfer of the laboring cultivators to the pay of capitalists.... Transfer of non-agricultural classes to the employ of capitalists"...* (pp. 52-53).

What Jones calls "transfer" here, is what I call "primitive accumulation". This is merely a formal difference. It is also in contradiction to the absurd notion of "savings".

* * *

Slavery: "Slaves may be divided into pastoral—predial—domestic—slaves of a mixed character, between predial and domestic.... We find them[a] as cultivating peasants;—as menials or artisans, maintained from the incomes of the rich;—*as laborers maintained from capital*" (p. 59).

But so long as slavery is predominant, the capital relationship can only be sporadic and subordinate, never dominant.

3. Richard Jones, "Text-book of Lectures on the Political Economy of Nations", Hertford, 1852

[a) Jones's Views on Capital and the Problem of Productive and Unproductive Labour]

[Jones writes in the *Text-book of Lectures on the Political Economy of Nations*:]

"The productiveness of the industry of nations really depends [...] on two circumstances. First, on the *fertility or barrenness of the original sources*" (land and water) "of the wealth they produce. Secondly, on the *efficiency of the labour* they apply in dealing with those sources, or fashioning the commodities they obtained from them" (p. 4).

"... the *efficiency of human labor* will depend—
"1st.—*On the continuity* with which it is exerted.
"2ndly.—*On the knowledge* and *skill* with which it is applied, to effect the purpose of the producer.
"3rdly.—On the *mechanical power* by which it is aided..." (p. 6).

"The *power* exerted by human labourers in producing wealth ... may be increased [....]
"1st.—By enlisting in their service, *motive forces* greater than their own....
"2ndly.—By employing any amount or kind of motive ||1134| forces at their command, *with increased mechanical advantage* [....] Let a steam-engine with a motive force of 40 horses be attached to a loaded train on a common turnpike road [and it will make but little way: level the road perfectly... and it will move at a rapid pace[b]]" (p. 8.)

"The best form of a plough [...] will do as much work, and as well, with two horses, as the worst with four" (p. 9).

"The steam-engine is not a mere *tool*, it gives *additional motive force*, not merely the *means of using forces* the labourer already possesses, *with a greater mechanical advantage*" (p. 10, note).

This is, therefore, according to Jones, the difference between a tool and machinery. The former provides the worker with means for employing the power he possesses to a greater mechanical advantage, the latter provides an increase of motive force. (?)

---

[a] In the manuscript, "slaves".—*Ed.*
[b] This part of the sentence is summarised by Marx.—*Ed.*

"*Capital* ... consists of wealth *saved from revenue*, and used *with a view to profit*" (p. 16). "The possible sources of capital [...] are obviously, all the revenues of all the individuals composing a community, from which revenues it is possible that any saving can be made. The particular classes of income which yield the most abundantly to the progress of national capital, *change at different stages of their progress*, and are therefore found *entirely different* in nations occupying different positions in that progress" (p. 16).

Profit is therefore by no means the only source from which capital is formed or augmented: it is even an unimportant source of accumulation, compared with wages and rents, in the earlier stages of society[a] (p. 20).

"... when a considerable advance in the powers of national industry has actually taken place, profits rise into comparative importance as a source of accumulation" (p. 21).

According to this, capital is a part of the wealth which constitutes revenue, the part which is expended not as revenue but for the purpose of producing profit. Profit is already a form of surplus-value which specifically presupposes capital. If the capitalist mode of production, i.e., capital, is postulated, then the explanation is correct; in other words, if one postulates what has to be explained. But here Jones means all revenue spent, not as revenue, but with the aim of enrichment, that is, productively.

Two aspects are, however, important in this context.

First: To a certain extent accumulation of wealth takes place in all stages of economic development, that is, partly an expansion of the scale of production and partly, the accumulation of treasure, etc. As long as wages and rents predominate—that is, according to what was said earlier, as long as the greater part of the surplus labour and surplus product which does not accrue to the worker himself, goes to the landowner (the State in Asia) and, on the other hand, the worker reproduces his labour fund himself, i.e., he not only produces his own wages himself, but pays them to himself, usually, moreover, (almost always in that state of society) he is also able to appropriate at least a part of his surplus labour and his surplus product—in this state of society, wages and rent are the main sources of accumulation as well. (In these circumstances profit is restricted to merchants, etc.) Only when the capitalist mode of production has become predominant, when it does not merely exist sporadically, but has subordinated to itself the mode of production of society; when in fact the capitalist directly appropriates the whole surplus labour and surplus product in the first instance,

---

[a] This paragraph represents a summary by Marx of the ideas outlined by Jones on p. 20 of his book. It is written almost entirely in English.—*Ed.*

although he has to hand over portions of it to the landowner, etc.—only then does profit become the principal source of capital, of accumulation, of wealth saved from revenue and used with a view to profit. This at the same time presupposes (as is implicit in the domination of the capitalist mode of production) that "a considerable advance in the power of national industry has actually taken place".

Jones thus answers those asses who imagine that no accumulation can take place without the profit yielded by capital or who justify profit by saying that the capitalist makes a sacrifice in order to *save* from his revenue for productive purposes, by pointing out that in this particular (capitalist) mode of production the function "of accumulating" devolves principally on the capitalist whereas, in previous modes of production, it was the labourer himself and, in part, the landlord who played the chief roles in this process and profit played hardly any part in it.

Naturally the function [of accumulating] always devolves on those, 1) who pocket the surplus-value and, 2) among those who pocket the surplus-value in particular on the person who also acts as agent in the production process itself. By saying, therefore, ||1135| that profit is justified *by the fact* that the capitalist "saves" his capital out of profit and that he fulfils the function of accumulating, one merely says that the capitalist mode of production is justified because it exists—this, however, applies equally to the modes of production which preceded it and those which will succeed it. If one says that otherwise accumulation would be impossible, then one forgets that this particular method of accumulation through the agency of the capitalist has come into existence at a certain historical stage and is moving towards the historical date when it will cease to exist.

Secondly, once so much accumulated wealth has been concentrated in the hands of capitalists *per fas.et nefas*[a] that they can dominate production, then the greater part of existing capital—after a certain lapse of time—can be considered as having been derived only from profit (revenue), that is, from capitalised surplus-value.

A point which Jones does not sufficiently emphasise, and which he really only implies tacitly, is this: If the labouring producer pays himself his own wages and if his product does not at first assume the "shape" of other people's revenue from

---

[a] By fair means or foul.—*Ed.*

which savings are made and then paid back by these people to the labourer, it is necessary that the labourer be in possession of his conditions of production (as property owner, or tenant, or hereditary occupier, etc.). In order that his wages and consequently the labour fund can confront him as alien capital, these conditions of production must have been lost to him and have assumed the shape of alien property. Only after his conditions of production together with his labour fund have been wrested from him and when, as *capital*, they are rendered independent in relation to him, does the further process begin, which is not concerned with the mere reproduction of these original conditions of production, but with their further development so that both the conditions of production and the labour fund confront the labourer as something "saved" from other people's revenue in order to be converted into capital. By losing possession of his conditions of production, and hence, of his labour fund, the labourer also loses the function of accumulating, and every addition he makes to wealth appears in the shape of other people's revenue which must first be "saved" by these people, that is to say, it must not be spent as revenue, if it is to perform the functions of capital and labour fund for the labourer.

Since Jones himself describes a state of affairs in which things have not yet reached this stage and where unity prevails, he certainly should have described this *"separation"* as the real generation process of capital. Once this separation exists, this process does indeed take place and it continues and extends, since the surplus labour of the worker always confronts him as the revenue of others, through the saving of which alone wealth can be accumulated and the scale of production extended.

The reconversion of revenue into capital. If *capital* ⟨i.e., the separation of the conditions of production from the labourer⟩ is the source of profit ⟨i.e., of the fact that surplus labour appears as the revenue of capital and not of labour⟩ then profit becomes the source of capital, of new capital formation, i.e., of the fact that the additional conditions of production confront the worker as capital, as a means for maintaining him as a worker and of appropriating his surplus labour anew. The original unity between the worker and the conditions of production ⟨abstracting from slavery, where the labourer himself belongs to the objective conditions of production⟩ has two main forms: the Asiatic communal system (primitive communism) and small-scale agriculture based on the family (and linked with domestic industry) in one form or another. Both are embryonic forms and both are equally unfitted to develop labour as *social* labour and the productive power of social labour. Hence the necessity for the separation, for the rupture, for the antithesis of labour and property (by which property in the conditions of production is to be understood). The most extreme form of this rupture, and the one in which the productive forces of social labour are also most powerfully developed, is capital. The original unity can be re-established only on the material foundation which capital creates and by means of the revolutions which, in the process of this creation, the working class and the whole society undergo.

Another point which Jones does not sufficiently emphasise is this:

Revenue which is exchanged as such against labour—if it is not the revenue of a labourer who works himself and employs an additional workman—is the revenue of the landowner, itself derived from the rent which the labourer pays him, and which the landlord does not entirely consume in kind, either by himself or together with his menials and retainers, but a part of which he uses to buy the products or services of additional workmen and so on. This always presupposes the first relationship.

||1136| ⟨In the same way as part of the profit is classified as interest, even if the industrial capitalist employs only his own capital, because this form [of revenue] has a separate mode of existence, so, given the capitalist mode of production, even if the labourer—who does not employ any other labourers—owns his means of production, they are regarded as capital and the part of his own labour realised by him over and above the ordinary wage appears to be profit yielded by his capital. He himself is then divided up into different economic categories. As his own workman, he gets his wages, and as capitalist, he gets his profits. This observation belongs to the chapter "Revenue and Its Sources".[121]⟩

"... there is a difference between the influence, on the productive powers of nations, of that *wealth which has been saved*, and is *dispensed as wages with a view to profit*; and of that wealth which is advanced out of revenue for the support of labour. With a view to this distinction, I use the word *capital* to denote that portion of wealth exclusively which has been saved from revenue, and is used with a view to profit" (op. cit., pp. 36-37).

"We might ... comprise, under the [...] term, capital, *all the wealth devoted to the maintenance of labour*, whether it has gone through any *previous process of saving or not*. ... we must, then, in tracing the position of the labouring classes and of their paymasters in different nations and under different circumstances, distinguish between *capital which has been saved*, and *capital which has undergone no process of accumulation*; between, in short, capital which is revenue, and capital which is not revenue..." (p. 36). "... in every country[a] of the Old World, except England and Holland, the *wages* of the agriculturists *are not advanced out of funds which have been saved and accumulated from revenues*, but are *produced by the labourers themselves*, and never *exist in any other shape than that of a stock for their own immediate consumption*" (p. 37).

What distinguishes Jones from the other economists (except perhaps Sismondi) is that he emphasises that the essential feature of capital is its socially determined form, and that he reduces the whole difference between the capitalist and other modes of production to this distinct form. It is that labour is directly converted into capital and that, on the other hand, this capital buys labour not for the sake of its use-value, but in order to increase its own value, to create surplus-value (i.e., a larger amount of exchange-value) and to use it "with a view to profit".

This shows, however, at the same time that the saving of revenue in order to convert it into capital and "accumulation" are distinguished from other methods only through the *form* in which "wealth is devoted to the maintenance of labour". The agricultural labourers in England and Holland who receive wages which are "advanced" by capital produce "their wages themselves" just like the French peasant or the self-supporting Russian serf. If the production process is considered in its continuity, then the capitalist advances the labourer as "wages" today only a part of the product which the labourer produced yesterday. Thus the difference [between the capitalist and other modes of production] does not lie in the fact that, in one case, the labourer produces his own wages and in the other case he does not produce them. The difference lies in the fact that [in one case] his product appears as *wages*; that in this case, the worker's product (i.e., the part of the product produced by the worker which makes up the labour fund) 1) appears as the revenue *of others*; 2) that then, however, it is not expended as revenue, and not spent on labour by means of which revenue is directly consumed, but, 3) that it confronts the worker as *capital* which returns to him this portion of the product, in exchange not merely for an equivalent but for more labour than the product he receives contains. Thus his product appears in the first place as revenue of others, secondly, as something which is

---

[a] In the manuscript, "nation."—*Ed.*

"saved" from revenue in order to be employed in the purchase of labour with a view to profit; in other words it is employed as *capital*.

And this process in which his own product confronts him as *capital*, is what is described as the labour fund which "has gone through a previous process of saving", which "... has undergone a process of accumulation" prior to being converted into the labourer's means of subsistence, "... exists in *another shape*" (here it is expressly stated that merely *a change of form* takes place) "than that of a stock for their" (the labourers') "immediate consumption". The whole difference lies in the *transformation* which the labour fund produced by the worker undergoes before it comes back to him in the form of wages. In the case of peasants or independent artisans, it therefore never assumes the form of "wages".

||1137| "Saving" and "accumulation"—as far as the labour fund is concerned—are mere *names* here for the transformations which the worker's product undergoes. The labourer working on his own account consumes his product just like the wage-labourer, or rather, the latter does so just like the former. But in the case of the wage-earner, his product *appears* to be something saved or accumulated from the revenue of *someone else*, i.e., from the revenue of the capitalist. In fact, however, it is this process that makes it possible for the capitalist to "save" or "accumulate" the labourer's surplus labour for his own purposes, and this is the reason why Jones places such great emphasis on the fact that, in non-capitalist modes of production, accumulation does not arise from profit, but from wages, in other words, from the income of the self-supporting cultivator or the artisan who exchanges his labour directly for revenue (otherwise how could the middle class have arisen out of the latter?) and from the rent of the landlord. But for the labour fund to undergo these transformations, the conditions of production must confront the labourer as capital, which is not the case in the other modes of production. The expansion of *wealth* does not appear to be due to the labourer in the latter case [the capitalist mode of production], but to the saving of profit, the reconversion of surplus-value into capital, in the same way as the labour fund itself (before its expansion as a result of new accumulation) confronts the labourer as capital.

"Saving", taken literally, only makes sense with regard to the capitalist who capitalises his revenue, in contrast to the capitalist who consumes his revenue, i.e., spends it as revenue, but it is meaningless when applied to relations between capitalist and labourer.

Two cardinal facts about capitalist production:

[First,] concentration of the means of production in a few hands so that they no longer appear as the immediate property of the individual labourer, but as factors of social production, even though in the first instance they appear as the property of the non-working capitalists, who are their trustees in bourgeois society and enjoy all the fruits of this trusteeship.

Second: Organisation of labour itself as social labour brought about by co-operation, division of labour and the linking of labour with the results of social domination over natural forces.

In both these ways, capitalist production eliminates private property and private labour, even though as yet in antagonistic forms.

The main difference between productive and unproductive labour noted by Adam Smith, is that the former is exchanged directly for capital and the latter for revenue—and the full meaning of this difference emerges first in Jones. His work shows that the first kind of labour is characteristic of the capitalist mode of production, and the second—where it is predominant—belongs to earlier modes of production, and, where it merely plays a subordinate role, is restricted (or ought to be restricted) to spheres which are not directly concerned with the production of wealth.

"... *capital* is the instrument through which all the causes which augment the efficiency of human labour, and the productive powers of nations, are brought into play. ... Capital is the stored-up results of *past labour* used to produce some effect in some part of the task of producing wealth" (p. 35).

(In the note on page 35, he says:

"It will be convenient, and it is reasonable, to consider the act of production as incomplete till the commodity produced has been placed in the hands of the person who is to consume it; all done previously has that point in view. The grocer's horse and cart which brings up our tea from Hertford to the College, is as essential to our possession of it for the purposes of consumption, as the labour of the Chinese who picked and dried the leaves.")

"But ... *this capital* ... does not perform in every community *all the tasks it is capable of performing*. It takes them up gradually and successively in all cases; *and it is a remarkable and an all-important fact, that the one special function*, the performance of which is *essential* to the *serious advance of the power of capital in all its other functions, is exactly that* which, in the case of the greater portion of the labourers of mankind, *capital has never yet fulfilled at all*" (pp. 35-36).

"I allude to the *advance of the wages of labour*" (p. 36).

"The wages of labour are advanced by capitalists in the case of less than one-fourth of the labourers of the earth [....] this fact ... of vital importance in accounting for the comparative progress of nations" (loc. cit.)

||1138| "Capital, or accumulated stock, after performing various other functions in the production of wealth, only takes up late that of *advancing* to the labourer his wages" (p. 79).

In the last sentence on page 79, capital is indeed described as a "relation", not merely as "accumulated stock" but as a quite definite relation of production. The "stock" cannot "take up the function of advancing wages". Jones, moreover, emphasises that it is *the basic form of capital*—the form which gives the whole process of social production its distinctive character, dominates it, leads to a quite new development of the productive forces of social labour, and revolutionises all social and political relationships—that confronts wage-labour, and pays wages. He emphasises that before capital performs this function, which is of decisive importance, it fulfils other functions and, appears in other, subordinate and historically earlier forms, but that its "power in all its functions" only develops fully when it steps forth as industrial capital. On the other hand, in the third lecture "On the gradual manner in which capital *or* capitalists" (there's the rub in this "*or*"; accumulated stock becomes capital only because of this personification) "undertake successive functions in the production of wealth", Jones does not indicate what the previous functions are. They can indeed only be those of capital engaged in commerce or banking. But although Jones comes so close to the correct concept and even expresses it in a certain fashion, nevertheless, being an economist, he is so enmeshed in bourgeois fetishism that not even the devil could be certain that he does not mean that "accumulated stock" as such, can perform different functions.

The sentence:

"Capital, or *accumulated stock*, after performing various other functions in the production of wealth, only *takes up* late that of *advancing* to the labourer his wages" (p. 79)

is the most complete expression of the contradiction; on the one hand, it expresses a correct historical conception of capital, but, on the other hand, a shadow is cast over it by the narrow-minded notion of the economist that "stock" as such is capital. Hence "the accumulated stock" becomes a person who "performs the function of advancing wages" to men. Jones is still rooted in economic prejudice when he solves [the problem], a solution becomes necessary as soon as the capitalist mode of production is regarded as a determinate historical category and no longer as an eternal natural relation of production.

One can see what a great leap forward there was from Ramsay to Jones. Ramsay regards precisely that function of capital which makes it capital—the advancing of wages—as accidental, due only to the poverty of the people, and irrelevant to the production process as such. In this narrow circumscribed manner, Ramsay *denies* the necessity for the capitalist mode of production. Jones, on the other hand, ⟨strange that they were both priests of the Established Church.[122] The ministers of the English Church seem to think more than their continental brethren⟩ demonstrates that it is precisely this function that makes capital capital and gives rise to the most characteristic features of the capitalist mode of production. He shows how this form occurs only at a certain level of development of the productive forces and that it then creates an entirely new material basis. Consequently, however, his comprehension of the fact that this form "can be superseded" and of the merely transitory historical necessity for this form, is quite different from that of Ramsay and more profound. He by no means regards capitalist relations as eternal.

"... a state of things may hereafter exist, and *parts of the world may be approaching to it,* under which the labourers and the owners of accumulated stock, may be identical; but in the progress of nations ... this has *never yet* been the case, and to trace and understand *that progress,* we must observe the labourers gradually transferred from the hands of a body of customers, who pay them out of their revenues, to those of a body of employers, who pay them by advances of capital out of the returns to which the owners aim at realizing a distinct revenue. This may not be as *desirable a state of things as that in which labourers and capitalists are identified,* but we must still accept it as *constituting a stage in the march of industry,* which has hitherto marked the progress of advancing nations. At that stage the people of Asia have not yet arrived" (p. 73).

||1139| Here Jones states quite explicitly that capital and the capitalist mode of production are to be "accepted" merely as a transitional phase in the development of social production, a phase which, if one considers the development of the productive forces of social labour, constitutes a gigantic advance on all preceding forms, but which is by no means the end result; on the contrary, the necessity of its destruction is contained in the antagonism between "owners of accumulated wealth" and the "actual labourers".

Jones was a professor of political economy at Haileybury and the *successor to Malthus*. One can see here how the real science of political economy ends by regarding the bourgeois production relations as merely *historical* ones, leading to higher relations in which the antagonism on which they are based is resolved. By analysing them political economy breaks down the apparently mutually independent forms in which wealth appears. This analysis (even in Ricardo's works) goes so far that:

1) The *independent, material form of wealth disappears* and wealth is shown to be simply the activity of men. Everything which is not the result of human activity, of labour, is nature and, as such, is not social wealth. The phantom of the world of goods fades away and it is seen to be simply a continually disappearing and continually reproduced objectivisation of human labour. All solid material wealth is only transitory materialisation of social labour, crystallisation of the production process whose measure is time, the measure of a movement itself.

2) The manifold forms in which the various component parts of wealth are distributed amongst different sections of society lose their apparent independence. Interest is merely a part of profit, rent is merely surplus profit. Both are consequently merged in profit, which itself can be reduced to *surplus-value*, that is, to unpaid labour. The value of the commodity itself, however, can only be reduced to labour-time. The Ricardian school reaches the point where it rejects one of the forms of appropriation of this surplus-value—landed property (rent)—as useless, insofar as it is pocketed by private individuals. It rejects the idea that the landowner can play a part in capitalist production. The antithesis is thus reduced to that between capitalist and wage-labourer. This relationship, however, is regarded by the Ricardian school as given, as a natural law, on which the production process itself is based. The later economists go one step further and, like Jones, admit only the *historical* justification for this relationship. But from the moment that the bourgeois mode of production and the conditions of production and distribution which correspond to it are recognised as *historical*, the delusion of regarding them as natural laws of production vanishes and the prospect opens up of a new society, [a new] economic social formation, to which capitalism is only the transition.[123] |1139||

||1139| We still have to consider a number of things in Jones's work.

1) In what way, in particular, the capitalist mode of production

—the advancing of wages by capital—alters the form and the productive forces.

2) His observations regarding accumulation and the rate of profit.

But, first of all, another point has to be emphasised.

||1140| "He[a] has been but an agent to give the labourers the benefit of the expenditure of the revenues of the surrounding customers, in a new form and under new circumstances..." (p. 79).

This refers to the non-agricultural labourers, whose earnings previously came direct from the revenue of the landowners, etc. Whereas previously they exchanged their labour (or the product of their labour) directly for that revenue, the capitalist exchanges the product of their labour—collected and concentrated in his hands—for that revenue, in other words, revenue is transformed into, exchanged for capital, in that it constitutes the returns on capital. Instead of being direct returns for labour, it constitutes direct returns for the capital that employs the labourers.[124] |1140||

||1144| After describing *capital* as a specific relation of production, the essence of which is that accumulated wealth takes over the function of advancing wages, and the labour fund itself appears as "wealth saved from revenue and used with a view to profit", Jones outlines the changes in the development of the productive forces characteristic of this mode of production. How the (economic) relations and consequently the social, moral and political state of nations changes with the *change* in the material powers of production, is very well explained.

"As communities *change their powers of production*, they *necessarily change their habits too*" (p. 48). "During their progress in advance, all the different classes of the community find that they are connected with other classes by *new relations*, are assuming *new positions*, and are surrounded by new moral and social dangers, and *new conditions* of social and political excellence" (loc. cit.).

He describes the influence of the capitalist form of production on the development of the productive forces in the following way. But before coming to this, a few passages connected with those already quoted.

"Great political, social, moral and intellectual changes, *accompany changes in the economical organization of communities*, and the agencies and the means, affluent or scanty, by which the tasks of industry are carried on.

---

[a] In the manuscript, "the capitalist".—*Ed.*

These changes necessarily exercise a commanding influence over the different political and social elements to be found in the populations where they take place; that influence extends to the intellectual character, to the habits, manners, morals, and happiness of nations" (p. 45).

"England is the only great country which has taken ... the first step in advance towards perfection *as a producing machine*; the only country in which the population, agricultural as well as non-agricultural, is ranged under the direction of capitalists, and where the effects of their means and of the peculiar functions they can alone perform, are extensively felt, not only in the enormous growth of her wealth, but also in all the economical relations and positions of her population.

"Now England, I say it with regret, but without the very slightest hesitation, is not to be taken as a safe specimen ||1145| of the career of a people so developing their productive forces" (pp. 48-49).

"The *general labour fund* consists 1st.—Of wages which the labourers themselves produce. 2ndly.—Of the revenues of other classes expended in the maintenance of labour. 3rdly.—Of capital, or of a portion of wealth saved from revenue and employed in advancing wages with a view to profit. Those maintained on the first division of the labour fund we will call *unhired labourers*. Those on the second, *paid dependants*. Those on the third, *hired workmen*" (wage-labourers). "The receipt of wages from any one of these divisions of the labour fund determines the *relations of the labourer with the other classes of society*, and so determines sometimes directly, sometimes more or less indirectly, the degree of continuity, skill, and power with which the tasks of industry are carried on" (pp. 51-52).

"The first division, *self-produced wages*, maintains more than half, probably more than two-thirds, of the labouring population of the earth. These labourers consist everywhere of peasants who occupy the soil and labour on it [....] The second division of the labour fund, *revenue expended in maintaining labour*, supports by far the greater part of the *productive* non-agricultural labourers of the East. It is of some importance on the continent of Europe; while in England, again, it comprises only a few jobbing mechanics, *the relics of a larger body*.... The third division of the labour fund, *capital*, is seen in England employing the great majority of her labourers, while it maintains but a small body of individuals in Asia: and in continental Europe, maintains only the non-agricultural labourers; not amounting, probably, on the whole, to a quarter of the productive population" (p. 52).

"I have not ... made any distinction as to *slave-labour*.... The *civil rights* of labourers do not affect their *economical position*. Slaves, as well as freemen, may be observed subsisting on each branch of the general fund" (p. 53).

Although the civil rights of the labourers do not affect "their economical position", their economical position does affect their civil rights. Wage-labour on a national scale—and consequently, the capitalist mode of production as well—is only possible where the workers are personally free. It is based on the personal freedom of the workers.

Jones quite correctly reduces Smith's productive and nonproductive labour to its essence—capitalist and non-capitalist

labour—by correctly applying the distinction made by Smith between labourers paid by capital and those paid out of revenue. Jones himself, however, apparently understands by *productive* and *unproductive* labour, labour which enters into the production of material [wealth] and that which does not. This follows from the passage quoted, where he speaks of the *productive labourers* who depend on revenue expended to maintain them [p. 52].
Further:

> "The portion of the community which is *unproductive of material wealth* may be *useful*, or it may be *useless*" (p. 42).

> "... it is reasonable, to consider the *act of production* as incomplete till the *commodity produced* has been placed in the hands of the person who is to consume it..." (p. 35, note).

The distinction made between the labourers who live on capital and those who live on revenue is concerned with the form of labour. It expresses the whole difference between capitalist and non-capitalist modes of production. On the other hand, the terms productive and unproductive labourers in the narrow sense [are concerned with] labour which enters into the production of *commodities* (production here embraces all operations which the commodity has to undergo from the first producer to the consumer) no matter what kind of labour is applied, whether it is manual labour or not ([including] scientific labour), and labour which does not enter into, and whose aim and purpose is not, the production of commodities. This difference must be kept in mind and the fact that all other sorts of activity influence material production and vice versa in no way affects the necessity for making this distinction.

[b) Jones on the Influence Which the Capitalist Mode of Production Exerts on the Development of the Productive Forces. Concerning the Conditions for the Applicability of Additional Fixed Capital]

||1146| We now come to the *development of the productive forces* by the capitalist mode of production.

[Jones writes:]

> "It may be as well to point out here how this fact" ⟨of the wages being advanced by capital⟩ "affects their *powers of production*, or the *continuity*, the *knowledge*, and the *power*, with which labour is exerted.... The capitalist who pays a workman may assist the *continuity of his labour*. First, by *making such continuity possible*; secondly, by *superintending* and *enforcing* it. Many large bodies of workmen throughout the world ply the street for customers, and depend for wages on the *casual wants* of persons who happen at

the moment to require their services, or to want the articles they can supply. The early missionaries found this the case in China. 'The artizans run about the towns from morning to night to seek custom. The greater part of Chinese workmen work in private houses. Are clothes wanted, for example? The tailor comes to you in the morning and goes home at night. It is the same with all other artizans. They are continually running about the streets in search of work, even the smiths, who carry about their hammer and their furnace for ordinary jobs. The barbers, too ... walk about the streets with an armchair on their shoulders, and a basin and boiler for hot water in their hands.'[125] This continues to be the case very generally throughout the East, and partially in the Western World.

"Now these workmen cannot *for any length of time work continuously*. They must ply like a hackney coachman, and when no customer happens to present himself they must be idle. If in the progress of time a change takes place in their economical position, if they *become the workmen of a capitalist who advances their wages beforehand*, two things take place. First, they *can* now labour continuously; and, secondly, an agent is provided, *whose office and whose interest it will be, to see that* they *do* labour continuously. ... the capitalist [...] has resources ... to wait for a customer.... Here, then, is an *increased continuity in the labour* of all this class of persons. *They labour daily from morning to night*, and are *not interrupted* by waiting for or seeking the customer, who is ultimately to consume the article they work on.

"But the *continuity of their labour*, thus made possible, is secured and improved by the *superintendence of the capitalist*. He *has advanced their wages*; he *is to receive the products of their labour*. It is *his interest and his privilege to see that they do not labour interruptedly or dilatorily*.

"The continuity of labour thus far secured, the effect even of this change on the productive power of labour is very great. ... *the power is doubled*. Two workmen steadily employed *from morning to night*, and from year's end to year's end, will probably produce more than four desultory workmen, who consume much of their time in running after customers, and in recommencing suspended labour" (pp. 37-38).

[With regard to the passages quoted]

Firstly. The transition from labourers who perform casual services—making clothes, coats, trousers, etc., in the landowner's house—to workers employed by capital, is already very well described by *Turgot*.

Second. Although continuity certainly distinguishes capitalist labour from the form described by Jones, it does not distinguish capitalist labour from slave production carried on on a large scale.

Third. It is incorrect to describe the *increased amount of labour* brought about by its long duration and continuity as an increase in productive power or the power of labour. This [occurs] only insofar as the continuity augments the personal skill of the labourers. By [increased] power, we understand the greater productivity of a given quantity of labour employed, not any change in the quantity employed. The latter belongs rather to the formal subordination of labour to capital and it only evolves fully with the development of fixed capital. (We shall deal with this soon.)

Jones correctly emphasises the fact that the capitalist regards labour as his property, no part of which must be wasted. With regard to labour which is maintained directly by revenue, this is a matter of the use-value of labour only.

||1147| Furthermore, Jones correctly emphasises that the continuous labour of the non-agricultural labourers lasting from morning to night is by no means something which arises spontaneously, but is itself a *product* of economic development. In contrast to the Asiatic form and to the Western form of labour (prevailing in former times, partly even today) in the countryside, the urban labour of the Middle Ages already constitutes a great advance and serves as a preparatory school for the capitalist mode of production, as regards the continuity and steadiness of labour.

⟨About this *continuity of labour*:

"The capitalist, too, keeps, as it were, an *echo-office* for labour; he *insures against* the uncertainty of finding a vent for labour, which uncertainty would, but for him, prevent the labour, in many cases, from being undertaken. The trouble of looking for a purchaser, and of going to a market, is reduced, by his means, to a comparatively small compass" (*An Inquiry into those Principles, respecting the Nature of Demand and the Necessity of Consumption, lately advocated by Mr. Malthus etc.*, London, 1821, p. 102).

In the same work:

"... where the capital is in a great degree *fixed*, or where it is sunk on land. ... the trader *is obliged* to continue to employ, much more nearly (than if there had been less fixed capital) the same amount of circulating capital as he did before, in order not to cease to derive *any* profits from the part that is fixed" (op. cit., p. 73).⟩

⟨[Jones says further:]

"... of the state of manners to which the dependence of the workmen on the revenues of their customers has given birth in China, you would, perhaps, get the most striking picture, in the Chinese Exhibition, so long kept open by its American proprietor in London. It is thronged with figures of artizans with their small packs of tools, plying for customers, and idle when none appear—painting vividly to the eye the necessary absence, in their case, of *that continuity of labour* which is one of the three great elements of its productiveness, and indicating sufficiently, to any well-informed observer, *the absence also of fixed capital and machinery*, hardly less important elements of the fruitfulness of industry" (Richard Jones, [*Text-book of Lectures on the Political Economy of Nations*, Hertford, 1852,] p. 73).

"In India, where the admixture of Europeans has not changed the scene, a like spectacle may be seen in the towns. The artizans in rural districts are, however, provided for there in a peculiar manner.... Such handicraftsmen and other non-agriculturists as were actually necessary in a village were maintained by an assignment of a portion of the joint revenues of the villagers, and throughout the country bands of hereditary workmen existed on this fund, whose industry supplied the simple wants and tastes which the cultivators did not provide for by their own hands. The position and rights of these rural artizans soon became, like all rights in the East, hereditary. The band found its customers in the other villagers. The villagers were stationary and abiding, and so were their handicraftsmen.....
"The *artizans of the towns* were and are in a very different position. They received their wages from what was substantially the same fund—surplus revenue from land—but modified in its mode of distribution and its distributors, so as to destroy their *sedentary permanence*, and produce frequent and usually disastrous migrations. ... such *artizans are not confined to any location by dependence on masses of fixed capital*" (as in Europe, for example, where cotton and other manufactories are "fixed in districts in which waterpower, or the fuel which produces steam, are reasonably abundant, and [...] considerable masses of wealth have been converted into buildings and machinery" etc.). "... the case is different when the ||1148| sole dependence of the labourers is *on the direct receipt* of part of the revenues of the persons who consume the commodities the artizans produce.... *They are not confined to the neighbourhood of any fixed capital.* If their customers change their location for long—nay, sometimes for very short—periods, the non-agricultural labourers must follow them, or starve" (pp. 73-74).
"... the [...] greater part of that^a fund" for the handicraftsmen in Asia is "distributed by the State and its officers. The *capital* was, necessarily, the principal centre of distribution..." (p. 75).
"From Samarcand, southward to Beejapoor and Seringapatam, we can trace the ruins of vanishing capitals, of which the population left them *suddenly*" (and not as in other countries [as a result of a gradual] decline) "*as soon as new centres of distribution of the royal revenues*, that is, of the whole of the surplus revenues of the soil, were established" (p. 76).

See *Dr. Bernier*, who compares the Indian towns to army camps.[126] This is due to the form of landed property which exists in Asia.⟩

* * *

We now proceed from the *continuity* to the division of labour, [the development of] knowledge, use of machinery, etc.
[Jones writes:]
"But the *effect of the change of paymasters* on *the continuity of labour* is by no means yet exhausted. The *different tasks of industry may now be further divided*. ... if he" (the capitalist) "employ more than one man, he can divide the task between them; he can keep each individual steadily at

---

^a In the manuscript, "this".—*Ed.*

work at the portion of the common task which he performs the best. ... if the capitalist be rich, and keep a sufficient number of workmen, then the task may be *subdivided* as far as it is capable of subdivision. The continuity of labour is then complete.... Capital, by assuming the function of advancing the wages of labour, has now, by successive steps, perfected its *continuity*. It, at the same time, increases the *knowledge* and *skill* by which such labour is applied to produce any given effect.

"The class of capitalists are from the first partially, and they become ultimately completely, *discharged from the necessity of manual labour*. Their *interest is that the productive powers of the labourers* they employ should be the greatest possible. *On promoting that power their attention is fixed*, and almost exclusively fixed. More thought is brought to bear on the best means of effecting all the purposes of human industry; *knowledge* extends, multiplies its fields of action, and assists industry in almost every branch....

"But further still, as to *mechanical power*. Capital employed not to *pay*, but to *assist* labour, we will call *auxiliary* capital."

⟨He therefore means by this term the part of constant capital which is not made up of raw material.⟩

"The *national mass of auxiliary capital may, certain conditions being fulfilled, increase indefinitely*: the number of labourers remaining the same. At every step of such increase, there is an increase in the third element of the efficiency of human labour, namely, its *mechanical power*. ... *auxiliary capital thus increases its mass relatively to the population*.... What conditions, then, must be fulfilled that the mass of auxiliary capital employed to assist them" ⟨the workers employed by the capitalist⟩ "may increase?

"There must concur three things —

"1st. The means of saving the additional mass of capital.

"2ndly. The will to save it.

"3rdly. Some invention by which it may be made possible, through the use of such capital, that the productive powers of labour may be increased; and increased to an extent which *will make it, in addition to the wealth it before produced, reproduce the additional auxiliary capital used, as fast as destroyed, and also some profit on it*....

"When the *full amount of auxiliary capital, that in the actual state of knowledge can be used profitably, has already been supplied ... an increased range of knowledge* can alone point out the means of employing more. Further, such employment is [...] only practicable if the means discovered *increase the power of labour sufficiently to reproduce the additional capital in the time it wastes away*. If this be not the case, the capitalist must lose his wealth.... But the increased efficiency of the labourers must, besides this, *produce some profit*, or he would have no motive for employing his capital in production at all. ... all the while, that *by employing fresh masses of auxiliary capital these two objects can be effected*, there is no definite and final limit to the progressive employment of such fresh masses of capital. They may go on increasing co-extensively with the *increase of knowledge*.But knowledge is never stationary; and, as it extends itself from hour to hour in all directions, from hour to hour some new implement, some new machine, some new motive force may present itself, which will enable the community profitably to add something to the mass of auxiliary capital by which it assists its industry, and *so increase the difference between the productiveness of its labour and that of poorer and less skilful nations*" (loc. cit., pp. 38-41).

||1149| First, with regard to the statement that the inventions, or appliances or contrivances must be of such a kind, "that the productive powers of labour may be increased; and increased to an extent which will make it,[a] in addition to the wealth it before produced, reproduce the additional auxiliary capital used, as fast as it is destroyed...", or "reproduce the additional capital *in the time it wastes away*". This means nothing more than that the wear and tear is replaced as it takes place, or, that on the average the additional capital is replaced in the same period during which it is consumed. A portion of the value of the product, or, what amounts to the same thing, a portion of the product, must replace the consumed auxiliary capital, and, at such a rate that if, in a given period of time, it is wholly consumed, it is reproduced wholly, or that a new capital of the same kind takes the place of the capital used up. But what is the condition for this? The productivity of labour must rise to such an extent through the application of the additional auxiliary capital that a part of the product can be deducted to replace this component part either in kind or by exchange.

The reproduction of the auxiliary capital takes place if the productivity is so great, in other words, if the increased amount of output produced during the working-day of the same length is such that a unit of a particular commodity is *cheaper* than a unit produced by the former method, although the aggregate price of the *total output* covers (for example) the annual depreciation of the machinery, that is, the amount of depreciation calculated per unit of the commodity is insignificant. If the part which replaces the depreciation, and secondly the part which replaces the value of raw material, are deducted from the total product, then there remains a part which pays for the wages and a part which covers the profit and even yields more surplus-value although the price [per unit] remains the same as it was previously.

An increase in the product could take place without fulfilling this condition. If, for example, the numbers of pounds of twist were to increase tenfold (instead of a hundredfold, etc.) and if the value of the wear and tear of the machinery which has to be

---

[a] In the manuscript, "the productive powers of labour are increased to such an extent as to make it".—*Ed.*

added to the price were to drop from one-sixth to one-tenth, then the twist spun by machinery would be dearer than that produced by spindle. If an additional £100 of capital in the form of guano were used in agriculture and if this guano had to be replaced in a year, and if the value of a quarter (produced by the old method) were £2, then 50 additional quarters would have to be produced merely to replace the depreciation. And without this the guano could not be used (profit is here disregarded).

Jones's remark that the additional capital must be "reproduced" (of course from the sale of the product or in kind), "in the time it wastes away" simply means that the commodity must replace the wear and tear embodied in it. In order to begin production anew, all the value elements contained in the commodity must be replaced by the time when its reproduction is to begin again. In agriculture, this reproduction time is given as a result of natural conditions, and the period of time in which the wear and tear must be replaced is given, in exactly the same way as the time in which all the other value elements of grain, for example, have to be replaced.

In order that the reproduction process can begin, i.e., that the renewal of the real process of production can take place, the commodity must pass through the process of circulation, that is, the commodity must be sold (insofar as it is not replaced in kind, like the seeds) and the money for which it is sold converted into elements of production again. In the case of grain and other agricultural products, there are certain specific periods for this reproduction dictated by the seasons, that is, extreme *limits*, definite limits are set to the duration of the process of circulation.

Second: Such definite limits to the circulation process arise in general from the nature of commodities as use-values. All commodities deteriorate sooner or later, although the extreme limit of their existence varies. If they are not consumed by people (either in the production process or individually), then they are consumed by elemental natural forces. They decay, and finally they disintegrate. If their use-value is destroyed, then their exchange-value goes down the drain and that puts an end to their reproduction. The final limits of their circulation time are therefore determined by the natural times and periods of reproduction proper to them as use-values.

Third: In order that the production process of the commodities may be continuous, ||1150| that is, so that one part of capital may be continuously in the production process and the other continuously in the process of circulation, very varied divisions of capital must take place, in accordance with the natural limits of the periods of reproduction, or the limits [of existence] of the different use-values, or the different spheres of operation of capital.

Fourth: This applies to all the value elements of the commodity simultaneously. But, in the case of commodities in the production of which a great deal of fixed capital is employed, there is, in addition to the limits which their own use-values impose on the circulation process, another determining factor, namely, the use-value of fixed capital. It wastes away in a certain time and, therefore, must be reproduced in a given period. Let us assume, for example, that a ship lasts ten years, or a spinning-machine twelve. The freight carried during the ten years, or the twist sold during the twelve years, must be sufficient for a new ship to replace the old one after ten years and for a new spinning-machine to replace the old one after twelve. If the fixed capital is used up in six months, then the product must be returned from circulation in this period.

Besides the natural mortality periods for commodities as use-values—periods which vary greatly amongst different use-values—and besides the requirements of the continuity of the production process, which set even more varied final limits to the circulation time, according to whether the commodities must remain in the production sphere or can remain in the circulation sphere for a longer or shorter period of time, a third factor is thus added, namely, the different mortality periods, and therefore different requirements of reproduction, of the auxiliary capital used in the production of commodities.

Jones declares that the second condition [for the use of auxiliary capital] is the "profit" which the auxiliary capital must produce, and this is the *conditio sine qua non* for all capitalist production, regardless of the particular form in which the capital is employed. Nowhere does Jones explain how he conceives the genesis of this profit. But since he merely derives it from labour, and the profit yielded by the auxiliary capital simply from the increased efficiency of the labour of the workmen, it must consist of absolute or relative surplus labour. It arises in general from the fact that after deducting the *part of the product* which either in kind or by exchange replaces the constituent parts of capital which consist either of raw materials or of means of production, the capitalist, firstly, pays wages from the remainder of the product, and secondly, appropriates a part of it as *surplus product*, which he either sells or consumes in kind. (This latter is not a significant factor in capitalist production and occurs only in a few exceptional cases, when the capitalist directly produces necessary means of subsistence.) This surplus product, however, just as the other parts of the product, consists of the workers' materialised labour, but labour which is not paid for; this product of labour is appropriated by the capitalist without any equivalent.

What is new in Jones's presentation is that the increase in the auxiliary capital over and above a certain level is contingent on an *increase of knowledge*. Jones declares that the necessary conditions are: 1) the means to save the additional capital, 2) the will to save it, 3) some inventions by means of which the productive power of labour is increased sufficiently to produce the additional capital and to produce a profit on it.

What is necessary above all is that there should be a *surplus product*, either in kind or converted into money.

In the production of cotton, for example, the planters in America (like those in India at the present time) were able to plant large areas, but did not have the means for converting the raw cotton into cotton by means of cleaning at the right time. Part of the cotton rotted in the fields. This kind of thing was ended by the invention of the cotton gin. Part of the product is now converted into cotton gin. But the cotton gin does not merely replace its own cost; it also increases the surplus product. New markets have the same effect; for instance, furthering the conversion of skins into money (likewise improved transport).

Each new machine which consumes coal is a means for converting surplus product existing in the shape of coal into capital. The conversion of a part of the surplus product into auxiliary capital can take place in two ways: [firstly,] increase in the auxiliary capital already in existence, that is, its reproduction on a larger scale; [secondly,] discovery of new use-values or of a new use for well-known use-values, and new inventions of machinery or of motive power leading to the creation of new kinds of auxiliary capital. In this context, extension of knowledge is obviously one of the conditions for increasing the auxiliary capital or, what amounts to the same thing, for the conversion of surplus product or surplus money (foreign trade is important in this connection) into additional auxiliary capital. For example, the telegraph opens up a whole new field for the investment of auxiliary capital, so do the railways, etc., and so does the whole gutta-percha and India rubber production.

||1151| This point about the extension of knowledge is important.

Consequently, accumulation does not have to set new labour in motion, it may simply direct the labour previously employed into new channels. For example, the same machine workshop which previously made hand-looms now makes power-looms, and some of the weavers are taken over by [mills using] the changed methods of production while the others are thrown on to the street.

When a machine replaces labour, it always demands less new labour (for its own production) than it replaces. Perhaps the old labour is simply given a new direction. In any case, labour is freed, which after a greater or lesser amount of trials and tribulations may be used in other ways. The human material for a new sphere of production is thus provided. As far as the *direct* freeing of capital is concerned, it is not the capital which buys the machine which becomes free, because it is invested in it. And even assuming that the machine is cheaper than the amount of wages it replaces, more raw material, etc., will be required. If the workers now dismiss dpreviously cost £500 and the new machine costs £500 too, then the capitalist previously had an outlay of £500 every year, whereas the machine may perhaps last ten years, so that in fact he now has an outlay of only £50 a year. But what at any rate becomes free (after deducting the [expenditure for] the larger number of workers employed in the manufacture of the machine and in auxiliary matters connected with it, such as coal [production], etc.) is the capital which constituted the income of the [dismissed] workers or that employed in the production of commodities which these workers bought with their wages. This continues to exist as it did previously. If workers are simply replaced as motive power without [the machinery] itself being substantially altered, for example, if wind or water [now operate the machinery] where this was done previously [by workers], two lots of capital are freed, the capital previously spent on paying the workers and the capital for which their money income was exchanged. This is an example used by Ricardo.[127]

But one part of the product previously converted into wages is now always reproduced as auxiliary capital.

A large part of the labour previously used directly in the production of means of subsistence is now used in the production of auxiliary capital. This too is in contradiction to Adam Smith's view, according to which the accumulation of capital is synonymous with the employment of *more* productive labour. Apart from the examples considered above, the result may be merely a change in the application of labour and a withdrawal of labour from the direct production of means of subsistence and its transfer to the production of means of production, railways, bridges, machinery, canals and so on.

* * *

(How important the existing amount of means of production and ·the existing scale of production are for accumulation [is described in the following]:

"The astonishing expedition with which a great cotton *factory*, comprehending spinning and weaving, can be erected in Lancashire, arises from the *vast c o l l e c t i o n* of patterns of every *variety* from those of gigantic steam engines, water wheels, iron girders and joists, down to the smallest member of a throstle or loom in possession of the engineers, mill-wrights, and machine makers. In the course. of last year Mr. Fairbairn equipped water wheels equivalent to 700 horses power and steam engines to 400 horses power from his engineer factory alone, independent of his mill-wright and steam-boiler establishment. Hence, whenever capital comes forward to take advantage of improved demand for goods, the means of fructifying it are provided with such rapidity, that it may realise its own amount in profit, ere an analagous factory could be set a-going in France, Belgium or Germany" (Andrew Ure, [*Philosophy of Manufactures*, London, 1835, p. 39,] *Philosophie des Manufactures etc.*, tome I, Paris, 1836, pp. 61-62).[a]

||1152| With development, machinery becomes cheaper, partly relatively—in comparison with its power—and partly absolutely; at the same time, however, a massive concentration of machinery takes place in the workshop, so that its value increases in proportion to the living labour employed, although the value of its individual components declines:

The driving force—the machine which produces the motive power—becomes cheaper as the machinery which transmits the power and the machine which the power operates, are improved, as friction is reduced, etc.

"The facilities resulting from the employment of self-acting tools have not only *improved the accuracy* and *accelerated the construction of the machinery* of a mill, but have also *lowered its cost and increased its mobility* in a remarkable

---

[a] This and the following quotation were taken by Marx from the French edition of A. Ure's work.—*Ed.*

degree. At present a throstle frame, made in the past manner, may be had complete at the rate of 9s. 6d. per spindle, and a self-actor at about 8s. per spindle including the patent licence for the latter. The spindles in cotton factories *move with so little friction that 1 horse power* drives 500 on the fine hand mule, 300 on the self-actor mule, and 180 on the throstle; which power includes all the subsidiary preparation machines as carding, roving, etc., a power of three horses is adequate to drive 30 large looms with their dressing machines" (Andrew Ure, [*Philosophy of Manufactures*, p. 40,] *Philosophie des Manufactures etc.*, tome I, Paris, 1836, pp. 62-63).⟩

* * *

[Jones says further:]

"Over by far the greater part of the globe, the great majority of the labouring classes do not even receive their wages from capitalists; they either produce them themselves, or receive them from the revenue of their customers. The great primary step has not been taken which secures the *continuity* of their labour; they are aided by *such k n o w l e d g e only*, and such an *amount of mechanical power* as may be found *in the possession of persons labouring with their own hands for their subsistence*. The skill and science of more advanced countries, the giant motive forces, the accumulated tools and machines which those forces may set in motion, are absent from the tasks of the industry which is carried on by such agents alone" ([Richard Jones, *Text-book of Lectures on the Political Economy of Nations*,] p. 43).

⟨In England herself:

"Take agriculture.... A knowledge of good farming is spread thinly, and with wide intervals, over the country. A very small part of the agricultural population is aided by all the capital which ... might be available in this branch of the national industry. ... the working in these" ⟨great manufactories⟩ "is the occupation of only a small portion of our non-agricultural labourers. In country workshops, in the case of all handicraftsmen and mechanics who carry on their separate task with little combination, there the division of labour is incomplete, and its continuity consequently imperfect.... Abandon the great towns, observe the broad surface of the country, and you will see what a large portion of the national industry is lagging at a long distance from perfection, in either continuity, skill, or power" (loc. cit., p. 44).

Capitalist production leads to separation of *science from labour* and at the same time to the use of science in material production.

* * *

With regard to *rent*, Jones remarks correctly:
Rent, in the modern sense of the term, which depends entirely on profit, presupposes:

"... *the power of moving capital and labour from one occupation to others*[a]

---

[a] In the manuscript, "to another".—*Ed.*

... the 'mobility' of capital and labour, and in countries where agricultural capital and labour have no such mobility ... we cannot expect to observe any of the results which we see to arise here from that mobility exclusively" (loc. cit., p. 59.)

This "mobility of capital and labour" is, in general, the *real* prerequisite for establishing the average rate of profit. It presupposes indifference to the *specific form* of labour. In reality friction takes place (at the expense of the working class) between the one-sided character which the division of labour and machinery impose on *labour-power* on the one hand, while on the other hand, it confronts capital ⟨which is thereby differentiated from its undeveloped form in craft-build industry⟩ merely as the living potentiality of any type of labour in general, which is given this or that direction according to the profit that can be made in this or that sphere of production, so that different masses of labour are transferable from one sphere to another.

In Asia, etc., "the body of the population consists [...] of labouring [...] peasants; *systems of cultivation imperfectly developed*, ||1153| *afford long intervals of leisure*. As the peasant produces his own food [...] he *also produces most of the other primary necessities which he consumes—his dress, his implements, his furniture, even his buildings*: for there is in his class little division of occupations. The *fashions and habits of such a people do not change*; they are handed down from parents to children; there is nothing to alter or disturb them" (p. 97).

On the other hand, the capitalist mode of production, whose characteristic features are mobility of capital and labour and continual revolutions in the methods of production, and therefore in the relations of production and commerce and the way of life, leads to great mobility in the habits, modes of thinking, etc., of the people.

Compare the following with the above-quoted passage about "the intervals of leisure" and the "imperfectly developed systems of cultivation".

1. Where a steam engine is employed on a farm; it forms *part* of a *system* which employs most labourers in agriculture, and is in all cases [associated] with a reduction [in the number] of horses[a] ("On the Forces used in Agriculture". A Paper read by Mr. John C. Morton at the Society of Arts on December 7, 1859[128]).

2. "... the *difference of time* required to complete the products of agriculture, and of other species of labour," is "the main cause of the great dependence of the agriculturists. They cannot bring their commodities to market

---

[a] This is not a quotation, but a summary of a passage from Morton's paper, which was published in the *Journal of the Society of Arts*. December 9, 1859, pp. 53-61.—*Ed.*

in less time than a year. For that whole period they are obliged to borrow of the shoemaker, the tailor, the smith, the wheelwright, and the various other labourers, whose products they cannot dispense with, but which[a] are completed in a few days or weeks. Owing to this natural circumstance, and owing to the more rapid increase of the wealth produced by other labour than that of agriculture, the monopolizers of all the land, though they have also monopolized legislation, have not been able to save[b] themselves and their servants, the farmers, from becoming the most dependent class of men in the community" (Thomas Hodgskin, *Popular Political Economy*, London, 1827, p. 147, note).

The capitalist differs from capital in that he must live, and therefore must consume part of the surplus-value as revenue, daily and hourly. Thus, the longer the period of production before the capitalist can bring his commodity to market, or the longer the period of time before he receives the proceeds from the sale of his commodities, the longer he must live either on credit during the intervening time—a matter we are not discussing here—or the larger must be the stock of money in his possession which he can expend as revenue. He must *advance* his own revenue for a longer period. His capital must be larger. He is obliged to leave a part of it always unused, as a consumption fund.

⟨In small-scale farming, therefore, domestic industry is combined with agriculture; supplies for the year, etc.⟩

[c) Jones on Accumulation and Rate of Profit. On the Source of Surplus-Value]

We now come to Jones's teaching on *accumulation*. His original contribution so far has been that it is by no means necessary for accumulation to arise from profit; and secondly, that the *accumulation of auxiliary capital* depends upon the *advance of knowledge*. He limits the latter to the discovery of new mechanical appliances, motive forces, etc. But it is true in general. For example, if corn is used as raw material in the preparation of spirits, then a new source of accumulation is opened up, because the surplus product may be converted into new forms, satisfy new wants and enter as a productive element into a new sphere of production. The same applies if starch, etc., is prepared from corn. The sphere of exchange of these particular commodities and of all commodities is thereby expanded. The same takes place when coal is used for lighting, etc.

---

[a] In the manuscript, "whose products they need, and which".—*Ed.*
[b] In the manuscript, "are unable to save".—*Ed.*

Foreign trade, too, is of course an important factor in the process of accumulation, because it tends to increase the variety of use-values and the volume of commodities.

What Jones says first of all is concerned with the *connection between accumulation and the rate of profit*. (He is by no means very clear about the origin of the latter.)

"The power of a nation to accumulate capital from profits *does not vary with the rate of profit*... on the contrary, the power to accumulate capital from profits, *ordinarily varies inversely as the rate of profit*, that is, it is great where the rate of profit is low, and small where the rate of profit is high" ([Jones, *Text-book of Lectures*,] p. 21).

Adam Smith says: ||1154| "Though that part of the revenue of the inhabitants which is derived from the profits of stock is always much greater in rich, than in poor, countries, it is *because the stock is much greater*; in *proportion to the stock*, the profits are generally much less" (Adam Smith, *Wealth of Nations*, Vol. II, Chapter 3 [quoted by Richard Jones in the *Text-book of Lectures*, p. 21, note]).

"In England and Holland, the *rate of profit* is lower than in any other part of Europe" ([Jones, loc. cit.,] p. 21).

"... during the period in which her" (England's) "wealth and capital have been increasing the most rapidly, the *rate of profits* has been gradually declining..." (pp. 21-22).

"... the *relative masses of the profits produced* ... depend *not alone on the rate of profit* ... but *on the rate of profit taken in combination with the relative quantities of capital employed*" (p. 22).

"The increasing quantity of capital of the richer nation ... is also usually accompanied by a decrease in the rate of profits, or a decrease in the proportion, which the annual revenue derived from the capital employed, bears to its gross amount" (loc. cit.).

"If it be said that *all other things being equal, the rate of profit will determine the power of accumulating from profit*, the answer is, that the case, if practically possible, is too rare to deserve consideration. We know, from observation, that a declining rate of profit is the usual accompaniment of *increasing differences in the mass of capital* employed by different nations, and that, therefore, while the rate of profits in the richer nations declines, *all other things are not equal.*

"If it be asserted that the decline of profits may be great enough to make it impossible to accumulate from profits at all, the answer [...] is that it would be foolish to argue on the assumption of such a decline, because long before the rate of profits had reached such a point, capital would go abroad to realize greater profits elsewhere, and that the power of exporting will always establish some limit below which profits will never fall in any one country, *while there are others in which the rate of profit is greater*" (pp. 22-23).

Apart from the *primary* sources of accumulation, there are *derivative* ones, such as, for example, the owners of the national debt, officials, etc.[a]

---

[a] This last sentence is a summary by Marx of an idea outlined by Jones on p. 23 of his book.—*Ed.*

All this is fine and good. It is quite correct that the *amounts accumulated* by no means depend solely on the rate of profit, but on the rate of profit multiplied by the capital employed, that is, just as much on the size of the capital advanced. If we call the capital employed C, and the rate of profit r, then accumulation will be Cr, and it is clear that this product can increase if C grows more quickly than r declines. And this is indeed a fact derived from observation. But this does not explain the *cause*, the *raison d'être* of this fact. Jones himself came very near to it when he made the observation that the auxiliary capital continuously increases relatively to the working population by which it is put into motion.

Insofar as the decline in [the rate of] profit is due to the cause mentioned by Ricardo—the rise of rent—the ratio of the total surplus-value to the capital employed remains unchanged. But one part of it—rent—increases, at the expense of the other part i.e., of profit; this leaves the proportion of the total surplus-value, of which profit, interest and rent are only categories, [to the total capital] unchanged. Thus, in fact, Ricardo denies the phenomenon itself.

On the other hand, the mere decline in the rate of interest proves nothing in itself, just as its rise proves nothing, although it does indeed always indicate the minimum rate below which profit *cannot* fall. For profit must always be higher than the average rate of interest.

||1155| Apart from the terror which the law of the declining rate of profit inspires in the economists, its most important corollary is the presupposition of a constantly increasing concentration of capitals, that is, a constantly increasing decapitalisation of the smaller capitalists. This, on the whole, is the result of all laws of capitalist production. And if we strip this fact of the contradictory character which, on the basis of capitalist production, is typical of it, what does this fact,this trend towards centralisation, indicate? Only that production loses its private character and becomes a social process, not formally—in the sense that all production subject to exchange is social because of the absolute dependence of the producers on one another and the necessity for presenting their labour as abstract social labour ([by means of] money)—but in actual fact. For the means of production are employed as communal, social means of production and therefore not [determined] by [the fact that they are] the property of an individual, but by their relation to production, and the labour likewise is performed on a social scale.

A separate section in Jones's work is headed *"On the causes which determine the inclination to accumulate"*. [He mentions the following]:

"... 1st.—Differences of temperament and disposition in the people.
"2ndly.—Differences in the proportions in which the national revenues are divided among the different classes of the population.
"3rdly.—Different degrees of security for the safe enjoyment of the capital saved.
"4thly.—Different degrees of facility in investing profitably, as well as safely, successive savings.
"5thly.—Differences in the opportunities offered to the different ranks of the population to better their position by means of savings" (p. 24).

All these five causes, in fact, boil down to this—that accumulation depends on the stage of the *capitalist mode of production* reached by a particular nation.

To begin with *No. 2*. Where capitalist production exists in a developed form, profit constitutes the chief source of accumulation, that is, the capitalists have concentrated the greater part of the national revenue in their hands and even a section of the landowners seeks to capitalise [their revenue].

No. 3. Security (in the legal and police sense) increases in proportion to the degree to which the capitalists secure control of the State administration.

No. 4. As capital develops, the spheres of production increase on the one hand, and, on the other hand, the organisation of credit [develops] in order to collect every farthing in the hands of the money-lenders (bankers).

No. 5. In capitalist production, the improvement of one's position depends solely on money, and everyone can delude himself into believing that he can become a Rothschild.

There remains *No. 1*. All people do not have the same predisposition towards capitalist production. Some primitive peoples, such as the Turks, have neither the temperament nor the inclination for it. But these are exceptions. The development of capitalist production creates an average level of bourgeois society and therefore an average level of temperament and disposition amongst the most varied peoples. It is as truly cosmopolitan as Christianity. This is why Christianity is likewise the special religion of capital. In both it is only men who count. One man in the abstract is worth just as much or as little as the next man. In the one case, all depends on whether or not he has faith, in the other, on whether or not he has credit. In addition, however, in the one case, predestination has to be added, and in the other case, the accident of whether or not a man is born with a silver spoon in his mouth.

* * *

The source of surplus-value and primitive rent:

"When land has been appropriated and cultivated, such land yields, in almost every case, to the labour employed on it, *more than is necessary* to continue the kind of cultivation already bestowed upon it. *Whatever it produces beyond this,* ||1156| we will call *its surplus produce.* Now this surplus produce is the *source of primitive rents,* and limits the extent of such revenues, as can be continuously derived from the land by its *owners,* as distinct from its *occupiers"* (p. 19).

These *primitive rents* are the first social form in which surplus-value is represented, and this is the obscure conception which forms the foundation of the theory of the Physiocrats.

Both absolute and relative surplus-value have this in common that they presuppose a certain level of the productive power of labour. If the entire working-day (available labour-time) of a man (any man) were only sufficient to feed himself (and at best his family as well), then there would be no surplus labour, surplus-value and surplus produce. This prerequisite of a certain level of productivity is based on the natural productiveness of land and water, the natural sources of wealth. It is different in different countries, etc. Needs are simple and crude in early times and the minimum produce required for the maintenance of the producers themselves is consequently small, and so is the surplus product. On the other hand, the number of people who live off the surplus product in those circumstances is likewise very small, so that they receive the sum total of the small amounts of surplus product obtained from a relatively large number of producers.

The basis for absolute surplus-value—that is, the real precondition for its existence—is the *natural fertility of the land,* of nature, whereas relative surplus-value depends on the development of the social productive forces.

And with this we finish with *Jones.* |XVIII-1156||

ADDENDA

REVENUE AND ITS SOURCES. VULGAR POLITICAL ECONOMY[129]

[1.] The Development of Interest-Bearing Capital on the Basis of Capitalist Production [Transformation of the Relations of the Capitalist Mode of Production into a Fetish. Interest-Bearing Capital as the Clearest Expression of This Fetish. The Vulgar Economists and the Vulgar Socialists Regarding Interest on Capital]

||XV-891| The form of revenue and the sources of revenue are the *most fetishistic* expression of the relations of capitalist production. It is their form of existence as it appears on the surface, divorced from the hidden connections and the intermediate connecting links. Thus the *land* becomes the source of *rent*, *capital* the source of *profit*, and *labour* the source of *wages*. The distorted form in which the real inversion is expressed is naturally reproduced in the views of the agents of this mode of production. It is a kind of fiction without fantasy, a religion of the vulgar. In fact, the vulgar economists—by no means to be confused with the economic investigators we have been criticising—translate the concepts, motives, etc., of the representatives of the capitalist mode of production who are held in thrall to this system of production and in whose consciousness only its superficial appearance is reflected. They translate them into a doctrinaire language, but they do so from the standpoint of the ruling section, i.e., the capitalists, and their treatment is therefore not naïve and objective, but apologetic. The narrow and pedantic expression of vulgar conceptions which are bound to arise among those who are the representatives of this mode of production is very different from the urge of political economists like the Physiocrats, Adam Smith and Ricardo to grasp the inner connection of the phenomena.

However, of all these forms, the most complete fetish is *interest-bearing capital*. This is the original starting-point of capital—money—and the formula M—C—M' is reduced to its two extremes—M—M'—money which creates more money. It is the original and general formula of capital reduced to a meaningless résumé.

The *land* or *nature* as the source of *rent*, i.e., landed property, is fetishistic enough. But as a result of a convenient confusion of use-value with exchange-value, the common imagination is still able to have recourse to the productive power of nature itself, which, by some kind of hocus-pocus, is personified in the landlord.

Labour as the source of *wages*, that is, of the worker's share in his product, which is determined by the specific social form of labour; labour as the cause of the fact that the worker by means of his labour buys the permission to produce from the product (i.e., from capital considered in its material aspect) and has in labour the source by which a part of his product is returned to him in the form of payment made by this product as his employer—this is pretty enough. But the common conception is in so far in accord with the facts that, even though labour is confused with wage-labour and, consequently, wages, the product of wage-labour, with the product of labour, it is nevertheless obvious to anybody who has common sense that labour itself produces its own wages.

Capital, insofar as it is considered in the *production process*, still continues to a certain extent to be regarded as an instrument for acquiring the labour of others. This may be treated as "right" or "wrong", as justified or not justified, but here the relation of the capitalist to the worker is always presupposed and assumed.

Capital, insofar as it appears in the *circulation process*, confronts the ordinary observer mainly in the form of *merchant capital*, that is, a kind of capital which is engaged only in this operation, hence profit in this field is in part linked with a vague notion of general swindling, or more specifically, with the idea that the merchant swindles the industrial capitalist in the same way as the industrial capitalist swindles the worker, or again that the merchant swindles the consumer, just as the producers swindle one another. In any case, profit here is explained as a result of exchange, that is, as arising from a social relation and not from a thing.

On the other hand, *interest-bearing capital* is the perfect fetish. It is capital in its finished form—as such representing the unity of the production process and the circulation process—and therefore yields a definite profit in a definite period of time. In the form of interest-bearing capital only this function remains, without the mediation of either production process or circulation process. Memories of the past still remain in capital and profit, although because of the divergence of profit from surplus-value and the uniform profit yielded by all capitals—that is, the general rate of profit—capital becomes ||892| very much obscured, something dark and mysterious.

Interest-bearing capital is the consummate *automatic fetish*, the self-expanding value, the money-making money, and in this form it no longer bears any trace of its origin. The social relation is consummated as a relation of things (money, commodities) to themselves.

This is not the place for a more detailed examination of interest and its relation to profit; nor is it the place for an examination of the ratio in which profit is divided into industrial profit and interest. It is clear that capital, as the mysterious and automatically generating source of interest, that is, source of its [own] increase, finds its consummation in capital and interest. It is therefore especially in this form that capital is imagined. It is capital *p a r e x c e l l e n c e*.

Since, on the basis of capitalist production, a certain sum of values represented in money or commodities—actually in money, the converted form of the commodity—makes it possible to extract a certain amount of labour gratis from the workers and to appropriate a certain amount of surplus-value, surplus labour, surplus product, it is obvious that money itself can be sold as capital, that is, as a commodity *sui generis*, or that capital can be bought in the form of commodities or of money.

It can be sold as the source of profit. I enable someone else by means of money, etc., to appropriate surplus-value. Thus it is quite in order for me to receive part of this surplus-value. Just as land has value because it enables me to intercept a portion of surplus-value, and I therefore pay for this land only the surplus-value which can be intercepted thanks to it, so I pay for capital the surplus-value which is created by means of it. Since, in the capitalist production process, the value of capital is perpetuated and reproduced in addition to its surplus-value, it is therefore quite in order that, when money or commodities are sold as capital, they return to the seller after a period of time and he does not alienate it [capital] in the same way as he would a commodity but retains ownership of it. In this way, money or commodities are not sold as money or commodities, but in their second power, as *capital*, as self-increasing money or commodities. Capital is not only increased, but is preserved in the total process of production. It therefore remains capital for the seller, and comes back to him. The sale consists in the fact that another person, who uses the capital as productive capital, has to pay its owner a certain part of his profit, which he only makes through this capital. Like land, it is rented out as a value-creating thing which in this process of generating value is preserved and continually returned, and therefore can also be returned to the original seller. It is only capital in virtue of its return to him. Otherwise he would sell it as a commodity or buy with it as money.

In any case, the form considered in itself (in fact, it [money] is alienated periodically as a means for exploiting labour, for making surplus-value) is this, that the thing now appears as capital and capital appears as a mere thing; the whole result of the capitalist production and circulation process appears as a property inherent in a thing, and it depends on the owner of money, i.e., of the commodity in its constantly exchangeable form, whether he expends it as money or rents it out as capital.

We have here the relation of capital as principal to itself as yield, and the profit which it yields is measured against its own value, which (in accordance with the nature of capital) is not diminished in this process.

It is thus clear why superficial criticism—in exactly the same way as it wants to maintain commodities and combats money— now turns its wisdom and reforming zeal against interest-bearing capital without touching upon real capitalist production, but merely attacking one of its consequences. This polemic against interest-bearing capital, undertaken from the standpoint of capitalist production, a polemic which today parades as "socialism", occurs, incidentally, as a phase in the development of capital itself, for example, in the seventeenth century, when the industrial capitalist had to assert himself against the old-fashioned usurer who, at that time, still [confronted] him as a superior power.

||893| The complete *objectification, inversion* and *derangement* of capital as interest-bearing capital—in which, however, the inner nature of capitalist production, [its] derangement, merely appears in its most palpable form—is capital which yields "compound interest". It appears as a Moloch demanding the whole world as a sacrifice belonging to it of right, whose legitimate demands, arising from its very nature, are however never met and are always frustrated by a mysterious fate.

The characteristic movement of capital, both in the production and in the circulation processes, is the return of the money or commodity to its starting-point—to the capitalist. This expresses, on the one hand, the real metamorphosis, the conversion of the commodity into its conditions of production, and the conversion of the conditions of production back into the form of the commodity—i.e., reproduction, and, on the other hand, the formal metamorphosis, the conversion of the commodity into money and of the money back into the commodity. Finally, the multiplication of value: M—C—M'. The original value, which is however increased during the process, always remains in the possession of the same capitalist. Only the forms change in which he possesses it: money, commodity, or the form of the production process itself.

In the case of interest-bearing capital, this *return* of capital to its starting-point acquires a quite *external* aspect, divorced from the real movement whose form it is. A spends his money not as money but as capital. No change takes place here in the money. It only changes hands. Its real conversion into capital takes place only while it is in the hands of B. But it has become capital for A as a result of the transfer of the money from A's hands into those of B. The real return of capital from the production and circulation process takes place for B. But for A, the return takes place in the same way as the alienation did. The money passes from B back again to A. He *lends* the money instead of spending it.

In the real production process of capital, each particular movement of money expresses an aspect of reproduction, whether it be the conversion of money into labour, the conversion of the finished commodity into money (the end of the act of production) or the reconversion of the money into commodities (renewal of the production process, recommencement of reproduction). The movement of money when it is *lent* as *capital*, that is, when it is not converted into capital but enters into circulation as capital, expresses nothing more than the transfer of the same money from one person to another. The property rights remain with the lender, but the possession is transferred to the industrial capitalist. For the lender, however, the conversion of the money into capital begins at the moment when he spends it as capital instead of spending it as money, i.e., when he hands it over to the industrial capitalist. (It remains capital for him even if he does not lend it to the industrial capitalist but to a spendthrift, or to a worker who cannot pay his rent. The whole pawnshop business [is based on this].) True, the other person converts it into capital, but this is an operation beyond that in which the lender and the borrower are involved. *This development is effaced*, is not visible, is not directly included in it. Instead of the real conversion of money into capital, there appears only the empty form of this process. Just as in the case of labour-power, *the use-value of money here becomes that* of creating exchange-value, *more exchange-value than it itself contains*. It is *lent as self-expanding value*, as a commodity, but a commodity which, precisely because of this quality, differs from commodities as such and therefore also *possesses a specific form of alienation*.

The starting-point of capital is the commodity owner, the owner of money, in short, the capitalist. Since in the case of capital both starting-point and point of return coincide, it returns to the capitalist. But the capitalist exists here in a dual form, as the owner of capital and as the industrial capitalist who really converts money into capital. The capital actually issues ||894| from him [the industrial capitalist] and returns again to him. But only as possessor. The capitalist exists in a dual form—juridically and economically. The capital as property consequently returns to the juridical capitalist, the left-handed Sam. But the return of the capital, which includes the maintenance of its value and establishes it as a self-maintaining and self-perpetuating value, is indeed brought about by intermediate steps for capitalist II but not for capitalist I. In this case therefore, the return is not the consequence and result of a series of economic processes but is effected by a particular juridical transaction between buyer and seller, by the fact that it is *lent instead of being sold, and therefore it is alienated only temporarily*. What *is sold is*, in fact, *its use-value*, whose *function in this case is* to produce *exchange-value*, to yield profit, in other words to produce more value than it itself contains. As money it does not change through being used. It is however expended as money and it flows back as money.

The form in which it returns depends on the mode of reproduction of the capital. If it is loaned as money, then it comes back in the form of circulating capital, that is, its whole value is returned plus surplus-value, in this case, that part of surplus-value or of profit which consists of interest; the sum of money loaned plus the additional amount which has arisen from it.

If it is loaned out in the form of machinery, buildings, etc., in short, in a material form in which it functions as fixed capital in the process of production, then it returns in the form of fixed capital, as an annuity, that is, for example, as an annual amount equal to the replacement of the wear and tear, i.e., equal to that part of the value which has entered the circulation process, plus that part of the surplus-value which is calculated as profit (in this case a part of the profit, interest) on the fixed capital (not insofar as it is fixed capital, but insofar as in general it is capital of a definite amount).

In profit as such, surplus-value, and consequently its real source, is already obscured and mystified:

1) Because, considered from the formal standpoint, profit is *surplus-value* calculated on the whole of the capital advanced, so that each part of capital—fixed and circulating—laid out on raw materials, machinery or labour, yields an equal amount of profit.

2) Because, just as in the case of a single given capital of 500, for example, every fifth part yields 10 per cent, if the surplus-value amounts to 50, so now, as a result of the establishment of the *general rate of profit*, every capital of 500 or 100, no matter which sphere it operates in, irrespective of the relative proportions of variable and constant capital, no matter how varied the periods of turnover, etc., will yield the same average profit—say 10 per cent—in the same period of time as any other capital under quite different organic conditions. Because, therefore, the *profit* of individual capitals regarded in isolation and the *surplus-value* which is produced by them in their own sphere of production become in fact different magnitudes.

It is true that point 2 merely develops further what has already been implied in point 1.

The basis of interest however is this already externalised form of surplus-value, i.e., its existence as *profit*. This form differs from its first simple aspect, in which it still reveals the umbilical cord of its birth, and is, at first sight, by no means recognisable as a form of surplus-value. Interest directly presupposes not surplus-value, but *profit*, of which it is merely a part placed in a special category or division. It is therefore much more difficult to recognise surplus-value in interest than in profit, since interest is directly connected with surplus-value only in the form of profit.

The time needed for the return of capital depends on the real production process; in the case of interest-bearing capital, its return as capital *appears* to depend merely on the agreement between lender and borrower. So that the return of the capital in this transaction no longer appears to be a result determined by the production process, but it seems that the capital never loses the form of money for a single instant. These transactions are nevertheless determined by the real returns. But this is not *evident* in the transaction.

||895| Interest, as distinct from profit, represents the *value of mere ownership of capital*—i.e., it transforms the ownership of *money* (of a sum of values, commodities, whatever the form may be) in itself, into ownership of capital, and consequently commodities or money as such into self-expanding values. The conditions of labour are of course capital, only insofar as they confront the labourer as his non-property and consequently function as someone else's property. But they can function in this way only in contradiction to labour. The *antagonistic existence of these conditions in relation to labour makes their owners capitalists*, and turns these conditions owned by them into capital. But capital in the hands of moneyed capitalist A does not have this contradictory character which turns it into capital and which therefore makes ownership of money appear as ownership of capital. *The concrete distinct form by means of which money or a commodity is converted into capital is obliterated.* Moneyed [capitalist] A does not confront the worker at all, but only another capitalist—capitalist B. What he sells him is actually the "use" of the money, the results it will produce when converted into productive capital. But in fact it is not the use which he sells directly. If I sell a commodity, then I sell a specific use-value. If I buy money with commodities, then I buy the functional use-value which money, as the converted form of commodities, possesses. I do not sell the use-value of the commodity along with its exchange-value, nor do I buy the particular use-value of the money along with the money itself. But money as money—before its conversion into and its function as capital, a function which it does not perform while it is in the hands of the moneylender—has no other use-value than that which it possesses as a commodity (gold, silver, its material substance) or as money which is the converted form of a commodity. What the moneylender sells in actual fact to the industrial capitalist, what really happens in the transaction, is simply this: he transfers the ownership of the money to the industrial capitalist for a certain period of time. He disposes of his ownership title for a certain term, and as a result the industrial capitalist has bought the ownership for a certain period. Thus his money appears to be capital before it is sold and the mere ownership of money or a commodity—

separated from the capitalist production process—is regarded as capital.

The fact that it becomes capital only after it has been disposed of, makes no difference, any more than the use-value of cotton is altered by the fact that its use-value only emerges after it has been disposed of to the spinner or that the use-value of meat only becomes apparent after it has been transferred from the butcher's shop to the consumer's table. Hence money, once it is not spent on consumption, and commodities, once they are not used as means of consumption by their owners, transform those who possess them into capitalists and are in themselves—separated from the capitalist production process and even *before* their conversion into "productive" capital—capital, that is, they are self-expanding, self-maintaining and self-increasing value. It is their immanent attribute to create value, to yield interest, just as the attribute of the pear tree is to produce pears. And it is as such an interest-bearing thing that the money-lender sells his money to the industrial capitalist. Because money preserves itself, i.e., is value which preserves itself, the industrial capitalist can return it at any time fixed by contract. Since it produces a definite amount of surplus-value, interest, annually, or rather since value accrues to it over any period of time, he can also pay back this surplus-value to the lender annually or in any other conventionally established period of time. Money as capital yields surplus-value daily in exactly the same way as wage-labour. While interest is simply a *part* of the profit *established under a special name*, it *appears here* as [the surplus-value specifically created by] capital as such, separated from the production process, and consequently [due] only to the mere ownership of capital, the ownership of money and commodities, separated from the relations which give rise to the contradiction between this property and labour, thus turning it into capitalist property. [Interest seems to be] a specific kind of *surplus-value* the *generation* of which is due to the mere ownership of capital and therefore to an intrinsic characteristic of capital; whereas on the contrary, *industrial profit* appears to be a mere addition which the borrower obtains by employing capital productively, that is, by exploiting the workers with the help of the capital borrowed (or, as people also say, by his work as a capitalist, the function of the capitalist being equated here with labour, and even identified with wage-labour, since the industrial capitalist, by really taking part in the ||896| production process, appears in fact as an active agent in production, as a worker, in contrast to the idle, inactive money-lender whose function of property owner is separate from and outside the production process).

Thus it is *interest*, not *profit*, which appears to be the *creation of value* arising from capital as such and therefore from the mere ownership of capital; consequently it is regarded as the specific revenue created by capital. This is also the form in which it is conceived by the vulgar economists. In this form all intermediate links are obliterated, and the *fetishistic feature* of capital, as also the concept of the *capital-fetish*, is complete. This form arises necessarily, because the juridical aspect of property is separated from its economic aspect and one part of the profit under the name of interest accrues to *capital* which is completely separated from the production process, or to the *owner of this capital*.

To the vulgar economist who desires to represent capital as an independent source of value, a source which creates value, this form is of course a godsend, a form in which the source of profit is no longer recognisable and the result of the capitalist process—separated from the process itself—acquires an independent existence. In M—C—M' an intermediate link is still retained. In M—M' we have the incomprehensible form of capital, the most extreme inversion and materialisation of production relations.

A general *rate of interest* corresponds naturally to the *general rate of profit*. It is not our intention to discuss this further here, since the analysis of interest-bearing capital does not belong to this general section but to that dealing with *credit*.[130] However the observation that the average rate of profit appears much less as a palpable, solid fact than does the *rate of interest* is important for the elaboration of this aspect of capital. True, the rate of interest fluctuates continuously. [It may be] 2 per cent today (on the money market for the industrial capitalist—and this is all we are discussing), 3 per cent tomorrow, and 5 per cent the day after. But it is 2 per cent, 3 per cent, 5 per cent for all borrowers. It is a general condition that every sum of money of £100 yields 2 per cent, 3 per cent or 5 per cent, while the same value in its real function as capital yields very different amounts of real profit in the different spheres of production. The real profit deviates from the ideal average level, which is established only by a continuous process, a reaction, and this only takes place during long periods of circulation of capital. The rate of profit is in certain spheres higher in some years, while it is lower in succeeding years. Taking the years together, or taking a series of such evolutions, one will *in general* obtain the average profit. Thus it never appears as something directly given, but only as the average result of contradictory oscillations. It is different with the rate of interest. In its *generality*, it is a fact which is established daily, a fact which the industrial capitalist regards as a pre-condition and an item of calculation in his operations. The average rate of profit exists indeed only as an ideal *average figure*, insofar as it serves to estimate the real profit; it exists only as an average figure, as an abstraction, insofar as it is established as something which is in itself complete, definite, given. In reality, however, it exists only as the determining tendency in the movement of equalisation of the real, different rates of profit, whether of individual capitals in the same sphere or of different capitals in the different spheres of production.

||897| What the lender demands of the capitalist is calculated on the *general* (average) *rate of profit*, not on individual deviations from it. Here the *average* becomes the *pre-condition*. The rate of interest itself *varies*, but does so for all *borrowers*.

A definite, equal rate of interest, on the other hand, exists not only on the average but in actual fact (even though it is accompanied by variations between minimum and maximum rates according to whether or not the borrower is first-rate) and the deviations appear rather as exceptions brought about by special circumstances. The meteorological bulletins do not indicate the state of the barometer more exactly than stock-exchange bulletins do the state of interest rates, not for this or that capital, but for the capital *available on the money market, that is*, capital *available for lending.*

This is not the place to go into the reasons for this greater stability and equality of the rate of interest on loan capital in contradistinction to the less tangible form of the general rate of profit. Such a discussion belongs to the section on credit. But this much is obvious: the fluctuations in the *rate of profit* in every sphere—quite apart from the special advantages which individual capitalists in the same sphere of production may enjoy—depend on the existing level of market prices and their fluctuations around cost-prices. The difference in the *rates of profit* in the *various* spheres can only be discerned by comparison of the market prices in the different spheres, that is, the market prices of the *different* commodities, with the cost-prices of these commodities. A decline in the rate of profit below the ideal average in any particular sphere, if prolonged, suffices to bring about a withdrawal of capital from this sphere, or to prevent the entry of the average amount of new capital into it. For it is the inflow of new, additional capital, even more than the redistribution of capital already invested, that equalises the distribution of capital in the different spheres. The *surplus profit* in the different spheres, on the other hand, is discernible only by comparison of the market prices with cost-prices. As soon as any difference becomes apparent in one way or another, then an outflow or inflow of capital from or to the particular spheres [begins]. Apart from the fact that this act of equalisation requires time, the average profit in each sphere becomes evident only in the average profit rates obtained, for example, over a cycle of seven years, etc., according to the nature of the capital. Mere fluctuations—*below* and *above* [the general rate of profit]—if they do not exceed the average extent and do not assume extraordinary forms, are therefore not sufficient to bring about a transfer of capital, and in addition the transfer of fixed capital presents certain difficulties. Momentary booms can only have a limited effect, and are more likely to attract or repel additional capital than to bring about a redistribution of the capital invested in the different spheres.

One can see that all this involves a very complex movement in which, on the one hand, the market prices in each particular sphere, the relative cost-prices of the different commodities, the position with regard to demand and supply within each individual sphere, and, on the other hand, competition among the capitalists in the different spheres, play a part, and, in addition, the speed of the equalisation process, whether it is quicker or slower, depends on the particular organic composition of the different capitals (more fixed or circulating capital, for example) and on the particular nature of their commodities, that is, whether their nature as use-values facilitates rapid withdrawal from the market and the diminution or increase of supply, in accordance with the level of the market prices.

In the case of money capital on the other hand, only two sorts of buyers and sellers, only two types of demand and supply, confront each other on the money market. On the one side, the borrowing class of capitalists—on the other, the money-lenders. The commodity has only one form—money. All the different forms assumed by capital according to the different spheres of production or circulation in which it is invested, are obliterated here. It exists here in the undifferentiated, always identical form, that of independent exchange-value, i.e., of money. Here competition between the different spheres ceases; they are all lumped together as borrowers of money, and capital too confronts them all in a form in which it is still indifferent to the way it is utilised. Whereas productive capital ||898| *emerges only in the movement of competition between the different spheres as the joint capital of the whole class, capital here actually—as regards the pressure exerted—acts as such in the demand for capital.* On the other hand, money capital (the capital on the money market) really possesses the form which enables it as a common element, irrespective of its particular employment, to be distributed amongst the different spheres, amongst the capitalist class, according to the production needs of each separate sphere. With the development of large-scale industry, moreover, money capital, insofar as it appears on the market, is represented less and less by the individual capitalist, the owner of this or that parcel of capital available on the market, but is concentrated, organised and is [subject] in quite a different way from real production to the control of a banker who represents the capital. So that insofar as the form of the demand is concerned, the pressure of a class confronts it [loan capital]; and as far as supply is concerned, it appears as loan capital *en masse*, the loan capital of society, concentrated in a few reservoirs.

These are some of the reasons why the *general rate of profit* appears as a hazy mirage in contrast to the *fixed rate of interest* which, although it fluctuates in magnitude, nevertheless fluctuates in the same measure for all borrowers and therefore always confronts them as something fixed, given; just as money despite the changes in its value has the same value for all commodities. Just as the market prices of commodities fluctuate daily, which does not prevent them from being *quoted* daily, so it is with the rate of interest, which is likewise quoted regularly as the *price* of money. This is the established price of capital, for capital is here offered as a special kind of commodity—*money*—and consequently its *market price* is established in the same way as that of all other commodities. The rate of interest is therefore always expressed as the *general rate of interest*, as a fixed amount [to be paid] for a certain amount of money; whereas the rate of profit within a *particular* sphere may vary although the market prices of commodities are the same (depending on the conditions under which individual capitals produce the same commodities; since the individual rate of profit does not depend on the market price of the commodity but on the difference between the market price and the cost-price) and it is equalised in the different spheres in the course of operations only as a result of constant fluctuations. In short, only in moneyed capital, the capital which can be lent, does capital become a *commodity*, whose quality of selfexpansion has a *fixed price*, which is quoted as the prevailing rate of interest.

Thus capital acquires its pure fetish form in *interest-bearing* capital, and indeed in its direct form of *interest-bearing money capital* (the other forms of interest-bearing capital, which do not concern us here, are in turn derived from this form and presuppose it). *Firstly*, as a result of its continuous existence as *money*, a form in which all its determining features are obliterated and its real elements invisible; in this form it represents merely independent exchange-value, value which has become independent. The money form is a transient form in the real process of capital. On the money market capital always exists in this form. *Secondly*, the surplus-value it produces, which [here] again assumes the form of money, seems to accrue to capital as such, consequently to the mere owner of money capital, i.e., of capital separated from its process. Here M—C—M' becomes M—M', and just as its form here is the undifferentiated money form (for money is precisely the form in which the differences between commodities as use-values are obliterated, consequently also the *differences between productive capitals, which are made up of the conditions of existence of these commodities, the particular forms of the productive capitals themselves are obliterated*) so the surplus-value it produces, the surplus money which it is or which it becomes, appears as a definite rate measured by the amount of the money. If the rate of interest is 5 per cent, then £100 used as capital becomes £105. This is the quite tangible form of self-expanding value or of money-making money, and at the same time the quite irrational form, the incomprehensible, mystified form. In the discussion of capital we started from M—C—M, of which M—M' was only the result.[131] We now find M—M' *as the subject*. Just as growth is characteristic of trees, so money-bearing (τόχος)[a] is characteristic of capital in this, its pure form as money [capital]. The incomprehensible superficial form we encounter and which has therefore constituted the starting-point of our analysis, is found again as the result of the process in which the form of

---

[a] *Tokos*—to bear, produce, the product; figuratively: interest on money lent.—*Ed.*

capital is gradually more and more alienated and rendered independent of its inner substance.

||899| We started with money as the converted form of the commodity. What we arrive at is *money as the converted form of capital*, just as we have perceived that the commodity is the pre-condition and the result of the production process of capital.

This aspect of capital, which is the most fantastic and at the same time comes nearest to the popular notion of it, is both regarded as the "basic form" by the vulgar economists and made the first point of attack by superficial critics; the former, partly because the inner connections are least apparent here and capital emerges in a form in which it *appears* to be an independent source of value, partly because its *contradictory* character is totally concealed and effaced in this form and no contradiction to labour [is evident]. On the other hand, [capital is subjected to] attack because it is the form in which it is at its most irrational and provides the easiest point of attack for the vulgar socialists.

The polemic waged by the bourgeois economists of the seventeenth century (Child, Culpeper and others) against interest as an independent form of surplus-value merely reflects the struggle of the rising industrial bourgeoisie against the old-fashioned usurers, who monopolised the pecuniary resources at that time. Interest-bearing capital in this case is still an antediluvian form of capital which has yet to be subordinated to industrial capital and to acquire the dependent position which it must assume— theoretically and practically—on the basis of capitalist production. The bourgeoisie did not hesitate to accept State aid in this as in other cases, where it was a question of making the traditional production relations which it found, adequate to its own.

It is clear that any other kind of division of profit between various kinds of capitalists, that is, increasing the industrial profit by reducing the rate of interest and vice versa, does not affect the essence of capitalist production in any way. The kind of socialism which attacks interest-bearing capital as the "basic form" of capital not only remains completely within the bounds of the bourgeois horizon. Insofar **as** its polemic is not a misconceived attack and criticism prompted by a vague notion and directed against capital itself, though identifying it with one of its derived forms, it is nothing but a drive, disguised as socialism, for the development of bourgeois credit and consequently only expresses the low level of development of the existing conditions in a country where such a polemic can masquerade as socialist and is itself only a theoretical symptom of capitalist development although this bourgeois striving can assume quite startling forms such as that of *"crédit gratuit"*[a] for example.[132] The same applies to Saint-Simonism with its glorification of banking (*Crédit mobilier*[133] later).

[2.] Interest-Bearing Capital and Commercial Capital in Relation to Industrial Capital. Older Forms. Derived Forms

The commercial and interest-bearing forms of capital are older than industrial capital, which, in the capitalist mode of production, is the *basic form* of the capital relations dominating bourgeois society—and all other forms are only derived from it or secondary: derived as is the case with interest-bearing capital; secondary means that the capital fulfils a special function (which belongs to the circulation process) as for instance commercial capital. In the course of its evolution, industrial capital must therefore subjugate these forms and transform them into derived or special functions of itself. It encounters these older forms in the epoch of its formation and development. It encounters them as *antecedents*, but not as antecedents established by itself, not as forms of its own life-process. In the same way as it originally finds the commodity already in existence, but not as its own product, and likewise finds money circulation, but not as an element in its own reproduction. Where capitalist production has developed all its manifold forms and has become the dominant mode of production, interest-bearing capital is dominated by industrial capital, and commercial capital becomes merely a form of industrial capital, derived from the circulation process. But both of them must first be destroyed as independent forms ||900| and subordinated to industrial capital. Violence (the State) is used against interest-bearing capital by means of compulsory reduction of interest rates, so that it is no longer able to dictate terms to industrial capital. But this is a method characteristic of the least developed stages of capitalist production. The real way in which industrial capital subjugates interest-bearing capital is the creation of a procedure specific to itself— the *credit system*. The compulsory reduction of interest rates

---

[a] Free credit.—*Ed.*

is a measure which industrial capital itself borrows from the methods of an earlier mode of production and which it rejects as useless and inexpedient as soon as it becomes strong and conquers its territory. The *credit system* is its own creation, and is itself a form of industrial capital which begins with manufacture and develops further with large-scale industry. The credit system originally is a *polemical form* directed against the old-fashioned usurers (goldsmiths in England, Jews, Lombards, and others). The seventeenth-century writings in which its first mysteries are discussed are all produced in this polemical form.

Commercial capital is subordinated to industrial capital in various ways or, what amounts to the same thing, [it becomes] a function of the latter, it is industrial capital engaged in a special function. The *merchant*, instead of buying commodities, buys wage-labour with which he produces the commodities which he intends to sell on the market. But commercial capital thereby loses the fixed form which it previously possessed in contrast to production. This was the way the medieval guilds were undermined by manufacture and the handicrafts confined to a narrower sphere. The *merchant* in the Middle Ages was simply a *dealer in commodities* produced either by the town guilds or by the peasants (apart from sporadic areas where manufacture developed, for instance in Italy and Spain).

The transformation of the merchant into an industrial capitalist is at the same time the transformation of commercial capital into a mere form of industrial capital. The *producer*, conversely, becomes a merchant. For example, the cloth producer himself buys material in accordance with the size of his capital, etc., instead of gradually obtaining his material in small amounts from the merchant and working for him. The conditions of production enter into the process [of production] as commodities which he himself has bought. And instead of producing for individual merchants or for particular customers, he now produces for the world of commerce.

In the first form, the merchant dominates production and commercial capital dominates the handicrafts and rural domestic industry which it sets in motion. The crafts are subordinated to him. In the second form, production becomes capitalist production. The producer is himself a merchant, merchant capital now acts as an intermediary only in the circulation process, thus fulfilling a definite function in the reproduction process of capital. These are the two forms. The merchant as such becomes a producer, an industrialist. The industrialist, the producer, becomes a merchant.

Originally, *trade* is the pre-condition for the transformation of guild, rural domestic and feudal agricultural production into capitalist production. It develops the product into a commodity, partly by creating a market for it, partly by giving rise to new commodity equivalents and partly by supplying production with new materials and thereby initiating new kinds of production which are based on trade from the very beginning because they depend both on production for the market and on elements of production derived from the world market.

As soon as manufacture gains strength (and this applies to an even greater extent to large-scale industry), it in turn creates the market, conquers it, opens up, partly by force, markets which it conquers, however, by means of its *commodities.* From now on, trade is merely a servant of industrial production for which a constantly expanding market has become a very condition of existence, since constantly expanding mass production, circumscribed not by the existing limits of trade (insofar as trade is only an expression of the existing level of demand), but solely by the amount of capital available and the level of productivity of the workers, always floods the existing market and consequently seeks constantly to expand and remove its boundaries. Trade is now the servant of industrial capital, and carries out one of the functions emanating from the conditions of production of industrial capital.

During its first stages of development, industrial capital seeks to secure a market and markets by force, by the *colonial system* (together with the prohibition system). The industrial capitalist faces the world market; [he] therefore compares ||901| and must constantly compare his own cost-prices with market prices not only at home, but also on the whole market of the world. He always produces taking this into account. In the earlier period this comparison is carried out only by the merchants, thus enabling merchant capital to dominate over productive [capital]. |901||

* * *

||902| *Interest* is therefore nothing but a part of the profit (which, in its turn, is itself nothing but surplus-value, unpaid labour), which the industrial capitalist pays to the owner of the borrowed capital with which he "works", either exclusively

or partially. Interest is a part of profit—of surplus-value—which, established as a special category, is separated from the total profit under its own name, a separation which is by no means based on its origin, but only on the manner in which it is *paid out* or appropriated. Instead of being appropriated by the industrial capitalist himself—although he is the person who at first holds the whole surplus-value in his hands no matter how it may be distributed between himself and other people under the names of rent, industrial profit and interest—this part of the profit is deducted by the industrial capitalist from his own revenue and paid to the owner of capital.

If the rate of profit is given, then the relative level of the rate of interest depends on the ratio in which profit is divided between interest and industrial profit. If the ratio of this division is given, then the absolute level of the rate of interest (that is, the ratio of interest to capital) depends on the rate of profit. It is not intended to investigate here how this ratio is determined. This belongs to the section dealing with the real movement of capital, i.e., of capitals, while we are concerned here with the general forms of capital.

The formation of interest-bearing capital, its separation from industrial capital, is a *necessary* product of the development of industrial capital, of the capitalist mode of production itself. Money (a sum of value, which is always convertible into the conditions of production) or the conditions of production into which it can be converted at any time and of which it is only the converted form—money employed as capital, commands a definite quantity of other people's labour, more labour than it itself contains. It not only preserves its value in exchange with labour, but increases it, produces surplus-value. The value of money or of commodities as *capital* is not determined by the value they possess as money or as commodities, but by the amount of surplus-value which they "produce" for their owners. The product of capital is profit. On the basis of capitalist production, whether money is spent as money or as capital depends only on the different ways in which money is *employed.* Money (a commodity) *in itself* is capital on the basis of capitalist production (just as *labour-power in itself* is labour) since, first, it can be converted into the conditions of production and is, as it exists, only an abstract expression of them, their existence as *value*; and secondly, the material elements of wealth in themselves possess the property of being capital because their opposite—wage-labour-which turns them into capital—is present as the basis for social production.

Rent is likewise simply a name for a part of the surplus-value which the industrialist has to pay out, in the same way as *interest* is another part of surplus-value which, although it accrues to him (like rent), has to be handed over to someone else. But the great difference here is the following: through landed property, the landowner *prevents* capital from making the value of agricultural products equal to their cost-price. Monopoly of landed property enables the landowner to do this. It enables him to pocket the difference between value and cost-price. On the other hand—as far as differential rent is concerned—this monopoly enables the landowner to pocket the excess of the market value over the individual value of the product of a particular piece of land· in contrast to the other spheres of production, where this difference in the form of surplus profit flows into the pockets of the capitalists who operate under more favourable conditions than the average conditions which satisfy the greater part of demand, thus determining the bulk of production and consequently regulating the market value of each particular sphere of production.

Landed property is a *means* for grabbing a part of the surplus-value produced by industrial capital. On the other hand, loan *capital*—to the extent that the capitalist operates with borrowed capital—is a means for producing the *whole* of the ||903| surplus-value. That money (commodities) can be loaned out as capital means nothing more than that it is *itself* capital. The abolition of landed property in the Ricardian sense, that is, its conversion into State property so that rent is paid to the State instead of to the landlord, is the ideal, the heart's desire, which springs from the deepest, inmost essence of capital. Capital cannot abolish landed property. But by converting it into rent [which is paid to the State] the capitalists as a *class* appropriate it and use it to defray their State expenses, thus appropriating in a roundabout way what cannot be retained directly. Abolition of interest and of interest-bearing capital, on the other hand, means the abolition of capital and of capitalist production itself. As long as money (commodities) can serve as capital, it can be sold as capital. It is therefore quite in keeping with the views of the petty-bourgeois Utopians that they want to keep commodities but not money, industrial capital but not interest-bearing capital, profit but not interest.

There are not two different kinds of capital—interest-bearing and profit-yielding—but *the selfsame* capital which operates in the process of production as capital, produces a profit which is divided between two different capitalists—one standing outside the process, and, as owner, representing capital *as such* ⟨but it is an essential condition of this capital that it is represented by a *private owner*; without this it does not become capital as opposed to wage-labour⟩, and the other representing operating capital, capital which takes part in the production process.

[3. The Separation of Individual Parts of Surplus-Value in the Form of Different Revenues. The Relation of Interest to Industrial Profit. The Irrationality of the Fetishised Forms of Revenue]

The further "ossification" or transformation of the *division* of profit into something independent appears in such a way that the *profit on e v e r y single* capital—and therefore also the *average profit* based on the equalisation of capitals—is split or divided into two component parts separated from, or independent of, each other, namely, interest and industrial profit, which is now sometimes called simply *profit* or acquires new names such as *wages of labour of superintendence*, etc. If the rate of profit (average profit) is 15 per cent and the *rate of interest* (which, as we have seen, is always established in the *general* form) is 5 per cent (the general rate being always quoted in the money market as the "value" or "price" of money), then the capitalist—even when he is the owner of the capital and has not *borrowed* any part of it, so that the profit does not have to be divided between two capitalists—considers that 5 per cent of the 15 per cent represents *interest* on his capital, and only 10 per cent represents the profit he makes by the productive employment of the capital. This 5 per cent interest, which he as an "industrial capitalist" owes to himself as "owner" of the capital, is due to his *capital as such*, and consequently it is due to him as owner of the *capital as such* (which is at one and the same time the existence of capital in itself, or the existence of capital as the capitalist, as property which debars other people from owning it), capital abstracted from the production process as opposed to operating capital, capital involved in the production process, and to the "industrial capitalist" as representative of this operating, "working" capital.

"Interest" is the fruit of capital insofar as it does not "work" or operate, and profit is the fruit of "working", operating capital. This is similar to the way in which the farming capitalist—who is at the same time also a landowner, the owner of the soil which he exploits in capitalist fashion—assigns that part of his profit which constitutes *rent*, this surplus profit, to himself not as capitalist but as landowner, attributing it not to capital but to landed property so that he, the capitalist, owes himself "rent" as a landowner. Thus one aspect of capital confronts another aspect of the same capital just as rigidly as do landed property and capital which, in fact, constitute the separate claims to appropriation of other people's labour which are based on two essentially different means of production.

If, on the one hand, five partners own a cotton mill which represents a capital of £100,000 and yields a profit of 10 per cent, that is, £10,000, then each of them gets a fifth of the profit or £2,000. On the other hand, if a single capitalist invested the same amount of capital in a mill and made the same amount of profit—£10,000—he would not consider that he received £2,000 profit as a partner and the other £8,000 company profit for the nonexistent four partners. Consequently, in itself the *mere division of profit* between different ||904| capitalists who have different legal claims on the same capital and who are in one way or another joint owners of *the same* capital, does not by any means establish different categories for the separate portions. Why then should the accidental division between lender and borrower of capital do so?

Prima facie it is simply a question of the division of profit when there are two owners of the capital with different titles—a *prima facie* legal, but not economic aspect. In itself it makes no difference at all whether a capitalist produces with his own or with other people's capital or in what proportion he uses his own capital to that of other people. How does it happen that this division of profit into [industrial] profit and interest does not appear as an accidental division, dependent on the accident whether or not the capitalist really has a share with *someone else*, or on whether he by chance is operating with his own or with someone else's capital, but that, on the contrary, even when he operates exclusively with his own capital, he in any case splits himself into two—into a mere owner of capital and into a user of capital, into capital which is outside the production process and capital which takes part in the production process, into capital which *as such* yields interest and capital which yields profit because it is *used in the production process?*

There is a real reason at the root of this. Money (as an expression of the value of commodities in general) in the [production] process appropriates surplus-value, no matter what name it bears or whatever parts it is split into, because it is already presupposed as *capital before* the production process. It maintains, produces and reproduces itself as capital *in* the process [of production] and moreover on a continually expanding scale. Once the capitalist mode of production is given and work is undertaken on this basis and within the social relations which correspond to it, that is, when it is not a question of the process of formation of capital, then even *before* the [production] process begins money as such is *capital* by its very nature, which, however, is only realised in the process ·and indeed only becomes a reality in the process itself. If it did not enter into the process as capital it would not emerge from it as capital, that is, as profity-ielding money, as self-expanding value, as value which produces surplus-value.

It is the same as with money. For example, this coin is nothing but a piece of metal. It is only money in virtue of its function in the circulation process. But if the existence of the circulation process of commodities is presupposed, the coin not only functions as money, but as such it is in every single case a pre-condition for the circulation process before it enters into it. Capital is not only the result of, but the pre-condition for, capitalist production. Money and commodities as such are therefore latent capital, potential capital; this applies to all commodities insofar as they are convertible into money, and to money insofar as it is convertible into those commodities which constitute the elements of the capitalist process of production. Thus money —as the pure expression of the value of commodities and of the conditions of labour—is itself as capital antecedent to capitalist production. What is capital regarded not as the result of, but as the prerequisite for, the process [of production]? What makes it capital before it enters the process so that the latter merely develops its immanent character? The social framework in which it exists. The fact that living labour is confronted by past labour, activity is confronted by the product, man is confronted by things, labour is confronted by its own materialised conditions as alien, independent, self-contained subjects, personifications, in short, as *someone else's property* and, in this form, as "employers" and "commanders" of labour itself, which they appropriate instead of being appropriated by it. The fact that value—whether it exists as money or as commodities—and in the further development the conditions of labour confront the worker as the *property of other people*, as independent properties, means simply that they confront him as the *property* of the non-worker or, at any rate, that, as a capitalist, he confronts them [the conditions of labour] not as a worker but as the *owner* of value, etc., as the *subject* in which these things possess their own will, belong to themselves and are personified as independent forces. *Capital* as the prerequisite of production, capital, not in the form in which it emerges from the production process, but as it is before it enters it, [is] the contradiction in which it is confronted by labour as the labour of other people and in which capital itself, as the property of other people, confronts labour. It is the contradictory social framework which is expressed in it and which, separated from the [production] process itself, ||905| expresses itself in *capitalist property as such*.

This aspect—separated from the capitalist production process itself of which it is the constant result, and as its constant result it is also its constant prerequisite—manifests itself in the fact that money [and] commodities are as such, *latently*, capital, that they can be *sold as capital*, and that in this form they represent the *mere ownership of capital*, and the *capitalist as the mere owner*, apart from his capitalist functions. Money and commodities considered as such constitute command over other people's labour, and therefore self-expanding value and a claim to the appropriation of other people's labour.

It is thus quite obvious that the title to and the means for the appropriation of other people's labour is this *relationship* and not some kind of labour or equivalent supplied by the capitalist.

Interest therefore appears as the *surplus-value* due to capital as capital, to the mere ownership of capital, as the surplus-value derived by capital from the production process because it enters it as capital, and therefore due to capital *as such* independently of the production process, although it is only realised *in* the production process; capital thus already contains the surplus-value in a latent form. On the other hand, *industrial profit* [appears] as the portion of surplus-value accruing to the capitalist not as the owner of capital, but as the operating owner representing the operating capital. In the same way as everything in this mode of production appears to be upside down, so likewise does the final reversal in the relation of interest to profit, so that the portion of profit separated under a special heading [interest] appears as the product intrinsically belonging to capital, and industrial profit appears as a mere addition appended to it.

Since the moneyed capitalist in fact receives his part of the surplus-value only as *owner of capital*, while he himself remains outside the production process; since the price of capital—that is, of the mere title to ownership of capital—is quoted on the money market as the rate of interest in the same way as the market price of any other commodity; since the share of surplus-value which *capital as such*, the *mere ownership* of capital, secures is thus of a *stable* magnitude, whereas the rate of profit fluctuates, at any given moment it varies in the different spheres of production and within each sphere it is different for the individual capitalists, partly because the conditions under which they produce are more or less favourable, partly because they exploit labour in capitalist fashion with different degrees of circumspection and energy, and partly because they cheat buyers or sellers of commodities with different degrees of luck and cunning (profit upon expropriation, alienation)—it therefore appears natural to them, whether they are or are not owners of the capital involved in the production process, that *interest* is something due to capital as such, to the ownership of capital, to the owner of capital, whether they themselves own the capital or someone else; industrial profit, on the other hand, appears to be the result of *their* labour. As operating capitalists—as real agents of capitalist production—they therefore confront themselves or others representing merely idle capital, as *workers* they consequently confront themselves and others as *property owners*. And since they are, as matters stand, workers, they are in fact wage-workers, and because of their superiority they are simply better-paid workers, which they owe partly also to the fact that they pay themselves their wages.

Whereas, therefore, *interest* and *interest-bearing capital* merely express the contradiction of materialised wealth as against labour, and thereby its existence as *capital*, this position is turned upside down in the consciousness of men because, *prima facie*, the *moneyed capitalist* does not appear to have any relations with the wage-worker, but only with other capitalists, while these other capitalists, instead of appearing to be in opposition to the wage-workers, appear rather as *workers*, in opposition to themselves or to other [capitalists] considered as mere owners of capital, representing the mere existence of capital. The individual capitalist, moreover, can either lend his money *as capital* or employ it *himself* as capital. Insofar as he obtains *interest* on it, he only receives for it the price which he would receive if he did not "operate" as a capitalist, if he did not "work". It is clear, therefore, that what he really gets from the production process—insofar as it is only interest—is due to capital alone, not to the production process itself and ||906| not to himself as a representative of operating capital.

Hence also the pretty phrases used by some vulgar economists to the effect that, if the industrial capitalist did not get any profit in addition to interest, he would lend his capital out for interest and become a rentier, so that all capitalists would stop producing and all capital would cease operating as capital, but nevertheless it would still be possible to live *on the interest*. In similar vein, Turgot has already [said] that if the capitalist received no interest, he would buy land (capitalised rent) and live off rent.[134] But in this case the interest would still be derived from surplus-value, since for the Physiocrats rent represents the real surplus-value. Whereas in that vulgarised concept things are turned upside down.

Another fact should be noted. Interest is part of the *costs* for the industrial capitalist who has borrowed money, the term costs is here used in the sense that it represents the value advanced. For example, a capital of £1,000 does not enter the capitalist production process as a commodity worth £1,000 but as *capital*, this means that if a capital of £1,000 yields 10 per cent interest per annum, then it enters into the annual product as a value of £1,100. This shows clearly that the *sum of values* (and the commodities in which it is embodied) becomes capital not only in the production process but that, as capital, it is antecedent to the production process and therefore already contains within itself the surplus-value due to it as mere capital. For the industrial capitalist who operates with borrowed capital, interest, in other words capital as capital—and it is this only insofar as it yields surplus-value (so that if it is worth £1,000 as a commodity, for example, it is worth £1,100 as capital, i.e., $1{,}000+\frac{1{,}000}{10}$, $C+\frac{C}{x}$)

—enters into his costs. If the product only yielded interest, this, though it would be a surplus over and above the *value* of the capital employed, regarded as a mere commodity, would not be a surplus over and above the value of the commodity considered as capital, for the capitalist has to pay out this surplus-value;

it is part of his outlay, part of the expenses he has incurred in order to produce the commodities.

As far as the industrialist who operates with his own capital is concerned, he pays the interest on his capital to himself and regards the interest as part of his outlay. In fact, what he has advanced is not simply a capital of £1,000 for example, but the value of £1,000 as capital, and this value would be £1,050 if the rate of interest were 5 per cent. This is moreover no idle consideration as far as he is concerned. For the £1,000 used as *capital* would yield him £1,050 if he lent it out instead of employing it productively. Thus, insofar as he advances the £1,000 to himself as capital, he is advancing himself £1,050. *Il faut bien se rattraper sur quelqu'un et fusse-t-il sur lui même!*[a]

The value of commodities worth £1,000 is £1,050 as capital. This means that capital is not a simple quantity. It is not a simple commodity, but a commodity raised to a higher power; not a simple magnitude, but a proportion. It is a proportion of the principal, a given value, to itself as surplus-value. The value of C is $C\left(1+\frac{1}{x}\right)$ (for one year) or $C+\frac{C}{x}$. It is no more possible by means of the elementary rules of calculation to understand capital, that is, the commodity raised to a higher power, or money raised to a higher power, than it is to understand or to calculate the value of x in the equation $a^x = n$.

Just as in the case of *interest*, part of the profit, of the surplus-value produced by capital, appears to have been *advanced* by the capitalist, so also in agricultural production another part of surplus-value—*rent*—appears to have been advanced. This seems to be less obviously irrational because in this case rent appears to be the annual price of the land which thus enters into production as a commodity. A "price of land" is indeed even more irrational than a price of capital, but this is not apparent in the form as such. Because in this case the land appears to be the use-value of a commodity and the rent its price. (The irrationality consists in this, that land, i.e., something which is not the product of human labour, has a price, that is, a value expressed in money and consequently a value, and is therefore to be regarded as materialised social labour.) Considered purely formally, land, just as any other commodity, is expressed in two ways,

---

[a] One must, after all, recover what is due to oneself, even if one takes it out of one's own pocket.—*Ed.*

as use-value and as exchange-value, and the exchange-value is expressed nominally as price, that is, as something which the commodity as use-value is absolutely not. On the other hand, in the statement: [a capital of] £1,000 equals £1,050, or £50 is the annual price of £1,000, something is compared with itself, exchange-value with exchange-value, and the exchange-value as something different from itself is supposed to be its own price, that is, the exchange-value expressed in money.

||907| Thus two forms of surplus-value—interest and rent, the results of capitalist production—enter into it as prerequisites, as *advances* which the capitalist himself makes; for him, therefore, they do not represent any surplus-value, i.e., any surplus over and above the advances made. As far as these forms of surplus-value are concerned, it *appears* to the individual capitalist that the production of surplus-value is a part of the *production costs* of capitalist production, and that the appropriation of other people's labour and of the surplus over and above the value of the commodities consumed in the process (whether these enter into the constant or into the variable capital) is a dominating condition of this mode of production. To a certain extent this applies also to average profit, insofar as it constitutes an element of cost-price, and hence a condition of supply, of the very creation of the commodity. Nevertheless, the industrial capitalist rightly regards this surplus, this part of surplus-value—although it constitutes an element of production—as a surplus over *his* costs; he does not regard it as belonging to *his* advances in the same way as interest and rent. In critical moments, profit too confronts the capitalist in fact as a condition of production, since he curtails or stops production when profit disappears or is reduced to a marked degree as a result of a fall in prices. Hence the nonsensical pronouncements of those who consider the different forms of surplus-value to be merely forms of distribution; they are just as much forms of production. |907||

* * *

||937| It might appear that in the trinity land—rent, capital—profit (interest), labour—wages, the last group is the most rational. At least it states the source from which wages flow. But it is on the contrary the most irrational of them all, and the basis for the other two, in the same way as *wage-labour* in general presupposes land in the form of *landed property* and the product

in the form of *capital*. Only when labour confronts its conditions [of production] in this form, is it wage-labour. As wage-labour it is defined by the formula labour—wages. Since wages here appear to be the specific product of labour, its sole product (and they are indeed the sole product of labour *for* the wage-worker), the other parts of value—*rent* and *profit* (*interest*)—appear to flow just as necessarily from other specific sources. And just as that part of the value of the product which consists of wages [is conceived] as the *specific* product of labour, so those parts of value which are made up of rent and profit must be regarded as specific results of agencies *for* which they exist and to which they accrue, that is, as offspring of the earth and of capital, respectively. |937||

[4. The Process of Ossification of the Converted Forms of Surplus-Value and Their Ever Greater Separation from Their Inner Substance—Surplus Labour. Industrial Profit as "Wages for the Capitalist"]

||910| Let us consider the road travelled by capital before it appears in the form of interest-bearing capital.

In the immediate process of production, the matter is fairly simple. Surplus-value has not as yet assumed a *separate* form, apart from the fact that it is surplus-value as distinct from the value which is equivalent to the value reproduced in the product. In the same way as value in general consists of labour, so surplus-value consists of surplus labour, unpaid labour. Hence surplus-value is only measured by that part of capital which really changes its value—the variable capital, i.e., the capital which is laid out in wages. Constant capital appears only as the condition enabling the variable part of capital to operate. It is quite simple: if with £100, i.e., the labour of 10 [men], one buys the labour of 20 [men] (that is, commodities in which the labour of 20 [men] is embodied), the value of the product will be £200 and the surplus-value will amount to £100, equal to the unpaid labour of 10 [men]. Or, supposing 20 men worked half a day each for themselves and half for capital—20 half-days equal 10 whole ones—the result would be the same as if only 10 men were paid and the others worked for the capitalist gratis.

Here, in this embryonic state, the relationship is still very obvious, or rather it cannot be misunderstood. The difficulty is simply to discover how this appropriation of labour without any equivalent arises from the law of commodity exchange—

out of the fact that commodities exchange for one another in proportion to the amount of labour-time embodied in them — and, to start with, does not contradict this law.

||911| The circulation process obliterates and obscures the connection. Since here the mass of surplus-value is also determined by the *circulation time of capital*, an element foreign to labour-time seems to have entered.

Finally, in capital as the finished phenomenon, as it appears as a whole, [as] the unity of the circulation and the production process, as the expression of the reproduction process—as a definite sum of values which produces a definite amount of profit (surplus-value) in a definite time, a definite period of circulation—in capital in this form the production and circulation processes exist only as a reminiscence and as aspects which determine the surplus-value *equally*, thereby disguising its simple nature. Surplus-value now appears as profit. This profit is, first, received for a definite period of circulation of capital, and this period is distinct from the labour-time; it is, secondly, surplus-value calculated and drawn not on that part of capital from which it originates directly, but quite indiscriminately on the total capital. In this way its source is completely concealed. Thirdly, although the mass of profit is still quantitatively identical in this first form of profit with the mass of surplus-value produced by the individual capital, the rate of profit is, from the very beginning, different from the rate of surplus-value; since the rate of surplus-value is $\frac{s}{v}$ and the rate of profit is $\frac{s}{c+v}$. Fourthly, if the rate of surplus-value is presumed given, it is possible for the rate of profit to rise or to fall and even to move in the opposite direction to the rate of surplus-value.

Thus, surplus-value in the first form of profit already assumes a form which not only makes it difficult to perceive that it is identical with surplus-value, i.e., surplus labour, but appears directly to contradict this view.

Furthermore, as a result of the conversion of profit into *average profit*, the establishment of the general rate of profit and, in connection with it and determined by it, the conversion of values into cost-prices, the profit of the individual capital becomes *different* from the surplus-value produced by the individual capital in its particular sphere of production, and *different*, moreover, not only in the way it is expressed—i.e., rate of profit as distinct from rate of surplus-value—but it becomes substantially *different*, that is, in this context, quantitatively *different*. Profit does not merely *seem* to be different, but *is* now in fact different from surplus-value not only with regard to the individual capital but also with regard to the total capital in a particular sphere of production. Capitals of equal magnitude yield equal profits; in other words, profit is proportional to the size of the capital. Or profit is determined by the amount of capital advanced. The relation of profit to the organic composition of capital is completely obliterated and no longer recognisable in all these formulae. On the other hand, it is quite obvious that capitals of the same magnitude which set in motion very different amounts of labour, thus commanding very different amounts of surplus labour and consequently producing very different amounts of surplus-value, yield the same amount of profit. Indeed, the basis itself—the determination of the value of commodities by the labour-time embodied in them—appears to be invalidated as a result of the conversion of values into cost-prices.

In this quite alienated form of profit and in the same measure as the form of profit hides its inner core, capital more and more acquires a material form, is transformed more and more from a relationship into a thing, but a thing which embodies, which has absorbed, the social relationship, a thing which has acquired a fictitious life and independent existence in relation to itself, a natural-supernatural entity; in this form of *capital and profit* it appears superficially as a ready-made pre-condition. It is the form of its reality, or rather its real form of existence. And it is the form in which it exists in the consciousness and is reflected in the imagination of its representatives, the capitalists.

This fixed and ossified (metamorphosed) form of profit (and thereby of capital as its producer, for capital is the cause and profit is the result; capital is the reason, profit is the effect; capital is the substance, profit is the adjunct; capital is capital only insofar as it yields profit, only insofar as it is a value which produces profit, an additional value)—and therefore also of capital as its cause, capital which maintains itself and expands by means of profit—the external aspect of this ossified form is strengthened even more by the fact that the same process of the equalisation of capital, which gives profit the form of average profit, separates part of it in the form of *rent* as something independent of it and arising from a different foundation, the land. It is true that rent originally emerges as a part of profit which the farmer pays to the landlord. But since this surplus profit is not pocketed by the farmer, and the capital he employs does not differ in any way as capital from other capitals (it is precisely because surplus profit is not derived from capital as such that the farmer pays it to the landlord), the land itself appears to be the source of this part of the value of the commodity (its surplus-value) and the landlord [appears to represent] the land only ||912| as a juridical person.

If the rent is calculated on the capital advanced, then a thread still remains which indicates its origin as a distinct part of profit, that is, of surplus-value in general. (The position is, of course, quite different in a social order where landed property exploits labour directly. In that case, it is not difficult to recognise the origin of surplus wealth.) But the rent is paid on a definite area of land; it is capitalised in the value of the land; this value rises and falls in accordance with the rise or fall of rent. The rise or fall of rent is calculated with regard to a piece of land which remains unchanged (whereas the amount of capital operating on it changes); the difference in the types of land is reflected in the amount of rent which has to be paid for a given yardage, the total rental is calculated on the total area of the land in order to determine the average rental, for example, of a square yard. Rent, like every phenomenon created by capitalist production, appears at the same time as a stable, given pre-condition existing at any particular moment, and thus, it is for each individual an independently existing magnitude. The farmer has to pay rent, so much per acre of land, according to the quality of the land. If its quality improves or deteriorates, then the rent he has to pay on so many acres rises or falls. He has to pay rent for the land quite irrespective of the capital he employs on it, just as he has to pay interest irrespective of the profit he makes.

The calculation of rent on industrial capital is another important formula of political economy which demonstrates the inner connection between rent and profit, its basis. But this connection does not *appear* in reality, for the calculation of rent is based on the real area of land, the intermediate links are thereby eliminated and rent acquires its externalised independent aspect. It is an independent form only in this externalisation, in its complete separation from its antecedents. So many square yards of land bring in so much rent. In this formula, in which rent, a part of surplus-value, *is represented in relation to a particular natural element, independent of human labour*, not only the nature of surplus-value is completely obliterated, because the nature of value itself is obliterated; but, just as the source of rent appears to be land, so now *profit* itself appears to be due to *capital as a particular material element of production*. Land is part of nature and brings in rent. Capital consists of products and these bring in profit. That one use-value which is produced brings in profit, while another which is not produced brings in rent are simply two forms in which things *produce value*, and the one form is just as comprehensible and as incomprehensible as the other.

It is clear that, as soon as surplus-value [is split up] into different, *separate* parts, related to various production elements— such as nature, products, labour—which only differ *physically*, that is, as soon as in general surplus-value acquires *special* forms, separate from one another, independent of one another and regulated by different laws, the common unit—surplus-value— and consequently the nature of this common unit, becomes more and more unrecognisable and does not manifest itself in the *appearance* but has to be discovered as a hidden mystery. This assumption of independent forms by the various parts — and their confrontation as independent forms—is completed as a result of each of these parts being related to a particular element as its measure and its special source; in other words, each part of surplus-value is conceived as the effect of a special cause, as an adjunct of a particular substance. Thus profit is related to capital, rent to land, wages to labour.

These ready-made relations and forms, which appear as pre-conditions in real production because the capitalist mode of production moves within the forms it has created itself and which are its results, confront it equally as ready-made pre-conditions in the process of reproduction. As such, they in fact determine the actions of individual capitalists, etc., and provide the motives, which are reflected in their consciousness. Vulgar political economy does nothing more than express in doctrinaire fashion this consciousness, which, in respect of its motives and notions, remains in thrall to the appearance of the capitalist mode of production. And the more it clings to the shallow, superficial appearance, only bringing it into some sort of order, the more it considers that it is acting "naturally" and avoiding all abstract subtleties.

||913| In connection with the circulation process dealt with above[a] it has to be added that the categories arising out of the

---

[a] See this volume, pp. 480-81.—*Ed.*

circulation process crystallise as attributes of particular sorts of capital, fixed, circulating and so on, and thus appear as definite material attributes of certain commodities.

In the final state in which profit, assumed as something given, appears in capitalist production, the innumerable transformations and intervening stages through which it passes are obliterated and unrecognisable, and consequently the nature of capital is also unrecognisable. This state becomes even more rigid owing to the fact that the same process which gives it its final finish causes part of the profit to confront it as *rent*, thus transforming profit into a *particular* aspect of surplus-value, an aspect based on capital as a special material instrument of production, in exactly the same way as rent is based on land; thus this state, separated from its inner essence by a mass of invisible intermediate links, reaches an even more *externalised* form, or rather the form of absolute *externalisation*, in interest-bearing capital, in the separation of interest from profit in interest-bearing capital as the simple form of capital, the form in which capital is antecedent to its own reproduction process. On the one hand, this expresses the absolute form of capital M—M', self-expanding value. On the other hand, the intermediate link C, which still exists in genuine merchant capital whose formula is M—C—M', has disappeared. Only the relation of M to itself and measured by itself remains. It is capital expressly removed, separated from the process, as an antecedent it stands outside the process whose result it is and through which alone it is capital.

{ [Here] the fact is disregarded that interest may be a mere transfer and need not represent real surplus-value, as, for example, when money is lent to a "spendthrift", i.e., for consumption. The position may be similar when money is borrowed in order to make *payments.* In both cases it is loaned as money, not as capital, but it becomes *capital* to its owner through the mere act of lending it out. In the second case, [if it is used to] discount [bills] or as a loan on temporarily not vendible commodities, it can be associated with the circulation process of capital, the necessary conversion of commodity capital into money capital. Insofar as the acceleration of this conversion process—such acceleration is a general feature of credit—speeds up reproduction, and therefore the production of surplus-value, the money lent is capital. On the other hand, insofar as it only serves to pay *debts* without accelerating the reproduction process, perhaps even limiting it or making it impossible, it is a mere *means of payment*, only money for the borrower, and for the *lender it is, in fact, capital independent of the process of capital*. In this case interest, like profit upon expropriation, is a fact independent of capitalist production—the production of surplus-value. It is in these two forms of money—money as means of purchase of commodities intended for consumption and as means of payment of debts— that interest, like profit upon expropriation, constitutes a form which, although it is reproduced in capitalist production, is nevertheless independent of it and [represents] a form of interest which belongs to earlier modes of production. It is in the nature of capitalist production, however, that money (or commodities) can exist as capital and can be sold as capital outside the production process, and that this can also be the case with the older forms, which are not converted into capital but only serve as money.

The third of the older forms of interest-bearing capital is based on the fact that capitalist production does *not* as yet exist, but that profit is still acquired in the form of interest and the capitalist appears as a mere usurer. This implies: first, that the producer still works independently with his own means of production, and that the means of production do not yet work with him[a] (even if slaves form a part of these means of production, for in these circumstances slaves do not constitute a separate economic category any more than draught animals do; there is at best a physical difference between them, i.e., dumb instruments, and speaking and feeling instruments); secondly, that the means of production belong only nominally to the producer; in other words, that because of some incidental circumstances he is unable to reproduce them from the proceeds of the sale of his commodities. These forms of interest-bearing capital occur, consequently, in all social formations which include commodity and money circulation, whether slave labour, serf labour or free labour is predominant in them. In the last-mentioned form, the producer pays the capitalist his surplus labour in the form of interest, which therefore includes profit. We have here the whole of ||914| capitalist production without its advantages, the development of the social forms of labour and of the productivity of labour to which they give rise. This form is very prevalent among peasant nations who already have

---

[a] This can also mean: "the means of production do not yet work with it", i.e., capital.—*Ed.*

to buy a portion of the necessaries of life and means of production as commodities (alongside whom, therefore, separate urban industries already exist) and who, in addition, have to pay taxes, rent, etc., in money.}

Interest-bearing capital functions as such only insofar as the money lent is really converted into capital and produces a surplus of which interest constitutes a part. This does not however invalidate the fact that interest and interest-bearing have become attributes of it independently of the [production] process. Any more than the use-value of cotton as cotton is nullified by the fact that it has to be spun or used in some other way, in order to demonstrate its useful properties. And thus capital [demonstrates] its capacity to yield interest only by becoming part of the production process. But labour-power likewise demonstrates its capacity to produce value when it functions as labour, is realised as labour in this process. This does not rule out that, in itself, as a faculty, it is a value-creating activity and does not merely become such as a result of the process, but rather is antecedent to the process. It is bought as such. A person can buy it without setting it to work (as, for example, when a theatre manager hires an actor not in order to give him a role in a play, but to prevent him from performing in a rival theatre). Whether or not a man who buys labour-power uses its faculty for which he pays, i.e., its faculty to create value, is of no concern to the man who sells it, and makes no difference to the commodity sold, just as it makes no difference whether the man who buys capital uses it as such, that is, employs the quality of creating value which is inherent in it, in the [production] process. What he pays for in these two cases is the surplus-value and the capacity of maintaining its own value—potentially, by the very nature of the commodity bought—contained in the capital in the one case and in the labour-power in the other. This is why the capitalist who operates with his own capital regards part of the surplus-value as interest, that is, as surplus-value which is yielded by the production process, because it has been brought into the production process by the capital independently of the process.

Rent and the relationship land—rent may appear as a much more mysterious form than that of interest, [and the relationship] capital—interest. But the irrational element in rent is not formulated in such a way that it expresses a *relation of capital itself*. Since land itself is productive (of use-value) and is itself a living productive force (of use-value or for the creation of use-values), it is possible either superstitiously to confuse use-value with exchange-value, i.e., to confuse it with a specific social form of the labour contained in the product. In this case, the reason for the irrationality lies in itself, since rent as a particular category is independent of the capitalist process as such. Or "enlightened" political economy may deny altogether that rent is a form of surplus-value, because it is not connected with either labour or capital, and declare that it is merely a surcharge which the landowner is able to make as a result of his monopoly of landownership.

The position is different in the case of interest-bearing capital. Here it is a question not of a relation which is alien to capital, but of the capital relation itself; of a relation which arises out of capitalist production, is specific to it, and expresses the essence of capital; of an aspect of capital in which it appears *as capital*. *Profit* is still related to operating capital, to the process in which surplus-value (and profit itself) is produced. Whereas in *profit* the form of surplus-value has become alienated, strange, so that its simple form and therefore its substance and source of origin are not immediately discernible, this is not the case in *interest-bearing capital*; on the contrary it is *precisely* this alienated form which is presupposed and declared to be the *essential* feature of *interest*. The alienated form has assumed an independent and rigid existence as something *antagonistic* to the real nature of surplus-value. The relationship of capital to labour is obliterated in interest-bearing capital. In fact, interest presupposes profit, of which it is only a part. The way in which surplus-value ||915| is divided into interest and profit and distributed between different sorts of capitalists is actually a matter of complete indifference to the worker.

Interest is definitely regarded as the offspring of capital, separate, independent and outside the capitalist process itself. It is due to *capital as capital*. It enters into the production process and therefore proceeds from it. Capital is impregnated with interest. It does not derive interest from the production process, but brings it into it. The surplus of profit over interest, the amount of surplus-value which capital derives solely from the production process, i.e., the surplus-value it produces as operating capital, acquires a separate form, namely, that of *industrial profit* (employer's profit, industrial or commercial, depending on whether the stress is laid on the production process or the circulation process), in contrast to interest, a value created by *capital in itself* and due to *capital*, to *capital as capital*. Thus even the last form of surplus-value, which to some extent recalls its origin, is separated and conceived not only as an alienated form, but as one which is in direct contradiction to its origin; consequently the nature of capital and of surplus-value as well as that of capitalist production in general is, finally, completely mystified.

Industrial profit, in contradistinction to *interest*, represents capital in the [production] process in contradistinction to capital outside the process, capital as a process in contradistinction to capital as property; it therefore represents the capitalist as functioning capitalist, as representative of *working capital* as opposed to the capitalist as mere personification of capital, as mere owner of capital. He thus appears as *working capitalist* in contrast to himself as *capitalist*, and further, as *worker* in contrast to himself as mere *owner*. Consequently, insofar as any relation between surplus-value and the process is still preserved, or apparent, this is done precisely in the form in which the very notion of surplus-value is negated. *Industrial profit* is resolved into labour, not into *unpaid* labour of other people but into *wage-labour*, into wages for the capitalist, who in this case is placed into the same category as the wage-worker and is merely a more highly paid worker, just as in general wages vary greatly.

Money is indeed not converted into capital as a result of the fact that it is exchanged against the material conditions required for the production of the commodity, and that in the labour process these conditions—materials of labour, instruments of labour and labour—begin to ferment, act on one another, combine with one another, undergo a chemical process and form the commodity like a crystal as a result of this process. The outcome of this would be no capital, no surplus-value. This abstract form of the labour process is common to all modes of production whatever their social form or their particular historical character. The process only becomes a capitalist process, and money is converted into capital only: 1) if *commodity production*, i.e., the production of products in the form of commodities, becomes the general mode of production; 2) if the commodity (money) is exchanged against labour-power (that is, actually against labour) as a commodity, and consequently if labour is wage-labour; 3) this is the case however only when the objective conditions, that is (considering the production process as a whole), the products, confront labour as independent forces, not as the property of labour but as the property of someone else, and thus in the form of *capital*.

Labour as wage-labour and the conditions of labour as capital (that is, consequently, as the property of the capitalist; they are themselves properties personified in the capitalist and whose property in them, their property in themselves, they represent as against labour) are expressions of the same relationship, only seen from opposite poles. This condition of capitalist production is its invariable result. It is its *antecedent* posited by itself. Capitalist production is antecedent to itself and is therefore posited with its conditions as soon as it has evolved and functions in circumstances appropriate to it. However, the *capitalist production process* is not just a production process pure and simple. The contradictory, socially determined feature of its elements evolves, becomes reality only in the process itself, and this feature is the predominant characteristic of the process, which it turns precisely into that socially determined mode of production, the *capitalist process of production.*

||916| The *formation process* of capital—when capital, i.e., not any particular capital, but capital in general, only evolves—is the *dissolution process*, the *parting product* of the social mode of production preceding it. It is thus a *historical process*, a process which belongs to a definite historical period. This is the period of its *historical genesis*. (In the same way the existence of the human race is the result of an earlier process which organic life passed through. Man comes into existence only when a certain point is reached. But once man has emerged, he becomes the permanent pre-condition of human history, likewise its permanent product and result, and he is *pre-condition* only as his own product and result.) It is here that labour must separate itself from the conditions of labour in their previous form, in which it was identical with them. It becomes *free* labour only in this way and only thus are its conditions converted into *capital* and confront it as such. The process of capital becoming capital or its development *before* the capitalist production process exists, and its realisation in the capitalist process of production itself belong to two historically different periods. In the second, capital is *taken for granted*, and its existence and automatic functioning is presupposed. In the first period, capital is the sediment resulting from the process of dissolution of a different social formation. It is the *product* of a different [formation],

not the product of its own reproduction, as is the case later. The existing basis on which capitalist production works is wage-labour, which is however at the same time reproduced continuously by it. It is therefore based also on *capital*, the form assumed by the conditions of labour, as its given prerequisite, a prerequisite. however which, like wage-labour, is its continuous presupposition and its continuous product.

On this basis, *money*, for example, is, as such, capital because the conditions of production in themselves confront labour in an alienated form, they confront it as someone else's property and thus dominate it. Then capital can also be sold as a *commodity* which has this attribute, that is, it can be sold as capital, as is the case when capital is loaned at interest.

But while thus the aspect of the specific social determination of capital and of capitalist production—a specific social determination which is expressed juridically in capital as property, in capital property as a special form of property—*is established*, and *interest*, therefore, appears as that *part of surplus-value* which is produced by capital in this determinate form, independent of this determination considered as the determination of the process as a whole, then the other part of surplus-value, the surplus of profit over interest, *industrial profit*, must obviously represent value which does not arise from capital as such, but from the production process separated from its social determination, which has indeed already found its special mode of existence in the formula, capital—interest. Separated from capital, however, the production process becomes *labour process* in general. [Consequently] the industrial capitalist as distinct from himself as capitalist, that is, the industrialist in contradistinction to himself as capitalist, i.e., owner of capital, is thus merely a simple functionary in the labour process; he does not represent functioning capital, but is a functionary irrespective of capital, and therefore a particular representative of the labour process in general, a *worker*. In this way, industrial profit is happily converted into *wages* and is equated with ordinary wages, differing from them only quantitatively and in the special form in which they are paid, i.e., that the capitalist pays wages to himself instead of someone else paying them to him.

The nature of surplus-value (and therefore of capital) is not only obliterated in this final division of profit into *interest* and *industrial profit*, but it is definitely presented as something quite different.

Interest represents part of surplus-value; it is merely a portion of profit which is separated and classified under a special name, the portion which accrues to the person who merely owns the capital, the portion he intercepts. But this merely *quantitative* division is turned into a *qualitative division* which transforms both parts in such a way that not even a trace of their original essence seems to remain. ||917| This is first of all confirmed by the fact that *interest* does not appear as a division which makes no difference to production, and takes place only "occasionally" when the industrialist operates with someone else's capital. Even when he operates with his own capital his profit is split into *interest* and *industrial profit*, thereby transforming the mere quantitative division into a *qualitative* one which does not depend on the accidental circumstance whether the industrialist owns or does not own his capital; the *qualitative* division arises out of the nature of capital and of capitalist production itself. There exist not simply two portions of profit distributed to two different persons, but two separate *categories* of profit which are related in different ways to capital and consequently to different determinate aspects of capital. Apart from the reasons mentioned earlier, this assumption of an independent existence is established all the more easily since *interest-bearing capital* appears on the scene as a historic form before industrial capital and continues to exist alongside it in its old form and it is only in the course of the development of industrial capital that the latter subordinates it to capitalist production by turning it into a *special form* of industrial capital.

The mere quantitative division thus becomes a qualitative one. Capital is itself divided. Insofar as it is a *prerequisite* of capitalist production, insofar, therefore, as it *expresses a specific social relation*, the *alienated form of the conditions of labour*, it is realised in *interest*. It realises its character as capital in interest. On the other hand, insofar as it operates in the process, this process appears as something separate from its specific capitalist character, from its specific social determination—as mere *labour process* in general. Therefore, insofar as the capitalist plays any part in it, he does so not as a capitalist—for this aspect of his character is allowed for in interest—but as a functionary of the labour process in general, as a *worker*, and his wages take the form of *industrial profit*. It is a special type of labour—labour of superintendence—but after all types of labour in general differ from one another.

Thus the nature of surplus value, the essence of capital and the character of capitalist production are not only completely obliterated in these two forms of surplus-value, they are turned into their opposites. But even insofar as the character and form of capital are complete [it is] nonsensical [if] presented without any intermediate links and expressed as the subjectification of objects, the objectification of subjects, as the reversal of cause and effect, the religious *quid pro quo*, the pure form of capital expressed in the formula M—M'. The ossification of relations, their presentation as the relation of men to things having a definite social character is here likewise brought out in quite a different manner from that of the simple mystification of commodities and the more complicated mystification of money. The transubstantiation, the fetishism, is complete.

Thus *interest* in itself expresses precisely the existence of the conditions of labour as *capital* in their social contradiction and in their transformation into personal forces which confront labour and dominate labour. It sums up the *alienated* character of the conditions of labour in relation to the activity of the subject. It represents the ownership of capital or mere capital property as the means for appropriating the products of other people's labour, as the control over other people's labour. But it presènts this character of capital as something belonging to it apart from the production process itself and by no means as resulting from the specific determinate form of the production process itself. Interest presents capital not in opposition to labour, but, on the contrary, as having no relation to labour, and merely as a relation of one capitalist to another; consequently, as a category which is quite extrinsic to, and independent of, the relation of capital to labour. The division of the profit amongst the capitalists does not affect the worker. Thus *interest*, the form of profit which is the special expression of the *contradictory character* of capital, is an expression in which this contradiction is completely obliterated and explicitly left out of account. Apart from expressing the capacity of money, commodities, etc., to expand their own value, interest, insofar as it presents surplus-value as something deriving from money, commodities, etc., as their natural fruit, is therefore merely a manifestation of the mystification of capital in its most extreme form; insofar as it at all represents a social relation *as such*, it expresses |'918| merely relations between capitalists, and by no means relations between capital and labour.

On the other hand, the existence of this form of *interest* gives the other part of profit the *qualitative form of industrial profit*, of wages for the labour of the industrial capitalist not in his capacity as capitalist, but as a *worker* (industrialist). The particular functions which the capitalist as such has to perform in the labour process and which are incumbent precisely on him as distinct from the workers, are represented as mere labour functions. He produces surplus-value not because he works as a *capitalist*, but because he, the capitalist, also *works*. It is just as if a king, who, as king, has nominal command of the army, were to be assumed to command the army not because he, as the owner of the kingship, *commands*, plays the role of commander-in-chief, but on the contrary that he is king because he *commands*, exercises the function of commander-in-chief. If thus one part of surplus-value, i.e., interest, is completely separated from the process of exploitation, then the other part, that is, industrial profit, emerges as its direct opposite, not as appropriation of other people's labour, but as the creation of value by one's own labour. This part of surplus-value is therefore no longer surplus-value, but its opposite, an equivalent given for labour performed. Since the *alienated character* of capital, its opposition to labour, is displayed outside the exploitation process, that is, outside the sphere where the *real action of this alienation* takes place, all the contradictory features are eliminated from this process itself. Consequently, *real* exploitation, the sphere where these contradictory features are put into practice and where they manifest themselves in reality, appears as its exact opposite, as a substantially different kind of labour, which belongs however to the same socially determined form of labour—wage-labour—to the same *category* of labour. The work of the exploiter is identified here with the labour which is exploited.

This conversion of one part of profit into *industrial profit* arises, as we have seen, from the conversion of the other part into *interest*. The social form of capital—that it is property—devolves on the latter part; on the former part devolves the economic function of capital, its function in the labour process, but detached, abstracted from the social form, the contradictory form in which it exercises this function. How this is further justified by learned reasoning is to be examined in greater detail in connection with the apologetic interpretation of profit as [remuneration for] labour of superintendence. Here the capitalist is equated with his *manager*, as Adam Smith already noted.[135]

Industrial profit does indeed include some part of wages—
in those cases where the manager does not draw them. Capital
appears in the production process as the director of labour, as
its commander (captain of industry) and thus plays an active
role in the labour process. But insofar as these functions arise
out of the specific form of capitalist production—that is, out of
the domination of capital over labour as *its* labour and, therefore,
over the workers as its instruments, out of the nature of capital,
which appears as the *social entity*, the subject of the social form
of labour personified in it [capital] as power over labour—this
work (it may be entrusted to a manager) which is linked with
exploitation is, of course, labour which, in the same way as that
of the wage-worker, enters into the value of the product; just
as *in the case of slavery, the labour of the overseer* has to be paid
for like that of a worker. If man attributes an independent existence, clothed in a *religious form*, to his relationship to his own
nature, to external nature and to other men so that he is dominated by these notions, then he requires *priests* and *their* labour.
With the disappearance of the religious form of consciousness and
of these relationships, the labour of the priests will likewise cease
to enter into the social process of production. The labour of
priests will end with the existence of the *priests* themselves and,
in the same way, the labour which the capitalist performs *qua*
capitalist, or causes to be performed by someone else, will end
together with the existence of the capitalists. (The example
of slavery has to be amplified by quotations.) [136]

Incidentally, these apologetics aimed at reducing profit to
wages, i.e., the wages of superintendence, boomerang on the
apologists themselves, for English ||919| socialists have rightly
declared: Well, in future, you shall only draw the wages usually
paid to managers. Your industrial profit should not be reduced
to wages of superintendence or direction of labour merely in
words, but in practice.

(It is of course impossible to examine in detail this nonsense
and twaddle with all its contradictions. For example, industrial
profit rises and falls in inverse [proportion] to interest or rent.
The *superintendence of labour*, the particular amount of labour
really performed by the capitalist, has however nothing whatever
to do with it, any more than with the *decline in wages*. This kind
of wages has the peculiarity that it falls and rises in inverse
proportion to real wages (insofar as the rate of profit is determined
by the rate of surplus-value, and insofar as all the *conditions of*

production remain unchanged, it is determined *exclusively* by this). But "little contradictions" of this kind do not prevent the apologetic vulgarian from regarding them as identical. The labour performed by the capitalist remains absolutely the same whether he pays low or high wages, whether the worker receives high or low wages. Just as the wages paid for a working-day do [not] affect the amount of labour involved. Moreover, the worker works more intensively when he gets better wages. The labour of the capitalist, on the other hand, is something strictly determined, it is determined both qualitatively and quantitatively by the amount of labour he has to direct, not by the wages paid for this labour. He can no more intensify his labour than the cotton operative can work up more cotton than is available in the mill.⟩

And they[a] add: the function of the manager, the labour of superintendence, can now be bought on the market in the same way as any other kind of labour-power, and is relatively just as cheap to produce and therefore to buy. Capitalist production itself has brought about that the labour of superintendence walks the streets, separated completely from the ownership of capital, whether one's own or other people's. It has become quite unnecessary for *capitalists* to perform this labour of superintendence. It is actually available, separate from capital, not in the sham separation which exists between the industrial capitalist and the moneyed capitalist, but that between industrial managers, etc., and capitalists of every sort. The best demonstration of this are the co-operative factories built by the workers themselves. They are proof that the capitalist as functionary of production has become just as superfluous to the workers as the landlord appears to the capitalist with regard to bourgeois production. *Secondly*: Insofar as the labour of the capitalist does not arise from the [production] process as a capitalist production process, and therefore disappears automatically with the disappearance of capital, i.e., insofar as it is not simply a name for the function of exploiting other people's labour, but insofar as it arises from the social form of labour—co-operation, division of labour, etc.—it is just as independent of capital as is this form [of labour] itself once it has stripped off its capitalist integument. To assert that this labour, as *capitalist labour*, as the function of the capitalist, is necessary, only shows that the vulgarian cannot

---

[a] The English socialists.—*Ed.*

conceive the social productive forces and the social character of labour developed within the framework¦ of capital as something separate from the capitalist form, from the form of alienation, from the antagonism and contradiction of its aspects, from its inversion and *quid pro quo*. (And this is precisely what we say.) |XV-919||

* * *

||XVIII-1142| ⟨The capitalist's real profit is largely profit upon expropriation and the "individual labour" of the capitalist has an especially wide scope in this field, where it is not a question of the creation of surplus-value but of the distribution of the aggregate profit of the whole class of capitalists among the individual members in the field of commerce. This does not concern us here. Certain kinds of profit, those based on speculation for example, are restricted merely to this field. It is therefore quite impossible to examine them here. It is an indication of the bovine stupidity of vulgar economy that (particularly in order to represent profit as "wages") it confuses this with profit insofar as it originates in surplus-value. See the worthy *Roscher*, for example. It is thus quite natural that, when dealing with the division of the aggregate profit of the whole capitalist class, such asses should mix up the items in the accounts and grounds for compensation of capitalists in different spheres of production with the grounds for the exploitation of the workers by the capitalists, with the grounds, so to speak, for the origin of profit as such.⟩ |XVIII-1142||

[5. Essential Difference Between Classical and Vulgar Economy. Interest and Rent as Constituent Elements of the Market Price of Commodities. Vulgar Economists Attempt to Give the Irrational Forms of Interest and Rent a Semblance of Rationality]

||XV-919| It is in *interest-bearing capital*—in the division of profit into interest and [industrial] profit—that capital finds its most objectified form, its pure fetish form, and the nature of surplus-value is presented as something which has altogether lost its identity. Capital—as an entity—appears here as an independent source of value; as something which creates value in the same way as land [produces] rent, and labour wages (partly wages

in the proper sense, and partly industrial profit). Although it is still the price of the commodity which has to pay for wages, interest and rent, it pays for them because the land which enters into the commodity produces the rent, the capital which enters into it produces the interest, and the labour which enters into it produces the wages, [in other words these elements] produce the portions of value which accrue to their respective owners or representatives—||920| the landowner, the capitalist, and the worker (wage-worker and industrialist). From this standpoint therefore, the fact that, on the one hand, the price of commodities determines wages, rent and interest and, on the other hand, the price of interest, rent and wages determines the price of commodities, is by no means a contradiction contained in the theory, or if it is, it is a contradiction, a vicious circle, which exists in the real movement.

True, the rate of interest fluctuates, but only like the market price of any other commodity in accordance with the ratio of demand and supply. This by no means invalidates the notion of interest being inherent in capital just as the fluctuations in the prices of commodities do not invalidate prices as designations appropriate to commodities.

Thus land, capital and labour on the one hand—insofar as they are the sources of rent, interest and wages and these are the constituent elements of commodity prices—appear as the elements which create value, and on the other hand, insofar as they accrue to the owner of each of these means for the production of value, i.e., insofar as he derives the portion of the value created by them, they appear as sources of revenue, and rent, interest and wages appear as forms of *distribution*. (As we shall see later, it is the result of stupidity that the vulgarians, as opposed to critical economy, in fact regard forms of distribution simply as different aspects of forms of production whereas the critical economists separate them and fail to recognise their identity.)

In interest-bearing capital, capital appears to be the *independent source of value* or surplus-value it possesses as money or as commodities. And it is indeed this source in itself, in its material aspect. It must of course enter into the production process in order to realise this faculty; but so must land and labour.

One can therefore understand why the vulgar economists prefer [the formula]: land—rent; capital—interest; labour—wages, to that used by Smith and others for the elements of price (or rather for the parts into which it can be broken down) and where [the relation] *capital—profit* figures, just as on the whole the capital relation as such is expressed in this form by all the classical economists. The concept of profit still contains the inconvenient connection with the [production] process, and the real nature of surplus-value and of capitalist production, in contradistinction to their *appearance*, is still more or less recognisable. This connection is severed when interest is presented as the intrinsic product of capital and the other part of surplus-value, industrial profit, consequently disappears entirely and is relegated to the category of wages.

Classical political economy seeks to reduce the various fixed and mutually alien forms of wealth to their inner unity by means of analysis and to strip away the form in which they exist independently alongside one another. It seeks to grasp the inner connection in contrast to the multiplicity of outward forms. It therefore reduces rent to surplus profit, so that it ceases to be a specific, *separate* form and is divorced from its apparent source, the land. It likewise divests interest of its independent form and shows that it is a part of profit. In this way it reduces all types of revenue and all independent forms and titles under cover of which the non-workers receive a portion of the value of commodities, to the single form of profit. Profit, however, is reduced to surplus-value since the value of the whole commodity is reduced to labour; the amount of paid labour embodied in the commodity constitutes wages, consequently the surplus over and above it constitutes unpaid labour, surplus labour called forth by capital and appropriated gratis under various titles. Classical political economy occasionally contradicts itself in this analysis. It often attempts directly, leaving out the intermediate links, to carry through the reduction and to prove that the various forms are derived from one and the same source. This is however a necessary consequence of its analytical method, ||921| with which criticism and understanding must begin. Classical economy is not interested in elaborating how the various forms come into being, but seeks to reduce them to their unity by means of analysis, because it starts from them as given premises. But analysis is the necessary prerequisite of genetical presentation, and of the understanding of the real, formative process in its different phases. Finally a failure, a deficiency of classical political economy is the fact that it does not conceive the *basic form of capital*, i.e., production designed to appropriate other people's labour, as a *historical* form but as a *natural form* of social production; the analysis carried out by the classical economists themselves nevertheless paves the way for the refutation of this conception.

The position is quite different as regards *vulgar political economy*, which only becomes widespread when political economy itself has, as a result of its analysis, undermined and impaired its own premises and consequently the opposition to political economy has come into being in more or less economic, utopian, critical and revolutionary forms. For the development of political economy and of the opposition to which it gives rise keeps pace with the *real* development of the social contradictions and class conflicts inherent in capitalist production. Only when political economy has reached a certain stage of development and has assumed well-established forms—that is, after Adam Smith—does the separation of the element whose notion of the phenomena consists of a mere reflection of them take place, i.e., its vulgar element becomes a special aspect of political economy. Thus *Say* separates the vulgar notions occurring in *Adam Smith*'s work and puts them forward in a distinct crystallised form. *Ricardo* and the further advance of political economy caused by him provide new nourishment for the vulgar economist (who does not produce anything himself): the more economic theory is perfected, that is, the deeper it penetrates its subject-matter and the more it develops as a contradictory system, the more is it confronted by its own, increasingly independent, vulgar element, enriched with material which it dresses up in its own way until finally it finds its most apt expression in academically syncretic and unprincipled eclectic compilations.

To the degree that economic analysis becomes more profound it not only describes contradictions, but it is confronted by its own contradiction simultaneously with the development of the actual contradictions in the economic life of society. Accordingly, vulgar political economy deliberately becomes increasingly *apologetic* and makes strenuous attempts to talk out of existence the ideas which contain the contradictions. Because he finds the contradictions in Smith relatively undeveloped, *Say*'s attitude still seems to be critical and impartial compared, for example, with that of *Bastiat*, the professional conciliator and apologist, who, however, found the contradictions existing in the economic life worked out in Ricardian economics and in the process of being worked out in socialism and in the struggles of the time. Moreover, vulgar economy in its early stages does not find the material fully elaborated and therefore assists to a certain extent in solving economic problems from the standpoint of political economy, as, for example, *Say*, whereas a Bastiat needs merely to busy himself with plagiarism and attempts to argue away the *unpleasant* side of classical political economy.

But Bastiat does not represent the last stage. He is still marked by a lack of erudition and a quite superficial acquaintance with the branch of learning which he prettifies in the interests of the ruling class. His apologetics are still written with enthusiasm and constitute his real work, for he borrows the economic content from others just as it suits his purpose. The last form is the *academic form*, which proceeds "historically" and, with wise moderation, collects the "best" from all sources, and in doing this contradictions do not matter; on the contrary, what matters is comprehensiveness. All systems are thus made insipid, ||922| their edge is taken off and they are peacefully gathered together in a miscellany. The heat of apologetics is moderated here by erudition, which looks down benignly on the exaggerations of economic thinkers, and merely allows them to float as oddities in its mediocre pap. Since such works only appear when political economy has reached the end of its scope as a science, they are at the same time the *graveyard* of this science. (That they look down in an equally superior manner on the phantasies of the socialists need hardly be stressed.) Even the genuine thought of a Smith or a Ricardo, and others—not just their vulgar elements—is made to appear insipid in these works and becomes a vulgarism. Professor *Roscher* is a master of this sort of thing and has modestly proclaimed himself to be the Thucydides of political economy.[137] His identification of himself with Thucydides may perhaps be based on his conception of Thucydides as a man who constantly confuses cause with effect.

In the form of *interest-bearing capital* it becomes quite obvious that capital *without* expending any labour appropriates the fruits of other people's labour. For it appears here in a form in which it is separated from the production process as such. But it can do this only because, in this form, it indeed enters by itself, without labour, into the labour process, as an element which in itself creates *value*, i.e., is a source of value. While it appropriates part of the value of the product without labour, it has also created it without labour, *ex proprio sinu*, out of itself.

Whereas the classical, and consequently the critical, economists are exercised by the form of alienation and seek to eliminate it by analysis, the vulgar economists, on the other hand, feel completely at home precisely with the *alienated form* in which the different parts of value confront one another; just as a scholastic is familiar with God the Father, God the Son, and God the Holy Ghost, so are the vulgar economists with land—rent, capital—interest, and labour—wages. For this is the form in which these relationships appear to be directly connected with one another in the world of phenomena, and therefore they exist in this form in the thoughts and the consciousness of those representatives of capitalist production who remain captive to it. The more the vulgar economists in fact content themselves with translating common notions into doctrinaire language, the more they imagine that their writings are plain, *in accordance with nature* and the public interest, and free from all theoretical hair-splitting. Therefore, the more alienated the form in which they conceive the manifestations of capitalist production, the closer they approach the nature of common notions, and the more they are, as a consequence, in their natural element.

This, moreover, renders a substantial service to apologetics. For [in the formula:] land—rent, capital—interest, labour—wages, for example, the different forms of surplus-value and configurations of capitalist production do not confront one another as alienated forms, but as heterogeneous and independent forms, merely different from one another but *not antagonistic*. The different revenues are derived from quite different sources, one from land, the second from capital and the third from labour. Thus they do not stand in any hostile connection to one another because they have no inner connection whatsoever. If they nevertheless work together in production, then it is a harmonious action, an expression of harmony, as, for example, the peasant, the ox, the plough and the land in agriculture, in the real labour process, work together *harmoniously* despite their dissimilarities. Insofar as there is any contradiction between them, it arises merely from competition as to which of the agents shall get more of the value they have jointly created. Even if this occasionally brings them to blows, nevertheless the outcome of this competition between land, capital and labour finally shows that, although they quarrel with one another ||923| over the division, their rivalry tends to increase the value of the product to such an extent that each receives a larger piece, so that their competition, which spurs them on, is merely the expression of their harmony.

Herr Arnd, for example, says in criticism of *Rau*:

> "Similarly, the author allows himself to be led by some of his predecessors to adding to the three elements of national wealth (wages, capital rent, land rent) a fourth, that of employers' profit. This entirely destroys the basis—constructed with such circumspection by Adam Smith—for any further development of *our science*" (!); "such a development is consequently quite out of the question in the work under consideration" (Karl Arnd, *Die naturgemäße Volkswirthschaft, gegenüber dem Monopoliengeiste und dem Communismus, mit einem Rückblicke auf die einschlagende Literatur*, Hanau, 1845, S. 477).

By "capital rent" Herr Arnd means *interest* (op. cit., p. 123). According to this one might think that Adam Smith reduces national wealth to *interest*, rent and wages, whereas on the contrary he quite expressly declares that *profit* results from the use of capital and repeatedly and expressly states that *interest*—insofar as it constitutes surplus-value at all—is only a form *derived* from profit. Thus the vulgar economist reads into his sources the direct opposite of what they contain. Where Smith writes "profit" Arnd reads "interest". It would be interesting to know what he supposes Adam Smith's "interest" to mean.

This same "circumspect" developer of "*our science*" makes the following interesting discovery:

> "In the natural course of the production of wealth, there is only *one* phenomenon which—in fully cultivated countries—seems to be destined to regulate the rate of interest to some extent, and it is the ratio in which the amount of wood in the European forests increases as a result of annual additional growth. This annual increase takes place quite *independently of their exchange-value*" (how strange that the trees arrange their additional growth "independently of exchange-value"!) "in the ratio of 3 to 4 per 100. Accordingly *therefore*" ⟨since this additional increase in the number of trees is "independent of their exchange-value", no matter how much their exchange-value may depend on their additional growth⟩, "a decline" (in the rate of interest) "below the level at present prevailing in the richest countries is not likely" (loc. cit., pp. 124-25).

This deserves to be called the "rate of interest originating in the forest", and in the same work its inventor has rendered another service to "our science" as the philosopher of the "dog tax".[138]

* * *

{Profit (including industrial profit) is proportionate to the amount of the capital advanced; on the other hand, the *wages* drawn by the industrial capitalist [stand] in inverse ratio to the amount of capital. [They are] considerable where the capital is small (because, in this case, the capitalist is something between an exploiter of other people's labour and a person who lives off his own labour), and insignificant where the capital is large, or they are quite independent of it in the case where a manager is [employed]. One part of the labour of superintendence merely arises from the antagonistic contradiction between capital and labour, from the antagonistic character of capitalist production, and belongs to the incidental expenses of production in the same way as nine-tenths of the "labour" occasioned by the circulation process. A conductor does not have to be the owner of the instruments used by the orchestra, nor is it one of his functions as a conductor to speculate on the subsistence costs of the members of the orchestra, or, in general, to have anything to do with their "wages". It is very remarkable that economists like John Stuart Mill, who cling to the forms of "interest" and "industrial profit" in order to convert "industrial profit" into wages for superintendence of labour, admit along with Smith, Ricardo and all other economists worth mentioning, that the average rate of interest is determined by the average rate of profit, [which according to] Mill stands in inverse ratio to the rate of wages, and it is therefore nothing but unpaid labour, surplus labour.

Two facts provide the best proof that the wages of superintendence do not enter [into the] average rate of profit at all.

||924| 1) That in co-operative factories, where the general manager receives a salary as in all other factories, and is responsible for the whole labour of superintendence—the overseers themselves are simply workers—the rate of profit is not below, but above, the average rate.

2) That where profit is continuously substantially above the average rate, as in individual, non-monopolised branches of business such as those of small shopkeepers, farmers, etc., this is correctly explained by the economists as being due to the fact that these people pay themselves their own wages. Where only the proprietor himself works, his profit consists of—1) the interest on his small capital; 2) his wages; 3) that part of the surplus time which, because of his capital, he is able to work for himself instead of for someone else; i.e., the part not already represented by interest. If, however, he employs workers, then their surplus labour has to be added.

Of course the worthy *Senior* (Nassau) also converts *industrial profit* into wages of superintendence. But he forgets this humbug as soon as it is a question, not of doctrinaire phrases, but of practical struggles between workers and factory owners. Thus, he opposes the *shortening of the working-day*, because in a working-day of say $11^1/_2$ hours, the workers allegedly work only one hour for the capitalist, and the product of this one hour constitutes the capitalist's profit (apart from the *interest* for which they also work an hour according to his own calculation). Suddenly here industrial profit is equal to the value added by the unpaid labour-time of the worker and not to the value added by the labour which the capitalist performs in the production process of commodities. If industrial profit were the product of the capitalist's own labour, then Senior should not have deplored that the workers work only one hour for the capitalist for nothing instead of two, and even less should he have said that, if the workers worked only $10^1/_2$ hours instead of $11^1/_2$, there [would be] no profit *at all*. He should have said that if the workers worked only $10^1/_2$ hours instead of $11^1/_2$, the capitalist would not receive wages of superintendence for $11^1/_2$ hours but only for $10^1/_2$ hours, he would thus lose one hour's wages of superintendence. In which case the workers would answer that if ordinary wages for $10^1/_2$ hours have to suffice for them, then the *higher wages* the capitalist receives for $10^1/_2$ hours should suffice for him.

It is incomprehensible how economists like John Stuart Mill, who are Ricardians and even express the principle that profit is equal to surplus-value, surplus labour, in the form that the rate of profit and wages stand in inverse ratio to one another and that the rate of wages determines the rate of profit (which is incorrect when put in this form), suddenly convert industrial profit into the individual labour of the capitalist instead of into the surplus labour of the worker, unless the function of exploitation of other people's labour is called labour by them, the result of this is indeed that the wages of this labour are exactly equal to the amount of other people's labour appropriated, in other words, they depend directly on the degree of exploitation, not on the degree of exertion that this costs the capitalist. (Insofar as this function of exploitation really requires labour in the course of capitalist production, it is represented by the wages of general managers.) I say that it is incomprehensible that, after they as Ricardians have reduced profit to its real element, they allow themselves to be misled by the antithesis of interest and industrial profit which is simply a *disguised form of profit* and is merely regarded as an independent form due to ignorance of the nature of profit. Only because one part of profit, *interest*, appears to be due to capital as a thing, an automatically functioning, automatically creating thing, apart from the production process, the other part appears as *industrial profit*, as arising from the activity taking place in the process (really the active process, this however also includes the activity of the operating capitalist) and *therefore* as due to the labour of the capitalist. Consequently, because capital and the surplus-value which arises from it and is called interest are considered *mysteries*. This view, which clearly arises from notions reflecting the most superficial aspects of the external form of capital, is the exact opposite of Ricardo's view and altogether inconsistent with his conception of value. Insofar as capital is value, its value is determined by the labour contained in it before it enters into the [production] process. Insofar as it enters the process as a thing, it does so as use-value, and as such, it can never create exchange-value, whatever its use. One can see how splendidly the Ricardians understand their own master. In relation to the moneyed capitalist, the industrial capitalist, who embodies functioning capital and therefore actually squeezes out surplus labour, is of course quite justified in pocketing a part of this surplus. In relation to the moneyed capitalist, he is a worker, but a *worker who is a capitalist, in other words, an exploiter of other people's labour.* ||925| But in relation to the workers it is *strange* to plead that the exploitation of their labour costs the capitalist labour and that, therefore, they have to pay him for this exploitation; it is the plea of the slave-driver addressed to the slave.}

* * *

Every pre-condition of the social production process is at the same time its result, and every one of its results appears simultaneously as its pre-condition. All the *production relations* within which the process moves are therefore just as much its products as they are its conditions. The more one examines its nature as it really is, [the more one sees] that in the last form it becomes increasingly consolidated, so that independently of the process these conditions appear to determine it, and their own relations appear to those competing in the process as objective conditions, objective forces, aspects of things, the more so as, in the capitalist process, every element, even the simplest, the commodity for example, is already an inversion and causes relations between people to appear as attributes of things and as relations of people to the social attributes of things.

⟨Interest is the remuneration for the productive employment of savings; profit, properly so called, is the remuneration for the *agency for superintendence during this productive employment*[a] (*The Westminster Review*,[139] Vol. V, January-April 1826, p. 107).

Thus interest here is declared to be remuneration for the fact that money, etc., is employed as capital; it therefore arises from capital as such, which is remunerated for its quality *qua* capital. Industrial profit, on the other hand, is remuneration for the function of the capital or capitalist "during this productive employment", i.e., in the production process itself.⟩ |925||

||925| *Interest* is only a part of profit, the part which is paid to the owner of capital by the industrial, functioning capitalist. Since he can appropriate surplus labour only by means of capital (money, commodities), etc., he has to hand over a portion of it to the man who makes capital available to him. And the lender, who wants to enjoy the advantages of money as capital without letting it function as capital, can do this only by being content with a part of the profit. They are in fact co-partners, one of them being the juridical owner of the capital, and the other, while he employs it, the economic owner. But since the profit only arises from the production process, is only its result and has first to be produced, *interest* is in fact merely a claim on part of the surplus labour which has yet to be performed, a title to future labour, a claim on a *portion of the value* of commodities which do not as yet exist, it is therefore only the result of a production process which takes place during the period at the end of which the interest only falls due.

||926| Capital is bought (that is, it is lent at interest) before it is paid for. Money functions here as means of payment as it does in relation to labour-power, etc. The price of capital—i.e., interest—enters therefore just as much into the advances made by the industrialist (and into the advances made to himself where a man is operating with his own capital) as the price of cotton which, for example, is bought today, but for which he has to pay perhaps in six weeks' time. This fact is in no way

---

[a] Marx gives this passage in his own words.—*Ed.*

altered either by the fluctuations in the rate of interest—the market price of money—or the fluctuations in the market prices of other commodities. On the contrary. The market price of money—the name for interest-bearing capital as money capital—is fixed on the money market by competition between buyer and seller, by demand and supply, like the price of any other commodity. The struggle between the moneyed and industrial capitalists is simply a struggle over the division of the profit, over the share which is to accrue to each of the two sections when the division is made. The relationship (demand and supply), like each of its two extremes, is itself a result of the production process or, in common parlance, [is determined] by the business situation existing at the time, the actual position in which the reproduction process and its elements find themselves. But, formally and apparently, it is this struggle which determines the *price* of capital (i.e., interest) before capital enters into the production process. This determination, moreover, occurs outside the real production process, and depends on factors independent of the process; this price determination appears rather as one of the conditions within which the process has to take place. Thus the struggle appears not only to establish the property title to a definite part of the future profit, but to cause this part not to emerge as a result of the production process, but on the contrary to enter into it as a pre-condition, as the price of capital, just as the prices of commodities or wages enter into it as pre-conditions, although in the course of the reproduction process they in fact continuously emerge from it. Each component of the price of a commodity, insofar as it appears as an advance—as an already existing commodity price which enters into the production price—ceases to represent surplus-value as far as the industrial capitalist is concerned. That part of the profit which thus enters into the production process as the price of capital is reckoned as part of the cost of the outlay; it therefore no longer appears to be surplus-value and is converted from a *product* of the process into one of its given pre-conditions—a *condition of production*—which as such enters into the process in an independent form and determines its result.

(If, for example, the rate of interest falls, and the situation obtaining on the market requires a reduction in the price of commodities below cost-price, the industrialist can lower the commodity price without reducing the rate of industrial profit; he can indeed lower the price and secure a higher industrial profit, which, however, will be regarded by the man operating only with his own capital as a fall in the rate of profit, a reduction in the gross profit. Everything which appears as a *given condition of production*, such as the prices of commodities, wages, capital—the market prices of these elements—affects the determination of the *market price* of the commodity at any particular time; the real *cost-price* of a particular commodity is established only within the fluctuations of the market prices, and is only the self-equalisation of these market prices, just as the *value* of commodities is only established as a result of the equalisation of the cost-prices of all the different commodities. Thus, the vicious circle of the vulgarian, whether he is a theoretician regarding matters from the capitalist standpoint or is in fact a capitalist—namely, that the prices of commodities determine wages, interest, profit and rent and that, on the other hand, the prices of labour, interest, profit and rent determine the prices of commodities—is merely an *expression of the circular movement* in which the general laws assert themselves in contradictory fashion in the real movement and in appearance.)

A part of the surplus-value—*interest*—thus appears as the *market price* of capital, which enters into the [production] process, and is therefore regarded not as surplus-value but as a condition of production. Thus, the fact that two sets of capitalists share the surplus-value, one set remaining outside the production process and the other participating in it, is presented in such a way that one part of surplus-value is due to capital outside the process and the other part to capital within the process. The fact that the division [of the surplus-value] is established beforehand is presented as the independence of one part from the other, as the independence of one part from the production process itself; and finally as the immanent attribute of things, *money, commodities*, but of these things as *capital*; this again appears not as the expression of a relationship, but in such a way that this money, these commodities are *technologically* intended for the labour process and because of this they become capital. Defined in this way, they are the simple elements of the labour process itself ||927| and *as such* they are *capital*.

There is nothing mysterious at all in the fact that the value of the commodity is made up partly of the value of the commodities contained in it, partly of the value of the labour—that is to say, the paid labour—partly of the unpaid but none the less salable labour, and that the part of its value which consists of unpaid labour—i.e., its surplus-value—is in turn divided into interest, industrial profit and rent; in other words, the person who "produces" and first of all takes possession of the whole of this surplus-value has to hand over portions of it to others, one portion to the landlord, another to the owner of the capital, and he keeps the third for himself; he does so however under a name—industrial profit—which distinguishes it from interest and rent, and from surplus-value and profit. The breakdown of surplus-value, that is, of part of the value of commodities, into these special headings or categories, is very understandable and does not conflict in the least with the law of value. But the whole matter is mystified because these different parts of surplus-value acquire an independent form, because they accrue to different people, because the titles to them are based on different elements, and finally because of the autonomy with which certain of these parts of surplus-value confront the production process as its conditions. From parts into which value can be divided, they become independent elements which *constitute* value, they become *component parts*. This is what they are as far as market prices are concerned. They really become the constituent elements of the market price. How their apparent independence as conditions of the process is regulated by the inherent law and that they are only *apparently* independent, does not become evident at any moment in the course of the production process, nor does it operate as a determining conscious motive. Exactly the opposite. The highest consistency which can be assumed by this semblance of results taking the form of independent conditions becomes firmly established when *parts of surplus-value*—in the form of prices of the conditions of production—are included in the price.

And this is the case with regard to both interest and rent. They are part of the outlay of the industrial capitalist and the farmer. They seem here to represent not unpaid surplus labour, but paid surplus labour, that is, surplus labour for which an equivalent is paid during the production process, although not to the worker whose surplus labour it is, but to other people, i.e., the owners of capital and of land. They constitute surplus labour as far as the worker is concerned, but they are equivalents as regards the capitalist [who lends the money] and the landowner to whom they have to be paid. Interest and rent therefore appear not as surplus-value, and still less as surplus labour, but as *prices* of the commodities "capital" and "land", for they are paid to the capitalist and the landowner only in their capacities as owners of commodities, only as owners and sellers of these commodities. That part of the value of the commodity which represents interest, therefore, appears as *reproduction* of the *price* paid for capital, and that part which represents rent appears as *reproduction* of the price paid for the land. These prices therefore become *constituent* parts of the total price. This does not merely *appear* to be the case to the industrial capitalist; for him interest and rent really constitute part of his outlay, and whereas, on the one hand, they are determined by the *market price* of his commodity—as the market price it is a determination of a commodity in which a social process or the result of a social process appears as a particular aspect belonging to the commodity, and the up and down of this process, its movement, appears as the fluctuations of the commodity price—on the other hand, the *market price* is determined by them, in just the same way as the market price of cotton determines the market price of yarn and, on the other hand, the market price of yarn determines the demand for cotton, hence the market price of cotton.

Since parts of surplus-value, i.e., interest and rent, enter into the production process as the *prices* of commodities—of the commodity land and the commodity capital—they exist in forms which not only conceal, but which disavow their real origin.

That surplus labour, *unpaid* labour, constitutes just as essential an element of the capitalist production process as *paid* labour, is expressed by the fact that factors of production—land and capital—distinct from labour have to be paid for, in other words, that *costs* besides the price of the commodities advanced and wages enter into the price. Parts of surplus-value—interest and rent—appear here as costs, as advances made by the exploiting capitalist.

Average profit enters into the production price of commodities as a determining factor and thus already here surplus-value [appears to be] not a result, but a condition, not one of the parts into which the value of the commodity is divided, but a component part of its *price*. But *average profit*, like the *production price* itself, acts rather as a determining ideal and at the same time appears as *surplus* over and above the advances made ||928| and as a price which is different from the cost-price properly speaking. Whether or not [average profit is obtained] and whether it is higher or lower than the profit corresponding *to the market price*—that is, corresponding to the direct result of the [production] process—determines the reproduction process, or rather the scale of reproduction; it determines whether more or less of the capital existing in this or that sphere of production is withdrawn or invested; it also determines the ratio in which newly accumulated capital flows into these particular spheres, and finally, to what extent these particular spheres act as buyers in the money market. On the other hand, as *interest* and *rent*, the separate portions of surplus-value in a quite definite form become pre-conditions for the individual production prices and are anticipated in the form of advances.

* * *

⟨*Advances*, that is, what is paid out by the capitalist, may be defined as *costs*. Profit accordingly appears as a surplus over these costs. This applies to the individual prices of production. And consequently, one can call the prices determined by the advances *cost-prices*.

Costs of production can be defined as prices determined by the average profit—that is, the price of the capital advanced plus the average profit—since this profit is the condition for reproduction, a condition which regulates the supply and the distribution of capital amongst the various spheres of production. These prices are *production prices*.

Finally, the real amount of labour (materialised and immediate labour) it costs to produce a commodity, is its *value*. It constitutes the real production cost of the commodity itself. The price which corresponds to it is simply the value expressed in money.

The term "cost of production" is used alternately in all three senses.⟩

* * *

If no surplus-value were produced, then of course together with surplus-value the part of it which is called interest would also cease to exist, and so would the part which is called rent; the *anticipation* of surplus-value would likewise come to an end, in other words, it would no longer constitute a part of the costs of production in the shape of the *price* of commodities. The existing value entering into the production process would not emerge from it as *capital* at all, and accordingly, could not enter into the reproduction process as *capital*, nor be lent out as *capital*. It is thus the continuous reproduction of the same relations—the relations which postulate capitalist production—that not only causes them to appear as the social forms and results of this process, but at the same time as its continual *prerequisites*. But they are these only as prerequisites continually *posited*, created, *produced* by the process itself. This reproduction is therefore not conscious reproduction; on the contrary, it only manifests itself in the continuous existence of these relations as *prerequisites* and as *conditions* dominating the production process. The parts, for example, into which the commodity value can be divided are turned into its *component* parts which confront one another as independent parts, and they are consequently also independent in relation to their *unity*, which on the contrary appears to be a *compound* of these parts. The bourgeois sees that the product continually becomes the condition of production. But he does not perceive that the production relations themselves, the social forms in which he produces and which he regards as given, natural relations, are the continuous product—and only for that reason the continuous prerequisite—of this specific social mode of production. The different relations and aspects not only become independent and assume a heterogeneous mode of existence, apparently independent of one another, but they seem to be the direct properties of things; they assume a material shape.

Thus the participants in capitalist production live in a bewitched world and their own relationships appear to them as properties of things, as properties of the material elements of production. It is however in the last, most derivative forms—forms in which the intermediate stage has not only become invisible but has been turned into its direct opposite—that the various aspects of capital appear as the real agencies and direct representatives of production. Interest-bearing capital is personified in the moneyed capitalist, industrial capital in the industrial capitalist, rent-bearing capital in the landlord as the owner of the land, and lastly, labour in the wage-worker. They enter into the competitive struggle and into the real process of production as these rigid forms, personified in independent personalities that appear at the same time to be mere representatives of personified things. Competition presupposes this externalisation. These forms conform to its nature and have come into being in the natural evolution of competition, and on the surface competition appears to be ·||929| simply the movement of this inverted world. Insofar as the inner connection asserts itself in this movement, it appears as a mysterious law. The best proof is political economy itself, a science which seeks to rediscover the hidden connection. Everything enters into competition in this last, most externalised form. The market price, for example, appears to be the dominant factor here, just as the rate of interest, rent, wages, industrial profit appear to be the constituents of value, and the price of land and the price of capital appear as given items with which one operates.

We have seen how Adam Smith first reduces value to wages, profit (interest) and rent, and then, conversely, presents these as independent constituent elements of commodity prices. [140] He expresses the secret connection in the first version and the outward appearance in the second.

If one comes still closer to the surface of the phenomenon, then, in addition to the average rate of profit, interest and even rent can be represented as constituent parts of commodity prices (that is, of *market prices*). Interest can be so represented quite directly, since it enters into the cost-price. Rent—as the price of land—may not determine the price of the product directly, but it determines the method of production, whether a large amount of capital is concentrated on a small area of land, or a small amount of capital is spread over a large area of land, and whether this or that type of product is produced—e.g., cattle or corn—the market price of which covers the rent most effectively, for the rent must be paid before the term stipulated by contract expires.

In order that rent should not bring about a reduction in industrial profit, pasture is turned into arable land and arable land into pasture, etc. Rent therefore determines the market prices of individual commodities not directly, but only indirectly, by influencing the proportions in which the various types of commodities are produced in such a way that demand and supply will produce the best price for each so that rent can be paid. Even though rent does not directly determine the market price of corn, for example, it determines directly the market price of cattle, etc., in short, of commodities produced in the spheres where rent is not regulated by the market prices of their products but where the market prices of products are regulated by the amount of rent borne by the grain-producing land. The price of meat, for example, is always too high in industrially developed countries, that is, it is not only far above its production price, but above its value. For the price must cover not only the cost of production, but also the rent which the land would carry if corn were grown on it. Otherwise, meat produced by large-scale stock-breeding—where the organic composition of capital approximates more closely [to the composition of capital in industry] or may have an even greater preponderance of constant capital over variable capital—could only pay a very small amount of *absolute rent*, or even none at all. The rent which it pays, and which enters directly into its price, is, however, determined by the absolute plus the differential rent which the land would pay as arable land. This differential rent, moreover, does not exist here in most cases. The best proof is that meat pays rent on the kind of land where corn does not.

If, therefore, *profit* enters into the production price as a determining factor, it can be said that wages, interest and, to a certain degree, rent constitute determining elements of the market price and certainly of the production price. Of course, ultimately everything can be reduced to value which is determined by labour-time, for on the whole the movement of interest is determined by profit, while corn rent on the other hand is determined partly by the rate of profit, partly by the value of the product and the equalisation of the different values produced on different kinds of land to the market value; the rate of profit, however, is determined partly by wages, partly by the productivity of labour in those spheres of production which produce constant capital—in the last analysis therefore by the level of wages and the productivity of labour; wages, however, are the equivalent of a part of the commodity (that is, [they are] equal to the paid portion of labour contained in the commodity, and profit is equal to the unpaid portion of labour contained in the commodity). Finally, the productivity of labour can affect the price of commodities only in two ways, either it affects their value, i.e., reduces it, or it affects their surplus-value, that is, increases it. Cost-price is nothing but the value of the capitals advanced plus the surplus-value they produce distributed amongst the different spheres according to the quota of the total capital which each sphere represents. Thus, cost-price resolves into value if one considers the total capital and not the individual spheres. On the other hand, the market prices in each sphere are continually reduced to the cost-price as a result of the competition between the capitals of the different spheres. Competition amongst the capitalists in each individual sphere seeks to reduce the market price of commodities to their market value. Competition between capitalists of different spheres reduces market values to common cost-prices.

Ricardo opposes Smith's establishment of value out of the parts of value which are determined by itself. But he is not consistent. Otherwise it would have been impossible for him to argue with Smith whether profit, wages and rent or, as he says, merely profit and wages, enter into price, that is, enter as *constituent* parts. Regarded analytically, they enter into it as soon as they are paid. He ought to have put it in this way: The price of every commodity is reducible to profit and wages, the prices of some commodities (and of very many, *indirectly*) are reducible to profit, rent and wages. But *no* commodity price is constituted by them ||930| for they are not independent factors acting of their own accord, having a definite magnitude, and *making up* the value of commodities; on the contrary, when the value is given, it can be divided into those parts in many different proportions. The magnitude of *value* is not determined by the addition or combination of given factors—i.e., profit, wages and rent—but one and the same *magnitude of value*, a given *amount of value*, is broken down into wages, profit and rent, and according to different circumstances it is distributed between these three categories in very different ways.

Assuming that the production process repeats itself continuously under the same conditions, in other words, that reproduction takes place under the same conditions as production, which presupposes that productivity of labour remains unchanged, or at least that variations in productivity do not alter the relationships of the different factors of production; thus, even if the value of commodities were to rise or fall as a result of changes in productivity, the distribution of the value of commodities amongst the different factors of production would remain the same. In that case, although it would not be theoretically accurate to say that the different parts of value determine the value or price of the whole [output], it would be useful and correct to say that they constitute it insofar as one understands by constituting the formation of the whole by adding up the parts. The value would be divided at a steady and constant rate into [pre-existing] value and surplus-value, and the [newly created] value would be resolved at a constant rate into wages and profit, the profit again being broken down at a constant rate into interest, industrial profit and rent. It can therefore be said that P—the price of the commodity—is divided into wages, profit (interest) and rent, and, on the other hand, wages, profit (interest) and rent are the constituents of the value or rather of the price.

This uniformity or similarity of reproduction—the repetition of production under the same conditions—does not exist. Productivity itself changes and changes the conditions [of production]. The conditions, on their part, change productivity. But the divergences are reflected partly in superficial oscillations which even themselves out in a short time, partly in a gradual accumulation of divergences which either lead to a crisis, [to a] violent, seeming restoration of the old relationships, or very gradually assert themselves and are recognised as a change in the conditions.

Interest and rent, which anticipate surplus-value, presuppose that the *g e n e r a l* character of reproduction will remain the same. And this is the case as long as the capitalist mode of production continues. Secondly, it is presupposed moreover that the *specific relations* of this mode of production remain the same during a certain period, and this is in fact also more or less the case. Thus the result of production *crystallises* into a *permanent* and *therefore prerequisite condition of production*, that is, it becomes a permanent *attribute of the material conditions of production*. It is *crises* that put an end to this apparent *independence* of the various elements of which the production process continually consists and which it continually reproduces.

(What *value* is for the genuine economist the *market price* is for the practical capitalist, that is, in each case the primary factor of the whole movement.)

The form of interest-bearing capital characteristic of and in accordance with capitalist production is *credit*. It is a form created by capitalist production itself. (The subordination of *commercial capital* [by the capitalist mode of production] does not in fact require such a new creation since commodity and money, and the circulation of commodities and money, remain the elementary prerequisites of capitalist production and are only turned into absolute prerequisites; commercial capital, on the one hand, is therefore the general form of capital and, on the other hand, insofar as it represents capital in a specific function—capital which operates exclusively in the circulation process—its determination by productive capital does not in any way alter its form.)

The equalisation of values to cost-prices occurs only because the individual capital functions as a commensurate part of the total capital of the whole class and, on the other hand, because the total capital of the class is distributed amongst the various individual spheres according to the needs of production. This is brought about by means of credit. Credit not only makes this equalisation possible and facilitates it, but one part of capital—in the form of moneyed capital—appears in fact to be the material common to the whole class and employed by it. This is one purport of credit. The other is the continual attempt made by capital to shorten the metamorphoses which it has to undergo in the circulation process, to anticipate the circulation time, its transformation into money, etc., and in this way to counteract its own ||931|| limitations. Finally, the function of *accumulating*, insofar as it is not conversion [of revenue] into capital but the supply of surplus-value in the form of capital, becomes, in part, the responsibility of a special class, in part everything *accumulated* by society in this sense becomes accumulation of capital and is placed at the disposal of the industrial capitalists. Operations of this kind take place at a very large number of isolated points in society, [their results] are concentrated and collected in certain reservoirs. Money which lies idle due to freezing of the commodities in the metamorphosis, is thus converted into capital.

* * *

Land—rent and capital—interest are irrational expressions insofar as rent is defined as the *price* of land and interest as the *price* of capital. The common origin [of all these different revenues] is still recognisable in the forms of interest-bearing capital, rent-bearing capital, profit-bearing capital, since, in general, *capital* involves appropriation of surplus labour; so that these different forms merely express the fact that the surplus labour produced by capital is, as concerns capital in general, divided between two types of capitalists, and in the case of agricultural capital, it is divided between capitalist and landlord.

Rent as the (annual) *price* of land and interest as the *price* of capital are just as irrational as $\sqrt{-3}$. The latter form contradicts the number in its simple, elementary form just as those do in the case of capital in its simple form of commodities and money. They are in the converse sense irrational. Land—rent, i.e., rent as the price of land, defines land as a commodity, a use-value which has a value whose monetary expression is its price. But a use-value which is not the product of labour cannot have a value; in other words, it cannot be defined as the materialisation of a definite quantity of social labour, as the social expression of a certain quantity of labour. It is nothing of the kind. Only if it is the product of concrete labour can use-value take the form of exchange-value—become a commodity. Only under this condition can concrete labour, for its part, be expressed as *social labour*, value. Land and price are incommensurable magnitudes, nevertheless they are supposed to bear a certain relation to each other. Here a thing which has no value has a price.

Interest as the price of capital, on the other hand, expresses the converse irrationality. Here a commodity which has no *use-value* has a dual value, it has a value in the first place and in addition a price, which is different from this value. For capital *is*, to begin with, nothing but a *sum of money* or a *quantity of commodities* equal to a certain sum of money. If the commodity is lent out as capital, then it is nothing but a *sum of money* in camouflaged form. For what is lent *as capital* is not so many pounds of cotton, but so much *money* whose value exists in the form of cotton. The *price* of the capital is therefore related to it only as the existence of a *sum of money*, that is, a certain value expressed in money and existing in the form of exchange-value. How is it possible for a value to have a price apart from the price which is expressed in its own money form? Price after all is the value of the commodity as *distinct* from its use-value. Price in contradistinction to the value of the commodity, price as the value of a sum of money (for price is simply the expression of value in money) is therefore a contradiction in terms.

This irrationality of expression (the irrationality of the thing itself arises from the fact that, as regards interest, capital as the prerequisite appears divorced from its own process, in which it becomes capital and consequently self-expanding value, and that, on the other hand, rent-bearing capital exists only as agricultural capital, as capital which only yields rent in a particular sphere, and this form in which it appears is *transmitted to the element that differentiates it in general from industrial capital*), this irrationality of expression is so much felt by the vulgarian that he falsifies both expressions in order to make them appear rational. He asserts that interest is paid on capital insofar as it is use-value, and therefore talks about the utility which the products or means of production have for reproduction and of the utility which capital has as a material element of the labour process.

But, after all, its utility, its use-value, already exists in its form as a commodity and without this it would not be a commodity and would have no value. As money, it is the expression of the value of commodities and is ||932| convertible into them in proportion to their own value. But if I convert money into a machine, into cotton, etc., then I convert it into use-values of *the same* value. The conversion is concerned only with the *value form*. As money, it has the use-value of being convertible into any other commodity, a commodity, however, of the same value. As a result of this transformation, the value of money changes no more than that of the commodity when it is converted into money. The use-value of the commodities into which I can convert money does not give the money, in addition to its value, a price which is different from its value. If, however, I presuppose the conversion and assert that the price is paid for the use-value of the commodities, then the use-value of the commodities is not paid for at all or is only paid insofar as their exchange-value is paid for. How the use-value of any commodity is utilised, whether it enters into individual or industrial consumption, has absolutely no bearing on its exchange-value. It only determines who will buy it—the industrial capitalist or the immediate consumer. The productive usefulness of a commodity can therefore account for the fact that the commodity has exchange-value at all, for the labour embodied in the commodity is paid for only if it has use-value. Otherwise it is not a commodity—it is a commodity only as the unity of use-value and exchange-value. But this use-value can by no means account for the fact that as exchange-value or as price, it has in addition another and different price as well.

One can see how the vulgarian wants to get over the difficulty here by seeking to convert *capital*—that is, the money or the commodity insofar as these have a *specifically different* form from themselves as money or commodity—into a mere *commodity*, in other words, by disregarding precisely the specific difference which has to be explained. He does not wish to say that capital is a means for the exploitation of surplus labour and that it therefore represents greater value than the value contained in it. Instead he says: It has more value than its own value because it is an ordinary commodity like any other, that is, it possesses a use-value. Here capital is identified with commodity, whereas the point to be explained is how the commodity can function as capital.

The vulgarian, insofar as he does not echo the Physiocrats, deals with land in the opposite way. In the previous case, he converted capital into a commodity in order to explain the *difference* between capital and commodity and the conversion of the commodity into capital. Now he converts land into capital because the capital relation as such is more in tune with his ideas than the price of land. Rent can be regarded as interest on capital. For example, if the rent is 20 and the rate of interest is 5, then it can be said that this 20 is interest on a capital of 400. And in fact the land then sells at 400, which simply amounts to the sale of the rent for a period of 20 years. This payment of the anticipated 20 years' rent is thus the price of the land. The land is thereby converted into capital. The annual payment of 20 merely represents 5 per cent interest on the capital which was paid for the land. And in this way, the formula land—rent is converted into capital—interest, which, for its part, is transmogrified into payment for the use-value of commodities, that is, into the relationship of use-value to exchange-value.

The more analytical vulgarians understand that the price of land is nothing more than an expression for the capitalisation of rent; [that] in fact [it is] the purchase price of rent for a number of years and that it is determined by the prevailing rate of interest. They understand that rent is antecedent to this capitalisation of rent and that, on the other hand, it is therefore impossible to explain rent by its own capitalisation. They therefore deny the existence of rent itself by asserting that it is interest on the capital invested in the land. This does not prevent them from admitting that land in which no capital is invested carries rent, any more than it prevents them from admitting that *equal amounts* of capital invested in land of different fertility yield *different* amounts of rent, or that *unequal amounts* of capital invested in land of unequal fertility may yield *the same* amounts of rent. [They admit] that likewise the capital invested in land—if indeed it is to account for the rent paid for the land—may yield perhaps five times as much interest, that is, five times as much rent, as is yielded by the same amount of capital invested as fixed capital in industry.

One perceives that here the difficulty is always eliminated by *disregarding* it and substituting a relationship expressing the opposite of the *specific difference* which has to be explained, and therefore, in any case, *not* expressing the difference at all. |932||

[6. The Struggle of Vulgar Socialism Against Interest (Proudhon). Failure to Understand the Inner Connection Between Interest and the System of Wage-Labour]

||935| Proudhon's polemic against Bastiat on the question of interest is characteristic both of the manner in which the vulgarian defends the categories of political economy and of the way in which superficial socialism (Proudhon's polemic hardly deserves the name) attacks them. We shall return to this in the section on the vulgarians.[141] Here only a few preliminary remarks.

The return movement [of money] should not have shocked Proudhon as being something peculiar if he understood anything at all about the movement of capital. Neither should the surplus-value contained in the returning amount. This is a characteristic feature of capitalist production.

⟨For Proudhon however, as we shall see, the surplus is a surcharge. Altogether his criticism is that of a novice, he has not mastered the first elements of the science he intends to criticise. Thus, he has never understood that money is a necessary aspect of the commodity (see Part I).[142] Here he even confuses money and capital because loan capital appears as money capital in the form of money.⟩

What might have struck him was not the surplus for which no equivalent was paid, since surplus-value—and capitalist production is based on it—is value which has cost no equivalent. This is not a specific feature of interest-bearing capital. The specific feature—insofar as we are considering the form of the movement—is only the first phase, that is, precisely the opposite of what Proudhon has in mind, namely, that the lender hands over the money without receiving an equivalent for it at the outset and that, therefore, the return of the capital with interest, as regards the transaction between borrower and lender, [is not related to] the metamorphoses which capital undergoes and which, insofar as they are mere metamorphoses of economic form, consist of a series of exchanges, conversion of commodities into money and conversion of money into commodities; insofar as they are real metamorphoses, that is, elements of the production process, they coincide with industrial consumption. Here consumption itself constitutes a phase of the movement of economic forms.

But what money in the hands of the lender does not do, it does in the hands of the borrower who really employs it as capital. It performs its real movement as capital in the hands of the borrower. It returns to him as money plus profit, money plus $\frac{1}{x}$ money. The movement between lender and borrower only expresses the starting-point and the final point of capital. It is money when it passes from the hands of A into those of B. It becomes capital in B's hands, and as such, after undergoing a certain revolution, it returns with profit. This interlude, the real process, which comprises both the circulation process and the production process, is not connected with the transaction between borrower and lender. It [the transaction] recommences only after the money *has been* realised as capital. The money now passes back into the hands of the lender along with a surplus, which, however, comprises only part of the surplus realised by the borrower. The equivalent which the borrower receives is industrial profit, that is, the part of the surplus which he retains and which he appropriates only by means of the money borrowed. All this is not visible in the transaction between him and the lender. This is limited to two acts. Transfer from A's hands into those of B. Interval during which the money remains in B's hands. After this interval the money along with interest returns into A's hands.

If one examines merely this form—the transaction between A and B—then one regards the mere form of capital without the intervening stage: a certain amount of money a is handed over and after a certain period returns as $a+\frac{1}{x}a$ without the assistance of any intermediate link apart from the period of time which elapses between the departure of the sum of money a and its return as $a+\frac{1}{x}a$.

And it is in this abstract form, which, indeed, exists as an independent movement alongside the real movement of capital, opens it and closes it, that Mr. Proudhon considers the matter in hand, so that everything inevitably remains incomprehensible to him. If instead of buying and selling, lending in this form were to be abolished, then, according to Proudhon, the surplus would disappear. In fact only the division of the surplus between two sets of capitalists would disappear. But this division can and must be constantly generated anew whenever it is possible to convert commodities or money into capital, and, on the basis of wage-labour, this is always possible. In order that it should be impossible for commodities and money to become capital and therefore be lent as capital *in posse*, they must not confront wage-labour. If they are thus not to confront it as *commodities* and *money* and consequently labour itself is not to become a commodity, then that amounts to a return to pre-capitalist modes of production ||936| in which it [labour] does not become a commodity, and for the greater part still exists in the form of serf or slave labour. On the basis of free labour, this is only possible where the workers are the owners of their means of production. Free labour develops within the framework of capitalist production as *social* labour. To say that they are the owners of the means of production amounts to saying that these belong to the united workers and that they produce as such, and that their own output is controlled jointly by them. But wanting to preserve wage-labour and thus the basis of capital, as Proudhon does, and at the same time to eliminate the "drawbacks" by abolishing a secondary form of capital, reveals the novice.

Gratuité du Crédit. Discussion entre M. Fr. Bastiat et M. Proudhon, Paris, 1850.

He regards lending as something evil because it is not a sale.

To lend at interest "is the ability to *sell* the same *object* again and again and always to receive a *price* for it without ever relinquishing ownership of the object which one sells" (op. cit., p. 9) (*First Letter* written by Chevé, one of the editors of *La Voix du Peuple*[148]).

What confuses him is that the "object" (money or a house, for example) does not change owners as in the case of buying and selling. But he does not see that when money is handed over, no equivalent is received in return; that, on the contrary, in the real [production] process, in the form and on the basis of exchange, not only an equivalent, but a surplus which is not paid for, is returned; insofar as exchange, exchange of things, takes place, no change of values occurs, the same person remains the "owner" of the same value, and insofar as there is a surplus, there is no exchange. When the exchange of commodity and money begins again, the surplus is already absorbed in the commodity. Proudhon does not understand how profit, and consequently interest as well, arise from the law of the exchange of values. "House", "money", etc., ought therefore to be exchanged not as "capital", but as "commodities ... at cost-price" (op. cit., pp. 43-44).

"Indeed the hatter, who sells hats ... gets back [...] their value, neither more nor less. But the capitalist who lends money, not only ... gets his capital back undiminished, he receives more than the capital, more than he put into the exchange; he receives interest in addition to the capital..." (op. cit., p. 69).

Mr. Proudhon's hatters do not appear to be *capitalists* but journeymen.

"Since in trade *the price of the commodity is formed* by adding *interest on capital* to the workers' *wages*, the worker is therefore unable to buy back the product of his own labour. To live by one's labour is a principle which, under the rule of interest, comprises a contradiction" (op. cit., p. 105).

The worthy Proudhon confuses money as a means of circulation with money as capital in Letter IX (pp. 144-52) and therefore concludes that "capital" in France yields 160 per cent, namely, 1,600 million interest annually in State debts, mortgages, etc., on a capital of one thousand million, i.e., "the amount of currency ... circulating in France...."
Further:

"Since, as a result of the accumulation of interest, *money capital* always returns to its source, from one exchange to another, it follows that re-lending is always undertaken by the same hand, always brings profit to the same person" (op. cit., p. 154).

Because capital is lent out in the form of money, Proudhon believes that money capital, that is, currency, possesses this specific attribute. Everything should be *sold* but nothing *lent*. In other words: In the same way as he wanted commodities to exist but did not want them to become "money", so here he wants commodities, money, to exist but they must not develop into capital. When all phantastic forms have been stripped away, this means nothing more than that there should be no advance from small, petty-bourgeois peasant and artisan production to large-scale industry.

"Since value is nothing but *a proportion*, and all products are necessarily *proportional to one another*, it follows that, from a social point of view, products are always values, and stable values at that. For society, the difference between capital and product does not exist. This difference is quite subjective, it exists only for individuals" (op. cit., p. 250).

What mischief is caused when such philosophical German terms as "subjective" fall into the hands of a Proudhon. The bourgeois social forms are "subjective" for him. And the subjective, and moreover erroneous, abstraction that, because the exchange-value of commodities expresses a *proportion*, it expresses every possible proportion between commodities and does not express a third thing to which the commodities are proportional—this false "subjective" abstraction is the social point of view ||937| according to which not only commodity and money, but commodity, money and capital are identical. Thus, from this "social point of view", all cats are indeed grey.

Finally there is also the surplus in the form of morality:

"All labour *must* produce a *surplus*" (op. cit., p. 200).

With which moral precept the surplus is naturally defined very nicely. |937||

[7. Historical Background to the Problem of Interest. Luther's Polemic Against Interest Is Superior to That of Proudhon. The Concept of Interest Changes as a Result of the Evolution of Capitalist Relations]

||937| Luther, who lived in the period of the dissolution of medieval civil society into the elements of modern society—a process which was accelerated by world trade and the discovery of new gold deposits—naturally knew capital only in its two antediluvian [forms] of interest-bearing capital and merchant capital. Whereas in its early phase capitalist production, having gained strength, seeks to subordinate interest-bearing capital to industrial capital by force—this was in fact done first of all in Holland, where capitalist production in the form of manufacture and large-scale trade first blossomed, and in England in the seventeenth century it was, partly in very naïve terms, declared to be the primary requisite of capitalist production—on the other hand, during the transition to capitalist

production, the first step is the *recognition* that "usury", the old-fashioned form of interest-bearing capital, is a condition of production, a necessary production relation; in the same way as later on its justification is recognised by industrial capital, which regards it as flesh of its own flesh, as soon as industrial capital subordinates interest-bearing capital to itself (eighteenth century, *Bentham*[144]).

Luther is *superior* to Proudhon. The difference between *lending* and *selling* does not confuse him, for he perceives that usury exists equally in both. The most striking feature of his polemic is that he makes his main point of attack the fact that *interest is an innate element of capital*.

I. Books *on trade and usury* written in 1524. [*Von Kauffshandlung und Wucher* in] Part VI of Luther's *Works*, Wittenberg, 1589.

(This was written on the eve of the Peasant War.)

[About] trade (merchant capital):

"There is now great outcry against the nobles or robbers amongst the merchants" (one can see why the merchants are for the princes and against the peasants and knights), "that they have to conduct their trade in great danger and that they are arrested, beaten, despoiled and robbed, etc., in consequence of trading. But if they suffered these things for the sake of righteousness, then, in truth, all merchants would be holy men.... But since such great unrighteousness and un-Christian thieving is rife throughout the whole world because of the merchants, and often enough amongst them themselves, why should we wonder if God wills it that such great wealth, gained by unrighteous means, is lost or stolen in its turn, and that because of it, the merchants are knocked on the head or arrested?... And it is the duty of the princes to punish such unrighteous commerce with due force and to see to it that their subjects are not fleeced so shamefully by the merchants. But because they do not do this, God uses the knights and the robbers and punishes the wickedness of the merchants through them; they must be His devils. Just as He plagues with devils or destroys with enemies the Land of Egypt and the whole world. Thus He causes one scoundrel to be flogged by another, but He does not indicate thereby that knights are lesser robbers than merchants, since the merchants rob the whole world every day while a knight only robs one or two people once or twice a year" (p. 296).

"... Follow the words of Isaiah: Your princes have become the companions of thieves. While they hang thieves who have stolen a guilder or half a guilder, they consort with those who rob the whole world and who steal. more safely than any others; truly, the proverb—big thieves hang ||938| little thieves—still holds good, and, as Cato, the Roman senator, said: Little thieves are put into dungeons and in the stocks, but great thieves parade in gold and silk. But what will God have to say in the end? He will do as He said when He spoke through the mouth of Ezekiel: He will crush and melt prince and merchant, one thief and another, into one another like lead and brass, just as happens when a town is burned down, so that there will be princes and merchants no longer, and I fear that this is not so far off" (p. 297).

[On] *usury. Interest-bearing capital:*

"I am told that nowadays 10 guilders, i.e., 30 per cent, are charged in any Leipzig market[145]; some add also the Neunburg market so that it comes to 40 per cent. I don't know whether it is even higher. Shame on you, where the devil will it end?... Whoever in Leipzig now has 100 florins, takes 40 in a year, this means that he has eaten up a peasant or a burgher in a year. If he has 1,000 florins, then he takes 400 in a year, that is, he eats up a squire or a rich gentleman in a year. If he has 10,000, he takes 4,000, that is, he eats up a rich count in a year. If he has 100,000, as must happen in the case of the great merchants, then he takes 40,000 in a year, that is, he eats up a great, rich prince in a year. If he has 1,000,000, then he takes 400,000 in a year, that is, he eats up some great king in a year. And he suffers not any danger in so doing, neither to his body nor to his treasure, labours not, sits by the fire and roasts apples; thus a chair thief may sit at home and eat up a whole world in 10 years" (pp. 312-13).[146]

⟨II. *Eyn Sermon auf das Evangelion von dem reichen Mann und armen Lazaro etc.*, Wittemberg, 1555 [A Sermon on the Gospel of the Rich Man and Poor Lazarus, etc.].

"We must not regard the rich man according to his outer bearing, for he wears sheep's clothing and his life shines and seems pretty and covers up the wolf most perfectly. For the Gospel does not charge him that he committed adultery, murder, robbery, sacrilege or anything that the world or reason would censure. Indeed he is as honest in his life as that Pharisee who fasts twice a week and is not as other men."⟩

Here Luther tells us how usurer's capital arises, [through] the ruination of the citizens (small townspeople and peasants), the gentry, the nobility and the princes. On the one hand, the usurer comes into possession of the surplus labour and, *in addition, the conditions of labour* of plebeians, peasants, members of craft guilds, in short, of the small commodity producers who need money in order, for example, to make payments before they convert their commodities into money, and who have to buy certain of their conditions of labour, etc. On the other hand, the usurer appropriates rent from the owners of rent, that is, from the prodigal, pleasure-seeking rich. Usury is a powerful means for establishing the pre-conditions for industrial capital— a mighty agency for separating the conditions of production from the producers, insofar as it has the twofold result, firstly, of establishing independent fortunes in the form of money, secondly, of appropriating the conditions of labour to itself, that is, ruining the owners of the old conditions of labour, just like the merchant. And both have the common feature that they acquire an independent fortune, that is, they accumulate in their hands in the form of money claims part of the annual surplus labour, [part] of the conditions of labour [and also part] of the accumulated annual labour. The money actually in their hands constitutes only a small portion of both the annual and the annually accumulated wealth and circulating capital. That they acquire *fortunes* means that a significant portion of both the annual production and the annual revenue accrues to them, and this is payable not in kind, but in the converted form, in money. Consequently, insofar as money does not circulate actively as currency, is not in movement, it is accumulated in their hands. They also hold some of the reservoirs of circulating money and to an even larger extent they hold and accumulate titles to products, but in the form of money titles, titles to commodities converted into money. ||939| On the one hand, usury leads to the ruin of feudal wealth and property; on the other hand, it brings about the ruin of petty-bourgeois, small-peasant production, in short, of all forms in which the producer is still the owner of his means of production.

The worker in capitalist production *does not own* the means of production, [he owns] neither the land he cultivates nor the tools with which he works. This alienation of the conditions of production corresponds here, however, to a real change in the mode of production itself. The tool becomes a machine, and the worker works in the workshop, etc. The mode of production no longer tolerates the dispersal of the means of production connected with small property, just as it does not tolerate the dispersal of the workers themselves. In capitalist production, usury can no longer *separate* the conditions of production from the workers, from the producers, because they have already been separated from them.

Usury *centralises* property, especially in the form of money, only where the means of production are scattered, that is, where the worker produces more or less independently as a small peasant, a member of a craft guild (small trader), etc. As peasant or artisan, whether the peasant is or is not a serf, or the artisan is or is not a member of a craft guild. The usurer here not only appropriates the part of the surplus labour belonging to the bondsman himself, or in the case of the free peasant, etc., the whole surplus labour, but he also appropriates the instruments of production, though the peasant, etc., remains their nominal owner and treats them as his property in the process of production. This kind of usury rests on this particular basis, on this *mode of production*, which it does not change, to which it attaches itself as a parasite and which it impoverishes. It sucks it dry, enervates it and compels reproduction to be undertaken under constantly more atrocious conditions. Thus the popular hatred of usury, especially under the conditions prevailing in antiquity, where this form of production—in which the conditions of production are the property of the producer—was at the same time the basis of the political relationships, of the independence of the citizen. This comes to an end as soon as the worker no longer possesses any conditions of production. And with it the power of the usurer likewise comes to an end. On the other hand, insofar as slavery predominates or [insofar as] the surplus labour is consumed by the feudal lord and his retainers and they fall prey to the usurer, the mode of production also remains the same, only it becomes more oppressive. The debt-ridden slave-holder or feudal lord squeezes more out because he himself is being squeezed dry. Or, finally, he makes way for the usurer, who becomes a landowner, etc., like the *eques*,[a] etc., in Ancient Rome. In place of the old exploiter, whose exploitation was to some extent a means of political power, there appears a coarse, money-hunting parvenu. But the mode of production itself remains unchanged.

The usurer in all pre-capitalist modes of production has a revolutionary impact only in the *political* sense, in that he destroys and wrecks the forms of property whose constant reproduction in the same form constitutes the stable basis of the political structure. [The usurer] has a centralising [effect] as well, but only on the basis of the old mode of production, thus leading to the disintegration of society—apart from the slaves, serfs, etc., and their new masters—into a mob. Usury can continue to exist for a long time in Asiatic forms of society without bringing about real disintegration, but merely giving rise to economic decay and political corruption. It is only in an epoch where the other conditions for capitalist production exist—free labour, a world market, dissolution of the old social connections, a certain level of the development of labour, development of science, etc.—that usury appears as one of the factors contributing to the establishment of the new mode of production; and at the same time

---

[a] Knight.—*Ed.*

causing the ruin of the feudal lords, the pillars of the anti-bourgeois elements, and the ruin of small-scale industry and agriculture, etc., in short, as a factor leading to the centralisation of the conditions of production in the form of capital.

The fact that the usurers, merchants, etc., possess "monetary fortunes" simply means that the wealth of the nation, insofar as it takes the form of commodities or money, is concentrated in their hands.

At the outset capitalist production has to fight against usury to the extent that the usurer himself does not become a producer. With the establishment of capitalist production the domination of the usurer over surplus labour, a domination which depends on the continued existence of the old mode of production, ceases. The industrial capitalist collects surplus-value directly in the form of profit; he has also already seized part of the means of production and he appropriates part of the annual accumulation directly. From this moment, and especially as soon as industrial and commercial wealth develops, the usurer—that is, the lender at interest—is a person who is differentiated from the industrial capitalist only as the result of the division of labour, but is subordinated to industrial capital.

||940|| III. *An die Pfarrherrn wider den Wucher zu predigen. Vermanung*, Wittemberg, 1540 (without pagination).

[Discusses] *trading (buying, selling) and lending*. (Unlike Proudhon, Luther is not deceived by these differences of form.)

"Fifteen years ago I wrote against usury since it had already become so widespread that I could hope for no improvement. Since that time, it has exalted itself to such a degree that it *no longer wishes to be a vice, sin or infamy* but extols itself as downright virtue and honour as if it conferred a great favour on and did a Christian service to the people. What will help and counsel us now that infamy has become honour and vice virtue? Seneca says with good reason: *Deest remedii locus, ubi, quae vitia fuerunt, mores fiunt.*[a] Germany has become what it had to become, accursed avarice and usury have corrupted it completely....

"First concerning *lending* and *borrowing*: Where money is lent and more or better is demanded and taken in return, that is usury, anathemised in all laws. Therefore all those who take five, six or more on a hundred on money lent are usurers, and they know they are acting as such and are called the idolatrous servants of covetousness and of Mammon.... And one should say the same in respect of corn, barley and other goods, where more or better is demanded in return, that it is usury, goods stolen and extorted. For lending means my handing over my money, goods or chattels to somebody for

---

[a] There is no remedy where that which was regarded as unvirtuous becomes the habit.—*Ed.*

as long as he needs them, or for as long as I can and wish to, and he returns the same things to me in his own good time, in as good a condition as that in which I lent him them."

"Thus *they also* make a *usury out of buying and selling.* But this is too much to deal with in one single bite. We must deal with one thing now, with usury as regards loans; when we have put a stop to this (as on the Day of Judgement), then we will surely read the lesson with regard to *usurious trade.*"

"Thus Squire Usurer says: Friend, as things are at present, I do my neighbour a great *service* in that I lend him a hundred at five, six, ten. And he thanks me for such a loan as a very special favour. He does, in truth, entreat me for it and pledges himself freely and willingly to give me five, six, ten guilders in a hundred.... Should I not be able without extortion to take this interest with a good conscience?...

"Let [whoever wants to do so] extol himself, put on finery and adorn himself [but pay no heed and keep firmly to the scripture] ... whoever takes more or better than he gives, that is usury and is *not a service, but a wrong* done to his neighbour, as when one steals and robs. All is not service and benefit to a neighbour that is called service and benefit. For an adultress and an adulterer do one another a great service and pleasure. A horseman does a great service to a robber by helping him to rob on the highway, and attack the people and the land. The papists do us a great service in that they do not drown, burn, murder all or let them rot in prison, but let some live and drive them out or take from them what they have. The devil himself does his servants a great, inestimable service.... To sum up: the world is full of great, excellent daily services and good deeds.... The poets write about the Cyclops Polyphemus, who said he would do Ulysses an act of friendship, namely, that he would eat his companions first and then Ulysses last. In sooth, this would have been a service and a fine favour. Such services and good deeds are performed nowadays most diligently by the high-born and the low-born, by peasants and burgesses, who buy goods up, pile up stocks, bring dear times, ||941| increase the price of corn, barley and of everything people need; they then wipe their mouths and say: Yes—one must have what one must have; I let my things out to help people although I might—and could—keep them for myself; and God is thus fooled and deceived.... The sons of men have become very holy.... So that now nobody can profiteer, be covetous or wicked; the world has really become holy, *everyone serves his fellows,* nobody harms anybody else....

"But if this is the kind of service he does, then he does it for Satan himself; although a poor needy man requires such service and must accept it as a service or favour that he is not eaten up completely....

"He[a] does and must do thee such a favour" ⟨pay interest to the usurer⟩ "if he wants to get *money.*"

⟨One can see from the above that usury increased greatly in Luther's time and was already justified as a *"service"* (Say, Bastiat [147]). Even the formulation of competition or harmony existed already: "Everyone serves his fellows."

---

[a] The poor man.—*Ed.*

In the world of *antiquity*, during the better period, usury was forbidden (i.e., interest was not allowed). Later [it was] lawful, and very prevalent. Theoretically the view always [predominated] that interest in itself is wicked (as was stated by *Aristotle*[148]).

In the *Christian Middle Ages*, it was a "sin" and prohibited by "the canon".

Modern times. Luther. The Catholic-pagan view still [prevailed]. Usury became very widespread (as a result partly of the monetary needs of the government, [partly] of the development of trade and manufacture, [and the] necessity to convert the products into money). But its civic justification is already asserted.

Holland. The first apologia for usury. It is also here that it is first modernised and subordinated to industrial or commercial capital.

England. Seventeenth century. The polemics are no longer directed against usury as such, but against the amount of interest, and the fact that it dominates credit. The desire to establish the form of credit. Regulations are imposed.

Eighteenth century. Bentham. Unrestricted usury is recognised as an element of capitalist production.⟩

[A few more extracts from Luther's *An die Pfarrherrn wider den Wucher zu predigen.*]

Interest as compensation for loss.

["The following case can happen and no doubt does happen often, that I, Hans, lend you, Baltzer, a hundred guilders on condition that I must have it back by Michaelmas when I shall need it urgently, otherwise (if you fail me) I shall be in dire trouble. Michaelmas comes and you do not give me the hundred guilders back. Thereupon the judge takes me by the throat, or throws me in the dungeon or prison, or some other trouble befalls me until I pay. There I sit, or remain locked away, missing my food and improvement to my great cost; and you with your delay have brought me to this pass and returned my good deed so badly. What shall I now do? My losses increase day by day and I suffer additional expenses because, and so long as, you delay and do nothing. Who is now to bear the loss or penalty? For my losses will remain an insufferable guest in my house until I am utterly ruined."]

"Well then, speaking in worldly and juridical fashion (we shall have to wait until later to speak about it theologically), you, Baltzer, are due to give me the hundred guilders along with all the losses and charges which have been added." ⟨By charges, he means legal charges, etc., which the lender has incurred because he himself could not pay his debts.⟩ "It is therefore right and proper and likewise according to reason and natural law that you make restitution to me of everything—both the *capital sum* and the loss.... In legal books, the Latin word for this indemnification is *interesse*....

"Something else can happen in the way of loss. If you, Baltzer, do not give me back my hundred guilders by Michaelmas and I have to make a purchase, say to buy a garden, a plot of land or a house, or anything from which I and my children could derive great use or sustenance, then I must forego it and you do me damage and are a hindrance to me so that I can never get such a bargain again because of your delay and inactivity, etc. But since I lent you the hundred guilders, you have caused me to suffer twofold damage *because I cannot pay on the one hand and cannot buy on the other* and thus must suffer loss on both sides. This is called *duplex interesse, damni emergentis et lucri cessantis*[a]....

"Having heard that Hans has suffered loss on the hundred guilders which he lent and demands just recompense for this loss, they rush in and charge *such double compensation on every 100 guilders*, namely, for expenses incurred and for the inability to buy the garden; *just as though every hundred could grow double interest naturally, so that whenever they have a hundred guilders, they loan them out and charge for two such losses which however they have not incurred at all*....

"Therefore thou art a usurer, *who makes good thine own imagined losses with your neighbour's money*, losses which no one has caused thee and which thou canst neither prove nor *calculate*. The lawyers call such losses *non verum, sed phantasticum interesse.*[b] *A loss which each man dreams up for himself*....

"It will not do ||942| to say I might incur a loss because I might not have been able to *pay* or *buy*. That would mean *ex contingente necessarium,*[c] making something that must be out of something which is not, to turn a thing which is uncertain into a thing which is absolutely sure. Would such usury not eat up the world in a few years....

"If the lender *accidentally* incurs a loss through no fault of his own, he must be recompensed, but it is different in such deals and just the reverse. There he seeks and *invents* losses to the detriment of his needy neighbours; thus he wants to maintain himself and get rich, to be lazy and idle and to live in *luxury and splendour on other people's labour* and worry, danger and loss. So that I sit behind the stove and let *my hundred guilders gather wealth for me throughout the land*, and, because they *are only loaned, I keep them safely in my purse* without any risk or worry; my friend, who would not like that?

"And what has been said about money which is loaned applies also to corn, wine and such like goods which are lent, for they also may occasion such double damage. But *such double damage is not something naturally accruing to the goods*, but may arise *by accident* only and cannot therefore be reckoned as damage unless it has actually occurred and been proved, etc. ...

"Usury there must be, but woe to the usurers....

"All wise, reasonable heathens have also inveighed against usury as something exceedingly evil. Thus Aristotle, in his *Politics*, says that usury

---

[a] Twofold compensation, for the loss incurred and for the gain missed.—*Ed.*

[b] Not real but imagined losses.—*Ed.*

[c] Making a necessity out of an accident.—*Ed.*

is against nature and for this reason: it always takes more than it gives. Thereby it abolishes the means and measure of all virtue, which we call like for like, *aequalitas arithmetica*,[a] etc. ...

"But taking from other people, stealing or robbing, is called a shameful way of maintaining oneself, and those who do so are called, by your leave, thieves and robbers, whom we are accustomed to hang on the gallows; a usurer however is a nice thief and robber and sits in a chair, therefore we call him a *chair thief*....

"The heathens were able, by the light of reason, to conclude that a usurer is a double-dyed thief and murderer. We Christians, however, hold them in such honour that we fairly worship them for the sake of their money.... Whoever eats up, robs and steals the nourishment of another, commits as great a murder (so far as in him lies) as he who starves a man to death or utterly undoes him. But such does a usurer, and sits the while, safe on his chair, when he ought rather to be hanging on the gallows and eaten by as many ravens as he has stolen guilders, if only there was so much flesh on him that so many ravens could stick their beaks in and share it....

"But the dealers and usurers will cry out that what is written under hand and seal must be honoured. To this the jurists have given a prompt and sufficient answer. *In malis promissis*.[b] Thus the theologians say that some people give the devil something under hand and seal signifies nothing, even if it is written and sealed in blood. For what is against God, Right and Nature is null and void. Therefore let a Prince who can do so, take action, tear up bond and seal, take no notice of it, etc. ...

"Therefore there is on this earth no greater *enemy of man*, after the devil, than a miser and usurer, for *he wants to be God over all men*. Turks, soldiers, tyrants are also bad men, yet they must let the people live and confess that they are bad and enemies, and can, nay must, now and then show pity on some. But a usurer and money-grubber, such a one would have the whole world perish of hunger and thirst, misery and want, so far as in him lies, so that he may have all to himself and everyone *receive from him as from a God and* ||943| *be his serf for evermore*. This is what gladdens his heart, refreshes his blood. And, at the same time, he can wear sable cloaks, golden chains, rings, gowns, wipe his mouth, be deemed and taken for a worthy, pious man, who is more merciful than God Himself, more loving than the Mother of God, and all the holy Saints....

"And they write of the great deeds of Hercules, how he overcame so many monsters and frightful horrors in order to save his country and his people. For usury is a great horrible monster, like the werewolf, who lays everything waste, more than any Cacus, Geryon or Antaeus, etc. And yet he decks himself out and wants to appear pious so that people may not see where the oxen have gone (*that he drags backwards into his den*)."

⟨An excellent picture, it fits the capitalist in general, who pretends that what he has taken from others and brought into his den, *emanates from him*, and by causing it to go *backwards* he gives it the semblance of having *come from his den*.⟩

---

[a] Arithmetical equality.—*Ed.*
[b] In evil promises.—*Ed.*

"But Hercules shall hear the cry of the oxen and of the prisoners and shall seek out Cacus even on the cliffs and among the rocks, and he shall set the oxen loose again from the villain. For Cacus means the villain that is a *pious usurer* who steals, robs and eats everything. And will not admit that he has done it and thinks no one will find him out, because the oxen, drawn backwards into his den, make it seem from their footprints that they have been *let out*. Thus the usurer wants to deceive the world, as though he were of use and gave the world oxen, *whereas, in reality, he seizes them for himself and consumes them....*

"Therefore, a usurer and miser is, indeed, not truly a human being, sins not in a human way and must be looked upon as a werewolf, more than all the tyrants, murderers and robbers, nearly as evil as the devil himself, but one who sits in peace and safety, not like an enemy, but like a friend and citizen, yet robs and murders more horribly than any enemy or incendiary. And since we break on the wheel and behead highwaymen and burglars, how much more ought we to break on the wheel and kill all usurers, and drive out, curse and behead all misers...."

A highly picturesque and striking description of both the character of old-fashioned usury, on the one hand, and of capital in general, on the other, with the "imagined loss", the "indemnification which naturally accrues" to money and commodities, the general phrases about usefulness, the "pious" air of the usurer who is not "like the rest of men", the appearance of giving when one is taking, and of letting out when one is pulling in, etc.

* * *

"The great premium attached to the possession of Gold and Silver, by the power it gives of selecting advantageous moments of purchasing, gradually gave rise to the trade of the *Banker.*" The Banker "differs from the old *Usurer* in this respect, that he lends to the rich and *seldom or never to the poor*. Hence he lends with less risk, and can afford to do it on cheaper terms; and for both reasons, he avoids the popular odium which attended the Usurer" (Francis William Newman, *Lectures on Political Economy*, London, 1851, p. 44).

The involuntary alienation of feudal landed property develops along with the development of usury and money.

"The introduction of money which buys all things, and in consequence of that, the favour due to creditors, who have lent their money to a possessor of land, brings in the necessity of legal alienation for the payment of what has been thus lent..." (John Dalrymple, *An Essay towards a General History of Feudal Property in Great Britain*, London, 1759, fourth ed., p. 124).

||944| "According to Thomas Culpeper (1641), Josiah Child (1670) and Paterson (1694) wealth depends on the self-imposed reduction in the rate of

interest on gold and silver." [This rule] "was observed in England for almost two centuries" (Charles Ganilh, [*Des systèmes d'économie politique...*, seconde éd., tome premier, Paris, 1821, pp. 58-59]).

When *Hume*—in opposition to Locke—declared that the rate of interest is regulated by the rate of profit,[149] he had a much higher development of capitalism in mind. This was even more true of Bentham when he wrote his defence of usury towards the end of the eighteenth century.

A reduction in the rate of interest was imposed by law from the time of Henry VIII to that of Queen Anne.

No country had a *general rate of interest* during the Middle Ages. Only the priests [prohibited all transactions involving interest] with great sternness. Legal measures safeguarding loans were unreliable. The rate of interest was consequently very high in individual cases. *The amount of money in circulation was small and it was necessary to make most money payments in cash*, for bills of exchange were not yet widely used. Hence interest and the concept of usury varied considerably. In Charlemagne's time it was regarded as usurious if 100 per cent was charged. The local burghers in Lindau on Lake Constance charged $216^2/_3$ per cent in 1344. The legal rate of interest in Zürich was fixed at $43^1/_3$ per cent by the Council. In Italy, 40 per cent had to be paid occasionally although the usual rate did not exceed 20 per cent from the twelfth to the fourteenth centuries. Verona decreed a legal rate of $12^1/_2$ per cent. Frederick II 10 per cent, but this only for Jews. He would not say what the rate should be for Christians. The usual rate in the Rhenish part of Germany was 10 per cent as early as the thirteenth century (Hüllmann, *Städtewesen des Mittelalters*, Zweiter Teil, Bonn, 1827, pp. 55-57).

The enormous rates of interest in the Middle Ages (insofar as they were not paid by the feudal aristocracy, etc.) were based in the towns, in very large measure, on the gigantic profits upon alienation which the merchants and urban craftsmen made out of country people, whom they cheated.

In Rome, as in the entire ancient world—apart from merchant cities, like Athens and others, which were particularly developed industrially and commercially—[high interest was] a means used by the big landowners not only for expropriating the small proprietors, the plebeians, but for appropriating their persons.

Usury was originally permitted freely in Rome. The Law of the Twelve Tables (303 A.U.C.[a]) "fixed interest on money at 1 per cent per year" (Niebuhr says 10 per cent). "This law was promptly infringed [...] Duilius" (398 A.U.C.) "reduced the rate of interest to 1 per cent again [...] *unciario foenore*[b] [...] It was limited to $^1/_2$ per cent in the year 408, and in 413 lend-

---

[a] A.U.C.—*anno urbis conditae*—in the year of the founding of the City, used to express the date since the foundation of Rome (753 B.C.).—*Ed.*

[b] Increase by one twelfth (one ounce).—*Ed.*

ing at interest was totally prohibited as a result of a referendum initiated by the Tribune Genucius [....] It is not surprising that in a republic in which the citizens were forbidden to carry on industry and both wholesale and retail trade, *trading in money should also be prohibited*" (Dureau de la Malle, [*Économie politique des Romains*,] t. II, [Paris, 1840,] pp. 259-61). "This lasted for 300 years until the fall of Carthage. It then [became legal to charge up to] 12 per cent, but the usual rate of annual interest was 6 per cent" (loc. cit., p. 261). "Justinian fixed the rate of interest at 4 per cent; in Trajan's time the legal rate of interest was 5 per cent, *usura quincunx*.[a] In Egypt the legal commercial interest was 12 per cent in 146 B.C." (loc. cit., pp. 262-63). |944||

* * *

||950a| *James William Gilbart* in his *The History and Principles of Banking* (London, 1834) says the following with regard to *interest*.

"That a man who borrows money with a view of *making a profit by it*, should give some portion of his profit to the lender, is a self-evident principle of natural justice. A man makes a profit usually by means of traffick. But in a country purely agricultural, and under such government as was the feudal system,[b] there can be but little traffick, and hence but little profit." Legislation against extortionate interest is therefore justified in the Middle Ages. "Besides, in an agricultural country a person seldom wants to borrow money except he be reduced to poverty or distress by misfortune" (p. 163).

"In the reign of Henry VIII, interest was limited to 10 per cent. James I reduced it to 8 per cent [...] Charles II [...] to 6 per cent [...] Anne [...] to 5 per cent" (pp. 164-65). "... in those times, the lenders [...] had in fact, though not a legal, yet an actual monopoly, and hence it was necessary that they, like other monopolists, should be placed under restraint. In our times, it is the rate of profit which regulates the rate of interest. In those times, it was the rate of interest which regulated the rate of profit. If the moneylender charged a high rate of interest to the merchant, the merchant must have charged a higher rate of profit on his goods. Hence, a large sum of money would be taken from the pockets of the purchasers to be put into the pockets of the money-lenders. This *additional price*, too, put *upon the goods*, would render the public less able and less inclined to purchase them" (p. 165).

In the seventeenth century, Josiah Child in his *Brief Observations concerning Trade and Interest of Money*, and Thomas Culpeper in his *Traité contre l'usure* (1621) likewise, attacks *Thomas Manley* (author of the tract *Interest of Money Mistaken*[150])

---

[a] Interest of five twelfths (five ounces).—*Ed.*
[b] In Marx's manuscript this sentence reads (in German) as follows: "But in the Middle Ages the population was wholly agricultural. And in this case, just as under a feudal government", etc.—*Ed.*

whom he calls the "champion of the usurers". Naturally the point of departure—like that of all the arguments of English economists of the seventeenth century—was the wealth of Holland where there was a low rate of interest. Child considers that this low rate of interest is the cause of wealth. Manley declares that it is only the result [of wealth].

"Insomuch that to know whether any Country be rich or poor ... no other question needs to be resolved, but this, viz. What Interest do they pay for Money?" ([Josiah Child, *Brief Observations concerning Trade and Interest of Money*, London, 1668, p. 9;] *Traités*, p. 74).[a]

"... the gentleman brings up his battalia, and, like a stout champion for the sly and timorous herd of usurers, plants his main battery against that part which I confessed to be weakest.... And he positively denies that the lowness of interest is the cause" (of wealth), "and affirms it to be only the effect thereof..." ([Josiah Child, *A New Discourse of Trade*..., London, 1775, p. 39;] *Traités*, p. 120).

"When interest is abated, they who call in their money must either buy land" (whose price goes up as a result of the number of buyers), "or trade with it..." ([*A New Discourse*..., p. 47;] *Traités*, p. 133).

"... whilst interest is at 6 per cent no man will run an adventure to sea for the gain of 8 or 9 per cent which the Dutch, having money at 4 or 3 per cent at interest, are contented with..." ([*A New Discourse*..., p. 47;] *Traités*, p. 134).

The low rate of interest and the high price of land force the merchant to stick to commerce. "... it" (a low rate of interest) "inclines a nation to thriftiness" ([*A New Discourse*..., p. 52;] *Traités*, p. 144).

"... if trade be that which enricheth any kingdom, and lowering of interest advanceth trade ... then the abatement of interest, or more properly restraining of usury ... is doubtless a primary and principal cause of the riches of any nation; it being not improper to say, nor absurd to conceive, that the same thing ||950b| may be both a *cause* and an effect" ([*A New Discourse*..., p. 58;] *Traités*, p. 155).

"... an egg is the cause of a hen, and a hen the cause of an egg."

"... [The like may be said of nations:] the abatement of interest causeth an increase of wealth, and the increase of wealth may cause a further abatement of interest. But that is best done by the midwifery of good laws..." ([*A New Discourse*..., p. 59;] *Traités*, p. 156).

"... I am an advocate for industry, he for idleness..." ([*A New Discourse*..., p. 71;] *Traités*, p. 179).

He appears here as the direct champion of industrial and commercial capital. |XV-950b||

---

[a] Marx quotes this and the following passages from the French translation of Child's work—*Traités sur le commerce et sur les avantages qui résultent de la réduction de l'interest de l'argent*, Amsterdam et Berlin, 1754.—*Ed.*

APPENDICES

QUOTATIONS IN FRENCH, GERMAN AND ITALIAN[a]

Words which Marx underlined are set in italics. Words and passages translated by Marx into German are set in spaced type.

27 «Des quantités égales de travail doivent nécessairement, dans tous les tems et dans tous les lieux, être d'une valeur égale pour celui qui travaille. Dans son état habituel de santé, de force et d'activité, et d'après le degré ordinaire d'habileté ou de dextérité qu'il peut avoir, il faut toujours qu'il donne la même portion de son repos, de sa liberté, de son bonheur. Quelle que soit la quantité de denrées qu'il reçoive en récompense de son travail, le prix qu'il paie est toujours le même. Ce prix, à la vérité, peut acheter tantôt une plus grande, tantôt une plus petit quantité de ces denrées; mais c'est la valeur de celles-ci qui varie, et non celle du travail qui les achète. En tous tems et en tous lieux, ce qui est difficile à obtenir, ou ce qui coûte beaucoup de travail à acquérir, est *cher*; et ce qu'on peut se procurer aisément ou avec peu de travail est à *bon marché*. Ainsi le travail, ne variant jamais dans sa valeur propre, est la seule mesure réelle et définitive qui puisse servir, dans tous les tems et dans tous les lieux, à apprécier et à comparer la valeur des toutes les marchandises.» (Adam Smith, *Recherches sur la nature et les causes de la richesse des nations.* Traduction nouvelle ... par Germain Garnier, t. I, Paris, 1802, pp. 65-66.)

27 « ... la valeur réelle de toutes les différentes parties constituantes du prix se mesure par la quantité de travail que chacune d'elles peut acheter ou commander. Le travail mesure la valeur, non-seulement de cette partie du prix qui se résout en *travail*, mais encore de célle qui se résout en *rente*, et de celle qui se résout en *profit*.» (ibidem, p. 100.)

62 «On a cru remarquer que les *cottagers*, qui ont des vaches, sont plus laborieux et mènent une vie plus régulière, que ceux qui n'en ont point... La plupart de ceux qui ont des vaches à présent les ont achetées du fruit de leur travail. Il est donc plus exact de dire que c'est leur travail qui leur a donné les vaches, qu'il ne l'est de dire, que ce sont les vaches qui leur ont donné le goût du travail.» (T. R. Malthus, *Essai sur le*

---

[a] See Publishers' Note.—*Ed.*

principe de population.... Traduit de l'anglais par P. Prévost, tome quatrième, Paris, 1836, pp. 104-05.)

62 « ... il *est évident que tous les hommes ne peuvent pas former les classes moyennes. Les* supérieures et les inférieures sont inévitables, et de plus très-utiles. Si l'on ôtoit de la société l'espérance de s'élever et la crainte de déchoir; si le travail ne portoit pas avec lui sa récompense et l'indolence sa punition; on ne verroit nulle part cette activité, cette ardeur avec laquelle chacun travaille à améliorer son état et qui est le principal instrument de la prospérité publique.» (ibidem, p. 112.)

63 «Plus le monopole s'étend, plus la chaine est lourde pour les exploités.» (Jean Jacques Rousseau.) [The source of this quotation has not been established.]

63 « ... on pourroit se livrer à l'espérance, qu'à quelque période future, les procédés par lesquels le travail est abrégé, et qui ont déjà fait un progrès si rapide, pourroient enfin fournir à tous les besoins de la société la plus opulente, avec moins de travail personel, qu'il n'en faut de nos jours pour remplir le même but: et *si l'ouvrir alors n'étoit pas soulagé d'une partie de la pénible tâche à laquelle il est assujetti aujourd'hui;* du moins *le nombre de ceux,* à qui la société impose un travail si rude, se trouveroit diminué.» (T. R. Malthus, *Essai sur le principe de population....* Traduit de l'anglais par P. Prévost, tome quatrième, Paris, 1836, p. 113.)

88 «De la Production.» (James Mill, *Elémens d'économie politique.* Traduit de l'anglais par J. T. Parisot, Paris, 1823, p. 7.)

88 «De la Distribution.» (ibidem, p. 13.)

88 «Des Exchanges.» (ibidem, p. 85.)

88 «De la Consommation.» (ibidem, p. 237.)

88 «T o u t e f o i s ,   a u   l i e u   d ' a t t e n d r e   q u e   l e s   p r o d u i t s   s o i e n t   o b t e n u s ,   e t   q u e   l a   v a l e u r   e n   a i t   é t é   r é a l i s é e ,   c e   q u i   e n t r a î n e   d e s   d é l a i s   e t   d e s   i n c e r t i t u d e s ,   o n   a   t r o u v é   q u ' i l   é t a i t   *p l u s   c o m m o d e*   p o u r   l e s   o u v r i e r s   d e   r e c e v o i r   l e u r   p a r t   à   *l ' a v a n c e .*   L a   f o r m e   s o u s   l a q u e l l e   o n   a   t r o u v é   p l u s   c o n v e n a b l e   q u ' i l s   l a   r e ç u s s e n t ,   e s t   c e l l e   d e   s a l a i r e s .   Q u a n d   l a   p a r t   d e s   p r o d u i t s   q u i   r e v i e n t   à   l ' o u v r i e r   a   é t é   r e ç u e   e n   e n t i e r   p a r   l u i ,   s o u s   f o r m e   d e   s a l a i r e s ,   c e s   p r o d u i t s   a p p a r t i e n n e n t   e x c l u s i v e m e n t   a u   c a p i t a l i s t e ,   p u i s q u ' i l   a   d e   f a i t   a c h e t é   l a   *p a r t   d e   l ' o u v r i e r*   e t   l a   l u i   a   p a y é e   d ' a v a n c e .»   (ibidem, pp. 33-34.)

93 «... ce qui détermine la part de l'ouvrier, ou la proportion suivant laquelle les produits [...] partagés entre lui et le capitaliste. Quelle que soit la part de l'ouvrier, elle règle le taux des salaires...» (ibidem, p. 34.)

93 « ...   l a   f i x a t i o n   d e s   p a r t s   e n t r e   l ' o u v r i e r   e t   l e   c a p i t a l i s t e ,   e s t   l ' o b j e t   d ' u n   m a r c h é   e n t r e   e u x

[....] Tous les marchés, lorsqu'on les fait librement, sont réglés par la concurrence, et les conditions changent selon que la *proportion* varie *entre l'offre et la demande.*» (ibidem, pp. 34-35.)

95 «... la fixation des parts entre l'ouvrier et le capitaliste, est l'objet d'un marché entre eux [....] Tous les marchés, lorsqu'on les fait librement, sont réglés par la concurrence, et les conditions changent selon que la proportion varie entre l'offre et la demande.» (ibidem, pp. 34-35.)

96 «... que si le rapport qui existe entre la masse des capitaux et la population reste le même, le taux des salaires restera aussi le même...» (ibidem, p. 37.)

96 «... la proportion suivant laquelle les produits sont partagés...» (ibidem, p. 35.)

96 «... *fixee* d'une *manière* quelconque.» (ibidem, p. 35.)

97 «... une manière quelconque.» (ibidem, p. 35.)

97 «... d'une manière quelconque.» (ibidem, p. 35.)

97 «... *offrir de travailler pour une moindre rétribution.*» (ibidem, p. 36.)

98 «... l'espèce *humaine,* la *perfectibilité,* ou le pouvoir d'avancer continuellement d'un degré de science et de bonheur à un autre plus grand, paraît en grande partie dépendre de l'existence d'une classe d'hommes qui sont *maîtres de leur temps,* c'est-à-dire, qui sont assez riches pour être exempts de toute sollicitude à l'égard des moyens de vivre dans un certain état de jouissance. C'est par cette classe d'hommes que le domaine des sciences est cultivé et s'agrandit; ce sont aussi ces hommes qui répandent les lumières; leurs enfans reçoivent la meilleure éducation, et se préparent à remplir toutes les fonctions les plus importantes et les plus délicates de la société; ils deviennent législateurs, juges, administrateurs, instituteurs, inventeurs, dans tous les arts, et directeurs de tous les grands et utiles travaux par lesquels la domination de l'espèce humaine s'étend sur les forces de la nature.» (James Mill, *Élémens d'économie politique.* Traduit de l'anglais par J. T. Parisot, Paris, 1823, p. 65.)

98 «Pour mettre une portion considérable de

la société à même de jouir des avantages que procure le *loisir*, il est évident que *l'intérêt des capitaux* doit être fort.» (ibidem, p. 67.)

98 «Il y a deux choses à observer à l'égard de ces deux *espèces de travail*: [...] elles *ne* sont pas toujours payées au même taux [...]» (ibidem, p. 100.)

100 «Ce que l'on consomme *productivement* est toujours capital. Ceci est une propriété de la consommation productive qui mérite d'être particulièrement remarquée. [...] que [...] ce qui est consommé productivement *devient* capital...» (ibidem, pp. 241-42.)

100 «Une demande signifie le *désir* et le *moyen d'acheter*... *L'objet équivalent* qu'un homme apporte est l'*instrument* de la demande. L'étendue de sa demande est mesurée par la valeur de cet objet. La demande et l'objet équivalent sont des termes qu'on peut substituer l'un à l'autre... Sa volonté d'*acheter* et ses *moyens de le faire* sont donc égaux, ou [...] sa demande est exactement égale à la valeur de ce qu'il a produit, et qu'il ne veut pas consommer.» (ibidem, pp. 252-53.)

102 «Il est évident que chaque homme apporte, à la masse générale des produits qui constituent l'offre, la totalité de ce qu'il a produit, et qu'il ne veut pas consommer. Sous quelque forme qu'une portion du produit annuel soit tombée entre les mains d'un homme, s'il se propose de n'en consommer rien lui-même, il veut se défaire du tout, et le tout vient, par conséquent, augmenter l'offre; s'il en consomme une partie, il veut se défaire de tout le reste, et tout le reste entre dans l'offre.» (ibidem, p. 253.)

103 «Ainsi, puisque la demande de tout homme est égale à la portion du produit annuel, ou, autrement dit, à la portion de richesse dont il veut se défaire, et que l'offre de chaque homme est exactement la même chose, l'offre et la demande de tout individu sont nécessairement égales.» (ibidem, pp. 253-54.)

103 «La demande et l'offre[a] ont entre elles une relation particulière. Une denrée ou marchandise offerte est toujours en même temps l'*objet* d'une demande, et une denrée ou marchandise qui est l'objet d'une demande fait toujours

---

[a] In the manuscript, "Offre and demande".—*Ed.*

en même temps partie de la masse générale des produits qui constituent l'offre. Toute denrée ou marchandise est toujours *à la fois* un objet de demande et un objet d'offre. Quand deux hommes font un échange, l'un ne vient pas pour faire seulement une offre, et l'autre pour faire seulement une demande; chacun d'eux a une offre et une demande à faire: *l'objet de son offre* doit lui procurer celui de sa demande, et par conséquent sa demande et son offre sont parfaitement égales. Mais si la demande et l'offre[a] de tout individu sont toujours égales l'une à l'autre, la demande et l'offre de tous les individus d'une nation pris en masse doivent être égales. Quel que soit donc le montant du produit annuel, il ne peut jamais excéder celui de la demande annuelle. La totalité du produit annuel est divisée en un nombre de portions égal à celui des individus entre lesquels ce produit est distribué. La totalité de la demande est égale à la somme de ce que, sur toutes les parts, les possesseurs ne gardent pas pour leur propre consommation; mais la totalité des parts est égale à tout de produit annuel.» (ibidem, pp. 254-55.)

104 «Voilà donc un cas au moins où le prix (le prix du travail) est réglé, d'une manière permanente, par le rapport de l'offre à la demande.» (J. R. McCulloch, *Discours sur l'origine, les progrès, les objets particuliers, et l'importance de l'économie politique*... Traduit de l'anglais par G^{me} Prévost, Genève et Paris, 1825, p. 187.)

104 « ... de donner une *déduction logique* des principes de l'économie politique...» (ibidem, p. 88.)

104 « ... expose presque tous les sujets de discussion. Il a su débroullier et simplifier les questions les plus compliquées et les plus difficiles, poser les divers principes de la science dans leur ordre naturel...» (ibidem, p. 88.)

104 «On peut élever un doute sur l'influence des *terres inférieures* pour régler les prix, en ayant égard, comme on le doit, à leur *étendue relative*.» (ibidem, p. 177.)

105 « ... '*Mr. Mill* use de cette comparaison: ‚Supposez que toutes les terres en culture dans un certain pays soient de même qualité et donnent les mêmes profits aux capitaux qu'on y applique, à l'exception d'un seul acre, qui donne un produit sextuple de celui de tout autre.' (Mill, *Elements etc.*, p. 71, 2de édit. angl.) Il est certain, comme M. Mill le prouve, que le fermier de ce dernier acre ne pourroit point élever son fermage, et que les cinq sixièmes du produit appartiendroient au propriétaire. Mais si l'ingénieux auteur avoit pensé à proposer une fiction

---

[a] In the manuscript, "But if offre and demande".—*Ed.*

semblable pour le cas inverse, il auroit reconnu que le résultat étoit différent. En effet, supposons toutes les terres au niveau, excepté un acre de terre inferieure. Que sur cet acre unique, le profit de capital soit la sixième partie du profit sur tout autre. Pense-t-on que le profit de quelques millions d'acres fût forcé de se réduire à la sixième partie de son profit habituel? Il est probable que cet acre unique n'auroit pas d'effet, parce que les produits quelconques (spécialement le blé) étant portés au marché, ne souffriroient point sensiblement de la concurrence d'une portion *minime*. Nous disons donc que l'assertion ricardienne sur l'effet des terres inférieures doit être modifiée par l'*étendue relative* des terres de fertilité inégale.» (ibidem, pp. 177-78.)

106 « ... nous reconnoissons qu'en général le taux des profits agricoles règle celui des profits industriels. Mais en même temps nous ferons remarquer que ceux-ci réagissent nécessairement sur les premiers. Quand le prix du blé vient à hausser à un certain point, les capitaux industriels s'appliquent aux terres et réduisent nécessairement les profits agricoles.» (ibidem, p. 179.)

106 « ... ne semble-t-il pas que, si la demande croissante des capitaux fait hausser le prix des ouvriers, c'est-à-dire le *salaire*, on n'a pas raison d'affirmer que l'offre croissante de ces mêmes capitaux ne peut point faire baisser le prix des capitaux, en d'autres termes le *profit?*» (ibidem, p. 188.)

107 « ... l'état prospère commence par faire hausser les profits, et cela long temps avant que l'on cultive les nouvelles terres; de sorte que, lorsque celles-ci exercent leur influence sur la rente en déduction des profits, ceux-ci, bien qu'immédiatement diminués, restent encore aussi élevés qu'ils étoient avant le progrès... Pourquoi à une époque quelconque, cultive-t-on les terres de qualité inférieure? Ce ne peut être qu'en vue d'un profit *au moins égal au profit courant*. Et quelle circonstance peut amener ce taux du profit sur de telles terres? L'accroissement de la population... Pressant ... sur la limite des subsistances, elle fait hausser le prix des alimens (du blé en particulier), du manière à donner de gros profits aux capitaux agricoles. Les autres capitaux affluent sur les terres; mais comme celles-ci sont d'une étendue bornée, cette concurrence a un terme; et il arrive enfin qu'en cultivant les sols plus ingrats, on obtient encore des *profits supérieurs à ceux du commerce ou des manufatures*. Dès lors (en supposant ces terres inférieures d'une étendue suffisante) les profits agricoles sont forcés de se régler sur ceux des derniers que l'on a versés sur les terres. C'est ainsi que prenant le taux des profits à l'origine du progrès divitial, on reconnoîtra que les profits non aucune tendance à diminuer. Ils haussent avec la population croissante, jusqu'au point où les profits agricoles ont tellement cru qu'ils peuvent éprouver (par des cultures nouvelles) une diminution notable, sans redescendre jamais au-dessous de leur taux primitif, ou (pour parler plus exactement) au-dessous du taux moyen déterminé par diverses circonstances.» (ibidem, pp. 190-92.)

108 «Les terres de qualité inférieure ... ne sont mises en culture que lorsqu'elles rendent des profits égaux ou supérieurs à ceux des capitaux industriels. Souvent, dans ces circonstances, malgré les nouvelles cultures, le prix du blé et des produits agricoles reste encore fort élevé. Ces hauts

prix gênent la population ouvrière, parce que la hausse des salaires ne suit pas exactement celle du prix des objets de consommation à l'usage des salariés. Ils sont plus ou moins à charge à la population tout entière, parce que presque toutes les marchandises sont affectées de la hausse des salaires et de celle du prix des objets de première nécessité. Cette gêne universell, jointe à la mortalité qu'occasionne une population surabondante, amène une diminution dans le nombre des salariés, et de suite une hausse dans les salariès et une baisse dans les profits agricoles. Dès lors toutes les opérations ont lieu en sens inverse des précédentes. Les capitaux se retirent des terres inférieures et se reversent sur l'industrie. Mais le principe de population agira bientôt de nouveau; dès que la misère aura cessé, le nombre des ouvriers croitra, leur salaire diminuera, et en conséquence les profits hausseront. Une suite de telles oscillations doit avoir lieu, sans que les profits moyens en soient affectés. Ils peuvent par d'autres causes hausser ou baisser, ou par cette cause même, ils peuvent changer alternativement en sens contraire, sans que leur baisse ou leur hausse moyenne puisse être attribuée à la nécessité d'entreprendre de nouvelles cultures. La population est le régulateur, qui rétablit l'ordre naturel et contient les profits entre certaines limites.» (ibidem, pp. 194-96.)

119 «O n n'achète des produits qu'avec des produits.» (Jean-Baptiste Say. *Traité d'économie politique...*, seconde édition, t. II, Paris, 1814, p. 382.)

180 «Services productifs [...] du capital» (ibidem, p. 474.)

180 « ... services productifs de la nature[a].» (ibidem, p. 53.)

180 « ... services productifs...» (ibidem, p. 53.)

186 «L'auteur ... énonce ainsi les craintes que la *baisse des profits* lui inspire. ‚L'apparence de prospérité que présente l'Angleterre, [...] est trompeuse; la plaie de la pauvreté a atteint secrètement la masse des citoyens, et les fondemens de la puissance et de la grandeur nationale ont été ébranlés... Là où le taux de l'intérêt est bas, comme en Angleterre, le taux des profits est également bas et la prospérité de la nation a dépassé le point culminant.' Ces assertions ne peuvent manquer de surprendre tous ceux qui connoissent l'état brillant de l'Angleterre.» (J. R. McCulloch, *Discours sur l'origine, les progrès, les objets particuliers, et l'importance de l'économie politique...* Traduit de l'anglais par Gme Prévost, Genève et Paris, 1825, p. 197.)

267 « ... è vera ricchezza ... l'uomo...» (Galiani, *Della Moneta* in: Scrittori Classici Italiani di Economia Politica. Parte moderna. Tomo III, Milano, 1803, p. 229.)

296 «*Wal* couvrir, fortifier; *vallo, valeo; vallus* couvre et fortifie, *valor* est la force elle-même. Comparez l'All. *walle*[b], walte, et l'Angl. *wall, wield.*» (Chavée, *Essai d'étymologie philosophique...*», Bruxelles, 1844, p. 70.)

362 «Les matières premières, l'instrument, l'approvisionnement.» (A. Cherbuliez, *Riche ou pauvre...*, Paris-Genève, 1840, p. 16.)

---

[a] In the manuscript, "la terre".—*Ed.*
[b] In the manuscript, "Wal" instead of "walle".—*Ed.*

362 « ... il n'y a aucune différence entre un capital et toute autre portion de richesse: c'est seulement par l'emploi qui en est fait qu'une chose devient capital; c'est-à-dire, lorsqu'elle est employée, dans une *opération productive*, comme matière première, comme instrument, ou comme approvisionnement.» (ibidem, p. 18.)

369 « Le profit mercantile est déterminé, comme on voit, par la *valeur des produits* comparée avec celle des *divers éléments* du capital productif...» (ibidem, p. 70.)

369 « ... les deux éléments principaux de cette détermination sont évidemment le prix des matières premières et la quantité d'approvisionnement nécessaire pour les mettre en œuvre. [...] le progrès économique des sociétés agit en sens *contraire* sur ces deux éléments [...] il tend à renchérir les matières premières en augmentant la valeur de tous les produits des industries extractives qui s'exercent sur des fonds appropriés et d'une étendue limitée...» (ibidem, p. 70.)

370 «La somme totale des produits, moins la somme totale du capital consommé pour les obtenir, donne la somme totale des profits pendant un espace de temps déterminé. Or, la somme totale des produits *s'accroît en raison du capital employé*, et non du capital consommé. Le *taux des profits, ou leur* rapport au capital, résulte donc de la combinaison de deux autres rapports, savoir: du *rapport entre le capital employé et le capital consommé, et du rapport entre le capital consommé et le produit.*» (ibidem, p. 70.)

371 « ... les deux *éléments passifs du capital*...» (ibidem, p. 59.)

372 « ... *la somme total des produits s'accroît* en raison de capital employé, et non du capital consommé.» (ibidem, p. 70.)

373 «Le *taux des profits*, ou leur *rapport* au capital, résulte donc de la combinaison de deux autres rapports, savoir: du *rapport entre le capital employé et le capital consommé*, et du rapport *entre le capital consommé et le produit.*» (ibidem, p. 70.)

374 «Soit P le produit total pendant une période écoulée, π le profit, C le capital employé, c le capital consommé, r le *rapport* du profit au capital. Dans équation $P-c=\pi$, substituons à π sa valeur$=rC$, nous obtiendrons cette $rC=P-c$, et $r=\dfrac{P-c}{C}$.» (ibidem, p. 70, note.)

375 «Le capital productif [...] est composé d'une partie consommable, [...] et d'une partie non consommable [...] A mesure que la richesse et la population font des progrès, la partie consommable tend à augmenter, puisque les industries extractives exigent une quantité de travail de plus en plus considérable. D'un autre côté, ce même progrès [...] augmente la *masse* du capital employé dans une proportion plus rapide que celle du capital *consommé*. Ainsi, quoique la masse totale du capital consommé tende à s'accroître, la masse des produits croissant selon une progression encore plus rapide, le premier effet se trouve neutralisé, et la *somme totale des profits* doit être considérée comme croissant dans une proportion au moins aussi forte que la *somme totale du capital emplyé*.» (ibidem, p. 71.)

375 «Je dis que la masse des profits va croissant non le taux, qui est le rapport de cette masse au capital employé, r étant représenté par $\frac{P-c}{C}$, il est clair que P—c, c'est-à-dire π, *peut* croître quoique r diminue, si C croit plus rapidement que P—C.» (ibidem, p. 72, note.)

376 «Après le prélèvement de la rente foncière, ce qui reste de cette *somme des profits*, c'est-à-dire de cet excédant des produits sur le capital consommé, se partage entre les producteurs capitalistes *en raison du capital que chacun a employé*; tandis que la portion des produits qui correspond au capital consommé, et qui est destinée à le remplacer, se partage en raison de celui qu'ils ont réellement consommé. Cette *double loi de partage* s'établit par l'*effet de la concurrence* [...] qui tend à égaliser les avantages de tous les emplois de capitaux. C'est cette double loi de partage qui assigne, en définitive, aux diverses espèces de produits leurs *valeurs* respectives et leurs *prix*.» (ibidem, pp. 71-72.)

377 «... obtiendront ce qui leur est nécessaire qu'en offrant leur *travail* aux capitalistes, par conséquent ils n'acquerront de droits que sur les choses qui leur seront allouées comme *prix de* leur *travail*, et non sur les *produits* de ce travail, ni sur la *valeur* qu'ils y auront ajoutée.» (ibidem, pp. 55-56.)

377 «Le prolétaire, en *donnant* son travail contre un approvisionnement déterminé [...] renonce complètement à tout droit sur les autres parties

du capital [....] L'attribution de ces produits reste ce qu'elle était auparavant; elle n'est en aucune façon modifiée par la convention dont il s'agit. Les produits [...] continuent d'appartenir exclusivement au capitaliste qui a fourni les matières premières et l'approvisionnement. *C'est là une conséquence rigoureuse de la loi d'appropriation*, de cette même loi dont le *principe fondamental était l'attribution exclusive à chaque travailleur des produits de son travail !*» (ibidem, p. 58.)

377 «Le travailleur a un droit exclusif sur la valeur résultant de son travail.» (ibidem, p. 48.)

378 «Les produits sont appropriés avant d'être convertis en capital, et cette conversion ne les dégage pas de l'appropriation.» (ibidem, pp. 53-54.)

379 «Chaque accumulation de la richesse fournit les moyens d'accélérer l'accumulation ultérieure.» (ibidem, p. 29.)

381 «L'hypothèse [...] d'un *rapport invariable* entre les divers éléments du capital ne se réalise à aucun stage du progrès économique des sociétés. Ce rapport est essentiellement *variable*, et cela par deux [...] causes, la division du travail et la substitution des agents naturels à la force humaine. Ces deux causes tendent à diminuer la *proportion* de l'approvisionnement aux deux autres éléments du capital.» (ibidem, pp. 61-62.)

381 « ... un *accroissement du capital productif* n'entraînera point nécessairement un accroissement de l'approvisionnement destiné à former le prix du travail; il pourra même, au moins temporairement, être accompagné d'une diminution absolue de cet élément du capital, et par conséquent d'une *baisse dans le prix du travail.*» (ibidem, p. 63.)

382 « ... le producteur qui veut introduire dans son industrie une nouvelle division des travaux, ou mettre à profit un moteur naturel, n'attendra pas qu'il ait accumulé assez de capital pour employer de cette manière *tous* les travailleurs dont il avait besoin auparavant. Dans le cas de la division du travail, il se contentera peut-être de produire avec cinq ouvriers ce qu'il produisait auparavant avec dix; dans le cas de l'emploi d'un moteur naturel, il n'occupera qu'une seule machine et deux ouvriers. L'approvisionnement sera par conséquent réduit, dans le premier cas, à 1,500; dans le second, à 600. Mais, comme le nombre des travailleurs reste le même, *leur concurrence* fera baisser le prix du

travail bien au-dessous de son taux primitif.» (ibidem, pp. 63-64.)

382 «Tel est un des résultats les plus frappants *de la loi d'appropriation*. L'augmentation absolue des richesse, c'est-à-dire des produits du travail, n'amène point une augmentation proportionnelle, et peut amener une diminution dans l'approvisionnement des travailleurs, dans la part qui leur revient de toutes les espèces de produits.» (ibidem, p. 64.)

382 «... les causes qui déterminent le *prix du travail* sont la quantité absolue du capital productif et le rapport qui s'établit entre les divers éléments du capital, deux faits sociaux sur lesquels la volonté du travailleur ne saurait exercer aucune influence.» (ibidem, p. 64.)

382 «... toutes les chances à-peu-près sont contre le travailleur...» (ibidem, p. 64.)

396 «Le progrès économique des sociétés, en tant qu'il est caractérisé par l'accroissement absolu du capital productif et par *un changement de proportion* entre les divers éléments de ce capital, offre bien aux travailleurs quelques avantages [....] D'abord, l'efficacité du travail [...] surtout par l'emploi des machines, amène un accroissement si rapide du capital productif, que malgré l'altération survenue dans le rapport de *l'approvisionnement* aux autres éléments du capital, cet élément lui-même ne tarde guère à recevoir un accroissement absolu, qui permet, non-seulement d'employer le même nombre de travailleurs qu'auparavant, mais d'en occuper un nombre additionnel; en sorte que [...] *et sauf quelques interruptions* [...] le résultat du progrès se résume, pour les travailleurs, en une augmentation du capital productif et de la demande de travail. Ensuite, la plus grande productivité du capital tend à diminuer considérablement la valeur d'une foule de produits, à les mettre par conséquent *à la portée du travailleur*, dont les jouissances par là se trouvent augmentées.» (ibidem, p. 65.)

397 «Cependant ... quelque peu durable, quelque partielle que puisse être la diminution temporaire de l'approvisionnement qui formait le prix d'une espèce de travail, elle n'en produit pas moins des effets désastreux... En second lieu, les circonstances qui favorisent le progrès économique d'une société sont en grande partie accidentelles, indépendantes du vouloir

des producteurs capitalistes. L'action de ces causes ne saurait donc être constante...» (ibidem, p. 66.)

397 «... c'est moins la consommation *absolue* du travailleur que la consommation *relative* qui rend sa condition heureuse ou malheureuse. Qu'importe à l'ouvrier de pouvoir se procurer quelques produits auparavant inaccessibles à ses pareils, *si le nombre des produits auxquels il ne peut atteindre s'est accru dans une proportion encore plus forte, si la distance qui le sépare des capitalistes* n'a fait qu'augmenter, si sa position sociale est devenue plus humble et plus désavantageuse? A part les consommations strictement nécessaires au maintien des forces et de la santé physiques, *la valeur de nos jouissances est essentiellement relative.*» (ibidem, p. 67.)

397 «On oublie trop souvent [...] que le travailleur salarié est un homme pensant, doué des mêmes facultés, mu par les mêmes mobiles, capable des mêmes sentiments que le travailleur capitaliste.» (ibidem, p. 67.)

397 «... quelques avantages que puisse procurer aux travailleurs salariés un rapide accroissement de la richesse sociale, *il ne remédie point à la cause de leur misère* ... ils demeurent *privés de tout droit sur le capital, obligés par conséquent de vendre leur travail et de renoncer à toute prétention sur les produits de ce travail...*» (ibidem, p. 68.)

397 «C'est là qu'est le vice principal de la loi d'appropriation... Le *mal gît dans ce défaut* absolu *de lien* entre le travailleur salarié et le capital que son industrie met en œuvre.» (ibidem, p. 69.)

397 «... si, dans l'état actuel [...] le profit reel provient [...] de l'épargne des capitalistes, il pourrait aussi bien provenir de celle des salariés.» (ibidem, p. 89.)

397 «... d'asseoir un impôt de manière à ce qu'il soit réellement prélevé sur la rente, et qu'il ne frappe que la rente...» (ibidem, p. 129.)

397 «... que ne fait-on un pas de plus *en abolissant l'appropriation* privée du sol?» (ibidem, p. 129.)

397 «Les propriétaires fonciers sont des oisifs entrenus aux dépens du public sans aucun avantage pour l'industrie, ni pour le bien-être général de la société.» (ibidem, p. 129.)

397 «Ce sont les capitaux appliqués à la culture qui rendent la terre productive; le propriétaire du sol n'y contribue en rien; il n'est là que pour recevoir une rente qui ne fait point partie du profit de ses capitaux, et qui n'est point le résultat du travail ni des pouvoirs productifs de la terre, mais l'effet du prix auquel la concurrence des consommateurs élève les produits agricoles...» (ibidem, p. 129.)

398 «Comme l'abolition de la propriété privée du sol ne changerait rien aux causes qui font naître la rente, cette rente continuerait d'exister; mais elle serait perçue par l'État, auquel appartiendrait tout le territoire, et qui en affermerait les portions cultivables aux particuliers munis des capitaux suffisants pour l'exploitation.» (ibidem, p. 130.)

398 «Enfin l'industrie émancipée, dégagée de toute entrave, prendrait un essor inouï...» (ibidem, p. 130.)

398 «C'est le capital qui finira par gouverner le monde, si aucun bouleversement ne vient arrêter la marche que suit le développement de nos sociétés sous le régime de la loi d'appropriation.» (ibidem, p. 152.)

398 «... partout le capital aura effacé les anciennes distinctions sociales, pour y substituer cette simple classification des hommes en riches et en pauvres, en riches qui jouiront et gouverneront, et en pauvres qui travailleront et obéiront.» (ibidem, p. 153.)

398 «L'appropriation universelle des *fonds productifs et des produits* avait, de tout temps, réduit la classe nombreuse des prolétaires à un état de sujétion et d'incapacité politique; mais cette appropriation était combinée jadis avec un système de lois restrictives qui, en *entravant le développement de l'industrie et l'accumulation des capitaux*, mettaient des bornes à l'accroissement de la classe déshéritée, restreignaient sa liberté civile dans des limites étroites, et contribuaient ainsi de plusieurs manières à rendre cette classe inoffensive. Aujourd'hui, le capital a brisé une partie de ces entraves; il s'apprête à les briser toutes.» (ibidem, pp. 155-56.)

398 «La démoralisation des prolétaires, tel est donc le second effet de la distribution des richesses...» (ibidem, p. 156.)

442 «L'étonnante rapidité avec laquelle une grande *factorie* de coton, comprenant la filature et le tissage, peut être établie dans le Lancashire, résulte des *immenses collections de modèles* de tout genre, depuis les énormes machines à vapeur, les roues hydrauliques, les poutres et les solives en fonte, jusqu'au plus petit membre d'un métier continu ou métier à tisser, dont les ingénieurs, les constructeurs et les mécaniciens ont un vaste assortiment. Dans le courant de l'année dernière M. Fairbairn fit des équipages des roues hydrauliques équivalents à la force de sept cents chevaux, et des machines à vapeur de la force de quatre cents chevaux, dans un seul de ses ateliers mécaniques, indépendant de ses grands ateliers de construction de machines et de chaudières à vapeur. Chaque fois qu'il s'offre des capitaux pour de nouvelles entreprises, les moyens de les faire fructifier s'exécutent avec tant de rapidité, que l'on peut réaliser un profit qui en double la valeur avant qu'une *factorie* du même genre puisse être mise en activité en France, en Belgique ou en Allemagne.» (Andrew Ure, *Philosophie des manufactures...*, tom premier, Paris, 1836, pp. 61-62.)

442 «Les facilités qui résultent de l'emploi des outils automatiques n'ont pas seulement *perfectionné la précision, et accéléré la construction* de *mécanisme* d'une fabrique, elles en ont aussi *diminué le prix* et *augmenté la mobilité* dans une proportion remarquable. Maintenant on peut se procurer un métier continu supérieurement fait, à raison de 9 schellings 6 pence par fuseau, et un mull-jenny automatique renvideur à environ 8 schellings par fuseau, y compris les droits de patente pour ce dernier. Les broches dans les factories de coton *se meuvent avec si peu de frottement, que la force d'un seul cheval* en chasse cinq cents sur le métier, enfin trois cents sur le mull-jenny renvideur automatique, et cent quatre-vingts sur le métier continu; cette force comprend toutes les machines préparatoires [...] telles que les cardes, les bancs à broches, etc. Une force de trois chevaux suffit pour chasser trente grands métiers à tisser avec leur métier à parer.» (ibidem, pp. 62-63.)

504 „Ebenso läßt sich der Verfasser von einigen seiner Vorgänger verleiten, den drei Elementen des Nationalreichtums (dem Arbeitslohne, der Kapitalrente und der Bodenrente) ein viertes Element in dem Unternehmergewinne anzureihen;—hierdurch wird die ganze, von Adam Smith mit so viel Umsicht gebildete, Grundlage jeder weiteren Entwicklung *unsrer Wissenschaft* zerstört, weshalb denn auch in dem vorliegenden Werke an eine solche Entwicklung gar nicht zu denken ist." (Karl Arnd, *Die naturgemäße Volkswirthschaft, gegenüber dem Monopoliengeiste und dem Communismus, mit einem Rückblicke auf die einschlagende Literatur*, Hanau, 1845, S. 477.)

504 „In dem natürlichen Gange der Gütererzeugung gibt es nur *eine* Erscheinung, welche—in ganz angebauten Ländern—den Zinsfuß einigermaßen zu regulieren bestimmt zu sein scheint;—es ist dies das Verhältnis, in welchem die Holzmassen der europäischen Wälder durch ihren jährlichen Nachwuchs zunehmen—dieser Nachwuchs erfolgt, *ganz unabhängig von ihrem Tauschwerte*, in dem Verhältnisse von 3 bis 4 zu Hundert.—Hiernach wäre *also* ein Herabsinken unter den Stand, welchen er gegenwärtig in den geldreichsten Ländern hat, nicht zu erwarten." (ibidem, S. 124-25.)

525 « ... est la faculté de *vendre* toujours de nouveau le même *objet* et d'en recevoir toujours de nouveau le *prix*, sans jamais céder la propriété de ce qu'on vend.» ([Bastiat-Proudhon] *Gratuité de crédit. Discussion entre M. Fr. Bastiat et M. Proudhon...*, Paris, 1850, p. 9.)

526 « ... marchandise ... à prix de revient.» (ibidem, pp. 43-44.)

526 «En effet, le chapelier qui vend les chapeaux..., r e c e v o i r [...] la valeur, ni plus ni moins. Mais le capitaliste prêteur, n o n - s e u l e - m e n t ... rentre intégralement dans son capital; il reçoit plus que le capital, plus que ce qu'il apporte à l'échange; il reçoit en sus du capital un intérêt...» (ibidem, p. 69.)

526 «Il est impossible [...] que, *l'intérêt du capital* s'ajoutant, dans le commerce, *au salaire* de l'ouvrier *pour composer le prix de la marchandise*, l'ouvrier puisse racheter ce qu'il a lui-même produit. Vivre en travaillant est un principe qui, sous le régime de l'intérêt, implique contradiction.» (ibidem, p. 105.)

526 «La somme de numéraire ... circulant en France...» (ibidem, p. 151.)

526 « ... comme, par l'accumulation des intérêts, le *capital-argent*, d'échange en échange, revient toujours à sa source, il s'ensuit que la relocation, toujours faite par la même main, profite toujours au même personnage.» (ibidem, p. 154.)

527 « ... Puisque la valeur n'est autre chose *qu'une proportion*, et que tous les produits sont nécessairement *proportionnels entre eux*, il s'ensuit qu'au point de vue social, les produits sont toujours valeurs et valeurs faites: la différence, pour la société, entre capital et produit, n'existe pas. Cette différence est toute subjective aux individus...» (ibidem, p. 250.)

527 « ... point de vue social...» (ibidem, p. 250.)

527 «Tout travail *doit* laisser un *excédant*...» (ibidem, p. 200.)

528 „Nun ist bei den Kaufleuten eine große Klage über die Edelleut oder Räuber wie sie mit großer Fahr müssen handeln, und werden drüber gefangen, geschlagen, geschatzt und beraubt etc. Wenn sie aber solches um der Gerechtigkeit willen litten: so wären freilich die Kaufleut heilige Leut ... Aber weil solch groß Unrecht und unchristliche Dieberei und Räuberei über die ganze Welt durch die Kaufleut, auch selbst untereinander, geschieht: was ist Wunder, ob Gott schafft, daß solch groß Gut, mit Unrecht gewonnen, wiederum verloren oder geraubt wird, und sie selbst dazu über die Köpfe geschlagen oder gefangen werden? ... Und den Fürsten gebürt, solche unrechte Kaufhändel mit ordentlicher Gewalt zu strafen und zu weren, daß ihre Untertanen nicht so schändlich von den Kaufleuten geschunden würden. Weil sie das nicht tun, so braucht Gott der Reuter und Räuber, und straft durch sie das Unrecht an den Kaufleuten, und müssen seine Teufel sein: gleich wie er Ägyptenland und alle Welt mit Teufeln plagt oder mit Feinden verdirbt. Also stäupt er einen Buben mit dem andren, ohne daß er dadurch zu verstehn gibt, daß Reuter geringere Räuber sind, denn die Kaufleut: sintemal die Kaufleut täglich die ganze Welt rauben, wo ein Reuter im Jar einmal oder zwei, einen oder zween braubt." (Martin Luther, *Von Kauffshandlung und Wucher*. In: *Der Sechste Teil der Bücher des Ehrnwirdigen Herrn Doctoris Martini Lutheri...*, Wittembergk, 1589, S. 296.)

528 „... Gehet nach dem Spruche Esaie: Deine Fürsten sind der Diebe Gesellen geworden. Dieweil lassen sie Diebe hängen, die einen Gulden oder einen halben gestohlen haben, und hantieren mit denen, die alle Welt berauben und stehlen sicherer denn alle andren, daß ja das Sprichwort wahr bleibe: Große Diebe hängen die kleinen Diebe; und wie der römische Ratsherr Cato sprach: Schlechte Diebe liegen in Thürmen und Stöcken, aber öffentliche Diebe gehn in Gold und Seiden. Was wird aber zuletzt Gott dazu sagen? Er wird thun, wie er durch Ezechiel spricht, Fürsten und Kaufleut, einen Dieb mit dem andren, ineinander schmelzen wie Blei und Erzt, gleich als wenn eine Stadt ausbrennt, daß weder Fürsten noch Kaufleut mer seien, als ich besorge, daß schon vor der Tür sei." (ibidem, S. 297.)

529 „Ich lasse mir sagen, daß man jetzt järlich auf einem jeglichen Leiptzischen Markt 10 Gulden, d.i. 30 aufs Hundert nimmt; etliche setzen

hiezu auch den Neumburgischen Markt, daß es 40 aufs Hundert werden: obs mer sei, das weiß ich nicht. Pfui dich, wo zum Teufel will denn auch. zuletzt das hinaus? ... Wer nun jetzt zu Leiptzig 100 Floren hat, der nimmt järlich 40, d.h. einen Bauer oder einen Bürger in einem Jar gefressen. Hat er 1000 Floren, so nimmt er järlich 400, das heißt einen Ritter oder reichen Edelmann in einem Jar gefressen. Hat er 10 000, so nimmt er järlich 4000; das heißt einen reichen Grafen in einem Jar gefressen. Hat er 100 000, wie es sein muß bei den großen Händlern, so nimmt er järlich 40 000, das heißt einen großen reichen Fürsten in einem Jar gefressen. Hat er 1 000 000, so nimmt er järlich 400 000, das heißt einen großen König in einem Jar gefressen. Und leidet darüber keine Fahr, weder an Leib noch an Wahr, arbeit nichts, sizt hinter dem Ofen und brät Aeppel: also möchte ein Stul-Räuber sizen zu Hause, und eine ganze Welt in 10 Jaren fressen." (Martin Luther, *An die Pfarrherrn wider den Wucher zu predigen.* In: *Der Sechste Teil der Bücher des Ehrnwirdigen Herrn Doctoris Martini Lutheri...,* Wittembergk, 1589, S. 312-13.)

529 „Den reichen Mann müssen wir nicht ansehn nach seinem äußerlichen Wandel, denn er hat Schaffskleider an, und sein Leben gleißt und scheint hübsch, und deckt den Wolff meisterlich. Denn das Evangelion schillt ihn nicht, daß er Ehebruch, Mord, Raub, Frevel oder irgend etwas begangen hab, das die Welt oder Vernunfft taddeln möcht. Er ist ja so erbarlich an seinem Leben gewesen, als jener Pharisäer, der zweimal in der Woche faßtet und nicht war wie ander Leutt." (Martin Luther, *Eyn Sermon auf das Evangelion von dem reichen Mann und armen Lazaro,* Wittemberg, 1555.)

532 „Ich habe vor fünfzehn Jahren wider den Wucher geschrieben, da er bereits so gewaltig eingerissen war, daß ich keiner Besserung zu hoffen wüßte. Seit der Zeit hat er sich also erhebt, daß *er nun auch kein Laster, Sünde oder Schande mehr sein will, sondern* läßt sich rhümen für eitel Tugend und Ehre, als thue er den Leuten große Liebe und einen christlichen Dienst. Was will nun helffen und raten, da Schande ist Ehre und Laster ist Tugend worden? Seneca spricht aus der natürlichen Vernunfft. Deest remedii locus, ubi, quae vitia fuerunt, mores fiunt. Deutschland ist gewest, was es hat sollen werden, der leidige Geitz und Wucher habens zu Grunde verderbet...
Erstlich von *Leihen* und *Borgen.* Wo man Geld leihet, und dafür mehr oder besseres fordert oder nimmt, das ist Wucher, in allen Rechten verdammt. Darum alle die jenen, so fünf, sechs oder mehr aufs Hundert nemen, vom geliehnen Gelde, die sind Wucherer, danach sie sich wissen zu richten, und heißen des Geitzes oder Mammons abgöttische Diener... Also eben soll man von Korn, Gerste und ander mehr Wahr auch sagen, daß, wo man mehr oder bessres dafür fordert, das ist Wucher, gestolen und geraubet Gut. Denn Leihen heißt, daß, wenn ich jemand mein Geld, Gut oder Geräte thue, daß ers brauche wie lange ihm Not ist, oder ich kan und wil, und er mir dasselbe zu seiner Zeit wider gebe, so gut als ichs im habe geliehen." (Martin Luther, *An die Pfarrherrn wider den Wucher zu predigen,* Wittemberg, 1540 [without pagination].)

533 „Machen also *aus dem Kaufen auch einen Wucher.* Aber das ist jetzt zu viel auf einen Bissen. Müssen jezt das eine Stück, als vom Wucher, im Leihen handeln, wenn wir dem hetten gesteuret (nach dem jüngsten

Tage), so wollten wir dem *Kaufwucher* auch seinen Text wol lesen." (ibidem.)

533 „Spricht Junker Wucher also: Lieber, als jetzt die Läufte sind, so thue ich meinem Nächsten einen großen *Dienst* darin, daß ich ihm leihe Hundert auf fünf, sechs, zehen. Und er dankt mir solchen Leihens, als einer sonderlichen Wolthat. Bittet mich wol drumb, erbeut sich auch selber willig und ungezwungen, mir fünff, sechs, zehn Gülden vom Hundert zu schenken. Solt ich das nicht on Wuchrer mit gutem Gewissen mögen nemen?...

Laß Du Rhümen, Schmücken und Putzen [wer da wil, kehre Dich gleich wol nichts daran, Bleibe fest bey dem Text]... Wer aber mehr oder besseres nimmt, das ist Wucher, und heißt *nicht Dienst, sondern Schaden* gethan seinem Nahesten, als mit Stelen und Rauben geschieht. Es ist nicht alles Dienst und wolgethan seinem Nahesten, was man heißt Dienst und Wolgethan. Denn eine Ehebrecherin und Ehebrecher thun einander großen Dienst und Wolgefallen. Ein Reuter thut einem Mordbrenner großen Reuterdienst, daß der ihm hilft, auf der Straßen rauben, Land und Leute bevehden. Die Papisten thun den unsren großen Dienst, daß sie nicht alle ertrenken, verbrennen, ermorden, im Gefängnis verfaulen lassen, sondern lassen doch etliche leben und verjagen sie, oder nemen jenen was sie haben. Der Teufel thut selber seinen Dienern großen, unermeßlichen Dienst ... Summa, die Welt ist voll großer, trefflicher, täglicher Dienste und Wolthaten ... Die Poeten schreiben von einem Cyclop Polyphemo, daß er dem Ulysse verhieß, er wollt ihm die Freundschaft thun, daß er zuvor seine Gesellen, danach ihn zuletzt, wollte fressen. Ja es ist auch ein Dienst und eine feine Wolthat gewest.

Solcher Dienst und Wolthat fleissigen und üben sich jezt Edel und unedel, Bauern und Bürger, kaufen auf, halten inne, machen theure Zeit, steigern Korn, Gerste und alles was man haben soll, wischen darnach das Maul und sprechen: Ja was man haben muß, das muß man haben, ich lasse es den Leuten zu Dienst, könnt und möcht ichs doch wol behalten, also ist dann Gott fein getauscht und genarret ... So gar heilig sind die Menschenkinder worden ... also kann jezt Niemand mehr wuchern, geitzen, noch böse sein, die Welt ist eitel heilig worden, *dient jedermann dem andren,* niemand thut dem andren Schaden...

Thut er aber damit einen Dienst, so thuts er dem leidigen Teufel, obgleich ein armer, benötigter Mann solchen Diensts bedarf, und wol muß solches für einen Dienst oder Wolthat annehmen, daß er nicht gantz und gar gefressen werde...

Er thut Dir und muß Dir thun solchen Dienst, will er anders *Geld* haben." (ibidem.)

534 [„Es kan geschehen oder geschicht auch wol offt dieser Fall, das ich Hans leihe dir Baltzer hundert Gülden, mit solcher masse, das ich sie mus auff Michaelis wider haben zur notdurfft, oder werde (wo du seumest) drob zu schaden komen. Michaelis kompt, du gibst mir die hundert Gülden nicht wider. So nimpt mich der Richter bey dem halse, oder setzt mich in Thurn oder Gehorsam, oder kompt der gleichen ander Unrat daraus uber mich, bis ich bezale. Da sitze oder bleibe ich stecken, verseume meine Narung und besserung mit großem schaden, da bringestu mich zu, mit deinem seumen, und lonest mir so ubel für meine wolthat. Was sol ich hie thun. Mein Schadewacht, weil du seumest und

schleffest, und gehet teglich unkost oder schaden drauff, so lange du seumest und schleffest. Wer sol nu hie den schaden tragen oder büßen? Denn der Schadewacht wird zuletzt ein unleidlicher Gast in meinem Hause sein, bis ich zu grund verterbe."] (ibidem.)

534 „Wolan, hie ist weltlich und juristisch von der Sache zu reden (die Theologia müssen wir sparen bis hernach), so bist Du Baltzer mir schuldig hienach zu geben über die hundert Gülden, alles was der Schadewacht mit aller Unkost darauf getrieben hat... Darum ists billig, auch der Vernunft und natürlichem Recht nach, daß Du mir alles widererstattest, beide die *Hauptsumme mit dem Schaden* ... Solchen Schadewacht heißen die Juristenbücher zu Latein *Interesse*...

Ueber diesen Schadewacht kann noch einer fürfallen. Wenn Du Baltzer mir nicht wiedergiebst auf Michaelis, die hundert Gülden, und stehet mir für ein Kauf, das ich könnte kaufen einen Garten, Acker, Haus oder was für ein Grund ist, davon ich großen Nutzen oder Narung möchte haben, für mich und meine Kinder, so muß ichs lassen faren, und du thust mir den Schaden und Hindernis, mit deinem Saumen und Schlafen, daß ich nimmer mer kann zu solchem Kauf kommen etc. Nu ich Dir sie geliehn habe, machest mir einen Zwilling aus dem Schadewacht, daß *ich hie nicht bezalen und dort nicht kaufen kann*, und also zu beiden Teilen muß Schaden leiden, das heißt man *duplex interesse, damni emergentis et lucri cessantis*...

Nachdem sie gehört, daß Hans mit seinen verliehnen Hundert Gülden hat Schaden gelitten, und billige Erstattung seines Schadens fordert, fahren sie plumps einhin und schlahen auf ein *jeglich Hundert Gülden, solche zween Schadewacht*, nemlich, des Bezalens Unkost, und des versäumten Gartens Kauf, *grade als weren den Hundert Gülden natürlich solche zween Schadewacht angewachsen, daß, wo Hundert Gülden vorhanden sind, die thun sie aus, und rechnen darauf solche zween Schaden, die sie doch nicht erlitten haben*...

Darum bist du ein Wucherer, *der Du selber deinen ertichten Schaden von deines Nehesten Gelde büssest*, den dir doch niemand getan hat, und kannst ihn auch nicht beweisen noch berechnen. Solchen Schaden heißen die Juristen *non verum, sed phantasticum interesse. Ein Schaden, den ein jeglicher ihm selber ertreumet*...

Es gilt nicht also sagen, Es köndten die Schaden geschehn, daß ich nicht habe können *bezalen noch kaufen*. Sonst heißts: *Ex contingente necessarium*, aus dem das nicht ist, machen das, das sein müsse; aus dem das ungewiß ist, eitel gewiß Ding machen. Solt solcher Wucher nicht die Welt auffressen in kurzen Jaren...

Es ist *zufällig* Unglück, das dem Leiher widerfaret, ohn sein Willen, daß er sich erholen muß; aber in den Handeln ists umgekehrt und gar das Widerspiel, da suchet und *ertichtet* man Schaden, auf den benetigten Nehesten, will damit sich neren und reich werden, faul und müßig, prassen und prangen von *ander Leut Arbeit*, Sorge, Fahr, und Schaden; daß ich sitze hinter dem Ofen und lasse *meine Hundert Gülden für mich auf dem Lande werben*, und doch, weil es *geliehen Geld ist, gewiß im Beutel behalte*, ohne alle Fahr und Sorge, Lieber, wer möchte das nicht?

Und was vom geliehen Geld gesagt ist, das sol auch vom geliehen Getreide, Wein und dergleichen Wahr verstanden sein, daß solche zween Schaden mögen darinnen fürfallen. Aber, *daß dieselben Schaden nicht solen der Wahr natürlich angewachsen sein*, sondern *zufälliglich* wider-

faren mögen, und darum nicht ehe für Schaden zu rechnen, sie seien denn geschehen und überweiset etc. ...
Wucher muß sein, aber wehe den Wucherern ...
Auch alle weise, vernünftige Heiden den Wucher überaus übel gescholten haben. Als Aristoteles Polit. spricht, daß Wucher sei wider die Natur, aus der Ursache: Er nimmt allzeit mehr denn er giebt. Damit wird aufgehoben das Mittel und Richtmaß aller Tugend, das man heißt, gleich um gleich, aequalitas arithmetica etc. ...
Das heißt aber sich schendlich neeren, wer andren Leuten nimmt, stilet oder reubet, und heißen, mit Vrlaub, Diebe und Reuber, die man an Galgen pfleget zu henken, indeß ein Wucherer ein schöner Dieb und Reuber ist, und auf einem Stuel sizt, daher man sie *Stulreuber* heißt ...
Die Heiden haben können aus der Vernunft rechnen, daß ein Wucherer sei ein vierfältiger Dieb und Mörder. Wir Christen aber halten sie in solchen Ehren, daß wir sie schier anbeten um ihres Geldes willen ... Wer einen andern seine Narung aussauget, raubet und stilet, der thut ebenso großen Mord (so viel an ihm liegt) als der einen Hungers sterbet und zu Grunde verterbet. Solches thut aber ein Wucherer und sitzet dieweil auf seinem Stuel sicher, so er billiger hengen solt am Galgen, und von so viel Raben gefressen werden, als er Gülden gestolen hatte, wo ander so viel Fleisches an ihm were, das so viel Raben sich drein stücken und teilen köunten...
Werden die Umschleger und Wucherer schreien, man soll Brieve und Siegel halten. Darauf haben die Juristen balde und reichlich geantwortet. *In malis promissis.* So sagen die Theolog, die Brieve und Siegel, so etliche dem Teufel geben, sind nichts, wenn sie gleich mit Blut versiegelt und geschrieben sind. Denn was wider Gott, Recht und Natur ist, das ist ein Nullus. Darum greife nur ein Fürst, wer es thun kann, frisch drein, zerreiße Siegel und Brieve, kehre sich nicht daran etc. ...
Also ist kein größer *Menschenfeind* auf Erden, nach dem Teufel, denn ein Geitzhals und Wucherer, denn *er will über alle Menschen Gott sein*. Türken, Krieger, Tyrannen sind auch böse Menschen, doch müssen sie lassen die Leute leben, und bekennen, daß sie Böse und Feinde sind, und können, ja müssen wol zuweilen sich über etliche erbarmen. Aber ein Wucherer und Geitzwanst, der wollt, daß alle Welt müßte in Hunger, Durst, Jammer und Not verderben, so viel an ihm ist, auf daß ers alles allein möcht haben, und jedermann *von ihm als einem Gott empfangen und ewiglich sein Leibeigener sein*. Da lachet ihm sein Hertz, das erfrischt ihm sein Blut. Daneben gleich wol daher tretten, in marderen Schauben, güldnen Ketten, Ringen, Kleider, das Maul wischen, sich für einen theuren, frommen Mann lassen ansehen und rhümen, der auch viel barmhertziger ist wie der Gott selbst, viel freundlicher wie die Mutter Gottes, noch alle Heiligen sind ...
Und was sie von des Herculis großen Thaten schreiben, wie er so viele monstra, ungeheure Greuel zwinget, Land und Leute zu retten. Denn Wucherer ist ein groß ungeheure Monstrum, wie ein Beerwolff, der alles wüstet, mehr denn kein Cacus, Gerion oder Anteus etc. Und schmückt sich doch und will fromm sein, daß man nicht sehen soll, wo die Ochsen (*so er rücklings in sein Loch zieht*) hinkommen. Aber Hercules soll der Ochsen und der Gefangenen Geschrei hören und den Cacum suchen, auch in Klippen und Felsen, die Ochsen wider lösen von dem Bösewicht. Denn Cacus heißt ein Bösewicht, der ein *frommer Wu-*

cherer ist, stilet, raubet, frißt alles. Und wills doch nicht gethan haben, und ihn soll ja Niemand finden, weil die Ochsen, rücklings in sein Loch gezogen, Schein und Fußtapfen geben, als seien sie *herausgelassen*. Also will der Wucherer auch die Welt effen, als nütze er und gebe er der Welt Ochsen, so *er sie doch zu sich allein reisst und frisst...*.
Darum ist ein Wucherer und Geitzhals warlich nicht ein rechter Mensch, sündiget auch nicht menschlich, er muß ein Beerwolff sein über alle Tyrannen, Mörder und Reuber, schier so böse als der Teufel selber, und nicht als ein Feind, sondern als ein Freund und Bürger in gemeinem Schutz und Frieden sitzet, und dennoch greulicher reubet und mordet, weder kein Feind noch Mordbörner. Und so man die Straßenreuber, Mörder oder Bevheder redert und köpffet, wie viel sollt man alle Wucherer redern und edern, und alle Geitzhälse verjagen, verfluchen und köpffen ..." (ibidem.)

537 «L o r s q u e [...] T h o m a s C u l p e p e r s e n 1 6 4 1, [...] J o s i a s C h i l d e n 1 6 7 0, P a t e r s o n e n 1 6 9 4 [...] l a r i c h e s s e d é p e n d d e l a r e d u c t i o n m ê m e f o r c é e d u t a u x d e l'i n t é r ê t d e l'o r e t d e l'a r g e n t. [...] s u i v i e e n A n g l e t e r r e p e n d a n t p r è s d e d e u x s i è c l e s...» (Charles Ganilh, *Des Systèmes d'économie politique...*, tome premier, seconde ed., Paris, 1821, pp. 58-59.)

538 «L a l o i d e s D o u z e-T a b l e s [...] avait fixé l'intérêt de l'argent à 1 pour % par an [....] Ces lois [...] promptement violées. [...] Duilius [...] réduisit[a] de nouveau l'intérêt de l'argent à 1 pour % [...], unciaria fœnere. [...] réduit à $1/2$ pour % en 408; et, en 413, le prêt à l'intérêt fut absolument défendu par un plébiscite q u' a v a i t provoqué le tribun Genucius. [...] il n'est pas étonnant que, dans une république où l'industrie, où le commerce en gros et en détail étaient interdits aux citoyens, on *défendit aussi le commerce de l'argent.*» (Dureau de la Malle, *Économie politique des Romains*, tome second, Paris, 1840, pp. 259-61.)

538 «Cet état dura trois cents ans, jusqu'à la prise de Carthage. [...] 12 pour %, mais 6 pour % était le taux commun de l'intérêt annuel.» (ibidem, p. 261.)

539 « ... J u s t i n i e n fixe l'intérêt à 4 pour % [...] usura quincunx [...] d e T r a j a n è s t [...] intérêt légal de 5 pour % [...] 12 pour % [...] était l'intérêt commercial en Egypte, 146 ans avant J.-C.» (ibidem, pp. 262-63.)

540 « ... q u e p o u r s a v o i r s i u n p a y s e s t r i c h e o u p o u v r e [...] i l n e f a u t p a s f a i r e d'a u t r e q u e s t i o n q u e c e l l e-c i: Quel y est le prix de l'intérêt de l'argent?» (Josias Child, *Traités sur le commerce...*, Amsterdam et Berlin, 1754, p. 74.)

540 « ... comme le champion de la troupe craintive & tremblante des usuriers, il établit sa principale batterie vers le côte que j'ai avoué être le plus foible... Il nie positivement que le bas intérêt en soit la cause, & il assûre qu'il n'en que l'effet...» (ibidem, p. 120.)

---

[a] In the manuscript "reduit".—*Ed.*

540 «Quand on réduit l'intérêt, ceux qui rappelent leur argent font forcés, ou d'acheter des terres, ou de le placer dans le commerce.» (ibidem, p. 133.)

540 «Car pendant que l'intérêt est à 6 pour cent, personne ne s'exposera à courir des risques dans le commerce par mer, pour ne gagner que 8 à 9 pour cent, profit dont les Hollandois qui ont l'argent à 4 & à 3 pour cent sont fort contens.» (ibidem, p. 134.)

540 « ... la réduction porte une nation à l'œconomie.» (ibidem, p. 144.)

540 «... si le commerce est ce qui enrichit un Royaume, & si la diminution de l'interêt augmente le commerce [...] dès-lors la réduction de l'intérêt, ou la restriction de l'usure [...] est sans doute une cause principale & productive des richesses d'une nation. Il n'est point absurde de dire que le même chose peut être en même temps *cause* dans certaines circonstances, & effet dans d'autres.» (ibidem, p. 155.)

540 « ... l'œuf est la cause de la poule, & la poule est la cause de l'œuf. La réduction de l'intérêt peut donc causer une augmentation de richesses, & l'augmentation des richesses causer une plus grande réduction de l'intérêt...» (ibidem, p. 156.)

540 « ... je suis l'avocat de l'industrie, & sa réponse, qu'il[a] plaide pour la paresse et l'oisiveté.» (ibidem, p. 179.)

---

[a] The manuscript has "et mon adversaire" instead of "& sa réponse, qu'il".—*Ed.*

NOTES

¹ In this chapter Marx examines those works of Malthus which were written after the publication in 1817 of David Ricardo's *On the Principles of Political Economy, and Taxation*. In these works Malthus attempts to counterpose a theory aimed at justifying exploitation and defending the interests of the most reactionary sections of the ruling classes in general to Ricardo's labour theory of value and his advocacy of "the most unrestricted development of the social productive forces, unconcerned for the fate of those who participate in production, be they capitalists or workers" (cf. this volume, pp. 51-52).

Malthus's "theory of population" is only incidentally referred to in this chapter. Marx gives a more general estimate of Malthus's *An Essay on the Principle of Population* in Part II of *Theories of Surplus-Value* in the chapter entitled "Notes on the History of the Discovery of the So-called Ricardian Law of Rent" (see *Theories of Surplus-Value*,[a] Part II, pp. 115, 116-17, 118-21, 144-45).   p. 13

² It was discovered later that the author of this anonymous work is John Cazenove.   p. 13

³ In earlier chapters of *Theories*, Marx criticises Adam Smith's view that the value of labour is the standard measure of value and shows that this view contradicts other, more profound concepts of value outlined by Smith. See *Theories of Surplus-Value*, Part I, pp. 75-76 and 147, and Part II, pp. 401-04.   p. 14

⁴ Ricardo's *On the Principles of Political Economy, and Taxation*, London, 1817.   p. 14

⁵ In Part II of *Theories of Surplus-Value* (pp. 395-99 and 404-17) Marx discusses the fact that Ricardo does not give any analysis of the origin of surplus-value and that the exchange of labour against capital is an insoluble problem for him.   p. 14

---

[a] References to the English edition of *Theories of Surplus-Value* are to the Progress Publishers edition of Part I (second printing), Moscow, 1969, and Part II, Moscow, 1968.—*Ed.*

⁶ See Note 35 in Part I of *Theories of Surplus-Value* with regard to the term "cost-price". p. 14

⁷ *"Profit upon expropriation"* or *"profit upon alienation"* are James Steuart's formulations which Marx quotes and analyses in Part I of *Theories of Surplus-Value* (see p. 42). p. 16

⁸ Marx is referring to the well-known book by Malthus, *An Essay on the Principle of Population*, the first edition of which was published anonymously in London in 1798. In this book Malthus asserts that the poverty of the working masses is due to the fact that the capacity of the population to increase is immeasurably greater than the capacity of the land to produce the wherewithal to feed mankind. If no restrictions are imposed, then population will increase in geometrical progression while food will increase only in arithmetical progression. p. 22

⁹ With regard to Ricardo's interpretation of the concepts *"value of labour"* and *"quantity of labour"*, see *Theories of Surplus-Value*, Part II, pp. 395-404. p. 25

¹⁰ Cazenove bases his formulation of the determination of value on statements made by Malthus and Adam Smith. The idea that the value of a commodity is determined by the quantity of living labour which this commodity will buy is borrowed by Malthus from Smith. p. 31

¹¹ For Ricardo's concept of *"relative wages"*, see *Theories of Surplus-Value*, Part II, pp. 417-24. p. 33

¹² For Ricardo's concept of *"real wages"*, see *Theories of Surplus-Value*, Part II, pp. 401, 404, 417, 423-24, 438, 558. p. 34

¹³ In this passage Malthus repeats almost literally Adam Smith's remarks quoted by Marx in Part I of *Theories of Surplus-Value* (pp. 155-56): "...the labour of a manufacturer *adds*, generally, to the value of the materials which he works upon, *that of his own maintenance, and of his master's profit*. The labour of a menial servant, on the contrary, adds to the value of nothing.... A man *grows rich* by employing a multitude of manufacturers: he grows poor, by maintaining a multitude of menial servants". Marx headed this passage with the characteristically Smithian formulation "Productive and Unproductive Labour", thus alluding to the fact that Malthus has borrowed the idea from Adam Smith. p. 34

¹⁴ Lord Dundrearyism—pretentious foppishness—a term derived from Lord Dundreary, a character in the comedy *Our American Cousin* by Tom Taylor (1817-1880), which was first performed in 1858. p. 37

¹⁵ In the manuscript, three sentences follow: "But $600:400=66^2/_3$ per cent. The value of the total product comes to 1,000 and the part laid out in wages is $6/_{10}$ of this. But what about Mr. Malthus's calculation?" The last sentence is the link with the text which follows, but the meaning of the first two sentences is not clear. p. 38

[16] Karl Marx, *Zur Kritik der Politischen Ökonomie*, Erstes Heft, Berlin, 1859 (*A Contribution to the Critique of Political Economy*, Part I, p. 68[a]). p. 40

[17] The author of the anonymous *Observations on certain Verbal Disputes in Political Economy* quotes from the first edition of Malthus's *Principles of Political Economy* which was published in London in 1820. p. 40

[18] The term *"surplus product"* is here used in the special sense defined by Marx on page 703 of his manuscript (see *Theories of Surplus-Value*, Part II, p. 490): "...surplus product, which means here, the excess of their product over that part of it which is equal to *their* constant capital...". Since it is assumed in this context that the constant capital amounts to zero, the words "surplus product" mean simply the product of *newly applied labour*. p. 48

[19] Setting forth his utopian projects of social reform, Owen sought to prove that from both the economic and the domestic point of view it was best to build settlements in the form of parallelograms or squares.
p. 55

[20] This section remained unwritten. p. 59

[21] A reference to Malthus, *An Inquiry into the Nature and Progress of Rent, and the Principles by which it is regulated*, published in London in 1815. p. 61

[22] Thomas Spence advocated the nationalisation of land and the equal distribution of rent—after the deduction of all taxes and communal expenses from it—among the inhabitants. p. 61

[23] Marx discusses James Mill's views regarding the "identity of demand and supply" in Part II of *Theories of Surplus-Value* (see pp. 493, 503-04, 504-05) and also on p. 58 of this volume. p. 65

[24] See Part II of *Theories of Surplus-Value*, pp. 550-51, with regard to this standpoint of Ricardo. p. 66

[25] The relevant passage from Adam Smith's *An Inquiry into the Nature and Causes of the Wealth of Nations* is quoted and analysed by Marx in Part I of *Theories of Surplus-Value* (see pp. 91-92). p. 69

[26] Regarding the concept *"period of production"* (as distinct from labour-time), see Note 8 in Part II of *Theories of Surplus-Value*. p. 71

[27] An allusion to *Zur Kritik der Politischen Ökonomie* (see Karl Marx, *A Contribution to the Critique of Political Economy*, pp. 59-60).
p. 74

[28] See *Theories of Surplus-Value*, Part II, p. 469. p. 79

---

[a] References to the English edition of *A Contribution to the Critique of Political Economy* are to the Progress Publishers edition of 1970.—*Ed.*

29	See *Theories of Surplus-Value*, Part II, pp. 27-30, 34-35, 66-71, 174-235, as well as Chapter X entitled "Ricardo's and Adam Smith's Theory of Cost-Price (Refutation)".	p. 81
30	In connection with the equalisation of the rate of profit Marx wrote: "in each particular sphere of production the individual capitalist, as well as the capitalists as a whole, take direct part in the exploitation of the total working-class by the totality of capital and in the degree of that exploitation...." "Here, then, we have a mathematically precise proof why capitalists form a veritable freemason society vis-à-vis the whole working-class, while there is little love lost between them in competition among themselves" (Karl Marx, *Capital*, Vol. III, Moscow, 1966, pp. 196 and 198).	p. 82
31	Marx probably took this passage from Bailey, *A Critical Dissertation etc.*, London, 1825, where it is quoted on p. 217.	p. 86
32	See **Karl Marx,** *A Contribution to the Critique of Political Economy*, pp. 96-97.	p. 88
33	Ibid., pp. 179-82.	p. 88
34	See T. R. Malthus, *The Measure of Value Stated and Illustrated*, London, 1823, pp. 17-18.	p. 93
35	See *Theories of Surplus-Value*, Part II, pp. 466-67.	p. 99
36	See *Theories of Surplus-Value*, Part II, especially pp. 164-69.	p. 104
37	According to the Errata slip in McCulloch's book printed in France under the title *Discours sur l'origine, les progrès, les objets particuliers, et l'importance de l'économie politique* (*A Discourse on the Rise, Progress, Peculiar Objects, and Importance of Political Economy*), translated by G. Prévost, this passage should read: "...le fermier de ce dernier acre ne pourroit point éluder son fermage..." ("...*the farmer of this last acre cannot avoid payment of rent...*").	p. 105
38	Marx is referring to Say's note to Chapter VII ("On Foreign Trade") in the French edition of Ricardo's *On the Principles of Political Economy, and Taxation*, translated by F. S. Constancio; in it Say cites as an example the fact that sugar imported into France from the Antilles is cheaper than sugar produced in France.	p. 105
39	In the first of his *Essays on some Unsettled Questions of Political Economy* (London, 1844), John Stuart Mill discusses "...Laws of interchange between Nations; and the Distribution of the Gains of Commerce among the Countries of the Commercial World" and remarks that "We may often, by trading with foreigners, obtain their commodities at a smaller expense of labour and capital than they cost to the foreigners themselves. The bargain is still advantageous to the foreigner, because the commodity which he receives in exchange, though it has cost us less, would have cost him more" (pp. 1, 2-3).	p. 106

[40] By *fictitious capital* Marx here means the capital of the National Debt which is brought into being by loans (of the bourgeois or bourgeois-landowner state) and never intended to be invested as capital and on which the creditors are paid interest out of the taxes imposed on the people (cf. *Capital*, Vol. III, Moscow, 1966, Chapter XXIX, pp. 463-75). p. 111

[41] See Karl Marx, *A Contribution to the Critique of Political Economy*, pp. 142-43. p. 114

[42] An analysis of this proposition of J. B. Say may be found in *Theories of Surplus-Value*, Part II, pp. 493-94, 499-503. p. 119

[43] Chapter XIX of David Ricardo's *On the Principles of Political Economy, and Taxation* is entitled "On Sudden Changes in the Channels of Trade". This chapter is discussed in Part II of *Theories of Surplus-Value*, pp. 497-98. p. 122

[44] In this notebook Marx had written down quotations from pp. 110 and 112 of the anonymously published work *An Inquiry into those Principles*. The anonymous author criticises and ridicules Say in these passages. p. 122

[45] Marx's notebook XII (on the cover of which he wrote—London, July 1851) contains further extracts from *An Inquiry into those Principles*. Page 13 of the notebook comprises passages from pp. 97, 99, 103-04, 106-08 and 111 of this work. On page 12, there are extracts from pp. 54-55 of this book concerning the landlords whose rent reduces the profits of the capitalists. p. 123

[46] At the top of page 12 of notebook XII, Marx reproduces a passage from *An Inquiry into those Principles* (p. 15), in which the author criticises Say's assertion that the reason for over-production in England is to be found in under-production in Italy. See *Theories of Surplus-Value*, Part I, p. 224, and Part II, p. 531. p. 123

[47] See Karl Marx, *A Contribution to the Critique of Political Economy*, pp. 34-35, 48-49. p. 130

[48] Ibid., pp. 66-68. p. 133

[49] If in place of the arbitrarily chosen figures "50, 60 or 70 quarters per man", figures are chosen which correspond to the example given by Bailey (see p. 152 of this volume), then we get the figures "$12^1/_2$, 25 or $37^1/_2$ quarters per man". p. 156

[50] See David Ricardo, *On the Principles of Political Economy, and Taxation*, third ed., London, 1821, pp. 13-15. p. 165

[51] In numbering the pages of the manuscript, Marx omitted the number 838. p. 166

[52] See David Ricardo, op. cit., pp. 1-12. p. 170

⁵³ An allusion to the words of a soldier in Schiller's drama *Wallenstein*, Part I, Scene 6:
„Wie er räuspert und wie er spuckt,
Das habt ihr ihm glücklich abgeguckt!
Aber sein Genie, ich meine, sein Geist
Sich nicht auf der Wachtparade weist." p. 171

⁵⁴ Marx is obviously referring here to the *second* edition of McCulloch's book *The Principles of Political Economy* published in 1830, since the first edition of this book—the one from which Marx usually quotes—was published in 1825, that is, three years before McCulloch's edition of Adam Smith's *An Inquiry into the Nature and Causes of the Wealth of Nations* was published. p. 172

⁵⁵ The relevant passage from the book by James Mill is quoted by Marx on page 792 of his manuscript (p. 86 of this volume). p. 178

⁵⁶ See J. B. Say, *Traité d'économie politique...*, seconde éd., tome I, Paris, 1814, pp. LI-LII. p. 180

⁵⁷ See *Theories of Surplus-Value*, Part I, p. 264. p. 181

⁵⁸ See Wilhelm Roscher, *System der Volkswirthschaft*, Erster Band: *Die Grundlagen der Nationalökonomie. Ein Hand- und Lesebuch für Geschäftsmänner und Studierende*, 3. Auflage, Stuttgart und Augsburg, 1858, pp. 82 and 191. p. 182

⁵⁹ As Marx himself wrote on the cover of notebook XIV, this passage about McCulloch as well as almost the whole chapter, "Disintegration of the Ricardian School", was written in October 1862. p. 185

⁶⁰ Regarding *Thucydides-Roscher*, see p. 502 of this volume as well as Note 49 in Part II of *Theories of Surplus-Value*. p. 185

⁶¹ The real author of this pamphlet was the publicist, John Wilson, who wrote under various pseudonyms. p. 185

⁶² *The Edinburgh Review, or Critical Journal*—a literary and political journal which appeared from 1802 to 1929. It was an organ of the Whigs in the twenties and thirties of the last century. Most of the economic articles which appeared in it during that period were written by McCulloch. p. 185

⁶³ *The Scotsman; or Edinburgh Political and Literary Journal* —a bourgeois paper which has been appearing since 1817. It was a Whig journal during the first half of the 19th century. Articles on economic questions by McCulloch appeared in it from its foundation until 1827. McCulloch edited it from 1818 until 1820. p. 185

⁶⁴ *Encyclopaedia Britannica*—this voluminous work, which has been appearing since 1768 in constantly new and revised editions, was published in Edinburgh until the end of the 19th century. p. 185

⁶⁵ Marx is referring here to the extensive digression about John Stuart Mill contained in his notebooks VII and VIII. In conformity with the table of contents found on the covers of his notebooks and on the basis of notes in his notebook VII, the section on John Stuart Mill has been transferred to Part III of *Theories of Surplus-Value* and can be found on pp. 190-237 of this volume. See also Note 63 in Part I of *Theories of Surplus-Value*. p. 187

⁶⁶ When Marx began to write *Theories of Surplus-Value*, in the beginning of 1862, he conceived it as the fifth, concluding part of the investigation of the production process of capital which was to follow immediately after the part dealing with absolute and relative surplus-value in their combination (see *Theories of Surplus-Value*, Part I, p. 14 and Note 2 on p. 473). However, in the course of his work Marx thought it necessary to insert the two additional sections, "Reconversion of Surplus-Value into Capital" and "Result of the Production Process", between the fourth part dealing with absolute and relative surplus-value in their combination and the fifth part, "Theories of Surplus-Value". This explains the reference to the section (not yet written in October 1862) entitled *"Conversion of Surplus-Value into Capital"*, in which, amongst other things, some of Wakefield's views were to be discussed; in particular Wakefield's thesis, contained in his book *England and America* (London, 1833, Vol. II, p. 110), that "labour creates capital before capital employs labour", which is also quoted in Vol. I of *Capital* (Moscow, 1965, p. 582, Note 2). (This chapter is likewise entitled "Conversion of Surplus-Value into Capital".) p. 187

⁶⁷ Wakefield uses the term *"surplus produce"* to denote that part of the product which is "over and above that portion of the produce which replaces capital with ordinary profit". See Wakefield's commentaries on Vol. II of Adam Smith's *The Wealth of Nations* (pp. 215, 217) which he published in 1843. p. 188

⁶⁸ John Stuart Mill's booklet entitled *Essays on some Unsettled Questions of Political Economy* (London, 1844) from which Marx quotes in the chapter "Theories of Productive and Unproductive Labour". See Part I of *Theories of Surplus-Value*, p. 182. p. 190

⁶⁹ By the "bulky compendium" Marx means John Stuart Mill's two-volume *Principles of Political Economy with some of their Applications to Social Philosophy*, London, 1848. p. 190

⁷⁰ In the section entitled "Conversion of Money into Capital" which is in notebook II of Marx's manuscripts of 1861-63, he formulates this difference as follows: "It consists in this, that production costs for the capitalist are only the sum of the values advanced by him, i.e., the value of the product is equal to the value of the capital advanced. On the other hand, the real production costs of the product are equal to the amount of labour-time embodied in it. But the amount of labour-time embodied in it is greater than the total labour-time advanced or paid for by the capitalist, and this surplus-value of the product over and above the value *advanced* or *paid for* by the capitalist is precisely what consti-

tutes surplus-value...." Marx returns to this question in notebook XIV in the section on Torrens (see pp. 79-84 of this volume), and in notebook XV (see p. 513 of this volume). p. 193

[71] Marx has in mind John Stuart Mill's work *A System of Logic, Ratiocinative and Inductive* published in two volumes in London in 1843.
p. 195

[72] Marx returns to the apparent variation in the rate of profit where one capitalist both produces constant capital and uses it, in the same notebook VIII, which comprises the end of the section on John Stuart Mill (see *Theories of Surplus-Value*, Part I, p. 220), and in notebook X in the chapter on Rodbertus (see *Theories of Surplus-Value*, Part II, pp. 49-55). p. 217

[73] Marx means that part of his work which grew into Vol. III of *Capital*. See Note 12 in *Theories of Surplus-Value*, Part I. p. 228

[74] This is a reference to the "digression" on John Stuart Mill. See Note 65. p. 236

[75] "This most incredible cobbler" is the description of McCulloch used by John Wilson in his pamphlet *Some Illustrations of Mr. McCulloch's Principles of Political Economy* (Edinburgh, 1826), which he published under the pseudonym of Mordecai Mullion. p. 238

[76] As can be seen from Marx's further comments, the author of the anonymous pamphlet *The Source and Remedy of the National Difficulties* understands by "*the value of capital*" the level of "interest on capital", that is, the ratio of the amount of surplus labour which the owner of the capital appropriates to the size of the capital he employs. By "interest on capital" the author understands what Marx calls surplus-value. But the anonymous author confuses the rate of surplus-value with the rate of profit. He relates the surplus labour squeezed out of the worker directly with the total capital advanced. p. 239

[77] The plan worked out by Marx in January 1863 shows that the section "Revenue and Its Sources" was meant to be included in the third part of *Capital* (see *Theories of Surplus-Value*, Part I, p. 415). This section is mentioned, however, on the cover of notebook XIV—written in October 1862—as "incidental" (that is, an episode), which was to follow the last chapter of *Theories* (see Part I, p. 39). In notebook XV written in October and November 1862, there is indeed a big section dealing with the problem of revenue and its sources in connection with a critique of vulgar political economy. But it contains nothing about "Price's fantasy". Marx makes a critical analysis of this fantasy in Vol. III of *Capital*, Chapter XXIV. p. 240

[78] A reference to John Elliot Cairnes's book *The Slave Power: its Character, Career, and Probable Designs*, which had just appeared at that time (1862) and from which Marx also quotes in notes to volumes I and III of *Capital*. p. 243

[79] See the section "Exchange of Revenue and Capital" in the chapter "Theories of Productive and Unproductive Labour" (Part I of *Theories of Surplus-Value*). p. 246

[80] The relevant quotations from Ricardo's book are reproduced and analysed in Part II of *Theories of Surplus-Value*, pp. 180-81, 182, 183, 400. p. 259

[81] Ravenstone understands by *"industry of consumption"* the production of luxury articles and the performance of various kinds of services for the owners of capital or property. p. 260

[82] The relevant section of Hopkins's book *On Rent of Land, and its Influence on Subsistence and Population* (London, 1828, p. 126) is dealt with in the chapter "Notes on the History of the Discovery of the So-called Ricardian Law of Rent" (see *Theories of Surplus-Value*, Part II, p. 138). p. 264

[83] Marx breaks off the consecutive numbering of the pages in his manuscript from this point until page 871. After page 864, the text carries over on to page 867, then pages 868, 869, 870 and 870a follow, then pages 865 and 866 and finally 870b, 871, 872 and so on. Marx himself indicates the sequence in which the pages follow one another.
p. 266

[84] Marx is referring to the section on primitive accumulation which had not yet been written at that time (October 1862) and which, according to his plan (see *Theories of Surplus-Value*, Part I, p. 414), was to precede *Theories of Surplus-Value*. Material for this section is contained in the economic manuscript written in 1857-58 (see *Die Grundrisse der Kritik der politischen Ökonomie*, Berlin, 1953, pp. 363-74). p. 271

[85] Marx deals with the chief factors of the reproduction process in the preceding chapters of *Theories of Surplus-Value*, where he gives a critical analysis of the views of Adam Smith and David Ricardo. The necessity for the *simultaneous* production and reproduction of all elements of this or that commodity is dealt with especially in Part I, pp. 114-15, 147, and Part II, pp. 471-72, 483-84, 485 of *Theories of Surplus-Value*.
p. 278

[86] Corbet's conception of the constant flooding of the market and that consequently supply always exceeds demand, is outlined in his *An Inquiry into the Causes and Modes of the Wealth of Individuals*, London, 1841, pp. 115-17. p. 286

[87] *The Economist*—a weekly journal dealing with economic questions and with politics. It has been published in London since 1843 and represents the standpoint of the big industrial bourgeoisie. p. 287

[88] Sismondi discusses the decline in the existing stock of commodities in consequence of the development of trade and of transport on page 49

et seq. of Vol. I of his book *Études sur l'économie politique*, Bruxelles, 1837. p. 287

[89] Marx describes money here as having "*merely a formal existence*" in the sense that "the use-value of this commodity, though real, seems in the exchange process to have merely a formal existence which has still to be realised by conversion into actual use-values" (Marx, *A Contribution to the Critique of Political Economy*, p. 48). p. 291

[90] See pp. 149-54 of *National Distress; its Causes and Remedies* by Samuel Laing (Junior), London, 1844. Marx quotes a passage from this book in *Das Kapital*, Band I, Kapitel 23, Note 115 (see Marx, *Capital*, Vol. I, Moscow, 1965, p. 658, Note 1), which describes the appalling housing conditions of workers in large towns in capitalist countries. p. 292

[91] Marx discusses the fetish character of commodities, money and capital in his *A Contribution to the Critique of Political Economy*, pp. 34-37, 48-49, 154-56. p. 296

[92] Marx mentioned in a letter to Engels (June 16, 1864) that he found this list of words from various Indo-European languages in a work of "a Belgian etymologist" and that he would like to know whether it is of any value. The "Belgian etymologist" in question was Honoré Joseph Chavée, author of *Essai d'étymologie philosophique*, Bruxelles, 1844. p. 297

[93] The sentence immediately following this passage in Hodgskin's pamphlet amplifies what he means by "A sort of balance ... is struck". This runs as follows: "The capitalists permit the labourers to have the means of subsistence, because they cannot do without labour, contenting themselves very generously with taking every particle of produce not necessary to this purpose", that is, for ensuring the physical minimum of wages. p. 298

[94] See *Theories of Surplus-Value*, Part II, pp. 439, 596. p. 302

[95] See pp. 88-89 of the second edition of Thomas Chalmers's *On Political Economy in Connexion with the Moral State and Moral Prospects of Society*, 1832. p. 311

[96] Marx is referring to his notebook IX written in 1851, on page 47 of which extracts from pages 252-56 of Hodgskin's *Popular Political Economy* are given. p. 319

[97] This section remained unfinished and is virtually just a collection of the principal passages from Bray which illustrate his attitude towards the economists. Marx has analysed Bray's utopian theory of "equality of exchanges" as early as 1847 in his *Misère de la philosophie* (see *The Poverty of Philosophy*, Moscow, 1962, pp. 66-75). p. 319

[98] A reference to the data which Gregory King, one of the first English statisticians, published under the title *Schema of the Income and Expense of the Several Families of England calculated for the year 1688* in his work *Natural and Political Observations and Conclusions upon the State and Condition of England* (1696). Charles D'Avenant later appended the list to his book *An Essay upon the Probable Methods of making a People Gainers in the Balance of Trade* (London, 1699). Marx also mentions this "scheme" in Part I of *Theories of Surplus-Value*. p. 325

[99] See Note 34 in Part I of *Theories of Surplus-Value* with regard to the term "average price". p. 331

[100] Marx means the section entitled "Capital and Profit", which later grew into Vol. III of *Capital*. Regarding the "exceptions" to the determination of value by labour-time mentioned by Ricardo, see *Theories of Surplus-Value*, Part II, pp. 173-203. p. 333

[101] See *Theories of Surplus-Value*, Part II, pp. 454-58. p. 346

[102] 1821 and 1822 are probably allusions to the pamphlet *An Inquiry into those Principles* published anonymously in 1821 in London and to Hopkins's book *Economical Enquiries relative to the Laws which regulate Rent, Profit, Wages, and the Value of Money*, London, 1822. The division of profit into "net profit of capital" and "profit of enterprise" is discussed on pp. 52-53 of *An Inquiry* and pp. 43-44 of Hopkins's work. p. 353

[103] See Storch, *Cours d'économie politique*, tome I, livre III, chap. XIII, Paris, 1823. p. 355

[104] See *Capital*, Vol. III, Moscow, 1966, pp. 85, 385-90, 440, with regard to the co-operative factories in England. p. 356

[105] See Thomas Corbet, *An Inquiry into the Causes and Modes of the Wealth of Individuals*, London, 1841, pp. 100-02. p. 357

[106] *The Morning Star*—a London daily paper which appeared from 1856 to 1869. Organ of Cobden and Bright, protagonists of Free Trade. p. 361

[107] Marx is referring here to the draft plan for *Theories of Surplus-Value*. Chapter XXIII is written in accordance with the plan for the last chapters of the *Theories* jotted down by Marx on the cover of notebook XIV, which includes the point "(n) Cherbuliez" (see *Theories of Surplus-Value*, Part I, p. 38). As far as Sismondi is concerned, Marx did not intend to analyse his views in *Theories* but in another part of his work intended to deal with "the real movement of capital (competition and credit)" (see pp. 53-54 of this volume). p. 362

NOTES 575

[108] *"Commercial profit"* ("profit mercantile") is, according to Cherbuliez, the profit of the individual capitalist as opposed to the profit of society as a whole. p. 369

[109] The term *"extractive industries"* (industries extractives) is used by Cherbuliez not only to denote the extraction of minerals, wood felling, fishing, hunting, etc., but also all kinds of agricultural activities which produce agricultural raw materials. p. 370

[110] At this point in the manuscript there follows the plan for Chapter II of Part III of *Capital* which is separated from the text by thick square brackets. Marx intended to deal with the formation of the general rate of profit in this chapter. See *Theories of Surplus-Value*, Part I, pp. 415-16. p. 376

[111] Marx has in mind the examination of merchant capital contained in notebooks XV and XVII of his manuscript, especially on pages 964 (notebook XV) and 1030 (notebook XVII). p. 395

[112] Marx is referring to the views contained in James Mill's *Elements of Political Economy* (first edition, London, 1821, Chapter 4, Section 5: "Taxes on Rent") in which Mill demonstrates the advantages of using the *whole* of rent to finance all government expenditure in cases where the land is not private property, and of using for this purpose the *increase* in rent where the land is already privately owned and an increase in rent in comparison with the previous position takes place. p. 397

[113] Cherbuliez declares that inequality between rich and poor is the first result of "the present distribution of wealth" ("de la distribution actuelle des richesses"). p. 398

[114] The article referred to is a review (printed in the August-December 1831 issue of the journal) of Richard Jones's *An Essay on the Distribution of Wealth*. p. 399

[115] *Ryot*—an Indian peasant. Jones uses this term to describe peasants in India and other Asian States who had to make payments in kind to their sovereign "as sole proprietor of the soil of his dominions" (see Richard Jones, *An Essay on the Distribution of Wealth*, London, 1831, p. 109 et seq.). p. 400

[116] See Adam Smith, *Wealth of Nations*, Vol. II, Chapter III. p. 410

[117] A short insertion follows here, it belongs to the chapter on Ramsay and is therefore given as a footnote on p. 353 of this volume. p. 413

¹¹⁸ What Richard Jones calls the *Labor Fund* is described by Malthus as "funds for the maintenance of labour". This term is already used a number of times in the first edition of *Essay on the Principle of Population* (London, 1798, pp. 303, 305, 306, 307, 312, 313, etc.) and especially in Book III, chapters 5 and 6, of the fifth edition (London, 1817). It also appears in Malthus's *Principles of Political Economy*. p. 414

¹¹⁹ Richard Jones says in his *Text-Book of Lectures on the Political Economy of Nations* (Hertford, 1852, p. 71): "...the Earl of Warwick alone fed daily, in his various castles, 40,000 men...." p. 416

¹²⁰ Marx quotes this passage also on the last page of his notebook XVIII (page 1157), where he adds the notes which are reproduced here.
p. 418

¹²¹ See Note 7 in Part I of *Theories of Surplus-Value* with regard to the chapter "Revenue and Its Sources". p. 423

¹²² Of the two economists mentioned in this paragraph only Richard Jones was a cleric, but Marx may have had in mind Malthus, to whom he refers on the following page of his manuscript, and who was indeed a divine of the Church of England. p. 428

¹²³ At this point of the manuscript there is an insertion, the draft plan for Part III or Section III of *Capital*, i.e., "Capital and Profit", which is separated from the rest of the text by thick square brackets. In this edition of *Theories of Surplus-Value*, the plan is reproduced in the Addenda to Part I, pp. 414-15. p. 429

¹²⁴ There follow (on pages 1140-1144 of the manuscript) a draft plan—under the title "The Production Process of Capital"—for Part I or Section I of *Capital* (see Part I of *Theories of Surplus-Value*, p. 414) as well as extracts from newspapers, magazines and books with regard to such questions as the rate of interest, the exploitation of the working class by the capitalists, the various interrelations of constant and variable capital. Some of these quotations are used by Marx in volumes I and III of *Capital*. A short passage, which deals with the apologetic views of the vulgar economists who regard profit as "wages" for the capitalists, from page 1142 of the manuscript is included in the Addenda to the present volume (see p. 498). p. 430

¹²⁵ Richard Jones here quotes the monthly magazine of the Physiocrats *Ephémérides du Citoyen*, Part III, p. 56, published in 1767. p. 433

¹²⁶ Marx is referring here to *Voyages ... contenant la description des États du Grand Mogol...* written by François Bernier, a French doctor and traveller. Marx quotes large extracts from this book in his letter to Engels of June 2, 1853, including the passage in which Bernier compares the Indian towns to army camps. p. 435

[127] See *Theories of Surplus-Value*, Part II, pp. 552-55. p. 441

[128] *Society of Arts*—a bourgeois philanthropical society founded in London in 1754. Morton's report was published in the Society's weekly, the *Journal of the Society of Arts*, on December 9, 1859. p. 444

[129] In the outline for the final chapters of *Theories* written on the cover of notebook XIV, there follows after "(o) Richard Jones. (End of this Part 5)", the "Episode: Revenue and its sources" (see *Theories of Surplus-Value*, Part I, p. 39). In the outline contained in notebook XV there is the heading—"Vulgar political economy" (ibid.). Notebook XV is occupied to a very considerable extent with these two themes—"Revenue and its sources" and "Vulgar political economy", both being treated in the closest interconnection with one another. In this notebook, written in October-November 1862, Marx broke off the analysis of Hodgskin's views at page 891 in order to write the "episode" as well as to deal with vulgar economy which is concerned with the superficial appearance of the fetishised form of revenue and its sources and builds on this basis its apologetic theory. Marx, while working on this "episode", proceeded to an analysis of loan capital which is closely linked with his critique of vulgar economy, and from this to an analysis of merchant capital as one of those spheres of the capitalist economy in which surplus-value is not created but only distributed. Therewith Marx gradually went beyond the limits of *Theories of Surplus-Value* as the historico-critical part of his work.

Marx continues his examination of merchant capital until the end of notebook XV. But he begins the next notebook—XVI—in December 1862 with the heading "Chapter III. Capital and Profit". This notebook is devoted mainly to the examination of the conversion of surplus-value into profit and of the rate of surplus-value into the rate of profit as well as the conversion of profit into the average profit. Marx utilised the material in this notebook extensively for the first and second sections of Vol. III of *Capital*, which he wrote in 1865. As Marx says, he proceeded to the most important question in this section at the end of notebook XVI, that is, the analysis of the causes which bring about a decline in the rate of profit as the capitalist mode of production develops. This exposition, which Marx later rewrote for the third part of Vol. III of *Capital* ("The Law of the Tendency of the Rate of Profit to Fall"), was concluded only at the beginning of the next notebook (XVII), written between December 1862 and the beginning of January 1863.

Marx returns to the analysis of merchant capital again in notebook XVII—beginning with page 1029—thus continuing the examination he interrupted in notebook XV. But once again, he breaks off his remarks about merchant capital, this time inserting the "episode"—"Reflux movement of money in capitalist reproduction". Marx concludes this fairly extensive "episode" in notebook XVIII (January 1863) with the words—"the further consideration of this point to be postponed", and takes up the analysis of merchant capital (on page 1075 of his manuscript) once again. This time he examines the views of various economists on this question. All this work on merchant capital contained in notebooks XV, XVII and XVIII was used extensively by Marx when he wrote the fourth part of Vol. III of *Capital* in 1865. After concluding his examination of merchant capital (on page 1084), Marx returns to *Theories of Surplus-Value*, i.e., to the section on Hodgskin broken off in notebook XV.

Of all the great mass of material contained in notebooks XV-XVIII of the manuscript of 1861-63 and described above, only "Revenue and Its Sources. Vulgar Political Economy" contained in notebook XV has been printed as Addenda to the present volume, in accordance with Marx's own plan. This concludes the historico-critical part of Marx's work. p. 453

[130] By "this general section" Marx means the section entitled "Capital in General" which, according to the plan outlined by Marx between 1858 and 1862, was to consist of three parts ("The production process of capital", "The circulation process of capital" and "The unity of the two, or capital and profit") which were to be followed by three sections of a more specialised character—"The competition of capitals", "Credit" and "Share Capital" (*Theories of Surplus-Value*, Part I, p. 14). As he worked on *Capital*, Marx included in the first three parts a great deal of material which according to the original plan was not intended for the section "Capital in General". This applies in particular to many problems connected with the treatment of credit and the credit system that found their way into Vol. III of *Capital*, which goes beyond the framework of the section "Capital in General". p. 462

[131] Marx is referring to notebook I of his manuscript of 1861-63 which begins with the section "The Conversion of Money into Capital". The first paragraph in this section is headed "M—C—M, the Most General Form of Capital". p. 466

[132] An allusion to Proudhon who in his polemic with Bastiat propagated the idea of "free credit". Marx criticises this idea on pages 935-37 of his manuscript (see pp. 523-27 of this volume). p. 468

[133] *Crédit mobilier*—Société générale du crédit mobilier—a French joint-stock bank founded by the brothers Péreire in 1852. It maintained very close connections with the government of Napoleon III, which encouraged it in its many speculative enterprises. It went bankrupt in 1867 and was liquidated in 1871. Marx wrote a number of articles about these speculative activities for the *People's Paper*, the Chartist newspaper published in London, and for the *New-York Daily Tribune*. p. 468

[134] Turgot, *Réflexions sur la formation et la distribution des richesses* (1766), §§ 73, 85. p. 478

[135] Adam Smith deals with this question in Chapter 6, Book I of his *Wealth of Nations*. p. 495

[136] Quotations regarding slave overseers are given by Marx in Chapter XXIII of Vol. III of *Capital*, which was written some two or three years after this. p. 496

137	The presumptuous reference to Thucydides by Roscher is to be found in the Preface to his *Die Grundlagen der Nationalökonomie* (1854).	p. 502
138	Arnd devotes a special paragraph to justifying the legality and expediency of the dog tax in his book *Die naturgemäße Volkswirthschaft* (S. 420-21, § 88).	p. 504
139	*The Westminster Review*—a bourgeois liberal quarterly which was published in London from 1824 to 1914.	p. 508
140	See *Theories of Surplus-Value*, Part I, pp. 93-97.	p. 515
141	In the plan for Part III of *Capital* drawn up in January 1863, the heading for the penultimate chapter—Chapter XI—was "Vulgar Economy" (see *Theories of Surplus-Value*, Part I, p. 415). This plan was drawn up some six weeks to two months after the section entitled "Revenue and Its Sources. Vulgar Political Economy" had been written in notebook XV of the manuscript of 1861-63.	p. 523
142	Karl Marx, *Zur Kritik der Politischen Ökonomie*, Erstes Heft. (See Marx, *A Contribution to the Critique of Political Economy*, pp. 55, 86.)	p. 523
143	*La Voix du Peuple*—a daily newspaper which reflected Proudhonist views and which appeared in Paris from October 1, 1849 to May 14, 1850.	p. 525
144	Marx is referring to Bentham's *Defence of Usury*, the first edition of which was published in London in 1787, the second in 1790.	p. 528
145	What is meant is a loan of 100 guilders on condition that the interest is paid in three instalments at the Leipzig fairs. At that time three fairs a year—at the New Year, at Easter and at Michaelmas—were held at Leipzig.	p. 529
146	This quotation is not from *Von Kauffshandlung und Wucher* (1524) but from Luther's later work—*An die Pfarrherrn wider den Wucher zu predigen* (1540) which Marx mentions later under point III.	p. 529
147	See *Theories of Surplus-Value*, Part I, p. 404.	p. 533
148	Aristotle's view that interest is unnatural, which he outlines in his *De Republica* (Book 1, Chapter 10), is quoted by Marx in *Capital*, Vol. I (see *Capital*, Vol. I, Moscow, 1965, pp. 164-65).	p. 534
149	See *Theories of Surplus-Value*, Part I, pp. 373-77.	p. 538

[150] Thomas Manley was not the author of the anonymous book, *Interest of Money Mistaken etc.*, which was published in London in 1668, but of a different one, with a very similar content, which was published in London in 1669 and entitled *Usury at 6 per cent examined and found unjustly charged by Sir Thomas Culpeper and J. C.* The author of *Interest of Money Mistaken* is unknown. p. 539

INDEX OF AUTHORITIES

A

ARISTOTELES. *De Republica.*—534, 535

ARND, KARL. *Die naturgemäße Volkswirthschaft, gegenüber dem Monopoliengeiste und dem Communismus, mit einem Rückblicke auf die einschlagende Literatur,* Hanau, 1845.—504

B

[BAILEY, SAMUEL.] *A Critical Dissertation on the Nature, Measures, and Causes of Value; Chiefly in Reference to the Writings of Mr. Ricardo and his Followers. By the Author of Essays on the Formation and Publication of Opinions, etc. etc.*, London, 1825.—28, 87, 111, 124, 133, 137, 140, 143-44, 146-48, 150-55, 159-63, 165-66

[BAILEY, SAMUEL.] *A Letter to a Political Economist; occasioned by an article in the Westminster Review on the Subject of Value. By the Author of the Critical Dissertation on Value therein reviewed,* London, 1826.—125

BANFIELD, THOMAS CHARLES. *The Organization of Industry, explained in a Course of Lectures, delivered in the University of Cambridge in Easter Term 1844.* Second Edition, London, 1848. (The first edition was published in London in 1845.)—325

[BASTIAT, FRÉDÉRIC et PIERRE-JOSEPH PROUDHON.] *Gratuité du crédit. Discussion entre M. Fr. Bastiat et M. Proudhon,* Paris, 1850.—525-27

BENTHAM, JEREMY. *Defence of Usury, showing the Impolicy of the Present Legal Restraints on the Terms of Pecuniary Bargains,* London, 1787.—528, 538

[BERNIER, FRANCOIS.] *Voyages de François Bernier, Docteur en Médicine de la faculté de Montpellier, contenant la description des États du Grand Mogol, de l'Indoustan, du royaume de Cachemire, etc. Où il est traité des richesses, des forces, de la justice, et des causes principales de la décadence des États de l'Asie, et de plusieurs événemens considérables; et où l'on voit comment l'or et l'argent, après avoir, circulé dans le monde, passent dans l'Indoustan, d'où ils ne reviennent plus.* 2 vols., Paris, 1830. (The first edition was published in Amsterdam in 1699.)—435

BRAY, JOHN FRANCIS. *Labour's Wrongs and Labour's Remedy; or, The Age of Might and the Age of Right*, Leeds, 1839.—319-25

C

CAIRNES, JOHN ELLIOT. *The Slave Power: its Character, Career, and probable Designs: being an Attempt to explain the real Issues, involved in the American Contest*, London, 1862.—243

CAREY, HENRY CHARLES. *Principles of Political Economy. Part the first: of the Laws of the Production and Distribution of Wealth*, Philadelphia, 1837. —182

[CAZENOVE, JOHN.] *Outlines of Political Economy; being a plain and short View of the Laws relating to the Production, Distribution, and Consumption of Wealth; to which is added a Brief Explanation of the Nature and Effects of Taxation; suited to the Capacity of every one*, London, 1832.—13, 63-68, 169

CAZENOVE, JOHN—see MALTHUS, THOMAS ROBERT. *Definitions in Political Economy...*, London, 1853.

CHALMERS, THOMAS. *On Political Economy in Connexion with the Moral State and Moral Prospects of Society.* Second edition, Glasgow, Edinburgh, Dublin and London, 1832.—56, 311

CHAVÉE, HONORÉ-JOSEPH. *Essai d'étymologie philosophique ou Recherches sur l'origine et les variations des mots qui expriment les actes intellectuels et moraux*, Bruxelles, 1844.—296-97

CHERBULIEZ, ANTOINE-ELISÉE. *Richesse ou Pauvreté. Exposition des causes et des effets de la distribution actuelle des richesses sociales*, Paris, 1841. (The first edition was published in Paris and Geneva in 1840 and entitled *Riche ou pauvre....*) —362, 369-78, 381-82, 396-98

CHILD, JOSIAS. *Traités sur le commerce et sur les avantages qui résultent de la réduction de l'interest de l'argent. Avec un petit traité contre l'usure; par le Chevalier Thomas Culpeper. Traduits de l'Anglois*, Amsterdam et Berlin, 1754. (The first edition of Child's work was published as a pamphlet in London in 1668. In 1669 and 1670 Child wrote ten additional chapters and the book was subsequently published several times. Culpeper's essay was first published in London in 1621; from 1668 onwards it appeared as a supplement to Child's work.)—539-40

CORBET, THOMAS. *An Inquiry into the Causes and Modes of the Wealth of Individuals; or the Principles of Trade and Speculation explained.* In two parts, London, 1841.—286, 357

CULPEPER, THOMAS. *Traité contre l'usure...*—see CHILD, JOSIAS. *Traités sur le commerce....*

D

DALRYMPLE, JOHN. *An Essay towards a General History of Feudal Property in Great Britain.* The fourth edition corrected and enlarged, London, 1759. (The first edition was published in London in 1757.)—538

[DE QUINCEY, THOMAS.] *Dialogues of Three Templars on Political Economy, chiefly in relation to the Principles of Mr. Ricardo. In: The London Magazine for April and May, Vol. IX, 1824.—123-24

DE QUINCEY, THOMAS. The Logic of Political Economy, Edinburgh and London, 1844.—124

DUREAU DE LA MALLE, ADOLPHE-JULES-CÉSAR. Economie politique des Romains, tome I et II, Paris, 1840.—538-39

E

Essay on the Application of Capital to Land...—see [WEST, SIR EDWARD.] Essay on the Application of Capital to Land....

G

GALIANI, FERDINANDO. Della Moneta (1750). In: Scrittori Classici Italiani di Economia Politica. Parte moderna. Tomo III, Milano, 1803.—267

GANILH, CHARLES. Des Systèmes d'économie politique, de la valeur comparative de leurs doctrines, et de celle qui paraît la plus favorable aux progrès de la richesse. Seconde édition. Tome I et II, Paris, 1821. (The first edition was published in Paris in 1809.)—537

GILBART, JAMES WILLIAM. The History and Principles of Banking. Second edition, London, 1835.—539

H

[HODGSKIN, THOMAS]. Labour defended against the Claims of Capital; or, the Unproductiveness of Capital proved. With Reference to the present Combinations amongst Journeymen. By a Labourer, London, 1825.—263, 266-67, 276-78, 294-95, 297-98, 302, 313-14, 316

[HODGSKIN, THOMAS.] The natural and artificial Right of Property contrasted. A series of Letters, addressed without Permission, to H. Brougham ... by the Author of "Labour defended against the Claims of Capital", London, 1832.—319

HODGSKIN, THOMAS. Popular Political Economy. Four Lectures delivered at the London Mechanics' Institution, London, 1827.—263, 315-19, 444-45.

HOPKINS, THOMAS. On Rent of Land, and its Influence on Subsistence and Population: with Observations on the operating Causes of the Condition of Labouring Classes in various countries, London, 1828.—264

HÜLLMANN, KARL DIETRICH. Staedtewesen des Mittelalters, 4 Teile, Bonn, 1826-29.—538

I

An Inquiry into those Principles, respecting the Nature of Demand and the Necessity of Consumption, lately advocated by Mr. Malthus, from which it is concluded, that Taxation and the Maintenance of unproductive Consumers can be conducive to the Progress of Wealth, London, 1821.—59-61, 117, 119-23, 306-07, 312-13, 353, 434

Interest of Money Mistaken, or A Treatise, Proving, that the Abatement of Interest is the Effect and not the Cause of the Riches of a Nation, and that six per cent is a Proportionable Interest to the present condition of this Kingdom, London, 1668.—539

J

JONES, RICHARD. *An Essay on the Distribution of Wealth, and on the Sources of Taxation*, London, 1831.—399-411, 414-15

JONES, RICHARD. *An introductory Lecture on Political Economy, delivered at King's College, London, 27th February, 1833. To which is added a Syllabus of a Course of Lectures on the Wages of Labor...*, London, 1833.—413-19

JONES, RICHARD. *Text-Book of Lectures on the Political Economy of Nations, delivered at the East India College, Haileybury,* Hertford, 1852.—419-20, 423-24, 426-28, 430-37, 443-44, 446-48

L

LAING, SAMUEL. *National Distress; its Causes and Remedies*, London, 1844.—292

LALOR, JOHN. *Money and Morals: A Book for the Times*, London, 1852.—263

LUTHER, MARTIN. *Von Kauffshandlung und Wucher*. In: *Der Sechste Teil der Bücher des Ehrnwirdigen Herrn Doctoris Martini Lutheri...*, Wittembergk, 1589.—528-29

LUTHER, MARTIN. *An die Pfarrherrn wider den Wucher zu predigen. Vermanung*. Wittemberg, 1540.—529, 532-37

LUTHER, MARTIN. *An die Pfarrherrn wider den Wucher zu predigen. Vermanung*. In: *Der Sechste Teil der Bücher des Ehrnwirdigen Herrn Doctoris Martini Lutheri...*, Wittembergk, 1589.—528

LUTHER, MARTIN. *Eyn Sermon auf das Evangelion von dem reichen Mann und armen Lazaro*, Wittemberg, 1555.—529

M

MALTHUS, THOMAS ROBERT. *Definitions in Political Economy, preceded by an Inquiry into the Rules which ought to guide Political Economists in the Definition and Use of their Terms; with Remarks on the Deviation from these Rules in their Writings*, London, 1827.—13-14, 16-17, 28, 30, 33-34, 58-59, 77, 168-69

Idem. A new edition with a preface, notes and supplementary remarks by John Cazenove, London, 1853.—13-14, 15, 17, 23-24, 29-31, 34-35, 58

[MALTHUS, THOMAS ROBERT.] *An Essay on the Principle of Population, as it affects the Future Improvement of Society, with Remarks on the Speculations of Mr. Godwin, M. Condorcet, and other Writers*, London, 1798.—22, 62-63, 414

Idem. The fifth edition in three volumes, London, 1817.—62-63, 414

MALTHUS, THOMAS ROBERT. *Essai sur le principe de population, ou Exposé des effets passés et présens de l'action de cette cause sur le bonheur genre humaine; suivi de quelques recherches relatives à l'espérance de guérir ou d'adoucir les maux qu'elle entraîne*. Traduit de l'anglais sur cinquième édition par Pierre et Guilleaume Prévost. 3ᵉ édition française très-augmentée. Tomes I-IV, Tome IV, Paris, 1836.—62-63

MALTHUS, THOMAS ROBERT. *An Inquiry into the Nature and Progress of Rent, and the Prin-

ciples by which it is regulated, London, 1815.—61

MALTHUS, THOMAS ROBERT. *The Measure of Value stated and illustrated, with an Application of it to the Alterations in the Value of the English Currency since 1790*, London, 1823.—13-14, 16, 24-25, 27, 29-30, 93

MALTHUS, THOMAS ROBERT. *Observations on the Effects of the Corn Laws, and of a Rise or Fall in the Price of Corn on the Agriculture and general Wealth of the Country*, London, 1814.—13-14

MALTHUS, THOMAS ROBERT. *Principles of Political Economy considered with a View to their practical Application*, London, 1820.—13-14, 40, 53, 61

Idem. Second edition with considerable additions from the author's own manuscript and an original memoire, London, 1836.—13-14, 35-36, 50-51, 53, 57-59

MARX, KARL. *Zur Kritik der Politischen Oekonomie. Erstes Heft*, Berlin, 1859.—40, 74, 88, 114, 130, 133, 296, 523

[McCULLOCH, JOHN RAMSAY.] Review of: *Considerations on the Accumulation of Capital, and its Effects on Exchangeable Value*, London, 1822. In: *The Edinburgh Review, or Critical Journal*, March 1824, Vol. XL, No. 79.—186

McCULLOCH (MacCULLOCH), JOHN RAMSAY. *Discours sur l'origine, les progrès, les objets particuliers, et l'importance de l'économie politique. Contenant l'esquisse d'un cours sur les principes et la théorie de cette science. Traduit de l'anglais par G^{me} Prévost*, Genève et Paris, 1825.—104-09, 186

McCULLOCH, JOHN RAMSAY. *The Principles of Political Economy: with a Sketch of the Rise and Progress of the Science*, Edinburgh, 1825.—168-69, 185, 187

Idem. Second edition, corrected and greatly enlarged, London, 1830.—172-73, 175

McCULLOCH, JOHN RAMSAY. Notes, and supplemental Dissertations to Smith's *Wealth of Nations*—see SMITH, ADAM. *An Inquiry into the Nature and Causes of the Wealth of Nations...*, Edinburgh, 1828.

MILL, JAMES. *Elements of Political Economy*, London, 1821.—76, 84, 97-98, 397

Idem. Second edition, revised and corrected, London, 1824.—84, 86, 99, 105

MILL, JAMES. *Éléments d'économie politique; traduit de l'anglais par J. T. Parisot*, Paris, 1823.—88-89, 93, 95-96, 98, 100, 101, 102-03, 104

MILL, JOHN STUART. *Essays on some Unsettled Questions of Political Economy*, London, 1844.—106, 190, 192, 194-96, 198, 207-08, 225-26, 228, 236

MILL, JOHN STUART. *Principles of Political Economy with some of their Applications to Social Philosophy*. In two volumes, London, 1848.—190

MILL, JOHN STUART. *A System of Logic, Ratiocinative and Inductive, being a connected view of the Principles of Evidence, and the Methods of Scientific Investigation*. In two volumes, London, 1843.—195

MORTON, JOHN CHALMERS. "On the Forces used in Agriculture." In: *Journal of the Society of Arts* (London), No. 368, Vol. VII, December 9, 1859.—444

MULLION, MORDECAI. *Some Illustrations of Mr. M'Culloch's Principles of Political Economy*, Edinburgh, 1826.—185-86, 238, 267

N

NEWMAN, FRANCIS WILLIAM. *Lectures on Political Economy*, London, 1851.—537

O

Observations on certain Verbal Disputes in Political Economy, particularly relating to Value, and to Demand and Supply, London, 1821.—39-40, 110-12, 113-17, 125-26, 128-29, 131-32, 137, 144, 146, 162, 166, 296

Outlines of Political Economy...— see [CAZENOVE, JOHN.] *Outlines of Political Economy*....

P

PRÉVOST, GUILLEAUME. *Réflexions sur le système de Ricardo*— see McCULLOCH, JOHN RAMSAY. *Discours sur l'origine, les progrès*....

PROUDHON, PIERRE-JOSEPH —see [BASTIAT, FRÉDÉRIC et PIERRE-JOSEPH PROUDHON] *Gratuité du crédit*....

R

RAMSAY, GEORGE. *An Essay on the Distribution of Wealth*, Edinburgh, 1836.—326-29, 330-31, 332, 334-40, 347, 349, 351, 353-60

RAVENSTONE, PIERCY. *Thoughts on the Funding System, and its Effects*, London, 1824.— 257-58, 260-63, 266, 309

RICARDO, DAVID. *On the Principles of Political Economy, and Taxation*, London, 1817.—14, 53, 69, 85, 122, 126, 256, 259

Idem. Second edition, London, 1819.—119-20

Idem. Third edition, London, 1821. —54, 114, 138, 165, 170, 181

RICARDO, DAVID. *Des Principes de l'économie politique, et de l'impôt. Traduit de l'anglais par F. S. Constancio, D. M. etc.; avec des notes explicatives et critiques, par M. Jean-Baptiste Say*. Tome premier et second, Paris, 1819.—95, 105

RICARDO, DAVID. *On Protection to Agriculture* (fourth edition), London, 1822.—55

ROSCHER, WILHELM. *Die Grundlagen der Nationalökonomie. Ein Hand- und Lesebuch für Geschäftsmänner und Studierende*, Dritte Auflage, Stuttgart und Augsburg, 1858.—182, 185, 353, 502

S

SAY, JEAN-BAPTISTE. *Traité d'économie politique, ou simple Exposition de la manière dont se forment, se distribuent et se consomment les richesses*. Seconde édition. Tome premier et second, Paris, 1814. (The first edition was published in Paris in 1803.)—119, 180

SENIOR, NASSAU WILLIAM. *An Outline of the Science of Political Economy*, London, 1836.— 353

SISMONDI, JEAN-CHARLES-LÉONARD SIMONDE DE. *Etudes sur l'économie politique*. Tome I et II, Bruxelles, 1837-38.— 287

SISMONDI, JEAN-CHARLES-LÉONARD SIMONDE DE. *Nouveaux principes d'économie politique, ou De la richesse dans ses rapports avec la population.* Seconde édition. Tome premier et second, Paris, 1827. (The first edition was published in Paris in 1819.)—42, 53

SMITH, ADAM. *An Inquiry into the Nature and Causes of the Wealth of Nations.* Two vols., London, 1776.—410, 446, 496

SMITH, ADAM. *An Inquiry into the Nature and Causes of the Wealth of Nations. With a Life of the Author, an introductory Discourse, Notes, and supplemental Dissertations. By J. R. McCulloch.* In four volumes, Edinburgh, 1828.—172-73, 179, 182-84

SMITH, ADAM. *An Inquiry into the Nature and Causes of the Wealth of Nations. With a Commentary, by the Author of "England and America"* (Edward Gibbon Wakefield). In six volumes, Vol. I, London, 1835.—187-88, 253

SMITH, ADAM. *Recherches sur la nature et les causes de la richesse des nations. Traduction nouvelle, avec des notes et observations; par Germain Garnier.* Tomes I-IV, Paris, 1802.—27

The Source and Remedy of the National Difficulties, deduced from Principles of Political Economy, in a Letter to Lord John Russell, London, 1821.—238-41, 252-57, 260, 266, 302, 313

STIRLING, PATRICK JAMES. *The Philosophy of Trade; or, Outlines of a Theory of Profits and Prices, including an Examination of the Principles which determine the relative Value of Corn, Labour and Currency*, Edinburgh, 1846.—188-89

STORCH, HENRI. *Cours d'économie politique, ou Exposition des principes qui déterminent la prospérité des nations. Avec des notes explicatives et critiques par J.-B. Say.* Tomes I-IV, Paris, 1823.—355

T

TORRENS, ROBERT. *An Essay on the Production of Wealth; with an Appendix, in which the Principles of Political Economy are applied to the actual Circumstances of this Country*, London, 1821.—24, 69, 71-74, 77

TORRENS, ROBERT. *A Letter to the Right Honourable Sir Robert Peel, Bart., M. P., (&c. &c. &c.) on the Condition of England, and on the Means of Removing the Causes of Distress.* Second edition, London, 1843.—222

U

URE, ANDREW. *Philosophie des manufactures, ou Économie industrielle de la fabrication du coton, de la laine, du lin et de la soie, avec la description des diverses machines employées dans les Ateliers anglais.* Traduit sous les yeux de l'auteur. Tome I et II, Paris, 1836.—442-43

W

[WAKEFIELD, EDWARD GIBBON.] *A Commentary to Smith's Wealth of Nations.*—see SMITH, ADAM. *An Inquiry into the Nature and Causes of the Wealth of Nations...*, London, 1835.

[WEST, SIR EDWARD.] *Essay on the Application of Capital to Land, with Observations shewing the Impolicy of any great*

Restriction of the Importation of Corn, and that the Bounty of 1688 did not lower the Price of it. By a Fellow of University College, Oxford, London, 1815.—306-07

PERIODICALS

The Economist, Weekly Commercial Times, Bankers' Gazette, and Railway Monitor: A political, literary, and general Newspaper, London, 1854.—287

The Edinburgh Review, or Critical Journal.—185-86
—Vol. XL, March-July 1824.—186
—Vol. LIV, August-December 1831.—399

The Morning Star, December 1, 1862.—361

The Scotsman; or, Edinburgh Political and Literary Journal.—185-86

La Voix du Peuple, Paris.—525

The Westminster Review, Vol. V, January-April 1826, London.—508

NAME INDEX

A

Abraham a Santa Clara (pseudonym of *Hans Ulrich Megerle*) (1644-1709)—Austrian preacher and writer.—53

Anderson, James (1739-1808)—British economist. Preceded Ricardo in the elaboration of the theory of rent.—39, 53, 61

Anne (1665-1714)—Queen of Great Britain and Ireland (1702-14). In her reign (in 1707) the Act of Union was passed which provided for the union of the English and Scottish parliaments.—538, 539

Aristotle (384-322 B.C.)—"... the most encyclopaedic intellect of them" [i.e., the ancient Greek philosophers], "had already analysed the most essential forms of dialectical thought" (Engels, *Anti-Dühring*). His philosophical views vacillated between materialism and idealism. He defended the natural economy of slave society and was the first to analyse value and the two primitive forms of capital (merchant capital and money-lending capital).—534, 535

Arnd, Karl (1788-1877)—German economist, advocate of Free Trade.—504

B

Bailey, Samuel (1791-1870)—British economist and philosopher. Attacked Ricardo's labour theory of value from the standpoint of vulgar political economy, but at the same time revealed a number of contradictions in Ricardo's views.—28, 87, 111, 124, 133, 137, 139-59, 161-66, 169, 177, 186, 259, 296

Banfield, Thomas Charles (1795-1880)—British economist.—325

Barton, John—British economist who lived between the end of the 18th and the early part of the 19th centuries. Exponent of classical bourgeois political economy.—242-43

Bastiat, Frédéric (1801-1850)—French economist who propagated the harmony of class interests in capitalist society. "The most superficial and therefore the best representative of vulgar economic apologetics" (Marx).—93, 501, 523, 525, 533

Bentham, Jeremy (1748-1832)—English sociologist, theoretician of utilitarianism. "A genius in bourgeois stupidity" (Marx).—528, 534, 538

Bernier, François (1625-1688)—
French physician and traveller.—435

Bray, John Francis (1809-1895)—
British economist, utopian socialist, adherent of Robert Owen; developed the theory of "labour money".—319-21, 323

Buchanan, David (1779-1848)—
British publicist and economist, disciple of Adam Smith and populariser of the latter's views.—403

Büsch, Johann Georg (1728-1800)
—German economist and writer, professor of mathematics and director of a commercial school in Hamburg.—243

C

Cairnes, John Elliot (1823-1875)—
Irish economist and publicist, opponent of slavery in the Southern States of the U.S.A.—243

Carey, Henry Charles (1793-1879)—
American economist, protectionist, protagonist of class harmony in bourgeois society.—182, 254

Cato. Marcus Porcius (The Elder) (234-149 B.C.)—Roman statesman and historian, defender of the privileges of the aristocracy.—528

Cazenove, John (19th century)—
British economist, supporter of Malthus.—13, 14, 15, 17, 23-24, 30-31, 33, 35-36, 58, 63, 168-69

Chalmers, Thomas (1780-1847)—
Scottish theologian and economist, "... one of the most fanatical Malthusians" (Marx).—56, 311

Charlemagne (or Charles the Great) (c. 742-814)—King of the Franks (768-814), Roman Emperor (800-814).—538

Charles II (1630-1685)—King of Great Britain (1660-85).—539

Chavée, Honoré Joseph (1815-1877)
—Belgian linguist and anthropologist.—296

Cherbuliez, Antoine Elisée (1797-1869)—Swiss economist, supporter of Sismondi; infused elements of Ricardo's ideas into Sismondi's teachings.—362-64, 369-79, 381, 382, 396-97

Chevé, Charles François (1813-1875)
—French journalist, Catholic socialist, supporter of Proudhon from 1848 to 1850; publisher of *La Voix du Peuple*.—525

Child, Sir Josiah (1630-1699)—
British merchant and economist, Mercantilist, "champion of industrial and commercial capital" against money-lending capital, "father of modern banking" (Marx).—467, 537, 539, 540

Constancio, Francisco Solano (1772-1846)—Portuguese physician; wrote various historical works and translated books by Godwin, Malthus, Ricardo and others into French.—105

Corbet, Thomas (19th century)—
British economist, supporter of Ricardo.—286, 287, 357

Culpeper, Sir Thomas (1578-1662)
—British economist, Mercantilist.—467, 537, 539

Custodi, Pietro (1771-1842)—Italian economist, publisher of the chief works of Italian economists written between the end of the 16th and the beginning of the 19th centuries.—267

D

Dalrymple, Hamilton Magill, Sir John (1726-1810)—Scottish economist and historian.—537

Darwin, Charles Robert (1809-1882)
—English naturalist; formulat-

ed the theory of evolution in his *Origin of Species by Means of Natural Selection*.—294

De Quincey, Thomas (1785-1859)— English writer and economist; his writings reflect the decline of the Ricardian school after Ricardo's death.—123, 124

Destutt de Tracy, Antoine Louis Claude, comte de (1754-1836)— French economist, supporter of the constitutional monarchy.— 138, 181

Duilius, Marcus (4th century B.C.) —Roman tribune.—538

Dureau de la Malle, Adolphe Jules César Auguste (1777-1857) —French poet and historian, translator of the works of Roman writers, author of a book on the Roman economy.—538

F

Fairbairn, Sir William (1789-1874) —Scottish manufacturer, engineer and inventor.—442

Fourier, François Marie Charles (1772-1837)—French utopian socialist.—238

Frederick II (1194-1250)—King of Sicily (from 1198), German King (1212-50) and Holy Roman Emperor (1215-50).—538

G

Galiani, Ferdinando (1728-1787)— Italian economist, opponent of the Physiocrats; propagated the view that the value of a commodity is determined by its usefulness, though he also advanced a number of correct views regarding the nature of commodities and of money.—267

Ganilh, Charles (1758-1836)— French politician and economist, follower of the Mercantilists.— 537

Garnier, Germain, comte de (1754-1821)—French economist and politician, monarchist; follower of the Physiocrats; translator of Adam Smith.—27

Genucius, Lucius (4th century B.C.) —Roman tribune.—538

Gilbart, James William (1794-1863)—British financier, wrote a number of books on banking.— 539

Godwin, William (1756-1836)—English philosopher and novelist.— 61

H

Henry VIII (1491-1547)—King of England (1509-47).—538, 539

Hodgskin, Thomas (1787-1869)— British economist and publicist; advanced the proletarian standpoint against classical bourgeois political economy. While utilising the theories of Ricardo, he defended the interests of the proletariat; criticised capitalism from the standpoint of utopian socialism.—260, 263-67, 270, 274-76, 280, 289-90, 292-97, 302, 304-07, 311, 313-16, 319, 445

Hopkins, Thomas (end of the 18th until the middle of the 19th centuries)—British economist; considered rent to be a consequence of the monopoly of land. —264, 403

Horace (Quintus Horatius Flaccus) (65-8 B.C.)—Roman poet.—23, 56

Hüllmann, Karl Dietrich (1765-1846)—German historian, wrote mainly about the history of finance and of trade.—538

Hume, David (1711-1776)—Scottish philosopher, subjective idealist, agnostic, historian and economist; friend and adviser of Adam Smith; propagated a quantitative theory of money and stood for free trade in matters of economic policy.—537

J

James I (1566-1625)—King of Great Britain (1603-25). He was proclaimed King of Scotland as James VI in 1567.—539

Jones, Richard (1790-1855)—English economist, one of the last exponents of classical bourgeois political economy.—399-403, 405-07, 409, 410, 412-35, 438-40, 443, 445-46, 448-49

Justinian I (c. 482-565)—Byzantine Emperor (527-65).—538

K

King, Gregory (1648-1712)—British statistician, genealogist and engraver.—325

L

Laing, Samuel (1810-1897)—British politician and publicist, Liberal MP; occupied many important posts in British railway companies.—292

Lalor, John (1814-1856)—British publicist and economist.—263, 287

Locke, John (1632-1704)—English philosopher, economist who "championed the new bourgeoisie in every way, taking the side of the industrialists against the working class and against the paupers, the merchants against the old-fashioned usurers, the financial aristocracy against the governments that were in debt, and he even demonstrated in one of his books that the bourgeois way of thinking was the normal one for human beings" (Marx).—537

Luther, Martin (1483-1546)—German reformer, founder of Protestantism (Lutheranism) in Germany; strongly supported the wealthy burghers, noblemen and princes against the peasants and poor townspeople during the Peasant War of 1524-25.—527, 528, 529, 532-34

M

McCulloch, John Ramsay (1789-1864)—British economist, vulgariser of Ricardo's teachings.—29, 67, 87, 93, 104, 168-76, 178-87, 238, 267

Malthus, Thomas Robert (1766-1834)—English economist, cleric, ideologist of the landed aristocracy which had become merged with the bourgeoisie, apologist of capitalism; advanced the reactionary theory of population, designed to justify the poverty of the working people under capitalism.—13, 14, 15-20, 22-34, 36-41, 45-48, 50-53, 56-64, 70, 71, 77, 83, 93, 97, 109, 110, 117, 120, 125, 149, 155, 169, 171, 177, 185, 242, 259, 266, 306, 330, 353, 414, 429

Manley, Thomas (1628-1690)—British lawyer and publicist; wrote on historic and economic questions.—539

Mill, James (1773-1836)—British economist and philosopher; vulgarised Ricardo's theory.—29, 30, 58, 65, 76, 84-105, 164, 166,

168, 172, 177-80, 182, 184, 185, 266, 331, 397

Mill, John Stuart (1806-1873)— British economist and positivist philosopher, vulgarised the classical economic teachings of Ricardo and advocated conciliation between the interests of the bourgeoisie and the vital interests of the working class; thought that the contradictions of capitalism could be overcome by reforming the methods of distribution; son of James Mill. —84, 106, 187, 190-96, 198-204, 206-08, 210, 213, 221, 223-26, 236, 505, 506

Morton, John Chalmers (1821-1888) —British agronomist.—444

Mullion, Mordecai—see *Wilson, John.*

N

Newman, Francis William (1805-1897)—English philologist and publicist, bourgeois radical, author of books on religious, political and economic questions.— 537

Niebuhr, Barthold Georg (1776-1831)—German historian.—538

O

Owen, Robert (1771-1858)—British utopian socialist.—55, 238, 261

P

Parisot, Jacques Théodore (b. 1783) —James Mill's *Elements of Political Economy* was translated by him into French.—89, 93, 96, 98, 100, 101

Paterson, William (1658-1719)— Scottish financier, one of the first directors (1694-95) of the Bank of England.—537

Peel, Sir Robert (1788-1850)—English statesman, Conservative Prime Minister (1834-35 and 1841-46).—222

Pindar (c. 522-c.442 B.C.)—Greek lyric poet.—275

Prévost, Guilleaume (1799-1883)— Swiss economist; translated, *inter alia*, one of McCulloch's books into French jointly with his father.—104-09, 186

Prévost, Pierre (1751-1839)—Swiss physicist and economist; translated books by Malthus and others into French; father of Guilleaume Prévost.—62

Price, Richard (1723-1791)—English radical publicist, economist and moral philosopher.— 240

Proudhon, Pierre Joseph (1809-1865)—French publicist, sociologist and economist, ideologist of the petty bourgeoisie, one of the founders of anarchism.— 468, 523, 525-28, 532

R

Ramsay, Sir George (1800-1871)— British economist, one of the last representatives of classical bourgeois political economy.— 326-32, 334-39, 342, 346, 347, 348, 349, 351, 353-60, 363, 364, 370, 428

Rau, Karl Heinrich (1792-1870)— German economist, "the German Say" (Marx).—504

Ravenstone, Piercy (d. 1830)—British Ricardian economist, opponent of Malthus and advocate of the interests of the working people.—257, 258, 260, 261, 266, 309

Ricardo, David (1772-1823)—English economist. His work represents the highest point reached by classical bourgeois political economy.—13, 14, 15, 16, 23, 25, 29-31, 33, 34, 51-56, 66, 69-71, 74, 75, 80, 84-86, 88, 89, 92, 93, 94, 95-100, 104-07, 109-11, 114-17, 119-26, 131, 137, 138, 139, 147, 148, 149, 152, 153, 159, 164-66, 168-72, 175, 176, 177, 179-83, 185-88, 190-92, 196, 200, 201, 207, 212, 226, 236, 237, 240-45, 253, 254, 256, 258-60, 263-67, 274, 313, 332, 333, 338, 351, 352, 353, 354, 379, 381, 396-99, 402, 403, 405, 406, 429, 441, 447, 453, 501, 502, 505, 506, 517

Rodbertus (-Jagetzow), Johann Karl (1805-1875)—Prussian landowner, economist, theoretician of Prussian Junker "state socialism".—304

Roscher, Wilhelm Georg Friedrich (1817-1894)—German vulgar economist, founder of the older historical school of German political economy; attacked utopian socialism and classical bourgeois political economy and substituted shallow empiricism for theoretical analysis, denying the existence of economic laws.—182, 185, 353, 498, 502

Rothschild, James, baron de (1792-1868)—head of the banking house of the same name in Paris.—448

Rousseau, Jean Jacques (1712-1778) —one of the great figures of the French Enlightenment, democrat, ideologist of the petty bourgeoisie.—63

Russell, Lord John (1792-1878)— British statesman, leader of the Whigs, Prime Minister (1846-52 and 1865-66).—238

S

Saint-Simon, Claude Henri de Rouvroy, comte de (1760-1825)— French utopian socialist.—468

Say, Jean Baptiste (1767-1832)— French economist; systematised and vulgarised Adam Smith's theory.—79, 93, 95, 105, 119, 121, 122, 123, 180-85, 252, 501, 502, 533

Seneca, Lucius Annaeus (c. 4 B.C. to A.D. 65)—Roman philosopher, one of the great representatives of Stoicism.—532

Senior, Nassau William (1790-1864)—English vulgar economist, one of the "economic spokesmen of the bourgeoisie" (Marx); apologist for capitalism, strongly opposed the shortening of the working-day.—30, 353, 506

Sismondi, Jean Charles Léonard Simonde de (1773-1842)—Swiss economist and historian; criticised capitalism "from the standpoint of the petty bourgeois" (Lenin).—42, 53, 54, 55, 56, 62, 84, 259, 261, 287, 362, 382, 396, 397, 398, 403, 424

Smith, Adam (1723-1790)—the most important British economist before Ricardo; generalised the experience of the period of capitalist manufactories and of the early factory system and gave classical bourgeois political economy its developed form.—13, 14, 16, 20, 23, 24-29, 31, 32, 39, 53, 61, 69, 70, 74, 83, 106, 110, 116, 119, 121, 123, 172, 173, 180, 181, 182, 185, 188, 202, 239, 253, 254, 264, 266, 269, 313, 335, 353, 379, 410, 414, 426, 431, 442, 446, 453, 495, 499, 501, 502, 504, 505, 515, 517

Spence, Thomas (1750-1814)—British utopian socialist.—61

Steuart, Sir James (1712-1780)— British economist, one of the last representatives of Mercantilism.—194, 243, 399

Stirling, Patrick James (1809-1891) —British economist.—188-89

Storch, Heinrich Friedrich von (Andrei Karlovich) (1766-1835)—economist, statistician and historian; vulgarised classical bourgeois political economy; member of the St. Petersburg Academy of Sciences.—355

T

Thucydides (c. 460-400 B.C.)— Greek historian.—185, 502

Torrens, Robert (1780-1864)—British officer and economist, Free Trader.—24, 58, 69, 71-77, 79, 80, 97, 165, 177, 186, 222, 259, 266

Townsend, Joseph (1739-1816)— British cleric, geologist and sociologist; propounded the theory of population, later expanded by Malthus. He "extolled poverty as the necessary condition of wealth" (Marx).—38, 53, 61

Trajan, Marcus Ulpius Trajanus (53-117)—Roman Emperor (98-117).—539

Turgot, Anne Robert Jacques, baron de l'Aulne (1727-1781)— French statesman and economist, Physiocrat, disciple of Quesnay; removed from his post as Comptroller-General of Finance because of his progressive economic policy.—270, 433, 478

U

Ure, Andrew (1778-1857)—British chemist and economist, Free Trader.—442-43

W

Wakefield, Edward Gibbon (1796-1862)—British statesman, colonial politician and economist.— 95, 187-88, 253, 289

Warwick, Richard Neville, earl of (1428-1471)—English feudal lord; played an important part in the Wars of the Roses. Because of his great influence which in 1461 he used to place Edward, son of Richard, Duke of York, on the throne, he received the nickname "the king-maker".—416

West, Sir Edward (1782-1828)— British economist; outlined a theory of rent.—306

Wilson, John (1785-1854)—British poet and publicist; wrote under various pen-names.—185, 186, 238

INDEX OF LITERARY, BIBLICAL AND MYTHOLOGICAL NAMES

Antaeus—a giant of Greek mythology, son of Poseidon, god of the sea, and Gaea, goddess of the earth. As long as he was in contact with his mother, the earth, nobody could vanquish him. Hercules lifted him off the ground and strangled him.— 536

Cacus—according to Roman mythology, Cacus, the son of Vulcan, was a fire-breathing giant, who was slain by Hercules.—536

Dundreary—a character in *Our American Cousin*, a comedy by the English dramatist Tom Taylor (1817-1880).—37, 48

Ezekiel(c. the 6th century B.C.)—a Hebrew prophet. A book of the Old Testament is named after him.—528

Geryon—according to Greek legend, a monster with three bodies who was slain by Hercules with an arrow.—536

Hercules—son of Zeus, the most renowned hero of Greek mythology.—536

Isaiah (c. 740-c. 700 B.C.)—a major Hebrew prophet. A book of the Old Testament is called Isaiah.—528

Odysseus (Ulysses)—a legendary king of Ithaca, the chief character of Homer's epic, *Odyssey*.—533

Polyphemus—a Cyclops who was blinded by Odysseus, according to Greek legend.—533

Ulysses—see *Odysseus*.

SUBJECT INDEX FOR THE THREE PARTS OF THIS WORK

A

Accumulation of capital—I, 59, 61, 107, 252, 303-04; II, 470, 479-80, 483-84, 485, 488, 490, 491, 492, 537, 542; III, 39, 59, 68, 271-72, 274, 315, 335, 380-81, 420-22, 425-26, 442
— conversion of revenue into capital—II, 476-77, 485, 486, 535; III, 38-39
— as a law of capitalist production—I, 169-70, 227; II, 483; III, 421
— as an aim of capitalist production—III, 48
— growth of population as its basis—I, 107; II, 137-38, 477, 492, 537-38; III, 241
— its qualitative limits—III, 241
— as a continuous process—II, 477, 479
— as a condition of the division of labour—III, 271-72
— and accumulation of labour—II, 480-81
— and the productivity of labour—I, 171; II, 537-38, 557; III, 121, 345
— and concentration of capital—I, 171; III, 315
— and the organic composition of capital—II, 472-73, 477, 537-38, 557, 562; III, 243-44
— and the value of constant capital—III, 345
— and simple reproduction—II, 481, 487; III, 380-81
— in agriculture and machine-building—II, 335, 485-89, 492; III, 379
— and credit—II, 482; III, 519
— and crises—II, 492, 494; III, 379
— and wages—III, 243-44, 421
— and exploitation of labour—II, 557, 565, 567-68; III, 250-51, 335, 352, 441
— and profit—I, 107-08; II, 537, 542-44; III, 39, 301-02, 420-22, 446-47, 448
— and rent—III, 420-21
— and foreign trade—III, 446
— and production of luxury goods—III, 246
— in the Middle Ages—II, 232
— and usury—I, 368-69; II, 232
— general law of capitalist accumulation—III, 335, 352, 441
— primitive accumulation of capital—III, 251, 272, 311-12, 314-15, 418

Agricultural labourers—see *Workers*

Agriculture—I, 46, 47-49, 50, 60, 136, 144, 170, 219; II, 19, 20, 24, 56, 59, 62, 63-64, 81, 95-96, 109-10, 141-42, 147, 159, 221, 237, 238, 303, 321, 360, 475-76; III, 289, 409-10, 444-45

— organic composition of capital—II, 20, 21, 69, 92, 298, 306-07, 315-16, 331, 376, 391, 394
— division of the spheres of production—II, 59
—replacement of constant capital—I, 127, 130, 136, 140, 142, 144, 187-88, 246, 247-48, 249; II, 54, 111-12, 159, 485-87
— difference between industry and—II, 48, 54, 55, 63-64, 93, 95-96, 101, 159, 303
— and capitalist methods of production—I, 43, 56; II, 56, 60-61, 64, 94, 110, 155-56, 243, 462, 467
— develops slower than manufacture under capitalist conditions—II, 18-19, 94; III, 300-01
— withdrawal of capital from—II, 378
— its productivity—II, 20, 81, 109-10, 112
— intensive and extensive—II, 82, 335
—' its scientific basis—II, 110
— accumulation of capital—II, 335, 486-87, 492
— and growth of population—II, 159
— decrease of variable capital—III, 235
— and' production of absolute surplus-value—II, 20
— formation of prices—II, 17-18, 100-01, 127, 209, 243, 300-01, 316, 332; III, 301
— excess profit—II, 71, 75-76, 93, 95-96, 126, 147, 240-41; III, 116-17, 399, 402. 413
— in advanced and undeveloped countries—II, 474
See also: *Stock-breeding*

Agrochemistry—II, 24, 59. 110, 159; III, 289
See also: *Chemistry*

Alienation—I. 51, 93, 345; II, 416; III, 259, 264, 272, 293, 296, 315, 466-67, 483, 489, 492, 493, 494-95, 498, 502-03, 530

America—I, 277; II, 228, 364, 557
See also: *United States of America*

American Civil War—I, 115; II, 328

Antiquity—I, 224, 287, 301, 302; II, 19, 152; III, 416, 531, 534, 538-39
See also: *Egypt (Ancient), Greece (Ancient), Rome (Ancient)*

Art and literature—I, 285, 298, 387, 401, 405, 410-11; II, 110, 528

Asia—III, 416, 417
— pre-capitalist relations of production—III, 414, 428, 431
— pre-capitalist forms of rent—III, 400, 401
— landed property—I, 277; III, 420, 435
— peasants—III, 416, 444
— handicrafts and manufacture—I, 157; III, 434-35

Australia (New Holland)—II, 301; III, 115

Austria—II, 16

Auxiliary materials—I, 135-36, 245, 247; II, 488

B

Bankers—I, 320; II, 123, 511

Banknotes—I, 324, 327-28, 343, 388; II, 494

Banks—I, 327; II, 484, 494, 525

Barter—II, 508-09, 527, 532; III, 120

Basis and superstructure—I, 284-85, 286-87, 288-89; III, 163
See also: *Relations of production, State*

Belgium—II, 23, 359

Bill-brokers—II, 123

Bill of exchange—I, 190, 319-20, 327-28; II, 511

Book-keeping—I, 145; III, 215, 217
— Italian book-keeping—I, 389; II, 48
— capitalist book-keeping—II, 48, 155

Bourgeoisie—see *Capitalists*

Building industry
— time of production in—III, 391-92

C

Capital—I, 45, 49, 93, 322-23, 392, 393; II, 528, 534-35, 548; III, 131, 137, 265, 272, 311, 373, 422, 424, 428, 455
— as a relation of production—I, 44, 92; II, 40, 400; III, 236, 264-65, 270, 327-28, 414, 422, 423-24, 427
— as the basis and necessary result of capitalist production—III, 260-61, 476
— antagonism between capital and wage-labour—I, 391, 394; II, 400, 416; III, 55-56, 271, 322-23, 423, 476
— wage-labour as its basis—I, 153, 200-01, 227, 293, 393, 396; III, 327-28, 427
— historical justification for—II, 405; III, 429
— its revolutionising role—I, 389; III, 427, 444
— and the development of productive forces—I, 389; II, 524; III, 427
— as a commodity—II, 510; III, 455-56, 457-58, 465-66, 491-92
— as money—I, 397; III, 137
— individual capital as a part of the aggregate capital of society—I, 416; II, 29, 69, 433; III, 81-82
— and revenue—I, 93-94, 219, 225, 228, 230, 234-35, 236-37, 240-41, 291, 311-12; II, 432, 476; III, 345

— in the process of production and circulation—III, 481-84
— capitalist as a personification of—I, 270, 282, 389, 409; III, 272, 296, 358, 514-15
— and crises—I, 38; II, 492-535
— movement of capital from one sphere to another—II, 206-11, 521
— its origin—I, 43, 56; II, 154, 462, 467
— and the separation of landed property from labour—I, 50, 51
— its primitive accumulation—III, 251, 272, 311-12, 314-15, 418
— usury as its old-fashioned form—I, 368-69; III, 527-28, 531-32
— its fetishist character—I, 389, 392, 394; III, 265, 296, 453, 454, 466-67, 494, 498-99
— bourgeois economists on—I, 44-45, 66, 93, 270, 307, 364, 369; III, 328, 362
— *centralisation of capital*—III, 311, 314-15
— *circulating capital*—I, 187
as a form of capital in circulation—I, 44
its reproduction—II, 471
its circuit—III, 393
wages as its part—I, 252
rate of profit influenced by its depreciation—I, 105
and fixed capital—II, 132, 195-96, 578-79
— *commercial (merchant) capital*—I, 250-52, 323, 410, 413; II, 485; III, 395, 420, 469-70
and industrial capital—I, 39; III, 468-70, 527, 529-30
and interest-bearing capital—I, 39
in the Middle Ages—II, 232
— *concentration of capital*—I, 170, 220; III, 447-48
and the development of the capitalist mode of production—III, 270-72, 315

in agriculture—II, 110
— *constant capital*—I, 104, 316-17; II, 21, 173-74, 297, 318-19, 414-16, 472-73; III, 92-93, 178, 211, 218, 249-50
   as a necessary condition of capitalist production—I, 109, 254; II, 415; III, 228
   and the production of surplus-value—I, 80, 395
   its elements—I, 245-47; II, 21, 62; III, 191
   its value and use-value—I, 106, 108-09, 219-20; II, 415-16; III, 178, 217-18
   profit as a source of its growth—I, 107-08
   its reproduction—I, 37, 99-102, 103-04, 106, 107-51, 187-98, 219-20, 242-52, 253-54, 323; III, 470-71, 473, 489-90
   its replacement in agriculture—I, 127, 130, 136, 142, 144, 187, 245-46, 248, 249; II, 54, 112, 159-60, 486-87
   its replacement in kind in other branches—I, 144-45, 147-49, 190-91, 195-96, 197, 219, 230-31, 244, 247-48, 250; II, 54, 454, 472-73, 479-80, 487-88
   its depreciation as a result of the growing productivity of labour—II, 415-16, 473-74
   and the rate of profit—II, 23
   variations in its value influence the rate of profit—I, 105-06; II, 22; III, 218, 226-28, 233-35, 346-47, 383
   and rent—II, 452-53, 457-58
   and variable capital—I, 147-48, 219; II, 579-80; III, 326-27
— *fixed capital*—I, 44, 187, 242-43, 327; II, 21, 62, 195-96, 212; III, 388, 437-38
   as a part of constant capital—II, 62
   its reproduction process—I, 103-04, 109, 242-43, 327; II, 28, 196, 470-71, 577
   and circulating capital—II, 132, 195-96, 578-79
   its depreciation—III, 389
   and the rate of profit—I, 105; III, 388-89
— *industrial capital*—I, 342; III, 468, 470
   as the most developed form of capital—III, 427
   and commercial capital—I, 39; III, 468-70
   and interest-bearing capital—I, 39; III, 467, 468-69
   and the credit system—III, 468-69
— *interest-bearing capital*—I, 39; III, 453, 454, 457, 460-62, 465, 466-67, 470-71, 472, 473, 477, 488-90, 498, 502
   its isolation from the production process—III, 461-62, 486, 523-24
   and the separation of juridical from economic ownership of capital—III, 462, 473, 474, 490, 508
   as a commodity—III, 455, 457-58, 465, 492
   its concentration—III, 465
   its pre-capitalist forms—III, 467, 487, 493, 528
   and industrial capital—I, 39; III, 467-69, 473-74, 493, 527-28
   and industrial profit—III, 461-62
   and accumulation of capital—II, 482
   and credit—III, 518
   and interest—III, 488, 493, 508
— *organic composition of capital*—I, 415; II, 96, 415-16, 433, 465, 490, 566; III, 363-64, 376, 387-88, 389, 396, 411-12, 418
   in different branches of production—II, 20, 69, 92-93, 298, 307, 315, 331, 376,

384, 391-92, 394; III, 516
and the productivity of labour—I, 219; II, 16, 28, 108-09, 251-52, 298, 415-16, 596; III, 300, 310-11, 364, 373, 383
and variations in the method of production—II, 252, 276, 279, 288, 380-82; III, 383
and the aim of capitalist production—II, 565-66
and productive forces—II, 415-16
and the process of circulation—II, 390-91
and surplus-value—II, 28, 47, 57-58, 297, 376-77; III, 228
and the rate of profit—II, 340-41, 374-75, 380-84; III, 302
and the tendency of the rate of profit to fall—II, 438-39, 596; III, 216, 302, 310-11
and surplus population—III, 306, 364
Barton and Ramsay on—II, 576-80; III, 326-28
— *physical composition of capital*—II, 288, 454, 455; III, 382
and the organic composition of capital—II, 279, 380, 381
and the mode of production—II, 282, 288
and the rate of surplus-value—III, 385
— *productive capital*—I, 342, 413; II, 137, 515, 517 III, 466
— *value of the component parts of capital*—I, 415-16; II, 28, 275-89; III, 383-87
and the organic composition of capital—I, 38; II, 275-89, 324, 380-81, 454-55; III, 383-88
— *variable capital*—I, 393, 395; II, 416; III, 242, 293, 371

its relative and absolute decrease—II, 557, 580; III, 235, 382-83, 418
and living labour—III, 327
and constant capital—I, 147, 219; II, 579; III, 326-27
— *wear and tear of constant capital*—II, 480; III, 59, 67-68
and its replacement—I, 113, 131, 135-36, 141, 145-46, 147-49, 242-43, 246; II, 58
and the value of commodities—I, 111-12, 214; II, 18, 433
and the quantity of labour employed—I, 169
and the demand for labour—III, 68
See also: *Accumulation of capital, Money-lenders' capital*

Capitalist mode of production—I, 285, 287, 301, 390, 409; II, 64, 152-53, 157, 247-48, 407; III, 53, 55-56, 74, 89-90, 112-13, 115, 170, 290, 359, 378, 420-21, 461-62, 476-77, 494-95
— general characteristics—I, 72, 199, 284, 293, 406-07; II, 152, 483-84, 501; III, 52, 55-56, 118, 126, 259, 377-78, 426, 444, 487
— its aim—I, 90, 213, 399-400, 406; II, 102, 495, 502, 503, 521, 547, 565-66; III, 258-59, 480
— conditions for—III, 490-91, 531
— its contradictions—I, 218, 231, 279-80, 283, 287, 305; II, 18, 118, 152, 492, 495, 500-01, 504-05, 510, 512-13, 519; III, 55-56, 84, 97-98, 120-21, 257, 259, 261, 315, 360, 423, 429, 476, 494, 498-99, 501-02
— as a barrier to the free development of the productive forces—II, 528, 565; III, 55-56, 84, 116, 119, 120
— and consumption—II, 502-03

— as a historical form of social development—I, 187, 296, 390-91, 409; III, 56, 84, 261, 315, 426, 447, 487
— its revolutionising role—I, 389; III, 427, 444
— its cosmopolitan character—III, 448
— accumulation of capital as its law—I, 170, 227-28; II, 483; III, 421
— and the development of productive forces—II, 117-18; III, 259, 487
— reproduction of capitalist relations of production—III, 271-72, 315, 514
— and surplus labour—I, 93, 346, 356, 389-90, 392, 394; II, 405-06
— and the law of value—III, 73-74
— and the productivity of labour—I, 70, 160-61, 187, 199, 218, 294
— and the scale of production—I, 231, 390, 392; II, 520, 521-22
— and necessary labour—I, 227, 231
— agriculture subjugated by—II, 237, 462; III, 99, 420
— and progress in agriculture—II, 24, 56, 60-61, 64
— and natural forces—I, 391; II, 552-55; III, 182, 300-01, 309
— its historical prerequisites—I, 45, 51, 78, 162, 201; II, 502; III, 272
— its genesis—III, 491-92
— its early stages—I, 52, 270, 276-77, 301; II, 157; III, 357
— industry as its starting-point—II, 18-19, 93; III, 99, 402
— the position of peasants and craftsmen—I, 407-09; II, 346-47; III, 423
— employment of slave labour—II, 302-03
— creates the material basis for communism—III, 265, 273, 423, 429
— bourgeois political economy as its theoretical expression—I, 45, 186-87; II, 36, 152-53, 238; III, 259, 265, 276
— regarded by bourgeois economists as the eternal and natural form of production—I, 44, 186-87, 361, 393; II, 18, 32, 153, 158, 504; III, 239, 259, 265, 274, 401-02
— Physiocrats' analysis of—I, 45-46, 49-50

Capitalist relations of production—I, 171, 389, 390-91, 403; II, 152, 400, 501; III, 82, 89, 93, 129, 137, 245, 251, 271-72, 275, 295-96, 315, 378, 425, 426, 453, 456, 460, 461, 481-83, 489, 494-95, 508-09, 510-11, 514-15
— in agriculture—I, 57
— relations between sellers and buyers—I, 296, 314-17, 397-98, 399, 406-07; II, 518-20; III, 174
— and bourgeois political economy—III, 88-91, 93-94, 245

Capitalists—I, 282-83, 300-01; II, 44, 152, 219, 328, 486; III, 272, 395, 448, 467-68, 496, 534
— as personified capital—I, 271, 282, 389, 409; III, 272, 296, 358, 514
— appropriation of surplus-value by—I, 85-86, 95, 108, 323; II, 152, 328, 373, 453; III, 251, 402, 420-21, 471
— and the other classes of bourgeois society—I, 175; III, 51-52
— exploitation of the working class by—II, 29; III, 82
— industrial bourgeoisie and the development of productive forces—II, 118
— small capitalists—I, 201; III, 311-12, 315, 356-57, 447
— capitalist and landowner united in one person—II, 15, 45, 302-03, 305, 306, 339, 362

— capitalist farmers—II, 17, 155, 157, 334-35, 377-78, 394
— and the struggle for the reduction of the rate of interest—I, 368; III, 456, 534, 538-39
— exploitation of the countryside by the urban bourgeoisie—II, 231-35
— radical bourgeois against private ownership of land—II, 44, 328
— their views on the source of profit—II, 69, 181
— their attitude towards unproductive professions—I, 175, 201, 287-88, 300-01; II, 44
— as they appear in the works of economists—I, 175-76, 271, 279-80; II, 421, 463; III, 315, 497-98

Chemistry
— its role in production—I, 247; III, 285, 392
— chemical processes—II, 177, 553; III, 64, 177, 229, 285, 349, 368, 392
— as a scientific basis of agriculture—II, 24, 59, 110, 159; III, 289

China—II, 557; III, 433, 434

Church—I, 210, 281, 283, 299-300, 301; II, 119; III, 311, 428

Circulation—I, 125, 142; II, 495
— as an intermediate stage between production and consumption—II, 483-84; III, 281-83
— and reproduction—I, 45, 106, 109, 128, 133-34, 136, 140, 142-43, 146-47; II, 510, 513
— and accumulation—I, 39; III, 281
— and exchange—II, 508
— reservoirs—I, 39; III, 280-89, 290-91
— its extention under capitalism—III, 289

— of commodities—I, 187, 273-74, 308; III, 291
— of money—I, 251-52, 273-74, 308, 325-27
— and the realisation of surplus-value—I, 55
— and relations between labour and capital—III, 482
— *circulation of capital*—I, 44, 308, 413; II, 28; III, 85-86, 326
of fixed capital—I, 242-43; III, 338
of circulating capital—III, 393
and surplus-value—III, 389-96
and profit—III, 71, 389-96
— circulation period —III, 85-86
See also: *Commodity circulation*

Classes
— and ownership of the conditions of production—I, 43, 50, 72
— class structure of capitalist society—I, 305; II, 152, 416, 419, 460, 468, 492-93, 561, 572, 573; III, 52, 62-63, 98, 352
— ruling class and its component parts—I, 175, 285-87, 300-01; II, 123
— and distribution of surplus-value—I, 42, 47-48, 83, 93-94, 108; II, 41, 151
— proletariat—I, 228; III, 62-63
— productive and unproductive —I, 177-80, 200-01, 228-29; III, 22, 52-53, 120
See also: *Capitalists, Farmers, Landlords, Peasants, Rentiers, Workers*

Class struggle—I, 301
— its economic basis—II, 29
— its reflection in bourgeois political economy—III, 501-02

Colonies—II, 239, 301-03
— two types—II, 301-02
— as markets for industrial capital—III, 470

— high profits derived from colonial trade—II, 228, 375, 436-37, 469
— landed property—II, 301-03 306, 308, 311-12, 315, 362, 436
— slavery—I, 229; II, 302-03, 436

Colonisation—II, 301, 310, 311-13
— Adam Smith and Ricardo on —II, 228, 239, 308-09, 311-13, 362, 436-37

Commodities—I, 72-73, 159, 160, 163-64, 171-73, 204, 232, 303-04, 312-14, 388; II, 15, 61, 64, 397, 403, 496, 500-02, 504, 514, 515, 517, 533, 539; III, 15-16, 20-21, 74, 112, 129, 288
— as a prerequisite and result of capitalist production—I, 158, 315, 411; II, 63, 264, 411, 423, 501-02; III, 74, 112, 167, 377-78, 467, 518
— their dual character—I, 303; II, 501, 507, 509; III, 88, 101, 128-31, 521
— their value—III, 127-28, 135, 160, 161
— dual character of labour contained in them—III, 130-31
— and money—I, 174, 303-04; II, 501-02, 504, 505, 509; III, 56, 88, 120
— exchange of commodities—I, 57-58, 62, 72-73, 204-06, 233, 235, 237-38, 315; II, 397; III, 129, 281-87
— production and realisation of commodities under capitalism—I, 124, 134-35, 232, 236, 327; II, 509; III, 17-18, 83
— labour-power as a commodity—I, 45, 51, 71, 73, 88, 94, 159, 167, 171, 314-16, 321-22, 356, 392, 397-98; II, 397; III, 89-90, 110, 114, 271, 290, 300
— their fetishist character—III, 130, 137, 295, 494, 508

Commodity circulation—II, 513; III, 112

— and capitalist relations—III, 378
— and circulation of money—I, 273-74, 308-09, 312-13, 333-43; III, 130
— and reproduction—I, 329, 342

Commodity production—I, 71-72, 171-72, 400; II, 454, 509; III, 112, 130, 137, 296, 494-95
— under capitalism—III, 288-90, 313
— and social labour—I, 207
— and circulation—III, 290
— and markets—II, 423; III, 268-69
— and the division of labour— III, 268

Communism—I, 217-18; II, 104, 105-06, 118, 580; III, 118, 271-72, 357-58, 360, 423
— as a result of the development of contradictions within capitalist production—III, 265, 273, 423, 429
— social form of labour—III, 496
— relations of production—III, 129, 273, 422-23, 429, 525
— extended reproduction—I, 107; III, 352-53
— consumption and accumulation—III, 337-38
— social needs determine production—II, 579-80; III, 118
— productive labour—I, 152-53
— labour-time and free time— III, 257
— and the division of labour— III, 273

Competition—I, 232; II, 18, 30-31, 38, 69, 94, 106, 164-65, 206-11, 217, 235, 266, 521; III, 32, 514-15
— within the same sphere of production—II, 101, 126-27, 155, 205-06, 209, 267, 306; III, 301
— between different spheres of production—II, 127, 206-09, 267, 332, 435; III, 86-87

— between capitalists—I, 155, 277; II, 41-42, 69, 94, 101-02, 205-06, 362, 484, 521; III, 355-56
— between workers—I, 388; II, 17, 435; III, 308
— between capital and labour—III, 354
— between unproductive labourers—I, 218
— between capitalist countries—II, 16, 19-20
— between sellers and buyers—II, 205
— and the formation of market value—II, 96, 204-07, 208, 267-68, 307; III, 301, 472
— and the formation of the general rate of profit—I, 416; II, 25, 27-30, 40-42, 68-69, 187, 206-09, 212, 297, 319, 332, 351; III, 69, 83, 463-64
— and credit—II, 211; III, 519
— obstacles in certain spheres of production—II, 29, 30, 127, 209, 332
— Physiocrats in favour of free competition in industry—I, 53, 65-66, 170, 380, 382

Conditions of production—see *Means of production, Production*

Consumption—I, 99, 103, 108, 255-56, 260, 298, 306, 311-12; II, 565; III, 250
— individual and industrial (productive)—I, 99, 102-03, 112-13, 114, 135, 141, 189-97, 231, 232, 236-40, 244, 248-49, 254, 298, 311, 329, 331; II, 470, 482-85, 486, 490, 516, 518-19; III, 274, 277-78, 524
— under capitalism—I, 90, 270; II, 492, 528-29, 534-35
— of workers—I, 282; II, 565-66; III, 352-53
— consumption of the mass of the people increases slower than the productivity of labour—II, 468
— of labour-power as a commodity—I, 45, 398; II, 136-37; III, 90-91
— of the ruling classes—II, 572
— and production—I, 103, 185-86, 283; III, 120, 288, 292
— and reproduction—I, 289-90, 311, 329; III, 283
— and accumulation—II, 490
— for the sake of consumption—I, 283
— and use-value—I, 298; III, 119
— and over-production—II, 468
— *cost of consumption*
as a component of cost of production—I, 47
its unproductive character—I, 210-11, 298-99
and services—I, 405

Contradiction—I, 51-52, 71, 87-88, 89, 92, 283; II, 32, 56-57, 106, 150, 165, 173, 396-97, 437, 492, 500-01, 504-05, 506-07, 508-10, 511-13, 519, 521, 534; III, 29, 70-71, 84-85, 88, 101, 120-21, 132, 137, 168, 256-57, 259-60, 276, 518
— in capitalist production—I, 218, 234, 280, 283, 287, 305; II, 18, 118, 152, 492, 495, 500-01, 505, 510, 512-13, 519; III, 56, 84, 87, 98, 120-21, 164, 256-57, 259-60, 261, 315, 361, 422-23, 429, 467, 494, 498, 501-02
— between labour and the objective conditions of labour—II, 416; III, 422-23
— in bourgeois political economy—II, 510, 512
— between living and materialised labour—III, 90, 276
— between use-value and value—III, 101-02, 130
— between concrete and abstract labour—III, 130, 136
— between individual and social labour—III, 136-37
— between growing wealth and growing poverty—III, 259

Co-operation—I, 164
— as a form of socially devel-

oped labour—I, 390; II, 521-22, 532
— and the division of labour—III, 270

Countryside
— development of capitalist production—II, 60-61
— its exploitation by the town—II, 232-35; III, 269
— parochialism of country life—II, 475

Credit—I, 337, 368; III, 122, 468-69, 486
— a condition and result of capitalist production—II, 211; III, 448, 468-69, 518
— and competition of capitals—II, 211; III, 519
— and accumulation of capital—II, 482; III, 519
— and economic crises—II, 496, 511-15; III, 122

D

Darwinism—III, 294-95
— refutes the Malthusian theory of population—II, 121

Differential rent—I, 359-60; II, 101, 105-06, 126, 142, 148, 240, 241, 255, 268-69, 273, 291, 293-95, 310, 311-13, 329, 452-53, 454, 457, 458, 459; III, 104-05, 472
— its amount and rate—II, 42-43, 95, 257; III, 405-07
— and excess profit—II, 207-08, 241, 242, 309
— and progress in agriculture—II, 241, 273
— and the labour productivity of agricultural workers—III, 361
— and prices of agricultural products—I, 359; II, 316; III, 105
— and nationalisation of land—II, 103-04, 152
— and communism—II, 105
— Petty on—I, 359-60

— Ricardo on—II, 94, 129-30, 162, 242, 244, 273-74, 315

Differential rent I
— and fertility of the cultivated land—II, 17-18, 42-43, 95, 240, 270, 310; III, 405-06
— and location of the land—III, 105

Differential rent II
— its origin—II, 42-43, 95, 270, 313, 332, 334; III, 405-06
— and landed property—II, 394

Distribution—I, 231
— relations of distribution and of production—I, 94; III, 56, 83-84, 480, 499
— of labour and capital—I, 217, 232; II, 483; III, 464
— of value—II, 134, 151, 152
— of surplus-value—I, 42, 83, 94, 108; II, 29, 41-42, 47-48, 68, 151-52, 199; III, 234, 357-58
— of excess surplus-value—II, 30-31
— of profit—I, 277; II, 453-54

Dividend—II, 433, 436; III, 82

Division of labour—I, 109, 180, 184, 259-60, 284, 294; II, 234; III, 216-17, 269, 279-80, 285, 349, 352-53, 448
— social—I, 143, 387; II, 23, 483-84, 502; III, 268-70
— within the workshop—II, 23; III, 269
— and the productivity of social labour—I, 297; II, 16, 234, 521-22, 532, 539-40; III, 270, 349
— accumulation of capital as its condition—III, 270-73
— and economy of time—I, 203
— manufacture as its form—I, 390; III, 271
— and co-operation—III, 271
— in agriculture—II, 59
— and the development of commodity production—I, 205; III, 268-69, 288-89, 290

— and mass production—III, 268-69, 271
— and density of population—III, 269
— and satisfaction of needs—II, 508

E

Economic crises—II, 495-96, 497-98, 500-02, 507-17, 521, 523, 524-25, 527-28, 533, 534-35; III, 122
— as a result of the capitalist production process—I, 38; II, 492-535; III, 54-55, 56, 84, 120-22
— and contradictions of bourgeois economy—II, 484, 492, 500, 503-05, 507, 509-10, 512-13, 516-17, 521, 534-35; III, 120, 518
— and disproportions in capitalist production—II, 495, 503-04, 510-11, 515-16, 520-21, 529
— their abstract forms—II, 492, 509-13, 514
— and separation of purchase and sale—II, 491, 494, 500, 502, 504-05, 508-10, 512, 514, 532
— and variations in value—II, 496, 514, 515, 517, 533
— and variations in prices—II, 494-95, 505, 515, 534
— and over-production—II, 516-17, 521, 524-25, 527-28; III, 122
— and credit—II, 494, 496, 511-13, 514-15; III, 122
— and accumulation of capital—II, 491, 492, 494; III, 379
— their periodic recurrence—II, 468, 497, 500; III, 56
— bourgeois economists on—I, 234, 268; II, 468, 493-94, 497-502, 503-05, 512-13, 514-15, 517, 528-35; III, 56, 100-01, 121-22
See also: *Over-production*

Egypt (Ancient)—III, 539

Enclosures—II, 143, 156, 157, 237-38

England—I, 50, 178, 179, 181, 220, 263, 269, 355, 356, 358, 360, 369; II, 119, 157-58, 237-39, 368, 474-76, 583-84; III, 61, 186, 402, 415, 424, 431, 443, 446, 469, 527-28, 533-34
— population—II, 474-75, 584-85; III, 323-25
— classes—I, 178, 200-01; II, 37, 482; III, 324-25, 416
— industry—II, 235, 437, 575-76; III, 287
— co-operative factories belonging to the workers—III, 356, 497, 505
— agriculture—II, 19-20, 45, 112-13, 116, 122, 139, 152-53, 157, 177, 237, 238, 241-42, 306, 330-31, 332-33, 359-60, 361, 377, 460-61, 474-75, 525-26, 542, 584; III, 405-06, 409-10
— colonies—II, 239, 301-02
— foreign trade—II, 133, 497-98; III, 222
— money and banks—I, 375-76, 385; II, 227-29; III, 354
— over-production and crises—II, 531-32; III, 121-22
— condition of the workers—I, 411; II, 17, 23, 201, 223-24, 408, 574, 580; III, 259
— feudal society—I, 408; III, 51-52
— enclosures—II, 143, 156, 157, 237-38
— rise in the rate of profit at the beginning of the nineteenth century—II, 459-60
— movement of wages and corn prices in the eighteenth century—II, 583-84
— *Corn Laws*—II, 118-19, 122-23, 236
and landed property—II, 116, 119, 121-23
See also: *Ireland, Scotland*

Europe—I, 154, 229, 262, 277, 385; II, 89, 234, 306, 308, 310, 357, 585; III, 277, 414, 424, 431, 433, 435, 446

Exchange
— of commodities—I, 57-58, 62, 72-73, 204-07, 233, 234-35, 237-38, 315; II, 397; III, 129, 281-87
— character of labour based on private exchange—III, 130
— of equivalents—I, 62, 169, 205-06, 255, 315, 317, 337, 398; III, 126-33, 135, 139-40, 146-47, 150-51, 377
— between labour and capital—I, 51-52, 56-57, 73, 77, 86-87, 156-57, 160, 187, 315, 389, 394-99, 403, 406-07; II, 397-99; III, 14-15, 19-20, 89-90, 93, 95-96, 170, 237, 377, 481-82
— of capital and capital—I, 145, 149, 188, 190, 197, 250, 252; II, 472, 489
— of revenue and revenue—I, 230-31, 233-34, 238, 252
— of revenue and capital—I, 236, 240, 251-52, 311-12, 322; II, 80, 489; III, 246-52
— and circulation—II, 508
— and the division of labour—I, 205
— its connection with production—I, 57-58, 296; II, 28
— source of surplus-value according to certain bourgeois economists—I, 41, 43, 49

Exchange-value—I, 204, 235-36, 270, 282, 302-03; II, 170, 172, 264, 503, 504; III, 54, 125-27, 130-31, 136-37, 149, 296
— as the immediate aim of capitalist production—III, 34
— and profit—I, 41
— and price—II, 264
— and labour-power as a commodity—I, 45
— and commodity exchange—I, 77-78, 158
— and crises—II, 496

Exploitation—I, 410
— of labour-power by capital—I, 72, 77-78, 79-81, 86-88, 153, 270, 278-79, 346, 391-92; II, 29, 438; III, 62-63, 301-02, 306, 308, 310, 352-53, 495

Export—see *Foreign trade*
Export of capital—II, 484; III, 122

F

Factories—I, 390; II, 37

Farmers—II, 23
— their constant capital—I, 100-01
— their real wealth—I, 101
— their transformation into industrial capitalists—II, 110; III, 289
— small farmers—II, 102

Fetishism
— of commodities—III, 130, 137, 295-96, 494, 507-08
— of money—I, 389; III, 295-96, 494
— of capital—I, 389, 392, 394-95; III, 265, 295-96, 453-55, 466, 494, 498
— in the works of bourgeois economists—III, 129, 147, 266-67, 274, 276, 427, 453, 462
— of capitalist relations—III, 295-96, 453, 494

Feudalism—I, 175
— feudal landed property—II, 42
— role of the landowner—II, 152-53
— feudal social relations—I, 408
— feudal character of landed property—II, 153, 237
— decline of the nobility—I, 368
— in Europe—I, 385, 408
— feudal relics in capitalist society—III, 52

— and the Physiocrats—I, 49-53, 381, 382, 385
See also: *Middle Ages*

Foreign trade—I, 48, 155, 170; II, 133, 478, 491, 560; III, 246, 446
— as a prerequisite and result of capitalist production—III, 253, 527
— and abstract labour—III, 253
— and law of value—III, 105-06
— and commodity production—II, 423
— and world money—III, 253
— and the rate of profit—II, 375, 436-37, 469
— and surplus product—II, 491; III, 241-43, 253
— and luxury articles—III, 245-46
— export of services—I, 166

France—I, 166, 325; II, 199; III, 416, 526
— agriculture—I, 50; II, 368; III, 410
— and the Physiocrats—I, 50
— tenant farming—II, 45
— rents, tithes and taxes—II, 137
— interest—I, 375-76; II, 227-28

French Revolution (1789-1794)—II, 119
— partial confiscation of landed property—I, 52, 66
— and the Physiocrats—I, 66, 344
— Malthus on—III, 61

G

Geometry—III, 143-44, 160-61

Germany—I, 166, 224, 376; II, 124, 157, 160, 237, 238, 239; III, 532

Gold (and silver)—I, 43, 154, 174, 282, 302-03, 327, 369; II, 199-200, 300; III, 135, 403-04, 527

Greece (Ancient)—II, 528
Guilds—III, 469

H

Handicrafts—I, 164; II, 232
— craftsmen as commodity producers—I, 407
— work to order—III, 286
— and machinery—II, 571
— under capitalism—I, 408-09

Holland—I, 181, 263, 376, 377, 384; II, 23, 112, 228, 541; III, 424, 446, 527, 534, 540

Home (domestic) industry—I, 159, 164; II, 583; III, 423, 445

Hungary—I, 302

I

Impoverishment of the working class—II, 565-66
— as an inevitable result of capitalism—III, 57, 126, 258-59, 306
— and overwork—III, 306
— paupers—I, 218, 257; II, 477-78; III, 259, 306
— and accumulation of capital—III, 335, 352-53
See also: *Accumulation of capital, Exploitation, Overpopulation, relative*

Incidental expenses of production (faux frais)—I, 167, 175, 289, 301, 381; III, 355-56, 505
See also: *Production*

India—I, 376; II, 16, 241, 407, 482; III, 188, 416, 435, 440

Industry—I, 43; III, 470
— as a branch of production—I, 46; II, 48, 54, 55
— as the truly bourgeois branch of production—II, 18
— its scientific basis—II, 110
— use of natural forces—I, 49, 60

— fixed capital as its product
—II, 62
— absence of fixed or circulating capital in some of its branches—II, 23, 45-46, 62-63, 92, 132; III, 388, 394
— and agriculture—I, 48; II, 18-19, 128; III, 300
— excess profit in—II, 95; III, 389
— Adam Smith and Ricardo on—I, 60
— manufacturing industry—II, 23, 45, 48, 63, 93
See also: *Mining*

Instruments of labour—see *Means of production*

Insurance—III, 357

Interest—I, 82-83, 276-77; II, 140, 142, 228; III, 462, 489, 493-95, 519, 520, 537-40
— a form of surplus-value—I, 82-83; III, 459, 470-71, 486-87, 493
— and the rate of profit—II, 227-28; III, 447, 471
— arising from the ownership of capital—III, 460, 476-77
— as the price of capital—III, 508, 519-23
— and the capitalist who uses his own capital—I, 408; III, 474-75, 479, 493
— as a component part of the costs of production—III, 83, 478-79, 509-10, 512
— and the capitalisation of rent—I, 358-59; III, 522
— in pre-capitalist modes of production—III, 487
— Physiocrats and Petty on—I, 47, 358-59; III, 478
— North, Hume and Massie on—I, 364, 373-74
— Proudhon's and Luther's arguments against—I, 323, 325; III, 456, 467, 523, 525-26, 527-37
— *rate of interest*—I, 358, 368, 375-76; II, 142, 227-28; III, 298-300, 354-55, 447, 462-64, 465-66, 508-09
and the rate of profit—II, 227-28; III, 447, 471
reduction of the rate of interest by the state—III, 468-69, 534, 538

Ireland—I, 300, 362, 385, 386; II, 31, 103, 137; III, 188, 324

Italy—II, 30, 137, 531-32; III, 469

L

Labour—I, 44, 157, 158, 186, 187, 390, 411; II, 492; III, 135-36, 264-65, 362, 376, 433-34
— and wealth—I, 280
— as the substance of value—I, 46, 48, 50, 84-85, 95, 204-05, 393; II, 130, 164, 172; III, 40, 128-29, 135, 155, 160-63, 260, 337, 481
— its forms under capitalism—I, 187, 390-91; III, 129, 130, 259, 264-65, 315, 426
— living and materialised—I, 72, 76-77, 80-82, 87, 98, 109-25, 126-28, 130-50, 171-72, 188-98, 220, 235, 239-41, 244-46, 248-49, 250, 255, 388, 395-96, 397-99; II, 80, 84, 152, 397-98, 399, 416, 421, 472-73, 485-86, 490; III, 72, 79-80, 89-90, 158, 274, 276, 278, 327, 371, 380-81
— simple and skilled—II, 15, 384; III, 165, 231, 308
— labour process and the formation of value—I, 103, 242, 245; II, 21, 48, 58-59, 80, 83-84, 112, 195-96, 414, 471; III, 111-12, 211, 372-73
— living labour as a source of value—I, 77, 394-95, 406-07
— controlled by capital—I, 391, 399-400
— its transformation into capital—I, 393, 394-96, 399-400
— its value—I, 397-98; II, 398, 401-02, 407

— its accumulation—II, 487; III, 75
— *abstract labour*—I, 399-401
  as a form of social labour—I, 48; II, 172, 504, 529; III, 130-31, 135-36, 253, 447
  as distinct from individual, concrete and particular labour—II, 504; III, 130, 131, 135-36, 138-39
— *child labour*—II, 408, 477
— *concrete labour*—I, 48, 156-58, 171-72, 366, 400; III, 253, 520
  and productive labour—I, 401, 404-05
— *female labour*—II, 408, 477
— *intensification of labour*—III, 307-09, 310, 497
— *labour of superintendence*—I, 81, 108, 297; III, 69, 355-57, 493, 495-98, 504-05, 507
— *mental and physical labour*—I, 156-57, 164, 175-76, 297-98, 307, 411-12; III, 432
  under capitalism—I, 412
  science as a product of mental labour—I, 353
— *necessary labour*—I, 107-08; III, 245-46
  socially necessary labour—I, 218, 232; II, 38, 130, 521; III, 113
  under capitalism—I, 227, 231-32
  and surplus labour—I, 213, 216
— *productive labour*—I, 46, 152, 157, 160, 161-63, 164-65, 172-73, 393, 394-401, 406, 409-10; II, 110, 547; III, 431-32
  as the basis of the capitalist mode of production—I, 152-53, 293, 399-400; III, 426
  productive workers—I, 156-57, 225, 226, 394, 411-12
  and the working class—I, 166, 397
  and the productivity of labour—I, 218-19, 289-90
  and the division of labour—I, 297
  in trade—I, 413
  as the material basis of unproductive labour—I, 184, 186, 211, 257, 289, 297; II, 561-62; III, 363
  and the concept of unproductive labour—I, 157, 158-60, 164-65, 171, 293-94, 401-07
  and the growth of the unproductive population—II, 561, 571-72
  in capitalist and non-capitalist production—III, 431-32
  under communism—I, 153
  Mercantilists on—I, 153-55
  Petty on—I, 179-80
  Physiocrats on—I, 46, 47, 49-50, 153
  vulgar conception of—I, 157, 175-76, 183, 184-85, 201, 204, 264-66, 270-71, 280, 388, 393
— *social labour*—I, 232
  its character under commodity production—I, 171-72, 207
  its specific form under capitalism—I, 187; III, 259, 314
  and the division of labour—I, 205
  concrete labour as its precondition—III, 520
  See also: *Exploitation, Labour-power, Productivity of labour, Surplus labour, Wage-labour*

Labour-power—I, 152-53, 217-19, 393; III, 165
— as a commodity—I, 45, 51, 71, 72-73, 87, 94, 158-59, 167-68, 171-72, 314-16, 321-22, 356, 392, 397-98; II, 397; III, 89-90, 110, 114, 271, 290, 300
— its use-value—I, 156, 400; III, 90, 178-79

— divorced from the conditions of production—I, 43, 45, 51, 56, 345; III, 271
— and capital—I, 390-91, 394-95, 396, 398; II, 400; III, 43, 90, 114, 308-10, 444
— its costs of production—I, 167-69, 210, 215, 282, 405; III, 148, 226-27
— and labour—I, 315; III, 471, 488
— and wages—I, 107-08, 210-11, 314-15, 397; II, 319; III, 43
— and the working-day—II, 408; III, 149, 309
— and the production of luxury goods—III, 349-50
— confusion of labour-power with labour—II, 404-05; III, 25, 89

Labour-time—I, 227; II, 16, 28
— and value—I, 45
— necessary—I, 305, 393-94; II, 19
— *socially necessary labour-time*—I, 231
as a measure of value—I, 75-76, 85
and individual labour-time —II, 38
and individually necessary labour-time—I, 218, 232, 393-94; II, 130, 521
and piece-work—III, 113-14

Land—I, 50; II, 18, 21, 43-44, 126, 139, 141-42, 147, 148, 245-46, 265, 301, 303, 306, 309, 333, 349, 491-92
— as a productive force—II, 18, 342; III, 488
— its natural and artificial fertility—II, 139-41, 142-43, 147-49, 158
— its industrial exploitation— III, 289
— its exploitation under capitalism—III, 301, 310
— private property in land as a condition of capitalist production—I, 50, 56; II, 44-45, 103-04, 152, 301-02
— value of land and rent—II, 129, 133; III, 110
— value of land and the rate of interest—I, 359, 369
— its price—I, 358, 361; II, 307; III, 479-80, 519-22
— Petty on its value—I, 357-58, 360-61
— nationalisation of land—I, 52, 59, 61; II, 44-45, 103-04, 155; III, 472

Landed property—I, 52-53, 59, 66, 384; II, 18, 117, 152, 158, 309, 365-66; III, 52, 85, 397-98, 429, 472
— its feudal character—II, 153, 237
— and the capitalist mode of production—I, 55-56; II, 44-45, 152-53, 237-38, 243, 301, 309, 310; III, 289, 360, 399
— rent as its economic form—I, 52; II, 17, 37, 94, 158, 163, 243, 247, 298, 301, 330-31, 336, 342-43, 361, 394; III, 401-02, 472
— its various forms—II, 42, 462
— as a source of revenue but not a source of value—I, 93-94; II, 42
— and the formation of prices in agriculture—II, 101, 127, 209, 243, 300-01, 316, 333; III, 301
— its separation from labour—I, 50, 55-56; II, 43-44, 103-04, 302
— nominal landed property—II, 37, 103, 237-38, 302, 305-06, 308, 319, 334-35, 339, 361, 362, 365, 393
— in the Physiocratic system— I, 49-53, 381, 382, 385
— in Ricardo's theory—II, 94, 96, 103, 117, 152, 237, 308-10, 316, 378

Landlords—I, 368; II, 306, 333, 349
— unproductive character under

capitalism—I, 175-76, 384; II, 44-45, 56, 152, 328, 519; III, 51
— appropriate agricultural excess profit—II, 21, 71, 246-47, 267, 328; III, 361
— manufacturers' interests opposed to those of landlords—II, 118, 121-23, 328
— against agricultural improvements—I, 368; II, 112
— appropriate the results of improved fertility of land—II, 103, 148, 372
— and tenant farmers—II, 152, 157
— in the ancient world and the Middle Ages—II, 44, 152
— Physiocrats on—I, 50, 53, 59, 384; II, 365

Law—I, 314
— criminal—I, 387
— Roman—I, 404
— and tenants—II, 103
— economic position and civil rights—III, 431
— influence of legislation on agriculture—II, 116, 119
— and landed property—II, 301-02, 316, 330-31
— and the sale of labour-power—I, 397; III, 114

Law of the diminishing rate of profit—I, 39; II, 111, 408, 438-39, 596; III, 240-41, 298-313
— and the productivity of labour—II, 438-39, 596
— and the organic composition of capital—II, 439, 596; III, 216, 302, 310-11
— and the exploitation of workers—II, 438, 439; III, 302, 310
— and the concentration of capital—III, 447
— in Ricardo's system—II, 313, 373, 438-39

"Law" of diminishing returns—II, 31-33, 89, 94, 162
— its refutation by bourgeois economists—II, 89, 116, 144-45, 159, 236, 595
See also: *Malthusianism*

Loans—I, 83, 228; II, 123, 335, 460, 484, 557

Luxury articles—I, 219, 305; III, 43, 243, 245-46, 252, 349-50, 363, 390

M

Machine-building industry—I, 132, 136-41, 145-49, 191, 196-97, 217-18; II, 487-89, 551-52; III, 366, 379

Machinery—I, 390-91; II, 479-80' 487-88, 571; III, 285, 366, 442
— its value and effectiveness (productivity)—I, 211, 243-44; II, 112, 551-52, 557; III, 221-22, 235, 365-67, 441-43
— and the value of commodity—II, 18, 554-55; III, 64, 366-67
— changes in its value affect the organic composition of capital and the rate of profit—I, 38; II, 554-55; III, 347
— its effect on variable capital and constant capital—II, 558-59, 562-63
— and labour—I, 217, 228, 391; II, 17, 551, 553-54, 556, 557-58, 561, 563, 571, 573, 583; III, 65, 250, 365, 441
— and lengthening of the working-day—II, 460
— and accumulation of capital—II, 583
— and growth of population—II, 555, 563; III, 245
— and manufacture—II, 556
— and science—I, 391-92
— and the productivity of labour—II, 16, 81; III, 366-67
— in the machine-building industry—II, 551; III, 366

Malthusianism—III, 16, 24-25, 29
— a misanthropic theory—II, 116, 117, 118-21; III, 61-63

— defends unproductive consumers—I, 172, 212; II, 115, 118-20, 122-23, 162; III, 14, 21-23, 40, 50-51, 52-53, 57, 62-63, 120, 242, 245
— justifies the poverty of the producers of wealth—II, 117, 119-20; III, 52, 57, 61
— "law" of diminishing returns—II, 31-33, 89, 94, 162
— population theory—I, 299, 354; II, 115-17, 119-21, 145, 223-24, 577, 589; III, 35, 40, 259, 299
— refuted by Darwin's theory—II, 121
— and the contradictions of capitalist society—II, 120-21; III, 14, 29, 57-58
— Malthus's plagiarism—II, 116-17, 119; III, 14, 27, 53-54, 56, 61
— critique of Ricardo's theory of value—II, 191; III, 13-14, 19-21, 29-31, 53, 63, 71, 171, 177
— vulgarises the theory of value—III, 16-17, 20, 24-29, 31-32, 46, 51-52, 63-64, 79, 306
— on the exchange between wage-labour and capital—III, 14, 17
— vulgar interpretation of profit—III, 16, 20-22, 23, 26, 32, 36-37, 40-41, 46, 64, 77
— theory of rent—II, 589
— on productive and unproductive labour—III, 34-35
— on crises—III, 50-51, 52-53
— its refutation by bourgeois economists—II, 89, 116, 121, 144-45, 159, 236, 595

Man—I, 288; II, 117-18; III, 378, 448
— pre-condition and result of human history—III, 491
— and nature—I, 285; III, 295

Manufacture—I, 157; II, 583
— as a form of the division of labour—I, 390; II, 583; III, 270-71
— effect of machinery on—II, 556
— work to order—III, 286
— in England in the first half of the eighteenth century—II, 583
— in the Middle Ages—III, 469

Market—I, 205, 257; II, 306, 332-33, 349, 482-84, 495, 525, 561; III, 17-18, 216-17, 269, 281, 288, 470
— and the growth of productive forces—II, 483-84, 524-25; III, 440
— commodity and labour market—III, 216
— and commodity production—II, 423
— and the division of labour—III, 268-69
— gluts—II, 18, 524
— and price fluctuations—II, 291-93, 322, 323; III, 284
— *internal market*—II, 561 and crises—II, 498, 524-25
— *world market*—I, 388; II, 423, 468, 497-98, 524-25, 583; III, 243, 253, 470, 531
See also: *Money market*

Market price—see *Price*

Market value—I, 232; II, 96, 126-27, 162-63, 194, 203-07, 208, 240, 266-67, 268, 270-71, 272, 307, 521; III, 301, 472, 517
— and individual value—II, 203-06, 268, 271-72, 293-94, 521
— and market price—II, 205, 268, 271; III, 517
— and excess profit—II, 206, 240-41
— and absolute rent—II, 268, 271, 293-95, 318-19
— and differential rent—II, 268-69, 293-95
— and distribution of the surplus product—II, 453
— and demand and supply—II, 272, 273-74
— in Ricardo's theory of rent—

II, 162-63, 193-94, 203, 205, 207, 242-43, 271, 306

Mathematics—I, 150; III, 87, 143-44, 160-61, 479, 519

Means of production—I, 103-04, 219, 408, 409; III, 352, 460
— and workers—I, 390; III, 115
— as an element of constant capital—II, 21
— their efficiency—I, 106
— and consumer goods—I, 235
— in primitive society—I, 108

Means of subsistence—I, 38; II, 298, 340-41, 580
— under capitalism—III, 290, 293
— their value—II, 417
— and the reproduction of labour-power—I, 46-47; II, 340, 404-05
— as variable capital—II, 579-80; III, 242, 293
— and the productivity of labour—III, 244
— and crises—II, 517
— and rent—II, 241-42, 291, 298, 304, 323, 342

Mechanics—II, 110

Mercantilism
— and the concept of surplus-value—I, 41, 43, 49, 62, 66, 173, 174, 178-79, 383-84; III, 77
— on productive labour—I, 153-55
— on value and money—I, 173
— on prodigality and frugality—I, 282-83
— its concepts in the works of later economists—I, 203-04, 209, 379-80, 384; III, 77, 171

Metamorphosis of capital—I, 328-31; II, 510-11, 515; III, 457, 519, 524

Metamorphosis of commodities—I, 62, 72, 86, 156, 204-05, 233, 309, 314, 329, 331, 340-41, 371; II, 500-02, 504, 507-10; III, 55, 88, 229, 268, 269, 279-80, 281-82, 283-84, 457, 519

Mexico—III, 115

Middle Ages—I, 276-77, 285, 289, 301, 369; II, 19; III, 434, 469
— accumulation of capital—II, 232
— guild system—III, 417
— monopoly prices—II, 316
— struggle for markets between town and country—III, 269
— taxes—II, 234-35
— usury—III, 534, 538
— dissolution of medieval society—III, 527
See also: *Feudalism*

Mining—I, 219, 220
— as a branch of industry—II, 48
— reproduction—I, 144-45; II, 62, 64
— absence of raw materials—II, 23, 47, 92, 132; III, 388, 394
— productivity of labour—II, 251
— rent—II, 249, 361-62
— abandoning of unproductive mines—II, 95-96, 251, 338

Mode of production—III, 507-08
— and mode of appropriation—III, 415
— and mode of accumulation—III, 420-22
— and forms of exchange—I, 295-96
— compulsion to perform surplus labour—I, 390
— its influence upon social relations—I, 407-08
See also: *Capitalist mode of production, Communism, Feudalism, Slavery, Society, primitive*

Monetary system
— and the concept of surplus-value—I, 43, 49, 173; III, 16
— formation of hoards as the

means of enrichment—I, 303-04
— on productive labour—I, 303-04
— its concepts in the works of later economists—I, 303-04; III, 16

Money—I, 270, 282, 303, 326, 370; II, 494; III, 162, 273-74, 276, 281-82, 467, 471
— as the expression of general labour—I, 50, 87, 205, 389; II, 509; III, 40, 135-36, 144-45
— value as its prerequisite—III, 161, 163
— as a general equivalent—III, 136, 466
— as an independent form of exchange-value—I, 66, 86-87, 95, 302, 319, 403; III, 130-31, 136, 371
— as a prerequisite of the capitalist mode of production—III, 518
— as a measure of value—II, 514; III, 39-40, 133, 136
— as the standard of prices—III, 161-62
— as means of purchase—I, 309, 311-13, 321; III, 487
— as means of circulation—I, 302-03, 312, 328-30, 336-37, 339, 343, 402; II, 514
— coin—I, 342
— as means of payment—I, 190, 309, 311-14, 315, 324, 328, 336, 339; II, 493, 510-12, 514; III, 114, 162, 486-87, 508
— world money—I, 371; III, 253
— its return flow—I, 278, 311, 321-28, 333, 342-43
— its value—I, 277; II, 202
— its depreciation—II, 133-34, 141, 460
— and the possibility of crises—II, 493
— as potential capital—III, 471-72, 475-76, 486-87, 492

— its transformation into capital—I, 394-97
— its fetishism—I, 389; III, 295-96, 494
— credit money—I, 324, 327; II, 494
See also: *Gold (and silver)*

Money circulation—I, 251-52, 341-42
— as the starting-point of capitalist production—III, 112
— and commodity circulation—I, 273, 308, 312-14, 333-34
— quantity of money in circulation—I, 371
— between capitalists and workers—I, 314-28
— law of money circulation—I, 341

Money-lenders' capital—I, 83, 368; II, 232; III, 469, 529, 531-32
— as a pre-capitalist form of interest-bearing capital—I, 368-69; III, 527-28, 531-32
— and industrial capital—III, 528, 532-33, 534, 537
— and centralisation of wealth—III, 530
— and compound interests—III, 303-04
— Luther on—III, 527-37
— Physiocrats on—I, 47
— Bentham's defence of—III, 528, 534, 538

Money market—II, 580-81; III, 463-65

Monopoly—II, 29-30; III, 182
— ownership of capital and surplus labour—II, 94
— in agriculture—II, 70, 94, 101, 155, 309-10, 328
— in land—II, 38, 94, 162, 163, 328, 342-43; III, 472
— in trade—I, 384
— and the law of value—II, 36, 94, 162
See also: *Monopoly prices*

Monopoly prices—I, 277; II, 34, 36, 332; III, 403

— and value—II, 36, 94, 162
— of agricultural products—II, 162-63, 387
— and rent—II, 30, 342-43, 387
— in the Middle Ages—II, 316
— Adam Smith and Ricardo on—II, 340, 387

Monopoly rent—II, 30, 34; III, 403

Mortgage—I, 409

Music—see *Art and literature*

N

National debt—I, 202, 281, 283, 368; II, 460; III, 309

Nature—I, 51
— as an element of production—II, 126, 245
— natural conditions of production—I, 49, 60; II, 40-41, 43-44, 245, 533; III, 86-87, 177
— and man—I, 285; III, 295
— ownership of the natural forces—II, 152
— natural forces and capitalist production—I, 391; II, 552-55; III, 182, 301, 309
— and excess profits in agriculture—II, 95, 135
— development of animals and plants—III, 294-95
— and explanation of surplus-value and wages by the Physiocrats—I, 46, 51, 55, 85

Needs—II, 508-09; III, 289
— and the productivity of labour—II, 16, 406-07; III, 449
— social—II, 407
— and effective demand—II, 506, 535
— workers' needs—II, 16-17; III, 292
— determine production under communism—III, 118

Norway—I, 409; II, 139

O

Over-population, relative
— reserve army of unemployed as a necessary condition of capitalist production—I, 257; II, 477, 554, 559-61
— as a result of capital accumulation—II, 557
— and the productivity of labour—III, 350
— in the countryside—II, 17

Over-production—II, 468, 506-07, 524, 528-29, 530-31, 534-35; III, 50-51, 52-53, 61, 121, 122, 282
— and crises—II, 528
— and the condition of the working class—II, 468, 506-07, 523, 528
— and accumulation—III, 379
— relative—II, 523, 527, 529-32
— and under-production—II, 531
— partial and general—II, 504-05, 506, 523
— of commodities and capital—II, 496-97, 533
— of fixed capital—II, 517, 521
— of circulating capital—II, 521
— impossible under communism—III, 118
— Ricardo's denial of—II, 468, 493, 496-97
See also: *Economic crises*

P

Paupers—I, 218, 257; II, 477-78; III, 259, 306

Peasants—I, 108, 409; II, 42, 462
— under capitalism—I, 407-09
— as commodity producers—I, 142, 149, 407
— their surplus product—III, 370
— production to order—II, 482
— in colonies—II, 301-02

Physiocrats—I, 44, 45, 46-47, 48,

49-53, 59, 60, 62, 64, 65-66, 153-54, 173; II, 150, 354-55, 578
— their role in the history of political economy—I, 44, 46, 49-52, 66, 67, 343-44, 383; III, 115-16
— concept of minimum wages— I, 45, 56, 67
— and exchange-value—I, 385
— analysis of capital and the capitalist mode of production—I, 44-46, 49-50, 55-59, 62, 66, 67
— concept of surplus-value—I, 50-52, 54, 55-58, 62, 66, 85, 153-54, 173-74, 382-83; II, 547; III, 115-16, 449
— on surplus-value and rent—I, 47, 50-51, 85, 180-81, 222-23, 356-58; II, 162, 547; III, 478
— concept of productive labour —I, 46, 47, 50, 53, 54, 84-85, 153, 384; II, 360
— their predecessors—I, 382
— bourgeois interpretation of feudalism—I, 49-53, 381, 382, 385
— and landed property—I, 52, 59, 66, 384; II, 365-66
— on the three classes of society—I, 54, 58; II, 162
— and the French Revolution— I, 66, 344
— their financial policy—I, 66, 384-85
— advocate free competition—I, 53, 66, 170, 380, 382
— on interest—I, 47; III, 478
— on accumulation—I, 59, 61
— vulgar conception of profit— I, 47, 59, 62, 63-64, 379-80, 382-84; II, 547
— Physiocratic views in the works of later economists— I, 44-45, 60-61, 64, 69-70, 85, 163, 202, 204, 356, 358, 362, 384-85; II, 161; III, 183
— critique of their system—I, 67-68, 162-63, 169; II, 161-62
See also: *Quesnay's tableau économique*

Poland—III, 243

Political economy—I, 157, 186-87; II, 116-17, 124, 165-66; III, 429, 501, 514-15
— its history—I, 344; II, 165; III, 22, 109, 500-02
— and moral considerations—I, 171, 185; II, 185; III, 527
— *bourgeois political economy as the theoretical expression of the capitalist mode of production*—I, 45, 186-87; II, 36, 152-53, 238; III, 259-60, 265, 276
Physiocrats and—I, 44
and contradictions of capitalism—III, 259-60, 272, 500-02
its evolution—I, 41, 44, 51, 53, 85, 88, 96-97, 153-54, 175
its vulgar character—I, 46-47, 59, 61; II, 347, 427, 468; III, 500-03
its apologetic character—I, 78, 264-65, 281, 307; II, 116-17, 119, 500-01, 519, 529, 571-73; III, 59, 168, 171-72, 453, 496-98, 501-02
bourgeois production regarded as a non-historical category—I, 44, 49, 361, 393; II, 18, 32, 153, 158, 504; III, 239, 259, 265, 274, 401-02, 416
its philosophical basis—I, 367
shortcomings of its method— I, 89; II, 106, 151, 168, 173-75, 191, 208, 270, 351, 374, 437
its empiricism and scholasticism—I, 89, 92, 97, 204-05; II, 191, 405; III, 29, 71-73, 84-85, 87-88, 372, 374
its fetishism—III, 129, 147, 267, 274, 276, 427, 453, 462
confuses social form and material content of the production process—I, 44, 204-05, 285, 307, 408; II, 215-16; III, 264, 265, 270, 271-73, 274-75, 295-96, 322, 362, 488-89, 495

confuses value with use-value—I, 46, 51-52, 154, 173-74, 267-68, 361, 366; II, 151; III, 488-89

turns capital from a relation into a thing—I, 93; II, 400; III, 267-68, 272-74, 275-76, 427

its basic error in examining surplus-value—I, 40, 92; II, 373; III, 377-78

confuses surplus-value with profit—I, 40, 89, 92; II, 410; III, 36-37, 85, 87, 191-92, 207, 221, 236-37, 254

confuses labour with labour-power—II, 404-05; III, 25, 89

on over-production and crises—I, 235, 268; II, 468, 493, 496-502, 504, 512, 514-15, 517, 528-34; III, 50, 52-53, 56, 100-01, 121-22

on the organic composition of capital—II, 577-80; III, 326, 334-35, 364, 381-82, 411-12, 418

search for a measure of value—I, 72-73, 74-75, 150-51; II, 366-67, 401-02; III, 13-14, 133-34, 145, 155-56

and money—I, 92; II, 125, 167, 200, 386, 437, 501-02, 504, 527; III, 55, 137-38

confuses values with prices of production—II, 25-28, 34, 129, 132, 154-55, 162-63, 175, 199, 208, 215, 217-18, 235, 242, 244, 300, 318-21, 329, 337, 373, 386, 393, 426, 434, 466-67; III, 29, 31-32, 70, 79, 159, 164, 179

and rent—II, 31-34, 161-63

and free competition—I, 53, 66, 170, 380, 382

theory of "savings"—I, 61, 63-64, 169; III, 414, 417, 418, 421-22

its bourgeois and petty-bourgeois critics—I, 325, 345; III, 259-60, 261, 398, 467

its proletarian opponents—III, 238-39, 254, 259-61, 265, 266-67, 274, 318-19

— *bourgeois political economy, method of*

Adam Smith and Ricardo—II, 106, 149-50, 153, 155, 164-69, 173-75, 191, 193, 208-09, 215-16, 217-19, 229-30, 235, 270, 347, 348, 351, 353-54, 374, 411, 437, 438; III, 15, 123-24

the Ricardian school—I, 89; II, 191, 405, 427; III, 29, 71-72, 84-85, 87-88, 91, 96-97, 101, 120-21, 124, 191-92, 196, 199, 201, 236-37

vulgar economists—II, 71, 347, 427; III, 130, 139, 145, 186-87, 453, 485, 499-500, 501-02, 510

— *classical political economy*—I, 44, 46, 47, 60, 61, 299, 343-44, 364, 370, 373, 377; II, 152, 165, 347, 427, 468, 504, 527-29; III, 55, 115, 125-26, 238-39, 259, 329, 360, 377, 399, 402, 414, 424, 427-28, 429, 453, 500-01, 502-03

as a reflection of capitalist contradictions—III, 84-85, 258-59, 501

shortcomings of its method—II, 106, 149-50, 164-66, 270; III, 377, 500

on the development of productive forces—II, 117-18; III, 258, 332, 427, 444

labour theory of value—I, 70-71, 79-80, 97; II, 164-67, 168-69; III, 258, 429

and surplus-value—I, 54, 97, 180-81; II, 405-06, 462-63, 566; III, 328-29

differentiates between constant and variable capital—II, 579; III, 326, 363-64

on the organic composition of capital—II, 577-79; III, 334, 381-82, 411, 418
— *vulgar political economy*—I, 61, 382-83; II, 69, 132, 266-67, 347-48; III, 265, 273-74, 453, 454, 462, 467, 478, 485, 499-500, 503
as an apologia for capitalism—I, 290, 299, 301; II, 116-17, 119, 124, 500-01, 519, 529, 571-74; III, 168, 171-72, 453, 496-98, 501-02
its plagiarism—II, 114-15, 116, 118; III, 14, 27, 53-54, 172-73, 183, 185, 501-02
tries to conceal the contradictions of capitalist production—II, 438, 495, 500-01, 519-20, 528-29, 531-32; III, 88, 91-92, 100-01, 118, 120, 131-32, 168, 503, 519-23
on competition—II, 71, 372; III, 130, 139, 187, 485, 502-03, 510
its fetishism—III, 129, 147, 267, 274, 276, 427, 453, 462
preaches harmony of interests—II, 120; III, 502, 533
and the relations between capital and labour—I, 403-04; II, 501; III, 88-91, 93-94
rejects the labour theory of value—III, 154, 155-56, 161, 163-64, 177
on cost of production—II, 133, 215, 469
on profit—I, 47, 59, 61, 63, 78-79, 81, 90-91, 94, 264-65, 273-74, 277-78, 314-17, 381-83; II, 418, 547; III, 16, 19-21, 174-75, 180
theories of money—II, 502; III, 101
on crises—I, 234, 268; II, 468, 493-94, 497-501, 503-04, 512, 514-15, 517, 528-35; III, 100-01, 121-22
identifies use-value with value, demand with supply, sellers with buyers, production with consumption—I, 299, 304; II, 493, 501, 503-05, 513, 519-20, 528-29, 532; III, 65, 100-04, 120, 185
on productive labour—I, 174, 202, 212, 279-80, 281, 286-87, 290, 296-97, 387-88
advocates unproductive expenditure—I, 203, 281; II, 115
on rent—II, 33-34, 94, 132, 144, 162-63, 342-43; III, 454, 489, 520-23
on the interrelation between wages and prices—II, 120, 192; III, 28
population theory—I, 299, 354; II, 115-17, 119-21, 145, 224, 577, 589; III, 35, 40, 259, 299
and classical economists—I, 46, 47, 59, 61; II, 347, 427, 468; III, 453, 498-503
See also: *Malthusianism, Mercantilism, Monetary system, Physiocrats, Quesnay's tableau économique, Ricardian school, `Ricardo, David; Smith, Adam*

Population
— productive and unproductive —I, 218-19, 222, 227, 289-90
— and accumulation of capital —I, 107; II, 137-38, 477, 492, 537-38; III, 241
— and the productivity of labour—II, 540-41; III, 244-45
— and machinery—II, 554-55, 563; III, 245
— as a source of labour-power —I, 257; II, 540, 553-54
— growth of labouring population and wages—II, 477, 581-84
— over-population—I, 388; II, 17, 553-54, 565, 573; III, 52-53

— and prices of agricultural goods—II, 133, 141, 142
— and rent—II, 138-39
— Petty's theory of—I, 354
— Malthus's theory of—I, 299, 354; II, 115-17, 119-21, 144, 223-24, 577, 589; III, 35, 40, 52, 259, 299
See also: *Over-population, relative*

Portugal—I, 376

Price—II, 161, 193-94, 235, 264-66, 286-87, 318-19, 333-34; III, 465, 509-10, 516-17
— and value—I, 42, 54-55, 95-96, 109, 124, 232; II, 17, 27, 263-64, 333; III, 111, 130-31, 518
— and market value—II, 33, 126-27, 205, 268, 270-71; III, 516-17
— its elements—III, 511-13, 515-17
— monopoly—I, 277; II, 34, 36, 94, 162-63, 316, 332, 343, 349, 387; III, 403
— and demand and supply—III, 508-09
— and technological progress—II, 26-27
— and variations in wages—I, 97, 154, 320-21
— and depreciation of money—II, 460
— history of prices—II, 110-11, 116, 125, 133-36, 141-44, 236, 408, 459-60

Price of land
— as a capitalised rent—I, 357-58, 361; II, 307; III, 479-80, 519-22

Price of production (cost-price, average price)—II, 126, 129-30, 146, 269, 319-20, 433; III, 100
— as a result of competition between different branches of production—I, 416; II, 25, 27-30, 41, 69, 187, 206-08, 212-13, 297, 319-20, 332-33, 351; III, 69, 83, 463-64

— as a prerequisite and result of the development of capitalist production—II, 332-33, 351; III, 167-68
— and value—I, 95, 416; II, 29-32, 34-35, 56-57, 70-71, 132, 183-84, 190, 193-94, 213-15, 235, 243-44, 277, 297; III, 81-82, 167, 377, 482, 509-10, 516-17
— and market price—II, 194, 235, 319; III, 510, 516-17
— and rent—II, 319-20; III, 100
— and variations in wages—II, 386-95; III, 333
— its historical character—II, 105-06, 243-44, 332-33
— confusion of value with price of production in bourgeois political economy—II, 25-28, 34-35, 129-30, 132, 154-55, 163, 174-75, 199, 208, 215-16, 217-18, 235, 241-43, 244, 300, 318-21, 329, 337, 373, 386, 393, 426, 434, 466-67; III, 29, 32, 70, 79, 80, 159, 164, 179
See also: *Production*

Private property—see *Landed property, Property (private)*

Production—I, 43, 45, 51, 53, 55-56, 102, 109, 232-33, 282, 288, 289, 345, 365; II, 18, 23, 40, 41, 137, 468, 512-13, 527-28; III, 271-72, 284, 293, 378-79, 415-16, 422-23, 426
— and the origin of surplus-value—I, 45-46, 50, 57-58
— of capital—II, 513, 578-80
— and the capitalist mode of production—I, 411-12; II, 64, 468, 483-84, 512-13, 520, 524, 527-29
— material—I, 159, 164, 175-76, 212, 218, 285-86, 288, 292, 409, 411-12; III, 432, 443-44
— non-material—I, 284-87, 288-89, 410-11
— interconnection of various

spheres of production—II, 48-49, 471-72, 484; III, 285
— industrial and agricultural—I, 46-47; II, 17-18
— and reproduction—II, 59; III, 285-86
— and wealth—I, 39, 270, 282
— mass production and growth of commodity production—III, 288-89
— forms of production and forms of distribution—III, 56, 83-84, 480, 499
— and exchange—I, 58, 296; II, 28
— and market—II, 468, 483, 524
— and consumption—I, 103, 185-86, 283; II, 519-24; III, 56, 278-79, 292
— Petty on—I, 360
— for the sake of production, according to bourgeois economists—I, 282-83; II, 117; III, 50, 84
— *concentration of production* under capitalism—III, 426 as a consequence of the division of labour—III, 270
— *cost of production*—II, 40, 50-54, 70, 139-42, 144, 148-49; III, 74-75, 79-82, 164-65, 193, 216-17, 478, 480, 513 as a component of value—I, 47, 193, 213, 233, 273, 322-23; II, 40
and production of surplus-value—III, 480
and transformation of surplus-value into profit—III, 80-81
and constant capital—I, 219
and price of production—II, 27, 40
and movement of prices—II, 26-27
of labour-power—I, 167-68, 210, 215, 252, 405; III, 148, 226
incidental expenses (*faux frais*)—I, 167, 175, 289, 301, 381; III, 355-56, 505

under conditions of simple commodity production—III, 74-75
vulgar economists on—II, 132-33, 215-16, 469
and value—I, 96, 109, 211; III, 194-95, 203-04, 217-18, 223, 226; III, 80-81, 513
— *period of production*—II, 28, 177-78; III, 85-86, 229, 256-57, 390-91
in various branches—III, 390-91
See also: *Capitalist mode of production, Means of production, Mode of production, Reproduction*

Productive forces—I, 280, 389, 390-91, 393-94; II, 539; III, 115
— under capitalism—I, 392, 409-10; II, 117-18, 524, 528-29, 572-73; III, 84, 300, 315
— and relations of production under capitalism—III, 55-56, 429-30
— and the organic composition of capital—II, 415-16
— and the restricted consumption of the workers—II, 528
— and accumulation of capital—III, 241
— and the cultivation of less fertile land—II, 20, 95-96, 141-43, 147, 236-37, 238, 321

Productive powers of labour—see *Productivity of labour*
Productivity of capital
— as the capitalist expression of the productivity of labour—I, 279-80, 389, 393-94; III, 265
— and compulsion to surplus labour—I, 93, 346, 356, 389-90, 392, 394; II, 406
— and the workers' means of subsistence—III, 244
— and production of use-values—I, 93; III, 264

Productivity of labour—I, 41, 109, 200-01, 203, 217-20, 228, 254,

393; II, 24, 81, 263, 265-66; III, 118, 227-28, 265, 349, 433-34
— absolute and relative—I, 153; II, 16
— from the capitalist standpoint—II, 44; III, 116
— under capitalism—I, 70, 160-61, 187, 199, 218, 280, 294, 305-06, 389, 391-92, 393-94, 409-10; II, 234, 521-22; III, 244-45, 264-65, 433-34
— and the material conditions of production—I, 289
— and growth of population— II, 541; III, 244
— and productive population— I, 217-18, 224, 227
— and unproductive population—I, 289-90; II, 406-07
— and the organic composition of capital—I, 219; II, 16, 28, 108-09, 252, 298, 415-16, 596; III, 300, 310-11, 364, 373-74, 382-83
— and the division of labour—I, 297-98; II, 16
— and reproduction—I, 69, 145, 192-98, 218-20, 243; II, 540
— and concentration of capital —I, 170, 228
— and accumulation of capital—I, 170; II, 537-38, 557; III, 121, 345
— and the employment of machinery—II, 16, 81; III, 366-67
— in industry and agriculture— I, 48-49, 169; II, 18-19, 43, 81, 85, 109-10, 128, 298, 299-300
— and surplus-value—I, 48-49, 64-65, 93, 152-53, 216, 305; II, 16, 86, 265-66, 406-07; III, 331-32, 449
— and value—I, 69, 71, 192-97, 203, 211, 232-33, 393-94; II, 262, 265-66
— and shortening of the necessary labour-time—I, 393-94
— and wages—I, 215-17; II, 16-17, 73-74, 265, 407

— and the conditions of the workers—I, 69-70, 216-18, 228-29, 289, 391-92; III, 64
— and the share of the capitalist and the worker in the total product—III, 149
— its influence upon price—III, 516
— and the rate of profit—I, 106; II, 438-39, 596

Profit—I, 85-86, 89; II, 296-97; III, 83-84, 459, 482-85, 489-90, 492-95
— its source—I, 79, 272-73, 278-79, 317, 323, 377; II, 296-97, 375, 379; III, 19, 81, 119-20, 175, 359
— as a form of surplus-value— I, 40, 92, 108; II, 319, 374; III, 85, 191, 459, 482-84, 486, 489
— as the direct aim of capitalist production—II, 333, 336; III, 17-18, 83, 120, 121-22
— and accumulation of capital —I, 107-08; II, 537, 542-44; III, 39, 301-02, 420-22, 447, 448
— its accumulation—I, 220; II, 487
— its rate and amount—II, 374-75, 376-77, 382-83, 426-27; III, 39, 237, 311
— industrial profit as a regulator of agricultural profit—II, 467; III, 99-100, 106
— its distribution—I, 277-78; II, 453-54
— the interrelation of profit, rent and interest—II, 453-54, 469; III, 359
— rent and interest are its parts —I, 47, 157, 235, 271, 278-79, 452-53, 457; III, 188
— Physiocrats on—I, 47-48, 59
— bourgeois economists confuse surplus-value with profit— I, 40, 89, 92; II, 410; III, 36-37, 85, 87, 191-93, 207, 221, 237, 254
— Adam Smith and Ricardo

on—I, 47, 78-81, 84-85, 94-95; II, 150, 222, 224, 233, 373-74, 415, 418-19, 429-31, 467; III, 99-100, 109, 504
— Ramsay on—III, 351, 355
— bourgeois economists' apologetic explanations of profit—I, 47, 59, 61, 63-64, 79, 81, 91, 94-95, 264-65, 274, 277-78, 314-18, 381, 382-83, 416; II, 468, 547; III, 16, 20-22, 175, 180, 189, 472, 476-77, 492, 495-96, 498, 506
— *average profit*—III, 83, 353-59, 403, 444, 473-79, 512-13
and surplus-value—I, 89; II, 34-35, 39-40, 184, 190; III, 85, 482
and costs of production—III, 512
and the law of value—II, 190
— *commercial profit*
its source—I, 251
and the general rate of profit —III, 395
in pre-capitalist modes of production—III, 420-21
— *excess profit*—II, 100, 453; III, 403
in industry and agriculture—II, 18, 32-33, 95-96, 103, 108, 240, 395; III, 389
and rent—II, 21, 71, 75-76, 93, 95-96, 126, 146-47, 240, 314, 394-95; III, 116-17, 399, 402, 412-13
and market value—II, 206, 240
in the colonies—II, 375, 436-37, 470
— *general rate of profit*—I, 92; II, 21, 47, 60, 175-76, 181-84, 187-88, 198-99, 316-17, 318-19, 433; III, 69, 234, 403, 444
the result of competition between different spheres of production—I, 416; II, 25, 27-30, 41, 69, 187, 206-08, 212-13, 297, 319, 332, 351; III, 69, 83, 463-64
and the law of value—II, 174

as a tendency—III, 462-64
and individual rate of profit—II, 34, 375, 431, 436-37, 469
and variations in wages—I, 416; III, 333
and prices of production—I, 91-92; II, 41-42, 56-57, 67-71, 201; III, 70-71, 164
and the theory of rent—I, 415; II, 92-94
— *rate of profit*—II, 21, 22, 34-35, 87, 134, 156, 459-60, 466-67; III, 99-100, 106, 191, 210-11, 212, 219, 228-29, 231-33, 301-11, 369, 465, 477
in different branches of production—I, 416; II, 20-21, 314-15, 374-75, 387, 391, 436-37, 469
and the value of the various elements of capital—I, 105; II, 23, 192-93, 276, 279-80, 282-83, 288-89, 374-75, 382-84, 391; III, 220, 225, 342, 369, 390, 417-18
and the rate of surplus-value —II, 426-27; III, 196, 211-12, 219-20, 225, 229-30
and the rate of absolute rent —II, 275, 289, 341, 387-88
and the rate of interest—II, 227-28; III, 447, 471
See also: *Profit upon alienation*

Profit upon alienation—I, 42, 50, 63, 66, 79, 83, 380, 384; III, 16, 20, 77, 79, 90, 171, 174, 189, 192, 194, 200-01, 477, 487, 489, 538

Proletariat—see *Workers*

Property (private)—I, 312-14, 346, 408; II, 15, 44-45, 302-03, 305, 306, 339, 362; III, 426
— means of production—I, 43, 54, 56, 365, 408, 409; II, 41
— capital—II, 153; III, 460, 462, 473, 474, 489, 508
— capitalist property and the working class—II, 416; III, 352

— landed property as a condition of capitalist production —I, 50, 56; II, 44-45, 103-04, 152-53, 301-02
— landed property becomes people's property under communism—II, 104
— Locke on communal and individual property—I, 365-67
See also: *Landed property*

Protectionism—I, 252; II, 115, 121-22; III, 470

Proudhonism—I, 323, 324-25; III, 456, 467-68, 472, 523, 525-27

Purchase and sale—I, 54
— in capitalist production and reproduction—I, 46, 250, 293, 296; II, 82, 491
— of commodities—I, 296-97, 340; III, 127, 130
— of labour-power—I, 315, 394, 397, 399; III, 113-14
— an exchange of equivalents—I, 62, 72, 237-38
— coincide in barter—II, 508, 532; III, 120
— contradictions between them —III, 56, 88, 119-20
— crises and separation of the acts of buying and selling— II, 491, 494, 500, 502, 505, 508-10, 511-12, 513-15, 532-33
— purchase and sale are treated as identical in bourgeois political economy—I, 380; III, 88
— vulgar economists explain surplus-value and profit from the sale of commodities above their value—I, 41, 42, 49, 63, 66, 173, 178-79, 272-73, 317-19, 383-84; III, 16, 17, 77

Q

Quesnay's tableau économique—I, 308, 378
— its significance in the history of political economy—I, 344
— Quesnay's wrong assumptions—I, 379
— Quesnay on the three classes of society—I, 54
— circulation of money and capital—I, 308-09, 344
— circulation between farmers and landowners—I, 308-14
— circulation between farmers and manufacturers—I, 328-33
— circulation of commodities and money—I, 308-09, 312-13, 333-43, 378

R

Railways—I, 219; III, 287

Raw materials—I, 220, 245; II, 515-17, 533; III, 345, 368-69
— as agricultural products—I, 170, 219; II, 62-63, 80-81
— demand for—III, 222-23
— the effect of variations in their value on the organic composition of capital—I, 38; II, 112, 379, 515-16
— the effect of variations in their value on the rate of profit—I, 105-06; II, 75-76, 379, 437, 515-16; III, 218-21, 225, 367-69
— and auxiliary materials—I, 135-36

Relations of production—I, 157, 285, 407-08; III, 55-56, 259, 264-65, 430, 507-08
See also: *Capitalist relations of production*

Religion—II, 528, 529; III, 276, 496
— and philosophy—I, 52
— Christianity—III, 448
See also: *Church*

Rent—I, 415; II, 17-18, 42-43, 94-95, 102, 136, 240, 269-70, 294-95, 586; III, 389, 413, 479, 484, 512

— and capitalist production—
II, 18, 96, 105-06, 361; III,
360, 401-02, 413
— a specific form of surplus-
value—I, 40, 47-48, 82, 92;
II, 18, 37, 77-78, 145, 360-61,
373, 547, 590
— a form of excess profit—II,
20-21, 71, 75-76, 93, 95-96,
126, 146, 240, 314, 395; III,
116-17, 399, 402, 413
— as an economic form of landed property—I, 52; II, 17,
37, 94, 158, 163, 243, 247-
48, 298, 301, 330-31, 336,
342-43, 361, 394; III, 401-02,
472
— its capitalisation—I, 358,
361; II, 307; III, 479-80,
519-23
— its source—II, 36, 39-40, 77-
78, 79-80, 161, 163
— and the organic composition
of capital—II, 103-04, 252-
53, 258-59, 307
— its historical character—II,
103-04, 105, 152-53, 243-44,
391-92, 393-94
— determined by the most fertile land (Storch's law)—II,
99, 142, 260, 292-93
— and improvements in agriculture—II, 104, 387-88, 392
— its amount and rate—II, 33,
42-43, 71, 90, 102-03, 104,
107-09, 112-13, 129, 251-53,
258-59, 275, 318, 330
— total rent—II, 269, 272, 293-
94
— its calculation—II, 17-18, 71,
113; III, 484-85
— agricultural rent in the strict
sense—II, 241-42, 245-46,
249-50, 270, 298, 336, 342,
356, 358, 365; III, 515-16
— in industry and ground-rent
—II, 37, 75-76, 365-66
— as a result of monopoly
price—II, 30, 343, 387
— its influence upon the value
and price of agricultural products—I, 359; II, 17-18, 316-
17; III, 105, 368, 405-06
— and the real wealth of society—II, 108, 341, 379, 549-50
— and interest on fixed capital
invested in the land—II, 140,
144, 342; III, 522-23
— pre-capitalist forms—III,
289, 399-40ა
— Physiocrats on—I, 47-48, 50,
85, 223, 356; II, 162, 547;
III, 478
— Petty on—I, 180, 356-58
— Anderson's theory of rent—I,
38; II, 34, 89, 114-17, 121,
125, 145-46, 148, 236, 244
— Ricardo on—II, 31-34, 94,
129-30, 162-63, 242, 244, 274,
300, 315, 393; III, 99, 402-03
— Rodbertus on—II, 47, 63,
71, 73, 86, 87, 92, 100, 105,
153, 154-60, 589
— vulgar concepts of—II, 33-
34, 94, 132-33, 144, 162,
163, 342; III, 454, 488-89,
520-21
— *absolute rent*—II, 100-01, 126,
142, 241-42, 255, 259, 267-
69, 293-95, 300, 329, 393;
III, 99-100, 403-04
as the expression of landed
property—I, 52; II, 17,
37, 94, 163, 243, 298, 301,
330-31, 336, 361, 394-95;
III, 472
conditions for its existence—
II, 37, 41, 43, 93, 94, 101,
103-04, 126, 163, 301, 303,
309-10, 329-30, 331, 332-33,
376, 394; III, 472
its historical character—II,
105, 243-44, 391-92, 393
-94
and the law of value—II, 36,
163
its amount and rate—II, 254,
259, 275
its independence of differential rent—II, 242, 309-10
and the price of agricultural
products—II, 316-17; III,
368

agricultural improvements and—II, 387-88, 392
productivity of labour and—II, 267
yielded by gold mines—III, 403-04
Ricardo denies its existence—II, 129-30, 162-63, 242, 244, 273-74, 300, 393
See also: *Differential rent*

Rentiers—III, 354-55, 359, 360

Reproduction—I, 106, 113-15, 123-24, 125-38, 141-42, 146-48, 167, 189-90, 219-20, 235-44, 292; II, 295, 454, 471-72, 482-83, 484, 494-96; III, 101-03, 251-52, 278-79, 284-85, 286-87, 337-38, 438-39, 513, 544-45
— as the unity of the production and circulation processes—I, 44, 106, 128, 133-34, 136, 140, 142-43, 308, 342, 343-44; II, 59, 63-64, 510, 513; III, 268, 282-83
— period of reproduction—I, 242-43; II, 470-71; III, 284-86, 390-93, 436-37, 438-39
— and labour productivity—I, 69, 145, 192-98, 218-19, 243; II, 540
— and the metamorphosis of commodities—I, 329, 342; III, 457
— of constant capital—I, 37, 99-102, 103-06, 107-51, 187-98, 219, 242, 243, 244-52, 323; II, 471-72, 473-74, 489-90
— of labour-power—I, 45, 73, 398
— and exchange between the capitalist and the worker—III, 92-93, 338
— of capitalist relations of production—III, 271-72, 315, 514
— and consumption—I, 289-90, 311, 329; III, 282
— and crises—II, 493, 494, 510
— and the return flow of money—I, 310-11, 321-28, 342-43
— in agriculture—II, 63

— simple and expanded reproduction—II, 481, 489; III, 380-81
— *expanded reproduction*—II, 524; III, 364, 381
its capitalist form—I, 252, 303; II, 483-84, 488; III, 272-73, 335, 380-81
of capitalist relations of production—III, 272, 315
and growth of the productivity of labour—II, 521-22
and replacement of the elements of production—III, 249-52, 380-81
and constant capital—I, 254
and circulation—I, 142
and exchange of commodities—I, 252
and simple reproduction—II, 481, 489; III, 380
— *simple reproduction*—II, 476-77; III, 518
and replacement of the annual product—I, 230-50
and replacement of capitals—III, 247-50
of constant capital—I, 107-51
and accumulation—II, 481, 489; III, 380-81

Reserve army of workers—see *Overpopulation, relative*

Reserve fund—I, 170

Revenue—II, 84
— its original sources—I, 93-94
— as a part of commodity value—I, 98-102, 123-24, 150, 221
— annual—I, 141, 148, 150, 221
— net income and gross income—II, 547
— its derivative forms—II, 84, 493
— exchange of revenue for unproductive labour—I, 157-58, 160, 163, 186-87, 407
— exchange of revenue for revenue—I, 230-31, 233-34, 235, 238, 326

— and capital—I, 94, 219, 224-25, 228, 230, 234, 236, 240, 291, 311-12; II, 432, 476, 477; III, 345
— of the capitalists—I, 255-56; II, 75
— and fetishism of capitalist relations—III, 453
— and the introduction of machinery—II, 558-59, 563, 568-69
— of unproductive labourers—I, 84, 235, 289-90; II, 561, 567
— and money circulation—I, 325

Ricardian school
— vulgarisation of Ricardo's economic theory—III, 22-23, 59, 72, 75, 76, 83, 84-85, 87, 88-91, 93-95, 97-98, 100-01, 120, 168, 170, 171-72, 183, 184-85, 191-92, 196, 200-02, 211, 236, 245, 429, 506-07
— scholastic methods—I, 89; II, 191, 405, 427; III, 29, 71-73, 84-85, 87, 91, 97, 124, 196, 199, 201
— and the law of value—III, 73, 80, 95-96, 176-77, 237
— vulgar conception of profit—III, 76-79, 201-02, 506-07
— confusion of surplus-value with profit—III, 85, 87, 191-92, 207, 221, 237
— on rent—III, 399
— nationalisation of landed property—I, 52-53, 59, 66; II, 152; III, 85, 172, 429, 472
— polemics with Malthusians—III, 22-23, 59
— its decline—I, 38; II, 398; III, 29, 84-85, 88, 92, 95, 110, 168, 171-72, 182, 185, 237

Ricardian socialists
— defend the interests of the industrial proletariat—I, 39; III, 239, 254, 260
— their views rest on bourgeois premises—I, 345; III, 238, 254, 260-61, 265, 274

— and the contradiction of capital and labour—III, 260-61, 296
— as adversaries of bourgeois political economy—III, 238-39, 254, 258-61, 265, 267, 274, 318-19, 500-01
— on surplus-value and surplus labour—III, 238-39, 254-55, 258, 266
— deny the inevitability of surplus labour—III, 254-57, 497
— on the nature of capital—III, 263-65, 297
— on the falling of the rate of profit—III, 240-41, 298-313, 316
— on the social character of labour—III, 313
— on the growth of the productive powers of labour—III, 266
— on free time—III, 255-56

Ricardo, David—I, 381; II, 118, 119, 125-26; III, 52
— his role in the history of political economy—II, 166, 238; III, 33, 259
— his criticism of Adam Smith—I, 71, 72-73; II, 169, 199-200, 235, 330-41, 375, 395-97, 498, 525; III, 24, 517
— argues from the standpoint of developed capitalist production—I, 61, 175, 225; II, 118, 155, 239, 418; III, 55, 85, 115, 239, 259
— radical conclusions drawn from his theory—I, 52, 59, 66; II, 152-53; III, 52, 85, 171-72, 254-57, 263-66, 397-98, 429, 472, 496-97
— his scientific honesty—II, 118-19, 125-26, 555; III, 52, 256-57
— describes the economic contradictions existing between the classes—II, 166, 419; III, 33
— his theory of value—I, 89; II, 129-30, 132, 150, 164-66,

168-69, 194, 395, 397-98, 424-25; III, 69-70, 74, 170, 175, 181, 258-59
— his theory of surplus-value— I, 222-23; II, 373-74, 395, 405-06, 423, 463, 566; III, 14, 15-16, 33, 238-39
— on the relations of capital and wage-labour—III, 92-93, 96, 99, 110, 148, 259
— value is resolved into labour and surplus-value into surplus labour—II, 406; III, 238-39
— concept of surplus product— II, 317, 418, 427; III, 238-39
— on the nature of capital— II, 421; III, 115
— his theory of profit—II, 374, 415-16, 419, 429-31, 467; III, 99, 109
— on machinery and the working class—II, 550-76, 577-78
— on productive and unproductive labour—I, 225, 227
— on landed property—II, 94, 96, 103, 152, 237-38, 378
— on landowners—I, 175; II, 16, 117, 122-23, 125, 152
— his theory of rent—II, 31-34, 94, 107, 129-32, 152-58, 162-63, 207, 215-16, 241-43, 244-50, 253, 270, 273-74, 300, 306, 308-18, 320-24, 327-28, 329-41, 350-51, 352, 371, 373, 379, 387, 391-95, 458-59; III, 99-100, 402-03
— on accumulation—I, 225, 228-29; II, 415, 467, 470, 485-86, 491, 535-46, 561-62; III, 274, 379
— on the productivity of labour—II, 44; III, 256-57, 265
— on the productivity of capital—III, 263-64
— on the productivity of agriculture—II, 43-44, 244, 299-300, 321, 438-39, 463, 467, 541
— on wages and the value of commodities—II, 120, 192, 199, 390, 418; III, 94

— on profit and wages—II, 73-74, 192-93, 373, 408, 417-19, 423, 427, 439; III, 94-95, 106, 149, 153
— on profit and rent—II, 74, 109, 439
— on value and cost-price—II, 25-27, 34-35, 129-30, 132, 154-55, 162-63, 175, 184, 196, 197-99, 208, 215, 217, 235, 242, 244, 299-300, 318-21, 329, 336-37, 373, 386, 393, 426, 434, 466-67; III, 29-30, 31, 69-70, 79-80, 159, 164, 179
— on the general rate of profit— II, 174, 179-82, 187-88, 190-91, 193, 195, 196-97, 222, 374-75, 427, 434; III, 14, 70
— on market value and market price—II, 33, 205, 207, 271-72, 435
— on the movement of capital— II, 210-11, 220, 240, 377-78, 434
— theory of colonisation—II, 228, 239, 308-09, 311-13, 437
— on foreign trade—II, 375, 436-37; III, 253
— on wages and the value of labour—II, 399-404, 417, 418-19, 423-24, 438, 558, 567; III, 33
— on gross and net income—II, 547-50, 564-65
— contradictions contained in his theory—I, 89; II, 32, 174-75, 249-50, 334, 403, 430-31, 573; III, 14, 19-20, 29, 84-85, 177, 259-60, 263-64
— shortcomings in his method of investigation—II, 106, 150, 153, 155, 164-65, 166-67, 173-75, 191, 193, 208-09, 215, 270, 373-74, 411, 437; III, 15, 123-24
— non-historical interpretation of the capitalist mode of production—II, 503-04, 527-29; III, 55, 115, 126, 230
— shortcomings in his theory of value—I, 71, 81-82, 88;

II, 164-65, 167-69, 170-72, 173, 201-02, 397-98, 399-401, 403, 411, 434, 503; III, 29, 95, 123-24, 131, 137-39, 159, 170, 176
— confusion of abstract with concrete labour—III, 138-39
— the effect changes in wages have on cost-prices—II, 175-76, 180, 191-94, 195-96, 197-98, 199; III, 70-71, 85-86, 333-34
— confusion of surplus-value with profit—I, 89, 92, 104; II, 32, 169, 174-75, 192-93, 215-16, 373-74, 376-77, 406, 426-27, 433-34, 438-39, 462-63, 467; III, 14, 69-70, 85, 149, 159, 191, 201, 254, 338-39
— capital is equated with accumulated labour—II, 400-01
— constant capital is disregarded—I, 104, 224; II, 182, 373, 413-14, 426, 463-64, 491, 535, 548-49, 564-65
— on changes in the "relative values" of commodities—II, 132, 174-89, 191, 193-95; III, 29, 70-71
— erroneous theory of money—II, 125, 164, 200, 386, 437, 502, 504, 527; III, 54-55, 137-39
— on over-production—II, 468, 493-94, 496-97, 501, 503-05, 527-28, 529; III, 54, 58
— shortcomings in the interpretation of competition—II, 207, 209, 211-12
— erroneous explanation of the falling rate of profit—II, 313, 373, 438-39, 461-69, 541-46; III, 313
— confusion of labour with labour-power—II, 404-05; III, 89
— fails to trace the source of surplus-value—II, 405-06, 408, 463

— the working-day is treated as a constant magnitude—II, 405, 408, 413, 416, 463
— criticism of his views in the works of bourgeois economists—I, 204-05, 222-23; II, 117-19, 157, 164, 166, 170, 172, 191, 240, 313, 378, 398-99, 405; III, 14, 110-11, 124-26, 149, 159, 164, 175
— criticism of his views from a pre-capitalist standpoint—II, 153, 156-58, 238-39
See also: *Ricardian school, Ricardian socialists, Ricardo's theory of rent*

Ricardo's theory of rent—I, 38, 175; II, 16, 33, 34, 89, 94, 96, 103-04, 105, 114-15, 117, 122-23, 125, 133, 152, 162-63, 237, 241-42, 245, 270, 273, 274, 310, 313, 315-16, 459
— its place in Ricardo's economic system—II, 115, 117, 313
— and the "law" of diminishing returns—II, 31-33, 89, 134, 236, 244, 273, 300, 310-11, 312, 337, 438-39, 464

Rome (Ancient)—I, 263, 409; II, 528; III, 304, 538

Russia—I, 104; II, 19
— agricultural population—II, 474-75

S

Savings—I, 221, 263, 273; II, 567; III, 273

Science—I, 176, 353, 391; II, 44, 110, 120, 124, 553; III, 443, 501
— as a productive force—I, 390, 392
— and the growth of productive forces—III, 440-41, 445
— and machinery—I, 391
— and the value of commodities—II, 553
— scientific honesty—II, 117, 118-21, 125-26 555; III, 52, 257

Scotland—II, 112, 121, 122, 228, 306, 322, 344, 359, 362

Serfdom—see *Feudalism, Middle Ages*

Services—I, 158-60, 163, 166-69, 172, 175, 186, 218, 266-67, 268, 269, 281, 287-88, 289, 293, 297, 303-04, 401, 403-06, 412-13; II, 501; III, 256, 293

Shares—II, 335, 496; III, 289-90

Silver—see *Gold (and silver)*

Slavery—I, 346; III, 422, 496
— appropriation of surplus-value in slave-owning societies —III, 400
— and landed property—II, 462
— value of slave labour—II, 224-25; III, 93
— unproductive use of surplus product—II, 528
— absence of crises—II, 502-03, 528
— and capitalist relations—III, 243, 419
— colonial—I, 228

Smith, Adam—I, 60, 61, 64, 81, 83-84, 87-88, 263, 280, 303-04; II, 150, 164-65, 217-18, 220-21, 321, 578
— his role in the history of political economy—I, 157, 199, 288, 300
— as a successor of the Physiocrats—I, 45, 60-61, 64, 69-70, 84-85, 162-63, 344; II, 161, 354-55, 357-58, 360, 365-66
— scientific concept of profit— I, 47-48, 78-81, 84-85, 94-95; II, 150, 222, 224, 233; III, 504
— on the nature and origin of surplus-value—I, 71, 74-75, 80, 82, 84-85, 87-88, 89-91, 97, 173, 258; II, 222, 232
— value is resolved into labour and surplus-value into surplus labour—I, 79-85; II, 405-06; III, 238-39

— on productive labour—I, 86, 152, 155-57, 159-74, 186, 225, 257-60, 264, 288-90, 292, 295, 300, 303, 304; III, 414, 426, 431-32
— on the division of labour—I, 295; II, 234; III, 65
— definition of the minimum wage—I, 69; II, 222-27, 233
— on the productivity of labour under capitalism—I, 69-70, 199
— on rent—I, 82, 84-85, 95; II, 150, 161, 222, 224, 238, 241, 246, 249, 308-09, 313, 320-21, 330, 334, 336, 338-39, 342-72
— on interest—I, 82-84
— on accumulation—I, 253-54, 259, 303; II, 467-68, 470, 525, 577; III, 335, 379, 442
— on the "natural price" of commodities—I, 86, 95; II, 318-21, 348-53, 363
— his theory of population—II, 224, 354
— his theory of colonisation— II, 227-28, 239, 308-09, 313, 362, 436
— on social classes—II, 372
— on the tendency of the rate of profit to fall—II, 438, 467-68, 497, 541; III, 313
— on crises—II, 525
— vulgar elements in his views —I, 61, 64, 78, 91, 96, 169-70; II, 347, 468; III, 502
— contradictions in his theory —I, 71-75, 77, 80, 84-85, 88, 89-91, 96, 103, 150-51, 153, 155-56, 161-63, 169, 171-72, 258-59, 264, 265; II, 106, 165, 222-23, 225, 347-48, 350, 352, 396, 402; III, 20
— his contradictory methods of investigation (exoteric and esoteric)—II, 106, 165, 169, 217-19, 229-30, 235, 347, 351, 353-54
— his different definitions of value—I, 70-71, 74-77, 85, 96-97, 173-74; II, 106, 200,

217, 226-27, 232-33, 318, 343-44, 345-46, 347-48, 366, 368-71, 395-98, 401-02; III, 24, 69, 515
— on the law of value under capitalism—I, 72-81; II, 191, 396-97, 401-02; III, 74
— the value of the annual product is resolved by him into revenue—I, 85-86, 97-102, 125, 147, 149-50, 251, 257; II, 150-51, 219, 414, 426, 491; III, 338
— confusion of surplus-value with profit—I, 85, 89-92
— his identification of values with costs of production—II, 25-29, 217-18, 235, 318-21, 337, 343-44; III, 31-32
— profit, rent and wages regarded as sources of value— I, 93-94, 103, 150; II, 106, 199, 216-19, 222-23, 226-27, 229-30, 235, 343-44, 348, 352-53, 370-71, 467
— on the measure of value—I, 150; II, 403
— critique of his views by bourgeois economists—I, 71, 73-74, 173-74, 183, 201-02, 204, 212, 253, 265-66, 281, 284, 285-86, 287-88, 299
— influence of his work on later economists—I, 88, 92, 151, 173, 176-77, 180, 182, 220-21, 224, 280-81, 286-87; II, 154, 165-66, 199, 210-11, 212, 215, 217-18, 228-29, 235, 238, 239, 308-09, 318, 351, 352, 413, 578; III, 20

Socialism, petty-bourgeois—III, 472, 525, 526-27
— its origin—III, 467-68
— attacks money-lending capital—I, 323, 325; III, 456, 467-68, 523, 525-27

Socialist revolution—II, 580; III, 271-72, 360, 423

Society, bourgeois—I, 409; III, 63

— its historical development— I, 44
— its social structure—I, 285, 289
— its antagonistic character— I, 409; III, 97-98, 261
— its functions—I, 287
— and the origin of private property—I, 245-46

Society, primitive—I, 108; III, 422-23

Spain—I, 179; III, 469

State—I, 277, 285; II, 496
— a tool in the hands of the bourgeoisie—I, 300-01; III, 448, 468-69, 534
— capitalists' attitude towards —I, 175, 281, 300-01
— *laissez faire*—I, 52, 53, 66, 170, 361
— and regulation of the working-day—II, 20, 435
— as a consumer of revenue—II, 561
— and nationalisation of land— I, 52, 59, 66; II, 44, 103-04, 152; III, 472

Statistics—I, 178; II, 231, 299, 459; III, 324-25

Stock-breeding—I, 191, 219; II, 241, 298, 342, 354-56, 554, 561; III, 168, 288, 379, 391, 516

Stocks of commodities—I, 254; III, 290-91
— their necessity—III, 276, 287
— their relative decrease—III, 286-87
— their fall in prices—II, 428-29
— and accumulation—II, 481
— and the division of labour— III, 269-70
— and the development of means of communication—II, 485; III, 286-87
— their storage—II, 491-92
— in the sphere of circulation— I, 39; II, 484-85; III, 280-82

Supply and demand—I, 96, 233; II, 26, 133, 271, 273-74, 493-94, 504-05; III, 65, 94-95, 97, 100-04, 312

Surplus labour—I, 82; II, 138, 384
— its specific forms—I, 82, 84-85
— as the basis of capitalist production—II, 284
— compulsion to perform it—I, 93, 346, 356, 389-90, 392, 394; II, 406
— and necessary labour—I, 213, 216
— and the productivity of labour—I, 48-49; II, 406; III, 449
— and profit—II, 379
— as a source of new constant capital—I, 107-08
— as a source of the capitalist's consumption fund—I, 108
— of the entire working class—III, 245-46
— in agriculture and industry—III, 386-87
— agricultural labour as its basis—I, 48, 170
— Physiocrats on—I, 54

Surplus product—I, 356; II, 138, 488
— and surplus-value—I, 213; III, 370
— and unpaid labour—III, 45
— and the productivity of labour—I, 290; III, 449
— as the source of profit—I, 278-79
— consumed by capitalists—III, 242
— its retransformation into capital—II, 485-89; III, 242, 243, 379-80
— its transformation into rent—II, 452-53
— and foreign trade—II, 491; III, 241-44, 253
— Ricardo on—II, 317, 418, 428; III, 238

Surplus-value—I, 46, 55, 79, 82, 173-74, 355, 383; II, 34-35, 190, 485-89, 542-43; III, 158, 255, 258, 485
— as unpaid labour—I, 55, 80, 83, 398-99; II, 40, 183; III, 15, 238-39, 241, 481-82
— as the purpose of capitalist production—I, 90, 213, 381, 399-400, 406-07
— its origin—I, 41-42, 45-46, 50-52, 54-55, 57-58, 62, 74-75, 79-81, 87, 89-91, 315, 355, 365, 383; III, 14-15, 63-64, 481-82
— its production and accumulation—I, 108, 383; II, 477, 485
— appropriated by the capitalist—I, 85-86, 95, 108; II, 152, 328, 373, 453; III, 402, 420-21, 471
— and the productivity of labour—I, 48-49, 65, 93, 153, 216, 305; II, 16, 86-87, 265-66, 406-07; III, 331-32, 449
— and labour—I, 46, 152, 213, 393, 396, 399
— and agriculture—I, 48; II, 360
— and surplus product—I, 213; III, 370
— in various branches of production—II, 20-21, 27-28
— and wages—II, 17, 278, 408; III, 149
— and the organic composition of capital—II, 28, 47-48, 57-58, 297, 376-77; III, 228
— and variable capital—III, 481
— its rate and amount—I, 213-14, 225-26; II, 190, 374-75, 376-77, 382, 409-10, 426-27; III, 229-31, 350-51
— its distribution—I, 42, 83, 84, 85-86, 93, 94, 95, 108; II, 29, 41, 47, 68, 74, 151, 152, 199, 433; III, 87
— its forms—I, 40, 47-48, 82, 85, 89; III, 254, 482, 485
— and profit—II, 409-10; III, 482

— its transformation into rent—
II, 452, 457-58
— Mercantilists on—I, 41, 43, 49, 62, 63, 66, 173, 178-79, 383; III, 16, 76-77
— bourgeois economists confuse it with profit and rent—I, 40, 89, 92; II, 410; III, 36, 85, 87, 191-92, 207, 221, 237, 254
— Petty on—I, 358
— Physiocrats on—I, 50-52, 53-54, 55-57, 62, 66, 85, 153-54, 173-74, 382-83; II, 547; III, 116, 449
— Adam Smith on—I, 71, 74-75, 79-80, 82, 83-84, 85-86, 87-88, 89-91, 97, 173-74, 258; II, 222, 232
— Ricardo on—I, 223; II, 373-74, 394-95, 405-06, 423, 462-63, 566; III, 14, 15, 34, 238-39
— Rodbertus on—II, 15-16, 63, 72-85, 91-92, 127
— *absolute surplus-value*—I, 48-49; II, 16, 406; III, 449
and lengthening of the working-day—II, 16, 408; III, 228
in industry and agriculture—II, 20
natural fertility of land and —III, 449
and relative surplus-value—I, 48-49; II, 16, 86, 438-39; III, 258, 449
— *excess surplus-value*
in industry and agriculture—II, 17-18
obstacles in its distribution among capitalists—II, 30
— *law of surplus-value*—I, 92; II, 410-11
and the volume of surplus-value—II, 47-48, 410
— *rate of surplus-value*
factors determining the rate of surplus-value—II, 86; III, 191
in different spheres of production—II, 207

and productivity in industry and agriculture—II, 19
and the rate of profit—II, 426-27; III, 196, 211-12, 219-20, 228-31
— *relative surplus-value*—II, 31, 406
depends on the productivity of labour—I, 48-49, 93, 305-06; II, 16, 44, 265-66, 406; III, 266, 350, 449
and absolute surplus-value—I, 48-49; II, 16, 86, 438-39; III, 258, 449

Switzerland—II, 139

T

Taxes—I, 84; II, 234-35; III, 289
— direct and indirect—I, 291; II, 234
— and money circulation—I, 311-12
— and the rate of profit—II, 384-85
— Physiocrats on—I, 52, 59, 66

Tithe—I, 384; II, 119

Town
— and the exploitation of the country—II, 232-35
— in the Middle Ages—II, 316; III, 269, 417, 434

Trade—I, 114, 175, 205, 218-19, 388; III, 498
— as a starting-point of capitalist production—III, 112, 470
— and the development of productive forces—II, 24
— and the distribution of profit—III, 498
— wholesale and retail—I, 342
— its balance—I, 43, 66
— Free Traders—I, 178-79
See also: *Barter, Foreign trade*

Transport industry—I, 412-13; II, 483-84, 491-92; III, 285-87, 440
— as a branch of material pro-

duction—I, 171-72, 412-13; III, 327
— labour employed—I, 412-13
— absence of raw materials—II, 45, 63, 92; III, 392-93

Turkey—I, 302, 376

U

Unemployment—see Over-population, relative

United Kingdom—see England, Ireland, Scotland

United States of America—I, 115, 409; II, 20, 38, 42, 96, 156, 301, 310, 311-12, 362, 574-76; III, 115, 242, 287, 417, 440
  See also: America

Use-value—I, 45, 158, 160; II, 489, 507; III, 252, 289, 296, 439, 463-64
— and value—I, 106, 113-14, 140-42, 167, 173-74, 203, 270, 282, 366; II, 263; III, 102, 119, 125, 127-29, 284, 296
— and the productivity of labour—I, 41-42, 109, 203, 228, 393; II, 263, 265-66; III, 119
— and consumption—I, 206, 234-35, 298; III, 292
— of capital—I, 106, 392; III, 439
— of labour-power—I, 156, 400; III, 90, 178
— in the process of production—II, 137; III, 264-65
— bourgeois economists on value and use-value—I, 46, 51-52, 154, 173-74, 267, 361, 366; II, 151; III, 488-89

Utopian socialism and communism—I, 345; III, 238
  See also: Ricardian socialists, Socialism, petty-bourgeois

V

Value—I, 46, 50, 71, 86, 94, 98-103, 105, 109, 116, 125, 147-48, 150, 173, 195, 221, 232, 242, 245; II, 21, 34-35, 48, 59, 80, 83-84, 112, 150, 195-96, 262, 333, 396, 414-15, 471, 473, 474, 496, 503, 513-14, 515, 517, 533, 540; III, 111, 113, 124, 125, 127-29, 131, 134-35, 160-61, 196, 211, 250, 253, 373
— as a social relation—III, 129, 147, 181
— its substance—I, 46, 48, 50, 84-85, 94-95, 204-05, 394; II, 130, 164, 172, 173; III, 40, 128, 134-35, 154-56, 162-63, 337, 482
— and the concept of surplus-value—I, 173-74, 355-56; II, 190
— self-expanding—I, 322-23, 392, 393-94; III, 131, 137, 424
— labour theory of value—II, 242, 333
— its form and amount—I, 50, 204-05, 317; III, 127-28, 130
— the measure of value—II, 164, 172, 202; III, 130, 138-39, 142-43, 144-45
— and price—III, 130
— its money form—I, 95; II, 137; III, 155-56, 161-62
— and use-value—I, 106, 113, 141-43, 167, 173-74, 203, 270, 282, 366; II, 263-64; III, 101-02, 118, 125, 126-29, 284, 296
— and the productivity of labour—I, 69, 71, 192-97, 203, 211, 232-33, 393-94; II, 262-63, 265-66
— individual and market—I, 232-33; II, 204, 262-66, 268-69, 270-71, 507-08, 520-21; III, 64
— relative and absolute—III, 132-33
— its distribution—I, 74, 84, 94, 97; II, 134, 152, 418
— and wages—I, 94-95; II, 15, 418, 551-52
— and the cost of production—I, 95, 416; II, 29, 30-32, 34-

35, 56-57, 70-71, 132, 183-84, 190, 193-94, 213-15, 235, 243-44, 277, 297; III, 81-82, 166-67, 377, 482-83, 510, 516

— and market price—I, 42, 54-55, 95, 109-10, 123-24, 232-33; II, 16, 27, 333; III, 111, 130, 518
— differential—II, 262, 268, 291
— its realisation—III, 126-27, 130-31
— Petty on—I, 355-56, 360-62
— Physiocrats on—I, 45-47, 60
— Steuart on—I, 41-43
— Ricardo on—II, 172
— value and use-value in bourgeois political economy—I, 46, 52, 154, 173-74, 267-68, 361, 366; II, 150-51; III, 489
— confused with price by vulgar economists—III, 154, 156, 161
— search for an "invariable measure of value" by bourgeois economists—I, 72, 74-75, 150-51; II, 366-67, 401-02; III, 13-14, 133-34, 145-46, 155
— law of value—II, 56-57, 201, 362; III, 69-71, 72-73, 74-75, 105-06, 164
as the basis of political economy—II, 242
and exchange of equivalents —I, 62, 169, 205, 256-57, 315, 317, 337-38, 398; III, 126-33, 134-35, 139-40, 147, 150-51, 377
and exchange between labour and capital—I, 73, 87, 315; II, 397-99; III, 14-15, 19-20, 90-91, 93, 377, 481-82
and cost of production—III, 82-83, 167-68
and rent—II, 36, 163
— *relative value*
as distinct from "absolute" value—II, 170-72
relative value of money—II, 201
See also: *Exchange-value, Market value, Price*

Village community (Asian)—III, 417, 423

W

Wage-labour—I, 93; II, 572, 573; III, 259, 271, 400-01, 431, 480-81
— as the basis of capitalist production—I, 229-30; II, 397; III, 289, 471, 491-92
— and commodity production— III, 290
— productive labour—I, 152, 156-57, 171, 200

Wages—I, 84-85, 93-94, 172, 252, 314-15, 320; II, 15, 17, 20-21, 38, 379, 392-93, 460; III, 92-94, 114, 338, 424-25, 481
— and value of labour-power— I, 314-15, 397-98; II, 318-19; III, 43
— and reproduction of labour-power—I, 84, 182-83
— as a part of circulating capital—I, 252
— and the value of commodities—I, 94; II, 15, 418, 552
— and surplus-value—II, 17, 278, 408; III, 149
— and profit—II, 73-74, 278-79
— and cost of production—II, 386-95; III, 333
— and market prices—I, 97, 154, 320-21
— and the productivity of labour—I, 215-17; II, 16-17, 73-74, 263, 406-07
— their forms—III, 114
— nominal and real—II, 17
— of industrial and agricultural workers—II, 17, 20-21, 231
— and growth of the labouring population—II, 477, 581-83
— and competition between workers—I, 388; II, 17
— level in different countries and at different periods—II, 17, 231, 476
— deduction from—I, 210

REQUEST TO READERS

Progress Publishers would be glad to have your opinion of this book, its translation and design and any suggestions you may have for future publications.

Please send your comments to 21, Zubovsky Boulevard, Moscow, U.S.S.R.

— of superintendance—I, 81, 108; III, 69, 356, 493, 495-97, 504-05, 507
— Physiocrats on—I, 45, 47, 56, 67
— Ricardo on—II, 401, 404, 417, 419, 423-24, 438, 558, 567; III, 33

War—I, 224; II, 118, 392; III, 51
See also: *American Civil War*

Wealth—I, 288
— bourgeois wealth—I, 174, 204, 223, 280; III, 54-55, 56, 429
— and the mode of production—I, 296
— commodity as its elementary form—I, 173, 204, 303
— socially necessary labour as its measure—I, 76
— as the goal of capitalist production—I, 270, 282
— and profit—I, 41, 101
— and productive labour—I, 225, 227, 279, 284
— and the prodigality of capitalists—I, 282
— idle wealth—I, 301
— and poverty—I, 305, 307; III, 56
— material—I, 161, 258, 284, 286-87, 288, 297-98, 409-10; 411-12; III, 129

West Indies—I, 376

Workers—I, 228, 381, 388; II, 152, 560, 561, 565-66, 573, 579-80; III, 63 261, 295, 352-53
— under capitalism—I, 93, 346, 356, 381, 390, 392, 394; II, 29, 42, 119, 224-25, 406, 416, 421, 548, 580; III, 97-98, 261, 271, 276, 331-32, 352-53, 530

— and the division of labour—II, 234; III, 352-53
— their share in the value of the product—III, 94
— and relative over-population—I, 388; II, 17, 554, 565, 573; III, 52-53
— and the contradictions of bourgeois economy—II, 506-07; III, 168
— and labour-power as a commodity—I, 45, 51, 71, 72-73, 87, 94-95, 159, 167-68, 171-72, 314-16, 321, 356, 392, 397-98, 409; II, 396-97; III, 89-91, 110, 114, 271, 300
— and productive labour—I, 166; II, 547; III, 119-20
— and the productivity of labour—I, 69-70, 217-18, 228
— as commodity buyers—I, 86-87, 404; III, 19-21
— and the cost of education—I, 167
— industrial and agricultural workers—I, 219; II, 15, 17, 20, 234

Workers' co-operative factories—III, 356, 497, 505

Working-day—II, 20, 406, 435, 439
— its natural and social limits—III, 300, 307-08
— and labour-power—II, 408; III, 149, 308-09
— its lengthening—II, 408-09; III, 228
— and absolute surplus-value—II, 16, 405-06
— and introduction of new machines—II, 460
— and accumulation of capital—III, 241

World trade—see *Foreign trade*

PUBLISHERS' NOTE

This translation has been made from Karl Marx, *Theorien über den Mehrwert*, Teil 3, Dietz Verlag, Berlin, 1962. The arrangement of the material and the notes correspond on the whole to the Russian edition of Marx-Engels, *Collected Works*, Vol. 26, Part III, Moscow, 1964, prepared by the Institute of Marxism-Leninism in Moscow, where the manuscript of the work is kept.

We have attempted to keep the translation as closely as possible to the original. When, for the sake of clarity, it has been found necessary to insert a few words these are enclosed in square brackets. In order to avoid confusion, the square brackets occasionally used by Marx in the manuscript have been replaced either by pointed brackets ⟨ ⟩ or, when the passages enclosed were longer, by braces { }.

Quotations from French, German and Italian authors are given in English in the text and are reproduced in the original language in the Appendix. In the case of British writers cited by Marx from a French source, the original English version appears in the text and the French translation used by Marx in the Appendix. Where an omission in a passage quoted has not been indicated by Marx, the ellipsis is enclosed in square brackets.

Other discrepancies between the quotations as recorded by Marx and as they appear in the original source, are mentioned in footnotes.

Words underlined by Marx, both in his own writing and in the extracts quoted by him, are set in italics, as are also titles of publications and foreign words customarily italicised (words underscored by two lines are set in spaced italics).

Chapter and section headings correspond in general to those of the Russian edition. Headings set in square brackets have been provided by the Institute of Marxism-Leninism in Moscow on the basis of formulations used by Marx in the chapter or section in question.

The numbers of Marx's notebooks are indicated by Roman numerals, those of the manuscript pages by Arabic numerals, which are separated from the text by vertical lines. As a rule these numbers are printed only at the beginning of the relevant portion of the manuscript, but where passages have been transposed the number of the manuscript page (and, when there is a change to another notebook, also the number of the notebook) is shown both at the beginning of the passage and at the end.

www.ingramcontent.com/pod-product-compliance
Ingram Content Group UK Ltd.
Pitfield, Milton Keynes, MK11 3LW, UK
UKHW022208141025
8391UKWH00003B/301